The Course of
MEXICAN HISTORY

The Course of

MEXICAN HISTORY

EIGHTH EDITION

Michael C. Meyer
University of Arizona

William L. Sherman
University of Nebraska-Lincoln

Susan M. Deeds
Northern Arizona University

New York   Oxford
OXFORD UNIVERSITY PRESS
2007

Oxford University Press, Inc., publishes works that further Oxford University's objective of excellence in research, scholarship, and education.

Oxford   New York
Auckland   Cape Town   Dar es Salaam   Hong Kong   Karachi
Kuala Lumpur   Madrid   Melbourne   Mexico City   Nairobi
New Delhi   Shanghai   Taipei   Toronto

With offices in
Argentina   Austria   Brazil   Chile   Czech Republic   France   Greece
Guatemala   Hungary   Italy   Japan   Poland   Portugal   Singapore
South Korea   Switzerland   Thailand   Turkey   Ukraine   Vietnam

Published by Oxford University Press, Inc.
198 Madison Avenue, New York, New York 10016
http://www.oup.com

Oxford is a registered trademark of Oxford University Press

Library of Congress Cataloging-in-Publication Data

Meyer, Michael C.
    The course of Mexican history / Michael C. Meyer, William L. Sherman, Susan M. Deeds. — 8th ed.
        p. cm.
    Includes bibliographical references and index.
    ISBN-13: 978-0-19-517835-7 (cloth : alk. paper)
    ISBN-13: 978-0-19-517836-4 (paper : alk. paper)
    1. Mexico—History.   I. Sherman, William L.   II. Deeds, Susan M.   III. Title.
    IV. Title: Mexican history.

F1226.M54   2007
972—dc21

                                                                    2006051741

Printing number: 9 8 7 6 5 4

Printed in the United States of America
on acid-free paper

Contents

Color plates follow p. 495

Maps and Charts

Preface

In 2003, *The Course of Mexican History* celebrated twenty-five years in print, an occurrence never contemplated when the original authors (Michael Meyer and William Sherman) sent their manuscript to press for the first time. Subsequent editions made it possible to correct errors, incorporate new findings, periodically update the history of colonial and modern Mexico, and remove recountings that seemed important or poignant at the time but proved to be of only fleeting significance in the larger historical scheme of things. In the eighth edition, Michael Meyer and Susan Deeds have streamlined the text in a number of places with the intent of providing an even more readable synthesis of Mexico's unique past. We also offer the addition of color images that vividly illustrate the links between Mexico's history and arts.

The book's longevity has, of course, allowed its authors to reach many more students than they were able to engage in their own classrooms. At the same time, we realize that no textbook can ever be a replacement for dedicated and enthusiastic college teachers, who not only draw upon their reservoir of historical knowledge but also provoke discussion, stimulate critical thinking, and share their individual experience as they stand in front of their students. We believe that the narrative approach we have undertaken in this text makes those tasks more attainable as it allows the individual professor the freedom and flexibility of pursuing special topics in greater depth and assigning different kinds of collateral readings without concern that the underlying narrative thread of the Mexican historical experience will have been lost. From the response of our own students, as well as those of many colleagues, we are convinced that this scheme works and that *The Course of Mexican History* has made at least a modest contribution in helping a generation of college undergraduates emerge from their Mexican history classes with a deeper appreciation of the Mexican past. We are confident that this, in turn, leads to a more nuanced understanding of the Mexican present. If this appreciation of the past and understanding of the present beget a degree of empathy for a country that has experienced more than its fair share of adversity through the centuries, the authors are then doubly rewarded.

As we send our manuscript to press for the eighth edition, Mexico has experienced economic and political changes unimaginable at the time of the first edition. The most dramatic transformation occurred when Vicente Fox, running under the label of the National Action Party (PAN), defeated the candidate of the Revolutionary Institutional Party in the 2000 presidential elections, ending seventy years of one-party rule. Fox's assumption of the office of chief executive gave rise to high and, as it turned out, unattainable national expectations.

Privatization of state-owned enterprises had begun even before his inauguration, and by the dawn of the new millennium the concept of the free market was no longer anathema to Mexico's mainstream economic thought. It had gained a strong foothold in sectors of the economy long dominated by the state. At the same time, those left behind in the new scheme have demanded that their critique of "progress" be heard. They remind us that the Indian communities of rural Mexico who identify with the "color of the earth" have not embraced an elite vision that disregards both their needs and their cultural difference. This edition permits us to address how these remarkable transformations evolved as Mexico moved cautiously into the twenty-first century.

The historical literature upon which we now rely to fashion our own scholarly judgments has grown immeasurably richer in the last several decades. If we have been able to keep abreast of changes and offer a fresh perspective in succeeding editions it is because we have profited and continue to profit from the diligence and scholarship of many other historians in Mexico, Europe, and the United States. The path of Mexican history might not yet be strewn with the rubbish of discarded hypotheses, but an increasingly rich corpus of new scholarship continues to confront many commonly held assumptions about the country's historical experience. A few landmark studies have actually undermined the tenets of conventional wisdom, while countless others have allowed us to refine our appreciation of the Mexican past. We are constantly challenged not only by new questions but also by new answers to old questions.

The task we set for ourselves here, as in all previous editions, is to present an up-to-date, engaging, and informed synthesis of Mexican history. While we naturally hope that our colleagues in both Mexico and the United States will find merit in our approach, we have directed our history not to them but to their students and the general reader. Like all survey texts, ours is intended to throw open the subject of Mexican history, certainly not to close it. Those wishing to pursue a topic in greater depth will find that we have updated the list of English-language works appended to each chapter. We have included works now considered standard with more recent interpretations that we found perceptive and interesting, including those whose conclusions differ from our own.

The understanding of Mexican history logically begins with an understanding of major political themes. These we have dutifully reconstructed, but we view them as a means to an end. They are, in effect, a foundation upon which to build. Political decisions influence the direction of the economy, the social structure, and even the cultural vitality of a country. Because we are persuaded that history properly encompasses the entire human experience, we have directed special attention to social and cultural developments, including population trends, lifestyles, the special role of women, literature, art, music, and intellectual life. We recognize that social and cultural patterns seldom fit neatly into political or economic periods, but as in the past, we have included a chapter on society and culture within each major chronological division in the belief that these sections help to provide a broader and more accurate representation of Mexican life in the crucial eras of Mexico's historical development.

Mexico's experience in the world community continues to be remarkable and unique. On some occasions, a national consensus has emerged, facilitating the tasks of exposition and interpretation, but on other occasions, uncompromising ideologies, differing views of national purpose, and competing articulations of problems and solutions render difficult our accounting of the Mexican experience. At those times where the air is not yet clear, where polemic threatens to offend our sensibilities, we can think of no better response than to offer the tempering context of historical perspective. Mexico's future inevitably will be tied to Mexico's past.

During our long relationship with the fine staff at the Higher Education Division of Oxford University Press we have had the opportunity to work with three editors: Nancy Lane, who supported our effort from its inception and who offered wise counsel for the first five editions; Gioia Stevens, who replaced her and skillfully guided us through the editorial process for the sixth edition; and Peter Coveney, whose sound editorial judgment left its positive mark on the seventh edition and continued into the eighth with the valuable efforts of John Challice, Brad Reina, and Lisa Grzan. It is a pleasure not only to acknowledge their contributions but also to offer our thanks. We also appreciate the efforts of Elsa Malvido in helping us obtain the credits for the new illustrations in this edition.

Tucson, Arizona   M.C.M.
Flagstaff, Arizona   S.M.D.
September 2006

The Course of
MEXICAN HISTORY

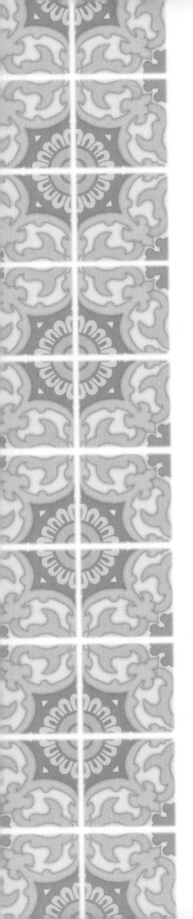

I

PRE-COLUMBIAN MEXICO

The First Mexicans

There is in Mexican society a pervasive awareness of the ancients. The Indian presence intrudes on the national psyche; it suffuses the art, philosophy, and literature. It is stamped on the face of Mexico, in the racial features of the sturdy mestizo. It lies within the marvelous prehistoric ruins among whose haunted piles the Mexicans seek their origins. It has not always been so. Following the Spanish conquest of the sixteenth century, a combination of the conquerors' ethnocentrism and excessive Christian zeal reduced all things Indian to a level of shame. At the end of the nineteenth century Mexican political elites saw that the grandeur of the Aztec empire could be invoked to validate their own ambitions, but the great push to revive the indigenous past occurred later during the Revolution, as leaders turned it to the service of a unifying national myth that could transcend the contradictions of an ethnically and culturally divided society. In their search for *mexicanidad*—the spirit of an inclusive Mexican cultural identity—revolutionary intellectuals looked to new configurations of stories, places, and heroes from the past. For several decades talented anthropologists, historians, painters, musicians, novelists, and craftsmen extolled native values. Then as cultural nationalism gave way to more nuanced representations of ancient cultures, so did the circumstances of contemporary indigenous peoples pose ever more stark contrasts to the depictions of stunning past achievements. The contradictions were startlingly manifested in the Chiapas insurrection of 1994.

PRE-AGRICULTURAL AND PROTO-AGRICULTURAL MEXICO

At what point or how the first Mexicans appeared on the scene is still debated. The long-standing academic theory is that they are descended from the intrepid hunters who crossed from the Asian mainland to Alaska. There may have been several waves of migrants, the first perhaps as early as 40,000 B.C., and at other times during the Wisconsin

3

(Pleistocene) Ice Age when sea levels were lower, and a land bridge over the Bering Straits facilitated the passage. When a melting trend began around 9000 B.C., the migrations very likely ceased.

More recent archaeological discoveries posit new hypotheses that support the idea of sea routes from Asia to North America and a coastal migration pattern down the Pacific coastline, as well as lithic connections with the Solutrean culture of western Europe, 24,000–16,500 years ago. Biological evidence from skeletons and mitochondrial DNA also suggest connections with Polynesian, Japanese, and European peoples. Native Americans offer their own explanations and oppose skeletal dating methods on religious grounds. As new archaeological, biological, and linguistic discoveries are made, changing and competing understandings about these matters will persist. Advances in the decipherment of hieroglyphic writing will also continue to alter how we divide pre-Hispanic Mexico into chronological periods with distinctive cultural characteristics. This chart provides a general overview, although not all cultures fit within it and dates vary by group and location.

The early human inhabitants of America were hunters, food gatherers, and sometimes fishermen. They were constantly on the move, searching for food and using crude stone tools. For thousands of years, these early hunters led a precarious existence, with little perceptible improvement in technology until about 10,000 B.C., when fine pressure-flaked stone points made hunting easier. At this time, the still moist conditions of the late Pleistocene supported lush grasslands

PERIODS IN MEXICAN PRE-HISTORY

40,000–8000 B.C.	*Pre-Agricultural:* Nomadic hunters and food gatherers.
8000–2000 B.C.	*Archaic (Incipient Agricultural):* Slowly evolving domestication of food plants; nascent village life; development of primitive skills.
2000 B.C.–A.D. 200	*Formative or Pre-Classic:* Elaboration of farming, villages, and pottery; appearance of chiefdoms, public architecture, solar calendar, and long-distance exchange.
A.D. 200–900	*Classic:* The florescence of ancient Mexican civilization with state-level societies ruled by kings and priests; elaboration of cities and monumental architecture; intensification of agriculture; increased social stratification; advancement in artistic expression, literacy, and science.
A.D. 900–1521	*Post-Classic or Historical:* Growth of city-states and empires; expansion of commerce; intensification of Late Classic trends in sacrifice and warfare; development of metallurgy; final destruction of Indian states by Spanish conquest.

and full foliage—ample fodder for animal prey—hairy mammoths, mastodons, giant armadillos, and early ancestors of the bison, camel, and horse. These animals were hunted by men who assailed their prey with missiles—including stone-tipped lances or darts propelled by the *atl-atl*, or spear thrower. Human remains dating to 13,000 years ago have been discovered in various Mexican sites, and other evidence of human habitation dates back even further. In an early find during the 1940s, the remains of a human were discovered at the village of Tepexpan, situated a few miles north of today's Mexico City on what was the edge of the old lake. "Tepexpan Man" (who, it turned out, was a woman) dates to about 8000 B.C. In 1952, not far distant at Santa Isabel Iztápan, another important discovery was unearthed: mammoth bones were found with a stone point lodged in the ribs, and there were clear indications that the beast had been butchered with flint knives that lay nearby. However, the earliest hunter-gatherer sites have been found in Oaxaca and Puebla.

Around 7500 B.C. a drying-up phase began: rainfall was less frequent, and the rich plant life gradually yielded to sparse vegetation; the lake shriveled up; and the huge beasts that had provided a plentiful supply of meat eventually became extinct as their sources of food and water disappeared. Ancient Mexicans were again back to eating insects, lizards, snakes, rodents, and anything else remotely edible, to supplement their diet of seeds, roots, nuts, berries, eggs, and shellfish. The audacious killer of mammoths gave way to the hunter of small game.

As meat consumption fell to less than 21 percent of the diet by 4000 B.C., collection of plants increased. And over several millenia maize cultivation developed as *teosinte* grass underwent genetic alteration to produce small corn cobs. Maize became the basis of the Mexican diet. We know, for example, that as early as 5000 B.C. primitive farmers practiced rudimentary agriculture at Tehuacán in the modern state of Puebla. By at least 2000 B.C., maize, along with previously domesticated beans and squash, had become a widespread source of human sustenance in Mesoamerica, or Middle America, as indicated by the presence of grinding stones for the making of meal.

The farmer was evolving, but there was great variation in this process throughout Mexico, and hunting and gathering continued to be practiced to differing degrees, even solely by some nomadic groups. But in central and southern Mexico, barring disasters common to all tillers of the soil, a fairly reliable source of food allowed populations to grow and to find leisure time for experimentation, to develop and refine skills and talents. Weavers of baskets and mats began to shape clay, a most important development.

THE FORMATIVE PERIOD

Ancient garbage dumps are to the archaeologist what documents are to the historian. From those piles of refuse scientific investigators patiently assemble pictures of primitive societies with a sophistication astonishing to the layman. Much has, of course, long been reduced to dust, and whatever use early inhabitants made of wood, hides, and woven reeds must be left to speculation. But instruments of flint, obsidian, and various kinds of stone survive, and some pottery has left us indelible traces of early cultures.

By 2000 B.C. the rough outlines of a Mesoamerican identity had begun to form. Mesoamerican refers to a loosely defined cultural tradition that characterized much of precontact Mexico and Central America. Its fundamental common characteristics were the dependence on maize agriculture and the evolution of an agricultural technology that used a wooden digging stick. Agriculture advanced during the Formative period with the beginning of irrigation, terracing, fertilizers and raised fields. Implements of stone and wood facilitated cultivation of fields by farmers, who built huts of branches, reeds,

Ceramic figurine of a dancer from Tlatilco, near Mexico City.

and mud nearby. A simple village life with incipient political and social orders evolved. Subsequently, cliques emerged to control both
power and wealth. Increased exchange of goods among different societies developed as a result of distinctive products and artisan spe-
cialties. In addition, varied climate and geography yielded regional
fruits, vegetables, woods, stone, and other items of value, such as
shells, jade, cotton, and turquoise. This spreading trade naturally led
to cultural exchanges as well.

Artists began to create ceramics that were both esthetically pleasing
and functional. Clay figurines, usually of females and more often than
not naked, were produced in great numbers. Among them were those
of Tlatilco, in the Valley of Mexico, where artists rendered charming
figurines of the type known as "pretty lady," with delicate and beautiful
faces. The eyes are almost slanting and the hairdos sometimes elaborate. The figures have tiny waists and bulging thighs. At the same time,
a fascination with the deformed manifested early the Mexican idea of
duality, for other small clay figurines represented dwarfs, hunchbacks,
and the diseased. Some figurines are of interest for their depiction of
everyday life—nursing babies, dancing, playing, and performing acro-
batics. Through them we gain some idea of popular pastimes, the use
of jewelry, and clothing. Still other pieces were made in the images of
animals and gods whose forms suggest ritual purposes related to natural forces and dependence upon the products of the earth.

During the Late Formative period agriculture was further enhanced
by the use of terracing and raised fields. One form of the latter was
the *chinampa*, the so-called floating garden, constructed by building
up layers of mud and aquatic vegetation from an adjacent lake.

Although textile manufacturing had evolved, it is likely that, in the
more temperate zones anyway, people went about nude, or almost so.
Clothing was apparently worn more among the upper classes than the
lower, as were sandals, jewelry, and other adornments. Individual expression and vanity were evident in the dyed hair and elaborate coiffures of aristocratic women.

As villages grew in size and society became more complex, serious
decisions had to be made by those who were most knowledgeable. Increasing reliance on agriculture made people aware that their security
depended upon the blessings of nature. The mysteries of the universe
were associated with the supernatural, and, as in other ancient cultures, gods of nature came to be worshipped. Vagaries of the elements
were equated with capricious gods. When rain failed, for example, sup-
plication was made to the angry deity through the agency of the priesthood. Among a credulous people, the priest, with his special powers,
acquired a predominant position. This presumed special relationship

with the gods, astutely cultivated by the priests, gave them a certain mystique and a hold over the community. In order to pay due reverence to the gods and to ensure their cooperation in providing rain and sunshine, priests ordered the construction of mounds, on top of which offerings were made. As the structures became larger and more elaborate, advanced permanent architecture evolved. By the Middle Formative (1200–400 B.C.) some impressive sites were already in evidence.

OLMEC CULTURE AND INFLUENCE

For many years archaeologists exclusively associated the early development of complex society in Mesoamerica with the Olmec culture of the Gulf coast lowlands. They believed it to have been the "mother culture" that profoundly influenced later Classic period civilizations. In the past few decades, scholars have learned more about the Olmecs whose sites of San Lorenzo, Veracruz, and La Venta, Tabasco, offered tantalizing clues for reconstructing their development. From simple village cultures, Olmecs and similar groups evolved into societies with exotic forms of pottery, economic specialization, new forms of religious life, and the building of large platforms and mounds with temples. Although Olmec culture evolved in the propitious natural setting of the coastal villages of the Gulf coast, it was distributed over several phases (dating from about 1500 B.C. to the Christian era) in areas outside its heartland to the south and west.

Massive public construction seems to have begun at San Lorenzo by 1350 B.C., where we find the Olmec "pudgy babies" or dolls, and motifs like the serpent mouth. The site also came to have a drainage system, a ball court, and the colossal stone heads for which the Olmecs are most well known. Some of these spectacular carved heads—embellished likenesses of rulers—were over nine feet high and weighed as much as forty tons. By about 850 B.C., San Lorenzo was eclipsed by the island site of La Venta, where elites mobilized labor and directed construction of this city of monumental architecture for over four hundred years. Their tombs have furnished many artifacts of Olmec culture including large mosaic masks and elegantly carved jade figurines. Early Olmecs worshipped the alligator, representing the earth, and the shark, representing the sea. Elites added the serpent as a symbol of rule, along with were-jaguars.

The Olmec and some contemporary cultures in the highland valleys of Mexico seem to have been the originators of the elite-commoner class divide that came to characterize Mesoamerican societies. Elites commanded resources from commoners who grew maize, another basic

This handsome basalt stone carving from the Gulf coast Olmec culture is known as "The Wrestler."

Representing a pudgy baby, or perhaps a eunuch, this Olmec piece is 13½ inches in height.

deity. Elites also developed the long distance trade in obsidian, jade, cacao, and other items that helped to spread Olmec influence. Their impact on surrounding and later cultures can also be seen in the advancement of terracing in agriculture and a calendrical system that meshed ritual and solar calendars. Although some archaeologists believed that glyphs on the great stone heads of the Olmecs might be names of rulers, there was little evidence to substantiate this hypothesis. But the 1998 discovery of a cylindrical ceramic stamp and greenstone fragments dated about 650 B.C. at a site subordinate to La Venta has added to speculation that the Olmecs were the first to invent writing.

Other Mesoamerican societies developed sophisticated polities in the late Formative period that had features in common with the Olmec: the building of public structures, the rapid growth of villages, the development of calendrical and writing systems, craft specialization, and long-distance trade. The nature of the exchanges between them is not well understood, but they shared elements of a belief system whose symbols are found in pottery designs and glyphs present at sites throughout central and southern Mexico.

Several colossal Olmec stone heads have been discovered. This one, more than 8 feet high, is covered with what appears to be a helmet.

New centers with temple-pyramid complexes like that at Cuicuilco, located on the outskirts of present-day Mexico City, and at lowland Maya locations to the south emerged in the Late Formative period (400 B.C.–A.D. 200). Some of the new sites would develop into great hubs of the Classic world in Mexico. On a hilltop in the Valley of Oaxaca, the site of Monte Albán expanded into an urban center administering much of the surrounding countryside. And in the Valley of Mexico, Cuicuilco's destruction by a volcano in the first century A.D. encouraged rapid urban growth at nearby Teotihuacán. Above an area of natural caves—considered sacred in Mesoamerican religion—its inhabitants constructed huge pyramids dedicated to the moon and the sun. By the end of the Formative period, the civic-religious complex at Teotihuacán had amassed the technology and central authority necessary for the creation of one of the splendors of the world.

Recommended for Further Study

Adams, Richard E. W. *Prehistoric Mesoamerica,* 3d ed. Norman: University of Oklahoma Press, 2005.

Adams, Richard E. W., and Murdo J. MacLeod, eds. *The Cambridge History of the Native Peoples of the Americas,* Vol. II: *Mesoamerica.* New York: Cambridge University Press, 1998.

Bernal, Ignacio. *The Olmec World.* Translated by Doris Heyden and Fernando Horcasitas. Berkeley: University of California Press, 1969.

Carmack, Robert M., Janine Gasco, and Gary H. Gossen. *The Legacy of Mesoamerica: History and Culture of a Native American Civilization.* Upper Saddle River, N.J.: Prentice Hall, 1996.

Coe, Michael, and Richard A. Diehl. *In the Land of the Olmec.* 2 vols. Austin: University of Texas Press, 1980.

Flannery, Kent V., ed. *The Early Mesoamerican Village.* New York: Academic Press, 1976.

Flannery, Kent V., and Joyce Marcus, eds. *The Cloud People: Divergent Evolution of the Zapotec and Mixtec Civilizations.* New York: Academic Press, 1983.

MacNeish, Richard S. *The Origins of Agriculture and Settled Life.* Norman: University of Oklahoma Press, 1991.

Miller, Mary Ellen. *The Art of Mesoamerica, from Olmec to Aztec.* London: Thames and Hudson, 1986.

Pohl, Mary E.D., K.O. Pope, and C. Von Nagy, "Olmec Origins of Mesoamerican Writing." *Science,* 298 (2002), 1984–1987.

Sharer, Robert J., and David C. Grove. *Regional Perspectives on the Olmec.* New York: Cambridge University Press, 1989.

Stark, Barbara L., and Philip J. Arnold III, eds. *Olmec to Aztec: Settlement Patterns in the Ancient Gulf Lowlands.* Tucson: University of Arizona, 1997.

Wolf, Eric. *Sons of the Shaking Earth: The People of Mexico and Guatemala—Their Land, History, and Culture.* Chicago: University of Chicago Press, 1974.

2

Mexico's Golden Age: The Classic Period

The Mesoamerican culture region flourished over the first millenium A.D., most visible in the monumental architecture of cities and the refinement of calendrical and astronomical knowledge. As the Roman Empire crumbled in Europe, Mesoamerica was resplendent.

THE FLOWERING OF CITIES

The period from A.D. 200 to 800 has been viewed as a Golden Age of intellectual and artistic endeavor. Because of the many societies under consideration, the Classic cannot be put into any simple chronological framework.[1] Some sites, such as Teotihuacán and Monte Albán, developed Classic features much earlier. Most Classic cultures declined in the ninth century, but some persisted as late as A.D. 1000.

One is struck by the grandiose scale of human endeavor in those centuries, most notable in the stunning architecture but also by the excellence of the ceramics, sculpture, and murals. Religion was the cohesive force in an increasingly stratified society, and kings invested with sacred power exacted both labor and tribute from the masses. It was a time of great vigor, with the proliferation of crafts and skills necessary to provide for complex communities. The leadership was dedicated to a sense of order in propitiating the gods, made possible by an apparently strict adherence to regimentation. Pressures to provide sustenance for a burgeoning population led to more careful consideration of planting cycles, which in turn produced exact calculations of the seasons. Even more important was the Mesoamerican belief that all things—gods, people, animals, plants, mountains, even cities—were alive, and that their movements could be timed to account for all life events. Consequently there

---

1. With only a tiny fraction of the thousands of known archaeological sites in Mexico having been scientifically excavated, the complexities of charting can be appreciated.

Why is this boy laughing? Such unrestrained joy is characteristic of the thousands of ceramic pieces found at the site of Remojadas in the state of Veracruz. Unique for their expressiveness, the figurines have triangular, flattened heads, and teeth that are often filed to points.

A howling coyote, another delightful piece from the Remojadas culture, A.D. 300–900. Indian artists frequently displayed a touch of whimsy in their works.

developed a very sophisticated knowledge of astronomy and mathematics, which made possible precise calendrical markings. Mesoamericans devised a highly sophisticated calendar system that included a 365-day solar count as well as a ritual calendar and counts of many other celestial bodies. Farming became scientific; abstract thinking soared. The intellectuals in ancient Mesoamerica apparently arrived at the revolutionary concept of the zero cipher well before its discovery by the fifth-century Hindus. Not until A.D. 1202 did Arab mathematicians introduce this concept to Europe. Yet, oddly enough, the accomplished scientists of the New World made almost no practical use of metals, nor had they stumbled onto the utility of the wheel!

It is therefore all the more admirable that in some places Mesoamericans were able to raise structures to the height of 230 feet that have stood for some fifteen hundred years. The magnitude of their technical limitations was equaled by their ingenuity. In lowland areas, massive blocks of cut stone were most likely transported on river rafts from quarries to distant cities, and for lifting the pieces high in the air some clever engineering devices, however crude in appearance, were utilized. Nature had provided Mexico no beasts of burden, so armies of laborers toiled for years on public works projects. An architectural design tradition evolved to take earthquakes into account in the highlands, but technical perfection in construction tends to be subordinated to an irresistible propensity for the esthetic. Though capable of exact measurements, they avoided harsh angles unpleasing to the eye. If the result was agreeable to humans, the purpose, it is clear, was to please the gods.

For many years archaeologists believed that these building complexes were not true cities but only ceremonial centers inhabited by priests, rulers, and their retainers. Today it is universally agreed that Classic centers were true cities. Elites lived in the most luxurious chambers of palace compounds nearest the primary ceremonial complexes or major avenues, which consisted of temple-pyramids, tombs, observatories, and acropoli. Other urban features include ball courts, steam baths, and causeways. Surrounding the city core in a concentric pattern were the apartment complexes of artisans who specialized in craft production as well as those of other middling occupational groups such as petty officials, soldiers, and merchants. Laborers, farmers, and others of the commoner class lived even further out, in modest thatched-roof huts of wattle and daub construction. There they farmed the land, hunted, fished, carried the burdens, and performed all sorts of tasks necessary to support the aristocracy. During festivals, religious in nature, or on market days, masses of people tended to gather in the central precincts.

These Mesoamerican cities functioned first and foremost as administrative and religious centers whose architecture and spatial design attempted to replicate the order of the universe and the hierarchical relationships that linked humans and supernaturals. Teotihuacán in central Mexico was truly remarkable for its size and religious importance. The marvelous stone cities of the Classic period were conceived for an impression of grandeur and laid out in breathtaking expanses. The architects were true artists, interposing grand courtyards to offset with horizontal lines the massive vertical projections. As Monte Albán dramatically testifies, they blended their creations with nature and composed with stone and textures that reflected the sunlight.

Although city size, population density, and spatial arrangements varied among Classic centers, there is no question that concentrated populations in so many sites had an incalculable impact on culture. The arts always thrive with greatest vigor in an urban milieu, and intellectual growth is enhanced as well. At the same time, the stratification of society is inevitable. So, too, is a central administration to maintain order, promote public works, provide justice, set regulations—to perform, in short, on a more simplified scale, the functions familiar to city administrators of our own times. Great plazas and avenues were paved, buildings were plastered and painted, subterranean tile drainage systems were provided, waste was disposed of, domestic water supplies were channeled, and the staggering problems of food supply were met.

Traditionally, the Classic period was viewed as having been devoted to moderation and comparative serenity, with order imposed by dominant centers such as Teotihuacán and Monte Albán. These powers, like city-states, carved out spheres of influence that were tolerated by others. We now realize that warfare and human sacrifice were very much a part of the Classic, and that conquest explains why certain city-states were able to exercise sway over surrounding territory. Although much of the evidence for the prevalence of sacrificial practices comes from the Maya area, excavations in central Mexico—even at Teotihuacán—testify to mass executions of warriors and other captives. Classic cities once thought to have lacked fortifications were often built on defensible hilltops. In the art of the Classic, we find images of soldiers, weapons, and slaves. The wide dispersion of a pan-Mesoamerican culture resulted not only from peaceful exchange but also from forceful impositions. The ruling class consisted not only of powerful priests but also of warriors.

The conventional view of relative tranquility has been most discredited in the case of the Classic Maya. Because of important revelations as a result of improved deciphering of Maya hieroglyphic script, the character of these people has been dramatically reassessed. The Maya genius in art, architecture, and science remains clear; nevertheless, the romanticized version of a society ruled by a benevolent and intellectual priesthood, shunning violence and conquest, now rings hollow. Scholars have revealed that aggressive Maya kings during the Classic period regularly made war on their neighbors for both ritualistic and materialistic motives. The most valued prize was another king, who would be humiliated over a period of time, subjected to exquisite tortures, and finally decapitated. These kings, with a profound sense of history, erected monuments to commemorate their victories and to record their lineage. Maya kingdoms tended to be small in scale, controlling limited territory, but at times regional states were able to subdue larger areas and exercise power over several hundreds of thousands. Various constellations of Maya states formed blocs or were interdependent in terms of trade and defense, but the Maya were not politically unified as a whole.

A unifying element in Classic societies was religion. Shaman-priest kings derived their authority from the gods. Priests were guardians of

scientific and genealogical knowledge, and, along with other cultural
leaders like scribes and painters, they held high social status and provided guidance to those below. The pantheon of gods included the omnipresent rain god Tláloc (Chac to the Maya) and Quetzalcóatl, the
Feathered Serpent. To the god of the sun and goddess of the moon
were added deities to celebrate the beneficence of fire, corn, and the
butterfly.

In these polities social cleavage was implicit. There was an order in
which everyone had his assigned place. The individual, unless of the
aristocratic class, counted for little. In this respect social stratification
was like that in other parts of the world, except that the commoners
who supplied tribute in goods and labor may have benefited more from
the calendrical knowledge of their rulers, which helped to ensure good
harvests. Families thus had their daily needs met, and rulers enjoyed
the surpluses. We cannot know how willingly the masses performed
their obligatory duties, but as warfare increased, states commanded
loyalty as long as they could provide a measure of security.

After a spectacular run of several centuries, the Classic world in
Mesoamerica began to deteriorate. Just why the great centers fell is
still a mystery, although some theories have wide acceptance; in the
case of the Maya drought has emerged as a main factor. While some
of the cities went into gradual decline, others, it appears, met a sudden, violent end. Pressures of various kinds impinged on ordered ways:
aggressive nomadic tribes on the peripheries and wars between king-

Small, hairless techichi *dogs from Colima were bred for the table and
were also used as foot-warmers. Molded in various poses, these ceramic pieces are usually in the form of a vessel.*

Poised for action, another Colima figure may represent either a warrior or an athlete.

A bearded musician sings and keeps rhythm with rasps. The clay figure, from the state of Nayarit (A.D. 300–900) is about 20 inches in height.

doms played a role in some cases; demand for increased food supplies, the result of population pressures, crop failures, and possibly soil exhaustion, was another cause. Perhaps an internal disruption was occasioned by a peasants' revolt against the ruling classes, bred by excessive demands or the parasitic priests' inability to mediate successfully with the all-important nature gods. Or were there plagues of some kind? The reasons no doubt vary from place to place, and there may well have been a combination of factors. Scholars lean more and more to explanations that stress overpopulation, environmental destruction, and increasing warfare. In any event, the Golden Age came apart after a long period of human intellectual and cultural achievement.

TEOTIHUACÁN AND ITS SUCCESSORS

Classic Mexico had many important centers, but at least three dominant polities exercised great influence over surrounding regions— Teotihuacán, Monte Albán, and the Maya. The most important city of its time was the immense urban complex of Teotihuacán, "the Place of the Gods," as the Aztecs were to call it. The overall expanse measured at least twelve square miles, in the core of which was the ceremonial center occupying about two square miles. Surrounding this precinct were the sumptuous quarters of the rulers and their retainers, and on the outer fringes the masses resided in apartments and rude dwellings that have long since disappeared. The population of the city at its height of prosperity remains in dispute, but it may have had as many as two hundred thousand inhabitants, making it one of the largest cities in the world at the time. Long after its fall the site was held in reverence and awe by succeeding cultures, and owing to the grandiose dimensions of its stuctures, the Aztecs considered it to have been built by a race of giants.

The origins of the Teotihuacanos are unknown, but by 200 B.C. they had begun to emerge as a powerful kingdom in the central Valley of Mexico. Exceptional urban planning created a colossal city of avenues, a grid system of streets, plazas, markets, temples, palaces, apartment complexes, waterways, and drainage systems. Its main thoroughfare was the Avenue of the Dead, 150 feet wide and stretching over two miles through the heart of the ceremonial center. The most striking monument is the splendid Pyramid of the Sun, measuring over 700 feet at the base lines and rising about 215 feet high. The truncated structure covered a sacred cave reminiscent of origin myths and served as a base for the elevation of a temple on top. It contains no inner chambers but is filled with over a million cubic yards of sun-dried bricks and rubble. The summit, reached after an ascent of 268 steps, offers the breathless viewer a commanding sweep of the surrounding valley. Even so, what we see today is a pale replica of the former magnificence of the Pyramid of the Sun. Its construction probably occupied ten thousand workers for two decades.

Teotihuacán must have been a bustling metropolis, teeming with porters carrying goods to the marketplace, laborers erecting temples, artisans busily engaged with their crafts, and here and there the sober presence of the elegant lords. Along the main avenue were various kinds of edifices covered with lime stucco, painted, and polished. Walkways and courts were paved. There were about one hundred palaces, the largest of which had an estimated three hundred rooms. Some of the salons contained bright frescoes. A ceremonial plaza where the rulers probably lived, covering about thirty-eight acres, now known as the Citadel, was flanked by fifteen low pyramid mounds. Near one end is the Temple of Quetzalcóatl, its incline studded with carved stone projections of the Feathered Serpent and Tláloc that are as phantasmic as medieval gargoyles.

The Pyramid of the Sun at Teotihuacán dominates the extensive ruins of the ancient city.

The dominance of Teotihuacán was so extensive that some scholars have discussed it in terms of an empire, believing its hegemony, based in part on its monopoly of obsidian, so necessary to daily life and ritual, to have been as broad as that of the later Aztecs. In any event, its trading network reached from parts of northern Mexico down into Guatemala, and artisans from Monte Albán and other distant places resided there, crafting exotic goods. Undoubtedly heavily influenced by Teotihuacán, nonetheless, Monte Albán and the Maya culture remained independent of this metropolitan power. Within its sphere the impact of that great city consisted not only in its cultural imperialism with respect to art and architecture but also in its religious dominance, for it was a mecca to which pilgrims traveled from far away. Ruling the pantheon of gods was Quetzalcóatl, by this time a deity almost universal in the Mexican world. Although the Feathered Serpent was venerated as a giver of learning and even of life, the construction of his temple at Teotihuacán was accompanied by mass human sacrifice, undermining the legend that Quetzalcóatl abhorred the practice.

Carved stone images of the rain god Tláloc and Quetzalcóatl on the Temple of Quetzalcóatl at Teotihuacán.

Detail of a plumed serpent head. The eyes at one time held red jewels, long since plucked out by vandals.

For some reason, perhaps related to an agricultural debacle, decline set in, inviting incursions by barbarians on the northern frontier. About A.D. 600 a weakened Teotihuacán suffered desecration and partial burning—apparently by its own inhabitants. The fall of the mightiest center was the first casualty in the gradual decay of the Classic world in Mexico.

With the Teotihuacano culture dissipated, central Mexico lost its focus. A number of other states emerged but commanded smaller spheres of influence. Cholula in the modern state of Puebla was a holy city and a large center of considerable importance. While tradition has it that 365 Christian chapels were later built over the ruins of pagan temples, the actual number is closer to seventy. The nature of the city's relationship with Teotihuacán is not entirely clear, but it seems to have been close. The center was dominated by its massive pyramid, the largest single monument in Indian America, with a total volume greater than that of Egypt's Pyramid of Cheops. It was a sanctuary of Quetzalcóatl, and many of the refugees from Teotihuacán fled to Cholula, which continued to flourish until it fell to invaders about A.D. 800.

Other successor states like Xochicalco in Morelos and Cacaxtla in Puebla were built on mountaintops and manifest the alarming escalation of militarism that developed in Mexico in the Late Classic period. Striking combinations of Teotihuacán and Maya influences are revealed at these sites, nowhere more graphically than in the beautifully painted murals that have been discovered at Cacaxtla since the 1970s.

El Tajín in Veracruz had extensive influence along the Gulf coast. A dramatic example of its unique architecture is the Pyramid of Niches, of which there is one for each day of the year. The vigorous life at Tajín included bloody rites that anticipated the terror of the Post-Classic period. The ball game *ollama* was an ancient tradition that became an obsession with these lowland peoples. Most of the prominent centers in Mexico had ball courts, and Tajín had no fewer than eleven. Along each side of the court (which could vary considerably in length, according to the culture) was a wall on which a stone ring was fixed. Two teams played, the object being to keep the seven- to eight-inch solid rubber ball out of the opponents' possession and, if possible, to hit the ball through one of the rings. Scoring was exceedingly difficult, not only because the ring was small and high but also because the players could not hit the ball with their hands. Often they were allowed to use only their hips, although rules differed according to time and place. The athletes wore padding in vulnerable spots, as the flying ball could kill if struck with sufficient force. Contests were played with great enthusiasm, and on some occasions large sums were wagered. Ollama was more than a game, however; it was a sacred ritual in imitation of the movement of celestial bodies and associated with human fate. On occasion the teams represented political factions. So seriously was the contest taken that the losing captain was sometimes sacrificed, as scenes on the architectural friezes depict. A variation on the agreement was that the losers became slaves of the victors.

Not as well researched and understood are the peoples who created monumental architecture and exquisite artifacts of ceramic, jade, and stone in the Occidente (west Mexico, including Nayarit, Jalisco, and Colima). Sharing characteristics and some gods with other pre-Hispanic Mesoamerican cultures, these groups also created very distinctive works, including shaft tombs, circular pyramidal structures and plazas, wetland gardens, and copper tools.

MONTE ALBÁN

From its lofty eminence thirteen hundred feet above the valley floor, Monte Albán, the creation of the Zapotecs, dominated surrounding Oaxaca for centuries. Less grand in scale than its contemporary

The Pyramid of the Niches, El Tajín, state of Veracruz.

Teotihuacán, it was nevertheless spacious, poised on a rocky shelf over three thousand feet long and half again as wide. Urban construction was carried out at great cost in human effort, because all materials, and even water, had to be hauled up the mountainsides. Grouped around its great paved plaza were many temples, platforms, and low pyramids, along with sunken patios. Surrounding the center were many separate *barrios* (neighborhoods) of houses terraced into the hillsides. The early evolution of Zapotec urban society at Monte Albán between 500 and 100 B.C. reflects Olmec influence. At the top of the social hierarchy that strictly separated nobles and commoners were a hereditary king and a hereditary high priest. The king controlled noble administrators who ruled the surrounding towns in Oaxaca. By the fourth century, higher population density and military strength had been employed through colonization, conquest, and alliance building to bring more distant provinces into Monte Albán's tribute-paying orbit. Skilled diplomacy enabled the Zapotecs to coexist peacefully with Teotihuacán, but between A.D. 400 and 700 Monte Albán lost its dominant position in Oaxaca, as subject towns—especially those in more defensible positions and better agricultural locations—grew in size and asserted their

A ball court at Monte Albán. The ball game of ollama (tlachtli) *was played in many different cultures, although the rules and courts varied somewhat.*

autonomy. In decentralized fashion, through Zapotec marriage alliances with neighboring Mixtecs at Mitla, both groups continued to exercise influence in Oaxaca for many centuries.

THE MAYA

Of all the Classic groups, the Maya have generally been considered the most brilliant. But while their luster is not diminished, they were not the first great civilization in Mesoamerica. Although the Maya in the Pacific coastal plain and highland areas created marketing and ceremonial centers with temple architecture as early as 400 B.C., their greatest florescence came later, occurring between A.D. 250 and 800, primarily in the southern lowlands of present-day Guatemala and Honduras.

An overview of Monte Albán in Oaxaca, showing its platforms and expansive plazas.

Incised on stone slabs, curious figures who seem to be dancing are a feature of Monte Albán. They are called danzantes and are believed to represent the bodies of slain enemies.

The Classic Maya had many important centers, no one of which completely dominated the others. A number of regional states, each composed of a capital city and subject towns, competed with each other, expanding and contracting over time in response to changing fortunes of war and trade. Defeated kingdoms supplied rulers for sacrifice and tribute in goods and slaves to conquering cities. Trade with Teotihuacán was accompanied by bride exchanges and the incorporation of art and architectural styles from this northern neighbor. The Petén in northern Guatemala could be said to be the heartland of the Classic Maya, but they also lived in the Mexican states of Chiapas, Tabasco, Campeche, and Yucatán, as well as in Quintana Roo. The development of Classic Maya centers reflected an increasing emphasis on the lineage of hereditary kings who were supported by a noble class of warriors and intellectuals; below them artisans, skilled laborers, and peasant farmers were responsible for producing the luxury items enjoyed by the aristocracy as well as the basic staples of maize, beans, and vegetables that sustained the entire society. We know much more about the lifestyles of elites who are depicted through a variety of Maya art forms. Their esthetic sensibilities appear in elaborate ornamentation in dress and jewelry (often

PRINCIPAL ARCHAEOLOGICAL SITES

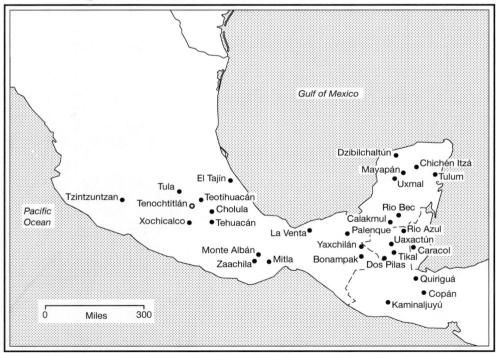

fashioned from jade), cranial deformation that flattened and slanted the head both front and back, filed teeth, and extensive body tattooing.

For many years, archaeologists believed the lowland Maya cities to have been primarily ceremonial, reasoning that the surrounding jungle could not have supported large populations with slash-and-burn agriculture. Extensive archaeological excavation demonstrated, however, that these areas were densely populated and that the Maya also used raised fields, terracing, and kitchen gardens to augment the production of corn and other foodstuffs. Like Teotihuacán and Monte Albán, the Maya had a vigorous ceramic tradition and produced lovely polychrome bowls and cylinders that recorded mundane events. In their exotic murals and bas-reliefs, however, they tended less to the geometric designs of central Mexico and more to the depiction of the human form, often rendered with superb draftsmanship. In 2001, archaeologists discovered in the northern Petén what is thought to be the oldest intact Maya mural. Over two thousand years old, its red, black, and yellow colors depict the resurrection of the corn god. The great fluidity and exuberance of Maya art gives it a baroque quality, whether in stone or stucco. Of the fascinating pictorial manuscripts, only four survived the ravages of time, climate, insects, and the fires of Spanish clergymen.

The Maya stand as the premier scientists of ancient America, noted for their independent invention of a positional numeration system based on the mathematical concept for zero. Just as impressive were their achievements in calendars and writing. Like other Mexican calendars, theirs had 365 days; in addition, a ceremonial calendar had 260 days. The Maya accurately observed the movements of celestial bodies and recorded them to aid in predicting future phenomena; they also inscribed hieroglyphic texts on stone pillars (stelae), facades, and stairways. These inscriptions recorded historical events and were intended to highlight the ancestral privilege of Maya kings (and occasionally queens) who were also the incarnation of local sacred knowledge. In ceremonies of self-mutilation, Maya rulers ritually shed blood from their own penis, ear, lips, and tongue, symbolically manifesting the life force that also substantiated their lineage and power. They were particularly obsessed with engraving their triumphs in stone. Recent progress in deciphering Maya writing has revealed that highly learned scribes, responsible for recording these histories, occupied the highest rank of Maya society.

The pantheon of Maya deities included four lords who held the earth and sky apart at the four cardinal directions. Life had emerged from an underworld of darkness and death due to the sun deity's daily travels through a triple-layered cosmos.

In dark hardwood, this unusual carving depicts a dignified worthy from the Tabasco Maya culture. It dates from the early Classic period.

The Temple of the Sun at Palenque is framed by thick jungle growth.

Although central Mexican pyramids are usually solid, without interior chambers, to the south temple-pyramids of the Maya sometimes contain tombs like the one shown here at Palenque's "Temple of the Inscriptions."

The metropolis of the Maya Classic was Tikal, with a population of about fifty thousand. It is one of the earliest sites, settled in the Formative period long before A.D. 292, the date of the earliest inscription. Set in a clearing of Guatemala's Petén jungle, Tikal is dominated by six great pyramids, including the tallest of any in the Maya civilization, towering 230 feet. The inner precinct covers more than a square mile, with other ceremonial edifices surrounding the core for a considerable distance. Aside from the usual temples, palaces, plazas, and ball courts, Tikal had ten reservoirs and was beautified by artificial lakes.

The Maya temple-pyramids were designed architecturally and artistically to proclaim the power of the site and glorify the rulers. Their

A superb stucco head with an elegant headdress found at the Temple of the Inscriptions at Palenque.

A pot-bellied, seed-filled ceramic rat-
tle from the Maya culture on the
small island of Jaina, off the coast of
Campeche.

Of the same Maya culture is this
whistle, in the form of an embracing
couple.

brilliantly decorated masonry, roof combs, statuary, and interior murals exhibit highly sophisticated craftsmanship. The cultural achievements of the Maya, from astronomy and calendars to architecture and
art, were fruits of their understanding and legitimation of a complex
cosmic order.

As the largest of the Classic Maya city-states, Tikal and Calakmul
were rivals in dominating large areas of the Maya lowlands in which
Dos Pilas played an important role. Recent excavations have also highlighted the importance of the affluent trading center of Cancuén on
the Pasión river in Guatemala. Other major Classic era kingdoms were
Copán in Honduras and Piedras Negras in Guatemala. Yaxchilán, in
the modern state of Chiapas, is known for its great central plaza, a
thousand feet long. Palenque (Chiapas), though relatively small, is considered the gem of the Maya cities because of its exquisite sculpture.
The bas-relief work there shows the art in its highest form. Although
of minor importance in most respects, Bonampak (Chiapas) contains

the most illustrious of the Maya murals, brilliantly depicting the aftermath of a battle, captives, and sacrifice. One of the earliest Maya
murals, discovered in 2001 in the Petén lowlands of Guatemala, dates
from A.D. 100 and reveals a complex iconography crucial for understanding Maya kingship and society.

There may have been no common cause for the decline of all the
Classic Maya centers, scattered as they were over considerable distances, although drought seems to have been the key factor. Explanations have tended to highlight demographic and ecological stress
resulting from rapidly growing populations and intensification of agriculture. Population densities may have been as high as six hundred per
square mile in some places. It is also possible that commoners rose up
in rebellion against increasing demands from their overlords. But there
is growing evidence that warfare—which escalated dramatically in the
Late Classic along with human sacrifice—was also a significant cause.
Foreign intrusion from other Maya areas probably capitalized on the
instability that prevailed after A.D. 800. By 900 most of the southern
lowland cities were abandoned as many Mayas fled north to the Yucatán Peninsula. Others moved back into the surrounding countryside
where they and their descendants have continued to farm for centuries.
Their "lost" cities were reclaimed by the jungle until archaeologists began to excavate the lichen-mottled ruins nearly a thousand years later.
Thus the Classic world in Mesoamerica folded, but in its demise were
alarming portents of what was to follow.

RECOMMENDED FOR FURTHER STUDY

Adams, Richard E. W., ed. *The Origins of Maya Civilization.* Albuquerque: Univer-
    sity of New Mexico Press, 1977.
Bassie-Sweet, Karen. *At the Edge of the World: Caves and Late Classic Maya World
    View.* Norman: University of Oklahoma Press, 1996.
Coe, Michael D. *Mexico: From the Olmecs to the Aztecs.* London: Thames and Hud-
    son, 1994.
Culbert, T. P., ed. *The Classic Maya Collapse.* Albuquerque: University of New Mex-
    ico Press, 1977.
Doolittle, William E. *Canal Irrigation in Prehistoric Mexico: The Sequence of Tech-
    nological Change.* Austin: University of Texas Press, 1990.
Florescano, Enrique. *The Myth of Quetzalcoatl.* Translated by Lisa Hochroth. Balti-
    more: Johns Hopkins University Press, 1999.
Foster, Michael S., and Shirley Gorenstein. *Greater Mesoamerica: The Archaeology
    of West and Northwest Mexico.* Salt Lake City: University of Utah Press, 2000.
Freidel, David, Linda Schele, and Joy Parker. *Maya Cosmos: Three Thousand Years
    on the Shaman's Path.* New York: William Morrow & Co., 1993.
Graulich, Michel. *Myths of Ancient Mexico.* Norman: University of Oklahoma Press,
    1997.

Joyce, Rosemary. *Gender and Power in Prehispanic Mesoamerica.* Austin: University of Texas Press, 2000.

Kubler, George. *Art and Architecture of Ancient America.* Harmondsworth and Baltimore: Pelican, 1984.

Marcus, Joyce, and Kent V. Flannery. *Zapotec Civilization: How Urban Society Evolved in Mexico's Oaxaca Valley.* London: Thames and Hudson, 1994.

Proskouriakoff, Tatiana. *Maya History.* Edited by Rosemary A. Joyce. Austin: University of Texas Press, 1993.

Scarborough, Vernon L., and David R. Wilcox. *The Mesoamerican Ballgame.* Tucson: University of Arizona Press, 1991.

Schele, Linda, and David Friedel. *A Forest of Kings: The Untold Story of the Ancient Maya.* New York: William Morrow & Co., 1990.

Sharer, Robert J., ed. *The Ancient Maya,* 6th ed. Stanford, Calif.: Stanford University Press, 2005.

3

Times of Trouble:
Post-Classic Mexico

The order imposed by Teotihuacán's dominance during the Classic period gave way to a fragmentation of power among the transition centers in areas north of the Mayas. Details of history in the Valley of Mexico are nebulous from A.D. 650 to 900, but one has the impression of confusion and a great shifting of peoples in the waning decades of the Classic, when aggressive city-states—Cholula, Xochicalco, and El Tajín—vied for control, but none succeeded in bringing about unity and order. Then gradually a new period emerges, with more secular and more martial characteristics.

The Post-Classic era began about A.D. 900 and lasted until the Spanish Conquest in the early sixteenth century. New states had significant commercial interests, as evidenced by the expansion of market systems. Long-distance exchange tended to make artistic styles more uniform and less imaginative. New technology could be seen in cotton quilted armor and the bow and arrow, but, in general, technological innovation slowed. Although metallurgy was introduced, probably from South America, its use was very limited. Gold and silver were fashioned into beautiful jewelry and copper was used in the manufacture of various tools and to cover the tips of arrow shafts.

An even more striking change during the Post-Classic was that the militaristic propensities of the Late Classic continued to grow, enhancing the prestige of warriors and fostering the conquest of tribute-paying subjects. Religion itself was marked by the rising importance of frightful gods thought to require ever-increasing quantities of the "divine liquid"—human blood. Human sacrifice proliferated as both elites and commoners became convinced that only the offering of massive and sustained quantities of this life force to the gods could prevent cosmic disaster.

Taking A.D. 900 as the pivotal date introducing the Post-Classic, we discern the emergence of historical central Mexico; for while earlier history must be deduced cautiously from archaeological evidence alone, there are in this period the beginnings of written records in which individuals appear with more clarity. But although there are now pegs upon which to drape our historical fabric, accounts are manifestly shot through with myths; thus some details vary with the telling, and many versions are vague and fragmentary at best.

THE TOLTECS

The great city of Teotihuacán, situated on the northern edge of the lake, had served as a buffer between civilized Mexico and the nomadic peoples of the north. With the fall of that stronghold, however, the frontier was breached by vigorous warriors from the arid lands beyond. The northern tribes, consisting of many diverse groups, were known by the generic term *Chichimecs,* which meant, literally, "People of Dog Lineage," a designation that could convey attributes both positive (skilled in fighting) and negative (lacking the culture of settled society and thus barbaric). Among these groups were the Tolteca-Chichimeca, or Toltecs, who may have come from southern Zacatecas. At the beginning of the tenth century legend has it that they swept into the central valley led by Mixcóatl (Cloud Serpent), a Mexican Ghengis Khan who swiftly scattered his demoralized opponents. After establishing his capital at Culhuacán and successfully extending his power, the resourceful Mixcóatl was assassinated by his brother, who seized leadership for himself.

Mixcóatl's pregnant wife fled into exile, where she died on giving birth to a son. The boy was given the name Ce Acatl Topiltzin (Ce Acatl meaning "One Reed," the year of his birth, perhaps A.D. 947, and Topiltzin meaning "Our Prince"), and he would become the cultural hero of foremost proportions in ancient Mexico. He became a devotee of the ancient god Quetzalcóatl and later, as a high priest of the cult, he assumed the name of his deity.

Upon reaching manhood, Topiltzin-Quetzalcóatl killed in single combat his uncle, Mixcóatl's assassin, and made himself lord of the Toltecs. Topiltzin-Quetzalcóatl eventually removed his capital some fifty miles northwest of the present Mexico City to a remote site on the frontier. There, around A.D. 968, he founded the splendid city of Tula, the most important city in the long interim between the fall of Teotihuacán and the later rise of Aztec Tenochtitlán. The Toltecs continued to incorporate northern nomads and gradually absorbed the more advanced ways of central Mexico. From their new capital they played a key role in the obsidian trade and asserted power over most of central Mexico and beyond. Although their hegemony lasted only about two centuries, their prestige was such that the name Toltec pervaded the consciousness of the land for five hundred years.

Less extensive than Teotihuacán, Tula was certainly more grandiose than its ruins today indicate. Palace interiors were decked with the brilliant plumage of exotic birds, while various salons were lined with sheets of gold, jewels, and rare seashells. Residents' ears were soothed by the sweet singing of pet birds. This version of paradise on earth was embellished in the retelling over the centuries; it accounts, in part, for the curiously persistent Toltec mystique.

The honeyed tradition notwithstanding, all was not peace and light at Tula. Two religious traditions evolved in the Toltec empire, emblematic of conflict in Mesoamerican society. The ancestral supreme deity of the Toltecs was Tezcatlipoca (Smoking Mirror, or Shining Smoke), an invisible and unpredictable god who was feared—and never crossed. His adherents resented the exaltation of the foreign god Quetzalcóatl introduced by Topiltzin. The deity-impersonator priests of Tezcatlipoca bided their time, conspiring against the heresy.

The Feathered Serpent is purported by legend to have been gratified only by modest sacrifices of butterflies, birds, or snakes and offerings of jade, incense, or merely tortillas. Tezcatlipoca, on the other hand, demanded human hearts. His followers sought by various deceits to discredit the high priest of Quetzalcóatl. According to one account, Tezcatlipoca, in disguise, gained entrance to the house of Topiltzin, who was ill. At first the ruler refused an offer of "medicine," which was, in fact, the strong drink of *pulque,* made from undistilled cactus juice. Finally persuaded to take a sip, the innocent Topiltzin found it pleasing and asked for more. At length inebriated by five cupfuls, the lord of Tula awoke the next morning on a mat beside his sister. Having broken his priestly vows and disgraced himself by the sins of drunkenness and incest, he prepared to go into exile after almost twenty years of enlightened rule.

The benevolent reign of Topiltzin-Quetzalcóatl at Tula thus came to a close, but he does not disappear from history. He and his followers traveled to the holy city of Cholula, and in 987 they are said to have sailed across the Gulf of Mexico to the land of the Maya. The legendary exit of the great Topiltzin-Quetzalcóatl is appropriate, if fantastic: he coasted down a river to the sea in a raft of serpents, after which he flashed into the heavens to become the morning star.

A more prosaic denouement, though heavily laden with the most serious implications, is the more credible version. When Topiltzin and his partisans left Tula for their long odyssey, they marked their way by shooting arrows through saplings, leaving crosslike signs. Later he sent

The ingenuous Topiltzin-Quetzalcóatl is deceived by the crafty Tezcatlipoca.

word that he would return from where the sun rose to take back his rightful throne in the year Ce Acatl, which recurred cyclically. By some accounts, he was of fair complexion and bearded. All of this would be of immense significance when, five centuries later, the Spaniards—white, bearded, and wearing crosses—appeared on the eastern horizon. The year was 1519—and Ce Acatl.

Meanwhile, with the success of the militant Tezcatlipoca faction at Tula, a new order of things evolved. While the reputation of the Toltecs as great architects was secure (the Aztecs named them Toltecs, meaning "Artificers"), a new and grotesque image of them was revealed in later works. Themes of death and destruction are evident in the Chacmools—reclining human figures with basins on their stomachs to receive human hearts—and a "serpent wall" that shows rattlesnakes devouring human skeletons. Towering statues of impassive warrior figures, sixteen to eighteen feet tall, appeared on top of temples, and friezes symbolized the military orders of the jaguar and eagle, the latter of which were shown devouring human hearts. Tula nourished two traditions that persisted until the coming of the Spaniards—an excess of human sacrifice and the forceful conquest of other states. Yet many questions persist about the size and nature of the alleged Toltec "empire."

From the late eleventh century to 1156, drought and famine struck the Toltecs. Wars and internal social conflict further weakened the state until, in desperation, the people even turned to the worship of their enemies' alien deities. Evidence of fire throughout the site may

Giant stone warriors at Tula were manifestations of the militaristic spirit that came to dominate the Toltecs.

explain the onset of the Toltec diaspora, with people spreading in many directions. The collapse of Tula was very significant for Mexico: once again the northern march between the sedentary peoples of the Valley and the northern "barbarians" was left unguarded. Not long after, new groups descended upon this wonder of the Post-Classic world and subjected Tula to brutal desecration.

THE ZAPOTECS AND MIXTECS

To the south, following the abandonment of Monte Albán in Oaxaca, the Zapotecs remained a vigorous culture with many important centers. Their capital was at Zaachila, but the site that interests us most is Mitla, built roughly the same time as Tula. Mitla was a comparatively small religious and military base. What one sees there, however, is a jewel of Mexican architecture. Surrounding a modest courtyard are white temples with walls of marvelous design—thousands of small pieces of cut stone, fitted together with a precision requiring no mortar, form mosaics of dazzling geometric patterns. Opening off the patios are subterranean passages leading to crypts. Although the site is in an exposed area, set apart some distance is the hill fortress, a grim reminder of the intense warfare that had overtaken Post-Classic Mexico.

A palace at Mitla.

Detail of the palace showing the intricate geometric designs formed by precision stone cutting.

To the areas west and north of the Zapotecs were a remarkable people who inhabited the mountainous regions, the Mixtecs, or Cloud People. The Mixtecs were certainly influenced by the Toltecs, some of whom apparently infiltrated after the fall of Tula. By the thirteenth century the Mixtecs were penetrating eastward into Zapotec territories, and, primarily by marrying into the Zapotec royalty, they eventually came to dominate their neighbors. At times they occupied many of the Zapotec sites, including Monte Albán and Mitla.

Mixtec artistic achievements are extraordinary in the exquisite decoration of their temple complexes. Among the treasures they gave us is the richest collection extant of picture *códices* in Mexico. These pictographic "books" are executed in brilliant colors on deerskin (the books of the Maya and others were made of vegetable fiber). They are also valuable historical sources. One gives data reaching back to A.D. 692, providing the earliest historical narrative of any society in the land. Mixtec códices also tell us that by the early years of the eighth century militaristic city-states had formed. Following the appearance of metallurgy around A.D. 1000, the Mixtecs became, in addition, the foremost jewelers in Mexico, fashioning delicate pieces in gold and silver.

THE POST-CLASSIC MAYA

Coincident with the final disintegration of the Maya Classic period by around A.D. 900 was a rising Maya cultural phenomenon on the peninsula of Yucatán. That peninsula is a limestone shelf, flat with some rolling, brush-covered hills, a land without surface rivers. With its thin soil and dependence for water on the *cenotes*, the sinkholes created by the collapse of underground caverns, it was an unlikely location for an agricultural people. Maya groups had inhabited Yucatán for many centuries B.C., but their achievements had not matched those of the southern Maya who flourished during the Classic era.

Beginning in the tenth century, the ancestral Yucatec Maya culture was adulterated by outside influences of peoples stigmatized as "foreigners." Some of the newcomers were undoubtedly refugees from the deserted Classic areas. The invigorating force that gave impulse to the new hybrid style in Yucatán appears to have been Toltec, but the nature of the relationship between Tula and the dominant early Post-Classic center of Chichén Itzá is still disputed. A prevalent explanation is that the banished Topiltzin-Quetzalcóatl and his followers actually made it to Chichén Itzá in 987 and imposed Toltec rule. Others believe

This unusual ceramic vessel, created in the Classic Period, is in the form of a stylized monkey wearing a startled expression.

A Mixtec vase from Zaachila. Representations of death were and still are common and are often treated lightly.

Zapotec bat god (Dios Murciélago).

that the northern attributes may have been brought earlier by coastal
Putun and Chontal Maya invaders who had been heavily influenced
by non-Maya cultures of the Gulf coast and central Mexico.

The "Toltec" period in the Yucatán peninsula lasted from about 900
to 1150. For much of that time, Chichén Itzá was allied with the cities
of Mayapán and Uxmal although it dominated the alliance as a result
of its successes in trade and military exploits. Warfare and human sacrifice were common, but whether they actually increased as a result of
central Mexican influence is unknown. Certainly these practices were
already widespread among the Yucatecan Mayas' neighbors to the
south in the Late Classic. The art and architecture of Chichén Itzá are

During the period of Toltec rule, curious Chacmool figures appeared at Chichén Itzá.

undoubtedly evocative of the militant spirit of Tula with warrior motifs, images of the Feathered Serpent, the forest of columns, and Chacmools. Among the monuments of Post-Classic Maya centers, those of Chichén Itzá are the most widely known. Like the sculptures, they are esthetically less pleasing than works of the Classic Maya. Uxmal, however, has structures of great beauty. Its Palace of the Governor is considered by many to be the most elegant of pre-Hispanic architecture.

Mesoamerican influence promoted the inclusion of Quetzalcóatl (called Kukulcán by the Maya) in the pantheon of local deities. Among

A great ball court in the Maya style at Chichén Itzá. Scores were seldom made by knocking the ball through the high ring. This city had six ball courts, one of which, the largest in Mesoamerica, measures 480 by 120 feet.

the most important were the fire god Itzamná, the rain god Chac, and the gods of corn and the sun. Into the great Sacred Cenote, a well measuring some two hundred feet across at the mouth, victims (although infrequently the virgins so dear to modern tradition) were cast, along with jewels and other valuables, to appease the rain god. Human sacrifice continued to increase in the Post-Classic period, but the practice never reached the excesses that were to overtake central Mexico.

Detail of the carved stone ring.

A heavily padded Maya ball player is portrayed in this graceful sculpture from Jaina.

A reconstruction of Chichén Itzá shows the broad thoroughfare leading from the Temple of Kukulcán to the Sacred Cenote (well).

Some authorities believe that the elitist priestly class lost considerable political and cultural influence to rising utilitarian merchants. But increasing repression by the militarists led to rebellion. In the subsequent fighting between Chichén Itzá and Mayapán, the latter emerged the victor. After some two centuries the Mayapán League broke apart, but the wonder is that it lasted as long as it did, considering its conflicting economic and political interests.

Henceforth a dozen cities of northern Yucatán were dominated by Mayapán, and, from 1200 or so until about 1450, a period of general decline set in. The new rulers established a strongly centralized regime maintained by Mexican mercenaries, by intermarriage, and by forcing all local chiefs from outlying areas to reside in Mayapán as hostages. Under this tyranny the capital was a walled city within which the inhabitants lived for security, while the economy was less oriented to agriculture and trade than to the parasitical dependence on tribute paid by subject towns. In the two and a half centuries there was a general lowering of standards: building construction was not only shoddy but devoid of beauty, hieroglyphic inscriptions ceased, and it seems that athletes even stopped playing the sacred ball game. Elsewhere, in the highland Maya areas of

The Temple of Kukulcán, also known as "El Castillo."

Guatemala, other groups claiming descent from the Toltecs established kingdoms. These Quiché and Cakchiquel warriors would pose a formidable challenge to the conquering Spaniards in the sixteenth century.

The shattering of Mayapán hegemony resulted in the decentralization of the Yucatec Maya, in which some sixteen petty city-states clung feebly to the vestiges of the distant past. The neglected cities fell into ruin, sometimes hastened by vicious and wanton destruction by marauders. To the casualties of war were added, during the last half of the fifteenth century, the victims of plagues and a disastrous hurricane. When the first Spanish adventurers arrived in the Yucatán Peninsula a few decades later, they found the descendants of the former grandeur that was the Maya civilization for so many centuries. These Maya commoners—having been let down once again by their own rulers—had taken refuge in their familiar traditions of maize cultivation, family, and community life. Could they imagine that the latest variation in the cyclical pattern of conquest would bring anything new?

Despite their amazing skills, the Maya architects never developed the true arch; however, a corbeled vault of the type pictured here served much the same purpose. This is the magnificent Palace of the Governor at Uxmal, measuring more than 320 feet in length and 25 feet in height.

RECOMMENDED FOR FURTHER STUDY

Byland, Bruce E., and John M.D. Pohl. *In the Realm of Eight Deer: The Archeology of Mixtec Codices.* Norman: University of Oklahoma Press, 1994.

Diehl, Richard A. *Tula: The Toltec Capital of Ancient Mexico.* London: Thames and Hudson, 1983.

Flannery, Kent V., and Joyce Marcus, eds. *The Cloud People: Divergent Evolution of the Zapotec and Mixtec Civilizations.* New York: Academic Press, 1983.

Fox, John W. *Maya Postclassic State Formation.* New York: Cambridge University Press, 1987.

Kelemen, Pál. *Art of the Americas, Ancient and Hispanic.* New York: Crowell, 1969.

Monaghan, John. *The Covenants of Earth and Rain: Exchange, Sacrifice, and Revelation in Mixtec Sociality.* Norman: University of Oklahoma Press, 1995.

Robertson, Donald. *Mexican Manuscript Painting of the Early Colonial Period.* Norman: University of Oklahoma Press, 1994.

Sanders, William T., Jeffrey R. Parsons, and Robert S. Santley. *The Basin of Mexico: Ecological Processes in the Evolution of a Civilization.* New York: Academic Press, 1979.

Schroeder, Susan. *Chimalpahin and the Kingdom of Chalco.* Tucson: University of Arizona Press, 1991.

Sharer, Robert J. *Daily Life in Maya Civilization.* Westport, Conn.: Greenwood Press, 1996.

Spores, Ronald. *The Mixtecs in Ancient and Colonial Times.* Norman: University of Oklahoma Press, 1985.

Thompson, J. Eric S. *The Rise and Fall of Maya Civilization.* Norman: University of Oklahoma Press, 1966.

4

The Rise of the Aztecs

The high Valley of Anáhuac—the Indian name for the Valley of Mexico, meaning "near the water"—was a compelling lure to wandering peoples seeking a more abundant life. With its equable climate and system of interconnecting lakes bordered by forests full of wild game, it was especially attractive to the nomads of the arid north. Because of its central location the Valley had been, from ancient times, a corridor through which tribes of diverse cultures passed—and sometimes remained. This cultural mélange produced a rich environment for the exchange of ideas and skills. Moreover, traders and merchants introduced exotic products from the coasts and other regions, thereby adding to the variety of life. At the same time, alien groups were frequently hostile, so that the lake country was periodically upset by violence. In the twelfth century, new city-states developed in the Valley of Mexico, interacting with each other, sometimes peacefully, sometimes aggressively. Throughout Mesoamerica, the links between polities multiplied in shifting relationships of exchange and political domination. In this network, central Mexico occupied the most influential position.

AZTEC PREDECESSORS

With the power vacuum created by the collapse of Tula in the twelfth century, several groups of Nahuatl-speaking Chichimecs entered the Valley from the north. By the early thirteenth century the Valley was teeming with activity and becoming increasingly crowded, with many of the attendant pressures so familiar to us today. It was an age of anxiety and tension. The first invader groups quickly staked out their claims, and later arrivals found little available space. The early Chichimecs settled in the proximity of established towns populated by remnants of Toltec refugees whose culture retained more complex Mesoamerican features. The phenomenon so familiar in history occurred: the recently arrived hunter-gatherers gradually adopted the more advanced ways of their sedentary neighbors.

Most prominent of the early invader chieftains was Xólotl (Monster), who arrived with his people in 1244. These Chichimecs established themselves at Tenayuca and came to dominate this northern part of the Valley through aggressive warfare based on the use of the bow and arrow. Under Xólotl (1244–1304), the crude northerners adopted features of the surrounding sedentary towns, imitating their dwellings, clothing, and agricultural practices. In 1246, they conquered the prestigious city of Culhuacán, and Xólotl married his son Nopaltzin (Revered Prickly Pear) to a princess of the vanquished Toltecs. Nahuatl was becoming the *lingua franca* of the Valley.

The Tepanecs, other invaders who had arrived in the Valley in 1230, recognized Xólotl as overlord. For their service as mercenaries, the Tepanecs received land grants enabling them to extend their influence from their capital of Atzcapotzalco on the western side of Lake Texcoco. The key figure of Tepanec expansion was Tezozómoc who made Atzcapotzalco the most powerful center in the Valley in the fourteenth century. Employing deceit, dynastic marriages, violence, and treachery, this tyrant expanded Tepanec territory with the conquests of Tenayuca, Culhuacán, Xochimilco, and Cuauhnáhuac (now Cuernavaca). Tezozómoc vanquished the city of Texcoco in the early fifteenth century and brutally skewered its ruler Ixtilzóchitl with spears in full view of his young son, Nezahualcóyotl (Fasting Coyote), who was concealed in a tree. Through the politics of terror, the Tepanecs broadened their sovereignty in the Valley.

THE AZTEC RISE TO POWER

The irruption of the Chichimecs from the arid north included one group that engages our attention above all others. While they called themselves the Mexica (pronounced "Mesheeka"), they have become more commonly known as the Aztecs. No tribe of record had more humble beginnings and rose to such heights in so short a time. Over the long view of pre-Hispanic Mexico, they must be regarded as upstarts, latecomers on the scene. The last of the important nomadic groups to enter the Valley, they were beginning to acquire some notoriety about two hundred years prior to the Spanish Conquest, but their rise to great power occurred less than a century before the advent of Cortés in 1519.

The origins of the Aztecs are apparently found on an island they called Aztlán, somewhere to the northwest of the Valley, from which many tribes wandered southward. Historical accounts for the first decades following their departure from Aztlán, evidently in A.D. 1111, are fragmentary and unreliable, for, once secure, the Aztecs destroyed all the records and reconstructed their history with accounts favorable to themselves. Like other Nahua groups who entered the Valley before them, the Aztecs eventually evolved official histories linking their migration stories with marriages that established (however spuriously) their prestigious Toltec connections.

The Aztecs' great search for the promised land logically enough led them toward the verdant intermontane basin of Anáhuac, but they arrived there only after many decades of wandering. Somewhere along the way they came to conceive of themselves as a messianic people, the chosen of the gods. They pressed on, inspired by visions of their imperial destiny and by the persistent twitterings of their strange hummingbird god. Their supreme deity was the terrible Huitzilopochtli (Hummingbird on the Left), god of war and the sun, who slew his sister Coyolxauhqui after she killed their mother, Coatlicue. He then proceeded to devour Coatlicue's heart.

At length these nomads made their way into the Valley of Mexico, where they found a cold reception. To begin with, all the lands were already carved up into various city-states. The Aztecs were perceived as unwelcome squatters, a boorish, uncouth lot, disposed to all sorts of vulgarities. They were held in disdain by the more refined farming residents of the Valley, who encouraged the newcomers to keep moving. It seems as if the Aztecs purposely sought to anger others with some repugnant habits (which included gruesome human sacrifices) and their outrageous practice of stealing their neighbors' wives. But however much the farming peoples of the Valley were repulsed by the interlopers, they also learned (sometimes the hard way) to entertain a healthy respect for them. The Aztecs were a young, vigorous people, hungry and ambitious. They were also superb warriors, whose fighting abilities did not go unnoticed by the ruling warlords of the Valley. Consequently, it was as mercenaries exploiting the tenuous balance of power in Anáhuac that the Aztecs first achieved recognition.

From the 1270s to the year 1319 the Aztecs maintained a precarious existence, occupying the hill of Chapultepec (now a park in Mexico City). They continued in their aggressive ways, and the leaders of some of the principal towns decided to deal with them once and for all. They drove the intruders from Chapultepec and sacrificed the Aztec chief and his daughter. The survivors escaped by concealing themselves in the rushes along the lake shore until it was safe to come out.

Now subject to Coxcox (Pheasant), the ruler of Culhuacán, the Aztecs were given some land to settle. But what land! They found themselves living in a gully acrawl with rattlesnakes, no doubt to the

The founding of the Aztec capital of Tenochtitlán, as depicted in the Codex Mendoza.

amusement of their enemies. But, according to legend, the Aztecs liked rattlesnake meat, and they devoured the vipers with gusto. Still, it was not the promised land, and the restless Aztecs bided their time. Their chance came when Coxcox agreed to give them their liberty and better land in exchange for assistance in a war against the town of Xochimilco. Aztec leaders delivered to the shocked Coxcox proof of their deeds—sacks containing eight thousand ears cut from the slain Xochimilcas.

Although the king of Culhuacán hastily gave them their freedom, the Aztecs did not go away. They asked the Culhúa lord for his daughter, who would be made the Aztec queen and would be treated as a goddess. Coxcox unwittingly agreed, whereupon the Aztecs, in a move calculated to assert independence from their overlords, sacrificed and flayed the princess. When her father attended the banquet in his honor, he was horrified to find that the entertainment included a priest-dancer dressed in the skin of his daughter. Having finally had enough, Coxcox raised an army that scattered the Aztecs, who took refuge once more among the reeds of the lake.

Again the Aztecs showed their adaptability and turned the situation to their advantage. They found that in the marshy edges of the lake no one bothered them, for the place was considered unsuitable for dwelling. It was, however, a region abundant in waterfowl, fish, and other edible creatures. Furthermore, it was of some strategic placement, located at a point where three kingdoms merged. Huddled in those swamps, the dogged Aztecs drew on their resources, and, finding strength and unity in adversity, they stiffened their resolve.

Unmolested, in about 1325 the Aztecs occupied a small isle, counseled by the prophecy of Huitzilopochtli that attributed significance to a place where an eagle with a serpent in its beak perched on a cactus. They began to acquire, through trade, the materials they needed to enlarge their foothold, and they dredged the lake bottom to form more surface soil. From such inauspicious beginnings, and with considerable ingenuity and great labor, they eventually created the great city of Tenochtitlán. From that island redoubt they later built connecting causeways, which could easily be defended, to the mainland. It was an inspired defensive concept, flawed only by the eventual dependence on mainland Chapultepec for drinking water. Aqueducts conveying water could be cut.

Meanwhile the furious activity of the Aztecs and the development of the island came to the attention of Tezozómoc, the strongman of Anáhuac, who brought them under his sway and used them in their traditional role of mercenaries. Tezozómoc made unreasonable demands of tribute from the Aztecs, and even humiliated them, but he was astute enough not to push them too far. Gradually they were accepted as minor partners, and in 1376 Tezozómoc allowed Tenochtitlán to establish a royal dynasty. In that year the young Acamapichtli became the first ruler of the Aztecs. By the time Tezozómoc finally died, in 1426, the Aztecs, his apt disciples, were flourishing.

About this time the Aztecs elected as their leader Itzcóatl (Obsidian Snake), whose energetic rule led to Aztec independence and the expansion of trade. Following a power struggle, Tenochtitlán allied itself with the *altepetl* (ethnic states) of Texcoco and the weaker Tlacopan. This Triple Alliance would soon control central Mexico.

Although the feverish drive of the Aztecs ultimately carried them to dominance of the alliance, Texcoco maintained its position of equality for some time. To considerable extent Texcoco's strength was owing to the brilliance of Nezahualcóyotl (ruled 1418–72), one of the most remarkable figures in the history of Mexico. While so many are remembered for their military exploits, the illustrious Nezahualcóyotl is recalled for his cultural refinement. He was too much a man of his times to be a pacifist, and he steadily increased his influence through military force, but he had esthetic sensibilities as well. Renowned for his philosophical verse, this "Poet King of Texcoco" was also a wise legislator and an impartial judge; he did not hesitate to condemn to death, for example, members of his own family who broke laws. In addition, he was an engineer who was instrumental in the construction of a great aqueduct, which brought water to Tenochtitlán from the mainland, and of a long dike across the lake. A scholar and bibliophile, his Texcoco, "the Athens of Anáhuac," had libraries housing thousands of manuscripts, which were, tragically, later destroyed. The city, with its gardens, royal baths, and beautiful temples, was the finest expression of culture in an age otherwise marred by cruelty, intrigue, and almost constant warfare. When Nezahualcóyotl died, in 1472, his son Nezahualpilli, who had many of his father's qualities, became ruler of Texcoco. But the city came increasingly under the influence of Tenochtitlán.

After Itzcóatl died, in 1440, his nephew, the mighty Moctezuma I (Moctezuma Ilhuicamina) became sovereign of the Aztecs. Even before taking power, Moctezuma was a prominent general, and during his reign of twenty-eight years he launched his armies to smashing victories, as the Aztec dominions were extended to the south and northeast. Beyond this explosive territorial growth, the Aztec state took on more formal characteristics and began to achieve remarkable cohesion. At the same time, a genuine Aztec art style evolved as one manifestation of fervent nationalism. On a less positive note, the pretension and arrogance for which the Aztecs were notorious became increasingly extravagant, as former allies were bullied and cheated in the extension of imperial ambitions.

Growth of the empire was checked in the middle of the fifteenth century by natural disasters that produced catastrophic famine. After several years of near-starvation, during which increasing resort to human sacrifice failed to placate the gods, Aztec rulers saw a greater need to expand their control over fertile lands. Moctezuma I's successor, Axayácatl (1469–81), conquered new provinces and established garrisons at frontier outposts. A brave leader who fought furiously alongside his common soldiers, Axayácatl lost a leg in one of his battles. He

PRINCIPAL LAKE CITIES IN THE VALLEY OF MEXICO DURING THE AZTEC PERIOD

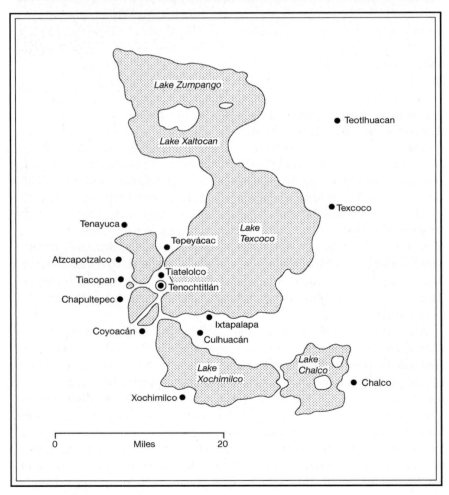

The sculpture of a female deity is reflected in an Aztec obsidian mirror with a wooden frame.

was succeeded by his brother Tizoc, a weak ruler overshadowed by the intrepid general Tlacaélel who shrewdly manipulated imperial affairs.

Under the leadership of Ahuítzotl (Water Dog) from 1487 to 1501, the Aztecs conquered the valley of Oaxaca, and pushed far down the Pacific coast to Guatemala. In the first year of his reign, Ahuítzotl oversaw the dedication of an impressive new temple erected to honor the god Huitzilopochtli. In a ceremony lasting four days sacrificial victims taken during campaigns were formed in four columns, each stretching three miles. By some estimates, as many as twenty thousand human hearts were torn out to please the god. Prominent guests, selected from allies and tributary towns, were invited to be impressed (and intimidated) by the might and glory of Tenochtitlán. In the frenzy of this ghastly pageant, the priests were finally overcome by exhaustion. The bloody reign of Ahuítzotl closed in 1502 when he accidentally struck his head on a stone lintel while trying to escape a flood. By this time, the Aztec yoke included several hundred city-states or ethnic kingdoms with varied arrangements in tribute obligations. While a city-state, or *altepetl*, acquiesced to Aztec tutelage in a material sense, its inhabitants retained a sense of cultural or ethnic distinctiveness, grounded in their singular tribal migration history and leadership.

THE AZTEC EMPIRE

The central basin of Mexico was firmly under Aztec control, but in some areas of the center and south where the Aztecs had won military victories, for example, in Oaxaca, rebellions by Mixtec and Zapotec city-states were common. Even closer to home, several mountainous zones to the east and south harbored independent states—most notably that of Tlaxcala. And to the west, the Tarascans never succumbed to Aztec domination.

The Tarascan empire comprised a score of city-states in the modern state of Michoacán with its capital at Tzinztuntzán on Lake Pátzcuaro. By trading with areas along the Pacific coast and becoming highly militarized, the Tarascans built a strong state capable of resisting the Aztecs. In 1479 Axayácatl invaded Michoacán with the intention of capturing sacrificial victims to celebrate the carving of the great Aztec calendar stone, and of course to get tribute. After his army was soundly defeated by a large Tarascan force relying heavily on archery and some copper weapons, the Aztecs pulled back from frontal assaults on the Tarascan empire.

The independent state of Tlaxcala was founded by one of the early Chichimec tribes in the region east of the mountains lining the Valley of Mexico. At various times the Tlaxcalans were allies of the Aztecs, but the relationship became increasingly hostile as Tlaxcala forged a confederacy with several other city-states and strengthened its army with mercenary soldiers from areas defeated by the Aztecs. In addition to preserving autonomy, the Tlaxcalans also wanted to keep the Aztecs from taking over their trade in salt, cotton, and other items with the Gulf coast. The Aztecs seem to have been content to try to keep the Tlaxcalans isolated and to engage them in periodic low-intensity warfare designed to obtain sacrificial victims.

In fact, these "Wars of Flowers," also practiced with other hostile states, came to form the main basis of the relationship between Aztecs and Tlaxcalans. A culture of war was not new to Mesoamerica, but the Aztecs had taken it to unprecedented levels. Warfare had two main purposes: to increase the number of tribute-payers and to obtain captives for sacrifice. Neither objective would be served by killing large numbers of foes in battle. As the Aztecs' hold on key areas intensified, Flowery Wars with recalcitrant city-states provided the opportunity for the revered class of warriors to gain experience. Military orders such as the jaguar and eagle knights accumulated prestige in these ritualized battles and obtained brave prisoners to be offered to the gods. Although these ceremonial engagements took place by invitation, the contests between Tlaxcalans and Aztecs only fed their enmity—a fact

A fine example of Aztec stone sculpture.

that would have ominous consequences with the arrival of the Spaniards in 1519.

In 1502 the ill-starred Moctezuma II was elected to succeed Ahuít-zotl. He reigned as the most absolute of Aztec lords, governing with great authority and enjoying the deference due a demigod. He was educated to be a high priest, but he later proved his valor on the field of battle. Moctezuma II undertook further expeditions to expand his suzerainty, and he laid the groundwork for an invasion of Central America. With the Aztec empire enjoying power and prosperity, there was a bustling commerce, a vigorous artistic style, and an advanced, well-organized society. From the meager beginnings, the Aztecs had created an astonishing capital city with a complex, sophisticated society. For seventeen years Moctezuma II ruled in splendor; then, quite suddenly, the Aztec world was turned upside down.

RECOMMENDED FOR FURTHER STUDY

Berdan, Frances F. et al. *Aztec Imperial Strategies.* Washington, D.C.: Dumbarton Oaks, 1993.

Caso, Alfonso. *The Aztecs: People of the Sun.* Norman: University of Oklahoma Press, 1958.

Clendinnen, Inga. *Aztecs: An Interpretation.* New York: Cambridge University Press, 1991.

Durán, Fr. Diego. *The Aztecs: The History of the Indians of New Spain.* Translated, with notes, by Doris Heyden and Fernando Horcasitas. New York: Orion Press, 1964.

Gillespie, Susan D. *The Aztec Kings: The Construction of Rulership in Mexican History.* Tucson: University of Arizona Press, 1989.

Hassig, Ross. "Aztec and Spanish Conquest in Mesoamerica," in *War in the Tribal Zone: Expanding States and Indigenous Warfare.* Edited by R. Brian Ferguson and Neil L. Whitehead, pp. 83–102. Santa Fe: School of American Research, 1992.

Hodge, Mary G., and Michael E. Smith, eds. *Economies and Polities in the Aztec Realm.* Austin: University of Texas Press, 1993.

León-Portilla, Miguel. *The Aztec Image of Self and Society: An Introduction to Nahua Culture.* Edited by José Jorge Klor de Alva. Salt Lake City: University of Utah Press, 1992.

Sahagún, Bernardino de. *Florentine Codex: General History of the Things of New Spain.* Translated by Arthur J. O. Anderson and Charles E. Dibble, 13 parts. Salt Lake City and Santa Fe: University of Utah Press and School of American Research, 1950–82.

Schroeder, Susan. "The Mexico That Spain Encountered," in *The Oxford History of Mexico.* Edited by Michael C. Meyer and William H. Beezley, pp. 47–77. New York: Oxford University Press, 2000.

5

Aztec Society and Culture

It is one of the paradoxes of history that violence and artistic development are entirely compatible within the same society; brutality coexists with refinement and justice. Aztec society is a good case in point. We have seen the emergence of a state committed to a policy of war and hostage to a bloodthirsty religion; it is also true that Aztec society and culture embodied some remarkably enlightened codes of conduct and justice, sensitive accomplishments in the arts, an orderly administration, and behavior that was strangely puritanical in outlook. In many respects it was civilization of the highest order.

AZTEC RELIGION

The mutually reinforcing relationship between Aztec cosmology and imperial policy bears examination. Aztec ideology certainly incorporated long-standing aspects of Mesoamerican religions, but it is probable that other elements were added by fifteenth-century rulers who recast migration history and myth in order to facilitate and legitimate their conquests. The Aztec rationale for human sacrifice had its origin in a cosmic view that encompassed the demands of their god Huitzilopochtli, lord of the sun and god of war, as well as a myth of solar struggle. They believed that the sun and earth had been destroyed in a cataclysm and recreated four times, and that in their age of the fifth sun, final destruction was imminent. That fate was, understandably, to be avoided as long as possible, and the Aztecs believed that special intervention through Huitzilopochtli would serve their interests.

Furthermore, the Aztecs accepted the view of a natural cycle: the sun, along with the rain, nourished the plant life that sustained human life, and therefore humans should give sustenance to the sun and rain gods. Ancient deities had sacrificed themselves to the sun, and mere mortals could hardly decline the same honor. The greatest offering that could be made, the highest expression of piety, was the giving of life itself. In practice, the ritual offering to the sun god involved the removal

A temple is burned in this Indian painting, signifying the end of a fifty-two-year cycle. From the Codex Telleriano-Remensis.

of a palpitating human heart for presentation to Huitzilopochtli. Without such expressions of reverence, it was feared that the sun might not rise to make its way across the sky. Of course, the need for sacrificial blood served militant expansionism.

Human sacrifice was not the sole preserve of Mesoamericans, as many ancient cultures of the Old World had also practiced it earlier. Sacrifice was to the Aztecs a solemn, and necessary, religious ceremony for the purpose of averting disaster. Victims were sent as messengers to the gods to demonstrate the reverence of the people, and it was often considered an honor to make the trip. Likewise, indulgence in

The New Fire ceremony is portrayed here much like a May Day frolic. The European artist had probably never seen an Indian in his native habitat.

ritual cannibalism as a means of acquiring the attributes of the enemy was not an Aztec novelty.[1]

These rituals followed strictly prescribed procedures. The most familiar sacrificial ceremony took place atop a high temple, where the victim was spread-eagled over a rounded stone, his back arched. While his limbs were held by four assistants, the priest went in under the rib cage with an obsidian knife to remove the heart. There were variations, according to the god to be honored. Those dispatched for the god of fertility were bound and shot full of arrows, the falling drops of blood symbolizing the falling of spring rain. Those honoring the fire god were drugged and then placed in fire. There was also a kind of gladiatorial combat that amounted to sacrifice, in which a captured warrior, usually one who had shown great skill and bravery, was tied by the ankle to a great round, flat stone. He was given dull wooden weapons to face a series of well-armed Aztec warriors, one at a time. In the unlikely event that the captive survived, he could have his freedom, but, in at least one notable case, a survivor insisted that he be honored as a warrior with a sacrificial death. Metaphors of warfare and

1. Frank Lestringant, *Cannibals* (New York, 1997), examines the universality of sacrifice and cannibalism in real and symbolic forms, including the Eucharist.

sacrifice pervaded Aztec thought, reinforcing one another and elevating militarism to virtue.

At the end of every fifty-two-year cycle (the Mesoamerican "century"), there was always the doubt that the sun would rise to begin a new cycle. Therefore, in fatalistic anticipation, on the last night of the cycle all dishes were broken and all fires put out. Then the priests assembled on a mountaintop to pray. When the sun did rise, a victim was sacrificed in appreciation and a New Fire ceremony was held; a new fire was kindled in the body of the sacrificed person, from which torches were carried to light all other fires.

The Aztecs perceived themselves as living in an insecure world, at the mercy of the elements and at the edge of doom. Natural calamities in their fragile universe were occasioned by the gods' displeasure. The Indians believed themselves surrounded by strange and harmful forces: as human beings were at one with nature, a person could suddenly be transformed into a hawk, a coyote, a fish, or even a tree or a rock. In such forms those who had passed on could haunt the living. There were demons and other strange apparitions in the nighttime, and in the dark one had to be especially careful of the noxious "airs." In an atmosphere heavy with symbolism, the apprehensive Aztec took no chances.

Huitzilopochtli was the predominant god, but there were many others to whom homage was paid. The ancient deities of Tláloc, Tezcatlipoca (the favorite of the warriors), and Quetzalcóatl (revered by the intellectual priests) were only a few of the more prominent gods worshipped for their special benefactions. Favored gods of conquered peoples were readily incorporated into a swelling Aztec pantheon of deities.

There was a version of afterlife, but it was not the same for all. Mothers who died in childbirth went to a special heaven. Warriors who fell in battle or who were sacrificed by the enemy went to a paradise with perfumed clouds, to accompany the sun in its daily passage; or they could find a new life as a hummingbird, destined to spend eternity among fragrant blossoms. Thus the warrior did not fear death any more than later Spanish priests feared the martyrdom that assured them a place in their heaven. Unless one was surprised by death, it was customary to confess late in life. Sins were related to the goddess Tlazoltéotl, "the Eater of Filth [sins]." After satisfying a penance imposed by a priest, the sinner was then cleansed.

Religion was all-pervasive in Tenochtitlán, and from birth to death there was daily religious observance. The Indians had many holy days during which celebrations, both solemn and joyful, took place. Some festivities included singing and dancing, along with children parading

In old age the Aztecs confessed to the goddess Tlazoltéotl, whose effigy is shown here giving birth to the God of Corn.

in garlands of flowers. Ritual activities included feasting, fasting, bloodletting, and human sacrifice—all part of Aztec beliefs that conjoined life and death in a continuous cycle.

Aztec Society

While Aztecs were nomadic and relatively few in number, their social structure was simple; the majority were peasants or warriors, and the handful of priests and war leaders enjoyed comparatively few perquisites. Following the settlement of Tenochtitlán, however, a rapidly expanding population, a diversified economy, and the organizational demands of the imperial system led to a more complex class structure.

Naturally, the royal family was the most noble of all, and it was a large group. While the supreme ruler or emperor had one principal (or "legitimate") wife, he had many others as well. The royal offspring were numerous, and they proliferated greatly. It is said that Nezahualpilli of Texcoco had two thousand wives and 144 children. Moctezuma II, with one thousand women, once had 150 pregnant at the same time. The royal wives had position and respect, and some were highly accomplished women whose views and talents were appreciated at court. Over a period of several generations the ruling dynasty had sufficient relations to be considered almost as a class apart. Emperors were always chosen from the royal family, but, unlike most monarchies, the heir apparent was not fixed. The best male candidate was chosen, whether he was a brother, nephew, or younger son of the previous emperor. Members of the royal family bore great responsibility; they were expected to serve as examples, to maintain dignity, and to lead warriors. Even as rulers embodied sacred power, they were strictly bound by the warriors ethos prescribed for all Aztec men.

Others in the noble category included high priests, prominent military officers, and influential government leaders such as judges and tax collectors. Sons of nobles were in an advantageous position to achieve their fathers' rank, but nobility (outside of the royal family) was not an inherited right. One had to distinguish himself in service in order to enjoy the privileges of the aristocracy. Nobles wore fine clothing, had commodious houses, servants, jewelry, and prestige—in sum, the best of everything that was available. Such luxuries went with the office, however; they were a consequence of achievement and were not sought for their own sake. In the late Aztec period, however, an elite class with landed estates, a kind of incipient feudal aristocracy, was apparently in process of formation.

All able-bodied males were expected to bear arms. As Inga Clendinnen made clear: "To be born a male in Tenochtitlán was to be designated a warrior. . . . What compelled the Mexican imagination were the men who were prepared to play the end game, to accept and embrace that final ritual of violent death. An imperishable glamour attended those warriors who vowed never to turn their backs in battle."[2] Distinction in battle was one way in which a commoner might rise to the nobility. In order to achieve the cherished rank of warrior, a youth had to take a prisoner. If he succeeded in capturing or killing four of the enemy he was entitled to share in the booty. Perhaps more important, he was allowed to dress in the distinctive adornments of the military elite. Conceivably, he could become a member of the prestigious military orders—the Eagle Knights or Jaguar Knights—and thus enjoy the luxuries of noble status. By encouraging upward mobility through performance, Aztec society remained flexible and vigorous.

Another avenue for mobility came through trade. The merchants of Tenochtitlán ranged far and wide. These traders, the *pochteca*, were one of the most interesting groups in Aztec society. They organized and led caravans as far as Central America, often passing through hostile country. The pochteca were as brave as they were shrewd and often depended on both their wits and courage to evade dangers. Some

---

2. Inga Clendinnen, *Aztecs: An Interpretation* (New York, 1991), pp. 112, 149.

of them knew foreign languages and customs and served as spies for the Aztec militarists. The pochteca imported to the capital exotic and profitable goods, which were displayed in the markets along with many tribute commodities demanded by the Aztecs. They lived in their own district and formed a separate group altogether. They had their own guild, their special deities, and their own courts. Within their section of the city they frequently gave sumptuous banquets and enjoyed other luxuries. Not of the nobility, they nevertheless had influence and respect.

High status was dominated by the most educated. Along with the ruling nobility, priests, scholars, artists, and scribes were all part of an educated elite that nurtured literary traditions within in the *altepetl*. They kept historical annals, genealogies of rulers, writings on philosophy and astronomy, and tribute records in their pictorial books. The sacerdotal life began with training young boys (or girls destined to be priestesses) in a monastery school, or *calmécac*. If suited to the life, a youth made the decision to enter the priesthood at about the age of twenty-one. Priests were expected to lead exemplary lives, and they spent long hours in prayer, fasting, and penance. Most of the priests led modest lives of service; those who advanced through the hierarchy, however, enjoyed the status of nobles and many of the perquisites that went with it. Aside from routine religious duties, each priest had a specialty, such as music, painting, teaching, dancing, or assisting at sacrificial rites. Some priests were also warriors. Priests were the guardians of morality, and some of their admonitions are not unlike Scriptural injunctions: "He who looks too curiously on a woman commits adultery with his eyes."

The great majority of the people formed the class of commoners (*macehualtin*). These farmers, laborers, minor craftsmen, servants, vendors, and petty functionaries of an altepetl were organized into wards or districts called *calpollis* (*barrios* to the Spaniards). Each of these subunits was made up of several households and had a temple dedicated to its patron deity and a school. It was a close-knit organization with loyalties much like those of an extended family. Each calpolli had lands apportioned to family heads who could use fields but did not own them. Members of the calpolli worked together, played together, and, in times of war, fought together as a unit. The people elected a captain who served as military commander of the district and was responsible for their welfare and good order.

At the bottom of the socioeconomic scale were the slaves. Aztec slavery differed from the slave system most familiar to us inasmuch as slaves had certain rights and bondage was not passed from parent to child. Some, in fact, served as slaves only for a specified term, either in payment of a debt or as punishment for a crime. In bad times people sometimes sold themselves or their children into slavery to avoid starvation. A gambler might bet his freedom on a ball game and end up as a slave. Some of the slaves were favored as concubines, and all slaves could intermarry with free persons. Little stigma was attached to some conditions of slavery; the mother of the emperor Itzcóatl, in fact, had been a slave. In a different category were those captured in war and destined for sacrifice. The class of slaves was increasing at the time of the Spanish Conquest, another sign of the widening social gap.

Aztec society's concern with education was singular for its time—school was compulsory for children. There were two main types of schools. Children of the nobility usually attended the *calmécac,* run by the scholarly priests, in preparation for the priesthood or some high office in the state. Occasionally a talented son of a commoner gained entrance. In a vigorous intellectual regimen young boys studied religion, astronomy, philosophy, history, poetry, rhetoric, and oratory, among other disciplines. Although the spoken language was rich and expressive and lent itself to fine subtleties, the picture writing was limited. History was passed on by oral traditions committed to memory. Written accounts depicted certain dramatic scenes that gave continuity and jogged the memory, but the fine details were transmitted from one generation to another by the retelling.

Most of the children attended one of the *telpochcallis* and found a less intellectual atmosphere. These students would become the class of commoners, or workers. Lay persons gave both boys and girls practical instruction in basic subjects. Here boys learned the rudiments of warfare, and those who went on to excel in the profession of arms could do very well for themselves; others had to be content with learning trades or lesser skills. Girls were instructed in the responsibilities of the household and motherhood. It should be noted that although Aztec society increasingly rewarded military skill, women maintained valued complementary roles, not only domestic, but also in agriculture, trade, and religion. The highest political and religious offices were restricted to men, but most deities had androgynous characteristics, and women and men inherited equally from their fathers and mothers. Women could own property and have productive activities outside the household, and childbirth was accorded a status equivalent to waging war.[3]

In the home parents imposed strict discipline. The birth of a child occasioned celebration and florid speeches. Babies received gifts

---

3. For more on women, see the articles by Louise Burkhart and Susan Kellogg in Susan Schroeder, ed., *Indian Women of Early Mexico* (Norman, 1997).

Pre-Hispanic Mexican women ground their corn with stone mano *and* metate, *and made tortillas much as many do today. From the Florentine Codex.*

according to gender: cooking utensils and weaving tools for females and farming tools and weapons for males. A child was named in hopeful anticipation of its character—the boys usually given names indicating military prowess and the girls names denoting beauty and delicacy, such as Rain Flower or Water Bird. In the home children were taught not only proper deportment but also the performance of daily tasks. While children were very young some indiscretions were tolerated, but by the age of eight they were considered to be responsible, and infractions brought harsh punishment. Although parents were ordinarily tender and loving, wayward children were castigated by whippings, scratching with thorns, or being forced to inhale the smoke of a fire into which chile peppers had been placed. It is reasonable to suppose that most children behaved themselves. Girls worked in the household until they were sixteen to eighteen, when they married; boys took mates in their early twenties. Marriage was sacred and monogamy was the rule, at least for commoners.

A peculiarly puritanical aspect of Aztec society has to do with the way in which the Aztecs conceptualized the sacred. Because alcohol and drugs provided paths for opening an individual up to the supernatural, ritual control of intoxicants such as pulque was deemed necessary to avoid dangerous displays of sacred power. Drunkenness could be a capital offense, although older people were allowed to become inebriated. Elites were permitted to ingest hallucinogenic mushrooms in order to procure visions of their destinies. Strictly prescribed behaviors also surrounded sexual activity and physical prowess—other vehicles of the sacred.

Aztec society demanded moral conformity, and violators of the code, as well as criminal offenders, were dealt with firmly. For minor offenses punishment was correspondingly light. But since personal dignity was highly prized, any public humiliation, such as the cutting of one's hair, was a great insult to pride. Several offenses, including lying, theft, and treason, brought the death penalty. The heads of adulterers were crushed between stones, homosexuals were hanged, and the lips of slanderers were cut off. Such penalties may seem unduly harsh to us, but it must be recalled that sentences in other parts of the world at that time were also excessive.

The Aztec legal system was complex, with high judges seated at both Texcoco and Tenochtitlán and lesser judges in localities. The legalistic society had need for many judicial officials to prepare the multitude of carefully documented lawsuits. There were judges in the great marketplaces to maintain fairness in business transactions and to settle disputes. Appointed by the emperor, judges were selected for their integrity and virtue. They had great authority and could arrest even the highest dignitaries, for before the law all were equal. The judge was expected to be absolutely impartial; if he accepted a bribe or favored a noble over a plebeian he could be executed.

Duty and responsibility, as well as danger, increased with one's rank, and they imposed special restraints. Because self-control was considered a mark of good breeding and nobility, the upper classes were subject to standards different from those of the lower classes. In contrast to most systems, where the upper classes have a favored position before the law, Aztec aristocrats were dealt with more harshly than plebeians. An offense that might bring a whipping or public humiliation for a commoner often brought death to a noble. A salient example of justice for the wayward nobility may be observed in the notorious case of one of Nezahualpilli's wives (a daughter of Axayácatl) who was unfaithful. She and three of her lovers were publicly executed.

Aztec medical practices were generally on a par with those in Europe, and were in some respects superior. Doctors knew how to set broken bones and dislocations and to treat dental cavities. They even performed brain operations. Like their European counterparts, Aztec healers were ill informed on the causes of disease but adept at effecting cures. The bleeding of patients, accepted medical practice in Europe until the end of the eighteenth century, was practiced by Aztec physicians as well. Aztec medicines were essentially extractions from plant life (and some animal life), from which were prepared a bewildering variety of brews, powders, poultices, purges, and pastes. Years after the Conquest a Spanish physician cataloged some fifteen hundred different plants whose medicinal properties were utilized by the Indians. The conquerors adopted native medicines, many of which are still popular in rural Mexico today.

Because Aztec society was largely agricultural in character, the daily routine of most people was directly involved in the growing of food. Aside from the many chinampas that ringed the island city, producing up to seven harvests annually, there were extensive plantings along the shores of the lakes. The diet remained much as it had been for centuries, with a base of corn, beans, chile, and squash. It also included a wide variety of other vegetables and melons, cactus fruit, and amaranth, in addition to many fruits imported from tropical regions. Commoners seldom ate meat, but the nobles, who liked to hunt for sport, consumed venison, peccary, pheasant, and turkey. A special treat was the small hairless dog fattened for the table. Cacao from the tropics was made into a chocolate drink, and avocados and many other exotic delicacies were brought in by the traders. Fish was a favorite when available.

THE AZTEC POLITICAL SYSTEM

The limited resources of the Valley were not sufficient to meet the needs of Tenochtitlán, Texcoco, Tlacopan, and other Valley communities. Moreover, there was an increasing demand for luxuries from other provinces. To satisfy the necessities and desires for both raw materials and consumer goods, Aztec realms were extended. The so-called Aztec empire was really a loose coalition of subject city-states that paid tribute to the imperial center. The Aztecs used marriage alliances to bolster the network of tribute obligations and discourage revolt, but they did not impose their own political system in conquered areas. Rather, the collection of tribute, which kept the Valley culture prosperous, was their main concern.

Tributes included a wide variety of commodities, among which were cacao, cotton, feathers, precious stones, jaguar skins, eagles, shells, dyes, cloth, gold, silver, sandals, and corn and other foodstuffs, as well as jewelry. Imperial tax collectors were stationed in tributary towns to ensure prompt payment. Towns conquered by the Aztecs were expected to provide soldiers and slaves and were required to recognize the imperial courts of appeal. But they were also allowed considerable autonomy. If the conquered peoples agreed to submit to Aztec sovereignty, the Aztecs did not much interfere with their internal affairs and their customs. Huitzilopochtli had to be recognized as the supreme deity; otherwise local religious practices and traditions were usually respected.

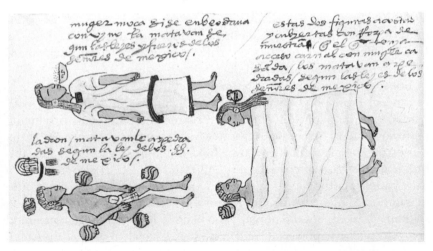

*A girl has been put to death for drunkenness and a thief has been exe-
cuted by stoning. Adulterers are shown wrapped together in a sheet
and then stoned to death. From the Codex Mendoza.*

Aztec political organization rested lightly on tributary towns, provided they were cooperative. In fact, it may be said that the Aztecs'
policy of generous autonomy for subject provinces was a weakness in
their political system. The subject peoples continued to be foreigners
within the empire, which remained a conglomeration of tributaries
with many different languages, customs, and religions. The provinces
paid tribute under duress but their primary allegiance was to their altepetl, or local polity. Thus the empire lacked genuine unity and was

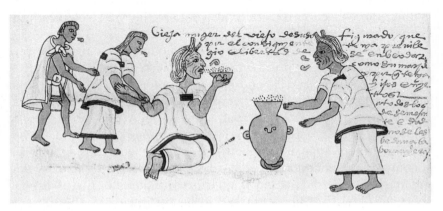

An older woman is legally allowed to partake of the intoxicant octli
(pulque). From the Codex Mendoza.

Aztec justice was strict, and it often imposed the harshest punishment on high officials. Here an erring functionary is being strangled. From the Florentine Codex.

honeycombed with discontent, a circumstance that would be fatal in the years ahead.

After the death of Nezahualcóyotl of Texcoco in 1472, the Triple Alliance had little significance, and Tenochtitlán gathered to itself almost all the power and most of the tribute. Consultation with other rulers became superfluous, and the emperor came to be elected from among the royal family by an increasingly elite group of military men with royal lineage. Surrounded by a small circle of military advisors, the monarch, whose selection was also seen as divinely ordained, grew even more powerful by the sixteenth century.

AZTEC ART, MUSIC, AND LITERATURE

The Aztecs borrowed much of their art from others and put their own stamp on it. The Mixtecs exerted strong influence on Aztec gold and silver work, pottery, and pictographs. We have few examples of Aztec murals. Aztec ceramic work was good but not superior. They did excel, however, in stone sculpture. "Aztec carvers created one of the world's strongest sculptural traditions with powerful conceptions that both impress and intimidate."[4] Monumental in size and weight, Aztec

---

4. Elizabeth Hill Boone, *The Aztec World* (Washington, D.C., 1994), p. 131.

This fearsome image of the goddess Coatlicue, mother of Huitzilopochtli, stands over 8 feet high.

stones adorned ritual precincts to commemorate victories and conquests, to hold sacrificial blood, and to represent the gods.

The artisans who made the gold and silver jewelry were also superb craftsmen. It is therefore lamentable that almost all of their work was either lost or destroyed during the Spanish Conquest, for the conquerors valued raw gold but all too often did not appreciate the fine workmanship. Equally impressive was the art of the lapidarists; from

A realistic stone sculpture of an Aztec Eagle Knight. His helmet is shaped like an eagle's head; knights of the orders of the Jaguar and Coyote were adorned with distinctive costumes, headgear, and insignia.

Careless musicians were sometimes punished by death.

Musicians played important roles in religious and civic observances. From the Florentine Codex.

precious jadeite, turquoise, and other stones they fashioned fine jewelry and mosaics. Most unusual were the artists who worked with feathers. The Aztecs put great value on the long green plumes of the quetzal bird that lived in the highlands of Chiapas and Guatemala, but the feathers of many other birds, too, were woven into mosaics of wonderful patterns and colors. Only rare examples remain, the most spectacular being the great headdress of Moctezuma II. The contemporary German artist Albrecht Dürer was lavish in his praise of Aztec artisans: "In all my life I have never seen anything that rejoiced my heart so much; I have found an admirable art in them, and I have been astonished by the subtle spirit of the men of these strange countries."[5]

Aztec music was composed primarily for ceremonial purposes, and it was accompanied by dancing. Instruments consisted of flutes, whistles, rasps, rattles, trumpets, conch shells, and drums vital for providing rhythm. Musicians were highly regarded because of their accompaniment in the religious rituals. Powerful lords were patrons to composers who created ballads recounting the nobles' military exploits. If they had prestige, musicians also bore great responsibilities. As no written form for recording music had developed, musicians had to memorize a very wide repertoire for the many ceremonies that often went on for hours. At the same time, as Robert Stevenson points out,

5. Quoted in Jacques Soustelle, *The Daily Life of the Aztecs on the Eve of the Spanish Conquest,* trans. Patrick O'Brian (London, 1961), p. 68.

"Imperfectly executed rituals were thought to offend rather than appease the gods, and therefore errors in the performance of the ritual music—such as missed drum beats—carried the death penalty."[6]

Neither in music nor in poetry was romantic love a popular theme. Aztec lyrics were often eloquent, moving, and sentimental. In this verse praising a goddess, the poet likened the blooming of a golden flower to the beginning of life itself:

> The yellow flower has opened,
> Our mother has opened like a flower.
> She came from Our Place of Beginning . . .
> Butterfly of Obsidian. . . .[7]

Like the short life of a bloom, however, life on earth was also fleeting. Poets sometimes addressed themselves to the proper role of artists and appealed to the public at large to assume a responsible and dignified posture. Like poets the world over, they often waxed philosophical and examined the meaning of life:

> Truly do we live on earth?
> Not forever on earth; only a little while here.
> Although it be jade, it will be broken,
> Although it be gold, it is crushed,
> Although it be quetzal feather, it is torn asunder.
> Not forever on earth; only a little while here.[8]

THE CITY OF TENOCHTITLÁN

Aztec architecture, like Aztec art, was essentially derivative. Buildings were basically elaborations of forms that went all the way back to Teotihuacán. But while many pre-Aztec structures survive in amazingly good condition, Tenochtitlán was thought to have been completely demolished by the Spaniards. However, excavations since 1978 have revealed important archaeological findings, including parts of the Templo Mayor (main temple) intact. We do have, moreover, enough descriptions of Tenochtitlán from both native and Spanish contemporary accounts to appreciate what the city looked like.

---

6. Robert Stevenson, *Music in Mexico: A Historical Survey* (New York, 1971), p. 18.

7. Quoted in Frances Gillmor, *Flute of the Smoking Mirror: A Portrait of Nezahualcoyotl, Poet-King of the Aztecs* (Albuquerque, 1949), p. 23.

8. Quoted in Miguel León-Portilla, *Aztec Thought and Culture: A Study of the Ancient Nahuatl Mind,* trans. Jack Emory Davis (Norman, 1963), p. 7.

By the time Moctezuma II was elevated to power in 1502, the island capital of Tenochtitlán was a most impressive city. With the estimate of 150,000 to 200,000 residents accepted by most scholars, the Aztec capital was one of the largest cities in the world. Only four cities of Europe—Paris, Venice, Milan, and Naples—had populations of one hundred thousand or more at the time. Seville, the city from which Spanish ships sailed for Mexico, had a population in 1520 of around forty thousand; and by 1580, when it was the largest city in Spain, it had only slightly over a hundred thousand. The amazement of the Spanish conquerors at their first sight of Tenochtitlán is therefore understandable. Cortés wrote of "the magnificence, the strange and marvelous things of this great city," which itself was "so remarkable as not to be believed."[9] In the Valley of Mexico, an area of some three thousand square miles, there were about fifty different cities by the second decade of the sixteenth century. If we take into account "greater" Tenochtitlán, with its many satellite communities on the lake shores (of which Texcoco was perhaps as large as the capital itself), the area surely held one of the heaviest concentrations of population in the world at the time.

By the early sixteenth century the island was an area comprising about five square miles, densely settled, and occupying much of the present center of Mexico City. It was a metropolis swarming with activity. Some sixty thousand people gathered daily in its buzzing market places, the most important of which was Tlatelolco, to barter for foodstuffs, cloth, and utilitarian wares. Cacao beans served as a form of currency. The core of the city, corresponding to the extensive plaza of today (the Zócalo), had the Templo Mayor, a great double pyramid dedicated to Huitzilopochtli and Tláloc, along with the royal palaces and other large structures. Among the shocks to the conquering Spaniards was a giant stone rack, the *tzompantli*, on which many thousands of human skulls were displayed.

From that central precinct enclosing about 125 acres, the city extended out to the residences of the nobles, which were often of two stories and contained as many as fifty rooms and patios. Beyond were districts with the modest dwellings of the commoners. The city was interlaced with stone-edged canals, which served as thoroughfares for thousands of canoes carrying people and goods. Paralleling the canals were streets for pedestrians. The Aztecs loved flowers, which with trees and other plants decorated many luxurious gardens. Aside from the royal botanical gardens, which displayed almost all species of plant life

---

9. Hernán Cortés, *Hernán Cortés: Letters from Mexico*, trans. and ed. A. R. Pagden, introd. J. H. Elliott (New York, 1971), pp. 101–02.

The center of Tenochtitlán, reconstructed by Ignacio Marquina from descriptions of Spanish conquerors and surviving Aztec monuments.

in the empire, there were also zoos, in which were represented practically all the animals and snakes of the country, as well as a large aviary full of all varieties of domestic birds. Large ponds were maintained for swans, ducks, and egrets. In special cages were Moctezuma's snakes, eagles, and jaguars, which consumed five hundred turkeys daily. Hundreds of people were kept busy in the maintenance of these gardens and zoos.

Five shallow lakes interconnected to form a network—two fresh water lakes in the south drained into the brackish water of Lake Texcoco. Three long causeways joined the island city to the shores: one stretched southward to Ixtapalapa, branching off with a road to Coyoacán; another causeway went west to Tlacopan, with an offshoot to Chapultepec; and a third made a connection to the north with Tepeyácac. These broad thoroughfares, twenty-five to thirty feet wide, were cut at intervals by drawbridges. Within the city itself many canals were spanned by stout bridges across which, according to Cortés, ten horsemen could ride abreast.

Compared to other cities in the world at the time, Tenochtitlán was very clean. There was good drainage, and night soil and garbage were hauled away in barges. A crew of a thousand men swept and washed down public streets every day. Cleanliness was considered

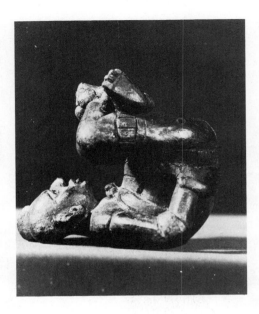

A ceramic foot juggler from Oaxaca, ca. A.D. 300.

essential, and people bathed often, many once a day. Owing at least in part to good sanitation and clean air, Aztec society was healthy.

MOCTEZUMA II

Moctezuma II reigned over a territory roughly the size of Italy. His domains included the modern states of Mexico, Morelos, Puebla, Hidalgo, most of Veracruz, much of Oaxaca and Guerrero, as well as the coast of Chiapas. They contained thirty-eight "provinces," stretching from arid highlands to the sweltering tropics. If, as some authorities believe, all of Mexico had a population approaching thirty million,[10] it was more populous than any country in Europe. France, the largest, had about twenty million, and Spain, ten at most.

With his immense authority, prestige, and luxurious style of life, Moctezuma II wielded enormous power. Three thousand servants attended him in his huge palace. Each day he was presented with a choice of one hundred different dishes, although he ate sparingly, taking his meals behind a screen. For his pleasure he had an unlimited number of women, and he was entertained by the antics of dwarfs, jesters, tumblers, acrobats, musicians, and dancers. No one dared look

---

10. Sherburne F. Cook and Woodrow Borah, *The Indian Population of Central Mexico, 1531–1610* (Berkeley, 1960); Cook and Borah, *The Aboriginal Population of Central Mexico on the Eve of the Spanish Conquest* (Berkeley, 1963).

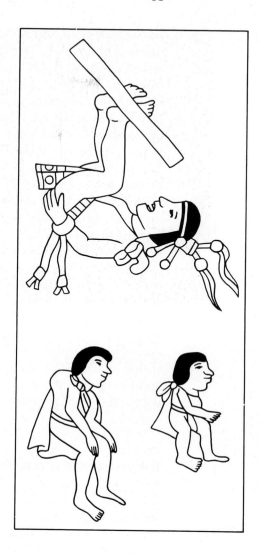

An Aztec foot juggler, from the Florentine Codex. Also shown are hunchbacks, a giant, and a dwarf, for whom the Indians had affection.

him in the face or touch him, and it was forbidden to turn one's back on him. Moctezuma was indeed the epitome of royalty, held as semidivine, exalted far above any of the earliest Aztec rulers. Nevertheless, he was an ultimately tragic figure, undone by historical forces with which he could not cope.

Yet before the Spanish arrived, Moctezuma was known for his bravery and successful military campaigns into Mixtec and Maya areas. In addition, his deep knowledge of Mexican history and his respect for tradition were factors in his successful rule and in the collapse of the Aztec state as well. Aside from his religious convictions, Moctezuma was superstitious and sensitive; he was also an amateur "wizard" who dabbled in astrology, perhaps as a means of lifting the shadow of historical inevitability. Or did he truly believe that the great Quetzalcóatl would return, as he had promised, to take back his rightful throne?

Just when Moctezuma learned of the presence of white men in the New World is not entirely clear. It is no doubt true that word of the Spaniards, who had been in the Caribbean for several years, drifted to the mainland. Perhaps he was not yet unduly concerned. Cuba, in fact, lay dangerously near—but it was not part of the Aztec world. Moctezuma was almost certainly informed by his agents that Spaniards had landed on the Yucatán Peninsula in 1517 and that others the following year were making their way up the Gulf coast. Indians reported seeing "towers or small mountains floating on the waves of the sea." Meanwhile, strange phenomena, construed by the emperor's priests as evil portents, had occurred. Lightning, unaccompanied by thunder, "like a blow from the sun," damaged a temple; a strange bird was found with "a mirror in its head," in which Moctezuma saw a host of foreign warriors. In 1517 a comet appeared "like a flaming ear of corn . . . it seemed to bleed fire, drop by drop, like a wound in the sky."[11] These and other unexplained signs heightened general anxiety. Then, in the spring of 1519 (the Aztec year Ce Acatl), the emperor was filled with apprehension when a courier arrived bearing ominous paintings—they depicted the encampment on Aztec shores of bearded white men with crosses.

RECOMMENDED FOR FURTHER STUDY

Anderson, Arthur J. O., and Susan Schroeder, eds. *Codex Chimalpahin: Society and Politics in Mexico Tenochtitlan, Tlatelolco, Texcoco, Culhuacan, and Other Nahua Altepetl in Central Mexico: The Nahuatl and Spanish Annals and Accounts Collected and Recorded by Don Domingo de San Antón Muñón Chimalpahin Quauhtlehuanitzin.* Norman: University of Oklahoma Press, 1997.

Berdan, Frances, and Patricia Anawalt, eds. *The Codex Mendoza,* 4 vols. Berkeley: University of California Press, 1992.

Boone, Elizabeth Hill. *Red and Black: Pictorial Histories of the Aztecs and Mixtecs.* Austin: University of Texas Press, 2000.

Broda, Johanna, David Carrasco, and Eduardo Matos Moctezuma. *The Great Temple of Tenochtitlan: Center and Periphery in the Aztec World.* Berkeley: University of California Press, 1987.

Gibson, Charles. *The Aztecs under Spanish Rule.* Stanford, Calif.: Stanford University Press, 1964.

---

11. Miguel León-Portilla, ed., *The Broken Spears: The Aztec Account of the Conquest* (Boston, 1972), pp. 13, 5, 6, 4.

Gillmor, Frances. *Flute of the Smoking Mirror: A Portrait of Nezahualcoyotl, Poet-King of the Aztecs.* Tucson: University of Arizona Press, 1968.

Keen, Benjamin. *The Aztec Image in Western Thought.* New Brunswick, N.J.: Rutgers University Press, 1971.

León-Portilla, Miguel. *Aztec Thought and Culture: A Study of the Ancient Nahuatl Mind.* Translated by Jack Emory Davis. Norman: University of Oklahoma Press, 1963.

———. *Fifteen Poets of the Aztec World.* Norman: University of Oklahoma Press, 1992.

Offner, Jerome A. *Law and Politics in Aztec Texcoco.* Cambridge: Cambridge University Press, 1983.

Ortiz Montellano, Bernard F. *Aztec Medicine, Health and Nutrition.* New Brunswick, N.J.: Rutgers University Press, 1990.

Pasztory, Esther. *Aztec Art.* New York: Harry N. Abrams, 1983.

Stevenson, Robert. *Music in Mexico: A Historical Survey.* New York: Crowell, 1971.

Zantwijk, Rudolf van. *The Aztec Arrangement: The Social History of Pre-Spanish Mexico.* Norman: University of Oklahoma Press, 1985.

Zorita, Alonso de. *Life and Labor in Ancient Mexico: The Brief and Summary Relation of the Lords of New Spain.* Translated, with an introduction, by Benjamin Keen. New Brunswick, N.J.: Rutgers University Press, 1962.

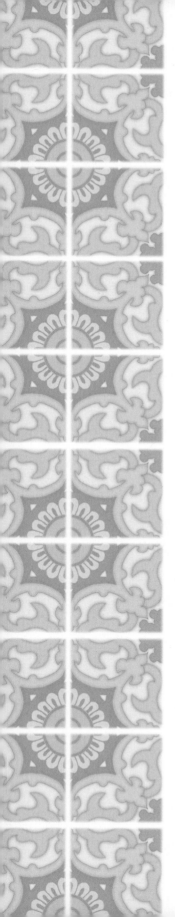

II

COLLIDING WORLDS

6

The Spanish Invasion

"Let us try for a moment to imagine," the late Ramón Iglesia wrote, "the astonishment of the inhabitants of a small island called Guanahaní one morning when they beheld three shapes out there in the water, three immense hulks, out of which issued several absurd beings who seemed human only in their eyes and movements, of light complexion, their faces covered with hair, and their bodies—if indeed they had bodies—covered with fabrics of diverse pattern and color."[1] We might surmise that, in 1492, the natives of the Caribbean fancied Columbus and his men to be exceedingly strange, even freakish, beings. The invaders were also surprised but even more disappointed, for they found little sign of the precious metals, valuable spices, and other wealth they had sought, and no indication of the fabulous kingdoms of the Orient they had anticipated. The native inhabitants, whom they nonetheless called Indians, were swiftly relegated to the status of "others," less worthy of respect.

SPANISH LEGACIES AND CARIBBEAN TRIALS

Later voyages to the "New World" (or the "Indies") dampened even the most optimistic spirits. Consequently the Caribbean Islands attracted relatively few settlers, as expeditions were financed with borrowed capital that could not easily be paid back in the absence of profitable trade goods. Columbus, who was always happier sailing about than governing waspish colonists, let administrative matters slide, thus giving the Spanish crown a pretext for removing him as governor of Santo Domingo, as the New World colony was called, and revoking the generous terms earlier granted him. Ultimately, the great discoverer was sent back to the mother country in chains.

---

1. Ramón Iglesia, *Columbus, Cortés and Other Essays,* trans. and ed. Lesley B. Simpson (Berkeley, 1969), p. 8.

Royal officials then took charge, but the bickering continued. Nearby islands were explored, some were settled, and Indians were put to work washing the streams for gold, which provided good income for only a few. Beyond that, and small profits from agriculture, there seemed little opportunity. Others began to explore elsewhere—up to the coast of Florida, to Central America, and down to South America.

Who were these Spaniards who came to conquer? Their own past embodied a history of conquest. Under the control of the Roman empire from the first to the fifth centuries A.D., Iberia underwent subsequent invasions by Visigoths and then Moors (Muslims) who arrived from North Africa in the eighth century. Over a period of nearly eight centuries Iberians reclaimed lands from the Muslims, but the kingdoms that emerged were diverse in cultural and linguistic traditions. At the dawn of the age of expansion, a single Spanish monarchy had not yet coalesced to unite the various Iberian kingdoms (except for Portugal, an independent polity since the twelfth century). The largest of these, Castile, provided much of the initiative that bound the future Spain loosely together by the sixteenth century, and it was from Castile that the New World ventures would be launched. Queen Isabella of Castile, strengthened by her marriage to King Ferdinand of Aragón in 1469, worked vigorously to mold judicial and administrative institutions intended to counter the power of the nobility as well as a strong tradition of municipal autonomy. Tensions between the monarchy, the nobility, and the towns would persist for some time in the peninsula while in the Americas the crown more rapidly curtailed the entitlements and autonomy of its early emissaries.

But even in the New World this was not at easy task. Spanish conquistadores were very much influenced by the legacies of the Reconquista (Reconquest) of the peninsula from the Moors, which had only recently been finalized in 1492 with the defeat of the Muslim rulers of Granada. The Reconquista had fostered a quasi-medieval cultural legacy in which military conquest, religious crusading, and the accumulation of booty and property were inextricably linked and mutually reinforcing. The legacy found expression in the New World, especially in the religious justification for military conquest and the strong role that would be played by the Roman Catholic Church in advancing the goals of the Spanish crown. Tales of chivalry and dreams of prizes to be won also traveled to the Americas in the minds of adventurers, but they were tempered by a changing economic milieu. By the end of the fifteenth century, the inroads made by mercantile capitalism meant that these aspiring conquistadores had to seek private funds to finance their expeditions. The need to recoup their investments provided even greater incentive for them to claim the customary material and political rewards from the monarchy they served.

In the peninsula privilege was reserved for the nobility, who comprised about 10 percent of the population, but only a small segment of this class held noble titles or great wealth. Most of the nobility consisted of untitled *caballeros* and *hidalgos*. Commoners made up the other major social subdivision, but they were also diverse in terms of income and status. The majority were peasants who worked for the nobility in agriculture and stock-raising, although some possessed their own land. The commoner group also included professionals, clerics, artisans, and merchants. People of all classes lived in and identified with towns and cities because civilized (politically ordered) living was exclusively urban. Society was also categorized in terms of religion: Christians, Jews, and Muslims. Where religious tolerance had once existed, however, it disappeared at the turn of the sixteenth century when the Catholic monarchs expelled Jews (1492) and Muslims (1502) who refused to convert to Christianity. The Castilian monarchy's efforts to consolidate power rested on a narrow agricultural economic base, with production concentrated in grain, sheep, olive oil, and wine. Economic contraction, in turn, led to greater search for guaranteed income via government and other bonds, which led to even less investment in productive enterprises and continuing contraction. The overall economic and social milieu encouraged the untitled nobility and even commoners to look elsewhere for social advancement, and their pretensions were fueled both by the past—the cultural heritage of the Reconquista—and the future—the potential offered by the New World "discoveries." The tensions between their ambitions, economic difficulties in Spain, and the slowly evolving bureaucracy of the crown dominated the early colony in Mexico.

From the Caribbean, the crown conducted the first experiments in imposing and inventing systems and institutions. The seat of royal government was on the island of Santo Domingo, but the larger island of Cuba held out more promise. Conquered in 1511, Cuba proved disappointing. But Spaniards remained in the islands, not only because they continued to hope that something exciting would turn up but also because they had little waiting for them back in Spain. At least in the Indies they had natives working their modest farms or, if they were lucky, mining for gold. However, one of the tragic consequences of the European occupation of the islands was a catastrophic loss of life among the Indians, partly because of fatigue and mistreatment but mostly because of their vulnerability to diseases to which they had no previous exposure or immunity. Epidemics of smallpox, measles, and other illnesses spread quickly among the natives, causing widespread death. With the great decline in the Indian population, a labor short-age ensued.

Governor Diego Velázquez of Cuba sent out an expedition in 1517 for the purpose of trading and finding other Indians to be enslaved. Under the command of Francisco Hernández de Córdoba, the party of three ships sailed west and touched the coast of Yucatán, thought at first to be an island. Further exploration revealed the existence of cultures more organized than those of the Caribbean, with people dressed in cotton fabric who tilled prosperous fields and lived in stone houses. In their brief contact with the natives the Spaniards heard of gold and silver in the land, and they also saw the first signs of human sacrifices. After a cautious initial reception, the Spaniards were at-tacked by a large and very fierce army of warriors and in the ensuing battle fifty of the Europeans were killed.

Despite the ferocity of the Yucatec warriors, the tantalizing refer-ences to gold fired the Spaniards' cupidity, and Governor Velázquez prepared to pursue the encouraging prospects. In 1518 he dispatched his nephew, Juan de Grijalva, with four ships and two hundred eager men to investigate further. After five months, the expedition returned home with some small gold objects and stories of a wealthy lake king-dom in the interior dominated by a great lord—Moctezuma of the Aztecs. Believing his nephew to have acted timorously and sensing the potential for riches and power, Velázquez commissioned the bolder, thirty-four-year-old Fernando[2] Cortés to undertake this venture.

FERNANDO CORTÉS

Cortés was a native of the arid Castilian province of Extremadura, the region from which so many of the prominent conquistadores came. Born in 1485 into an old, honorable family of slender means, the frail boy grew into a robust youth, often into mischief. Not much interested in the law career his family wished for him, he chose to seek his for-tune in the Spanish Indies, and he prepared to sail with a large fleet. An amorous adventure frustrated his plans, however; he fell off a wall outside a bedroom and narrowly escaped death from a wrathful hus-band. Injured and ill, he missed the sailing. Later, when he did catch a ship to the New World, it was 1504, and Cortés was nineteen.

After accompanying Velázquez in the conquest of Cuba in 15II, Cortés settled there in Santiago de Baracoa, where he raised livestock.

---

2. Cortés's first name is often shown as Hernán or Hernando, but he seems to have preferred Fernando.

The chapel-de-fer, or kettle-hat, was a helmet popular with the Spanish infantry.

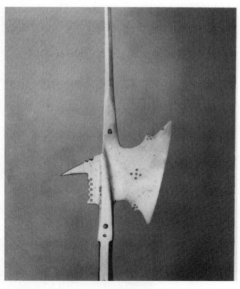

A halberd of the type used by the conquistadores.

An elaborate Spanish stirrup of the seventeenth century.

A warhorse of the sixteenth century was sometimes fitted with a chamfron, like the one shown here.

His Indian servants mined enough gold for him to enter into a trading partnership. With an official position in local government, Cortés was a secure and respected member of the community. Had it not been for the indecision of the governor's nephew, Fernando Cortés would very likely have ended his days in obscurity.

As Cortés began recruiting men and acquiring ships and supplies for the expedition to Yucatán, Velázquez grew apprehensive about mounting expenses. Worse, the ambitious Cortés assumed pretentious airs, leading the governor to wonder if he could control the headstrong captain. He ordered the expedition canceled and Cortés arrested. Alerted to the danger, Cortés addressed his men, promised them riches and glory, and then prepared to sail immediately. At muster, he counted 550 men, perhaps a hundred of whom were sailors, along with several Cuban Indians and some blacks. The soldiers were divided into eleven companies, each with a captain, and put aboard eleven small vessels. Sixteen scarce and expensive horses were put on board, as well as some small cannon. All of this had put Cortés heavily in debt, and there was no money to pay the men wages. But on February 18, 1519, they set sail as adventurers, to gamble on the potentially lucrative outcome.

THE INITIAL RECEPTION

After weathering stormy seas, the ships put in at the island of Cozumel, where friendly natives told them of two white men who lived in nearby Yucatán. Cortés made contact with one of them, Jerónimo de Aguilar, a survivor of a shipwreck in 1511 en route from Panama to Santo Domingo. The other was thoroughly assimilated into Indian society, but Aguilar was overjoyed to be among his own again. His knowledge of the native language and local customs would be of great assistance to the Spaniards in the months ahead.

Later, at Potonchán (Tabasco), the local natives resisted Cortés's overtures for peace and attacked with abandon. After a bloody contest, Cortés took the city by force. In this and other fights the Spaniards suffered many wounded, and several men were killed. The Indians, on the other hand, lost two hundred men and were convinced that the Spaniards were invincible. Little gold was found, but the natives said that people to the west had great amounts of it. After lecturing the Indians on their need for salvation through Christianity and describing

---

Fernando Cortés (1485–1547) dressed in the half armor used in battle. Full armor was not as heavy as one might think, but it did make the wearer very warm. Most Spaniards eventually adopted use of Indian layered-cotton protection.

the magnificence of the king of Spain, Cortés accepted a gift of twenty young maidens and continued up the Gulf coast.

When they got near the present city of Veracruz, the Spaniards met people who spoke a tongue foreign to Aguilar. However, one of Cortés's young maidens, baptized Marina, was able to communicate with them. Her role in the Conquest proved to be of great significance. Doña Marina, as she became known to her contemporaries (and Malinche to many Mexicans who consider her part in the Conquest as treasonous) became Cortés's interpreter and adviser. More than that, she was later his mistress and bore him a son. As a small child she had been given to or stolen by merchants who sold her to people of the south, and consequently she knew not only her native Nahuatl but one of the Maya languages as well. She communicated with the Indians, passed on the words in Maya to Aguilar, who then translated into Spanish for Cortés.

Realizing that the Indians would report to Moctezuma, Cortés had his men perform a mock battle to impress them. He then asked the local chief to send greetings to Moctezuma and to tell the Indian ruler that the Spaniards had a disease of the heart that could be cured only by gold. Although Tenochtitlán lay two hundred miles to the interior, swift runners quickly relayed the report to Moctezuma, who had already received drawings of their ships. The cautious emperor, perhaps fearful that Quetzalcóatl, or his emissaries, had returned to take the throne, now gave careful thought to his next move. For the moment, he sent word that he rejoiced in the coming of the strangers. He sent rich presents but declined to meet with Cortés because he was ill and could not make the long journey. Moreover, it was out of the question for Cortés to come to see him because the trip through rugged mountains and deserts was too rigorous. Beyond these hardships, the Spaniards would have to pass through dangerous enemy territories. In this fashion Moctezuma wished Cortés well, as if to dismiss him—all of which disheartened the Spanish captain not one bit. He replied by message that he would not think of missing the opportunity of greeting the great emperor to deliver a message from his king.

Meanwhile, Cortés was well aware of his own tenuous legal position. Spaniards were not allowed to go off exploring on their own, but only with royal permission. Since Cortés had ignored the revocation of the governor's commission to him, he was dangerously close to treason. Consequently, he sought to clothe his actions with a veneer of legality, gambling that all would be forgiven in the event of a glorious conquest.

With that in mind, he founded a settlement called La Villa Rica de la Vera Cruz (today Veracruz), according to established ceremony, in the king's name, with the procedure duly noted by witnesses. Cortés appointed town councilmen and other appropriate municipal officials and resigned his leadership. The officials of Veracruz then proceeded to elect him captain and *justicia mayor* with authority in military matters, pending royal orders to the contrary.

To gain the loyalty and affection of his men, Cortés turned over to them all the supplies and equipment, which, he said, had put him seven thousand ducats in debt. He already had enemies among the troops, but by this magnanimous, if calculated, gesture he gained considerable goodwill. In keeping with the generosity of the moment, the men agreed that, after the king's share of 20 percent—the *quinto*—was deducted, their captain would receive one-fifth of the remaining spoils.

THE TOTONACS AND A MUTINY SUPPRESSED

Pushing on to the Totonac city of Cempoala, the Spaniards were enthusiastically greeted by citizens bearing flowers and fruit. The obese ruler, who had sent regrets that he was too heavy to travel to meet them, complained of the Aztec tyranny and gave Cortés a detailed description of Tenochtitlán. He suggested an alliance of the Spaniards with the victims of the oppressors.

Cortés agreed to stand by the Totonacs and told them to send word to potential allies to be prepared. Cortés then directed other Indian towns to stop tribute payments to the Aztecs. His army strengthened by the arrival of a ship from Cuba bearing sixty Spaniards and nine horses, Cortés made plans to press inland. In order to maintain a coastal base, a fortress and houses were built at Veracruz, to be staffed by the ill, wounded, and older men. Cortés wrote the king, telling of his progress to date, assuring him of his devotion, and sending most of the treasure accumulated to that point. He added that he needed help, requesting financial assistance. The town council wrote another letter to the king, asking that the election of Cortés be confirmed. A ship with the letters, treasure, and two delegates sailed for Spain in late July 1519.

Anticipating the dangers and hardships that lay ahead, some men, especially the followers of Cuban governor Velázquez, plotted mutiny. Cortés learned of the conspiracy, and, after a trial and confessions, he hanged two of the leaders and severely punished others.

The companions of Cortés were not soldiers but soldiers-of-fortune, and only firm leadership based on respect (and fear) could maintain discipline and prevent mutiny under stressful conditions. Cortés was both intelligent and tactful, but his great authority stemmed most of all from his own fearlessness; he was in the front ranks of battle, and he shared with his men all the fatigues, privations, wounds, fevers, and narrow escapes from death and sacrifice. Now determined to drive to the highlands as soon as possible, Cortés arranged to give the weakhearted no alternative and the disloyal no opportunity to desert. Alleging the unseaworthiness of the ships, he instructed loyal pilots to strip the vessels and then scuttle them as quietly and quickly as possible. His audacity brought the army close to mutiny, and some no doubt questioned his sanity, but by this bold stroke he cut off all means of retreat. There was now no question of the Spaniards' course—they would have to conquer the mighty Culhúa-Mexica or die in the attempt. So Cortés led his men into the heart of the Aztec empire, initiating what would become, from the European perspective, one of the greatest epic adventures of all times. For the natives, the outcome was scarcely heroic.

THE TLAXCALANS AND REPORTS TO MOCTEZUMA

Moctezuma's depiction of the hardships before the Spaniards was only slightly exaggerated, for the march upcountry would take them some two hundred miles, on a rough and twisting path, from the steamy tropics to the chilling highlands, where they would find the Aztec capital at seventy-five hundred feet. Aside from the wild terrain, there was indeed danger from enemies—both those hostile to the Aztecs and those who acted under the orders of the wily emperor himself.

Leaving 150 men and two horses at Veracruz, Cortés departed the city in the middle of August with four hundred troops, a thousand Cempoalan bearers, the remaining horses, and three cannon. As they pushed inland the Spaniards were well received by towns subject to Moctezuma, for the emperor had ordered them to be friendly. Cortés sent some of the Cempoalans ahead to make amicable contact with the Tlaxcalans, known to be dedicated enemies of the Aztecs. But the Tlaxcalans, aware of the communications between Cortés and Moctezuma, were suspicious and engaged in several skirmishes with the intruders, killing two of their horses. The word now spread that the beasts were mortal, a loss of great psychological advantage for the invaders.

Meanwhile, noble envoys from Moctezuma arrived to reaffirm the emperor's friendship and willingness to pay a yearly tribute to the king of Spain, provided Cortés halted his ascent to the interior. Moctezuma remained fearful and perplexed as to the best way to treat with the strangers, for he was unsure of not only who but what they were. Hoping to appease the white men, who appeared to be some kind of invincible deities, the Aztec emperor ordered his agents to sacrifice captives whose blood the "gods" might wish to drink; the Spaniards reacted with revulsion to this practice so linked with Huitzilopochtli.

The European animals with Cortés were terrifying to the natives. Indians could only equate horses with deer, but later descriptions graphically depicted creatures of a more fearful aspect, as beasts who snorted and bellowed and sweated heavily, whose muzzles spilled over with foam. Although Cortés seems to have utilized war dogs very little in battle, the swift greyhounds and huge mastiffs, which weighed as much as two hundred pounds, intimidated the natives, one of whom recorded that

> their dogs are enormous, with flat ears and long, dangling tongues. The color of their eyes is a burning yellow; their eyes flash fire and shoot off sparks. Their bellies are hollow, their flanks long and narrow. They are tireless and very powerful. They bound here and there, panting, with their tongues hanging out. And they are spotted, like an ocelot. . . . They raised their muzzles high; they lifted their muzzles to the wind. They raced on before with saliva dripping from their jaws.[3]

Receiving descriptions of all these strange and unnerving things, the emperor ordered his magicians and warlocks to work their magic on the Spaniards, to send an evil wind their way. He called for more human sacrifices to the gods. And finally, when these strategies failed to halt the Spaniards' advance, he commanded his people to give the strangers whatever they desired. But Moctezuma was surrounded by warriors who counseled resistance, and the emperor had not ruled out force.

As much as Cortés had tried to manipulate Indian rivalries and the discontent of tributaries, he still did not fully understand the complexities of native governance. Quite aware of the precariousness of the Spaniards' situation, he must have breathed a sigh of relief when the Tlaxcalans finally pledged their support. What he did not know was how close Xicoténcatl, the commander of the Tlaxcalan forces, had come to convincing the other nobles to oppose the newcomers. This would not be the first or the last time that the Spaniards would be saved by a fortuitous political decision in a factionalized situation over which they had no control.

THE CHOLULA MASSACRE

Moctezuma, who had been kept abreast of these developments by his agents, warily waited to see what the Spaniards would do next. His seeming reluctance to attack the invaders stemmed not only from Aztec fears that the Spaniards might be gods, but also from military and

---

3. Miguel León-Portilla, ed., *The Broken Spears: The Aztec Account of the Conquest of Mexico,* trans. Lysander Kemp (Boston, 1972), pp. ix, 31, 41.

logistical weakness. It was now late September 1519, a few months short of the harvest necessary to sustain the imperial economy and provide food to supply large armies and of the dry season that could make roads passable.

At this point Cortés chose to proceed with his Indian supporters to Cholula, a former Tlaxcalan ally only recently brought into the Aztecan orbit. Cortés may have been manipulated by Tlaxcalan and Cempoalan allies into attacking the Cholulans who initially received him in friendship. The main version of the story holds that the Cholulans secretly planned to bottle up the Spaniards in the city and attack them. Warned either by Tlaxcalan allies or by Doña Marina who had been informed of the plot by a Cholulan woman, the Spanish captain now moved to a preemptive strike; he gave a prearranged signal to his men, who were poised for the attack, and the guns raked the main plaza, cutting down the unsuspecting citizens. Cortés gave orders to spare women and chil-

The Cholula Massacre as depicted by a sixteenth-century Indian artist in the Lienzo de Tlaxcala.

dren, but in the ensuing five-hour battle some six thousand Cholulan warriors were killed. Much of the ancient holy city was burned and then put to the sack by the Spaniards' Indian allies, who richly savored the defeat of their old enemies.

Whatever the reasons for Cortés's decision to attack, certainly the massacre at Cholula was a turning point, for Moctezuma, stunned at the Spaniards' prescience, now despaired of stopping them, although more halfhearted attempts would be made. The tragedy of that day is the blackest mark against Cortés in the minds of most Mexicans, who believe that, without provocation, he planned the slaughter.

INTO THE VALLEY OF ANÁHUAC

The emperor reluctantly invited Cortés to an audience. The Spanish commander and his men made their way toward the Valley, observed by incredulous natives, one of whom later preserved the striking impression made by the aliens.

> They came in battle array, as conquerors, and the dust rose in whirl-winds on the roads; their spears glinted in the sun, and their pennons fluttered like bats. They made a loud clamor as they marched, for their coats of mail and their weapons clashed and rattled. Some of them were dressed in glistening iron from head to foot; they terrified everyone who saw them.[4]

The Spaniards climbed to the high pass between the spectacular volcanic peaks of Popocatépetl and Iztaccíhuatl. As they began the descent into the Valley, they saw laid out in the distance before them the grand prospect of the lake cities. In that breathless moment, viewing one of the most awe-inspiring sights man has ever seen, the soldiers experienced a tense excitement from the drama of the occasion and all that it promised but also a chilling realization of the audacity of their scheme. None was more alive to the peril than the captain.

As the army moved toward the lake, an embassy of prominent lords, including the young Cacama, lord of Texcoco, approached to escort the Spaniards, expressing Moctezuma's regrets that he was unable to be there because of illness. Cacama announced that the Spaniards' way would be resisted and blocked, a threat that now rang hollow since there had been no serious military opposition on the part of the Aztecs. In

---

4. León-Portilla, ed., *The Broken Spears*, p. 41.

ROUTE OF CORTÉS

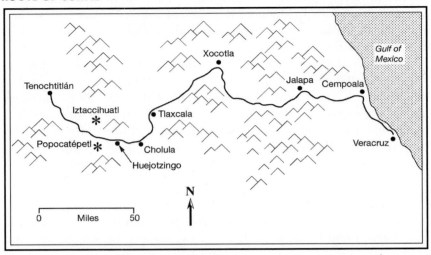

the end, the emperor, seemingly demoralized by prophecies and qualms about the origins of the intruders, resigned himself to face Cortés.

On November 8, 1519, Indians of the Valley flocked to observe the entrance of the newcomers, who descended on Ixtapalapa, which anchored the longest causeway. From that beautiful city the Spaniards could look straight down the thoroughfare to where the red and white towers of Tenochtitlán rose out of the water and the torches of the temples shimmered on the lake. Proceeding down the causeway, the Spanish force of about four hundred, with their six thousand native allies, moved through throngs of the curious who lined the way with their canoes. At length the party crossed a drawbridge that gave access to the city, and there, under a canopy of green, gold, and silver, and attended by a splendid retinue, was the lord of the Aztec empire. Moctezuma leaned on the arms of two nephews. Clothed in gorgeous finery, the fifty-two-year-old emperor was of dignified mien, slender, of average height with longish hair and a very sparse moustache and chin whiskers. As he walked forward, servants placed mantles on the ground so that the royal sandals did not touch the earth. Following him was a magnificent procession of two hundred courtiers.

The bearded captain, dressed in shiny armor and bright European fabrics, dismounted and strode forth to embrace Moctezuma, but the nobles restrained him, signifying that the emperor's person was not to be touched. Instead, the leaders saluted each other and exchanged gifts. Then Moctezuma received Cortés in a manner befitting a god and offered the Spaniards palatial accommodations.

A Test of Wills

By incredible good fortune, having made their way into the Mexica stronghold, the Spaniards spent several days wandering about the city, taking in the marvelous sights, much like any tourists in a foreign land. They admired the palaces with their cedar-lined chambers, the gardens, and the canals. Other scenes had quite the opposite effect: they were aghast at the great rack festooned with human skulls, and the priests, their long hair matted with dried blood, were repulsive to them. The visitors were properly fascinated by the zoo, as Bernal Díaz del Castillo noted, but, as for "the infernal noise when the lions and tigers roared, and the jackals and foxes howled, and the serpents hissed, it was horrible to listen to and it seemed like a hell."[5]

Moctezuma and his nobles visited their guests' quarters often to provide for all their needs. This attention and gracious hospitality notwithstanding, the peril of the situation was not lost on Cortés, who perceived with the greatest clarity that they were in fact trapped—if Moctezuma chose to make it so. Outside their luxurious palace the Spaniards were surrounded by a multitude of Indians who could rise on signal to ensnare them. The Spanish soldiers manifested their anxiety to Cortés, who now resolved on a bold and desperate course— he would seize as hostage Moctezuma himself. He accused Moctezuma of preparing to massacre the Spaniards in Tenochtitlán. The emperor would continue to rule his people and would be treated with the greatest respect. Meantime he was to counsel calm and patience among his people, because any outbreak of hostilities would result in his death.

To check the rising anger among his people, Moctezuma announced that he was not a prisoner; rather, he resided with the strangers at his pleasure, because it was the will of the gods. Though kept under guard, Moctezuma was treated with kindness. His servants, women, and advisers were free to visit him, and he was allowed to leave his chambers to worship at the great temple. The emperor, however, seemed resigned to remaining with his captors. To a greater extent than previous rulers, he was an intellectual, like his grandfather, Nezahualcóyotl. He was a man of sentiment and reason, both of which Cortés played on with consummate skill. Furthermore, if Moctezuma feared the defection of nearby city-states from their alliance with Tenochtitlán, Cortés could provide the best means of coercing their allegiance.

The general populace of Tenochtitlán abided by the ruler's wish for peace out of respect for his exalted rank, but some of the leaders did

---

5. Bernal Díaz del Castillo, *The True History of the Conquest of New Spain, 1517–1521*, trans. A. P. Maudslay, introd. Irving Leonard (New York, 1966), p. 213.

so only grudgingly. They were incensed at Cortés's demands that human sacrifice cease and pagan idols be smashed, to be replaced by crosses and images of the Virgin Mary. After some six months, outraged priests roused the populace and joined the warriors in calling for an armed offensive against the Spaniards. Moctezuma advised Cortés, with the greatest urgency, to leave the city. The pleased ruler told Cortés that the Spaniards could leave immediately—a fleet of eleven ships, bearing nine hundred men, stood off the shore at Veracruz.

THE NARVÁEZ EXPEDITION

In Cuba, Diego Velázquez seethed with anger against Cortés and grew more bitter with news of his protégé's success. To Velázquez, Cortés's deeds represented a blatant act of rebellion. He assembled a large force to pursue the rebel captain and arrest him. Under the command of Pánfilo de Narváez, the expedition included not only a very sizable complement of foot soldiers but also eighty horses.

Making port at Veracruz, Narváez ordered two soldiers and a priest to the garrison, now under the command of the capable Gonzalo de Sandoval, to demand submission. Sandoval arrested the three of them and sent them off to Cortés. Narváez then landed his troops and proceeded instead to Cempoala, where the Totonacs, assuming the newcomers to be associates of Cortés, lavished gifts and provisions on them. Narváez convinced the Cempoalans and agents of Moctezuma that Cortés and his men were traitors. He assured them that, after Cortés was taken, all Spaniards would leave the country and the emperor would again rule as before. Moctezuma, unknown to Cortés, responded with presents and encouragement to Narváez, shrewdly exploiting the quarrel between the two Spanish forces. For the first time since the strangers arrived, the hapless ruler found himself in a favorable position. With good fortune, the white men might kill each other off.

On first learning of the large Spanish expedition on the coast, Cortés had a sense of foreboding—it was an army roughly twice as large as his own. After failing to win Narváez to his side, Cortés mustered his followers. He told them that Narváez and his men had dishonored them by insults and were trying to steal what they had won with their sweat and blood. The captain selected some volunteers to accompany him to Veracruz and asked Moctezuma to assure the safety of the Spaniards left behind. The emperor agreed, offering the use of Aztec warriors to Cortés. Leaving Pedro de Alvarado in command of about 140 men in the city, Cortés departed for the coast with the same number. In Cholula he was joined by 120 of his men who had been settling a town on the lower Gulf coast.

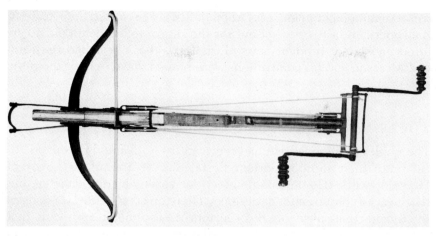

A crossbow with windlass of the type used in the Conquest. Because of its devastating force, popes forbade its use against Christians; but it was used very effectively in wars against Muslims and natives of the New World.

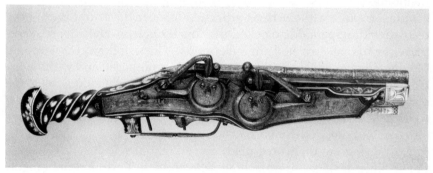

A wheel-lock pistol of the sixteenth century. This one belonged to Charles V.

In a rapid march Cortés soon put his men on the outskirts of Cempoala, arriving under cover of darkness. He attacked suddenly, at midnight during a driving rainstorm, and in the confusion and darkness he gained the advantage. It appears that many of the newcomers were less than anxious to resist Cortés. After a frenzied skirmish Narváez took a pike in the eye and surrendered.

The swift and decisive action of Cortés. against a much larger force, served to enhance his prestige among the Indians as well as with the men of Narváez. A diplomat of genius, Cortés now showed generosity to the defeated soldiers, most of whom he had known in Cuba. They were eager enough to join him when they were promised their share of the spoils. But as Cortés set out for the return to Tenochtitlán, a battered messenger brought news of disaster—the Aztecs had risen up, and Alvarado and his companions were pinned down in their quarters.

THE SPANIARDS BESIEGED AND THE SAD NIGHT

The nobles of Tenochtitlán had received from Alvarado permission to celebrate their most important fiesta, that of Toxcatl, in honor of Huitzilopochtli. The Spaniard agreed to the singing and dancing, but there was to be no human sacrifice. There are conflicting versions of the tragedy that subsequently occurred. We assume, in any event, that the reduced Spanish garrison was edgy, especially since Narváez had sent provocative messages to the Aztecs, inciting them to rebel against the men of Cortés.

According to Alvarado, he was informed that the ceremonial dance to the war god was a prelude to an attack on the Spaniards, who were to be sacrificed. Therefore he determined to strike first. Others have maintained that he was moved by bloodlust, or that he simply overreacted to rumors without basis in fact. Whatever the truth, during the festivities the Spaniards blocked the four exits from the square, drew their swords, and rushed the celebrants. There followed a wild and bloody scene in which the Indians, caught unprepared and without escape, had little chance. In a short time hundreds of Aztec nobles, the cream of the warriors, fell under Spanish steel. After the Spaniards retreated to their quarters they were besieged by thousands of grief-stricken and enraged Indians.

Cortés, fearing the worst, made forced marches to the Valley in order to lift the siege. Approaching Tenochtitlán, he found a strangely silent city, showing little sign of activity. He fired a cannon and was heartened to hear a return boom. He entered Tenochtitlán unopposed with about one thousand soldiers and one hundred cavalrymen. Although he gained the palace without difficulty, it soon became clear that the Aztecs had simply allowed him to walk into a trap.

The Spaniards preferred fighting in wide open spaces where they could deploy their guns to advantage and charge their horses into enemy ranks. Confined in the city, hemmed in by buildings that afforded protection to the Indians, they were less effective. The Aztecs made repeated assaults on the Spanish position, finally resorting to what resembled suicide squads. The cannon put shot into them at close range, while the harquebuses, falconets, and crossbows took a frightful toll—and still fresh relays came. As the defenders grew weary, Cortés persuaded Moctezuma, who was still held hostage, to urge the Aztecs to desist. The ruler mounted the rooftop to draw attention and began to speak. He was struck down and died three days later.

There are two versions of his death. The best documented is that he was stoned, perhaps accidentally, by his own people. But it is just as likely that Moctezuma was strangled or stabbed to death on orders from Cortés. Because of his failure to effectively oppose the Spanish invasion, Moctezuma is viewed in Mexican histories as less than heroic. The ruler was not a coward (his bravery had been tested on the field of battle), but his true sentiments and motives remain enigmatic.

Surrounded by tens of thousands of their adversaries, with food and powder almost depleted and his men badly mauled from the fighting, Cortés decided to make a break for it that night. The chosen avenue for escape was the Tacuba causeway, which, though said to have been two miles long, was the shortest of them. The Aztecs had removed the bridges spanning the gaps in the causeways, so Cortés ordered the construction of a portable bridge, which was to be carried by forty Tlaxcalan warriors. The treasure acquired earlier from Moctezuma was divided, with each man allowed to take what he wished for his share. Some foolishly weighted themselves down with precious metals and jewelry, which later hampered their movements and contributed to their capture or death.

Sandoval, who had returned to Tenochtitlán with Cortés, was put in charge of the lead columns, while Alvarado was given command of the rear guard. Cortés elected to lead a flying squad of one hundred men, ready to shift to any weak point. At midnight they stole quietly out of the palace, the horses' hooves wrapped in cloth to muffle their movements. A heavy fog and light rain helped obscure the figures but made the footing treacherous. It was early in the morning of July 1, 1520, the *Noche Triste*, or Sad Night, as it has come down in history.

Moving carefully over the causeway the Spaniards were able to place their bridge over the first channel and cross. Then suddenly an old woman drawing water from a canal spotted them and cried out. Sentries sounded the alarm with blasts on their conch shells, and the Aztecs came pouring out of the darkness. Thousands of warriors fell on the escapees, and some Spaniards in the rear were cut off and seized. Other Indians flanked the causeway in their canoes and shot into the mass. The Spanish formations broke as each man tried to save himself.

With great effort the bridge was thrown across the second breach, but under the strain of fleeing cavalry and foot soldiers, the bridge collapsed, throwing into confusion and panic those who followed. Cortés and his cohorts raced for the mainland, forced to swim the remaining breaks in the causeway. The unit in gravest danger was the rear guard, for it was taking the brunt of the Aztec charge. Alvarado's mare had fallen under him, and he now stumbled over the masses of the dead choking the breaches and crossed on the bodies. As the enemy closed, Alvarado, who was a powerful athlete, sprinted toward the last open channel, placed the point of his lance, and, according to some contemporary accounts, made a tremendous vault that carried him over to safety.

In that terrifying night, the most drastic reversal of Spanish arms in the conquests of the New World, at least 450 of Cortés's men died[6] and more than four thousand of the steadfast Indian allies fell. Forty-six of the horses lay sprawled along the littered causeway. The survivors gained the mainland where, according to tradition, Fernando Cortés was so moved by the disaster that he sat under a great tree and wept.

THE SPANIARDS REGROUP

Because of their catastrophic defeat at Tenochtitlán, the Spaniards were uncertain of their reception from the various Indian groups that had previously sworn them allegiance. But once again disagreements among contending native factions were resolved in their favor when lords from Tlaxcala and Huejotzingo offered consolation and warriors. Had it not been for these allies Cortés and his men would have been lost.

It required all of Cortés's force of personality and subtle blandishments to prevent mass defections and rebellion among his men. Cortés began to lay plans for the return. He conceived an ingenious plan for securing the island city: he would assault it by water as well as by land. To that end he set carpenters to work constructing launches in sections, which could be carried across the mountains by native porters and assembled on the lake shore. The vessels would be fitted for both sails and oars.

Following the victory in Tenochtitlán, the elated Aztecs raised to the throne a nephew of Moctezuma, Cuitláhuac, lord of Ixtapalapa. The Aztecs now geared up for total war with no moderate voice at their court. The Indians knew that the strangers were not deities—they had slain them, sacrificed them to their gods, and even tasted of their flesh. Nor did the horses inspire the same terror; it was futile to attempt outrunning them, but they bled, too, and the Indians learned that they could be hamstrung. All things considered, it appeared that the Aztecs had gained the advantage.

---

6. Bernal Díaz del Castillo, who was present, wrote that on the Sad Night and in the next five days, during which the Aztecs pursued them, over 860 Spaniards died. Ibid., p. 321.

Cuauhtémoc (1502?–1525), the last Aztec emperor, as he appeared to a post-Conquest Indian artist.

But the Spaniards had a silent, deadly, and totally unexpected ally in the land: one of Narváez's men came to Mexico infected with smallpox, which spread quickly with devastating consequences to the Indians. Tens of thousands were carried off by the disease. It was, some Spaniards noted with satisfaction, only just, for the Indians had introduced them to new infectious illnesses as well. Although syphilis was long believed to have been one of these, because a virulent form of it appeared in Europe soon after conquest, it is now thought to have been a mutation of a related form of yaws already present in Europe. In any event, Europeans were not decimated by New World diseases. The pox was contracted by Emperor Cuitláhuac within a short time, and when he succumbed, the lords chose the last Aztec ruler. He was the eighteen-year-old Cuauhtémoc, another nephew of Moctezuma. Cuauhtémoc has become a symbol of valor, the cultural hero of Indian Mexico.

The Fall of Tenochtitlan

In late December 1520, Cortés made headquarters at Texcoco and succeeded over the next few months in isolating the island city of Tenochtitlán by winning over the surrounding population with diplomacy or force. Meanwhile Sandoval proceeded to Tlaxcala to escort the launches. Sections of the thirteen vessels were carried over the mountains by eight thousand porters, while another two thousand bore provisions. The long procession, stretching out almost six miles, arrived at the Spanish camp at Texcoco without grave incident. Cortés reviewed his forces, now augmented by the arrival of additional adventurers from the Caribbean. He counted 900 Spaniards, of whom 86 had horses, 118 carried crossbows and harquebuses, and all were armed with swords and daggers. Some wielded pikes and halberds, most had shields, and many wore some form of protective armor. There were fifteen bronze cannon and three heavy guns of cast iron. Supporting the Spaniards were native legions numbering some hundred thousand warriors.

The small Spanish fleet was crucial to their strategy, for if the causeways could be commanded, all transportation and communication to the island could be cut off. Moreover, the Aztecs could be prevented from attacking the Spaniards from their canoes. Cortés chose to command the fleet in person. Those fighting on land were assigned to three commanders, each of whom was to secure a causeway. On May 10, 1521, they began the siege, and with help from favorable winds they overpowered hundreds of Aztec canoes. Spanish boats penetrated canals on the edges of the city, after which the attackers set fire to many houses. With the success of the operation on water, Alvarado and Cristóbal de Olid charged down the causeways to engage the defenders of the barricades and bridges.

Furious fighting continued for weeks, for although the attackers were able to penetrate sections of the city, they could not easily hold positions. They were assailed by warriors who rained arrows and stones on them from the flat rooftops while others engaged them in hand-to-hand combat. The advantages of horse and cannon were greatly reduced in the close street fighting. Cortés concluded, to his regret, that he must level the city. Accordingly, his men began the systematic destruction of the great temples and palaces that afforded his adversaries protection.

Early on, the aqueducts had been cut, and the launches swept the lake to prevent water, food, and reinforcements from reaching the besieged defenders. Still, in the face of heavy casualties, illness, and a lack of food and drinking water, the Aztecs held out, resigned to the warrior's death. Attempts to effect a truce failed. Finally, in a last concerted offensive, the Spaniards and their native allies overran the Aztec position. In the savage finale Cortés and Alvarado backed the survivors to the wall, and Tenochtitlán fell on August 13, 1521.

Taken by Cortés, Cuauhtémoc then touched the dagger in his adversary's belt and spoke: "I have done everything in my power to defend myself and my people, and everything that it was my duty to do,

An Aztec Jaguar Knight dressed for battle, wearing a pelt and wielding an obsidian-edged war club.

A mounted Spaniard in full armor.

to avoid the pass in which I now find myself. You may do with me whatever you wish, so kill me, for that will be best."[7]

When the tumult subsided and the dust settled, there remained a scene of desolation: the beautiful metropolis effectively smashed, the gardens flattened, and the canals filled with rubble. The destruction of one of history's grandest cities was accompanied by great heroism and suffering on both sides. Aside from their superior weapons and armor, the Spaniards derived great advantage from some 200,000 Indian allies, their horses, the spread of smallpox, and a favorable psychological atmosphere. They benefited enormously from their deployment of native allies in tactics of all-out warfare that ignored the traditional ceremonial formalities of Aztec combat.

Brilliant as it was in certain respects, Aztec civilization thrived on militarism; therefore, the character of its fall was consistent with its rise. And it was poetically apt that its last great warrior-king was Cuauhtémoc, whose name translates "Falling Eagle" or, in another sense, "Setting Sun."

RECOMMENDED FOR FURTHER STUDY

Cerwin, Herbert. *Bernal Díaz, Historian of the Conquest.* Norman: University of Oklahoma Press, 1963.

Chance, John K. *Conquest of the Sierra: Spaniards and Indians in Colonial Oaxaca.* Norman: University of Oklahoma Press, 1989.

Cortés, Hernán. *Hernán Cortés: Letters from Mexico.* New York: Orion Press, 1971.

Cook, Noble David, and W. George Lovell, eds. *Secret Judgments of God: Old World Diseases and Colonial Spanish America.* Norman: University of Oklahoma Press, 1991.

Crosby, Alfred W. *The Columbian Exchange: Ecological and Cultural Consequences of 1492.* Westport, Conn.: Greenwood Press, 1972.

Cypess, Sandra. *La Malinche in Mexican Literature from History to Myth.* Austin: University of Texas Press, 1991.

Díaz del Castillo, Bernal. *The True History of the Conquest of New Spain, 1517–1521.* New York: Farrar, Strauss, and Giroux, 1966.

Elliot, John H. *Imperial Spain, 1469–1716.* New York: St. Martin's Press, 1962.

Gardiner, C. Harvey. *The Constant Captain: Gonzalo de Sandoval.* Carbondale: Southern Illinois University Press, 1961.

———. *Naval Power in the Conquest of Mexico.* Austin: University of Texas Press, 1956.

Hassig, Ross. *Aztec Warfare: Imperial Expansion and Political Control.* Norman: University of Oklahoma Press, 1988.

---

7. Quoted in Francisco López de Gómara, *Cortés: The Life of the Conqueror by His Secretary* (Berkeley, 1964), p. 292.

————. "The Collision of Two Worlds," in *The Oxford History of Mexico*. Edited by Michael C. Meyer and William H. Beezley, pp. 79–112. New York: Oxford University Press, 2000.

Kamen, Henry. *Philip of Spain*. New Haven, Conn.: Yale University Press, 1997.

Karttunen, Frances. *Between Worlds: Interpreters, Guides, and Survivors*. New Brunswick, N. J.: Rutgers University Press, 1994.

León-Portilla, Miguel, ed. *The Broken Spears: The Aztec Account of the Conquest of Mexico*. Boston: Beacon Press, 1972.

Liss, Peggy. *Isabel, the Queen: Life and Times*. New York: Oxford University Press, 1992.

Lynch. John. *Spain, 1516–1598: From Nation State to World Empire*. Oxford: Blackwell, 1992.

Nader, Helen. "The Spain That Encountered Mexico," in *The Oxford History of Mexico*. Edited by Michael C. Meyer and William H. Beezley, pp. 11–45. New York: Oxford University Press, 2000.

Padden, Robert C. *The Hummingbird and the Hawk: Conquest and Sovereignty in the Valley of Mexico, 1503–1541*. New York: Harper & Row, 1970.

Prescott, William H. *History of the Conquest of Mexico*. New York: Bantam Books, 1967.

Restall, Matthew. *Seven Myths of the Spanish Conquest*. New York: Oxford University Press, 2003.

Schwartz, Stuart, ed. *Victors and Vanquished: Spanish and Nahua Views of the Conquest of Mexico*. New York: Bedford/St. Martin's, 2000.

Todorov, Tzvetzan. *The Conquest of America: The Question of the Other*. New York: Harper & Row, 1984.

Vigil, Ralph H. "A Reappraisal of the Expedition of Pánfilo de Narváez to Mexico in 1520." *Revista de Historia de América* 77–78 (1974): 101–25.

7

The Settlement of New Spain

The conquerors withdrew to nearby Coyoacán, leaving the Aztecs to remove their dead. The Spaniards decided to build a new city over the ruins of Tenochtitlán, and soon armies of native laborers under the direction of Spanish architects and artisans laid the foundations for the splendid city of Mexico. It would be the capital of New Spain, by which name the country would be officially known for the next three centuries.

THE ENCOMIENDA SYSTEM

The Conquest had been the result of a great effort by individual adventurers who received no pay for their work. Many had gone into debt to outfit themselves for the enterprise; all had suffered great hardships and had seen companions die horrible deaths; almost all had been wounded. But the treasure for which they had endured so much proved to be a pittance. Some of the survivors of the Noche Triste had escaped with a few valuable objects, but the bulk of the riches had been lost in the lake waters.[1] Of the spoils, a horseman received as his share only about a hundred gold pesos, one-fifth of the cost of a horse. Foot soldiers, who constituted the bulk of the army, received even less. As the mood of his companions grew more ugly, Cortés relented and allowed the torture of Cuauhtémoc and other lords, hoping thereby to learn the location of any remaining hoard of riches. The royal feet of the nobles were oiled and held over fire. Despite their agonies, they gave no information, for there was no cache—or at least none has ever been found.

One of Cortés's first concerns was to secure the tribute rolls of the Aztec treasurer, which contained paintings identifying the subject towns along with the kinds and amounts of tribute paid to Tenochtitlán. There

---

1. In 1981, several feet underground in Mexico City a crude gold bar was found. Quite possibly it was dropped on the retreat.

were 370 such towns, each having yielded to the Aztec emperor one-third of its production. Thus the Spanish captain acquired knowledge of the population, the geography, and the economy—not to mention the tribute that the conquerors could now enjoy. In order to calm his irate soldiers, Cortés agreed, with some misgivings, to distribute the Indian towns to them as rewards.

There was a precedent for this practice; in the Caribbean Islands, Spaniards had been granted native villages for their profit. As originally conceived, this system, the *encomienda*, was seen as the best solution for all concerned. The individual deserving Spaniard (the *encomendero*) received the tribute of the Indians, as well as their free labor, in return for which the natives were commended to the encomendero's care. He was to see to their conversion to Christianity, to ensure good order in the village, and in all ways to be responsible for their welfare. It was hoped that by this system the Indians would be more easily acculturated, better controlled, and protected. What happened in practice was quite another matter, as the system, subjected to every imaginable abuse, kept the Indians in a state of serfdom. Indians were overworked, separated from their families, cheated, and physically maltreated. The encomienda in early decades was responsible for demeaning the native race and creating economic and social tragedies that persisted in one guise or another into modern times.

The tremendous loss of Indian lives, attributable at least in part to this system, was a grim warning against awarding encomiendas in other lands. Moreover, the Spanish crown wanted the tribute for itself and thus sought to maintain direct control over the Indians to retain them as royal vassals. The thought of the conquered multitudes being subject to the whims of the conquerors was unsettling to the sovereign. Yet the crown could not—or would not—compensate those who had won extensive territories and millions of people for Spain. And so the king grudgingly allowed the awarding of encomiendas for New Spain. Nonetheless, he was never at ease with the arrangement and from the first sought the means to bring all Indian towns under royal control. The struggle between the crown and the individuals who held encomiendas was a dominant theme for much of the sixteenth century.

THE SPREAD OF CONQUEST

Even before the fall of Tenochtitlán, Cortés had sent small parties to explore the land's resources. They returned with information on sources of gold and silver and reported on the location of natural ports and timber for the construction of ships. Once he had secured the Valley, Cortés lost no time in dispatching expeditions in all directions to

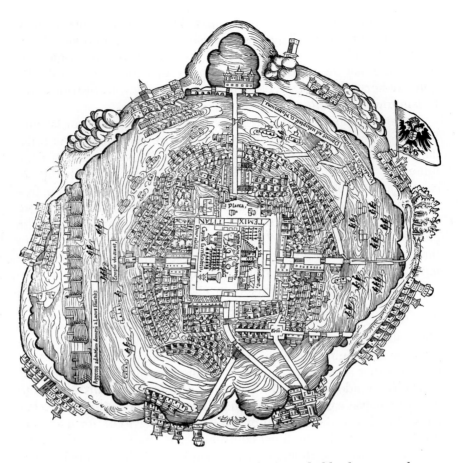

*An early map of "Temixtitan" (Tenochtitlán). Probably drawn at the re-
quest of Cortés, it appeared in the Latin edition of his Second Letter,
printed in Nuremburg in 1524. In order to ingratiate himself, Cortés
wrote five long letters to the king in which he related the progress of
the Conquest.*

bring under Spanish control other inhabitants in the country. He was
impelled to do so for various reasons: to gather more information about
the people and the land, to satisfy a consuming interest in the existence of a strait through the continent to Asia, and to dominate as
much territory as possible before rivals staked their claims. His time
was short, for the crown had ordered an agent to take over the government and to arrest him. By August 1521 Cristóbal de Tapia had arrived, but he was intimidated by partisans of Cortés and withdrew. The
conqueror meanwhile sent the king word of his defeat of the Aztecs,
after which Cortés was forgiven his insubordination.

During the course of the next several years Spanish forces under many different lieutenants overran Mexico, parts of Central America, and much of what is now the southwestern United States. And although the Conquest of the Mexica-Aztecs had taken a relatively short time, the Spaniards soon discovered that bringing under their sway the entire land was a vastly more difficult enterprise.

Highly centralized states strongly dependent on a dominant capital are vulnerable, tending to disintegrate quickly when the center falls. Hence the collapse of the imperial capital of Tenochtitlán was tantamount to the surrender of almost all towns under the city's control, and, therefore, much of central Mexico automatically fell to the invaders. There were many other areas of Mexico, however, outside the Aztec pale. Some threw in with the Spaniards early, and some came around as the Spaniards gained in reputation. But other groups that had successfully resisted the Aztecs rejected Spanish overlordship as well. While none could command forces comparable to those of the Aztecs, their more fragmented political structure made conquest difficult. Fighting the loosely organized tribes of Mexico presented the same frustrations and vexing problems that confront those dealing with guerrilla tactics in modern warfare.

Cortés was eager to plant settlements with a view to legitimizing his actions. In 1521 he sent Gonzalo de Sandoval to Coatzacoalcos (later called Puerto México but now known also by its Indian name) to settle that region and establish better communications with the islands. The same year Luis Marín departed for Oaxaca, where he encountered little success in his attempt to pacify the Zapotecs in hill country. He was more fortunate farther south in Chiapas, remaining until 1524 to establish a town; however, in 1527, the Chiapanecos rebelled, and the territory had to be reconquered by Diego de Mazariegos.

The governor of Jamaica, Francisco de Garay, had earlier been granted a royal commission to govern the Pánuco region north of Veracruz on the Gulf coast. Hoping to prevent what they considered an incursion, Cortés and Alvarado used force and diplomacy to convince Garay to withdraw. Meanwhile Cristóbal de Olid, one of Cortés's closest friends and confidants, was sent to western Mexico in 1522. After a cordial reception in Michoacán, he explored the Pacific coast, but in Colima he was stiffly opposed and forced to pull back.

Aware that expeditions from Panama were pushing northward up into Central America, Cortés moved to seize control first. Rumors circulated of cities rivaling Tenochtitlán in size and wealth, and in late 1523 Alvarado was ordered into the old Maya territory of Guatemala. After some arduous campaigns, he drove into El Salvador and conquered that region as well. For Alvarado's brilliant, though bloody, accomplishments, a grateful Spanish king appointed him governor and captain general of the lands he had won.

Shortly after Alvarado's departure from Mexico, Olid set sail to secure Honduras, stopping by Cuba for provisions. At this point Olid threw off loyalty to his captain and made common cause with the enemy, Governor Velázquez. When Cortés learned that Honduras was to be taken in the name of Olid and Velázquez, he was furious. He dispatched a punitive expedition, then decided to go down himself. It was the most costly decision the conqueror ever made.

Departing Mexico with a party of Spaniards mostly mounted, along with many Indian allies, musicians, tumblers, acrobats, and some young Spanish noblemen, Cortés headed to the Gulf coast and then cut southward across unknown country. The journey took them through Tabasco, Campeche, and the base of Yucatán. Because they were not following native trade routes, they encountered few settlements and had to survive off the wilderness. Great numbers of the porters collapsed from exhaustion, and many of the horses perished also. Indians and Spaniards alike contracted fevers and dysentery, and all suffered from

PRINCIPAL EXPLORATIONS AND CONQUESTS IN THE SIXTEENTH CENTURY

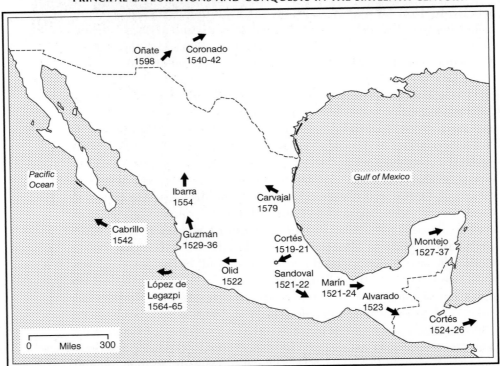

The flamboyant Pedro de Alvarado (1485–1541), Cortés's lieutenant and the conqueror of Guatemala.

near starvation. Though lacking the drama of the Aztec Conquest, the Honduras march exceeded the earlier enterprise in sheer hardship. For months the expedition cut its way through thick jungles, waded in swamps, and crossed swollen rivers. Once, within a distance of fifty miles, the Spaniards were forced to build fifty bridges, one of which, by Cortés's account, required a thousand trees. During this disastrous march a tragic episode occurred. Cuauhtémoc and several other high Indian lords had been taken along as hostages lest, in the absence of Cortés from Mexico, they encourage a native rebellion. When they allegedly attempted to foment an uprising among the Indians on the expedition, all, including Cuauhtémoc, were summarily tried and hanged.

At last Cortés and his men stumbled into Honduras, only to find that all had been in vain, for the advance punitive party had beheaded the rebel Olid and returned to Mexico. After spending some time trying to establish a settlement in his name, the captain set about returning, this time wisely traveling by sea. The nineteen-month venture was a remarkable achievement of exploration and endurance but a fiasco in all else.

CORTÉS IS DISCREDITED

Before departing for Honduras, Cortés had entrusted the government to the hands of royal treasury officials, with Alonso de Estrada in charge. Estrada was an honorable judge, but he found it difficult to govern the various factions that had formed and finally lost control. Because the expedition to Honduras remained out of contact with civilization so long, the rumor spread in Mexico that Cortés and the others had perished. Encouraged by word of Cortés's death, various factions moved to dispossess his followers of their encomiendas and other privileges, which were then handed over to supporters of corrupt treasury officials. A time of anarchy for all, Indians were especially maltreated.

The usurping governors ordered funeral ceremonies for Cortés and his men and then granted permission for the "widows" to remarry. When one of the wives, Juana Ruiz de Marcilla, criticized the action and heaped scorn on the officials, she was given one hundred lashes in public. Cortés later paid her great honors, carrying her on his horse and addressing her as "Doña." Most damaging for the captain (irreparably damaging, as it turned out) were the accusations made against him in dispatches sent to Spain, in which he was charged with having hidden Aztec treasure for himself, misusing crown funds, and cheating the royal treasury in other respects. The reports also cast doubt on his loyalty to the king. The dramatic news that Cortés was alive caused his men to rise up and seize the usurpers, who were thrown in cages and put on public display. Cortés's return to Mexico had a calming effect on political strife, but his reputation was not so easily restored.

The charges against the conqueror were never substantiated, but they planted seeds of suspicion, further nourished by partisans of the treasury officials in Spain. Moreover, the allegations provided a convenient pretext for which the crown may well have been thankful. At precisely the time Cortés was campaigning against the Aztecs, Emperor Charles V, the king of Spain, faced a revolt of his nobles at home, and although he was able to prevail, he retained a distrust of the fractious Spanish nobility. Thus Charles viewed with some concern the concentration of so much prestige and power in the hands of a budding aristocracy in the New World, especially since these "nobles" were rough adventurers and far distant from his royal armies in Europe. Crown policy had been to ease explorers and conquerors from political power, but, for the sake of appearances, the crown sought pretexts to void earlier signed agreements. Hence, Columbus's maladministration of Española had given the crown an excuse to replace him. And now the accusations against Cortés would serve the same purpose.

Receiving word of the defeat of the Aztecs, the king had appointed the conqueror as governor and captain general of New Spain in 1522. As an administrator, Cortés demonstrated many attributes of a statesman and a responsible colonizer. In addition to moving energetically to explore the land and seek ports for further discoveries, he also began to develop the economy. He undertook the search for mines, introduced European plants and livestock, and promoted commerce. He issued intelligent ordinances for the good order of the colony, sought ecclesiastics and educators, promoted justice, and in most respects acted as an enlightened governor should. And while he probably commanded sufficient respect and fear among both Spaniards and Indians to seize the land as his own, the evidence is that he remained stoutly loyal to his sovereign. The king and his council did not, however, ignore the allegations made against the conqueror both by enemies at court and in Mexico, and they decided to suspend him, for the time being at least. Royal officials were sent to supplant Cortés's authority. Growing increasingly frustrated and disgusted, he resolved to lay his case before the king in person.

With a grand retinue of Indian nobles, exotic Mexican plants and animals, and rich gifts for Charles V, Cortés arrived in Spain in 1528. His entrance caused a great sensation, and he was received with considerable fanfare. Charles V, pleased with his gifts and charmed by the conqueror's gallant manner, was satisfied that most of the rumors of misconduct were false or exaggerated. He allowed Cortés to choose for his encomiendas twenty-two towns, and the captain proceeded to select some of the richest settlements in the land. He was granted

Charles V (1500–58), King of Spain and Holy Roman Emperor, reigned during the decades of the Spanish conquests of the New World.

twenty-three thousand Indians as his vassals, confirmed as captain general, and awarded the grand title of the Marqués del Valle de Oaxaca. Nonetheless, he was not confirmed as governor of New Spain, and he took this slight as a special rebuke.

THE ADMINISTRATION OF NEW SPAIN

Prior to the settlement of Mexico there were few Spaniards in the Indies. The territories under Spanish control were small and required little attention from Spain. Ferdinand and Isabella appointed counselors for matters pertaining to the New World and turned their full attention to more pressing matters in Europe. In 1503, shortly before her death, Isabella created the Casa de Contratación, a house of trade to deal with affairs of the Indies, especially with regard to commerce, shipping, and emigration to the colonies. Juan Rodríguez de Fonseca, the bishop of Burgos, was given prime authority for making overseas policy.

The situation changed considerably, however, following the Conquest of Mexico, with its extensive lands and millions of people. Shortly thereafter Central America was penetrated, and early reports on Peru and other South American lands promised even more far-flung colonies. Affairs in the New World now clearly required a more broadly organized administration. Consequently, in 1524 Charles V created a supreme body called the Council of the Indies. This committee, composed of able, high-ranking Spaniards, would oversee all aspects of the colonies, both counseling the king and acting in his behalf.

Earlier, in 1511, there had been created in Santo Domingo a court of appeals so that matters of justice could be handled in the Indies instead of being referred to Spain. But the three judges of that body, called the *audiencia*, came to have broader duties. Traditionally, audiencias in Spain were courts of justice only, but in the New World they assumed executive and legislative functions as well. The judges (*oidores*) in Santo Domingo were the most powerful individuals in the Indies. With the lack of good government in New Spain, it was determined by the crown in 1527 that a similar court was needed in Mexico. Four experienced judges in Spain were appointed, but two died before taking office. The president of the audiencia was Nuño de Guzmán, a lawyer from a noble family with powerful connections.

Guzmán joined the two surviving judges in Mexico in early 1529. The rule of these three judges proved to be of the worst sort and a low point in the history of government in Spanish Mexico. As an adherent of Governor Velázquez of Cuba, Guzmán was a dedicated enemy of Cortés, and, with the conqueror absent in Spain, the audiencia moved against his followers. Once again their encomiendas were taken, and some were removed from official positions. It was a time of graft, corruption, and injustice for Indians and Spaniards alike.

Meanwhile, a bishop, Juan de Zumárraga, had arrived in Mexico City. Although he bore the title "Protector of the Indians," the judges refused to recognize his authority and prevented the Indians from seeking help from him or any other clergyman. Angered by the chaos and iniquities engendered by the misrule, Zumárraga bravely preached a sermon condemning the oidores, which brought threats against his life. All correspondence critical of the government was intercepted before it reached Spain, until the bishop traveled to Veracruz and entrusted a letter to the crown to a faithful sailor who smuggled the message aboard a departing vessel. As it became clear to Guzmán that his days were numbered, and fearing imminent arrest by royal agents, he set off in late 1529 for the west of Mexico, hoping to regain the royal confidence by a spectacular conquest of new territories.

Guzmán invaded Michoacán with a large force of Spaniards and thousands of native auxiliaries. He cut a bloody path through the west, burning villages, murdering chiefs, enslaving the Indians, and abusing them in every manner. One of the most brutal incidents saw the Tarascan king dragged behind a horse until he was almost senseless and then burned alive. The soldiers pressed north, lured by tales of a bountiful island ruled by attractive amazons, tales fabricated by the natives to induce their tormentors to move on. Quite aside from

Juan de Zumárraga (1468–1548), a Franciscan, was the first bishop and archbishop of Mexico.

his depredations, Guzmán explored and conquered a large area, all the way up to southern Sonora. Altogether he founded five cities.

The extensive western region was isolated from central Mexico and was later created as the separate administrative territory of New Galicia, over which its conqueror was appointed governor. But Guzmán's dark deeds caught up with him at length. After his long odyssey, notable for its duration no less than its savagery, Guzmán was ordered in 1533 to appear before a new audiencia to answer charges. In 1538 he was sent to Spain, where he spent the next two decades of his life as a virtual prisoner of the court.

While Guzmán was terrorizing the hinterlands of the west, the southeast region of Yucatán, the areas first sighted in 1517 by Spaniards from Cuba, remained outside Spanish control. Its conquest had been unsuccessfully attempted in 1527 by Francisco de Montejo, an early companion of Cortés. The enterprise went badly because of unfavorable terrain and a lack of local provisions, but mostly because of the indomitable spirit of the Maya. After nine years of stalemate in Yucatán, the conquest was renewed in 1537, and Montejo's son and nephew, both of whom were also named Francisco, brought most of the region under Spanish control by 1542, when the city of Mérida was founded. In 1547 a serious insurrection broke out, and many Spanish settlers were killed before calm was restored. After two decades of conflict, the conquest of Yucatán was finally effected.

After the fiasco of the first audiencia, the king and the Council of the Indies were more circumspect in their choice of oidores. They chose wisely in the appointment of Sebastián Ramírez de Fuenleal, who had served as both president of the Audiencia of Santo Domingo and bishop of that island. A man of highest integrity and proven abilities, he stood much in contrast to his predecessor in Mexico. He was joined in Mexico City by fellow judges of uniformly high quality, including Vasco de Quiroga, who would distinguish himself later in other undertakings. Within five years (1530–35) these learned magistrates wrought significant changes in the troubled colony. Bringing to bear the full weight and authority of the crown and maintaining a busy schedule, they proceeded to correct many abuses. A semblance of good order was restored, and ordinances were passed to improve the conditions of the Indians. The crown also moved to eliminate any threat from the powerful Cortés. Under investigation for encomienda abuses, he was deprived of various properties and privileges. Cortés remained the most prestigious individual in New Spain, but in 1535 even that status was challenged with the arrival of a viceroy.

The king and Council of the Indies had decided by 1528 that New Spain needed a ruler who would personify the dignity and authority of the crown and offset the affection of the people for Cortés. Such a person would have to be a great nobleman, jealous of his honor and above staining his name with acts of avarice and injustice, one whose competence and loyalty to the king were beyond question. After all, he would literally be a "vice-king." Many—and no doubt Cortés himself—assumed that the conqueror of New Spain would be the obvious choice for the post of viceroy. But Cortés had neither the desirable lineage nor the administrative experience for the high honor. Furthermore the very qualities that brought him success as a conqueror—audacity, independence of thought, and imagination—were anathema to the centralized bureaucracy of an absolute monarch. And there were too many disturbing and unanswered questions about his past actions.

The first three noblemen offered the august appointment declined the honor. The fourth, Don Antonio de Mendoza, the count of Tendilla, accepted, and he proved to be an excellent choice. An able ambassador to Rome, Mendoza was scion of one of Spain's most distinguished families and related to the royal house itself. He received his commission as viceroy in 1530, but the press of personal affairs prevented his arrival in Mexico until 1535. The viceroy's charge was to observe all matters of consequence affecting the colony except judicial matters, which would continue as the province of the audiencia. He had special orders to increase crown revenues and to ensure good treatment of the Indians. He was also vice-patron of the Church and responsible for the defense of New Spain. Allowing the viceroy a good salary as well as perquisites that included a palace and a personal guard, the crown purposely sought to enhance the prestige of the office.

Don Antonio de Mendoza
(1492?–1552) served as first viceroy in
New Spain, from 1535 to 1550.

In Search of Fabled Cities

During the 1520s and 1530s many fantastic tales circulated about wondrous lands in the New World. Among the more intriguing was the so-called Northern Mystery, which embraced not only the persistent myth of the amazons but also stories of the Seven (Golden) Cities of Cíbola. Speculation about fabulously rich kingdoms in other parts of the New World was rife, and it is not strange that men were ready to believe them. Had not the first rumors of Tenochtitlán and the dazzling Inca empire (conquered in the early 1530s) appeared just as fanciful?

Pánfilo de Narváez, the one-eyed casualty of Veracruz, commanded a fleet to Florida in 1528, hoping to discover the fabled lands of Apalachee. After an overland expedition, Narváez failed to make contact with his supply ships, and he and his men tried to reach Mexico by sailing makeshift boats down the Gulf coast. Most of them perished, but a few made the Texas coastline. In the end only four survived: Alvar Núñez Cabeza de Vaca, two other Spaniards, and Estéban, a black slave. For years they wandered among the Indians of the present-day Southwest of the United States, sometimes as slaves, sometimes as respected medicine men. In 1536, after many travails, they reached the northern Mexican outpost of Culiacán, where they were received with astonishment by their fellow countrymen.

Having spent so much time in the north, they were plied with questions about the Seven Cities, of which they had heard vaguely. That was enough to cause excitement, and prominent men scrambled for the privilege of undertaking the great search. The viceroy sensed an opportunity for an expedition that might overshadow the achievements of Cortés, and so of course he kept the rights for himself. But he took the precaution of sending an advance party, guided by Estéban and under the command of a Franciscan friar named Marcos de Niza. Pushing ahead of the main party, Estéban met an ironic end, for, having survived so long among the northern tribes, he apparently angered some Indians, who killed him.

Distraught by this news, Marcos de Niza proceeded with extreme caution. He seems to have viewed from a distance one of the Zuni villages in New Mexico, which he later reported as being larger than Tenochtitlán. Moreover—so he said—local chiefs told him that the city he saw was the smallest of the seven. In kindness to the friar, it must be said that sometimes, toward sunset, the fading light in that part of the country casts a rosy glow, and there may have been pieces of reflective quartz stuck in the adobe walls of the two-story dwellings he saw from afar; and so it is possible that he imagined he saw something truly marvelous. In any case, the Spaniards in Mexico wanted to believe

ROUTE OF CORONADO'S EXPEDITION, 1540–42

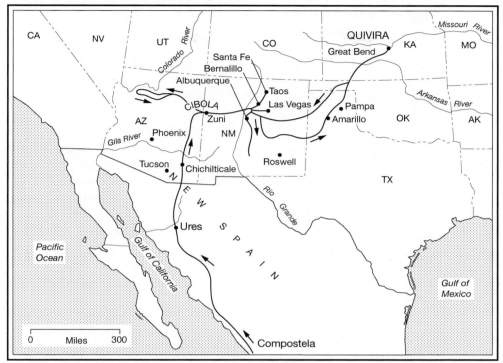

the existence of such cities, and preparations were eagerly made for the adventure. Those who had missed the earlier conquests would now have their chance.

Mendoza chose his friend, Francisco Vázquez de Coronado, the governor of New Galicia, to lead the well-equipped expedition. In 1540, 336 Spaniards, with hundreds of Indian allies and about a thousand horses and swine, moved out with high expectations. When they saw the mud village at the end of a grueling march, they vented their frustration by slaughtering Zunis unwilling to cooperate with them during a time of ritual celebration. From other Pueblo Indians, they learned of "the Land of Quivira," some distance away but even more wonderful than the legendary cities of Cíbola. Their hopes raised, off they went.

The natives, whose villages were being destroyed, soon found that the best way to get rid of the unwelcome intruders was to tell them that, while they had no wealth, there were abundant riches *más allá*— farther on. Because of such information the Spaniards wandered aimlessly for months, finally reaching the vicinity of Wichita, Kansas. Now greatly disheartened, having seen only a few villages scattered over a vast prairie and some "shaggy cows" (buffalo), the miserable survivors dragged themselves back to Mexico.

In 1542 a party commanded by Juan Rodríguez de Cabrillo sailed up along the beaches of California. The modern attractions of the area, however, had little appeal for the Spaniards, and they would not settle California for a very long time. That same year Mendoza dispatched Ruy López de Villalobos to the Philippines (named for prince Philip), but the expedition failed to return to Mexico.

The Vázquez de Coronado mission occasioned serious problems of another sort. When the expedition left western Mexico a good number of Spaniards who had settled New Galicia went along, leaving the frontier sparsely occupied by Christians and militarily weakened. Conscious of the situation, the Indians, who harbored resentments going back to the cruelty of Nuño de Guzmán, were roused by their shamans to rebel. The ensuing Mixtón War (1540–41) was the most serious revolt prior to the struggle for Independence. The whole frontier was aflame. Natives attacked isolated Spanish ranches and then fortified themselves on well-stocked hilltops called *peñoles*, from which they could not be dislodged.

When the governor of New Galicia failed to subdue the rebels, he turned for assistance to Pedro de Alvarado, who had sailed up from Guatemala on his way to explore the Pacific. Courageous to a fault, Alvarado rashly ignored the advice to wait for reinforcements. A furious counterattack by the Indians produced a panicky Spanish retreat, during which a horse fell on Alvarado, crushing him. The great rebellion ended only after the viceroy himself took the field at the head of a strong army, comprised primarily of central Mexican Indian allies.

THE LAST YEARS OF CORTÉS

Meanwhile Cortés, having been excluded from the search for the Northern Mystery and feeling insulted by his treatment from the viceroy and the audiencia, returned to Spain in 1540 to put his grievances once again before the king. Charles V was abroad, however, and crown representatives gave the Marqués a cool reception. The crisis of instability appeared to have been resolved in the colony, and with the royal bureaucracy entrenched and functioning well, government officials saw no need to humor the conqueror. Beset by invidious rivals in Mexico and an indifferent sovereign in Spain, he spent his last years in frustration, then resignation. He was about to return to New

Spain when, in 1547, he fell ill. Shortly thereafter, in his sixty-second year, he died in a village outside Seville. In 1556 his bones were deposited in Mexico, according to his wishes.

Though the last two decades of Cortés's life were fraught with disappointment, there is no greater example of rise to fame and fortune in the history of the New World. Through his diverse talents he gained immortality as one of the greatest military figures of the ages. He married into one of Spain's most noble families, was awarded a high title himself, and became one of the richest men in the Spanish empire. As a symbol of Spain's might and the exploitation of indigenous peoples, his image later became tarnished, first with Mexico's independence from Spain and later with the Revolution of 1910, which aspired to rehabilitate the indigenous past. The image of destroyer displaced that of heroic leader.

Few of his fellow conquerors attained Cortés's status and wealth in the colonial period, but many established themselves as part of New Spain's upper class. When the immediate wealth they had hoped to carry home to support a life of leisure did not materialize, they comforted themselves by acquiring native labor and property locally. For most of them, the new lifestyle represented a significant step up from their modest origins.

STABILITY UNDER VICEROY MENDOZA

Despite the reversals of the ill-fated Coronado expedition and the costly Mixtón War, by 1542 the colonial government was finally ready to achieve stability and order. There was good cause for optimism, for Mendoza was a firm and capable viceroy and the audiencia he worked with was responsible. Bishop Zumárraga was an energetic and positive complement to civil government. Yet there was brewing in Spain a reform movement that was destined to inflame passions once again. Bartolomé de Las Casas, a powerful Dominican friar and an indefatigable lobbyist on behalf of Indian liberties, had successfully convinced the crown to introduce legislation aimed at curtailing abuses of the natives, whose numbers had declined drastically. These New Laws of 1542–43 called for, among other things, the freedom of natives who had been unjustly enslaved and the easing of labor requirements. Most threatening from the standpoint of the Spanish conquerors, the laws eroded the encomienda system, for encomiendas awarded to conquerors and first settlers were to escheat to the crown on the death of the original encomendero. News of the provision caused a great outcry among the encomenderos, who remonstrated bitterly that they would have nothing to leave their children. Surely, they insisted, the king could not be so ungrateful to those who had won and settled lands larger than Spain itself.

The continuance of the encomienda system was regarded in Mexico, even by many royal officials, as vital to the maintenance of the colony's prosperity, for without it, it was feared, many Spaniards would leave. In fact, most ecclesiastics also favored its retention, seeing it as the best instrument for control of the Indians. Furthermore, tribute and labor helped support various charities, educational facilities, and religious institutions. The bishop himself held an encomienda. Many Spaniards agreed that natives under crown control were abused more by royal agents than by encomenderos. When an official investigator, Francisco Tello de Sandoval, was sent from Spain to help implement the New Laws, he found widespread opposition in the colony.

Tello de Sandoval and Viceroy Mendoza, assessing the situation and fearing a general revolt, exercised the prerogative of withholding the laws. Under the circumstances, they probably chose wisely: when the viceroy in Peru insisted on imposing the ordinances a serious insurrection ensued, which took his life and embroiled the colony in civil war for years. Finally giving way to the outraged encomenderos, the crown modified the laws in 1545 by removing the offending limitation to the encomiendas.

Although the crown had retreated, it still intended to reform the encomienda system. In 1549 it ordered that encomenderos could no longer avail themselves of the free labor of their Indians but would have to be content with their tributes only. In the same year there was a flurry of excitement when a small group of Spaniards plotted to overthrow the government. They were tried, found guilty, and summarily hanged.

By 1550, as Mendoza's rule of nearly fifteen years came to a close, the colony was well implanted and thriving. In the crown's view Mendoza was the ideal administrator. His dreams of extending Spanish realms into rich areas (that did not exist) were unrealized, but his contributions in other respects were impressive. The part played by Mendoza was of crucial importance, because, as the first viceroy, he established patterns that would be followed by his successors. He left a flourishing economy and a capital that had already assumed the appearance of a beautiful city distinguished for its cultural life. He established order and stability; he founded schools, hospitals, and charitable foundations; he attempted to foster religion and justice for all. Because of his government, royal authority began to be stamped on New Spain. The colony had survived the turbulent first three decades of its life.

RECOMMENDED FOR FURTHER STUDY

Adorno, Rolena, and Patrick Charles Pautz. *Alvar Núñez Cabeza de Vaca: His Account, His Life, and the Expedition of Pánfilo de Narváez*. Lincoln: University of Nebraska Press, 1999.

Aiton, Arthur S. *Antonio de Mendoza, First Viceroy of New Spain*. Durham, N.C.: Duke University Press, 1927.

Altman, Ida. *Emigrants and Society: Extremadura and America in the Sixteenth Century*. Berkeley: University of California Press, 1989.

———. *Transatlantic Ties in the Spanish Empire: Brihuega, Spain, and Puebla, Mexico, 1560–1620*. Stanford, Calif.: Stanford University Press, 2000.

Bolton, Herbert E. *Coronado: Knight of Pueblos and Plains*. Albuquerque: University of New Mexico Press, 1949.

Chamberlain, Robert S. *The Conquest and Colonization of Yucatán, 1517–1550*. Washington, D.C.: Carnegie Institute of Washington, 1948.

Chipman, Donald. *Nuño de Guzmán and Pánuco in New Spain, 1518–1533*. Glendale, Calif.: Clark, 1966.

Clendinnen, Inga. *Ambivalent Conquests: Maya and Spaniard in Yucatán, 1517–1570*. Cambridge: Cambridge University Press, 1987.

Gruzinski, Serge. *Images at War: Mexico from Columbus to Blade Runner, 1492–2019*. Durham, NC: Duke University Press, 2001.

Hirschberg, Julia. "Social Experiment in New Spain: A Prosopographical Study of the Early Settlement at Puebla de los Angeles, *1531–1534*." *Hispanic American Historical Review* 59 (1979): 1–33.

Jones, Grant D. *The Conquest of the Last Maya Kingdom*. Stanford, Calif.: Stanford University Press, 1998.

———. *Maya Resistance to Spanish Rule: Time and History on a Colonial Frontier*. Albuquerque: University of New Mexico Press, 1989.

Krippner-Martínez, James. *Rereading the Conquest: Power, Politics, and the History of Early Colonial Michoacán, 1521–1565*. University Park: University of Pennsylvania Press, 2001.

Pupo-Walker, Enrique. *Castaways: The Narrative of Alvar Núñez Cabeza de Vaca*. Berkeley: University of California Press, 1993.

Restall, Matthew. *Maya Conquistador*. Boston: Beacon Press, 1998.

Warren, J. Benedict. *The Conquest of Michoacán: The Spanish Domination of the Tarascan Kindgom in Western Mexico, 1521–1530*. Norman: University of Oklahoma Press, 1985.

Weber, David J. *The Spanish Frontier in North America*. New Haven, Conn.: Yale University Press, 1992.

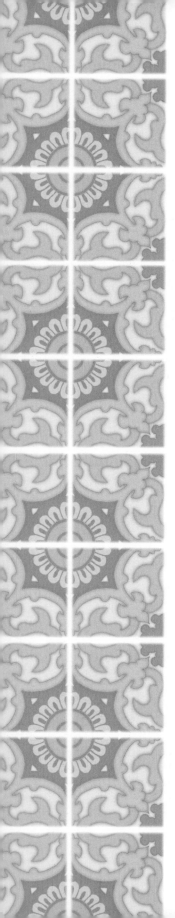

III

THE COLONY
OF NEW SPAIN

8

The Imperial System Entrenched

THE POLITICAL ADMINISTRATION OF NEW SPAIN

"Do little and do it slowly" had been Viceroy Mendoza's stated philosophy of administration. It was an attitude less than acceptable to reformers but consistent with royal wishes. The sixteenth-century viceroys, facing many crucial situations, were allowed considerable latitude, but their successors in the seventeenth century were reined in. Later kings and their councils increasingly gathered authority to themselves, discouraging the viceroys and audiencias from independence of thought and action.

Yet given the difficulty of communication and the time lapse between a request for instructions and the response from Spain, a certain amount of autonomy was implicit. Correspondence between colonial officials and the crown was necessarily slow, because for most of the colonial period ships sailed only once a year between Mexico and Spain. It was common for authorities in New Spain to wait many months for guidance. Consequently high officials often made important rulings on their own, pending royal approval. When a crown order seemed contrary to the best interests of the local situation, a viceroy sometimes noted, in all deference, *Obedezco pero no cumplo* (I obey but do not execute). The process of government was further bogged down by the endless detailed reports, requiring action, sent to Spain by officials, clergymen, and private subjects.

Colonial policy of the Hapsburgs was ponderous and inefficient. But sluggish as the bureaucracy was, the crown concerned itself less with competence than with loyalty. Unable to micromanage a far-flung empire, the Hapsburgs were willing to relinquish considerable control to local elites who could keep the peace in the crown's name. The preoccupation with conformance and fidelity also manifested itself in the system of checks and balances. Officials were encouraged to comment on and criticize the performance of others. The viceroy was the most powerful individual, but as the judges of the audiencia reported directly to the king and the Council of the Indies and were often at odds

with the viceroy, they were a restraint on the viceroy's actions. Moreover, treasury officials and various other bureaucrats, as well as clergymen, members of town councils, and private individuals, contributed
their complaints, and as a result, the crown was exposed to a wide spectrum of opinion on the operation of colonial administration.

To ascertain the true state of affairs, the crown occasionally sent a
royal inspector (*visitador*) to make an on-the-spot investigation (*visita*).
The crown visitador had great authority on arrival; he usually assumed
rule of the colony for the tenure of his inspection, which could take
weeks or months. The visita was sometimes undertaken in response to
a specific set of charges emanating from the colony, but in other instances it was more routine in nature. In some instances the visitador
traveled incognito, taking officials by surprise, before adequate cover-
ups could be arranged. At other times the imminent arrival of the inspector became known in time for precautionary measures on the part
of local officials.

Visitadores, usually men trained in the law, were responsible for cor-
recting abuses and instituting reforms. Moreover, their charges included judging the performance of the viceroy and other high functionaries. Such a judicial review, or trial, was known as a (*juicio de*)
residencia. A residencia usually came at the end of an official's term
of office. Notice of an impending review was made public, so that all
within the official's jurisdiction with grievances could bring charges.

The admirable institutions of the visita and the residencia were models that might well profit all governments. Unfortunately, like so much
in Spanish administration, there existed a wide breach between theory and practice. Witnesses were sometimes bribed or intimidated;
perjury and obfuscation were common; and judges were occasionally
bought. Furthermore, despite the long lists of allegations posted—and
testimony that often convincingly established the official's guilt—relatively few were punished in accordance with their crimes. Heavily re-
liant on the allegiance of far-removed colonial officials, the crown frequently winked at their greed and misdeeds.

Various restrictions were imposed on officials with a view to averting corruption. They were forbidden to hold encomiendas or to participate in commercial activities as well as other activities that presented a conflict of interest. Although certainly one finds many officials
of integrity, the infractions were numerous. In essence, a weak Hapsburg state governed informally through mechanisms that rewarded
New Spain's elites by allowing them to exploit Indians and maximize
profits. The crown was satisfied as long as they kept the peace and re-
mitted a modicum of returns to the imperial government. Corruption
was furthered by the introduction in the sixteenth century of the sale

of public office. At first limited to local appointments, the practice was extended in the seventeenth century to include the highest positions, including treasury officials, oidores, and even viceroys.

Of the sixty-two viceroys who served in New Spain, almost all came from the high nobility and were born in Spain. Men born in the New World could attain this highest office (Mexico had three in the seventeenth century), but as sons of high nobles serving as viceroys themselves, they were not identified as locals. Most viceroys proved reasonably good rulers; a few were truly outstanding. The colony was fortunate that the first two viceroys, Mendoza (1535–50) and Luis de Velasco (1550–64), were wise administrators who set New Spain on firm footing. Mendoza was a superb politician who carefully played off troublesome factions to achieve order. Velasco abolished Indian slavery and implemented other measures to ease the suffering of the natives. These first two viceroys served many years, but there was no specified term for a viceroy, and most remained in office for shorter periods. The quality of the viceroys declined in the seventeenth century, but the following century saw the emergence of some great talent in the office.

It is more difficult to assess the character of the oidores of the audiencias. As the functions of the courts expanded, more judges were added. With the settlement of western lands, a new audiencia, that of Nueva Galicia, was created in 1548. It usually had four or five oidores, while the Audiencia of Mexico counted ten by late eighteenth

Luis de Velasco I (1511–64), the second viceroy of New Spain, served until his death. He continued the prudent policies established by his predecessor Mendoza.

century, plus other lawyers. Since the appointments of judges were for life, they developed strong local ties, prompting speculation as to their impartiality.

The same cannot be said for the provincial officials. As new territories were colonized and towns founded, it became impossible to govern outlying provinces from the capital. Subdivisions of administration were, therefore, formalized, and many smaller administrative districts were created within the audiencia jurisdictions. Such districts were administered by officials known variously as *corregidores, alcaldes mayores*, or *gobernadores*, whose territories of jurisdiction were called *corregimientos, alcaldías mayores*, or *gobiernos*. There was little difference among the duties of these officials, and a brief discussion of the position of corregidor serves, in essence, to describe the others as well. Corregidores were responsible for the good order of their districts, but their judicial and legislative responsibilities were limited, as they were subject to higher authorities in all matters. In the early years of the system these positions often went to conquerors or their sons, or other early settlers, as a form of pension in lieu of encomiendas. As can be imagined, most appointees had little or no training for administrative posts and were poorly paid. It came to be accepted that these provincial officials would supplement their salaries where they could—which usually meant cheating the natives or other lower-class groups.

Most notorious were *corregidores de indios*, whose responsibility it was to administer Indian towns. The natives had been gathered into new villages to facilitate their conversion and acculturation, and the corregidor de indios was charged with the good order of those under his jurisdiction, in those towns paying tribute to the crown rather than to individual encomenderos. These Spanish supervisors, or their agents, collected the king's tributes in the "crown towns" and supposedly guaranteed justice. In fact, they were the greatest enemies of the Indians, defrauding them in a variety of ways, often in collusion with the native governors. In addition to forcing Indians to produce cloth, which they then sold at a profit, corregidores also acted as petty traders, compelling natives to buy goods from them at elevated prices. These practices were known as the *repartimiento de mercancías*.

Distinct from the royal authorities were those in municipal government. Beginning with the founding of Veracruz in 1519 by Cortés, as Spanish towns were established a town council was immediately formed. In the earliest years Cortés simply appointed many local administrators, but it became customary for them to be elected annually. The municipal council, called the *cabildo* (or *ayuntamiento*), consisted of members known as *regidores*. These councilmen numbered anywhere from four or five in smaller communities up to fifteen in late colonial Mexico City. A council usually had two senior officials, called *alcaldes ordinarios*, who had some judicial powers and more importance than the regidores, who were simply councilors.

The cabildos were responsible for such purely local matters as defending the town, keeping the peace, controlling prices, allocating lots, cleaning streets, and seeing to drainage, water supplies, public food, and a multitude of other concerns. Generally speaking, the cabildos of the various towns represented the interests of the local elites, which were frequently in conflict with the wishes of the crown.

Positions in the cabildos were awarded to the highest bidders, even though consideration was supposed to be given to those with the best credentials. Such posts were cherished because of the distinction they offered in the community, not to mention the opportunities for making profits on the side. The result was that membership in the cabildos came under the control of certain families, who held proprietary interest in them for generations. Since the seats were often sold in perpetuity, they were passed on from father to son. By the late colonial period fifteen regidores in Mexico City owned their positions. Cabildos tended to be composed largely of elite *criollos*, or Mexican-born Spaniards.

Administration of Indian towns was modeled after that of the Spanish communities, but practices varied widely. In areas where an Indian nobility existed before contact, regidores were commonly chosen from among them. Indian towns also had a local governor (*gobernador*) who oversaw the activities of the cabildo and aided it in collecting tribute, apportioning village lands, and dispensing justice. Native leaders had to engage in a delicate balancing act in order to satisfy the demands of the local Spanish officials or clergymen without alienating their fellow Indians. Failure to maintain this balance could result in their removal by Spanish authorities or violence against them by local villagers. As time went on, in most parts of central and southern Mexico hereditary leaders found their political and/or economic privileges eroded in some measure.

In other areas where Indians had not lived in permanent pueblos before the conquest, Spanish civil and religious officials congregated them in villages and exerted strong influence over their government. It was not uncommon to find outsiders and even individuals of mixed race occupying the position of governor after a couple of generations. Despite the constant drain on Indian economies, local Indian leaders consistently sought ways to keep control of their own resources and production. Sometimes they were able to do this through *cofradías*, confraternities dedicated to the cult of a saint, which owned property and livestock. In addition to keeping some of their foodstuffs in the community, cofradías also served as a source of local credit.

DISTURBANCES DURING THE "COLONIAL SIESTA"

By the middle of the sixteenth century the Spanish imperial system was established, and the bureaucracy was spreading its net. Even though order was steadily imposed, the next two and a half centuries cannot accurately be depicted as a "colonial siesta." Challenges to Spanish hegemony came from both outside and inside New Spain. Internal contestation emanated from all levels of society.

Even elites plotted rebellion when their interests were threatened, as an episode of the 1560s demonstrates. Anticipating the eventual loss of their encomiendas, a group of young criollos in Mexico City began to talk loosely of assassinating oidores and other high officials, throwing off allegiance to the crown, and making Martín Cortés king of Mexico. Don Martín was the only legitimate son of the conqueror and his heir. Because his active role in the conspiracy could not be proven, Martín escaped the fate of its leaders whose heads were cut off and displayed on pikes. The severity of the punishment for young men believed by most to have been foolish rather than treasonous shocked the elites. For most of the colonial period, however, the upper classes sought redress or influence through cooperation with the royal officials or through the courts. At least until the middle of the eighteenth century, they tended to enjoy considerable autonomy as long as they could maintain local order and furnish the crown its share of the colonial goodies.

Intra-elite squabbles occasionally erupted in violence. For example, in 1624, as a result of bitter animosities, the viceroy and the religious orders arrayed against a coalition of the archbishop and the audiencia. The archbishop excommunicated the viceroy, who responded by ordering the prelate banished from Mexico. The lower classes, fiercely loyal to their spiritual leader, formed a rampaging mob that threatened the viceroy. Their demonstration ended in violence and in some seventy deaths. So bitter were the denunciations that the viceroy was recalled.

More common were the urban protests over food shortages, prices, or taxation in Mexico City and provincial capitals. In 1692, a crisis brought on by severe food shortages, the result of crop failures, was exacerbated by the rumor that authorities had connived to corner the grain market to their profit. The resentment of the Indians and mestizos—persons of mixed Spanish and Indian blood—burst into destructive riots during the celebration of Corpus Christi in which the viceregal palace was burned and looted. Other government buildings were destroyed, along with 280 shops and stalls, before the viceroy's troops finally restored order through harsh measures.

Authorities also had to contend with various natural calamities over which they had little control. Very destructive were the many floods that plagued the capital in the colonial period. The dike whereby the Aztecs had controlled the lake waters was destroyed by the Spaniards and never replaced. From the middle of the sixteenth century on, the city was inundated at intervals, with very serious losses. Officials were equally helpless in dealing with such periodic disasters as earthquakes, pestilences, and crop failures, even though some minimal precautions were taken.

Although urban riots were not a daily occurrence, violence was. For the growing numbers of mixed race and marginalized peoples, poverty could serve as a powerful motivation for petty theft. Racial and gender tensions frequently erupted in domestic abuses, crimes of passion, and personal violence. In the colonial Mexican countryside, insecurities, tensions, and resistance to exploitation were also vented in personal violence, witchcraft, village riots, and even rebellions in peripheral areas.

EXPANSION INTO NORTHERN MEXICO

Violent resistance to Spanish intrusion was the primary response of the nomadic and semi-sedentary indigenous groups in northern Mexico. While much of central and southern Mexico was under Spanish control by the middle of the sixteenth century, the wide expanses of the north remained unsettled by the newcomers. Interest in the northern frontiers had quickened, however, with the discovery of silver ore in the 1540s, setting off a rush into the Zacatecas region. Within a few years mining camps appeared in many locations, but bellicose Chichimec warriors made supplying the camps difficult and dangerous. The long distances between Spanish settlements and the isolated mining camps offered the Indians ample opportunity to strike the mule trains. For half a century the indomitable northern tribes resisted the Spanish advance, and the fighting subsided only in the last decade of the sixteenth century when Viceroy Luis de Velasco II, with the help of missionary clergy, inaugurated a policy of conciliation. In return for annual supplies of cattle and clothing, many of the natives were persuaded to put down their arms.

Although some Franciscans had preceded them, in the seventeenth century the Jesuits forged northward, following Spanish explorers and miners like Francisco de Ibarra into the northwestern areas of Sinaloa, Durango, and Chihuahua that became known as Nueva Vizcaya (New Biscay). Eventually they pushed all the way to Baja California and

Arizona. Their attempts to resettle semi-sedentary Indians in permanent villages invariably met with rebellion, either within a generation or two, or later in the colonial period. In the 1570s Luis de Carvajal was given a commission to pacify the northeast of the country. Finding little mineral wealth, the settlers of that land enslaved the local Indians, who were sold as miners to north central Mexico. Carvajal founded the city of Monterrey and settled other towns in the new province, which was named Nuevo León.

In the 1590s the viceroy of New Spain sent out more expeditions to the far north earlier traversed by Vázquez de Coronado. Following the march of Juan de Oñate in 1598, an outpost was established and Franciscan friars began converting Indians at San Juan, Taos, and other pueblos. In 1609, two years after the English colonized Jamestown, the northern capital was planted at Santa Fe. Nevertheless, the extensive region of New Mexico remained sparsely populated; there were some friars, a few soldiers, and a scattering of miners, traders, and ranchers, along with various officials. The harsh land yielded little revenue and offered hardly more to the imperial system than Indian souls and a tenuous hold on the land in the face of French expansion.

Expeditions by sea continued to explore new lands for the Spanish empire. After earlier attempts to plant colonies in the Pacific had failed, the historic voyage in 1565 by Miguel López de Legazpi and the friar Andrés de Urdaneta led to settlement. Most important, Urdaneta discovered a satisfactory route back to the western hemisphere, sailing for the California coast and then turning southward to Mexico. Manila was founded, and shortly thereafter the fabulous trade between the Orient and New Spain began, with one ship a year—the Manila Galleon—making its way from the Philippine capital to Acapulco and back. Vast amounts of Mexican silver reached Asia in payment for such prized goods as Chinese silk and porcelain, Indonesian spices, and Indian cotton.

The Manila trade piqued new interest in the coast of California, where the galleons first sighted the mainland of America. In the 1590s Sebastián Vizcaíno explored the coastline with indifferent success. In 1602 another expedition under his command produced a commendable chart of California waters, and Vizcaíno founded the port of Monterey, but there was still no compelling reason to make serious attempts at colonizing California.

RIVALS IN THE NEW WORLD

A growing concern of Spanish authorities was the encroachment of foreigners on the fringes of New Spain, both by land and sea. A French force led by the Chevalier de La Salle journeyed southward from

Canada in the 1680s into the region of Texas, where, it was rumored, a settlement was planted. In response Spaniards began to occupy Texas, and in 1698 a Spanish fort was established on the Gulf coast at Pensacola (Florida).

A more serious threat was posed by foreigners on the seas. North European powers had never accepted the pope's division of the New World, which gave most of it to Spain, and, especially following the growth of Protestantism, they challenged Spain's hegemony. Pirates, often with the blessings of their sovereigns, aggressively attacked Spanish property. French interlopers were cruising the eastern coastline of South America little more than a decade after Columbus's first voyage. The ship sent by Cortés carrying Aztec treasure to Charles V had been seized by French corsairs when it was in sight of Iberian shores. Later the French moved closer to the source, attacking Spanish ships in American waters and looting ports. Along the Gulf coast, from Yucatán to Tampico, French filibusters raided with little opposition.

The Pacific port of Acapulco in a 1671 Dutch engraving.

In 1561 they sacked the town of Campeche and a decade later seized valuable treasures from a Franciscan convent in Yucatán.

Somewhat later the English, too, appeared off Mexican shores. In 1567 John Hawkins sailed boldly into the port of Veracruz under pretext of repairing his ships, but he actually planned to sell his cargo of black slaves in defiance of laws that forbade Spanish trade with foreigners. Hawkins was trapped by an incoming Spanish fleet bearing a new viceroy. Despite a gentleman's agreement for a truce, the viceroy brought his ships to bear and peppered the English vessels, allowing only two of Hawkins's nine ships to escape. The captured English corsairs were given sentences at labor, and later some were tried and burned by the Inquisition, not for piracy but for heresy. The defeat of Hawkins was a great feather in the viceroy's cap, but the Spaniards would pay dearly for it, for escaping on one of the English ships was Hawkins's cousin, Francis Drake. Before long *El Draque* took his

A Spanish shield of the seventeenth century.

vengeance, becoming the terror of the Spanish Indies, raiding with considerable success in both the Caribbean and the Pacific, and driving the Spaniards to distraction.

From the middle of the sixteenth century until the end of the eighteenth century, English and French corsairs attacked the coasts of Yucatán and Campeche many times, though the rewards were often modest. Some of the small, isolated ports were so poorly defended that they could be taken by a handful of pirates. In Pacific waters both the English and Dutch were active, the most successful being Thomas Cavendish, who captured a richly laden Manila Galleon.

The most vicious attack, however, was not on sea but on land. In 1683, after laying careful plans, a Frenchman known as Lorenzillo led a force of about a thousand ruffians of mixed nationalities to the strongly fortified port of Veracruz and invested the city under cover of night. Over six thousand local citizens were rounded up, held inside the churches, and denied food and water for three days and nights. Many were horribly tortured, and most of the females, of all ages, were raped. The pirates carried off about a million dollars worth of loot.

By the end of the seventeenth century the viceroyalty of New Spain stretched out over a vast expanse of territory. It embraced all land on the mainland north of Panama, extending up to New Mexico, the islands of the Caribbean, and even the Philippines. Ostensibly all these far-flung regions were under the control of the viceroy; in actual practice, his authority was nominal, for the more remote areas were effectively beyond his reach. Central America, the islands of the Caribbean, and the Philippines had their own audiencias, which were for all intents and purposes autonomous.

Spain itself, after boasting the richest and most powerful empire in the world during the sixteenth century, began to decline in the early decades of the seventeenth century. But the Spanish empire remained intact and relatively prosperous, thanks to an administrative system that, despite its flaws, held the immense territories together.

RECOMMENDED FOR FURTHER STUDY

Bolton, Herbert E. *Rim of Christendom: A Biography of Eusebio Francisco Kino, Pacific Coast Pioneer*. New York: Macmillan, 1936.

Borah, Woodrow. *Justice by Insurance: The General Indian Court and the Legal Aides of the Half-Real*. Berkeley: University of California Press, 1983.

Burkhart, Louise M. *The Slippery Earth: Nahua-Christian Moral Dialogue in Sixteenth Century Mexico*. Tucson: University of Arizona Press, 1989.

Burkholder, Mark A. "An Empire beyond Compare," in *The Oxford History of Mexico*. Edited by Michael C. Meyer and William H. Beezley, pp. 115–49. New York: Oxford University Press, 2000.

Cline, S. L. *Colonial Culhuacan, 1580–1600: A Social History of an Aztec Town.* Albuquerque: University of New Mexico Press, 1986.

Farriss, Nancy M. *Maya Society under Colonial Rule. The Collective Enterprise of Survival.* Princeton, N.J.: Princeton University Press, 1984.

Gerhard, Peter. *The North Frontier of New Spain.* Princeton, N.J.: Princeton University Press, 1982.

Gibson, Charles. *The Aztecs under Spanish Rule: A History of the Indians of the Valley of Mexico, 1519–1810.* Stanford, Calif.: Stanford University Press, 1964.

Gruzinski, Serge. *The Conquest of Mexico: The Incorporation of Indian Societies into the Western World, 16th–18th Centuries.* Cambridge: Polity Press, 1993.

Haring, Clarence H. *The Spanish Empire in America.* New York: Oxford University Press, 1947.

Haskett, Robert. *Indigenous Rulers: An Ethnohistory of Town Government in Colonial Cuernavaca.* Albuquerque: University of New Mexico Press, 1991.

Himmerich y Valencia, Robert. *The Encomenderos of New Spain, 1521–1555.* Austin: University of Texas Press, 1991.

Horn, Rebecca. *Postconquest Coyoacan: Spanish-Nahua Relations in Central Mexico, 1519–1650.* Stanford, Calif.: Stanford University Press, 1997.

Jones, Oakah L. *Nueva Vizcaya: Heartland of the Spanish Frontier.* Albuquerque: University of New Mexico Press, 1988.

Kellogg, Susan. *Law and the Transformation of Aztec Culture, 1500–1700.* Norman: University of Oklahoma Press, 1995.

Lane, Kris E., *Pillaging the Empire: Piracy in the Americas, 1500–1750.* Armonk, N.Y.: M.E. Sharpe, 1998.

Liss, Peggy Korn. *Mexico under Spain, 1521–1556: Society and Origins of Nationality.* Chicago: University of Chicago Press, 1975.

Lockhart, James: *The Nahuas after the Conquest: A Social and Cultural History of the Indians of Central Mexico, Sixteenth through Eighteenth Centuries.* Stanford, Calif.: Stanford University Press, 1992.

Mecham, J. Lloyd. *Francisco de Ibarra and Nueva Vizcaya.* Durham, N.C.: Duke University Press, 1927.

Naylor, Thomas H., and Charles W. Polzer, eds. *The Presidio and Militia on the Northern Frontier of New Spain: A Documentary History.* Vol. 1: *1570–1700.* Tucson: University of Arizona Press, 1986.

Poole, Stafford. *Juan de Ovando: Governing the Spanish Empire in the Reign of Philip II.* Norman: University of Oklahoma Press, 2004.

Powell, Philip W. *Soldiers, Indians, and Silver.* Berkeley: University of California Press, 1969.

Terraciano, Kevin. T*he Mixtecs of Colonial Oaxaca: Nudzahui History, Sixteenth through Eighteenth Centuries.* Stanford, Calif.: University of California Press, 2001.

Vigil, Ralph H. *Alonso de Zorita, Royal Judge and Christian Humanist, 1512–1585.* Norman: University of Oklahoma Press, 1987.

Weber, David J. *The Spanish Frontier in North America.* New Haven, Conn.: Yale University Press, 1992.

Wood, Stephanie. *Transcending Conquest: Nahua Views of Colonial Mexico.* Norman: University of Oklahoma Press, 2003.

9

The Colonial Economy

SPAIN'S ECONOMIC POLICIES

Mexico, as the colony of New Spain, existed for the benefit of the mother country. At least that was the view of the Spanish crown's economic advisers. Like other European colonial powers, Spain subscribed to the economic philosophy of mercantilism, which held that the purpose of a colony was to make the mother country stronger and more self-sufficient. If a colony did not return such advantages to the mother country it could be more of a liability than an asset. There were other considerations, both religious and strategic, but profit was no doubt the primary consideration.

Spain's colonial economic policies were protectionist in the extreme, which meant that the economy in New Spain was very much restricted by limitations imposed by the imperial system. Thus the natural growth of industry and commerce was significantly impeded, because manufacturers and merchants in Spain were protected from the competition of those in the colony. In accord with the classic pattern, the Spanish Indies were to supply Spain with raw products, which could be made into finished goods in the mother country and sold back to the colonists at a profit. In the case of Mexico, silver would become the main export to Spain, where it promoted inflation and Spanish imperial wars.

In early years of the colony whites lived parasitically off many Indians and a few blacks, but the picture changed considerably after a time. The importance of the encomiendas in the overall economy of New Spain did not last long, for not many of those who came after the conquerors received grants of Indian villages. Within a short time the encomenderos formed but a small minority of the Spaniards in Mexico. Of perhaps eight hundred first-generation encomenderos, their numbers dropped to just over five hundred by mid-sixteenth century, and at the beginning of the seventeenth century, there were only about fifty left in central Mexico. Most of the encomienda towns escheated to the crown for lack of legitimate heirs.

In all events, even in the palmy decades of the sixteenth century the majority of the encomenderos had encomiendas that offered only modest incomes. It is true, however, that the more prominent conquerors had large numbers of tributaries, and such men were prosperous, especially if they diversified their interests. The wealthiest of all was Fernando Cortés, who had many rich towns. He held real estate and engaged in commercial transactions in New Spain as well as in other colonies; he raised blooded horses and other stock and experimented with the production of silk; and he had interests in mining, shipbuilding, sugar processing, and farming.

Meanwhile many more Spaniards poured into the colony, and, contrary to the view often held, most of them had to work. True, most had the preferred occupations in society, but as officials, clergymen, merchants, artisans, miners, ranchers, lawyers, physicians, teachers, sailors, or whatever, they were productive. While it was certainly advantageous to be white, a light complexion by no means guaranteed a life of ease. Indeed, some Spaniards of low socioeconomic status were reduced to menial labor and occasionally became beggars or brigands. Enterprising mestizos, on the other hand, might be more prosperous than the less energetic of lower-class Spaniards.

Despite official attempts to encourage Spanish farmers and laborers to emigrate to America, almost none did. As a consequence, the necessary physical labor was performed by Indians, blacks, and those of mixed races. It has often been noted that the true wealth discovered by the Spaniards consisted of the millions of natives whose labor kept the colonies functioning. In the years following the Conquest a good number of Indians were slaves, either because they were already in that category in their own societies or because they were enslaved by Spaniards for continued resistance to Spanish authority. Slaves were often worked to the point of exhaustion and usually had short lives. Owing to the bitter protests of Spaniards of conscience—most notably the Dominican friar Bartolomé de Las Casas—Indian slavery was finally abolished in the 1550s, but it persisted long after in New Spain's far north.

The percentage of Indians who were truly chattels was relatively small; those assigned to encomiendas constituted a far greater number. In addition to the tribute owed to their encomenderos, Indians were also required to contribute labor under a regulated system. Often the encomendero rented the services of his Indians to merchants and others who drove them mercilessly. In 1549 the labor obligation was abolished, and labor in lieu of tribute was forbidden. Without slaves and forced labor, who was then to carry out the necessary tasks of labor? The policy makers in Spain reasoned that if Indians were paid a fair wage for their work, and if they were treated humanely, they would

A Spanish overseer directs Indian laborers on a sugar plantation in this painting by the modern muralist Diego Rivera (1886–1957).

volunteer. But few among the dwindling number of Indians stepped forward to assume the burden.

Consequently the crown decreed a system of forced labor called the *repartimiento*, or *cuatequil* (the Nahuatl name for a similar structure employed by the Aztecs to extract labor). Under this system each adult male Indian had to contribute about forty-five days of labor a year, usually a week at a time at various intervals. Only a small percentage of the men from any village were to be absent simultaneously, and the head of a family was to have time free to cultivate his own fields. Provisions stipulated that each laborer was to be paid for his work and treated with consideration. In practice, however, Indians were mistreated, forced to work excessive hours, and cheated of their pay. Labor drafts often took entire villages away from their own fields at planting or harvest times. Laws in the early seventeenth century decreed the abolition of repartimiento, but it persisted, especially in the northern and southern fringes of New Spain, until the end of the colonial period.

In central Mexico, the frequent labor shortages caused by Indian population decline were met with a variety of labor practices that included repartimiento, black slavery, sharecropping, and wage labor. Wage labor sometimes turned into debt peonage when money or goods were advanced to individuals by an employer and not repaid quickly. In some cases, employers could hold these workers in perpetual servitude by continuing to advance credit, but the system could also work to the advantage of laborers who could accumulate debt and resources and then move on to another place. The degree of force that employers could exert varied according to time, place, and the available labor pool, but coercive debt peonage was probably not widespread in the colonial period.

One onerous labor practice was a carryover from pre-Hispanic times when everything that had to be moved was transported on the backs of porters, called *tamemes*. Despite a legal limit of fifty pounds for each load, it was not uncommon for tamemes to be forced to carry twice that weight over mountain passes. Prominent Spaniards arriving at Veracruz were conveyed to the capital two hundred miles distant in sedan chairs carried by Indians. So many carriers succumbed to fatigue that a royal decree ordered the increased use of mules and horses and the opening of roads for carts. But the sight of men bent under staggering loads remained familiar.

MINING

The lands of the Spanish Indies belonged to the Spanish sovereigns personally, but their subjects were allowed to exploit the land at the pleasure of the rulers. The royal quinto of American riches applied to

Indian tamemes *were the traditional bearers of cargo, transporting goods to all corners of the colony. From the Florentine Codex.*

Indian treasure, precious metals and jewels, and the sale of slaves, to cite a few examples. The crown was, therefore, no less anxious to promote the search for gold and silver than the most avaricious colonist. The search for precious minerals continued unabated and ultimately succeeded. It was silver, however, not gold, that provided the great wealth of colonial Mexico. By the early 1530s silver was being mined in various locations, but not until a quarter century after the fall of Tenochtitlán was a great strike made. Between 1546 and 1548 the fabulous silver deposits of Zacatecas were revealed, and within a few years more rich mines were found at Guanajuato, San Luis Potosí, Pachuca, and other sites. Later silver strikes in Parral and Chihuahua spurred settlement in the far north during the seventeenth and eighteenth centuries.

The great wealth of the mines dramatically transformed the economy of the colony. Mining camps, some of which became the important cities we see today, sprouted in many locations in northern Mexico. By the early years of the seventeenth century Zacatecas had become the third largest city in the colony, surpassed only by the capital and Puebla. A few miners became very wealthy and lived in ostentation. Other entrepreneurs made their fortunes by supplying those who flocked to the mining camps seeking silver. Commerce was profitable for merchants who risked taking their goods over the dangerous trails, past the Chichimecs. Others established stores and provided diverse services for the miners. Equally prosperous were farmers who furnished the food that was so much in demand in the barren north. At first cattle and sheep were driven north in herds, but eventually ranchers saw the wisdom of establishing ranches in the vicinity of the

mines, and this was the genesis of the great livestock spreads of northern Mexico.

Until the eighteenth century when Guanajuato became the chief
producer, most silver was mined in Zacatecas and areas further north
where no large sedentary Indian populations existed. Paid mining labor was recruited primarily in indigenous areas to the south. Indians
labored far underground in the dark, damp shafts, breathing the noxious airs; some were drowned by floods or killed in explosions. They
hauled ore out of the mines by climbing up notched logs that served
as crude ladders, carrying their heavy loads in the same blankets with
which they covered themselves at night. Poor diets, fatigue, and the
unhealthful conditions in the mines made the workers susceptible to
disease and early death. Yet, because the pay was good, at least in later
years, there seems to have been enough labor for the mines. The mines
of Zacatecas, producing one-third of Mexico's silver, required some five
thousand laborers at the height of production and suffered no serious
labor shortage.

Spaniards embraced the theory of bullionism—that is, they believed
that true wealth consisted of precious metals. So intent were they on
stockpiling bullion that they neglected other important aspects of the

A panoramic view of a silver-mining operation.

economy, retarding their own industrial development. Silver apparently stimulated Mexico's internal economy because so much of it—perhaps half—was used to buy goods produced in New Spain. Through the mixed use of smelting and mercury amalgamation processes, mining output increased slowly throughout the colonial period. Less silver apparently reached the coffers of the crown, as it was increasingly employed in the local economy, used to purchase European or Far Eastern trade goods, or siphoned off in contraband trade.

AGRICULTURE AND RANCHING

Although mining was the most salient enterprise, agriculture remained the basic occupation in all parts of New Spain. It was, of course, absolutely essential for the sustenance of the colony, and most agricultural production was for domestic consumption. To the variety of foods native on the land, the Spaniards introduced an assortment of plant life—citrus and other fruits, wheat, sugarcane, and many edibles to enrich the colonial diet. Early Spanish settlers were given, in addition to town lots for residences, small garden plots outside of town for their own needs, to be cultivated by Indian farmers. The natives had their own personal lands, held privately or in common, to provide food for themselves.

This graceful aqueduct at Querétaro was built between 1729 and 1739. With seventy-four arches, it is 85 feet high at one point and carried water to the city over a distance of 5 miles.

Colonists were allowed to grow what they wished as long as their production did not conflict with interests in Spain. Often they ended up having to pay inflated prices for imported necessities that could easily have been grown in Mexico. Wine and olive oil, for example, were not luxuries, but staples. They were considered essential to the traditional Spanish table, and wine was necessary for mass. Yet so great were the profits to producers and middlemen in Spain that the growing of vines and olive trees was largely forbidden in the colonies. As a supplemental beverage, beer was brewed in Mexico as early as 1544.

Export crops were an important part of royal income. Essential to the booming textile industry in Europe were good dyes, and Mexico produced one of the best with the native product called cochineal. This red dye was of considerable value and convenient for export because of its compact nature. It was extracted from tiny insects found in the nopal cactus, which was soon planted in extensive tracts. Another profitable dye was the blue extracted from the indigo plant. Cacao, from which chocolate was made, had long been a favorite food with the Indians, and eventually it caught the fancy of Europeans, providing yet another valuable export for Spain. Both vanilla and henequen were additional products of some importance. Finally, sugar was introduced into Mexico by Cortés in 1524, and soon there were many plantations and mills in the warmer climes of the colony. Even though Mexican exports of sugar were comparatively modest, they added to the diversity of New Spain's economy. Black slave labor was commonly employed in sugar and indigo production.

Most agricultural produce was consumed locally, and the staple crops were corn and wheat. Indians continued to produce corn for subsistence and for the market, but eventually Spanish haciendas (agricultural estates) supplied the bulk of maize consumed in urban areas. They also produced large quantities of wheat in the areas of Puebla and the Bajío (Guanajuato and Querétaro). At the same time, Indians could also be required to plant fruits, vegetables, and grains introduced by the Spaniards.

The Spanish introduction of livestock had the most far-reaching implications for indigenous peoples. They were most likely to raise chickens, pigs, and sheep for themselves, and their cofradías often owned at least a few head of cattle. While animals introduced more protein into the Indian diet, in the predominantly unfenced terrain, they also caused great harm to Indian crops. The ranching industry developed throughout Mexico, but the largest livestock spreads evolved in the north where the land was marginal for cultivation. Multiplying herds were branded and regulated by the stockmen's guild, the *mesta*.

Travelers reported seeing herds of as many as 150,000 head, and in the region of Zacatecas over two million sheep grazed in summer pastures. Even though beef was inexpensive, colonists consumed much more of the costlier mutton. Sheep thrived better in the north than cattle, and their wool brought very good returns on investments.

Large Mexican estates are usually associated with the vast haciendas of the north, but in central and southern Mexico there were important, though smaller, landholdings devoted to the growing of sugar, henequen, and other agricultural products. The conquerors were often rewarded with tracts of land consisting of twenty to a hundred acres, and many were able to add to their holdings. Thus the acquisition of large estates began in earnest in the late sixteenth century, especially after the devastating epidemic of the 1570s that took thousands of Indian lives and facilitated the claiming of their lands. Individuals with the capital necessary for an enterprise appealing to royal interests were either given land outright or allowed to purchase it at a low price. Large acreage was necessary for cattle and sheep to forage. One entrepreneur of the northern frontier began putting together parcels in 1583, and by his death, in 1618, the family estates stretched over 11,626,850 acres. In many instances hacienda owners acquired land from Indians, either by purchase, fraud, or coercion.

While it is traditional to assume that a large percentage of Indian lands were lost to the Spaniards, in fact, the natives retained sufficient ancestral holdings at least until the population began to rebound at mid-seventeenth century. After that, land and water disputes multiplied between Indian towns and between Indian towns and Spanish haciendas. The colonial court dockets were crowded with disputes over water and the Indians were at a decided disadvantage in litigation with the Spaniards. Gradually the mechanisms for conflict resolution were defined and water disputes were generally resolved by some form of compromise Although there were regional variations, haciendas and villages coexisted in a kind of synergy that allowed Spaniards to profit modestly in a chronically weak domestic market and Indian villages to preserve some autonomy and land.

It should be noted that both mining and agriculture had significant impacts on Mexican ecosystems. Livestock were particularly invasive, as they proliferated in ungrazed grasslands and overran Indian fields and commons. Erosion and damage from overgrazing and the transhumance of sheep were already apparent by the end of the sixteenth century. In the Valle de Mezquital, north of Mexico City, desert vegetation quickly took over from the grasslands that had supported what has been termed a plague of sheep. Reduction in pasturelands curbed the raising of livestock for a time in the seventeenth century, but production climbed again in the eighteenth to supply the mines and growing urban populations with meat and leather. Furthermore, silver production required great quantities of charcoal for smelting, resulting in the almost total deforestation of mining areas.

INDUSTRY AND COMMERCE

With industry so closely regulated to prevent competition with Spain, Mexico produced very little in the way of manufactured goods for export. Almost all luxury goods had to be imported from Spanish merchants, even though most were not Spanish in origin, for Spain had neglected her own domestic industries and commerce. Expensive fabrics were imported by Spain from northern Europe, while the production of fine cloth was forbidden to the colonies. Silk, for example, flourished for a while in Mexico, especially during the sixteenth century. But its production was discouraged following objections of Spanish silk merchants in the mother country and ultimately by the competition of inexpensive silk from China.

Still there were many products for everyday use coming out of small industries in Mexico. Cotton and woolen cloth were manufactured in *obrajes*, the textile mills that existed in various locations, especially Mexico City, Puebla, and Querétaro. Since few could afford imported finery, local mills were numerous, more than eighty by 1571. Until the eighteenth century, when the powered mills of Europe flooded the markets with cheap cloth, Mexican obrajes employed thousands of workers to meet the growing demand for textiles. Conditions in the obrajes varied, but in some cases workers were virtually imprisoned in sweatshops.

Other manufactured items were produced by the many artisans in the colony—the tailors, blacksmiths, cobblers, candlemakers, goldsmiths, and so on. There were guilds, or *gremios*, for each of these crafts. Well established by the late sixteenth century, the guilds fixed both the quality of goods and the prices of work. Non-Spaniards were allowed to join the gremios, but only whites were allowed to attain the rank of master. In a more positive sense, the gremios were protective of their members, making provisions for those who suffered accidents and illness as well as extending help to widows. They were also active in promoting religious celebrations and philanthropic undertakings for the community. Eventually there were about a hundred guilds in Mexico City. A professional merchants' guild, the Consulado, was established in the capital in 1592. Its function was to arbitrate commercial disputes, to protect the interests of merchants, to establish rules of business conduct, and to foster the interests of the community.

The city of Puebla was (and is) famous for its excellent ceramic products. Pots and tiles are richly decorated and glazed in the styles known as majolica *and* talavera. *Above right,* a typical seventeenth-century Puebla bowl. *Above left,* Moorish influence *is evident in this vase.* Right, *this flowerpot is of a Chinese type.*

Commerce was supervised by the imperial system through the agency of the Casa de Contratación. This house of trade was located in Seville, which served as the official entrepôt for all traffic with the Indies. As in industry, tight controls were imposed on commerce in order to benefit the merchants in Spain. Everything and everyone going to or coming from the colonies passed through officials who checked all papers with care. Traders in the city of Seville sent to the colonies a wide variety of goods—expensive fabrics, hats, wax for candles, wine, liquors, vinegar, olive oil, paper, steel and iron implements, fruit preserves, and other items. The masses rarely enjoyed such luxuries, however, and had to rely on native products sold in open markets. The main plaza of Mexico City was crowded with shoppers who could make their selections among the 323 stalls that existed in 1686. Villages throughout Mexico had their own small public markets, but Indians were limited consumers of Spanish goods. They continued to weave their own cloth and produce utilitarian wares, prompting the forced sale of goods (*repartimiento de mercancías*), practiced so venally by the corregidores.

All products destined for the Spanish Indies were required to go on Spanish ships with Spanish crews, and, to facilitate the collection of duties, cargoes were channeled through the one official port of Veracruz. Because of pirates, after the 1560s ships sailing to and from the New World went in annual convoys with armed escort vessels. One of the big events in New Spain was the arrival of the fleet in the spring, at which time merchants purchased their supplies for the coming months. The prevalence of yellow fever and malaria discouraged any sizable permanent population in Veracruz, but when the fleet arrived tents bristled on the beach almost overnight, as great numbers of buyers came to negotiate in the colorful trade fair that ensued. In some

Muleteers (arrieros) *were a familiar sight on the roads of New Spain.*

years the cargoes were taken to Mexico City rather than remaining in the pestilential airs of the port. Eventually the fair was relocated inland at the higher, more salubrious climate of Jalapa, which had the added advantage of being a safer depository for silver destined for Spain.

A similar, though smaller, scene was presented on the Pacific coast at Acapulco. Once a year the Manila Galleon arrived at the port city laden with rich luxuries of the Orient, including silks, jade, ivory, perfumes, incense, and other goods. This trade was especially lucrative for the great Mexico City silver merchants who also served as brokers in the exchanges of Peruvian silver and Asian goods.

THE RESULTS OF SPAIN'S POLICIES

In addition to its profits through mining and agricultural exports, the Spanish crown realized revenues through retention for itself of monopolies on such items as mercury, gunpowder, salt, pulque, and, in the eighteenth century, tobacco. The crown's quinto was eventually reduced to a tenth, but it still constituted a substantial source of royal income. As the encomienda system withered away, more Indian villages came under the crown, to whom tribute was paid. Although tribute in the early years was rendered in kind, Spaniards increasingly demanded it in coinage as a way of forcing the Indian economy into the marketplace. Indians then had to sell their produce or their labor to

A piece-of-eight minted in Mexico in 1609. Such coins were used mainly for trading with Spain for manufactured goods or purchase of Oriental spices and silks carried by the Manila Galleon.

get cash. The king's treasury also benefited from the sale of licenses, offices, and land, and from the various taxes paid by the colonists. Altogether there were about sixty different taxes, of which the most detested was the *alcabala*, a sales tax payable on almost everything sold. At first only 2 percent of the item's value, the alcabala went as high as 14 percent during Spain's wars of the eighteenth century. The *almojarifazgo* was a tax of 7.5 percent on all imports and exports, so the crown was paid twice for goods moving between Spain and its colonies, for a total income of 15 percent.

Despite the reduction in the labor force that resulted from the Indian demographic decline, production of silver apparently did not drop drastically in the seventeenth century. Nor did the excessive and arbitrary economic controls of the Hapsburgs necessarily stifle local incentive and growth. A greater share of royal revenues remained in the colony, and population revival after 1630 contributed to a rise in craft production as well as more regional specialization in agriculture and manufacturing. A growing transoceanic trade with Europe and Asia in the end did not foster a profound capitalist transformation in New Spain's primarily agrarian economy where domestic relations of production changed little and an oligarchy controlled limited markets. Spain's great glory, wealth, and power receded into the past. The Spanish Bourbon kings would make a forceful attempt to restore them in the next century.

RECOMMENDED FOR FURTHER STUDY

Bakewell, Peter J. *Silver Mining and Society in Colonial Mexico: Zacatecas, 1546–1700.* Cambridge: Cambridge University Press, 1971.

Barrett, Elinore M. *The Mexican Colonial Copper Industry.* Albuquerque: University of New Mexico Press, 1987.

Barrett, Ward. *The Sugar Hacienda of the Marqueses del Valle.* Minneapolis: University of Minnesota Press, 1970.

Borah, Woodrow. *Early Trade and Navigation between Mexico and Peru.* Berkeley: University of California Press, 1954.

———. *New Spain's Century of Depression.* Berkeley: University of California Press, 1951.

Boyer, Richard. "Mexico in the Seventeenth Century: Transition of a Colonial Society." *Hispanic American Historical Review* 57 (1977): 455–78.

Brockington, Lolita Gutiérrez. *The Leverage of Labor: Managing the Cortés Haciendas in Tehuantepec, 1588–1688.* Durham, N.C.: Duke University Press, 1989.

Chevalier, François. *Land and Society in Colonial Mexico: The Great Hacienda.* Berkeley: University of California Press, 1963.

Dusenberry, William. *The Mexican Mesta: The Administration of Ranching in Colonial Mexico.* Urbana: University of Illinois Press, 1963.

Frank, Andre Gunder. *Mexican Agriculture, 1521–1630. Transformation of the Mode of Production.* New York: Cambridge University Press, 1979.

Harris, Charles H., III, *A Mexican Family Empire: The Latifundio of the Sánchez Navarro Family, 1765–1867*. Austin: University of Texas Press, 1975.

Hassig, Ross. *Trade, Tribute, and Transportation: The Sixteenth-Century Political Economy of the Valley of Mexico*. Norman: University of Oklahoma Press, 1985.

Israel, J. I. "Mexico and the 'General Crisis' of the Seventeenth Century." *Past and Present* 63 (1974): 33–57.

Kicza, John E. *Colonial Entrepreneurs: Families and Business in Bourbon Mexico City*. Albuquerque: University of New Mexico Press, 1983.

Konrad, Herman W. *A Jesuit Hacienda in Colonial Mexico: Santa Lucia, 1576–1767*. Stanford, Calif.: Stanford University Press, 1980.

Ladd, Doris. *The Making of a Strike: Mexican Silver Workers' Struggles in Real del Monte, 1766–1775*. Lincoln: University of Nebraska Press, 1988.

Leiby, John S. *Colonial Bureaucrats and the Mexican Economy*. New York: Peter Lang, 1986.

Lipsett Rivera, Sonya. *To Defend Our Water with the Blood of Our Veins: The Struggles for Resources in Colonial Puebla*. Albuquerque: University of New Mexico Press, 1999.

Melville, Elinor G.K. *A Plague of Sheep: Environmental Consequences of the Conquest of Mexico*. Cambridge: Cambridge University Press, 1994.

———. "Disease, Ecology, and the Environment," in *The Oxford History of Mexico*. Edited by Michael C. Meyer and William H. Beezley, pp. 213–43. New York: Oxford University Press, 2000.

Meyer, Michael C. *Water in the Hispanic Southwest: A Social and Legal History, 1550–1850*. Tucson: University of Arizona Press, 1984.

Patch, Robert W. *Maya and Spaniard in Yucatan, 1648–1812*. Stanford, Calif.: Stanford University Press, 1993.

Radding, Cynthia. *Landscapes of Power and Identity: Comparative Histories in the Sonoran Desert and the Forests of Amazonia from Colony to Republic*. Durham, N.C.: Duke University Press, 2006.

Riley, G. Micheal. *Fernando Cortés and the Marquesado in Morelos: A Case Study in the Socioeconomic Development of Sixteenth Century Mexico*. Albuquerque: University of New Mexico Press, 1973.

Salvucci, Richard J. *Textiles and Capitalism in Mexico: An Economic History of the Obrajes, 1539–1840*. Princeton, N.J.: Princeton University Press, 1988.

Schurz, William L. *The Manila Galleon*. New York: Dutton, 1939.

Semo, Enrique. *The History of Capitalism in Mexico: Its Origins, 1521–1763*. Translated by Lidia Lozano. Austin: University of Texas Press, 1993.

Simpson, Lesley B. *The Encomienda in New Spain*. Berkeley: University of California Press, 1960.

Super, John C. "Querétaro Obrajes: Industry and Society in Provincial Mexico." *Hispanic American Historical Review* 56 (1976): 197–216.

Taylor, William B. *Landlord and Peasant in Colonial Oaxaca*. Stanford, Calif.: Stanford University Press, 1972.

Van Young, Eric. *Hacienda and Market in 18th-Century Mexico. The Rural Economy of the Guadalajara Region, 1675–1820*. Berkeley: University of California Press, 1981.

West, Robert C. *The Mining Community in Northern New Spain: The Parral Mining District*. Berkeley: University of California Press, 1949.

10

The Colonial Church

A traveler in colonial Mexico approaching the outskirts of a town first saw in the distance a bell tower rising over all other structures. Before long he would hear the tolling of bells resounding over town and countryside. In the streets priests, friars, and nuns mingled prominently in the crowds. If the physical presence of the church was everywhere, in other ways, too, it was the most pervasive of colonial institutions, and none left its imprint more deeply on the culture.

CHURCH ORGANIZATION

Because of its expulsion of the Muslims in Spain and its discovery of the New World, the Spanish crown was granted extraordinary privileges by the papacy. In effect, through the royal patronage (*patronato real*) Spanish kings were heads of the Roman Catholic Church in their domains. While this conferred great power and prestige, it also imposed many responsibilities. And, significantly, it meant that the church became an arm of the state.

Church organization consisted of two distinct branches—the secular clergy and the regular clergy. The secular group was composed of priests who served under their bishops. The regulars were missionaries under the separate authority of the superiors of their various orders—the Franciscans, Dominicans, Augustinians, and others. The Spanish conquest undoubtedly was fueled by a desire for status and wealth, but it was also legally justified by its Christian mission—the saving of souls. And the Spanish conquerors were devout in their religious observances, confessing their sins and praying frequently, especially in times of danger. Cortés demonstrated his pious fervor in his adamant insistence, even in threatening circumstances, that Indians cast down their idols, forbear human sacrifices, and abandon their old gods. His zeal more than once jeopardized the safety of the Spaniards, and he had to be restrained by his own priests.

Typical fortress-like construction is apparent in this sixteenth-century Dominican monastery at Tepoztlán, Morelos. There are some striking Renaissance details in this important structure.

In 1527 the Dominican Julian Garcés arrived in Tlaxcala to assume his duties as the first bishop in the land. That same year another bishopric was created for the city of Mexico, and the following year Juan de Zumárraga, a Franciscan friar, arrived as bishop. With the additional title "Protector of the Indians," Zumárraga not only established the form of the early secular church but also took an active part in alleviating the sufferings of the Indians, a policy that brought him into conflict with encomenderos and Spanish officials. A Christian humanist and wise administrator, Zumárraga was a stabilizing factor in the early years of the colony. He was elevated to archbishop of Mexico shortly before his death in 1548.

An event of considerable significance was said to have occurred in 1531. According to tradition, a newly converted Indian by the name of Juan Diego beheld a vision of the Virgin, who commanded him to have a temple built in her honor.[1] After this legend was popularized in the mid-seventeenth century, first criollos and later Indians embraced the devotion of the Virgin of Guadalupe. The latter occurred when the church undertook a deliberate evangelization campaign in the eighteenth century that emphasized the Virgin's indigenous, dark-skinned features. Since modern times, Guadalupe has become a symbol of liberation and of cultural fusion, not only in Mexico but in all of Latin America. The shrine to Guadalupe at Tepeyac in the northern part of Mexico City attracts many thousands of pilgrims each year.

As the Spaniards spread out over the land, new bishoprics were formed: seven were established in the sixteenth century, one in the seventeenth century, and two in the eighteenth. They were staffed by large numbers of priests who ministered to the needs of all segments of society.

THE RELIGIOUS CONQUEST

Meanwhile the important work of the regular orders had begun. In 1521 Cortés requested that missionaries be sent, and in 1523 three lay brothers arrived, the most remarkable of whom was Pedro de Gante. The following year twelve Franciscan friars landed at Veracruz and walked barefoot to the capital. One of them, lame and tattered, was Father Toribio de Benavente, called affectionately by the Indians Motolinía, "the Poor Little One." He became one of the most renowned churchmen in Mexico's history. As monasteries were built to accommodate their activities, other Franciscans traveled to the colony. Friars of the Dominican Order arrived in 1525. Distinguished for their intellectual discipline, the Dominicans had long been powerful in Spain, where they were associated with the Inquisition. In the colonies, Dominicans like Las Casas campaigned for more just treatment of Indians.

The Augustinians reached Mexico in 1533 and proceeded to construct some of the finest monasteries in the land. All of these orders flourished early: by 1559 there were thirty Franciscan houses with 380 religious; 210 Dominicans labored out of forty houses; and there were 212 Augustinians with forty houses. Other orders had convents as well, in addition to those for nuns. The fruit of their activity is astounding;

---

1. Despite controversy regarding his existence, Juan Diego received papal approval for canonization in December 2001.

The Virgin of Guadalupe as protectress of Mexican children in twentieth-century barrio art, Ciudad Juárez.

Motolinía claimed (no doubt with considerable exaggeration) that as early as 1537 some nine million Indians had been baptized, four million of them by the Franciscans alone.

Founded years after the Conquest, the Jesuits entered Mexico only in 1571, when other religious groups were well established in the center and the south. In their first years they occupied themselves with teaching the sons of Spaniards and soon won the reputation of being superior teachers. But they also taught Indian children, and within a few years they undertook the arduous task of converting natives on the northern frontiers. After establishing their first missions in Sinaloa, Durango, and Chihuahua, later Jesuits, such as Fathers Eusebio Francisco Kino and Juan Manuel de Salvatierra, carried their evangelization efforts to Sonora, Arizona, and Baja California. In addition to teaching Indians the Christian doctrine, by resettling them in villages, missionaries hoped to get them to adopt Spanish agriculture, animal husbandry, and crafts. Eventually missions could sell their surplus production to local markets, and the congregated Indians could be drafted for repartimiento labor. Franciscans continued this work in New Mexico, Texas, and California until after the end of the colonial period.

Throughout Mexico, then, the clergy took up the challenge of conversion. Initial efforts in any given region were undertaken with great dedication and zeal as priests learned local languages and often faced hostility. The clergy's efforts to train selected young native men in Spanish and Christian doctrine meant that very early the church was able to produce confessional manuals and other religious writings in Indian languages. Native elites also staffed the offices that assisted the clergy. Still, many Indians clung with tenacity to their traditional beliefs and rituals. The elimination of "idolatry" was only achieved over time, and then as a new creation of local religion that blended and layered the Christian and the native. If Indians acknowledged the power of the Christian god who had been influential in their defeat, they more eagerly took up the cult of saints, perhaps identifying their patron saint with a local deity. In particular, Saint James (Santiago) and the Virgin Mary came to have powerful connotations as protectors of Indians. At the same time, Christian images (for example, the Crucifixion) could easily be misconstrued by the natives as they sought to place them in familiar contexts.

In churches and in religious celebrations, native ritual, myth, and history continued to be layered with Catholic themes and motifs. By the end of the colonial period, indigenous peoples probably did not distinguish between what was native and imported in their local religion. But for many of them, the ability to borrow and blend had served as protection and resistance against the complete eradication of their cultures.

Indians were generally keen to adopt those introductions of the clergy that could enhance their material conditions, such as tools and additions to the diet. Local fiestas or feast-day celebrations were especially popular, as they liberated Indians from their labors and were often accompanied by lavish feasts that enabled them to consume more of their own production. Religious plays, music, and dancing often accompanied these festivals. Accustomed to public ritual, indigenous people embraced these ceremonies and were especially attracted to those of Corpus Christi, Todos Santos, and Holy Week.

Indian cofradías, created to promote particular religious devotions, also served the purpose of enabling Indians to manage their own economic resources. Although cofradía holdings varied widely, they commonly included some livestock and perhaps small properties that were rented out. In some places, they functioned as credit institutions, lending modest amounts to members. Conflicts between parish priests and cofradías over control of these resources were frequent. Many priests complained that Indians used cofradía assets for unauthorized purposes and that the fiestas they sponsored were too extravagant and libertine.

RELIGIOUS DISPUTES AND COLONIAL PIETY

From the beginning, clergymen in Mexico became embroiled in bitter disputes. Ecclesiastics and encomenderos competed for control of the Indians. Friars and priests tried to protect the natives from abuses of

An anonymous Mexican artist of the early eighteenth century rendered this St. Michael.

Spaniards, while the latter resented the interference of the clergymen in the encomienda towns. Men of the church saw the colonists as examples of bad Christians who corrupted Indian morals in addition to mistreating them physically and exacting exorbitant tributes. The encomenderos, in turn, regarded many of the ecclesiastics as hypocrites who were guilty of the same crimes of which they accused others. Within the church itself there were other quarrels over evangelical methods and territorial jurisdiction. On occasion the disputes ended in violence.

There were, moreover, some acrimonious quarrels between ecclesiastical and civil authorities, involving not only lesser figures in the provinces but even archbishops and viceroys. One of the most notorious and scandalous episodes took place in the 1640s between the Jesuits and the bishop of Puebla, Juan de Palafox, who also held a number of high civil posts and served briefly as viceroy. This contest involving the wealth and power of the Jesuits became a *cause célèbre* in which several important people were excommunicated and a Jesuit school was almost burned. For the moment the Jesuits were victorious and the powerful bishop was withdrawn. Eventually, however, the secular arm of the church gained the upper hand in Mexico, as the crown consciously strove to weaken the influence of the regular orders.

Finally, some clergymen felt discriminated against because of the social circumstances of their birth. As in the civil bureaucracy, most of the higher positions were denied to those of Spanish blood born in Mexico. Yet, by the seventeenth century the majority of Mexican clerics were criollos. Nearly all elite families provided at least one son or daughter to some branch of the church, along with the income to support him or her. For some women, life as a nun provided a desired alternative to marriage as well as a means to devote themselves to God and perhaps even acquire an education. Since most Spaniards were faithful Catholics, they also left pious bequests to the church. Thus the church became wealthy, the owner of extensive rural and urban properties (which it rented out) throughout Mexico. In the absence of banks, the church became a major lending institution, extending credit to elites. In addition, a good deal of church wealth went into the construction of opulent places of worship, but it was also used to finance the colony's only social services: the charitable institutions such as hospitals, schools, and orphanages that were run by the various orders and cathedral chapters.

The good works of the church must be measured against the personal behavior of clerics. In general, the regular orders were regarded as more dedicated—primarily because they were better educated—than the secular clergy. Reports accused priests of taking mistresses, imbibing to excess, gambling, soliciting in the confessional, and engaging in commerce. Others were charged with exacting excessively

*The eighteenth-century baroque Sanctuary of Nuestra Señora de
Ocotlán, Tlaxcala. Its richly decorated interior is a prime example of
the Churrigueresque.*

high fees for the sacraments and subjecting Indians to harsh punishments. As the primary agents of social control, at least until the eighteenth century, parish priests and missionaries were expected to use
or condone corporal punishment to compel the obedience of their
charges. And although the majority of priests observed their vows, lived
modestly, and worked to foster improvements in the physical plant of
their domains, charitable activities were less in evidence. They cus-
tomarily extracted resources from their parishioners, serving to benefit not only the church but often themselves.

By the seventeenth century, the humility and simplicity evident in
earlier decades yielded to a more material and increasingly profane
mode of behavior that may be attributed to a decline in interest as the
novelty of the crusading spirit wore thin and routine set in. Then, too,
in a practical sense the challenge was less in terms of numbers, for the
Indian population had declined drastically. The humanistic efforts of
the early church to provide education and social services to Indians
gradually gave way to less zealous, more avaricious priests, who, along
with corregidores, conspired to extract resources from the native. Still,

Detail of San Francisco Acatepec. The tiles are green, yellow, and blue, bordered by red brick.

The tiled domes of Iglesia del Carmen in Mexico City.

some priests played a broker role, defending their flocks either out of common interests or altruism.

Throughout the colonial period, the organized church continued to provide a vocation and income for thousands of Mexican clerics. At no time, however, did they constitute more than a fraction of a percent of the total population. Perhaps more than half lived in Mexico City and other sizeable cities like Puebla and Valladolid. At the end of the colonial era, there were about two thousand nuns and slightly over seven thousand priests (of whom about 40 percent belonged to the regular orders).

THE INQUISITION

Religious affairs assumed a more somber cast in 1571 with the entrance of the Holy Office of the Inquisition. With its roots in the Middle Ages, the Inquisition was employed in Spain when Ferdinand and Isabella were striving to achieve political and cultural unity in the state. Under those "Catholic Kings" conformity was seen as essential, Christianity was equated with the very soul of Spain, and heresy was akin to treason. Jews were forced to convert or leave, and later on Protestants were forbidden in Spanish realms. The essential function of the Inquisition was to maintain the purity of the faith, to preserve religious orthodoxy. Since proper morality was so inseparable from correct religious behavior, the Inquisition's broader mandate was the enforcement of social conformity.

Although emigrants to the New World were screened with care, some heretics slipped by. Particularly suspect were *conversos*, or New Christians, that is, those of Jewish origins who had converted to Christianity, and the Inquisition was determined to root out "crypto-Jews" in New Spain. Some unfortunate Protestant corsairs were also tried for heresy. Moreover, many colonists, including clergymen and even persons in high official positions, were tried for purely moral offenses.

The Inquisition also exercised control over printed matter that entered the colony, being concerned primarily with works that dealt with liberal, "dangerous" ideas, which, it was feared, would corrupt and lead astray the unsophisticated Indians as well as Spaniards. In fact, however, many prohibited writings, including those of the eighteenth-century French and English Enlightenment, found their way into the private libraries of educated people, among whom were a good number of clergymen.

Before the formal establishment of the Inquisition, bishops had exercised inquisitorial powers and their jurisdiction included Indians charged with idolatry. The most notorious case involved Don Carlos of Texcoco, who was accused of idolatry, though his outspoken statements allegedly contained political and social overtones. Bishop Zumárraga found the noble guilty and, in 1539, had him burned at the stake. This and other examples of excessive zeal, along with the realization that conversion would not occur overnight, helped convince the crown that the conquered peoples should not be tried as heretics. Instead suspicion of idolatry was to be investigated by local clerics, and royal officials would administer suitable punishments, short of the death penalty.

The great majority of Inquisition cases involved more mundane aspects of the lives of the non-Indian population. Thousands of cases investigated the misappropriation of supernatural power through the fraudulent manipulation of Christianity or practices of magic, witchcraft, and superstition. Another large portion pertained to sexual transgressions such as bigamy, solicitation in the confessional, cohabitation, fornication, and sodomy. For historians, Inquisition cases provide rich information about social and ethnic relationships, popular beliefs, and petty rivalries. They also show that magical customs from Indian and African religions as well as local religion in Spain were often manifest in the popular piety of diverse ethnic groups. In trying to correct popular and traditional practices, the Inquisition applied a range of punishments (including floggings, fines, and forms of public humiliation), but as the colonial period progressed, charges were often thrown out and penalties were lightened through confession and penitence.

Those who paid the extreme penalty had been convicted, in most cases, of the serious crime of heresy, often compounded by "obstinancy"—that is, the refusal to recant. Prisoners sentenced to burning at the stake were often strangled first. The solemnity of official proceedings notwithstanding, *autos da fé* assumed a carnival spirit for which elaborate preparations were made. People came from near and far to jeer the parade of those who carried candles and wore penitential garb with pointed hoods, as well as to regard the special ceremony reserved for those consigned to the stake. From the reviewing stand the viceroy, bishops, and other high dignitaries, with their ladies, viewed the macabre spectacle.

The first auto da fé in the colony took place in 1574. Sixty-three prisoners had been judged, of whom five were burned and most others flogged. Eight more autos occurred in the next twenty years. In 1528, long before the formal tribunal was established, two Spaniards died at the stake, accused of being crypto-Jews. But perhaps the most sensational proceeding involving crypto-Jews concerned Don Luis de Carvajal, the colonizer and governor of Nuevo León, who was accused

The Inquisition headquarters in Mexico City.

of harboring relatives who practiced Jewish rites. In an auto that included sixty-seven persons, some of his family were burned.

Always coercive in religious and moral affairs, the Inquisition became, in later times, less concerned with spiritual matters. As an instrument of royal policy, it was utilized in the eighteenth century to check dissident political elements. Both of the liberal priests who led the struggle for Independence from Spain in the early nineteenth century were tried by the Inquisition before being turned over to secular

The frontispiece of a treatise against heresy printed in Spain in 1519.
Much of colonial publishing dealt with religious subjects.

Baroque façade of the Jesuit seminary of San Javier, Tepotzotlán.

authorities for execution. The tribunal persisted almost to the end of the colonial period and was not abolished until 1820.

The church touched the lives of those in New Spain from baptism to burial. Altogether some twelve thousand churches were built in the colony during the three centuries of Spanish rule. To the Spaniards the church was a link with the mother country, a familiar and comforting association that made them feel less alien in the New World. It has been argued that considerations of honor and piety motivated them to support the church lavishly "almost to the point of their own economic

*Carved wooden mask used in a dance
celebrating the Christian victory over the
Moors.*

suicide."[2] A deep spirituality also inspired local Catholicism in Indian
communities. Indians were lured by the solemn ceremonies that connected them with whatever sense of the cosmic they had evolved; the
tolling of chimes and tinkling of bells, the incense, and the burning candles aroused a sense of reverence and awe. Outside the churches, native peoples savored the singing, dancing, eating, and drinking of the
fiestas with their noisy and colorful displays of fireworks and pageantry.
Above all, "local religious practices sought to explain and domesticate
Spanish colonial rule. Indians sought access to the Spaniards' spiritual
knowledge and power in order to fortify the connection between the
sacred and profane in ways that responded to the overshadowing importance of natural forces in their lives."[3] For indigenous peoples, the
new religion was a source both of travail and solace.

---

2. Arnold J. Bauer, "The Colonial Economy," in Louisa S. Hoberman and Susan M.
   Socolow, eds., *The Countryside in Latin America* (Albuquerque, 1996), p. 46.

3. William B. Taylor, *Magistrates of the Sacred: Priests and Parishioners in Eighteenth-
   Century Mexico* (Stanford, 1996), p. 62.

RECOMMENDED FOR FURTHER STUDY

Brading, D. A. *Mexican Phoenix, Our Lady of Guadalupe: Image and Tradition across Five Centuries.* New York: Cambridge University Press, 2001.

Brescia, Michael M. "Liturgical Expressions of Episcopal Power: Juan de Palafox y Mendoza and the Tridentine Reform in Colonial Mexico." *The Catholic Historical Review* 90 (2004): 497–518.

Burkhart, Louise M. *Before Guadalupe: The Virgin Mary in Early Colonial Nahuatl Literature.* Austin: University of Texas Press, 2001.

Cervantes, Fernando. *The Devil in the New World: The Impact of Diabolism in New Spain.* New Haven, Conn.: Yale University Press, 1994.

Clendinnen, Inga. "Disciplining the Indians: Franciscan Ideology and Missionary Violence in Yucatán." *Past and Present* 94 (1982): 27–48.

Curcio-Nagy, Linda A. "Faith and Morals in Colonial Mexico," in *The Oxford History of Mexico.* Edited by Michael C. Meyer and William H. Beezley, pp. 151–182. New York: Oxford University Press, 2000.

Deeds, Susan M. *Defiance and Deference in Colonial Mexico: Indians under Spanish Rule in Nueva Vizcaya.* Austin: University of Texas Press, 2003.

Farriss, Nancy. *Crown and Clergy in Colonial Mexico, 1759–1821.* London: University of London Press, 1968.

Greenleaf, Richard E. *The Mexican Inquisition of the Sixteenth Century.* Albuquerque: University of New Mexico Press, 1969.

———. *Zumárraga and the Mexican Inquisition, 1536–1543.* Washington, D.C.: Academy of American Franciscan History, 1961.

Gruzinski, Serge. *Man-Gods in the Mexican Highlands: Indian Power and Colonial Society, 1520–1800.* Stanford, Calif.: Stanford University Press, 1989.

Hackel, Steven W. *Children of Coyote, Missionaries of Saint Francis: Indian–Spanish Relations in Colonial California, 1769–1850.* Chapel Hill: University of North Carolina Press, 2005.

Hanke, Lewis. *Bartolomé de Las Casas: Bookman, Scholar, and Propagandist.* Philadelphia: University of Pennsylvania Press, 1952.

Hordes, Stanley M. "The Inquisition as Economic and Political Agent: The Campaign of the Mexican Holy Office against the Crypto-Jews in the Mid-Seventeenth Century." *The Americas* 39 (1982): 22–38.

Hu-Dehart, Evelyn. *Missionaries, Miners and Indians: Spanish Contact with the Yaqui Nation of Northwestern New Spain, 1533–1820.* Tucson: University of Arizona Press, 1981.

Lamb, Ursula. "Religious Conflicts in the Conquest of Mexico." *Journal of the History of Ideas* 17 (1956): 526–39.

Lavrin, Asunción. "The Role of the Nunneries in the Economy of New Spain in the Eighteenth Century." *Hispanic American Historical Review* 46 (1966): 371–93.

Megged, Amos. *Exporting the Catholic Reformation: Local Religion in Early-Colonial Mexico.* Leiden: E.J. Brill, 1996.

Phelan, John L. *The Millennial Kingdom of the Franciscans in the New World: A Study of the Writings of Gerónimo de Mendieta.* Berkeley: University of California Press, 1956.

Poole, Stafford. *Our Lady of Guadalupe: The Origins and Sources of a Mexican National Symbol, 1531–1797.* Tucson: University of Arizona Press, 1995.

———. *Pedro Moya de Contreras: Catholic Reform and Royal Power in New Spain, 1571–1591.* Berkeley: University of California Press, 1987.

Ricard, Robert. *The Spiritual Conquest of Mexico*. Berkeley: University of California Press, 1966.

Riley, James D. "The Wealth of the Jesuits in Mexico, 1670–1767." *The Americas* 33 (1976): 226–66.

Sandos, James A. *Converting California: Indians and Franciscans in the Missions*. New Haven, Conn.: Yale University Press, 2004.

Schwaller, John F. *The Church and Clergy in Sixteenth-Century Mexico*. Albuquerque: University of New Mexico Press, 1987.

Sigal, Peter. *From Moon Goddesses to Virgins: The Colonization of Yucatecan Maya Sexual Desire*. Austin: University of Texas Press, 2000.

Taylor, William B. *Magistrates of the Sacred: Priests and Parishioners in Eighteenth-Century Mexico*. Stanford, Calif.: Stanford University Press, 1996.

11

Colonial Society:
Race, Class, and Gender

RACIAL GROUPS

The conquistadores of Mexico were adventurers, not true colonists. They sought no religious haven, nor were they searching for fields to cultivate or shops to tend. Heirs of a military tradition, they responded to the allure of danger and the promise of wealth in the New World. Not for them the prosaic toil of the pioneer.

The married among them left their wives and children in Spain; thus the restraints of domesticity were absent, and few felt any moral qualms about their sexual behavior in the Indies. From the beginning Spaniards mixed freely with female natives, leaving offspring of a new ethnic type. Just as readily they had relationships with black women, fathering more progeny of mixed blood. Later cohabitation of the mixed children themselves resulted in additional racial distinctions, so that within a couple of generations the ethnic pattern was quite diverse.

Society in New Spain was composed of three basic ethnic groups: Spanish, Indian, and African. Miscegenation, however, produced offspring of mixed bloods who were called *mestizos*. Commonly, a mestizo is considered to be of Spanish-Indian parentage, but it is helpful to distinguish the racial categories more precisely:

> *Euromestizos:* those of a Spanish–Indian mixture, with European (Spanish) ethnic and cultural characteristics predominating. Such persons in the early colony were often considered as *Spanish* and later as *criollo*.
>
> *Indomestizos:* persons of a Spanish–Indian mixture, with Indian ethnic and cultural characteristics predominating. They formed the bulk of those termed *mestizo*.
>
> *Afromestizos:* persons of mixed bloods in which a black strain was evident. If Spanish–black, the designation was *mulatto*; if black–Indian, the designation was *zambo*.

Because all of the preceding combined in further strains, racial and cultural traits often became hopelessly confused; by the end of the colonial period mixed race groups were often designated collectively as *castas*. Generalizations about the different groups of colonial society can be misleading, however, because conditions and identities did not remain static. Some of the nonwhite castes could not hold official positions in royal government or become clerics, carry arms, serve in the military, or dress like Spaniards, but such prohibitions were by no means always in force. Anyone who relies extensively on published Spanish legislation will have a distorted view of the reality of colonial life; not only did laws change frequently, but in many instances they were not enforced. Although a fairly rigid class system was defined in the sixteenth century, by the eighteenth century society was quite different in several respects. The most notable change was the greatly increased number of those of mixed blood, who were diverse in character and socioeconomic circumstances. The majority of the castas were in a disadvantaged position, but enough of them achieved a measure of prosperity and recognition for their abilities and accomplishments to make facile generalizations invalid. Within certain constraints of hierarchy and patriarchy, colonial identity was mobile, fluid, and highly contentious.

THE SPANIARDS

The elite of society in the post-Conquest colony was made up of the more than two thousand Spaniards in Mexico in 1521. As the conquerors and first settlers, they were undisputed lords of the land, yet few were born with the proverbial silver spoon in the mouth. While a considerable number of conquerors were hidalgos from the nobility, more often than not they had little wealth. Partible inheritance law throughout most of Spain resulted over time in the subdivision of land into smaller parcels, leaving sons and daughters of the landed classes with smaller legacies. At the beginning of the sixteenth century, the high nobility was permitted to create entailed estates that passed larger properties intact to the eldest son. In either situation, lesser endowed sons sought other outlets, but their options were limited because their pretensions to hidalgo status prevented them from taking employment deemed unworthy of their class. A career in law might enable one to find a place in the royal bureaucracy, but it required a university education. Alternatives lay in the church or the army. Owing to the long history of warfare in Spain, by the early modern period the warrior was a figure of assured social standing, associated with the nobility. In the colonial world a military occupation continued to be honorable, but one's social status also depended on other factors. Elites developed a system of honor in which attitudes regarding occupation, lineage, and behavior were prescribed and adjusted to ensure their superior social status. Although the social hierarchy tightened over time, the Conquest provided opportunity for both hidalgos and commoners to acquire prestige, and even those of ignoble birth were quick to assume the title of "Don."

The majority of the conquerors, in fact, came from the working class, and many of them had trades. Suddenly, tailors, carpenters, masons, cobblers, seamen, and the like found themselves part of the new post-Conquest aristocracy. History offers few comparable examples of such rapid upward social mobility. Aside from the true hidalgos, the conquerors were an unlikely lot of "nobles." Many were coarse in speech, unrefined in manner, half literate (if indeed they were lettered at all), ignorant of the social amenities, and altogether possessing few of the attributes associated with even the minor nobility.

The needs of these Spaniards were taken care of by Indian servants and laborers, and their time was free to enjoy the simple diversions available in the developing society. Even though most of them groused about their pinched circumstances, individual economic well-being varied so much as to render generalizations difficult. Some of them ended up isolated in remote provinces with very few Indians, while others were favored with large Indian towns near one of the main Spanish settlements. A few found official positions, either in local government or in the royal bureaucracy, both of which could open the way to profiteering. It is probably safe to say that all enhanced their pre-Conquest socioeconomic status.

The natural leader of this early society was Fernando Cortés, who wielded great power and authority. He had a house in Coyoacán, another large residence built on the site of Moctezuma's demolished palace in Mexico City, a palace in Cuernavaca, and a house in Oaxaca, as well as other dwellings. With his many tributaries and powers Cortés resembled one of the great feudal lords of Europe.

The heyday of the conquerors was short lived. Soon the colony was invaded by a different type of Spaniard, educated and well connected in the mother country. Royal officials with legal training entered to look after the crown's interests, and private lawyers (despite Cortés's plea that they be excluded) arrived to involve themselves with the interminable lawsuits that arose. Cultured men of the church came to set a higher moral and intellectual tone. Most of these newcomers were of a more elevated social status than the conquerors, and they were favored at the royal court. Spanish immigrants were not of one mind or loyalty as they brought with them their regional and local customs and prejudices. For example, the Basques who were instrumental in the colonization of northern Mexico strove to preserve ethnic distinctions that they believed set them apart from other Spaniards.

A number of the conquerors, dissatisfied with the spoils in Mexico, left for the conquests of Central America and Peru and other ventures. Following the restraints imposed on Cortés, the symbol of enco-mendero power, and the seating of royal control through the audien-cia and viceroy, the first settlers were further hurt by the passage of the New Laws of 1542. Although important parts of the legislation were not implemented, the laws were symptomatic of the trend to erode the encomenderos' position.

With the phasing out of Conquest society, the remainder of the colo-nial period would be dominated in circles of influence by men sent from the Spanish peninsula—the *peninsulares*, or *gachupines*, as they were derisively called by those born in Mexico. The peninsulares held the best positions in the civil and ecclesiastical hierarchies for much of the colonial period. They also were found, along with criollos, in the most lucrative occupations as miners, merchants (especially long-dis-tance traders), and landowners, but as time wore on, emigrant Spaniards of modest means only attained those levels through wealthy relatives or marriage into influential criollo families. It is estimated that during the three centuries of colonial rule between 250,000 and 300,000 Spaniards entered Mexico, but their numbers were never large at any one time.

THE CRIOLLOS

The second level of colonial society was formed by those of Spanish blood born in Mexico. These criollos were by physical appearance in-distinguishable from the peninsulares, but the mere fact of their New World birth was sufficient to prejudice their status. It was commonly held by those born in Europe that America's environment was some-how detrimental, that the climate was enervating and corrosive, and that the atmosphere produced beings who were physically, mentally, and morally inferior. Thus the criollos were viewed by many peninsu-lares as innately lazy, effete, irresponsible, and lacking in both vigor and intelligence. To these defects were joined all the social and cul-tural limitations of life in the colony. Such opinions formed a conve-nient pretext for the gachupines to justify their favored position.

The criollos, despite their secondary rank, were in a relatively fa-vorable position in the society of New Spain; merely by virtue of their light skins they were considered superior to the darker masses below

WHITE POPULATION OF NEW SPAIN

Year	Whites	Comments
1521	2,329	peninsulares
1529	8,000	peninsulares
1560	20,211	peninsulares and criollos
1570	57,000	peninsulares and criollos
1646	114,000–125,000	mostly criollos
1770	over 750,000	mostly criollos
1793	1,095,000	70,000 of these were peninsulares

them. They could rise to respectable levels in church organization and to lower- and middle-rank posts in the royal bureaucracy, and they were able to dominate the cabildos. In fact, during the seventeenth and early eighteenth centuries some criollos were successful in attaining the highest offices of both church and government, and eventually a number also held high military rank. Nevertheless, distance from the power centers in Spain and the less prestigious academic degrees of the colony prevented their having equal opportunity.

Still, criollos made up the largest segment of New Spain's economic elite as *hacendados*, or owners of large agricultural estates, miners, and merchants. Their dominance in the cabildos abetted their economic pursuits, especially in provincial areas. The special social prestige attached to landholding also helped to confer upon criollos a prominent place in the social hierarchy. Despite their superior numbers, that prominence would be eroded in the latter decades of late eighteenth century, with fateful results. But for the most part property-owning Spaniards, regardless of birthplace, were united in their resolve to dominate the rest of society.

THE MESTIZOS

During the Conquest friendly caciques gave women to the Spaniards, and other native females either joined the conquerors by choice or were taken forcibly. These women cooked for their men, nursed their wounds, carried their belongings, and shared their beds. Informal unions of Spaniard and native resulted in the new physical type of the mestizo. Many such liaisons were fleeting, but others ripened into long, comfortable arrangements. In the early, hopeful years the conquerors visualized advantageous marriages with Spanish women. But when, as happened in most cases, circumstances prevented their returning to

Spain in desirable style, they remained in Mexico, where their relative positions were sounder. Other Spaniards already had wives in Spain or in the Caribbean, and, although by law they were obligated to send for them, by one pretext or another many avoided doing so. In 1551, according to the bishop of Mexico, there were five hundred married Spaniards in his diocese whose wives languished outside the colony. Meantime most of these men took native partners, and some even remarried, thereby risking trial for bigamy.

In the early post-Conquest years, crown and church encouraged unmarried Spaniards to wed Indian noblewomen and to legitimize their illegitimate children, but as the numbers of Spanish women arriving in Mexico with their fathers, brothers, and uncles slowly increased, the situation changed. By midcentury, there were also a number of mestizo daughters of conquistadores of marriageable age, and after that time, few Spaniards or criollos married Indian women.

Financial considerations were important factors in marriage; a woman of property had a decided advantage, often to the exclusion of certain other qualities. A widow of an encomendero, for example, seldom remained unmarried very long. If she happened to be an Indian or mestiza she might well be more attractive to a poor Spaniard than a penniless Spanish woman. If an encomendero died leaving no son or widow to inherit his Indian villages, the encomienda passed to his eldest daughter. If single, she was required to marry within a year in order to keep the encomienda. As time went on, however, it was much less likely that non-Spanish women would possess such high status.

The proportion of mestizos and other mixed blood castas increased rapidly in Mexico, surpassing the number of Spaniards in the seventeenth century. It is very difficult to generalize about their status, which varied according to time and place and was influenced by such factors as physical characteristics, gender, the ability to acquire skills or property, and cultural identity. The mestizo children who were legitimized by their conquistador fathers fared the best in terms of rank.

To take a notable case, Don Martín Cortés was the son of the captain and Doña Marina. Technically he was a mestizo, but such was the standing of his father that he was certainly considered to be a Spaniard and entitled to every honor—except of course the inheritance of the estate of the Marqués del Valle, which went to his younger but legitimate criollo brother (who was also named Martín). Fernando Cortés took his mestizo son with him to Spain when the boy was only five. While still a young child, Martín was made a knight of the prestigious Order of Santiago and a page to the prince (later Philip II). He fought with distinction in Spanish armies in Algeria and Germany and later fell in crown service battling the Moriscos in Granada. Pedro de Alvarado's

mestizo daughter also had high social status; she married a cousin of
the duke of Albuquerque, one of Spain's most powerful nobles.

The majority of the mestizos, however, could not aspire to high status. A high percentage were illegitimate (not infrequently the result
of rape) and the term *mestizo* was synonymous with bastard for most
of the colonial period. Informal liaisons between Spanish men and
casta or Indian women continued to be commonplace. Mexico (as elsewhere in Spanish America) had a very high rate of illegitimate births
across all racial groups in urban areas. At the same time, Indians in
rural zones had the highest ratio of legitimate births.

Castas (along with some poor Spaniards) could be found in a wide
variety of occupations, working as domestic servants, apprentices, artisans, petty entrepreneurs and traders, muleteers, and common laborers. Being lower on the social scale did not necessarily translate into
deference to whites. In fact, the record is replete with examples of individuals who challenged their subordination by protesting unfair treatment in the courts, in occasionally attempting to "pass" to a different
ethnic category by asserting a corresponding occupational or cultural
identity, by verbally and physically abusing superiors, by calling on
magic to bring retribution against oppressors, or by migrating to other
regions.

THE INDIANS

Central Mexico alone (roughly equal to the size of France) may have
had a pre-Conquest population as high as twenty-five million, and for
many decades the Indians of Mexico vastly outnumbered all other racial groups in New Spain. Then their numbers were catastrophically
reduced. Waves of devastating plagues swept over the land, and after
a century of Spanish occupation, during which many died from over-
work and maltreatment, there were only about one million natives left.
From their lowest number around 1630 they began to increase slowly.
By the end of the colonial period the Indians were still the largest ethnic group, but not by so vast a percentage.

As a conquered people the natives were exploited by the victors. At
first Spaniards used the Indian nobility to do their bidding, and noble
caciques were able to maintain higher status within indigenous societies at least for a time. For the most part, however, the Spaniards saw
the Indians as an inferior people. There were some enlightened ecclesiastics and a few royal officials who pleaded the Indian cause; they
appealed to Christian ethics, emphasized the natives' positive qualities, and pressed for humane treatment. All too many Spaniards, however, considered the Indians simply pagans, cannibals, and sodomites.

Natives were frequently described as lazy, disposed to vices, devious, and backward.

Legally Indians were considered as minors and wards of crown and church. Their care and supervision were commended to clergymen, corregidores, and encomenderos. Yet, because of their tutelary status, the Indians were, at least in some respects, protected and given consideration. The crown and the church showed concern for the Indians' welfare, and many laws were passed for their benefit. Lawyers eagerly encouraged Indians to file lawsuits, and a surprisingly large number were settled in the Indians' favor in the General Indian Court or in other tribunals. Ultimately, however, the colony's welfare depended upon the labor of the Indians, and so they were doomed to serve the interests of the Spaniards.

But they hardly did so with total acquiescence. The responses of native peoples to Spanish colonialism were so varied as to defy categorization, but whether the response was aggressive or accommodative, the intent was to preserve familiar structures and to maintain whatever balance was necessary for living in harmony with the natural world and for assuring an adequate material subsistence. We know, for example, that Nahua peoples resisted linguistic and other forms of acculturation for generations while asserting their rights to ancestral lands through fabricated "titles" that would have resonance in the Spanish legal system. In general, indigenous groups in central and

INDIAN POPULATION OF CENTRAL MEXICO: CONTACT TO MID-SEVENTEENTH CENTURY

Year	Indians	Plague Years	Comments
1519	25,200,000		
		1520	smallpox
		1529	measles
1532	16,800,000		
		1545	matlazáhuatl (typhus?); Indian deaths est. 800,000
1548	6,300,000		
1568	2,650,000		
		1576	matlazáhuatl; Indian deaths est. 2,000,000
1580	1,900,000		
1595	1,375,000		
1605	1,075,000		
1625–50	1,000,000 (or less?)		lowest point of Indian population

Sources: Figures to the year 1605 are based on the research of Sherburne F. Cook and Woodrow Borah: *The Indian Population of Central Mexico, 1531–1610* (Berkeley, 1960), and *The Aboriginal Population of Central Mexico on the Eve of the Spanish Conquest* (Berkeley, 1963). Their counts, especially those prior to 1568, are considered much too high by some scholars.

Eighteenth-century "casta paintings" depicted the many combinations of mixed race marriages and their children. This one, from an anonymous artist, is entitled Español e india, mestizo.

southern Mexico were successful in using the courts to protect substantial portions of their land. They were less effective in resisting recruitment of their labor and the variety of means devised by Spaniards for extracting resources from their communities. Corregidores or alcaldes mayores collected tribute through Indian middlemen, forced sales of unwanted merchandise on Indian communities, and exacted graft payments. To moderate these outlays, Indian villages often devised inventive ways to manipulate local resources through "broker" institutions like the cofradía and the *caja de comunidad* (community chest), both borrowed from Spanish society.

In peripheral areas, more aggressive resistance was initially the response of less sedentary peoples to Spanish intrusion. Some, like the Apaches in the north, adopted the Spanish horse and preyed upon Spanish cattle to successfully avoid subjugation. Eventual defeat and resettlement in pueblos followed for most northern Indians, but even then, they chose flight and other evasive tactics such as foot-dragging, false deference, sabotage, pilfering, gossip, and slander to resist total incorporation. Rebellion continued to be an option, either for resisting the early stages of incorporation when their worlds were turned upside down (the case of the Tepehuanes and Tarahumaras of Durango and Chihuahua in the seventeenth century), or for peoples who found the accommodations they had worked out with their oppressors for generations to have been violated.

No widespread rebellion affected Mexico in the colonial period, and aggressive resistance was mostly restricted to single village riots, which increased as the eighteenth century progressed and burgeoning Indian populations put new strains on resources, including land and water. These protests were often directed against the excessive demands of individual Spanish officials or priests. Some villagers struggled to maintain cohesive communities, remaining in the pueblos where they cultivated small plots of land and retained many traditional linguistic and cultural practices. Growing numbers, however, left to find work in Spanish haciendas and mines. In some cases, they found advantageous situations under the protection of their *patrones* (bosses), but the loss of communal ties and the failure to substitute compensatory social relationships could also result in despair and alcoholism.

In varying degrees, then, indigenous communities and peoples survived conquest and epidemic disease and went on to conserve features of their cultural patrimony by deliberately and selectively taking from European techniques and beliefs what could be most usefully adapted to indigenous ways. Of course, the effectiveness of resistance could be thwarted when native populations declined drastically, when natural resources were valuable enough to bring heavy Spanish might to bear, or when indigenous middlemen sided with their exploiters.

THE BLACKS

During the Conquest there were half a dozen blacks with the Spanish forces. In the Caribbean an expanding sugar economy resulted in the importation of large numbers of African slaves, and eventually many were taken to Mexico. At first most slaves were personal servants imported by prominent men, who often had three or four in their household staffs. Less fortunate were those slaves assigned to hard labor, especially in the mines. As a consequence of the declining Indian population, 120,000 or more slaves entered Mexico between 1519 and 1650. But blacks were expensive, while natives cost little. Accordingly, slaves from Africa used for labor were put where they could produce returns justifying their high purchase price. In the early years of silver mining, they made up a substantial portion of the labor force. Later they were used extensively in the tropical sugar-producing regions. Considered more reliable than Indians, blacks were often trained for important skilled positions and sometimes put in charge of native workers as overseers in mining operations, small factories, and ranches. In the latter capacity, they were frequently accused of exploiting the Indians. Other blacks became accomplished artisans, bringing their masters good profits. It was not uncommon for the slave to be given a share of the profits, which eventually allowed him to purchase his freedom. And although treatment of slaves was arbitrary and often unjust, owners frequently manumitted slaves in their wills.

Mulattoes, offspring of the union of Spaniards and blacks, could also improve their circumstances, both because they were thoroughly Hispanicized and because their Spanish fathers could ease the way for them by making sure they were free. Otherwise the mulatto would inherit the status of his mother according to law and would be a slave if she were one. By late sixteenth century there were many free blacks and mulattoes.

Perhaps two hundred thousand Africans entered Mexico during the colonial period. It appears that by around 1560 there were almost as many blacks as whites in New Spain. Especially in urban areas, elites enhanced their social prestige by having a retinue of black and mulatto slaves engaged in domestic service and craft production. Slaves were often rented out to other Spaniards. There was always a shortage of black women (the usual ratio of slaves introduced being two males for every female), which led many black men to take Indian wives. After the importation of slaves diminished at mid-seventeenth century, mulattoes increasingly took Indian and mestizo partners, and in Mexico City Africans "began to lose their identity as a separate racial category." The children of the frequent mestizo-mulatto unions tended

BLACK POPULATION OF NEW SPAIN

Year	Blacks	Blacks and/or Afromestizos	Comments
1521	6		
1553	20,000		Afromestizos uncounted
1560	17,312		Afromestizos uncounted
1570	18,535	1,465	Perhaps 2,000 blacks or mulattoes were escaped slaves
1580	18,500	1,500	Figures are probably low
1600		140,000	
1646	35,089		Afromestizos uncounted
1650		130,000	Including 20,119 black and mulatto slaves
1793	6,000		Afromestizos uncounted
1810	10,000	624,461	

to gravitate to the "social network of one parent or the other, whichever was more advantageous."[1] In rural areas, where they worked as cowboys and agricultural workers or overseers, slaves were more likely to form unions with Indian women.

From the early years of Spanish occupation black slaves in Mexico had frequently run away from their masters, sometimes joining Indians in isolated regions. There were apprehensions that blacks would incite a general rebellion, and many instances of black resistance worried settlers. Blacks were forbidden to carry arms; they were forced to observe a curfew; and no more than three could gather in public. Few slave insurrections occurred, but both slaves and free blacks were often accused of inciting natives to raid ranches and assault mule trains in remote areas. In response, runaway slaves (maroons, or *cimarrones*) were hunted down by bounty hunters and punished with floggings, castration, or hanging if they had committed serious crimes.

Around the beginning of the seventeenth century the threat of black resistance centered in the eastern region, especially near Veracruz. There an elderly slave named Yanga had held out in the mountains for thirty years. In 1609 the viceroy sent an army of six hundred men against Yanga, whose camp had eighty men and some women and children. The viceroy's soldiers were given some lessons in guerrilla maneuvers by Yanga, and, when the skirmishing finally ended in a standoff, the government agreed to treat with the black rebel. It was an extraordinary concession on the part of royal authority, and Yanga's struggle was surely one of the most successful instances of black resistance in the New World. He and his followers remained free by agreeing to cause no more trouble and to help track down other runaways. Not long afterward an independent black town, San Lorenzo de los Negros, was founded near modern Córdoba.

Through miscegenation, manumission, and the purchase of freedom by slaves themselves, black slavery declined considerably over the generations. Although toward the end of the colonial period there were many Afromestizos, only around ten thousand could be considered blacks. Of those, perhaps only six thousand or so were slaves by 1800, mainly congregated in the environs of Veracruz and Acapulco. By far the majority of Afromestizos were integrated into the larger casta segment of society, and their relationships with Indians and other mixed-race peoples varied widely. Free-colored (Afromestizo) militias served the crown throughout New Spain.

---

1. R. Douglas Cope, *The Limits of Racial Domination: Plebeian Society in Colonial Mexico City, 1660–1720* (Madison, 1994), pp. 83–84.

OTHER GROUPS

The crown's policy on immigration severely restricted the flow of foreigners into the Mexican colony. However, during the union of the Spanish and Portuguese crowns (1580–1640), a substantial number of Portuguese crossed the Atlantic to New Spain. Included in their ranks were some converted and crypto-Jews. A few other Europeans—Italian, French, German, English, and Greek—also went to New Spain. Some were specialists and scientists invited by royal officials, but others sneaked in, usually by bribing officials. Asians—Filipinos and Chinese for the most part—entered the country on the Manila galleons. One authority believes that in some decades of the seventeenth century as many as six thousand may have arrived.[2]

The diversity of race in Mexico was well advanced before the close of the sixteenth century. White remained the color of privilege, but the number of castas far outstripped the European population before the eighteenth century. Since even the criollo sector was not free of race mixture, money could sometimes buy status regardless of color. And although elites endeavored to maintain a race-based hierarchy, the racially mixed castas habitually contested the boundaries of their subordination creating a popular culture that transcended ethnic divisions, as they simultaneously reinforced and challenged colonial prescriptive norms.

WOMEN AND FAMILY

Subordination was also a tenet of the Spanish Catholic patriarchal system through which men theoretically exercised control over the sexuality, reproductive capacities, and labor power of women. The ideal woman was chaste, pious, and submissive, living under the supervision and protection of her father or husband. While women who defied these norms stained the honor and threatened the racial purity of the family, the promiscuous sexual behavior of men was seen as a natural component of male virility and authority (*machismo*). Domestic abuse not infrequently was a result of patriarchal and honor codes.

Despite the arbitrariness of this system, Spanish women could inherit from their fathers, and they enjoyed control over property they owned before they married. For elite families, carefully arranged marriages were crucial to enhancing status and wealth. Widows and

---

2. J. I. Israel, *Race, Class and Politics in Colonial Mexico, 1610–1670* (London, 1975), p. 76.

unmarried older women not infrequently administered estates and businesses. Some women elected not to marry, choosing instead the religious vocation of the convent. Other Spanish women transgressed the norms by engaging in informal liaisons, but they often did so in the hope of securing a promise of marriage.

Lower-class casta women were even less easily held to the rules, not surprisingly because they were often objects of men's sexual advances. Unmarried mestizas and mulattas—frequently single heads of households—worked as street vendors, maids, cooks, washerwomen, midwives; some were petty merchants with their own stalls in the markets. In urban areas, Indian women also occupied these roles.

Rural indigenous women were more likely to be married and engaged in performing agricultural labor, domestic chores, and perhaps a skill like weaving or potting. Although Indian women had held significant religious and political positions in earlier precontact societies, those who came under the more stratified organization of imperial rule found their roles circumscribed even before Spanish contact. At contact, Indian women throughout Mexico performed crucial social and economic functions that paralleled and complemented those of men. The tendency of native societies to recognize and even venerate women's contributions to shared duties was eroded in the colonial period, resulting in diminished legal status and influence, if not necessarily economic power.

Nonetheless, across the ethnic spectrum, women were typically engaged in contesting and negotiating their status through a variety of channels including the church, the courts, and petty witchcraft. Moreover, their activities contributed importantly to the maintenance of families—the critical social unit in all sectors of society. Families were a site for the transmission of cultural values and a supportive base for forging political and social connections. Extended families and godparents (*compadres*) constituted networks that could provide access to advantageous marriages and economic influence for elites, as well as a safety net for the lower classes. In the final analysis, the complexities of the intersections of race, class, and gender determined the lived experiences of women and men in colonial society.

POPULATION FIGURES

Tenochtitlán had a population of perhaps two hundred thousand at the advent of the Spaniards, but the Christian city that arose on its ruins began with far fewer people. In 1560 Mexico City had about eight thousand Spaniards. By 1574 there were around fifteen thousand

Spaniards, in addition to a large Indian population and significant numbers of blacks and mixed bloods. By 1800 Mexico City had approximately 137,000 souls; it was the largest city in the Western Hemisphere, but still had a much smaller population than that boasted by the Aztec capital at the time of the Conquest.

Population figures for the colony as a whole are especially suspect because of the difficulty of counting people in so many isolated villages. Some generalizations can be made. From its nadir of about one million in 1630, the Indian population of central Mexico began to recuperate and probably tripled by the end of the colonial period. In southern Mexico (especially in Oaxaca and in Maya areas), the indigenous population also continued to constitute the largest segment, while in the north some indigenous groups disappeared altogether and the rest were outnumbered by non-Indians.

Castas rapidly increased in numbers after the mid-seventeenth century to compose nearly a third of the total at the end of the eighteenth. As noted earlier, few pure blacks remained, although many Afromestizos could be counted within the mestizo sector. Analyses of a major census undertaken in 1793 suggest that a substantial number of mestizos claimed criollo status. At Independence in 1821, almost exactly three hundred years after the Conquest, the total population of Mexico was around six million. About 60 percent were Indians; mixed races made up nearly a fourth; blacks less than 1 percent; and Spaniards (predominantly criollos) between 15 and 20 percent. Of course, regional variations in those proportions were striking, with marked differences between rural and urban areas and between central-southern Mexico and the north.

RECOMMENDED FOR FURTHER STUDY

Anderson, Arthur J. O., Frances Berdan, and James Lockhart, eds. *Beyond the Codices: The Nahua View of Colonial Mexico*. Berkeley: University of California Press, 1976.

Bennett, Herman L. *Africans in Colonial Mexico: Absolutism, Christianity, and Afro-Creole Consciousness, 1570–1640*. Bloomington: University of Indiana Press, 2003.

Boyer, Richard. *Lives of the Bigamists: Marriage, Family, and Community in Colonial Mexico*. Albuquerque: University of New Mexico Press, 1995.

Carrera, Magali M. *Imagining Identity in New Spain: Race, Lineage, and the Colonial Body in Portraiture and Casta Paintings*. Austin: University of Texas Press, 2003.

Carroll, Patrick J. *Blacks in Colonial Veracruz: Race, Ethnicity, and Regional Development*. Austin: University of Texas Press, 1991.

Chance, John K. *Conquest of the Sierra: Spaniards and Indians in Colonial Oaxaca*. Norman: University of Oklahoma Press, 1989.

Chandler, D. S. *Social Assistance and Bureaucratic Politics: The Montepíos of Colonial Mexico, 1767–1821*. Albuquerque: University of New Mexico Press, 1991.

Cook, Noble David, and W. George Lovell, eds. *Secret Judgments of God: Old World Diseases and Colonial Spanish America*. Norman: University of Oklahoma Press, 1991.

Cook, Sherburne F., and Woodrow Borah. *The Aboriginal Population of Central Mexico on the Eve of the Spanish Conquest*. Berkeley: University of California Press, 1963.

———. *The Indian Population of Central Mexico, 1531–1610*. Berkeley: University of California Press, 1960.

Cooper, Donald. *Epidemic Disease in Mexico City, 1761–1813*. Austin: University of Texas Press, 1965.

Few, Martha. *Women Who Live Evil Lives: Gender, Religion and the Politics of Power in Colonial Guatemala*. Austin: University of Texas Press, 2002.

Franco, Jean. *Plotting Women: Gender and Representation in Mexico*. New York: Columbia University Press, 1989.

Gosner, Kevin, and Deborah E. Kanter, eds. *Women, Power, and Resistance in Colonial Mesoamerica*. Special Issue, *Ethnohistory* 42 (1995).

Gradie, Charlotte M. *The Tepehuan Revolt of 1616: Militarism, Evangelism, and Colonialism in Seventeenth-Century Nueva Vizcaya*. Salt Lake City: University of Utah Press, 2000.

Gutiérrez, Ramón. *When Jesus Came, the Corn Mothers Went Away: Marriage, Sexuality, and Power in New Mexico, 1500–1846*. Stanford, Calif.: Stanford University Press, 1991.

Haslip-Viera, Gabriel. *Crime and Punishment in Late Colonial Mexico City, 1692–1810*. Albuquerque: University of New Mexico Press, 1999.

Herrera, Robinson A. *Natives, Europeans, and Africans in Sixteenth-Century Santiago de Guatemala*. Austin: University of Texas Press, 2003.

Hoberman, Louisa. "Bureaucracy and Disaster: Mexico City and the Flood of 1629." *Journal of Latin American Studies* 6 (1974): 211–30.

———. *Mexico's Merchant Elite, 1590–1660*. Durham, N.C.: Duke University Press, 1991.

Israel, J. I. *Race, Class and Politics in Colonial Mexico, 1610–1670*. London: Oxford University Press, 1975.

Jackson, Robert H. *Indian Population Decline: The Missions of Northwestern New Spain, 1687–1840*. Albuquerque: University of New Mexico Press, 1994.

Johnson, Lyman L., and Sonya Lipsett-Rivera, eds. *The Faces of Honor: Sex, Shame and Violence in Colonial Latin America*. Albuquerque: University of New Mexico Press, 1998.

Kellogg, Susan, and Matthew Restall, eds. *Dead Giveaways: Indigenous Testaments of Colonial Mesoamerica and the Andes*. Salt Lake City: University of Utah Press, 1998.

Landers, Jane. *Black Society in Spanish Florida*. Urbana: University of Illinois Press, 1999.

Lavrin, Asunción, ed. *Sexuality and Marriage in Colonial Latin America*. Lincoln: University of Nebraska Press, 1989.

———. "Women in Colonial Mexico," in *The Oxford History of Mexico*. Edited by Michael C. Meyer and William H. Beezley, pp. 245–73. New York: Oxford University Press, 2000.

Lewis, Laura A. *Hall of Mirrors: Power, Witchcraft, and Caste in Colonial Mexico*. Durham, N.C.: Duke University Press, 2003.

Martin, Cheryl E. *Governance and Society in Colonial Mexico: Chihuahua in the Eighteenth Century*. Stanford, Calif.: Stanford University Press, 1995.

Mörner, Magnus. *Race Mixture in the History of Latin America*. Boston: Little, Brown, 1967.

Palmer, Colin A. *Slaves of the White God: Blacks in Mexico*. Cambridge: Cambridge University Press, 1976.

Patch, Robert W. "Indian Resistance to Colonialism," in *The Oxford History of Mexico*. Edited by Michael C. Meyer and William H. Beezley, pp. 183–211. New York: Oxford University Press, 2000.

Powers, Karen V. *Women in the Crucible of Conquest: The Gendered Genesis of Spanish American Society, 1500–1600*. Albuquerque: University of New Mexico Press, 2005.

Radding, Cynthia. *Wandering Peoples: Colonialism, Ethnic Spaces, and Ecological Frontiers in Northwestern Mexico, 1700–1850*. Durham, N.C.: Duke University Press, 1997.

Reff, Daniel. *Disease, Depopulation, and Cultural Change in Northwestern New Spain*. Salt Lake City: University of Utah Press, 1991.

Restall, Matthew. *The Maya World: Yucatec Culture and Society, 1550–1850*. Stanford, Calif.: Stanford University Press, 1997.

Schroeder, Susan, ed. *Native Resistance and the Pax Colonial in New Spain*. Lincoln: University of Nebraska Press, 1998.

Schroeder, Susan, Stephanie Wood, and Robert Haskett, eds. *Indian Women of Early Mexico*. Norman: University of Oklahoma Press, 1997.

Seed, Patricia. *To Love, Honor, and Obey in Colonial Mexico: Conflicts over Marriage Choice, 1574–1821*. Stanford, Calif.: Stanford University Press, 1988.

Socolow, Susan M. *The Women of Colonial Latin America*. New York: Cambridge University Press, 2000.

Stern, Steve J. *The Secret History of Gender: Women, Men, and Power in Late Colonial Mexico*. Chapel Hill: University of North Carolina Press, 1995.

Tuñón Pablos, Julia. *Women in Mexico: A Past Unveiled*. Austin: University of Texas Press, 1999.

Twinam, Ann. *Public Lives, Private Secrets: Gender, Honor, Sexuality, and Illegitimacy in Colonial Spanish America*. Stanford, Calif.: Stanford University Press, 1999.

Vinson, Ben, III *Bearing Arms for His Majesty: The Free-Colored Militia in Colonial Mexico*. Stanford, Calif.: Stanford University Press, 2001.

12

Culture and Daily Life in New Spain

EDUCATION

When Don Antonio de Mendoza arrived in Mexico fourteen years after the fall of Tenochtitlán, he was greeted by, among others, an Indian boy who recited in classic Latin. The amused viceroy soon learned that the energetic friars had already made a significant impact, Hispanicizing the natives through education. It was a plan encouraged by both crown and church, for quite aside from sentiments of altruism, there were practical considerations. The sincere design to Christianize the conquered people was feasible only through their understanding Spanish; moreover, it hastened their assimilation of Spanish ways, which was essential to the goal of a more settled society.

In Spain a broad educational system was not seen as a responsibility of the state. Education was, rather, an individual concern, usually involving only those of the privileged class, while instruction itself was the province of the church. Only on the university level did the crown evince strong interest, primarily to prepare young men for careers in the bureaucracy. The church was equally concerned with higher education in order to instruct clergymen, who would in turn run the schools in the colonies, as in Spain. But in Mexico there developed the curious irony of at least a few well-educated Indians being held inferior by some illiterate Spaniards.

One is struck by the cultural vitality in the early years of a Conquest society that was in so many ways both turbulent and rustic. The impulse to refinement came from learned clergymen primarily because educated laymen were usually involved in government, law, or other professional interests. Therefore the intellectual and cultural attainments of the Spanish colony are attributable primarily to the religious orders.

The first prominent educator in Spanish Mexico was Pedro de Gante, a Franciscan lay brother and illegitimate relative of Charles V.

By 1524 he was teaching Indian boys, and later he founded the famous school of San José, where under his direction hundreds of native youths were given primary instruction and adults were taught trades. While the children were drilled in Latin, music, and other academic subjects, the elders became the colony's masons, carpenters, blacksmiths, painters, and sculptors. Their skills were put to good use by Gante, who claimed to have supervised personally the building of one hundred chapels and churches.

The school of Santa Cruz de Tlatelolco was founded in 1536 by Viceroy Mendoza and Bishop Zumárraga. With such powerful patrons it became the outstanding Indian school and aimed at the higher instruction for the sons of nobles, through whom it was thought Spanish culture would more easily be passed on to commoners. Aside from the fundamentals of reading and writing, courses were offered in Latin, rhetoric, logic, and philosophy, as well as music and native medicine. Taught by learned humanists, the youths received excellent instruction, and they in turn aided the friars in schools and church.

The most appealing figure in early education was Vasco de Quiroga, whose practical approach to education was distinct. A man of varied interests, Quiroga was a humanist, lawyer, and a judge in the second audiencia. But his fame rests on his personal crusade to benefit the conquered peoples. Using his own capital, the aging lawyer established his first hospital-school of Santa Fé in 1531–32, on the outskirts of Mexico City. Shortly thereafter he moved to Michoacán, near Lake Pátzcuaro in the area of the old kingdom of the Tarascans. There, in the region so troubled since the depredations of Nuño de Guzmán, the benevolence of Quiroga (Tata Vasco) inspired trust from the natives. Intrigued by Thomas More's *Utopia*,

The Colegio de Santa Cruz de Tlatelolco.

Quiroga attempted, with considerable success, to create an ideal society in the New World. He formed communities in which the Indians received training not only in religion but also in practical arts and crafts as well as in the rudiments of self-government. Each person worked six hours a day, sharing and contributing equally to the common welfare. Under Quiroga's tutelage the Indians became self-sufficient in agriculture and increased their prosperity through the preservation of traditional crafts. Appointed bishop of Michoacán in 1537, Quiroga continued to lead a productive life until he was nearly ninety. With his death the utopian villages declined, but he had established some fine traditions that persisted, and descendants of his specialized artisans ply their crafts still.

There were various other Indian schools. The Jesuit San Gregorio Magno was started in 1586. Concern for abandoned or orphaned mestizos led to the opening in 1547 of the orphanage school of San Juan de Letrán. But in the end the attempts to educate young Indians and mestizos, however congenial to the best interest of the young colony, were limited in scope. What had begun on such an auspicious note fell largely into neglect, as the cultural transition passed and apathy set in. After several decades of association with their conquerors, many of the Indians naturally absorbed the language and customs of the Spaniards, and the danger of large-scale rebellion seemed past. Now educating Indians and mestizos was perceived as not only unwarranted but socially undesirable.

The Franciscans are most identified with early education of Indians, and, similarly, the Jesuits and Augustinians were foremost in instructing criollos. Though many Spanish conquerors were uncultured, their sons inherited a social position that called for some measure of refinement. Consequently, there were primary schools, at least, in all Spanish communities of any size, and several advanced institutions in the colony. The most prestigious of such schools was the elite Jesuit Colegio de San Pedro y San Pablo, founded in 1576 and supported by profits from efficient Jesuit haciendas. Its graduates were equal, and sometimes superior, to those of the University of Mexico. An Augustinian institution, established a year earlier by the prominent intellectual Alonso de la Veracruz, also provided superior studies. There were in addition excellent seminaries where a high level of scholarship was maintained, perhaps the best being those of San Ildefonso and Tepotzotlán, both of which belonged to the Jesuits.

The most notable institution of learning was the Royal and Pontifical University of Mexico, created at the petition of Viceroy Mendoza and Bishop Zumárraga. The crown authorized it in 1551, and classes began in 1553, making it the first university to function in the New

World. Founded with the aim of educating criollos for the clergy, the University was modeled on the Spanish University of Salamanca, with which it was supposed to be equal in rights and privileges. With an excellent faculty, it would produce many of New Spain's leading literary figures, scientists, lawyers, medical doctors, and theologians. During the colonial period the University granted around thirty thousand bachelors' degrees and over one thousand masters' and doctorates. Late in the colonial period, in 1791, another university was founded in Guadalajara.

Females were not completely ignored in the educational system, although, to be sure, they were given fewer opportunities. As early as 1534 women teachers arrived in Mexico and opened a school for girls, and soon nuns of various orders continued the tradition. Indian girls, under the tutelage of Gante, were taught mainly how to be good wives in the Spanish manner. In 1548 the Caridad school was established for orphaned *mestizas*, and in the late sixteenth century schools were founded for young criolla women.

SCHOLARSHIP AND LITERATURE

Perhaps the most remarkable aspect of scholarship in the colony began not long after the Conquest with the diligent studies made by friars, among whom were a number of non-Spanish Europeans educated in France, Flanders, or other countries. Their inquiries into the nature of the native peoples and the land were truly phenomenal.

The Conquest itself was described by Cortés in his famous letters to the king, which have been translated into several languages and appear in many editions. A more popular account, however, remains the *Historia verdadera de la conquista de la Nueva España*, written by Bernal Díaz del Castillo, a footsoldier in Cortés's army. Díaz later moved to Guatemala, where he wrote his delightful, personalized account years after the events. He has left us a work that, with its simple prose and graphic descriptions, has become a classic of its kind.

Especially noteworthy are scholarly studies of the Indians: Motolinía's *Historia de los indios;* the Spanish judge Alonso de Zorita's *Breve y sumaria relación de los señores de la Nueva España;* and the magisterial *Historia general de las cosas de la Nueva España* by Father Bernardino de Sahagún, a compendium of Aztec life that forms the basis for our knowledge of Nahua peoples. Anticipating modern anthropological practice, Sahagún worked with native informants to record their history in Náhuatl and Spanish. Many other important works of the sixteenth century, including church histories, are eloquent

Carlos de Sigüenza y Góngora (1645–1700) was an eminent scholar of wide-ranging scientific and historical interests.

testimony to the intellectual curiosity, industry, and painstaking scholarship of these early historians.

Although the scholarly studies of the sixteenth century were outstanding, valuable works were written in the seventeenth and eighteenth centuries as well. The most significant work is the *Historia antigua de México* by the celebrated Jesuit Francisco Javier de Clavijero, a native-born Mexican considered to be the founder of modern Mexican historiography. Another erudite Jesuit was Francisco Javier Alegre, accomplished in many fields but best known for his history of the Jesuits in New Spain.

Like early anthropologists and ethnohistorians, clergymen preserved Indian histories, customs, and languages. They created dictionaries and grammars so that Indians could read and write in their own languages. Many of the friars became proficient in three or four native tongues. There were fewer scholars of note in other disciplines, although some excelled in studies of the flora, fauna, and medicines of Mexico. Occasionally research was sponsored by the crown: in 1571 the royal cosmographer was ordered to take a census, study eclipses, and undertake both a general and a natural history. The towering figure in scientific thought was Carlos de Sigüenza y Góngora, a criollo of universal renown during the seventeenth century. He studied to be a Jesuit at Tepotzotlán but was expelled for an infraction of the strict rules. Poet, historian, mathematician, astronomer, and antiquarian, he exemplifies the scientific curiosity in the colonial period.

Leaving aside chronicles of the Conquest, the literary achievements in New Spain began with the *Dialogues* of Francisco Cervantes de Salazar, who extolled the beauty of Mexico City and the quality of the university. The brightest literary light of all, however, and holding first place in the hearts of Mexicans, was a woman, *Sor* (Sister) Juana Inés de la Cruz (1651–95). Apparently of high but illegitimate birth, Sor Juana grew from a child prodigy who amazed intellectuals at the viceregal court into a beautiful, graceful young woman with astonishing talents. An early exponent of women's rights, she lamented the disdain with which female efforts were greeted and the subordinate position of women generally. Her disenchantment was well expressed in one of her poems:

> Hombres necios que acusáis
> a la mujer sin razón,
> sin ver que sois la ocasión
> de lo mismo que culpáis;
>
> . . . .
>
> ¿Cuál mayor culpa ha tenido,
> en una pasión errada:
> la que cae de rogada
> o el que ruega de caído?
> ¿O cuál es más de culpar,
> aunque cualquiera mal haga:
> la que peca por la paga,
> o el que paga por pecar?[1]

At the age of eighteen she stunned her admirers by ignoring favorable prospects of marriage and her privileged position at court and

---

1.   Ah stupid men, unreasonable
     In blaming woman's nature,
     Oblivious that your acts incite
     The very faults you censure.

     . . . .
       Which has the greater sin when burned
     By the same lawless fever:
     She who is amorously deceived,
     Or he, the sly deceiver?
       Or which deserves the sterner blame,
     Though each will be a sinner:
     She who becomes a whore for pay,
     Or he who pays to win her?

Translated by Robert Graves, in Joseph Sommers and Antonia Castañeda Shular, eds., *Chicano Literature: Text and Context* (Englewood Cliffs, N.J., 1972), pp. 10–11.

entering a convent. She devoted the rest of her life to contemplation, intellectual exercises, and the writing of prose and lyric poetry that was surpassed in the Spanish-speaking world at the time perhaps only by Calderón de la Barca. This nun-poetess, the first great poet in the New World, composed passionate, almost erotic, love poems of great beauty.

The eighteenth century, so full of conflicting ideologies and intellectual ferment, did not produce creative writers comparable to those of the seventeenth century. Late in the colonial period, however, Mexico had a major figure in José Joaquín Fernández de Lizardi. His satirical *El Periquillo Sarniento* (translated as *The Itching Parrot*) [1816], a picaresque depiction of life in early nineteenth-century Mexico, is widely considered to be the first true novel written in Spanish in Latin America.

Mexico City had a printing press by 1537–39. In the latter year the first book was printed in the colony, a religious tract written in both Náhuatl and Spanish by Bishop Zumárraga. Before the century was out, about 220 books had been produced in the capital, although no other Mexican city had a press until a century later. It is estimated that during the colonial period some fifteen thousand books were printed in Mexico, among them books in at least nine different Indian languages. In addition to many religious studies, there were dictionaries, grammars, accounts of navigation, descriptions of natural phenomena like earthquakes, and works on medicine, methods of teaching reading, and simple arithmetic. In the second half of the sixteenth century at least twelve liturgical books containing music were published; in the same period only fourteen came out of presses in Spain.

Various obstacles were placed in the way of authors; permission for publication had to be obtained from both viceroy and bishop, and books treating American subjects required authorization from the Council of the Indies. Despite such impediments and the restrictions of the Inquisition, books were available in considerable variety, and there were some large and excellent private libraries in New Spain. When Vasco de Quiroga died, in 1565, he had accumulated more than six hundred volumes, and in her convent Sor Juana was surrounded by four thousand of her own books. By the seventeenth century the College of Discalced Carmelites had twelve thousand volumes. Probably the finest library in the New World, however, at least by the eighteenth century, was the one originally started by Bishop Juan de Palafox y Mendoza in Puebla.

The literate public without means, however, had limited reading material, for there were no public libraries and, until late in the colonial period, no newspapers. Communication within the colony was, for the general populace, mainly rumor, gossip, and the information brought by travelers. In early times official announcements were made in the public square by a town crier, following the ringing of church bells, drum beats, or the blast of trumpets. Eventually broadsides were tacked up in public places. The curious were drawn to such places no more by official pronouncements than by the graffiti that showed up mysteriously. These *pasquines* were a way of venting displeasure with government or scoring personal enemies. Usually in rhyme, they were witty, sarcastic, and frequently risqué. No one was safe from these lettered shafts, and the more prominent the victim the sweeter the vengeance. Although illegal, they could no more be prevented than the scrawls that decorate our public walls today.

News from Spain and other parts of Europe came with the annual fleet, at which time enterprising printers published sheets with the "latest" information. For domestic events of high interest, such as a pirate attack in Campeche or a destructive earthquake in Oaxaca, a special sheet might be run off. Sigüenza y Góngora published a periodical, *Mercurio Volante*, beginning in 1693. It was not until 1805, however, that a daily newspaper—the *Diario de México*—was offered to the public.

MUSIC

Spanish musicians had entertained Cortés and his men during the Conquest, and as life in the colony became more sedate, others performed more formally in the viceregal court and before bishops and wealthy, cultured ladies and gentlemen of various occupations. Elegies were composed to mourn the deaths and celebrate the lives of kings and viceroys. The clergymen, aside from using music in solemn religious ceremonies, also staged plays written in prose in which music had a place. The performers were often Indians.

Music had been important to the Aztecs, especially for ritual ceremonies, and musicians had very respectable status in the Indian community. Spanish clergymen soon found that the Indians' love of music was an expedient through which the natives could be attracted to Christianity. Hearing the mass sung, neophytes came to identify the Spaniards' religion with music. Natives were also pleased to perform, not only because of the enjoyment and the prestige involved but also because performers were, at least part of the time, exempt from paying tribute. By 1576 there were about ten thousand Indians singing services.

In the beginning, Indians sang a capella or accompanied by native instruments, but organs were later introduced from Spain. Before long the variety of European instruments arrived, and local musicians became familiar with sackbuts, clarinets, rebecs, viola, bassoons, lutes,

guitars, cornets, and so forth. Indians quickly learned to make such instruments, including even the great organs. Native artists also reproduced choirbooks, complete with illuminated letters. In addition, Spanish masters encouraged Indians to compose music, which they did with
considerable skill.

The church discouraged some Indian music identified with pagan-
ism. Clergymen were horrified by the "obscene motions and lewd
gestures" of native dances, in which "the ultimate intricacies of the
conjugal act" were pantomimed. To complicate matters, uninhibited
dancing found new life with the introduction by black slaves of dances,
such as the *porto rico*, from the Caribbean. And clerical admonitions
notwithstanding, the dances continued to be popular, especially in rural
areas where it was almost impossible to impose control. In the eighteenth century the Inquisition protested the *jarabe gatuno*, "so inde-
cent, lewd, and disgraceful, and provocative, that words cannot encompass the evil of it. The verses and the accompanying actions,
movements, and gestures, shoot the poison of lust directly into the
eyes, ears, and senses."[2]

Yet the church did not discourage many forms of frivolous amusement, including some of the popular songs. Enjoying sensational popularity was the *villancico*. Originally a type of traditional Spanish
Christmas carol usually sung in church, the villancico developed in
Mexico as a popular song for festive occasions. In the seventeenth century it emerged, like the contemporary baroque taste in art, as an exuberant display of lightheartedness. Felicitous lyrics celebrated not
only saints' days but also the rites of spring and the emotions of profane love in startlingly modern form. There was at least a flirtation with
a higher form of secular composition in the early eighteenth century
when Manuel Zumaya wrote the New World's first opera, *La
Parténope*, which was staged in 1711.

ARCHITECTURE

The highest form of creative expression in colonial Mexico was
achieved in architecture through European styles and by Indian laborers and craftsmen. The Catholic church dominated building projects designed to evangelize, glorify God, and provide solace as well as
preparation for salvation. Naturally enough, Spaniards tried to create
buildings in the colony similar to those in Spain, and in the very early
years an essentially Gothic medieval style predominated. It was,

---

2. Robert Stevenson, *Music in Mexico: A Historical Survey* (New York, 1971), p. 184.

nevertheless, modified in Mexico: churches assumed a fortresslike appearance because of the threats of Indian attacks; dangers of earthquakes called for buildings with very thick walls, often supported by great flying buttresses; and the humid tropics required provision for better ventilation. The apocalyptic views of the Franciscans are also evident in the defensive elements. As the sixteenth century progressed, Renaissance styles, plateresque and mannerist, were the norm. Moreover, architecture in Mexico took on a distinctively local character because building materials in the colony offered more color. In wide use

The church and convent of San Agustín, Hidalgo.

was the red, porous *tezontle* pumice, the local whitish limestone, and a green stone found in Oaxaca. As the bright Puebla (*poblano*) style emerged, polychrome tiles came to be used extensively and in some cases dominated the façades of buildings. Indian influence crept in as native craftsmen insinuated their motifs in carvings and paintings. And because even the large churches could not accommodate the great crowds of Indian worshipers, broad courtyards, and "open-air chapels," were a familiar sight.

The first century of architecture in Mexico saw a *mestizaje* of styles, in which Gothic, Renaissance, and *mudéjar* (Moorish) features merged. The intricate plasterwork of the plateresque resembled the art of silversmiths. Monasteries of the friars had a simplicity that contrasted with the massive, richly ornate cathedrals. The great cathedrals stand out by virtue of sheer bulk, but those of Mexico City and Puebla, designed by the same architect and competing in excellence, are especially noteworthy structures. Begun in 1563, the cathedral of Mexico City occupied teams of craftsmen for a century and even then was not completed until the late colonial period. That of Puebla, considered by many the finer of the two, was laid out around 1575 and dedicated in 1649. Its dome provided more light to accent the interior ornamentation, and this pattern was widely copied throughout New Spain. Other features of the evolving Mexican baroque were the distinctive *retablo* facades with twisted columns and brightly colored stone and plaster work.

Civil architecture fared less well over the centuries. We know that splendid buildings arose—palaces of the viceroy and bishops, offices of the audiencia and ayuntamiento, and various other government structures. But some were destroyed, and the original forms of others were altered by later constructions. It is sad, too, that the Renaissance mansions of the conquerors have almost all disappeared, although we gain some appreciation of their elegance from the residence of Francisco de Montejo in Mérida and the modified palace of Cortés in Cuernavaca. The monumental palace of the Condes de San Mateo de Valparaíso in Mexico City has an impressive central courtyard framed by four huge, lowered arches.

The Mexican baroque has been called an art of paradox by Mexican cultural critic, Carlos Fuentes—a "criollo" style that fuses elements of the Old World and the New. As it developed, it gave way to what some have called "ultra" baroque—that is, a style dominated by a profusion of decorative effects. Surfaces were encrusted with decoration, and façades and altarpieces were stifled with riotous detail. It was, in a way, the glorious celebration of the optimism and prosperity of criollo

Cathedral of Mexico.

society; although too busy for some tastes, it nevertheless produced some of the finest examples of religious architecture and is held by many to be the highest form of the builder's art in colonial Mexico.

Such excesses inevitably exhaust the senses, and it is not surprising, therefore, that the next phase of architecture was a reaction. The severe, formal neoclassic was a sober turn. Reflecting the stern realities of late colonial life, it was cold and devoid of the color and fantasy that have generally characterized Mexican art from the marvelous Maya façades to the brilliant murals of the twentieth century.

SCULPTURE AND PAINTING

Sculpture was, to great extent, an adjunct to architecture. Sculptors, many of whom were Indians and mestizos, rendered in stone and plaster the incredibly complex designs of ceilings and façades, and they carved wooden altarpieces, images of saints, and other adornments that contributed to the grandeur of the art of New Spain. Most of these artists remain anonymous, but one prominent sculptor deserves mention. Manuel Tolsá, a Spaniard, created the admirable equestrian statue of Charles IV that is affectionately known as "the Caballito." Prominently on display in Mexico City today, it is regarded as one of the finest works of its kind in the world.

The first European painter in Mexico was a companion of Cortés who painted his captain at prayer. With the construction of churches and monasteries, friars and Indians trained in Gante's school painted tempura murals on their walls. Good examples of these early efforts have been preserved at Acolman, Cuernavaca, and Actopan. Also to the first decades belong the post-Conquest códices, painted, with official encouragement, by Indian artists. The códices that survive have not only invaluable historical importance but genuine artistic qualities as well. For the most part, however, native painters shed earlier artistic traditions as they were pressed into studios for training in the realism of the Spanish school.

Painting advanced in quality with the arrival in 1566 of the Flemish master Simón Pereyns. He gathered around him a talented group of criollo artists who painted canvases in the Spanish manner. Euro-

A water tower at Teoloyucan, with its flared buttresses, one of the many remaining monuments to colonial artisans.

Second-story façade of the sixteenth-century residence of Francisco de Montejo in Mérida, Yucatán.

pean mannerist and baroque styles evolved in the second century of colonial rule. One of the best-known of seventeenth-century painters is Cristóbal de Villalpando, whose brilliantly colored and shadowed paintings of religious themes grace churches throughout Mexico. Some of the canvases, such as those in the sacristy of the Cathedral of Mexico, cover entire walls. Although Villalpando was influenced by Peter Paul Rubens, many of his compositions have inventive features. Luis Juárez also painted many images for convents and monasteries. In the seventeenth century more opportunities opened for the studio artist who prospered through rich patrons. The prominent and wealthy adorned their residences with paintings, and portraits were in great demand. One may weigh the skills of those portraitists in the paintings of the viceroys, most of whom stare down from the walls with grim and baleful countenance. Many such portraits by Nicolás Rodríguez Juárez and his brother Juan were produced at the end of the seventeenth century. By the eighteenth century painters like Miguel Cabrera prospered, satisfying the egos of the silver barons and others who sought to be preserved for posterity.

The most originally Mexican category of painting can be seen in the casta paintings that depicted the myriad of hybrid racial classifications that resulted from mestizaje. They typically show a male from one ethnic group with a female partner from a differing ethnicity, and their racially blended offspring, with a label that states these categories. These images reveal a great deal about colonial racial attitudes and behavioral prescriptions.

As part of the "progressive" trend in Spain, the Art Academy of San Carlos was dedicated in Mexico City in 1785, and academic training was introduced to give equal opportunity to aspiring artists of all races. The stiff formal approach gave impulse to a controlled, less Mexican, school of art, consonant with the neoclassic in architecture.

DAILY LIFE

The poverty, exploitation, injustices, and general misery of the lower classes notwithstanding, colonial life was not a scene of unrelieved tragedy. Religious festivals and public spectacles honoring Spanish rulers provided welcome diversions for many. Colonial elites intended to use ritual performances to inculcate the correct forms of religious observance and to demonstrate to subordinates their proper place in the social hierarchy. Nonetheless, popular celebrations had a way of taking on a life of their own. They often fostered unruly behavior and veiled forms of social protest, and occasionally they became the sites of riots—for example, the 1692 tumult in Mexico City that took place during the celebration of Corpus Christi. Even in less agitated moments, the viceregal capital offered a variety of diversions.

Visitors to Mexico City who recorded their impressions usually commented on its fine buildings and broad, straight avenues. In the seventeenth century, travelers asserted that everything one could desire was available, including abundant supplies of foods that were both delicious and inexpensive. Daily more than one thousand boats and three thousand mules carried in provisions from outlying provinces. Foreigners remarked on the excellence of the city's construction, laid out in a grid pattern with plazas, fountains, and sidewalks. An Englishman living in Mexico City in 1625 estimated that the capital had fifteen thousand coaches, some of which were trimmed with gold, silver, and Chinese silk.

Color, of which Mexicans have always been almost excessively fond, was what struck the foreigner's eye. Color was everywhere, from the flower gardens and blossoming trees, to the textured hues of walls, to the kaleidoscope of the great open markets where bright exotic fruits and vegetables vied with polychrome tiles and pottery, brilliant native textiles, and jewelry. There was an astonishing variety of goods available in the marketplace, where thousands of people gathered to bargain and exchange gossip. A motley population thronged the streets, their rich skin tones adding to the mosaic of color. Dark habits of the ecclesiastics heightened the bright sashes of university students and the dress of criollo dandies who paraded in plumed, scarlet taffeta hats, ruffled laces, and velvet capes. A dignified worthy clothed in severe ebony might be accompanied by black slaves attired in blue or yellow breeches, with white silk stockings.

Both men and women wore jewels in the street, and it was not uncommon to see hatbands set with pearls and diamonds. Occasionally the procession of the viceroy or archbishop with his retinues passed, causing a mild sensation. Women, who were just as fashion conscious as men, flaunted exquisite cloths from Asia and the richest textiles from Europe. Wealthy ladies frequently observed modesty by making their way through the streets in veiled palanquins, sedan chairs borne by slaves. But other females enjoyed the approval (or jealousy) provoked by scanty dress. Visitors were especially taken by beautiful mulatta women wearing expensive silks and sparkling gems, despite sumptuary laws that were passed from time to time to prevent them from dressing like whites. Women of various classes applied rouge and eye makeup.

Beneath all the finery and cosmetics, however, were people who aged quickly and who enjoyed fewer of the beauty aids available to serve the vanities of our times. In close conversation with a colonist one would become aware of a strong musty odor, a smile marred by missing or rotting teeth, and a face scarred and pitted. At least on social occasions some were considerate: a strong perfume might disguise the infrequency of bathing, and offensive breath could be tamed by chewing cloves or licorice.

Among the more unfortunate elements of society were the many vagabonds who roamed the colony. They lounged around city streets, living by their wits and making a general nuisance of themselves in both urban and provincial areas. These *pícaros*, so charmingly presented in literature, were a threat to the colonial order, much to the dismay of the authorities. They were seen as a disruptive element and potentially dangerous.

Some of the beggars (later called *léperos*) were lads in their early teens who made their way to the Spanish Indies, where they picked up vices and venereal diseases. Much of their time was spent molesting Indian girls and spoiling for adventure, and they often ended up as petty criminals. Moreover, the colony produced its own domestic vagabonds, of all racial groups. Many suffered from disease, poverty, and official neglect. Dressed in filthy rags, syphilitic victims displayed open sores, grotesque tumors, and maimed limbs. The blind joined other indigents outside churches to collect alms. Modest attempts were made to provide care for them, and the church regularly dispensed food and small sums of money. In the countryside vagabonds often lived illegally in Indian villages, forcing villagers to support them and sometimes seizing their women. As early as 1560 there were three to four thousand of these vagrants in New Spain without visible means of support.

All of these social types, elegant and rustic, were part of daily scenes in streets that were alternately muddy or dusty, depending on the season. Cursing mule drivers prodded their braying beasts along, stirring up clouds of dust or making quagmires, while other herders pushed swine, sheep, or turkeys through the crowds. Peddlers hawked their wares, Indian servant women carried jugs of water from the public fountains, and tamemes bent under the loads that almost obscured them. Eventually some streets had cobblestones, but gutters remained like open sewers, strewn with garbage and an occasional dead dog. If color delighted the eye, stench assailed the nostril. But such aromas and unsanitary conditions were, after all, not much different from those

Late seventeenth-century ceramic fountain from Puebla suggesting Chinese influence.

Glazed pottery was introduced to Mexico from Talavera de la Reina, Spain, in the sixteenth century. In the first half of the seventeenth century, about forty potters were registered in the city of Puebla. Other examples are shown on the following page.

A Puebla vase decorated in Oriental
style, late seventeenth century.

Flower pot of the style commonly used in
the halls and patios of colonial houses.

Tiles from Puebla were commonly used
on building façades.

in other parts of the world at the time. The filth did pose a serious health problem, however, and the government moved to keep the capital cleaner. The pigs that ran loose in the streets and scavenged for food were relied upon less fully after an ordinance of 1598 provided for twelve teams of two Indians, with mule carts, to collect refuse from city streets every day. Public buildings, including storehouses and jails, were to be cleaned every four months. There was little improvement in sanitary conditions throughout the colonial period, however, and swine, mongrel dogs, and vultures continued to be counted on to help keep streets clean, at least until they themselves fouled them.

At the center of social life was the viceregal court, although bishops and wealthy laymen often rivaled the court in extravagant entertainment. For the cultured elite there were the latest plays, music, and literature from Spain and clever conversation in the salons. Some recitals and performances were private, but a great many were for the general public. Dancing was popular with all, from the formal balls of the wealthy to the more spontaneous, often earthy, dances of the lower classes. Bullfighting, introduced shortly after the Conquest, found wide favor with all segments of society. An archbishop in the early seventeenth century was such as *aficionado* that he had his own private bullring on the grounds of the archiepiscopal palace. The more intellectual enjoyed chess, and cards were played by all classes. Gambling was a vice to which almost everyone was addicted, as wagers were made at dice, cards, horse races, cockfighting, or any contest available for betting purposes. Such diversions were indulged in mainly by men, but new arrivals to the colony were shocked to see criolla women of presumed high social standing dealing cards with males. For the aristocrats there were jousting and other games played on horseback, and they rode to the hunt with their greyhounds and falcons.

Leisure time was abundant for many urban dwellers; colonists enjoyed many holidays, with eighty-five religious festivals annually. Individuals celebrated their saints' days, and towns had their special saints to be honored as well. These and other holy days were enjoyed to the fullest. Solemn religious rites, processions, and sometimes penance were followed by fireworks, feasting, singing, dancing, and no small amount of drinking—which in turn often led to fighting. Gentlemen might settle accounts of honor with a duel; the lower classes would more likely find satisfaction informally and immediately with knives or machetes. A favorite—and healthier—diversion at parties (during which daughters were watched by hawk-eyed chaperones) was the throwing of eggshells filled with confetti or of hollow wax balls containing perfume water. All of this was conducted with great merriment and a consuming interest in sweetmeats and the opposite sex.

A cherished ritual of the elite youth was the daily *paseo*, in which the young men gathered around five o'clock in Mexico City's Alameda Park. These popinjays arrived in fancy carriages or perhaps mounted on purebred horses and were attended by black slaves suitably dressed to display their young masters' elegance. Young ladies arrived in much the same fashion, for the same purpose.

Other events demanded celebration. The birth of a royal child, a royal marriage, the coronation of a new king, the arrival of a new viceroy or archbishop, or a great victory over one of Spain's enemies, all called for displays and merrymaking. The most glorious of spectacles were the *mascaradas*, often planned far in advance and summoning the most creative talents to assure sensational (and sometimes bizarre) effects. The essential part of the show was the grand parade. It might lead off with Indian caciques decked out in traditional native garb, followed by dignitaries of the church in their rich vestments, high royal officials mounted on superb horses with silver trappings, and faculty members of the university in their gaudy robes. There were also decorated floats, clowns, acrobats, jugglers, and musicians. Some individuals were masked (from which the ceremonies took their names),

The picturesque Alameda Park in the center of Mexico City was first laid out in 1593 during the rule of Viceroy Luis de Velasco. Now much enlarged, it is still the scene of promenades under the tall trees and along the pathways past fountains and bright flower gardens.

wearing costumes representing mythical or historical figures, while others personified Pride, Greed, Lust, or perhaps one of the virtues.

Sometimes the mascarada was sponsored, at great cost, by a wealthy individual and other times by the state, but the aim of the organizers was always to surpass previous extravaganzas. No expense or labor was spared—even to the extent of importing camels and ostriches for the parade, to the great delight of the spectators. In the eighteenth century Mexico City officials, increasingly alarmed by the profanity and disorder of these spectacles, began to severely curtail celebrations. Public ritual no longer served the interests of state authority and social control.

The impression should not be left that colonial society witnessed a continual round of parties and sport. The foregoing observations of colonists at play pertain mostly to large centers like Mexico City and Puebla. Smaller towns had similar amusements, but they were on a scale less grand and carried off with less flair. Occasions such as saints' days in small communities called for celebrations and processions that were simple but lively, and the custom of the paseo—which has persisted into modern times—saw the gathering of young people of more humble aspect in village plazas. Local celebrations might consist of little more than a mass followed by fireworks and drinking to stupefaction.

Life in the colony also had its grim aspects. Throughout most of the colonial period streets were dark at night, with no provisions for lighting. Thus assaults were not unusual, and few went out late at night without arms and companions. Thievery was widespread, and so were crimes of passion. Rural brigandage was a plague to all. In the sixteenth century there were almost no inns, and Indian villages were required to furnish food and lodging for travelers. Later on, crude facilities for those on the road were maintained.

A common sight was that of criminals hanged by the roadside and left as a warning to others. Death by hanging was decreed for many crimes, and for especially serious offenses, such as treason, the body of the culprit was drawn and quartered, with the head and limbs prominently and gruesomely displayed. Mutilation of limbs, the severing of a hand or foot, the crushing of a foot in a diabolical device known as "the boot," and other tortures were employed on occasion. Floggings of one or two hundred lashes were not uncommon. Those of high social position, however, were usually spared humiliating and cruel punishment, escaping with fines or sometimes jail sentences. Nobles found guilty of treason, however, could not avoid the severest penalty, but they were given the preferred death of decapitation, for hanging was considered too undignified for one of high rank.

The plagues that so devastated the Indian population by no means left Spaniards untouched, even though they had better resistance. One of the most virulent of the diseases was *matlazáhuatl*. All ethnic groups were susceptible to epidemics of this malady, identified variously by historians as typhus or plague. Smallpox continued to be a great killer, and when it struck Mexico City in 1779–80, nearly 20 percent of the capital's population perished. Toward the end of the colonial period an extensive vaccination program succeeded in checking the spread of smallpox. But life expectancy for the colonists was half that of ours today.

When Spaniards landed at the port of Veracruz their first thought was to get out of the fever-ridden town and up into higher altitudes where the climate was more salubrious. The same unhealthful conditions prevailed at the Pacific port of Acapulco. Both ports were populated in the majority by blacks and mulattoes. Colonists suffered from intestinal parasites and all sorts of digestive disorders, from leprosy, kidney stones, rheumatism, gout, and a variety of other complaints that were only vaguely diagnosed. There was little to relieve suffering, although bleeding and purging were widely used as standard cures for many complaints.[3]

Bishop Zumárraga established a hospital in the capital for those ailing from venereal diseases. Later an asylum for the insane was opened. At first there were hospital facilities for Spaniards only, but a royal order of 1553 made provision for a hospital for ill and indigent Indians. By 1580 Mexico City had six hospitals—four for Spaniards, one for Indians, and another for blacks and mestizos. Facilities were minimal, and these hospitals were actually what we might today call rest homes.

Medical practitioners, identified as surgeons, were usually barbers as well and no doubt more skilled in the latter practice. Details of surgical operations may be left to the imagination—the doctors probably killed as many patients as they saved. They were, however, skillful in performing Caesarean sections. Medical doctors often had their own bags of tricks, with favorite cures of dubious merit. People of all ethnicities frequently sought out Indian healers, who were apparently just as effective, if not more so.

At least some attempts were made by the crown to impose controls over the qualifications of doctors; after 1535 those practicing medicine were supposed to have been examined by university specialists. A professorship of surgery and anatomy was established at the University in 1621, and a medical board was formed a quarter century later. Medical inspectors were sent to the colony from time to time to improve

---

3. See Michael C. Meyer, "Health and Medical Practice on the Northern Frontier of New Spain, 1550–1821," *Locus* 2 (1993): 111–30.

medical practices, especially with regard to better training for surgeons and druggists. By 1790 there were fifty-one medical doctors in Mexico, along with 221 "surgeons and barbers," most of whom resided in the capital or other large centers. Despite modest attempts of authorities to improve medical services, the state of the profession advanced very little throughout the eighteenth century. People in Mexico learned to be familiar with death, to dwell upon it, and sometimes to make light of it; they were fatalistic and anxious to make their peace with God.

Far from being the vulgar backwater peninsular Spaniards supposed, New Spain had a vibrant and diverse cultural life, especially in the larger cities. Scholarship and learning were advanced primarily by the clergy with support from viceregal and church officials. At the same time a rich patchwork of popular culture and popular piety evolved throughout the viceroyalty, often linking people of diverse ethnic groups. By 1700 it had a uniquely Mexican character, with customs and traditions so firmly impressed on society that the patterns are still evident today.

RECOMMENDED FOR FURTHER STUDY

Bailey, G. A. *Art of Colonial Latin America*. London: Phaidon Press, 2005.

Beezley, William H., Cheryl E. Martin, and William E. French, eds. *Rituals of Rule, Rituals of Resistance: Public Celebrations and Popular Culture in Mexico*. Wilmington, Del.: Scholarly Resources, 1994.

Charlot, Jean. *Mexican Art and the Academy of San Carlos, 1785–1915*. Austin: University of Texas Press, 1962.

Curcio Nagy, Linda. *The Great Festivals of Colonial Mexico City: Performing Power and Identity*. Albuquerque: University of New Mexico Press, 2004.

Gibson, Charles. "Writings on Colonial Mexico." *Hispanic American Historical Review* 55 (1975): 287–323.

Gutiérrez, Ramón et al. *Home Altars of Mexico*. Albuquerque: University of New Mexico Press, 1997.

Haskett, Robert S. " 'Our Suffering with the Taxco Tribute': Involuntary Mine Labor and Indigenous Society in Central New Spain." *Hispanic American Historical Review* 71 (1991): 447–76.

Hernández Saenz, Luz María. *Learning to Heal: The Medical Profession in Colonial Mexico, 1767–1831*. New York: Peter Lang, 1997.

Katzew, Ilona. *Casta Painting: Images of Race in Eighteenth Century Mexico*. New Haven, Conn.: Yale University Press, 2004.

Kubler, George. *Mexican Architecture of the Sixteenth Century*. 2 vols. New Haven, Conn.: Yale University Press, 1948.

Lanning, John Tate. *Academic Culture in the Spanish Colonies*. London: Oxford University Press, 1940.

León-Portilla, Miguel. *Bernardino de Sahagún: First Anthropologist*. Norman: University of Oklahoma Press, 2002.

Leonard, Irving. *Baroque Times in Old Mexico: Seventeenth-Century Persons, Places, and Practices*. Ann Arbor: University of Michigan Press, 1971.

————. *Don Carlos de Sigüenza y Góngora, A Mexican Savant of the Seventeenth Century.* University of California Publications in History, vol. 18. Berkeley: University of California Press, 1929.

McAndrews, John. *The Open-Air Churches of Sixteenth-Century Mexico.* Cambridge, Mass.: Harvard University Press, 1965.

Martin, Cheryl E. *Rural Society in Colonial Morelos.* Albuquerque: University of New Mexico Press, 1985.

Meyer, Michael C. "Health and Medical Practice on the Northern Frontier of New Spain, 1550–1821," *Locus* 2 (1993): 111–30.

Mullen, Robert J. *Architecture and Its Sculpture in Viceregal Mexico.* Austin: University of Texas Press, 1997.

Paz, Octavio. *Sor Juana. Or, The Traps of Faith.* Translated by Margaret Sayers Peden. Cambridge, Mass.: Harvard University Press, 1988.

Robertson, Donald. *Mexican Manuscript Painting of the Early Colonial Period: The Metropolitan Schools.* New Haven, Conn.: Yale University Press, 1959.

Ronan, Charles E., S.J. *Francisco Javier Clavijero: His Life and Works.* Chicago: Loyola University Press, 1977.

Taylor, William B. *Drinking, Homicide and Rebellion in Colonial Mexican Villages.* Stanford, Calif.: Stanford University Press, 1979.

Toussaint, Manuel. *Colonial Art in Mexico.* Translated and edited by Elizabeth W. Weismann. Austin: University of Texas Press, 1967.

Warren, Fintan B. *Vasco de Quiroga and His Pueblo Hospitals of Santa Fé.* Publications of the Academy of American Franciscan History, vol. 10. Washington, D.C.: Academy of American Franciscan History, 1963.

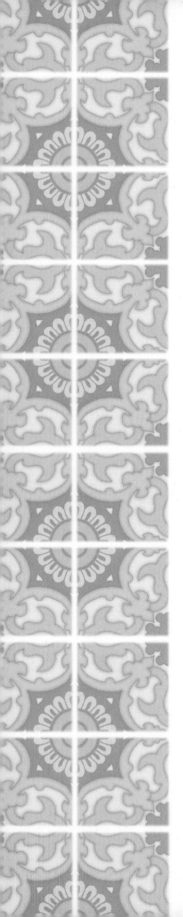

IV

REFORM AND REACTION

The Move to Independence

13

The Bourbons Restructure
New Spain

EARLY BOURBON REFORMS

The nadir of Spain's fortunes by the late seventeenth century was nowhere better exemplified than in the person of the king himself. Inheriting the throne in 1665 at age four, Charles II was feeble in mind as well as body and was even in maturity clearly incompetent to rule. This wretched king, called in all kindness *El Hechizado,* "the Bewitched," sought desperately in off moments to hang himself with his bedclothes. His retainers, in dubious service to the nation, put a stop to that. He was, after all, the monarch, and so his idiosyncrasies were accommodated by an indulgent people. While exorcists tried to drive out his devil, advisers made policy of sorts.

Charles was the last of the Spanish Hapsburgs, and there was justifiable concern over the matter of succession. Despite two marriages, the king did not sire an heir. Who, then, would rule the Spanish empire after his anticipated early demise? While Spaniards weighed their fate with apprehension, others in Europe schemed to exploit the situation. Then, as now, there was considerable intermarriage among the various royal families of Europe, and relatives floated their pretensions to the Spanish throne. In the end the Austrian and French factions emerged as the two strongest claimants, and their diplomats maneuvered for years. To the exasperation of almost all concerned, Charles II refused to die. Finally, as his days grew short, he named as his successor Philip of Anjou, a grandson of Louis XIV of France. Charles joined his ancestors in 1700, and a new dynasty, the line of Spanish Bourbons, began with the rule of Philip V (1701–46). The Austrian party and their allies contested Philip's crowning during the long War of the Spanish Succession (1701–13), but the final outcome saw the Bourbons established in Spain.

Philip inherited a debilitated Spain, wracked by foreign wars and internal revolts. The economy was in shambles, and the demoralized Span-

Charles II (1661–1700). The death of this unfortunate king, the last Spanish Hapsburg, precipitated the War of the Spanish Succession.

iards lived in an age of cynicism, their proud intellectual and cultural tradition now barren. The new king was beset by further strains on revenues and manpower because of the war, but he approached the country's problems with vigor and intelligence. He applied many of the administrative policies that other Bourbons had used in France, and his centralization of authority proved effective in some areas. An immediate concern was the strengthening of the Spanish army and navy. Philip undertook a program of rehabilitation with some success.

Equally shattered at the time of Philip's coronation was the internal economy. Its treasury diminished, its industry and agriculture deteriorated, Spain was beholden to foreigners. Trade with the colonies was to a great extent in the hands of non-Spanish merchants who enjoyed extraordinary concessions from the Spanish crown. Furthermore, silver remittances to the metropolis from New Spain had declined throughout the seventeenth century.

As his government began to bring some order to Spain, Philip also looked to his colonies with an eye to improving their economies for the financial benefit of the empire and as compensation for Spain's territorial losses in Europe. In 1702 a royal decree allowed two ships a year, instead of one, to sail from Manila to Acapulco. The antiquated trading system was further improved in 1717 when the official port for the New World trade was formally changed from Seville to Cádiz, which had better facilities. This was an important break in the monopoly of vested interests. Then, in 1740 the fleet system, which had operated so inefficiently for two centuries, was suspended. With the threat of piracy having subsided and smuggling rampant, there seemed little point in restricting both merchants and consumers. In case of war, however, privateers could freely attack Spanish shipping, and, in fact, the fleets were revived later, sailing off and on until their final abolition in 1789. Although these colonial economic reforms were modest enough, along with other changes they were indicative of the Bourbon interest in economic development that would benefit the imperial state.

REVIVAL OF THE COLONIAL ECONOMY

In the second half of the century momentous change took place. Following the relatively calm reign of Ferdinand VI (1746–59), Spain had a dramatic resurgence under one of its greatest sovereigns, Charles III (1759–88). A devotee of the Enlightenment philosophies then current in Europe, Charles not only introduced important reforms within Spain but also moved to restructure the colonies. To that end, in 1765 he dispatched to New Spain José de Gálvez with the powers of visitor general. Gálvez energetically undertook a long tour of the colony, and over the next five years he compiled important information that led to the formulation of several new policy initiatives in New Spain. The Bourbons determined to extract more wealth from the colony by stimulating mining production, creating a loyal but efficient bureaucracy to collect taxes, and appropriating a share of the Church's immense assets in money and rural and urban properties.

Not the least of New Spain's economic woes stemmed from the monopolies held by merchants and guilds of the two official ports of Veracruz and Acapulco. Their privileges were prejudicial to competition and kept prices unnaturally high; consequently, the economy was sluggish. In the 1760s Charles relieved this stifling situation by opening other official ports in Campeche and Yucatán, and before the end of the century additional ports in Mexico were given similar rights of trade. About the same time a different royal decree permitted New Spain to trade with other Spanish colonies. In 1764–65 the monopoly of Cádiz was broken when certain other ports in Spain were allowed to trade freely with the colonies. Finally, in 1790 the Casa de Contratación, having tightly controlled shipping and commerce for 287 years, was abolished. The crown also stimulated the economy by lowering some taxes, revising offensive customs duties, making mercury more easily available for miners, and organizing a miner's guild.

The cause of most rejoicing was the rise in silver production throughout the century, except for a slight dip in the 1720s. The silver boom was partially attributable to royal policies, but probably derived more from improved technology, stable or declining labor costs, the discovery of new lodes (especially in Guanajuato), and a rise in the value of silver. From slightly more than 3.25 million pesos in 1700, silver production rose to over 13.5 million by 1750, and by 1804 it had reached the substantial figure of 27 million pesos. Mexico alone produced about as much silver as the rest of the world. Between 1690 and 1822 Mexico minted over 1.5 billion pesos in silver and some 60 million in gold.

By the late colonial period there were about three thousand mines in the colony, although most had been abandoned and many of those being worked were small operations. In 1774 thirty-five sizable mining camps existed, of which only a few produced most of the silver. Mines could be worked with increased efficiency because of more scientific refining techniques and better drainage facilities. Modernized technology also permitted deeper mine shafts, and that of the great Valenciana (Guanajuato) reached into the earth some two thousand feet, deeper than any other mine in the world.

Important as precious metals were, however, the general production of the colony increased considerably in other ways, too. Always very profitable, cochineal dye was the second most valuable export during the eighteenth century. It was produced primarily in Oaxaca, where as many as thirty thousand Indians were employed in the industry. Another important commodity was sugar; by 1774 the town of Córdoba

(Veracruz) alone had more than fifty sugar mills, employing mostly black slaves. Toward the close of the century the colony produced around twenty-five thousand tons of sugar annually, of which some two-thirds were exported. The city of Puebla was a manufacturing center of note, specializing in both textiles and ceramics. It sent more than a million pounds of cloth a year to the capital and in 1793 had forty-six shops producing pottery and glass. Native cotton had been cultivated over the centuries, and in 1803 Mexico exported more cotton to Europe than did the United States. A very lucrative crop by late eighteenth century was tobacco; Mexico City and Querétaro each had factories employing about seven thousand workers. Among the many other export commodities were hemp, cacao, vanilla, and hides. Few manufactured goods were exported from the colony; 93 percent of exports consisted of silver, cochineal, and various agricultural products.

By the second half of the eighteenth century New Spain had become by far the most prosperous of Spain's holdings. Around 1800 the port of Veracruz had a trade in excess of thirty million pesos annually. By 1810 New Spain contributed nearly three-fourths of the profits from all the Spanish American colonies. Nevertheless, the domestic market had become increasingly important in Mexico, due to phenomenal demographic growth in the eighteenth century. The population apparently tripled in size between 1700 and 1821. The need to boost production of staple crops put pressure on the land, and larger owners began to encroach upon the tracts of weaker owners in some areas. More workers were employed in the production of goods for Mexican consumption—in agriculture, ranching, minor industry, and local commerce—than in export commodities. The chart on the following page indicates how the main economic sectors contributed to overall production.

Royal income derived from Mexican taxes, duties, and monopolies increased steadily over the eighteenth century by more than 2 percent each year. In the last three decades of colonial rule royal receipts rose even higher as the Spanish crown borrowed heavily from individuals and institutions in the colony to pay for its involvement in European conflicts. Although the Bourbon reforms channeled more capital to the metropolis, the gains were limited by persistent mercantilist structures in trade and manufacture. Spain itself never moved beyond a primarily agrarian economy and narrow tax base.

REFORM OF COLONIAL ADMINISTRATION

International rivalries among colonial powers in the eighteenth century led to wars that were fought in various theaters, including the

VALUE OF NEW SPAIN'S ANNUAL PRODUCTION, CA. 1810

Source	Value in Pesos	Percentage
Agriculture	106,285,000	56
Manufactures	55,386,000	29
Mining	28,451,000	15

Source: David A. Brading, *Miners and Merchants in Bourbon Mexico, 1763-1810* (Cambridge, 1971), p. 18.

New World. The power of Great Britain and its expanding colonies in North America was perceived in Madrid as a threat to the Spanish Indies, and not without reason. Thus, in 1762, during the Seven Years' War, Charles III authorized a professional standing army for New Spain. The troops were few in number, but the addition of various militia groups brought the armed forces in 1810 up to roughly thirty-three thousand, of whom no more than a third were regular soldiers.

During his inspection tour José de Gálvez became acutely conscious of the defenseless northern borders. Spanish settlement had pushed northward slowly during the seventeenth century, but even by the mid-eighteenth century, Spaniards had barely penetrated Arizona and Texas with a handful of missions and even fewer presidios. Problems with hostile Indians—especially Comanches and Apaches who had become more mobile and aggressive with Spanish horses and firepower—inhibited colonization. Franciscans under Fray Junípero Serra began founding missions in California in 1769, but in general the northern lands remained very sparsely settled and vulnerable to encroachments by other powers. Even though the French threat to Texas ended in 1762 when Spain acquired Louisiana from France, British expansion presented a menace, as did the appearance of Russian ships in California waters. One result of the increasing international tensions was that viceroys and other high officials appointed in the last decades of the colonial period were often men with military training and experience. But even they were too far removed from the distant north to render effective defense of the frontiers. Therefore Gálvez planned an independent military government. After he returned to Spain and was appointed to the powerful post of minister of the Indies, he created, in 1776, the position of commandant general of the Interior Provinces. The new territorial organization of the commandancy general embraced the Interior Provinces of the present north Mexican states as well as Texas, greater New Mexico, and California. The commandant general oversaw the military and political administration of this large area, and in the early years he was independent of the viceroy, reporting directly to the king. His main goals were to increase Spain's military presence in order to stem foreign incursions and to bring frontier Indian groups under Spanish control. Despite considerable bureaucratic wrangling, the second goal was partially achieved in the 1780s when the commandant and his officers succeeded in using diplomacy and gifts ("peace by purchase") to fashion temporary alliances with Comanches, Navajos, Utes, and Apaches. Relative peace with Indians and the failure of a serious European threat to materialize facilitated modest settlement of the borderlands.

The flaccid and corrupt bureaucracy of the colony also came under the careful scrutiny of Gálvez, and he did effect some profound changes for New Spain's administration. Since the first decades of settlement, alcaldes mayores and corregidores had been notorious as the worst tormentors of the Indians. Their inadequate salaries had always encouraged extralegal commercial activities, and by the early eighteenth century these officials received no salaries at all. Instead they were expected to engage in business ventures. In effect, they were petty merchants who lived by purchasing the products and labor of the natives cheaply and forcing them to buy, at inflated prices, goods that they neither needed nor wanted. Gálvez proposed that such officials be replaced by others called *intendants* and their lieutenants or *subdelegados*. Intendants had served well in France and were subsequently utilized by the Bourbons in Spain. In 1786 Charles III agreed to the appointment of twelve intendants and over a hundred subdelegados to replace some two hundred governors, alcaldes mayores, and corregidores in Mexico.

Implicit in the reforms decreed by the Bourbons was centralization and the imposition of unity, order, and efficiency. And paramount to the reorganization was the firm and effective management of crown revenues. The intendants sent to New Spain were charged with controlling royal monopolies, collecting taxes, and overseeing the whole range of treasury interests in the colony, including suppression of smuggling. More than that, however, they had broad responsibilities to improve general administration in their districts, called intendancies, including such matters as justice, public facilities, and defense. Peninsulares would now be the exclusive candidates for the positions of intendant and audiencia judge, and for the most part they were experienced, educated, and capable administrators. They enjoyed considerable prestige and had ample authority in their large districts. The same could not be said for the subdelegados who, unlike the intendants, did not receive adequate pay and resorted to the tactics of

INTERIOR PROVINCES (LATE EIGHTEENTH CENTURY)

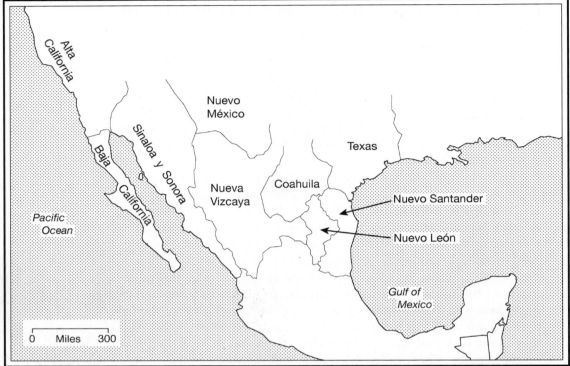

extortion that had been employed by the corregidores. Indians, therefore, did not find the change to be beneficial, but more importantly, the creation of the new offices engendered the resentment of both the oidores and the viceroys, many of whom saw their own authority vitiated as a consequence.

CHURCH REFORMS

If the Catholic church had always functioned as an arm of the state, the Bourbons determined that it must do so more as an underling than as a privileged associate. The change in policy was not an attack on the spiritual power of the church. Rather the crown was concerned about the extent to which the various branches of the church had come to monopolize control of land and property in Mexico.

Above all, it was the Jesuits who stuck in the monarch's craw. The Society of Jesus had distinguished itself in various ways, especially in educating and missionizing, but it had also grown very powerful and wealthy. The Jesuits were also believed to be too closely aligned with the pope and susceptible to political intrigue against monarchies. For these reasons, the Portuguese and French kings had expelled the Jesuits from their realms at mid-century.

In 1766 the Jesuits were accused of fomenting a popular riot against Spain's prime minister. The following year, without warning, they were suddenly expelled from all Spanish kingdoms. Sealed orders were opened throughout the Spanish empire on the same day in 1767, ordering the expulsion of the Jesuits forthwith and decreeing the confiscation of their properties. Colonists were stunned by this bold move of the crown. Initial shock gave way to outrage on the part of many criollos who had been educated in Jesuit colegios, and in a half dozen communities violent demonstrations by criollos and Indians protested the action.

New Spain was notably affected by the expulsion. The crown took over Jesuit assets, reported to be worth some ten million pesos. The Jesuits had maintained the best schools in the colony, with twenty-three colleges and many seminaries staffed by distinguished faculties. Their graduates, especially those of San Ildefonso, were some of the most prominent men in Mexico, including audiencia judges.

The Jesuits were not the only target of clerical reforms. Bourbon decrees eroded some of the powers of Inquisition and, perhaps more significantly, the authority (both temporal and moral) of local parish priests. In a broader attempt to wrest functions of social control from the clergy and to impose orthodoxy on popular religiosity, the crown imposed restrictions on the frequency of public celebrations and the lavish spending on public ritual.

THE EFFECTS OF BOURBON REFORMS

A confluence of factors brought about significant change in the colony of New Spain by the time of the death of Charles III, in 1788. Still, change is not necessarily progress, and it is necessary to consider who actually benefited from the "reforms." On the whole, the economic reforms stimulated increased production in the colony, but they not constitute a profound capitalist transformation in the primarily agrarian economy. Market demand grew along with demographic recuperation as the Indian population doubled in the eighteenth century while non-Indian numbers tripled. At the same time, rural working people experienced a drop in real wages and incomes as the century progressed. At the top of the social hierarchy wealth was somewhat redistributed as a result of the broken monopolies of Mexico City merchants and the

Consulado interests. But the crown gave itself, at the same time, certain monopolies that inevitably hurt other groups. The king's exclusive control over tobacco, for instance, took great sums of money out of private hands and displaced a large number of individuals involved in its production and marketing. But the monopoly was an important part of the imperial policy of restructuring, since these new crown revenues went to the support of the professional army. The pulque monopoly also put local merchants out of business, while the surtax imposed on this drink of the plebeian class outraged the populace.

And one must not attach too much significance to the so-called free trade policies that emerged under the Bourbons. Despite the growth of the Mexican economy, new strictures in the form of taxes were imposed. Moreover there was a flood of peninsulares to the colony, and they were the ones who all too often profited from the rejuvenated business climate. The essence of mercantilism survived; the Bourbons had simply made it more efficient. Mexico's economy was increasingly manipulated for the benefit of Spain. Dependency of the colonists on the mother country remained a fundamental tenet of the imperial system.

The Mining College (Colegio de Minería), designed by Manuel Tolsá, was constructed at great cost between 1797 and 1813. One of Mexico's handsomest colonial buildings, it has 238 rooms, 13 stairways, 11 fountains, and 7 courtyards. Its grandeur is an indication of the importance of silver mining in the late Spanish period.

Political reforms were equally mixed blessings. What had been envisioned as a more centralized, tighter colonial administration became in the end an expanded bureaucracy, in which the number of highly paid officials quadrupled. Furthermore almost all the intendants were Spaniards, and they replaced many criollos who were persons of importance in their localities and who had come to regard the positions as criollo sinecures. The result was increased resentment on the part of criollos against the peninsulares. The commandancy general brought slightly better administration to the borderlands without, however, effecting any profound change. Throughout the colony power, like wealth, was redistributed, creating new vested interest groups. As the prerogatives of the viceroys and audiencia judges were diminished, the intendants and tax collectors assumed considerable influence. One administrative reform may have countered the effects of excluding criollos from high political office. The creation of new local militias to repel foreign threats and control local disturbances provided an opportunity for Mexican-born Spaniards to acquire prestige and power.

In summary, the Bourbons were successful in extracting more resources from the colony of New Spain, but they were unable to capitalize on them. Although Bourbon Spain wished to create a modern nation-state, it did not have the will or means to make the necessary changes in modes of production and labor relations. Nor did it help that Spain squandered much of its new wealth in European political and military machinations. Charles III was succeeded by a son lacking in wisdom; political affairs on the European continent would ultimately engulf Spain; and these and other events would foster a growing disenchantment among the colonists in New Spain. Since the royal intent was to benefit Spain, not the colonists, tradition-bound monarchs of the eighteenth century saw no plausible benefits in social reform. Quite to the contrary: the year following the death of Charles III the French masses rose up in the name of social justice, beheaded their king, and went on the rampage. The shudder that passed through the royal courts of Europe was felt in Madrid as well.

RECOMMENDED FOR FURTHER STUDY

Archer, Christon I. *The Army in Bourbon Mexico, 1760–1810.* Albuquerque: University of New Mexico Press, 1977.

Arnold, Linda. *Bureaucracy and Bureaucrats in Mexico City, 1742–1835.* Tucson: University of Arizona Press, 1988.

Baskes, Jeremy. *Indians, Merchants, and Markets: A Reinterpretation of the Repartimiento and Spanish-Indian Economic Relations in Colonial Oaxaca, 1750–1821.* Stanford, Calif.: Stanford University Press, 2001.

Booker, Jackie R. *Veracruz Merchants, 1770–1829: A Mercantile Elite in Late Bourbon and Early Independent Mexico*. Boulder, Colo.: Westview Press, 1993.

Brading, David A. *Miners and Merchants in Bourbon Mexico, 1763–1810*. Cambridge: Cambridge University Press, 1971.

Burkholder, Mark A. "The Council of the Indies in the Late Eighteenth Century: A New Perspective." *Hispanic American Historical Review* 56 (1976): 404–42.

Cutter, Charles R. *The Legal Culture of Northern New Spain, 1700–1810*. Albuquerque: University of New Mexico Press, 1995.

Deans-Smith, Susan. *Bureaucrats, Planters, and Workers: The Making of the Tobacco Monopoly in Bourbon Mexico*. Austin: University of Texas Press, 1992.

De la Teja, Jesús Frank. *San Antonio de Béxar: A Community on New Spain's Northern Frontier*. Albuquerque: University of New Mexico Press, 1995.

De la Teja, Jesús F. and Ross Frank, eds. *Choice, Persuasion, and Coercion: Social Control on Spain's North American Frontiers*. Albuquerque: University of New Mexico Press, 2005.

Frank, Ross. *From Settler to Citizen: New Mexican Economic Development and the Creation of Vecino Society, 1750–1820*. Berkeley: University of California Press, 2000.

Garner, Richard L., and Spiro E. Stefanou. *Economic Growth and Change in Bourbon Mexico*. Gainesville: University Press of Florida, 1993.

Hamnett, Brian R. *Politics and Trade in Southern Mexico, 1750–1821*. Cambridge: Cambridge University Press, 1971.

Jackson, Robert H., ed. *New Views of Borderlands History*. Albuquerque: University of New Mexico Press, 1998.

Jacobsen, Nils, and Hans-Jürgen Poole. *The Economies of Mexico and Peru during the Late Colonial Period, 1760–1810*. Berlin: Colloquium Verlag, 1986.

McAlister, Lyle N. *The "Fuero Militar" in New Spain, 1764–1800*. Gainesville: University of Florida Press, 1967.

Mörner, Magnus. *The Expulsion of the Jesuits from Latin America*. Boston: Little, Brown & Co., 1967.

Offutt, Leslie F. *Saltillo, 1770–1810: Town and Region in the Mexican North*. Tucson: University of Arizona Press, 2001.

Ouweneel, Arij. *Shadows over Anáhuac: An Ecological Interpretation of Crisis and Development in Central Mexico, 1730–1800*. Albuquerque: University of New Mexico Press, 1996.

Stein, Stanley J. and Barbara H. *Apogee of Empire: Spain and New Spain in the Age of Charles III, 1769–1789*. Baltimore, Md.: Johns Hopkins University Press, 2003.

Thomas, Alfred B. *Teodoro de Croix and the Northern Frontier of New Spain, 1776–1783*. Norman: University of Oklahoma Press, 1941.

Thomson, Guy C. P. *Puebla de los Angeles: Industry and Society in a Mexican City, 1700–1850*. Boulder, Colo.: Westview Press, 1989.

Viqueira Albán, Juan. *Property and Permissiveness in Bourbon Mexico*. Translated by Sonya Lipsett-Rivera and Sergio Rivera Ayala. Wilmington, Del.: Scholarly Resources, 1999.

Voekel, Pamela. *Alone before God: The Religious Origins of Modernity in Mexico*. Durham, N.C.: Duke University Press, 2002.

Weber, David. J. *Bárbaros: Spaniards and Their Savages in the Age of Enlightenment*. New Haven, Conn.: Yale University Press, 2005.

14

Society and Stress in the Late Colonial Period

DISTRIBUTION OF WEALTH

Wealthy colonials seemed even less attuned to the tensions of the late colonial period as they accumulated greater riches. A disproportionate number of the wealthiest were peninsulares who had made good in America, but there were many prosperous criollos as well. Great fortunes were made in mining, such as those of the counts of Valenciana, Regla, and Bassoco. Regla's staggering wealth (the greatest fortune in the colony) is difficult to assess, but in the late eighteenth century Valenciana sometimes took a net profit of more than a million pesos annually, quite aside from his millions tied up in land and various other interests. Bassoco, elevated to count only in 1811 after a gift to the government of two hundred thousand pesos, accumulated assets worth some three million pesos.

These mining barons, along with some wealthy ranchers and merchants, frequently made generous gifts to the crown, which in gratitude conferred on the donors cherished titles of nobility—usually that of *conde*, less often that of *marqués*. Some prominent men had to be content with knighthood in one of the prestigious military orders. During the eighteenth century about fifty titles of nobility were granted to residents of New Spain, most of them after 1750.

But while these dignitaries appealed to the vanity of the recipients, many of the rich were more genuinely philanthropic. They contributed large sums of money to religious organizations, funded charities, and financed the construction of schools, hospitals, and lovely churches. They also financed festivals and cultural events for the enjoyment of the community. In times of pestilence the rich often paid for medicines, and when famine struck they distributed large supplies of grain and other foods. Unfortunately these gestures were often little more than tokens, for some catastrophes were overwhelming. A subsistence crisis in 1785–86 resulted in hundreds of thousands of deaths due to starvation and disease.

Considered the most complete example of Mexican baroque is the exquisite church of Santa Prisca in Taxco. Built between 1751 and 1759, its cost was underwritten by the mining baron Don José de la Borda.

Among the most powerful men of Mexico were a number of rich hacendados in the north. As missionaries, miners, and soldiers penetrated the frontier, the Indians were gradually pushed back and land came into the possession of wealthy and influential ranchers. Much of the region consisted of desert and could be acquired at low cost; in 1731 the marqués de Aguayo purchased 222,000 acres from the crown for a paltry 250 pesos. Within four decades his family controlled over

This magnificent colonial residence, rising four stories, is a good example of baroque architectural style. Built in the eighteenth century for the Count of San Mateo de Valparaíso, it was later used as a palace by Emperor Agustín I (Iturbide). Subsequently it served as a hotel and today it is beautifully maintained by a bank.

14.5 million acres, some of which were patrolled by the marqués's private cavalry to protect the livestock from marauding Indians. By the late colonial period some northern haciendas, sprawling and isolated, were like private fiefdoms. Yet the stereotype of the hacienda as an operation little concerned with profit and efficiency, a self-sufficient enterprise maintained primarily for the status inherent in the ownership of vast expanses of land, does not always survive examination. A study of the huge holdings of the Sánchez Navarro family, for example, shows the owners to have been capitalists who diversified their interests. Aside from running sheep, cattle, and horses, they were also involved in mining, agriculture, and commerce. They were hard-working men who were by no means cut off from the outside world, although their *latifundio,* eventually covering an area almost as large as the country of Portugal, was the largest ranch in Spanish America.

The increased prosperity of some was reflected not only in ornate religious edifices but also in the many impressive public buildings. In Mexico City today one can still see enough of those surviving to appreciate the grandeur of the capital in the late colonial era. There also

A rural scene of an hacendado and his foreman.

A spirited mount and fine clothing typify this scene of rural landowners in the early nineteenth century. The Mexicans' equestrian skill and love of fine horses have long been known.

This imposing residence, built in 1528, had been altered by the counts of Santiago de Calimaya by 1779. Today it is the Museum of the City of Mexico.

remain about thirty of the magnificent mansions belonging to the wealthy of that period, some preserved either by the government or commercial firms. The spectacular House of Tiles, covered on the exterior and the interior with tiles said to have been brought expressly from China, is a modern landmark. Once the residence of the conde del Valle de Orizaba, it is today a restaurant. The stately townhouse of the counts of San Mateo de Valparaíso (also known as the Palace of Iturbide) has been restored by a bank, while the large residence of the

The Casa de Alfeñique ("Sugar-candy House"), an eighteenth-century showplace in Puebla, a city of many colonial treasures.

counts of Santiago de Calimaya is now the interesting Museum of the City of Mexico.

The colony, and especially the capital, benefited from the improvements made by one of the greatest viceroys, the second count of Revillagigedo (1789–94). Among his many intelligent innovations was the lighting of streets, which lowered the rate of crimes and accidents. He also paved the streets and authorized the first public transportation system, and when that added to the crowded traffic in the capital, he set speed limits, restricted parking, and issued laws against shrill whistling and shouting imprecations at pedestrians and riders. He is remembered also for having ordered an important census, for improving the postal service, and for sponsoring scientific and artistic projects.

In rural New Spain, where Indians predominated, new tensions were appearing. Many of the natives in remote areas, and particularly in southern Mexico, had scarcely been acculturated into Spanish society, but in the rural communities there was increasing conflict between indigenous and nonindigenous peoples. Village riots had long been commonplace, but they took on new urgency at the end of the eighteenth century as outsiders expanded their political and economic influence in predominantly Indian villages.

At the other end of the social scale, the aristocracy of the eighteenth century differed from its counterpart of the two preceding centuries primarily in the matter of style rather than attitude. Later aristocrats were wealthier and more cosmopolitan. Some had studied and traveled in Europe. They adopted continental fashions, the women appearing on festive occasions in expensive gowns and elaborate coiffures, the men in knee breeches, tricorn hats, and, on formal occasions, powdered wigs. To some extent Mexican high society had, like that of Spain, become "Frenchified" through tastes acquired with the Bourbon accession. Also in imitation of European styles were the fancy dress balls and salons in which the elite discoursed on the new philosophies emanating from France and England and conversed about art, literature, music, and, inevitably, the economy and politics. Poetry was read and scientific papers were presented. All this was spiced with gossip and expressions of horror at the vulgarities of the masses.

SOCIAL UNREST

The proliferation of wars during the eighteenth century, far from the shores of Mexico, occasioned little more than casual notice, enlivened perhaps by the personal account of a Spanish veteran. But interest increased with the successful revolt of the English colonists to the north and the outbreak of the French Revolution. Later came news of the alarming success of black slaves who overthrew their French masters in Haiti and declared their independence. Informed criollos could hardly fail to observe that in both revolts in the hemisphere, colonial populations smaller than Mexico's had thrown over imperial powers greater than Spain. But criollos also recognized that their own society was far more heterogeneous than either the United States or Haiti.

A portrait of an aristocratic lady by Miguel Cabrera (1695–1768).

The opulent extreme of the rich was in glaring contrast to the majority, who lived in poverty as real wages declined in the eighteenth century. Nearly all of the five-sixths of the population who were not white (five million Indians and castas) were experiencing economic hardship. The lot of the castas had improved somewhat over the centuries. They were less abused physically and were usually paid for their labor. Indians still bore the humiliating obligation of paying tribute to the crown and being subjected to labor coercion. Those who still lived in villages sought to preserve community solidarity. When their populations dropped after conquest, their lands became more vulnerable to sale, rental, or other forms of appropriation by outsiders. Demographic recuperation created new tensions by the mid-eighteenth century, and land values rose. Pueblos increasingly came into conflict with each other and with neighboring estates over access to land and water. Local grievances over land and the payment of taxes (tribute, tithe, and other ecclesiastical duties) frequently erupted in violence, although it was usually confined to the village level. Food shortages and rising prices after 1808 aggravated local tensions, but indigenous protest centered primarily on the defense of local community identity. By this time, the demographic recovery among Indians most likely had slowed due to increased pressures on land.

Scarcity of land could drive Indians to seek work outside their pueblos. A considerable number were attracted to the expanding economy of the Bajío region (parts of Guanajuato, Querétaro, Michoacán, and Jalisco). The cities of this fertile wheat-producing area also boasted a sizable textile industry and some of the richest silver mines. But even there subsistence crises and inflated prices limited opportunities toward the end of the eighteenth century, and indigenous miners, hacienda workers, and artisans found their wages insufficient to meet

A typical scene along a provincial road.

their needs and obligations. They became much more aware of the legal discrimination that isolated them racially.

Lower-end castas also suffered from the economic vagaries of the late eighteenth century, which included rising unemployment and inflation. Along with blacks and Indians, many mestizos and mulattoes shared the indignities of poverty and discrimination. Together this underclass nursed deep resentments against the privileged Spanish colonists. Because they were so dispersed, their occasional violent protests did not represent a cohesive threat before the nineteenth century. Some of the disaffected harbored a vague hope that the Spanish king would intervene to punish their local oppressors. They were occasionally attracted by messiahs who wandered the countryside, making millenarian prophecies of a better future and often extorting money from community funds. Popular ideology in Indian communities drew on a mixture of indigenous and imposed traditions, but it clearly differentiated between Indians and outsiders in ethnic and cultural terms. In the face of social change that threatened rural community values, collective anxieties multiplied to produce more protest and violence, still very localized.

Criollo grievances, on the other hand, lent themselves to more coordinated expression through local societies and literary clubs that were established in the eighteenth century to discuss economic innovations that might boost colonial production as well as other enlightened ideas of the day. Criollos had from the beginning been forced into a secondary position by those born in Spain. The peninsulares, or gachupines, had always enjoyed special privileges and occupied the favored positions in church and state. There was a certain logic in this, for the peninsulares receiving high office were usually well educated and had more administrative experience and polish than the criollos. Beyond that, an official with strong ties to the mother country was likely to be more loyal to the interests of Spain. Few criollos, on the other hand, had ever seen Spain, and by birth, education, cultural milieu, property, and familial relationships they naturally identified strongly with the colony. As officials, they might succumb to the temptation of favoring their countrymen, perhaps at the expense of royal interests.

Still, in the seventeenth and early eighteenth centuries the crown appointed some criollos to high office, and others were able to purchase posts put up for bidding. A number even served as judges in the audiencias as well as in other powerful positions. By 1769 at least eight of the twelve members of the Audiencia of Mexico were criollos. They were even more successful in obtaining rank in the church. This promising state of affairs came under some change during the reign of Charles III, who agreed with Gálvez that the colonists' participation in government should be restricted. As a result the number of criollos in the audiencia of the capital had declined by 1780 to only four of sixteen, and later there were even fewer. Criollos were, however, able to secure rank in the military; by the close of the eighteenth century of a total of 361 officers in the regular regiments 227 were criollos, and in the militia they held 338 commissions of 624 officer positions.

The distinctions they perceived between the gachupines and themselves were increasingly galling to the criollos. Far from accepting the stigma of congenital inferiority that Spaniards had placed on them, however, the criollos asserted their self-worth more vocally in the eighteenth century. Charges of colonial degeneracy supported by some of the pseudoscientific theories of European naturalists were energetically refuted by criollo patriots in the *Gaceta de Literatura*. Creoles also drew on the work of the exiled Jesuit Father Clavijero, who accurately described New Spain's geography, flora, and fauna and extolled the region's positive characteristics and achievements. Among these he included Mexico's magnificent Indian past. There was reason for pride in their land; foreign travelers had affirmed that Mexico City compared favorably with Spanish cities, even Madrid. Colonists praised the unique charm of Mexico, a country with its own flavor and a society with its own character, more exotic and colorful than Spain.

One immediately noticeable difference was in the language, now losing its Castilian lisp and enriched by Indian words and diminutives. The Mexican diet was distinctive; the architecture of Spain had been modified; customs and dress had acquired their own traits. The Mexican ambience had colored the literature, art, and music. The people, the landscape, the flora, and the fauna were all peculiar to Mexico. What was originally Spanish had been altered, and while the Spaniards showed disdain at the corruption of Spanish culture, the native-born began to celebrate their *mexicanidad*. Shunning the socially tainted designation of *criollo*, they considered themselves *americanos* or *mexicanos* and took to satirizing the inequities and absurdities of colonial policies in verse and song.

Despite the grumbling, serious consideration of rebellion against Spain was entertained by only the most radical of colonists. There were complaints about the imposition of new taxes, and the general tightening of administration pinched here and there. Colonists were displeased with the ubiquitous officials of the swollen bureaucracy, and some resented attempts to press them into the militia. But while some criollos had been hurt by royal economic policies, others had prospered, and, all things considered, the colonists were better off than ever before. They still felt a personal relationship to the monarchy and most were devoted to the church, which, in addition to attending to their spiritual needs, had been lending them money.

What the criollos really wanted was to be on an equal footing with the peninsulares, or, better yet, somehow to replace them altogether. Aristocrats by virtue of complexion and lineage, the criollos wanted to maintain the class system. Their attitudes toward the lower masses were no less haughty than the peninsulares' opinion of the criollos. In no way did the criollos advocate social equality for those below them. As the visiting German scientist Alexander von Humboldt observed in the late colonial period, "In America, the skin, more or less white, is what dictates the class that an individual occupies in society. A white, even if he rides barefoot on horseback, considers himself a member of the nobility of the country."[1] Rebellion evoked the specters of anarchy and race war, in which the colored masses, who made little distinction between gachupín and criollo, might rise against all white persons.

CHURCH AND STATE

The provincial conservatism of many colonists was offended by the conscious crown policy of diminishing the traditional power, wealth, and prestige of the church. Criollos were particularly rankled by the crown's expulsion of the Jesuits—those teachers and defenders of their *patria chica* (local world). In the end, some criollos benefited from the opportunity to acquire former Jesuit properties, but many more would be affected negatively by the Act of Consolidation of 1804.

After the expulsion of the Jesuits, the crown continued to complain about the extensive urban and rural properties held by branches of the church. Royal officials claimed these holdings were not being used to their potential, thus obstructing government efforts to stimulate the economy. Therefore, in 1804 the crown required the church to call in all the loans it had made using charitable funds. Royal officials would receive the principal and pay interest on it. Many of these loans had been made to criollos in the form of mortgages, and most colonists were hard-pressed to come up with the cash to pay them off. The Act of Consolidation represented a serious threat to the economic stability of Mexico, since about half of the colony's available capital was tied up in these loans. Nonetheless, several million pesos were collected within a few years, and some criollos were reduced to financial ruin.

---

1. Quoted in Magnus Mörner, *Race Mixture in the History of Latin America* (Boston, 1967), pp. 55–56.

The act also severely constrained the activities of the church and embittered many clerics in the process. In particular, the lower echelon of parish priests became alienated as their perquisites were threatened, and they communicated their disillusionment with crown policies to their flocks. Another source of disenchantment for the masses was the church hierarchy's cooperation with Bourbon officials in curtailing popular religious celebrations and devotions.

CONSPIRACIES IN NEW SPAIN AND CONFUSION IN SPAIN

Resistance to Spanish domination took many forms throughout the colonial period. Most often it transpired through small acts of defiance, but a number of rebellions and conspiracies also challenged Spanish rule before the outbreak of insurgency in 1810. Some posed serious threats to Spain's hegemony, while others were trivial affairs. At least in a few there was mention of independence, but such movements were considered aberrations and slightly insane by the general populace. Most of the disturbances found their origins in local grievances and lacked broad support. However, some of the Indian rebellions found numerous ardent followers—with violent and bloody consequences. Examples of native rebellions that occurred many generations after contact are rare, but they did occur. In the northern province of New Mexico, the Pueblo Revolt of 1680 drove out the Spaniards for more than a decade; Tzeltal Mayas shook the colonial system in Chiapas in 1712; the Yaqui Rebellion of 1740 slowed Spanish expansion in Sonora; and a Maya insurrection led by Jacinto Canek threatened Yucatán in 1761. In each of these cases, discontent spilled outside the village to encompass larger ethnic groups when Indians saw their way of life overwhelmingly threatened. The excesses and abuses of elites had violated the many accommodations they had already made to colonial rule. Messianic leadership that drew on native and Christian beliefs also played a role in these revolts.

Grievances abounded in the last decades of the eighteenth century, but sporadic and localized late colonial protests by castas and Indians did not yet provide the catalyst for widespread rebellion. Neither were criollos ready for a complete break with Spain.

In 1794, the popular Viceroy Revillagigedo was replaced by the vain, corrupt marqués de Branciforte. His appointment aroused anger, which was ventilated in September in wall posters appearing in the capital. The messages acclaimed the ideals of the French Revolution, and rumors of a plot spread throughout the city. A conspiracy had, in

María Luisa of Parma, the queen of Spain, painted by Goya. At age fourteen she married her cousin, who became Charles IV.

fact, formed, with plans to seize the government, release eight hundred prisoners from jail, free the Indians from the tribute obligations, and liberate Mexico. The plotters, including a priest, were taken into custody, but the trials were delayed for years and in the end the prisoners were incarcerated in exile. Curiously enough, these intriguers were not criollos but peninsulares.

Hardly had their cases been disposed of when, in 1799, an ill-conceived conspiracy of criollos was discovered in Mexico City. Their plan was so naive that their cache of arms consisted only of machetes, and their plot became known, therefore, as the Machete Conspiracy. The plotters were arrested quietly to avoid a sensation. After languishing in prison, some died, but others were eventually released, escaping execution because of official fears that the affair would create criollo martyrs. The leniency toward rebels, including some Indian conspirators in 1801, suggests the crown's concern with the festering discontent in New Spain. Ironically, royal forbearance served only to underscore Spain's impotence. The weak response did little to discourage further plots.

Ultimately the deterioration of Spain's position in Europe brought on a crisis. At the death of his father, in 1788, Charles IV had become king, and he quickly lent weight to the commonplace that great men seldom beget sons of their equal. He was inept and had little apparent interest in ruling the empire. His subjects grew weary of him and impatiently awaited the succession of Prince Ferdinand. The queen also tired of him and found solace in the intimate company of a handsome provincial guardsman named Manuel de Godoy. The clever, ambitious Godoy maneuvered himself at the age of twenty-five into the rank of prime minister. He then proceeded to make a series of unwise alliances, which finally encouraged the invasion of Spain in 1808 by the troops of Napoleon Bonaparte. When Madrid fell to the French army, Charles IV and his son became prisoners, and shortly thereafter the king abdicated in favor of the prince. But the new Ferdinand VII was a king without a throne. Napoleon appointed his own brother Joseph to rule over Spain, while much of the country resisted. Some Spanish patriots formed a government in exile in the fortified city of Cádiz.

When news of the king's capture and the occupation of Spain by the French reached New Spain there was confusion as to who was to rule the colony. Joseph Bonaparte as sovereign was unthinkable, but what was the logical alternative? Although a few saw the situation as a golden opportunity to gain independence, the majority of the colonists advocated the formation of a caretaker government to run affairs in the name of Ferdinand VII until such time as the king was released. The viceroy seemed the obvious person to assume rule in Mexico, but the audiencia insisted on sharing power. Eventually, in cities throughout the Spanish American colonies, the cabildos asserted their own claims. They argued that historically, when a legitimate ruler was lacking, provisional bodies, or *juntas*, formed to manage local affairs. Following such a bold proclamation, several members of the cabildo of Mexico City were arrested.

The great central plaza of Mexico City, popuarly known as the Zócalo. It is bordered by the cathedral, the viceregal (now the national) palace, the cabildo quarters, and other public buildings.

Viceroy José de Iturrigaray had shrewdly assessed the developments: if he played his cards right he might see a Mexican crown on his head. He decided that the criollos had the best prospects, and he played to their interests by allowing them to form a junta. A group of peninsulares now made their move, viewing Iturrigaray's actions as both stupid and treasonous. On the evening of September 15, 1808, a small band of Spaniards forcibly removed the viceroy from his palace and packed him off to Veracruz to await passage to Spain, where he was later imprisoned. The peninsulares also arrested half a dozen prominent criollo leaders. Replacing Iturrigaray was Pedro Garibay, a senile field marshal in his eightieth year who had to contend with various militant factions.

The instability of government in 1809 only added to the anxieties arising from a threatening economic picture. Insufficient rain fell that summer, and the resulting shortage of corn caused prices in some areas to inflate to four times their normal level. The consequences were far-reaching, affecting, for example, mining production, since there was too little food for draft animals, and workers had to be laid off. Interrupted commerce with the occupied mother country further dislocated the Mexican economy. Taken altogether, it was a time of confusion and stress, with all segments of society growing restless.

Among the more sophisticated criollos in Mexico City the mood remained conservative. They might question the traditional order, but rebellion against the crown was a painful and perhaps frightening thought, since it evoked the possibility of mob rule. Attitudes in the provinces were somewhat different. More isolated from ritual and pomp, more independent, and more closely identified with the land, the criollos in smaller communities had a more fully developed sense of the patria chica where they wanted to run their own affairs. Provincial criollos, often under the auspices of the new intendants, had already been meeting to discuss ways to modernize the economy and expand production and trade. They undertook scientific surveys of local resources and adopted some new technologies. Along with these innovations, they could not help but be aware of the notions of freedom and equality espoused by the Enlightenment and the French Revolution. The disruption of ties with Spain now made them more conscious of the possibilities for political change. Their gatherings were watched closely by royal officials who suspected that they were conspiratorial. One plot, which included clergymen, military officers, and Indian groups, was exposed in Vallodolid in 1809. Although the principals were imprisoned for a while, most were in the vanguard of the insurrection that was to follow shortly.

In 1810 the important cities of southern Spain fell to French troops, compromising without question the sovereignty of the nation. The colonists were bewildered and apprehensive. In that same year it also came to the attention of royal authorities in Mexico City that a conspiracy had formed in Querétaro. Its ringleaders included an aging, dissident priest named Hidalgo. Once again troops were dispatched to deal with yet another provincial incident.

RECOMMENDED FOR FURTHER STUDY

Archer, Christon, ed. *The Birth of Modern Mexico, 1780–1814.* Wilmington, Del.: Scholarly Resources, 2003.

Arrom, Silvia Marina. *The Women of Mexico City, 1790–1857.* Stanford, Calif.: Stanford University Press, 1985.

Brading, David A. *Church and State in Bourbon Mexico: The Diocese of Michoacán, 1749–1810.* Cambridge: Cambridge University Press, 1994.

———. *Haciendas and Ranchos in the Mexican Bajío: León, 1700–1860.* Cambridge, Eng.: Cambridge University Press, 1978.

Burkholder, Mark A., and D. S. Chandler. *From Impotence to Authority: The Spanish Crown and the American Audiencias, 1687–1808.* Columbia: University of Missouri Press, 1977.

Cooper, Donald B. *Epidemic Disease in Mexico City, 1761–1813.* Austin: University of Texas Press, 1965.

Couturier, Edith B. *The Silver King: The Remarkable Life of the Count of Regla in Colonial Mexico.* Albuquerque: University of New Mexico Press, 2003.

Deeds, Susan M. "Indigenous Rebellions on the Northern Mexican Mission Frontier: From First-Generation to Later Colonial Responses," in *Contested Ground: Comparative Frontiers on the Northern and Southern Edges of the Spanish Empire.* Edited by Donna J. Guy and Thomas E. Sheridan. Tucson: University of Arizona Press, 1998.

Gosner, Kevin. *Soldiers of the Virgin. The Moral Economy of a Colonial Maya Rebellion.* Tucson: University of Arizona Press, 1992.

Hamnett, Brian R. *Roots of Insurgency, Mexican Regions, 1750–1824.* Cambridge: Cambridge University Press, 1985.

Humboldt, Alexander von. *Political Essay on the Kingdom of New Spain.* Edited, with an introduction, by Mary Maples Dunn. New York: Knopf, 1972.

Knaut, Andrew L. *The Pueblo Revolt of 1680: Conquest and Resistance in Seventeenth-Century New Mexico.* Norman: University of Oklahoma Press, 1995.

Ladd, Doris M. *The Mexican Nobility at Independence, 1780–1826.* Austin: University of Texas Press, 1976.

Lafaye, Jacques. *Quetzalcóatl and Guadalupe: The Formation of Mexican National Consciousness, 1531–1813.* Translated by Benjamin Keen, with an introduction by Octavio Paz. Chicago: University of Chicago Press, 1976.

Lavrin, Asunción. "The Execution of the Law of Consolidation in New Spain: Economic Gains and Results." *Hispanic American Historical Review* 53 (1973): 27–49.

Lindley, Richard B. *Haciendas and Economic Development: Guadalajara, Mexico, at Independence.* Austin: University of Texas Press, 1983.

MacLachlan, Colin M. *Criminal Justice in Eighteenth Century Mexico: A Study of the Tribunal of the Acordada.* Berkeley: University of California Press, 1974.

Scardaville, Michael C. "Alcohol Abuse and Tavern Reform in Late Colonial Mexico City." *Hispanic American Historical Review* 60 (1980): 643–71.

Schroeder, Susan, ed. *Native Resistance and the Pax Colonial in New Spain.* Lincoln: University of Nebraska Press, 1998.

Sheridan, Thomas E., ed. *Empire of Sand: The Seri Indians and the Struggle for Spanish Sonora, 1645–1803.* Tucson: University of Arizona Press, 1999.

Stein, Stanley J., and Barbara H. Stein. *The Colonial Heritage of Latin America: Essays on Economic Dependence in Perspective.* New York: Oxford University Press, 1970.

Tutino, John. *From Insurrection to Revolution in Mexico: Social Bases of Agrarian Violence, 1750–1940.* Princeton, N.J.: Princeton University Press, 1986.

Van Young, Eric. "Agrarian Rebellion and Defense of Community: Meaning and Collective Violence in Late Colonial and Independence-Era Mexico." *Journal of Social History* 27 (1993): 245–69.

Whitaker, Arthur P. "The Elhuyar Mining Missions and the Enlightenment." *Hispanic American Historical Review* 31 (1951): 557–85.

Zeitlin, Judith Francis. "Ranchers and Indians on the Southern Isthmus of Tehuantepec: Economic Change and Indigenous Survival in Colonial Mexico." *Hispanic American Historical Review* 69 (1989): 23–60.

15

The Wars for Independence

HIDALGO AND EARLY SUCCESS

Born in 1753 of moderately well-to-do criollo stock, Miguel Hidalgo y Costilla spent his first twelve years on the Hacienda de San Diego Corralejo in Guanajuato, where his father served the owner as *mayordomo* (resident manager). Encouraged by his father, the boy moved with his older brother, José Joaquín, to Valladolid (today Morelia) and matriculated at the Jesuit College of San Francisco Javier. The brothers had been at their studies only two years when shocking news reached the city: King Charles III of Spain had banished the Jesuits from New Spain and all Spanish possessions in the New World. Left without teachers, the boys had to interrupt their schooling, but within a year they had enrolled in the diocesan College of San Nicolás Obispo, also in Valladolid, and one of the nineteen colleges and seminaries in Mexico that prepared students for degrees eventually to be awarded by the Royal and Pontifical University in Mexico City. Young Miguel Hidalgo steeped himself in rhetoric, Latin, and Thomistic theology, and, in the tradition of generations of Mexican priests before him, found time to study Indian languages. His bachelor's degree was awarded by the University of Mexico in 1774, and he immediately began preparations for the priesthood. The bishop celebrated his sacrament of ordination in the fall of 1778.

Enthusiastic and self-assured, the twenty-eight-year-old priest returned to Valladolid to teach at the College of San Nicolás Obispo, where he eventually became rector. But he was scarcely exemplary from the church's point of view. Before the turn of the century the Holy Office of the Inquisition had been apprised, by rumor and fact, of a curate whose orthodoxy was suspect, who questioned priestly celibacy, who read books proscribed by the *Index Expurgatorius,* who indulged in gambling and enjoyed dancing, who challenged the infallibility of the Most Holy Father in Rome, who doubted the veracity of the virgin birth, who dared to suggest that fornication out of wedlock was not a sin, who referred to the Spanish king as a tyrant, and who—

alas—kept María Manuela Herrera as a mistress and procuress. Hidalgo was hailed before the Inquisition in 1800, but nothing could be proved. The testimony was carefully filed, however, to be used later.

Hidalgo's future fortunes and misfortunes were cast when, in 1803, he accepted the curacy of the small parish of Dolores. Devoting only minimal time to the spiritual needs of his parishioners, Father Hidalgo concerned himself primarily with improving their economic potential. He introduced new industries in Dolores: tile making, tanning, carpentry, wool weaving, beekeeping, silk growing, and wine making. He preferred to spend his spare time reading and engaging his fellow criollos in informed debate rather than listening to the confessions of his Indian charges. A few years after his arrival in Dolores, Hidalgo's path crossed that of Ignacio Allende, a thirty-five-year-old firebrand who was a captain in the Queen's Cavalry Regiment in nearby Guanajuato. Allende took the priest into his confidence and introduced him to a coterie of friends: Juan de Aldama, also a military man; Miguel Domínguez, a former corregidor of Querétaro, and his wife, Doña Josefa Ortiz de Domínguez, remembered in Mexican history as *La Corregidora*; Epigmenio González, a grocer; Marino Galván, a postal clerk; and a few others.

The group had organized a "literary club," but the members were less interested in disputing the latest tour de force of Goethe, Schiller, Wordsworth, or Chateaubriand than in plotting the separation of the New Spain from the old. As converts were attracted and the plans matured, a date was set for the uprising—December 8, 1810. Although the conspirators were all admonished to hold their tongues, Marino Galván, the postal clerk, leaked the news to his superior who, in turn, informed the audiencia in Mexico City. The forewarned Spanish authorities moved on September 13, when they searched the house of Epigmenio González in Querétaro, found bountiful arms and ammunition, and ordered the arrest of the panic-stricken owner. The events of the next few days are known to every Mexican schoolchild, for they are repeated every September 16 amidst a wide array of Independence Day celebrations.

Doña Josefa entrusted Ignacio Pérez with the task of carrying the news of the arrest to Ignacio Allende in San Miguel. Not finding him at home, the messenger relayed the news to Juan de Aldama, who immediately set out to inform Father Hidalgo in Dolores. When, about two o'clock on the morning of September 16, he arrived at the priest's house, Aldama found Allende there also. The three realized that orders for their own arrest had probably been issued and decided to strike out for Independence at once. Hidalgo rang the church bells summoning his parishioners to mass earlier than usual that morning.

Miguel Hidalgo y Costilla (1753–1811). One of the most renowned individuals in nineteenth-century Mexican history, Father Hidalgo provided the initial spark for the Independence movement.

Assembled at the little church in Dolores the Indians and mestizos, including a group of prisoners already released from the local jail, were harangued about matters of this world, not the next. The exact words of this most famous of all Mexican speeches are not known, or, rather, they are reproduced in almost as many variations as there are historians to reproduce them. But the essential spirit of the message is this:

> My children: a new dispensation comes to us today. Will you receive it? Will you free yourselves? Will you recover the lands stolen three hundred years ago from your forefathers by the hated Spaniards? We must act at once. . . . Will you not defend your religion and your rights as true patriots? Long live our Lady of Guadalupe! Death to bad government! Death to the gachupines!

The immediate response to the *Grito de Dolores* was enthusiastic. With Hidalgo at their head, the motley band of poorly armed Indians and mestizos struck out for San Miguel, picking up hundreds of recruits along the way. When they stopped for a rest about noon at the hamlet of Atotonilco, Hidalgo entered the local church and emerged carrying a banner of the Virgin de Guadalupe—the dark-skinned lady who had appeared to Juan Diego almost three centuries before. The priest adopted this Virgin as the emblem of his crusade, but for reasons less religious than political. How better appeal to the masses who would make up the rank and file of his revolutionary army? The devotion to the Virgin of Guadalupe as the patron of all

New Spain had expanded in the eighteenth century, especially into Indian communities.

By dusk Hidalgo's band had taken San Miguel without difficulty, for the local militia joined the rebels. The day's dramatic events should have ended with the imprisonment of the local Spanish populace, but as night fell the unpredicted happened. The Indians were not ready to rest on their laurels and bed down for the night. If it were true that the Spaniards were to blame for everything that had befallen the aboriginal population of Mexico since the arrival of Cortés in 1519, then it was time that they be held accountable. Hidalgo's army became a mob. Bent on destruction, they moved through the streets with their clubs, slings, machetes, bows and arrows, lances, and occasional firearms, and they pillaged in blind despair. Hidalgo could not reason with them, and only Ignacio Allende, racing through the streets on horseback and warning prompt retribution, was able to contain the passions of the crowd. By morning chaos had begun to subside, but the problem would prove monotonously recurrent during the next few months. From San Miguel the rebels moved on Celaya, and after taking the town the mob again subjected the gachupín population to pillage. But Celaya was merely a rehearsal for a major encounter at Guanajuato, where the rebel army would be seriously opposed for the first time.

Hidalgo asked the intendant of Guanajuato, Juan Antonio de Riaño, to surrender the city, and he offered full protection to the Spanish citizenry in return. But the news from San Miguel and Celaya had already reached Guanajuato, and Riaño knew that Hidalgo could give no such assurance. He felt it better to make a stand and congregated the Spanish population in the Alhóndiga de Granaditas, the public granary. Although his people were greatly outnumbered, he believed they could hold out until reinforcements from Mexico City arrived.

Shortly before noon on September 28 Hidalgo began his approach to Guanajuato. He was joined by hundreds of workers from the surrounding silver mines. As the first wave of Indian foot soldiers rushed the improvised fortress, Riaño gave the order to open fire. Hundreds of Indians were cut down by the intendant's artillery. Before the second assault began, Riaño led a group of soldiers outside the wall to position them strategically. Just as he was about to re-enter the granary through the huge wooden gate, he took a musket ball on the side of the head and fell dead on the spot. But it would not have mattered at any rate. The attackers, led by Juan José Martínez (known affectionately by his nickname El Pípila), gathered up a bunch of soft pine torches used in the mines and laid them at the foot of the wooden gate. They set fire to them, and, as the gate was consumed, a few Indians charged through into the central patio. They were quickly followed by hundreds, perhaps even a thousand. Within the hour most of the gachupines were dead. They were stripped, and their naked bodies were dragged unceremoniously through the streets to the nearby cemetery of Belén, where they were buried in makeshift graves. It was then time for the looting.

An eyewitness to the events of that day was eighteen-year-old Lucas Alamán, later one of Mexico's most renowned conservative statesmen and historians. In his multivolume history of Mexico he recollected:

> This pillage was more merciless than would have been expected of a foreign army. The miserable scene of that sad night was lighted by torches. All that could be heard was the pounding by which doors were opened and the ferocious howls of the rabble when the doors gave way. They dashed in in triumph to rob commercial products, furniture, everyday clothing, and all manner of things. The women fled terrorized to the houses of neighbors, climbing along the roof tops without yet knowing if that afternoon they had lost a father or husband at the granary. . . . The plaza and the streets were littered with broken pieces of furniture and other things robbed from the stores, of liquor spilled after the masses had drunk themselves into a stupor.[1]

It took a day and a half to restore order. The casualty figures were tremendous: over five hundred Spaniards and two thousand Indians killed. Hidalgo and Allende now felt strong enough to split their army into two striking forces, and within a month they had captured Zacatecas, San Luis Potosí, and Valladolid. By late October Hidalgo had an army of about eighty thousand marching on Mexico City. The anticipated battle took place on October 30 at the Monte de las Cruces, and there Hidalgo proved that sheer numbers could overcome a small, well-equipped, and disciplined professional army. The Spaniards were forced to retreat back into the city, and as Hidalgo camped on the hills overlooking the capital, he pondered what to do next.

A decisive strike at the capital might have ended the Wars for Independence after only a month and a half of fighting. But Hidalgo had taken heavy losses at Las Cruces, he was short on ammunition, and he was uneasy about turning his mob loose on Mexico City—they would have devastated the capital. Over Allende's objections he therefore decided to order a retreat rather than follow up his victory; as a consequence the Wars for Independence would drag on for eleven more years.

---

1. Lucas Alamán, *Historia de México* (Mexico City, 1942), 1: 403–04.

Moving northwest toward Guadalajara many of the rebel troops, their greatest opportunity denied, began to desert. At the same time Spanish forces under General Félix Calleja started to regroup. Guadalajara fell to the insurgents unopposed, but in January 1811 the royalist troops from the south caught up with the rebels and engaged them at the Puente de Calderón on the Río Lerma. Again Hidalgo and Allende had the numerical superiority, but General Calleja conducted his operations superbly and, in addition, was aided by a battlefield accident. A Spanish artillery shot hit a rebel ammunition wagon, and the resulting explosion caused a grass fire in the midst of Hidalgo's army. Panic ensued, and thousands of rebels broke rank and fled. The retreat turned into a rout. Hidalgo, Allende, and a number of other leaders recognized the futility of trying to regroup their forces and so moved northward, hoping to obtain relief in Coahuila and Texas. But their days were numbered. In March 1811, near the scorched desert town of Monclova (Coahuila), they were ambushed by a Spanish detachment that had been forewarned they were going to pass that way. Captured by Governor Manuel Salcedo of Texas, the rebels were marched in chains to Chihuahua, where Allende and the other nonclerical leaders were immediately executed as traitors. Hidalgo, because he was a priest, was subjected to an arduous trial conducted under the auspices of the Holy Office of the Inquisition. Finding him guilty of heresy and treason, the court defrocked him and turned him over to the secular arm for execution. At dawn on July 31 the firing squad did its job. Hidalgo's corpse was decapitated, and his head, fastened to a pole, was displayed on the charred wall of the granary in Guanajuato as an object lesson to potential rebels.

MORELOS AND THE DECLINE OF REBEL FORTUNES

With the death of Hidalgo the rebel leadership was assumed by another parish priest, José María Morelos y Pavón, a mestizo. But by this time sympathy for the cause of Independence had waned considerably. Many wealthy criollos had become alarmed at the radical twist the revolution seemed to be taking. The mob attacks on aristocratic property made some apprehensive and others openly hostile. Shut off for centuries from the decision-making positions in both church and state and obliged to compete for minor posts, the criollos favored the elimination of their Spanish rivals (and realized that Independence was the way to do it) but not at the expense of being swept up in some kind of social revolution. They recognized that to the downtrodden Indians and mestizos their white skin, if not their social position, was indistinguishable from that of the gachupines.

When the mantle of insurgent leadership fell on Morelos he knew full well that he could not count on criollo support. Unlike his predecessor, he trained a small but effective army that relied primarily on guerrilla tactics to keep the enemy off guard. Dividing his attention almost equally between military and political matters, he devised a strategy that called for the encirclement of Mexico City. By the spring of 1813 the circle was completed, and the capital was isolated from both coasts. Morelos then called for a congress to meet in Chilpancingo (Guerrero) to discuss plans for the nation once the Spaniards were driven out.

Some of the conservative criollos were still unsure of the direction in which Morelos wished to move, but his speech to the delegates at Chilpancingo cleared the air. If the Conquest of Mexico by Cortés represented a negation of Indian values by the Spanish, the Wars for Independence represented a negation of Spanish values by the Indians. Morelos invoked the names of the ancient emperors, Moctezuma and Cuauhtémoc, and implored the delegates to avenge the shameful disgrace of the last three centuries. The chains that enslaved the native population in Tenochtitlán in 1521 would be broken in Chilpancingo in 1813.

The congress formally declared independence and agreed upon a series of principles that should be incorporated into a new constitution: sovereignty should reside in the people and male suffrage should be universal; slavery and all caste systems should be abolished; gov-

José María Morelos (1765–1815). With Hidalgo's execution in 1811, Morelos assumed the leadership of the Independence movement. Although a strong supporter of Hidalgo, he had very different ideas about how to wage a war and how to constitute a new nation.

ernment monopolies should be abolished and replaced by a 5 percent income tax; all judicial torture should be abolished. The nineteenth-century liberalism of the delegates was tempered only by their insistence that Roman Catholicism should be made the official religion of the new state.

But while the delegates at Chilpancingo engaged in political debate, General Calleja and his Spanish army assumed a new military offensive. In six months' time the Spaniards broke the circle around Mexico City and captured Valladolid, Oaxaca, Cuernavaca, Cuautla, Taxco, and even Chilpancingo itself. The delegates hurriedly packed their bags and moved to the more secure environs of Apatzingán, where they promulgated the constitution they had already largely agreed upon. But what the Constitution promised Mexicans on paper the viceroy's army denied them on the field of battle. Morelos became more of a fugitive than the commander of an organized rebel force. And in the fall of 1815 he was captured by an enemy detachment and escorted to Mexico City, where he was tried for treason and, like Hidalgo before him, shorn of his religious vestments and executed by a firing squad.

For the next five years the Independence movement consisted of little more than sporadic guerrilla fighting. A number of independent bands, inadequately supplied and without any meaningful coordination, operated in isolated mountain pockets and the heavy foliaged areas of the coast. They did not always share a broad common vision for the future of Mexico, but they did agree on the need to refine the political relationship between the patria chica and the larger state. The Spanish army was unprepared to conduct an effective counterinsurgency campaign, and the rebels' lack of organization proved to be a strength. Not even the viceroy's newly introduced "flying brigades" (cuerpos volantes) could match the mobility of guerrillas conducting hit-and-run warfare. While never able to capture major cities, or to turn back the viceregal army, the two most effective Independence leaders, Guadalupe Victoria (with two thousand ragged troops in the mountains of Puebla and Veracruz) and Vicente Guerrero (with a thousand men in Oaxaca), seemed themselves invulnerable to defeat. While guerrilla bands of two hundred or three hundred insurgents proliferated and began dominating more and more of the countryside, the chore of the counterinsurgency army became impossible. Lack of military success took its toll as the viceroy's troops became increasingly despondent and demoralized; defections followed defections. Nevertheless, in 1819 the Spanish viceroy in Mexico City, Juan Ruiz de Apodaca, reported to the Spanish king, Ferdinand VII, that the situation was so well under control that he anticipated no further need for reinforcements. To hasten the final victory he published an *indulto* (par-

TERRITORY UNDER INSURGENT CONTROL, 1811–13

don) for all those who would lay down their arms. The most generous interpretation that can be made of his assessment is that he was badly misinformed. His position had steadily deteriorated while that of the enemy had improved.

ITURBIDE AND THE PLAN DE IGUALA

King Ferdinand VII was not concerned only with events in Mexico. He found himself facing insurrection in Central America, the Caribbean, and South America as well. To quell all of these movements he assembled a powerful fighting force for service in the New World. While the troops underwent the final preparations, Colonel Rafael Riego proclaimed himself in revolt against his sovereign and was promptly seconded by thousands of troops. The Spanish insurgents demanded that Ferdinand swear allegiance to the Spanish Constitution of 1812, a liberal document that affirmed the sovereignty of the people, contained several mildly anticlerical provisions, and enunciated a liberal bill of rights. When the conservative criollos in New Spain learned that King Ferdinand had yielded to Riego's demands and accepted the Constitution, many for the first time decided to cast their lot with the revolution for Independence. Ironically, a conservative colony would thus gain independence from a temporarily liberal mother country.

Of the numerous defections from the cause of Spain to that of an independent Mexico the most significant was that of Agustín de Iturbide. Born in Valladolid of conservative Spanish parents in 1783, Iturbide early displayed an interest in pursuing a military career. He entered the army at the age of fourteen and soon received a royal commission as a lieutenant in the infantry regiment of Valladolid. When Father Hidalgo issued his Grito de Dolores in 1810, Lieutenant Iturbide decided to support the crown in its fight against the rabble that followed the banner of Guadalupe. For almost a decade he fought against the insurgents and on several occasions distinguished himself in the zeal with which he persecuted the enemy.

In the fall of 1820 Viceroy Apodaca invited Iturbide, by then a colonel, to discuss plans for a new offensive against Vicente Guerrero. Iturbide was placed in charge of twenty-five hundred men and left Mexico City for the south in late November. After a few indecisive skirmishes he asked Guerrero to a meeting during which he proposed to make peace—not war. Iturbide's price for the treason he was contemplating was to dictate the terms of Independence. But Guerrero was not easily convinced of either Iturbide's sincerity or his ideas for an independent Mexico. A series of conferences had to be held before the guerrilla warrior and the new convert could issue, on February 24, 1821, their *Plan de Iguala*.[2] Unlike the United States Declaration of Independence, which berated the mother country in a tirade of denunciations, the Plan de Iguala had an entirely different orientation and appeal. To attract conservative support it praised the Spanish endeavor in the New World and held out Spain as the most Catholic, holy, heroic, and magnanimous of nations. But after three hundred years of tutelage it was time for Mexico to strike out on its own. The plan contained twenty-three articles but only three major guarantees: first, the independent Mexican nation would be organized as a constitutional monarchy, and the crown would be offered to King Ferdi-

---

2. In Mexican history revolutionary movements are almost always preceded by a plan that outlines the principles to be embraced and seeks to widen the base of support.

nand or some other appropriate European prince; second, the Roman Catholic religion would be given a monopoly on the spiritual life of the country and its clergymen would retain all the rights and privileges they currently enjoyed; and, third, criollos and peninsulares would be treated equally in the new state. To uphold the promises a new army, the *Ejército de las Tres Garantías* (the Army of the Three Guarantees) would be placed directly under Iturbide's command.

In the Plan de Iguala, Iturbide played his cards with consummate skill. The proposal was imaginative, even brilliant, in its conception. Mexicans were weary of a decade of war, and many of stout heart had given up hope. The liberal Constitution of Apatzingán had failed to attract sufficient support, and it was clear that to succeed the movement needed help from the conservatives. With liberalism temporarily manifesting itself in the mother country, the timing was perfect. In seeking to reconcile the interests of opposing factions, the plan changed the nature of the fight for Independence. Instead of urging death to the gachupines, Iturbide curried their favor. He recognized and capitalized upon the fact that both liberals, who favored the establishment of a republic, and conservatives, who preferred an absolute monarchy, could compromise on this plan as it held out the best hope for Independence, something that both groups wanted most.

Within several weeks the broadly based plan began to yield its first dividends as converts began to arrive. Military contingents throughout the country joined the Army of the Three Guarantees; priests urged cooperation from the pulpits; Masonic groups pledged support; and thousands of drifters again took up the cause. But, most importantly, the community of Spaniards, some fifty thousand strong, found in the Plan de Iguala the promise of a good future in a newly independent Mexico; as a result they, too, pledged support. When Guanajuato, Puebla, Durango, Oaxaca, Querétaro, and Zacatecas all fell to the insurgents, Viceroy Apodaca tendered his resignation. The Spanish crown, however, was unprepared to accept the inevitability of a rebel victory and appointed a replacement, Juan de O'Donojú, as Captain-General of New Spain. O'Donojú quickly perceived that Apodaca had assessed the situation correctly. New Spain was irrevocably lost, and there was little to be gained by not recognizing the fact. At the town of Córdoba, Iturbide and O'Donojú affixed their signatures to a treaty that, for the most part, accepted the terms of the Plan de Iguala. The highest-ranking Spanish official in New Spain had thus recognized Mexican Independence. But Iturbide, thinking of the future, incorporated into the Treaty of Córdoba one important modification. If no suitable European monarch could be persuaded to accept the Mexican crown, a Mexican congress could choose a New World emperor instead. The commander of the Army of the Three Guarantees had begun to feather his own nest.

THE EFFECTS OF THE WARS FOR INDEPENDENCE

Iturbide's triumphal entry into Mexico City in September 1821 marked the end of eleven years of war. The *Gaceta Imperial de México* proclaimed theatrically that not even Rome in its days of grandeur had ever witnessed such an exultant spectacle. Upon receiving gold keys to the city the commander-in-chief explained that they would be used to lock the doors of irreligion, disunion, and despotism and to open the doors of general happiness. But the first door Iturbide opened in Mexico City was that of the great cathedral on the central plaza. Cementing his future relationship with the archbishop, he received communion and listened to a Te Deum offered in his honor.

From the campaigns, Mexico acquired not only its share of heroes and traitors but also a legacy of political violence and economic devastation. The wars exerted an incalculable influence on Mexico's future. The army had converted the dream of Independence into reality and was by no means ready to step aside and allow civilians to control the nation's destiny. For a full century the Mexican military would be very much involved in the political processes of government and would bargain with opposing factions for a greater and greater share of the nation's wealth. The military clique would constitute a ready instrument for unscrupulous politicians to use for their own purposes. More important yet, the basic issues separating different segments of society had not been resolved. Competing groups had cooperated long enough to achieve a common end, but, once Independence was achieved, the alliance called together by the Plan de Iguala proved very transitory. For some the revolution was simply anticolonial in nature and therefore it was over; others wanted its momentum to be carried into the arena of political and economic reform. The internal struggles between liberals and conservatives, between republicans and monarchists, between federalists and centralists, and between anticlericals and proponents of clerical privilege would consume the energies of the neophyte nation for much longer than the most pessimistic political analyst would have dared to predict.

If in 1821 it was difficult to predict the instability that was about to ensue, the roots of discord could be traced back into the colonial past, both for creoles and indigenous groups. The armies of the independence period were made up of Indians (more than half) and castas (just under a fourth). Although their goals were very different from those of the elites, the rural masses had been active in the fighting, mostly in pursuit of resolving their local grievances over the preservation of their communities and traditions, culturally mixed as they were by the end of the colonial period. Their participation garnered them little advantage as their concerns were ignored and their privations increased after independence. They could take little solace in the fact that the politically articulate groups in Mexico City demonstrated precious little ability to govern even themselves.

RECOMMENDED FOR FURTHER STUDY

Almaraz, Felix D. *Tragic Cavalier: Governor Manuel Salcedo of Texas, 1808–1813.* Austin: University of Texas Press, 1971.

Anna, Timothy E. *The Fall of Royal Government in Mexico City.* Lincoln: University of Nebraska Press, 1978.

Archer, Christon I. *The Birth of Modern Mexico, 1780–1824.* Wilmington, Del.: Scholarly Resources, Inc., 2003.

Benson, Nettie Lee, ed. *Mexico and the Spanish Cortes, 1810–1822.* Austin: University of Texas Press, 1966.

Ducey, Michael T. "Village, Nation, and Constitution: Insurgent Politics in Papantla, Veracruz, 1810–1821." *Hispanic American Historical Review* (1999): 463–93.

Guedea, Virginia. "The Old Colonialism Ends, the New Colonialism Begins," in *The Oxford History of Mexico.* Edited by Michael C. Meyer and William H. Beezley, pp. 277–99. New York: Oxford University Press, 2000.

Hamill, Hugh M. "Caudillism and Independence: A Symbiosis?" in *The Independence of Mexico and the Creation of the New Nation.* Edited by Jaime E. Rodríguez O., pp. 163–74. Los Angeles: UCLA Latin American Center, 1989.

———. *The Hidalgo Revolt: Prelude to Mexican Independence.* Gainesville: University of Florida Press, 1966.

Hamnett, Brian R. "Royalist Counterinsurgency and the Continuity of Rebellion: Guanajuato and Michoacán, 1813–20." *Hispanic American Historical Review* 62 (1982): 19–48.

Lombardi, John V. *The Political Ideology of Fray Servando Teresa de Mier, Propagandist for Independence.* Cuernavaca: Centro Intercultural de Documentación, 1968.

Robertson, William S. *Iturbide of Mexico.* Durham, N.C.: Duke University Press, 1952.

Rodríguez O., Jaime E. "From Royal Subject to Republican Citizen: The Role of the Autonomists in the Independence of Mexico," in *The Independence of Mexico and the Creation of the New Nation.* Edited by Jaime E. Rodriguez O., pp. 19–43. Los Angeles: UCLA Latin American Center, 1989.

Rydjord, John. *Foreign Interest in the Independence of New Spain.* Durham, N.C.: Duke University Press, 1935.

Timmons, Wilbert H. *Morelos: Priest, Soldier, Statesman of Mexico.* El Paso: Texas Western College Press, 1963.

Van Young, Eric. *The Other Rebellion: Popular Violence, Ideology, and the Mexican Struggle for Independence, 1810–1821.* Stanford, Calif.: Stanford University Press, 2001.

16

The First Mexican Empire

POMP AND CIRCUMSTANCE

In the best of circumstances nation building is a precarious business, but how does one create a nation out of a newly independent state when the economy is in shambles and the political atmosphere is pervaded by acrimony and mistrust? How does one fashion a set of national contours when ideological fissures and profound regional differences tear at the heart of the body politic? These questions obsessed many Latin American leaders in the nineteenth century once parental authority had been successfully challenged. Iturbide did not have all of the answers, but he felt that he had one reliable formula. Identify the head of government with the state, subsume the two into one, and by some miraculous metamorphosis a nation will emerge. But the crucial element in the process, he believed, was to identify a dynamic, resourceful, and charismatic leader. Not worried about overstepping the bounds of modesty, he could identify only one Mexican possessed of all these redeeming prerequisites—himself.

As provided by the Plan de Iguala, Iturbide named a provisional junta to govern the country. This junta, completely dominated by conservative criollo interests, in turn named him to serve as its presiding officer. The first order of business was to select a five-man regency to exercise executive functions until an emperor could be designated. The junta chose Iturbide as one of the five. But the presidency of the junta and membership on the regency was deemed an insufficient tribute to the leader of the Independence movement, so the group awarded him a new military title, *Generalísimo de Tierra y Mar*, and, to go along with it, a salary of 120,000 pesos annually.

While the junta, the regency, and Iturbide threw flowers in each other's path, an independent Congress, also dominated by conservatives, debated Mexico's future. Although a small group of recalcitrants tried to muster sympathy for a republic, Iturbide's conservative cohorts controlled the organizational proceedings. While they beat back all attempts at republicanism they began to waver on a series of economic and military issues. When the Congress, though divided, decided to cut back on the size of the Army of the Three Guarantees and decreed that no member of the regency could simultaneously hold military office, Iturbide realized that his ranks were being thinned and that time was no longer on his side. If he failed to act decisively the crown he wanted so desperately might be denied him.

On the evening of May 18 the Generalísimo staged a dramatic demonstration in his own behalf. Troops were ordered out of the barracks and into the streets. Firing muskets and rockets into the air and shouting "Viva Agustín I, Emperor of Mexico!" they enticed other soldiers to join them. As the frenzy grew in the downtown business district, thousands of civilians accompanied the mob on its way to Iturbide's residence. Once there, the multitudes demanded that their favorite declare himself emperor at once. Iturbide told friends who were in his home at the time that although he wanted to go out on his balcony and turn them down, he yielded for the sake of the public good.

With good reason historians have concluded that Iturbide's reluctance was feigned, that his submission to the inevitable was not so stoic, and that the sergeant orchestrating the event had acted under his explicit instructions. The following morning Iturbide appeared personally before the Congress, and, with his mob in the galleries shouting, the intimidated body named him constitutional emperor of Mexico. He demonstrated no concern that a legal quorum was missing. In his oath of office he swore before God and the Holy Evangels to uphold and defend the Roman Catholic religion at the exclusion of all others and to enforce all laws and decrees promulgated by the Congress that chose him.

With the throne thus occupied, the Congress set to work, not on the conspicuous demands of the Mexican nation, but on defining proper etiquette and protocol in an obvious attempt to emulate the greatest imperial regime the world had ever known. It would not only appropriate for the emperor all of the prerogatives of the Spanish nobility but would add to them. In June the Congress refined the organizational structure of the monarchy, declaring it to be hereditary. The heir was Iturbide's eldest son, Señor Don Agustín, who was designated "Prince Imperial," while the other sons and daughters of the emperor were to be Mexican princes and princesses. Iturbide's father would carry the title "Prince of the Union" and his sister, Doña Nicolasa, "Princess of Iturbide." May 19, the day of Iturbide's proclamation, was declared a national holiday, as were his birthday and the birthdays of his children. Defining the accouterments of regality took months and at times prompted the most ludicrous debate, such as that concerning whether the motto appearing below Iturbide's bust on the new metal coinage should be in Latin or Spanish. The Congress opted for *Augustinus Dei Providentia* on one side and *Mexici Primus Imperator Constitutionalis* on the other.

The greatest preparations of all were made for the official coronation ceremonies in July. Although several liberal deputies argued that kissing of the hand and bending of the knee were repugnant to the dignity of free peoples, their voices were lost to the monarchist majority. The efforts were all based on a French model, and the Congress hired a French baroness who had designed the costumes for Napoleon Bonaparte some twenty-two years before. Serious thought was given to ordering a national fast for the three days prior to the ceremonies, but the idea was finally dismissed as impractical to enforce outside of prisons and convents. The Congress did, however, authorize a new Mexican order, the Knights of Guadalupe, to participate in the coronation. As the day of the coronation approached, jewelry was borrowed, thrones were erected, banners and flags were hung from church towers, and teams of peasants were engaged to scour the streets. The citizenry of the capital were being prepared for the most pretentious spectacle ever to occur in Mexico City.

At 8:00 A.M. on Sunday, July 21, 1822, amidst the din of artillery salvos and the clamor of several military bands, the imperial cortège worked its way along a carpeted and flower-strewn path to the provisional palace, and the royal family was escorted to the central cathedral by an honor guard recently designated by the Congress. At the door the emperor and empress were met by two bishops who blessed them with holy water and led them to the two thrones placed on the altar. When the lesser dignitaries, including the diplomatic corps, were seated according to the complicated body of protocol, the bishop of Guadalajara celebrated high mass and consecrated the emperor and empress with sacred oil. With tremendous solemnity the president of the Congress placed the crown on Iturbide's head and he, in turn, placed a slightly smaller one on the head of the empress. The bishop then intoned *Vivat Imperator in aeternum*. It was time for the bishop of Puebla to participate, and his contribution, ending the ceremony, was a long eloquent speech eulogizing the new emperor.

While the outer trappings of the empire were pretentious to the absurd, they were not entirely without purpose and meaning. Iturbide's understanding of Mexico's past, while by no means profound, was acute enough. He realized that the entire governmental system of the colonial period had been predicated upon loyalty to the king and the crown. Even provincial and local officials decreed and implemented ordinances in the king's name. Independence obviously undercut the per-

Agustín de Iturbide (1783–1824). Changing allegiance from the Spanish to the insurgent cause, Iturbide successfully concluded the fight for Independence and had himself named emperor of Mexico.

sonal loyalty that sealed Mexican society together, but the emperor wanted to capitalize upon the time-tested tradition. He wanted to reap advantages from the fact that Mexico was not immune to the forces of history. While he became emperor in name, in fact he became a *caudillo*, a military leader with a personal following. The Congress had given him the legal base he considered vital; the ostentation that engulfed his person helped to reinforce the mystique of his indispensability and to blur the distinctions between the man and the office. The words *Augustinus Dei Providentia Mexici Primus Imperator Constitutionalis*, even if they were not understood, sounded enough like the unintelligible locutions of the Sunday mass to inspire awe in the large unsophisticated portion of the citizenry. Iturbide worked hard to identify the new state with his own person and, for a while, seemed to be succeeding.

PROBLEMS FACING THE NEW EMPIRE

The empire was huge. Embracing much of the old viceroyalty of New Spain, it stretched in the north to California and the present-day Southwest of the United States and the south included all of Central America with the exception of Panama. Long subject to what they considered the autocratic rule of Guatemala, many Central Americans favored union with the Mexican empire, but when rebellious elements in Honduras, El Salvador, and Costa Rica demurred, Iturbide sent in an army of six hundred men to ensure adhesion. That was sufficient.

A more serious problem occurred with the neighbor to the north. The new regime quite naturally wished to secure the official recognition of the United States. The cultivation of harmonious relations was deemed vital to the security of Mexico's northern provinces (the United States had already exhibited expansionist tendencies) and could lead to extensive commerical ties. In addition, the boundary between the two countries had never been properly defined and needed to be drawn. Most of all the Mexican monarch hoped for a loan of $10 million to help his new government meet its obligations. But President James Monroe's explicit purpose in extending diplomatic recognition to the newly independent Latin American states was to promote the establishment of free republican governments. When the Mexican Congress named Iturbide emperor, Monroe was discouraged and ventured the opinion that the monarchy could not last long.

Iturbide took the lead when he dispatched Manuel Zozaya as minister to Washington. Reception of the Mexican would, in effect, recognize the Mexican regime. With mixed emotions the United States president urged the Congress to authorize recognition in December of 1822. To reject Zozaya would impair relations with Mexico from the beginning, and business interests in the United States wanted to cultivate trade relations. In January 1823 Monroe appointed Joel Poinsett as minister to Mexico even though Poinsett had expressed serious reservations about the Mexican regime. Iturbide, through no concerted effort of his own, had won a minor diplomatic victory.

But all was not well in Mexico City. The showy imperial façade rested on vulnerable socioeconomic foundations. Mexico's eleven years of war had cost more than most governmental officials, the emperor not excepted, were willing to admit. Most serious of all was the perilous state of the Mexican economy.

Mexico's colonial economy was overwhelmingly dependent upon the gold and silver mines in the central part of the country. But it was in precisely this area that the Wars for Independence had exacted their highest toll. During the years of internecine strife mine workers left their jobs to join the fight, mine owners and operators were killed, machinery was damaged, and many of the mines were flooded. Without sufficient bullion reaching the mints, coinage was curtailed. Over $26 million was minted in 1809; in 1821, less than $6 million. Without operation of the mines, unemployment was rampant in the mining centers, and the situation was aggravated by the mustering out that began shortly after the military campaigns ended.

The impact of the wars on Mexico's agricultural output was similar. Both Spanish troops and insurgents destroyed fields, commandeered crops, and killed off cattle and sheep that might have been of benefit to the enemy. Many an hacendado was killed, and those who escaped could likely have seen their haciendas in flames if, during their flight, they had time to glance over their shoulders. Mexico was a rural country at the time of Independence, but thousands in Mexico City (population 155,000), Puebla (population 60,000), Guadalajara (population 50,000), and other cities suffered as the price of agricultural products rose steadily in 1822.

The average citizen in the city felt the impact of the economic decline, and the government did too. In an attempt to make the cause of Independence even more popular, the Congress lowered many old taxes, such as those on pulque and tobacco, and eliminated others altogether. But commerce and the revenues to be derived therefore stagnated as trade with Spain ended and free trade with new areas was slow to take up the slack.

To ensure loyalty soldiers and bureaucrats had to be paid and officers promoted, but the depleted revenues could not begin to cover the extravagant expenses of the imperial regime. Month after month expenses exceeded income. Virtually nobody was willing to invest in the shaky economy or loan money to the government. Available capital was largely in the hands of the Spaniards, and most of them began to depart soon after Independence. The few moneylenders around proposed interest rates that were nothing short of exorbitant. In response to the growing crisis the Congress decreed a forced loan on ecclesiastical properties, but this measure was no more than a temporary expedient. Several issues of paper currency, not backed by hard reserves and not trusted by anyone, caused more problems than they solved, and, as the wheels of the economy ground into ominous stagnation, Mexicans became more and more critical of their new regime.

Criticism was leveled at the emperor from many quarters: from disgruntled veterans who found no employment, from deputies in the Congress who really never accommodated themselves to the concept of monarchy, and from a number of courageous journalists who exposed the burlesque aspects of Mexico's empire. Sensitive to criticism, in the summer the emperor suppressed several liberal newspapers that espoused republican ideals and even one conservative one that favored monarchy but argued that the throne should be offered to a European prince. With the newspaper suppressions a group of liber-

270 REFORM AND REACTION: THE MOVE TO INDEPENDENCE

als in the Congress, led by Fray Servando Teresa de Mier, an accomplished orator, and Carlos María de Bustamante, began to conspire. Through a government spy who infiltrated congressional circles Iturbide was able to secure an accurate list of his leading enemies and, on August 20, 1822, had them all arrested. The Congress protested, and even some of Iturbide's staunchest supporters in the legislative body defended their arrested colleagues. The opposing positions were irreconcilable, and the debates in the fall were heated; their substance was less significant than the fact that they demonstrated a steadily growing majority against the emperor and the imperial concept itself. Even Guadalupe Victoria, Iturbide's erstwhile ally, denounced him as a tyrant with all the fiery eloquence he could command. On October 31 Iturbide became the first Mexican chief executive to dissolve the legislative branch of government. The precedent, once established, would be repeated many times before the nineteenth century ran its course.

The reaction in both Mexico City and the provinces was resolute. The antimonarchists found their ranks swelling, and a specific plot crystalized in Veracruz. The self-acclaimed leader was Iturbide's commander in the port city, Antonio López de Santa Anna. Although it is possible that Santa Anna had been schooled in the virtues of republicanism by Carlos María de Bustamante, whom he had met and befriended a few years before, his decision to lead a revolt against the monarchy seems to have had a more fundamental root. As commander of Veracruz, Santa Anna had been assigned the task of driving the last remaining Spanish troops from San Juan de Ulloa, the harbor fortress they still held. But Iturbide believed that Santa Anna was not pursuing the enemy forcefully enough and was even considering turning Veracruz over to them. As a result he ordered Santa Anna to Mexico City where he could be closely observed. But Santa Anna would countenance no such move. On December 1, 1822, at the head of some four hundred troops, he rode through the streets of Veracruz proclaiming a republic. A few days later he formally launched his revolt under the Plan de Veracruz. Within a month Vicente Guerrero, Nicolás Bravo, and Guadalupe Victoria had joined the movement, enhancing its prestige. Iturbide recognized the seriousness of the problem; it was one thing for deputies in the Congress to attack the regime with words and quite another for army officers to attack it with arms and ammunition.

Placing José Antonio Echáverri, the captain general of Veracruz, in charge of the imperial campaigns, Iturbide felt that he had little to fear. Echáverri and Santa Anna had been at each other's throats for months over the most expeditious means for driving the Spaniards out of San Juan de Ulloa. But Echáverri decided to give the emperor a little of his own medicine. Much as Iturbide had made common cause with Vicente Guerrero when dispatched to engage him, Echáverri joined Santa Anna. On February 1, 1823, Echáverri and thirty-three cohorts proclaimed the *Plan de Casa Mata*. Santa Anna, not having encountered much military success in recent months, and realizing that the Plan de Casa Mata was not inconsistent with his own Plan de Veracruz, accepted the new plan. Two anti-imperial movements now became one.

One military contingent after another swore allegiance to the Plan de Casa Mata. One province after another fell to the insurgents, and they began marching on Mexico City. They did not have to take the capital by force, however. Realizing that his experiment with monarchy had ended in failure, Iturbide abdicated his throne in the middle of February 1823, some ten months after coming to office, and accepted a generous pension that would have enabled him to live comfortably. In his resignation address he stated he did not desire to have his name become a pretext for civil war. Then with his family he made his plans to go into European exile. The rebel army marched into Mexico City unopposed.

AN ASSESSMENT

The first Mexican empire had been a dismal failure. In conception it had merely substituted a new criollo oligarchy for the old gachupín oligarchy and indeed had satisfied many Mexicans hostile to the innovations of nineteenth-century liberalism. The royal household, with all of its gaudy trappings, underscored that very little had changed since New Spain won control of its own destiny. The diplomatic initiatives, the loan from the United States, and an equitable settlement of the boundary had languished.

With the advantage of historical hindsight, the revolt, fought under the banner of the Plan de Casa Mata, is laden with irony. The entire antimonarchy fight was made in the name of the Congress, which Iturbide had emasculated from the day it accepted his oath of office. One would have thought that at best legislative supremacy, and at worst legislative equality, would have been the political dictum of the nineteenth century. In fact, just the opposite was true. Executive dominance and legislative subservience may have been bequeathed to Mexico during the three centuries of colonial tutelage, but they were sufficiently enforced during the empire never to be successfully challenged again. Few practical lessons in nation building derived from the empire. Administrative and legislative experience was still in short supply. The Mexican elite did not yet consider the fact that successful leadership in the Wars for Independence was by no means synonymous with statesmanship. In the period following the empire Mexico would once again turn to military heroes who had emerged from the campaigns with more than life-sized stature.

But in at least one respect the collapse of the empire marked the beginning of a new day. It brought to power for the first time the criollo middle class, which had early supported the Independence movement only to be outflanked by the conservatives after the Riego revolt in Spain. These criollos were not social revolutionaries in any sense. While on occasions they attacked entrenched interests, their objectives were political, not social. In all innocence they seemed to believe that the docility of the lower classes had no bounds and that the poor would endure their privations forever.

As Mexico prepared to embark upon its second experiment as an independent nation, only one major question had been answered. The monarchists had been so thoroughly discredited that virtually nobody, at least for a while, harbored serious notions about reviving the concept. Iturbide's wasteful pomp had converted more monarchists to republicans than could have been persuaded by a team of skillful rhetoricians. Mexico would be organized as a republic; the nature of that republic would now be the issue at stake. It would provoke violent debate, near anarchy, and finally civil war.

RECOMMENDED FOR FURTHER STUDY

Anna, Timothy E. *Forging Mexico, 1821–1835.* Lincoln: University of Nebraska Press, 1998.

———. *The Mexican Empire of Iturbide.* Lincoln: University of Nebraska Press, 1990.

Benson, Nettie Lee, and Charles R. Berry. "The Central American Delegation to the First Constituent Congress of Mexico, 1822–1823." *Hispanic American Historical Review* 49 (1969): 679–702.

Brading, D. A. *The First America: The Spanish Monarchy, Creole Patriots and the Liberal State, 1492–1866.* Cambridge: Cambridge University Press, 1993.

Cotner, Thomas E. *The Military and Political Career of José Joaquín de Herrera, 1792–1854.* Austin: Institute of Latin American Studies, 1949.

Harrison, Horace V. "The Republican Conspiracy against Agustín de Iturbide," in *Essays in Mexican History.* Edited by Thomas E. Cotner and Carlos E. Castañeda, pp. 142–65. Austin: Institute of Latin American Studies, 1958.

Lewis, William Francis, III. "Xavier Mina and Fray Servando Mier: Romantic Liberals of the Nineteenth Century." *New Mexico Historical Review* 44 (1969): 119–36.

Lombardi, John V. *The Political Ideology of Fray Servando Teresa de Mier, Propagandist for Independence.* Cuernavaca: Centro Intercultural de Documentación, 1968.

Poinsett, Joel R. *Notes on Mexico Made in the Autumn of 1822, Accompanied by an Historical Sketch of the Revolution.* New York: Praeger, 1969.

Robertson, William S. *Iturbide of Mexico.* Durham, N.C.: Duke University Press, 1952.

Tenenbaum, Barbara. "Taxation and Tyranny: Public Finances during the Iturbide Regime," in *The Independence of Mexico and the Creation of the New Nation.* Edited by Jaime E. Rodríguez O., pp. 201–14. Los Angeles: UCLA Latin American Center, 1989.

Villoro, Luis. "The Ideological Currents of the Epoch of Independence," in *Major Trends in Mexican Philosophy.* Edited by Mario de la Cueva et al., pp. 185–219. Notre Dame, Ind.: University of Notre Dame Press, 1966.

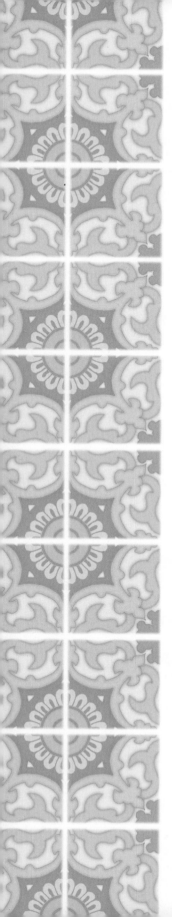

V

THE TRIALS OF NATIONHOOD, 1824–55

17

The Early Mexican Republic, 1824–33

THE CONSTITUTION OF 1824

With the collapse of the empire, a three-man junta governed Mexico provisionally. All three—Nicolás Bravo, Guadalupe Victoria, and Pedro Celestino Negrete—were military men. The precedent of miscasting soldiers as statesmen was now well established. The first order of business was to call elections for delegates to a constitutional congress that would be charged with framing the new charter. The constituent body met for the first time on November 27, 1823, and before the week was out the lines of combat had been drawn. The focus narrowed to a question that on the surface seemed simple enough: should the new republic be federalist or centralist?

Although there were some exceptions to the general alignment of forces, the centralists found their strength among the clergy, the hacendados, and the army officers, while the federalist firebrands drew support from those liberal criollos and mestizos who considered themselves intellectual heirs of the French and American revolutions and students of the United States Constitution and the liberal Spanish document of 1812. The chief spokesmen for the federalists were Miguel Ramos Arizpe from Coahuila and Valentín Gómez Farías from Zacatecas. The centralist cause was championed by Fray Servando Teresa de Mier and Carlos María de Bustamante. When Ramos Arizpe presented the body with a working paper modeled very closely after the Constitution of the United States, Fray Servando, an iconoclast who once questioned the authenticity of the Virgin of Guadalupe, responded with an eloquent speech. He observed that the experience of the northern neighbor had been entirely different from that of Mexico, and, while a federal system might well be suited to the needs of the United States, it could not work in Mexico for it would weaken the country just when strength from union was required. Speaking of the thirteen colonies to the north, Fray Servando argued:

> They were already separate and independent one from another. They federalized themselves in union against the oppression of England; to federalize ourselves, now united, is to divide ourselves and to bring upon us the very evils they sought to remedy with their federation. They had already lived under a constitution that, when the name of the king was scratched out, brought forth a republic. We buckled for three hundred years under the weight of an absolute monarch, scarcely moving a step toward the study of freedom. We are like children barely out of diapers or like slaves who have just unshackled their chains. . . . We might say that nature itself has decreed our centralization.[1]

Fray Servando was not speaking for rhetorical effect. But his arguments, although having much to commend them, failed to persuade. Ramos Arizpe and his federalist cohorts also drew upon the irrefutable lessons of history but interpreted them quite differently. Centralism they equated with despotism. As examples they pointed to the three hundred years of colonial rule, which were centralistic and despotic, and the ten months of monarchy, which were also centralistic and despotic. They preferred the dispersion of powers inherent in the federal structure and argued that such a system was more in harmony with Mexico's recently won liberties. A would-be dictator could be thwarted in his nefarious attempts to subject the people only if the states and localities enjoyed a respectable measure of independent power. Arizpe's plea appealed more to emotion than to rigorous logic, but nevertheless he carried the day. It was simply too irresistible for some to attribute the tremendous progress recorded by the United States since its independence to its federal form of government.

Under the Constitution of 1824 the Estados Unidos Mexicanos were organized as a federal republic composed of nineteen states and four territories. In the separation-of-powers clause delineating governmental authority into the executive, legislative, and judicial branches, the philosophical influence of Montesquieu and the practical influence of the United States Constitution of 1787 are both patent. The legislature was made bicameral, the upper house designated as the Senate and the lower house as the Chamber of Deputies. Each state was represented by two senators and one deputy for every eighty thousand inhabitants. In at least one respect the federal system established in 1824 went beyond its United States model and gave the states even greater power than those to the north: both the president and the vice-

---

1. Quoted in *Antología del pensamiento social y político de América Latina* (Washington, D.C., 1964), pp. 242–43.

THE MEXICAN REPUBLIC IN 1824

States		Territories
1. Chiapas	11. Querétaro	20. New Mexico
2. Chihuahua	12. San Luis Potosí	21. Old California
3. Coahuila y Texas	13. Sonora y Sinaloa	22. New California
4. Durango	14. Tabasco	23. Tlaxcala
5. Guanajuato	15. Tamaulipas	
6. México	16. Veracruz	
7. Michoacán	17. Jalisco	
8. Nuevo León	18. Yucatán	
9. Oaxaca	19. Zacatecas	
10. Puebla		

Adapted from Romeo Flores Caballero, Counterrevolution: The Role of the Spaniards in the Independence of Mexico (Lincoln: University of Nebraska Press. 1974), p. 85.

president were to be elected not by popular vote or an electoral college but by the state legislatures, for a term of four years.

While the federalists thus won on the major points of governmental organization, in an important sense they gave up as much as they gained. The centralists regrouped and scored at least three victories of their own. First and foremost, the Catholic Church retained its three-hundred-year monopoly on Mexico's spiritual life. Many Mexican conservatives still held that religious toleration was somehow incompatible with public morality. In addition, the president of the country was given extraordinary powers in times of emergency, powers that could convert him into a dictator while at the same time investing him with the sanction of law. The word *emergency* in the nineteenth century came to be interpreted rather loosely. Finally, the Constitution guaranteed members of the clergy and the military their special *fueros*. This time-worn Spanish institution exempted clergymen and military personnel from having to stand trial in civil courts, even if they were charged with the violation of civil law.

THE VICTORIA PRESIDENCY

In Mexico's first presidential election the state legislatures chose as president Guadalupe Victoria and as vice-president Nicolás Bravo. The new president, a man of goodwill, was honest and unassuming. He always had time to meet the public and had proven his courage on the battlefield, but he was not a particularly talented individual. In a mood of compromise he invited several conservatives to serve in the cabinet. They accepted, not for purposes of reconciliation but to secure a power base within the government. The president sought to be impartial, but his attempts at fairness degenerated into indecision. Those in whom he placed trust took advantage of him. The problems that beset him were immense. Woefully unprepared by education or temperament, he was not only unable to kindle popular imagination but proved unequal to the task.

The debates of the empire and over the nature of the new republic had bequeathed an intensely political atmosphere, pervaded by mistrust, self-righteousness, rancor, and despair. Those in high office, including the president himself, found a constant friend a rare thing. While exaggerated jealousies magnified trifles, basic ideological cleavages emerged as well and began to manifest themselves in a unique manner. Both of the major political factions identified themselves and their efforts with a branch of freemasonry. The federalists attached themselves to the York Rite Masons (*Yorquinos*) and the centralists to the Scottish Rite (*Escoseses*). Masonic meetings, of course, were held in secret, and, because the lodges were inviolable, all manner of cabal could be plotted behind closed doors with little fear of exposure.

One of the more unfortunate incidents to occur during the Victoria presidency was the execution of the former emperor, Agustín de Iturbide. Taking up residence first in Italy and later in England, the exiled monarch heard rumors that the restored Spanish king, Ferdinand VII, backed by the Holy Alliance, was about to undertake a reconquest of Mexico. Early in 1824 he offered his services to the republican government. He had defeated the Spanish army once and was prepared to do battle again in the name of Mexican Independence. Congress turned down his good offer and, in fact, passed legislation stipulating that should he dare return to Mexico he would be considered a traitor and, as such, would face immediate execution. Impatient and imprudent as ever, Iturbide did not wait for an answer. On May 11, 1824, he left England with his family and retainers for the New World. Disembarking at Soto la Marina, north of Tampico, he was soon recognized by the local military commander. The Tamaulipas state legislature met in hurried session and decreed that it must enforce the order of treason handed down by the national Congress the month before. On July 19, 1824, standing before a firing squad at the small town of Padilla, Iturbide could not resist making one final rambling and emotional speech protesting his innocence to his executioners: "Mexicans! Even in this act of my death I recommend to you love of our fatherland and observance of our holy religion. . . . I die for having come to assist you, and I die happy because I die among you. I die with honor, not as a traitor."[2]

The execution of Iturbide was really incidental to the Victoria presidency. The administration scored high marks in foreign policy. Not only was Mexico's Independence formally recognized by most of Europe, but several treaties of amity and commerce were concluded as well. A treaty with the United States pledged both countries to accept the Sabine River as the eastern boundary of Texas, thus ostensibly settling the boundary question. But President Victoria found representatives of foreign nations to be more reasonable than his opponents at home and international problems more soluble than domestic imbroglios.

The Victoria adminstration was unable to do much about the new nation's steadily worsening financial situation. For years prior to Independence the criollos had argued that the weakness of Mexico's economy was a result of poor management by the gachupines. But now in power themselves, the criollos could do no better. Citizens long accustomed to hard specie were reluctant to accept paper money. Domestic commerce, already vulnerable to banditry, burned bridges, and unsafe roads, suffered as a result. The president, not concerned that a large standing army could be a menace to civil liberties, to any hope of future civilian governments, and to a healthy economy kept over fifty thousand men under arms at all times. The new government assumed

---

2. Quoted in Lucas Alamán, *Historia de México* (Mexico City, 1942), 5: 736–37.

Guadalupe Victoria (1785–1843). Mexico's first president, Victoria found his term disrupted by the internal chaos that came to dominate the country's political life in the first half of the nineteenth century.

all national debts from the late colonial period and the monarchy (over 76 million pesos) and sought to support itself by means of import taxes, sales taxes, and new government monopolies. The import duties were largely circumvented by rampant smuggling; the sales taxes were largely avoided by failure to report transactions; and the monopolies, after collection expenses, brought in little cash. Not only were the revenues insufficient to pay installments on the debt, but they were unequal to the day-to-day costs of government. Yet the deficit was less significant than the fact that the entire fiscal structure was unsound. Loans from England were deemed to be the salvation and small amounts were received. These minor infusions of foreign capital were insufficient to stimulate the economy but did mark the first step of Mexican economic dependency.

While efforts to heal the breach between rival factions foundered, the political and economic pressures merged in 1827 and expressed themselves in an armed revolt against President Victoria. The leader of the insurrection was none other than Vice-President Nicolás Bravo, who drew upon the Scottish Rite lodges for support. The Yorquinos rallied around the president, and ultimately the revolt was suppressed by Generals Santa Anna and Guerrero. But the precedent of the military coup had been set.

DOMESTIC TURMOIL AND A SPANISH INVASION

Passions had not yet subsided when the new presidential elections were held in September 1828. The liberal candidate, Vicente Guerrero, an uneducated hero of the wars, was opposed by conservative Manuel Gómez Pedraza, an accomplished scholar who had served in the Victoria cabinet as secretary of war. The election results showed that Gómez Pedraza carried ten of the nineteen state legislatures, but the liberals, feeling no obligation to pay homage to the Constitution, charged that he had used his influence with the army to intimidate the legislators. Rather than turn the government over to their enemies, the liberals opted instead for revolution. Once again they found their champion in Antonio López de Santa Anna, but on this occasion the odds were strongly against him. Through persuasion and deception he gradually won others over to the liberal cause. When Juan Alvarez rose up in Acapulco and Lorenzo de Zavala in the environs of Mexico City, the government army had to disperse its forces and the rebels made such headway that the president-elect, already disgusted with partisan abuse, announced that he was giving up the fight. As a result the defeated candidate, Vicente Guerrero, became president and Anastasio Bustamante, a compromise conservative, vice-president. Santa Anna, for his efforts, was awarded a division generalship, the highest military rank in the country.

The second president of Mexico was much more active and decisive than the first. He was not the least troubled that he alienated various segments of the population in pursuit of goals he considered worthwhile. The most progressive measure he undertook was the abolition of slavery. The bill, signed in September 1829, was accepted without protest except in Texas, where the institution of slavery had actually been encouraged by previous Mexican legislation.

Scarcely comfortable in the presidential chair, the new president received word that Spain, which had not yet recognized Mexico's independence, was indeed planning a reconquest of Mexico. The Spanish timing seemed to be excellent. The same day that the Congress named Guerrero president it decreed the enforcement of a law, passed under the previous administration, expelling almost all remaining Spaniards from Mexico. The country was rent with factionalism and considerably weakened. Just as the first Spanish conquest in 1519 had been served admirably by internal dissension, maybe the second, three hundred and ten years later, could profit as well.

The Spanish expedition of some three thousand troops left Havana, Cuba (one of the few remaining Spanish possessions in the New World), in July 1829 under the command of General Isidro Barradas. Landing on the coast of Tamaulipas at the height of summer, the

Spaniards were exhausted and demoralized by intense heat, yellow fever, and an acute scarcity of water. To their amazement, however, they found that Tampico had been evacuated in anticipation of a much larger expedition, and they took the forfeited prize.

President Guerrero decided to place government operations in the hands of the man who had ostensibly saved the nation several times, the new division general, Antonio López de Santa Anna. On August 21 Santa Anna attacked Tampico but was repulsed by Barradas's well-intrenched forces. But the Spaniards had not established any sure line of supply, and Santa Anna opted for a long siege, which, he reasoned, would take its toll. As inadequate provisions and yellow fever taxed Spanish resistance, General Barradas decided to surrender. By October most of the Spanish troops were on their way home. The attempted reconquest was Spain's last Mexican hurrah. It touched off a series of reprisals against the few remaining Spaniards in the country, and they began leaving hurriedly. The exodus of these middle-class Spanish merchants further weakened Mexico's economy.

Santa Anna had saved Mexico again. By 1830 there were few in the country who could rival his popularity. Honorific but unremunerative titles began to flow in from all corners of the republic: *Vencedor de Tampico* (Victor of Tampico) and *Salvador del País* (Savior of the Country). And the national Congress authorized a medal inscribed "At Tampico he defeated Spanish arrogance" and officially named him *Benemérito de la Patria* (Benefactor of the Fatherland). Undoubtedly, he could have taken advantage of his position immediately if he had wanted to. But he was not quite ready.

THE FEDERALIST–CENTRALIST STRUGGLE CONTINUES

With the Spanish threat removed, the Mexican liberals and conservatives now returned to anathematizing one another. When President Guerrero refused to relinquish the extraordinary powers Congress gave him to cope with the threat, Vice-President Bustamante posed as the champion of constitutionalism. For the second time in Mexico's brief republican history a conservative vice-president led an armed revolt against a liberal president. But where Nicolás Bravo had failed, Bustamante, largely because of his influence with the army, succeeded.

With Bustamante in the presidential office, the conservatives were back in power for the first time since the overthrow of the empire. But their promises would be so totally unredeemed as to imply that promises were made only for the pleasure of breaking them. All along the conservatives had been substituting catchy syllogisms for penetrating analyses of Mexico's problems, and when they found themselves in power they did not know what to do. Although they cut back on the size of the army and renegotiated the English loan, Bustamante was no more able to bring about stability and progress than had his liberal predecessors. And he compounded his shortcomings by giving his fellow Mexicans their first real lessons in military dictatorship.

Repressions taken against the Yorquinos were grossly intemperate. Freedom of the press was suppressed as only those presses upholding the government were allowed to roll. The federal legislature and the judiciary were badgered into acquiescence. Political corruption, not unknown in Mexico's past, reached new heights. But the incident that occasioned the greatest public outrage was the capture and execution of the former president, Vicente Guerrero. After his ouster by the Bustamante army, Guerrero gradually made his way to Acapulco, where he accepted passage on the *Colombo*, a ship flying the Italian flag. But Captain Picaluga, a Genoese citizen, had already made a trip to Mexico City and for $50,000 had agreed to sell Guerrero to the government. As soon as the former president boarded the *Colombo*, he was bound hand and foot and turned over to federal authorities. He was subsequently tried, convicted of treason, and on January 14, 1831, executed.

The execution had a sobering effect as Mexicans began to tally up. Of the five outstanding leaders of the Wars of Independence, four— Miguel Hidalgo, José María Morelos, Agustín de Iturbide, and now Vicente Guerrero—had died before the firing squad. Only Guadalupe Victoria escaped this fate. The word *traitor* had come to be used too easily and the charge invariably carried the supreme penalty. As a nation, Mexico was unsure of itself. It had drifted and vacillated since Independence. National, state, and local governments were plagued by civil disorder and insolvency. The state was still little more than an abstraction, and the criollo leadership had not served it well. The social structure had not changed in any meaningful way. Executing Vicente Guerrero might have satiated the political vengeance of a few but did nothing to stem devastating epidemics, repair pitted roads, or nurture a national healing process. Abolishing the caste system scarcely abolished poverty. Emancipating the slaves did not eliminate malnutrition and illiteracy. It seemed time for a change of direction, and there was one Mexican now ready to seize the opportunity. Santa Anna marshaled his forces once again, overthrew the Bustamante government, and returned to Veracruz to revel in his latest victory and await the outcome of the 1833 presidential elections.

RECOMMENDED FOR FURTHER STUDY

Archer, Christon I. "Fashioning a New Nation," in *The Oxford History of Mexico.* Edited by Michael C. Meyer and William H. Beezley, pp. 302–37. New York: Oxford University Press, 2000.

Arrom, Silvia M. "Popular Politics in Mexico City: The Parián Riot, 1828." *Hispanic American Historical Review* 68 (1988): 245–68.

Callcott, Wilfrid H. *Church and State in Mexico, 1822–1857.* Durham, N.C.: Duke University Press, 1926.

Costeloe, Michael P. *Bonds and Bondholders: British Investors and Mexico's Foreign Debt, 1824–1888.* Westport, Conn.: Praeger, 2003.

Flores Caballero, Romeo. *Counterrevolution: The Role of the Spaniards in the Independence of Mexico.* Lincoln: University of Nebraska Press, 1974.

Fowler, Will. *Mexico in the Age of Proposals, 1821–1853.* Westport, Conn.: Greenwood Press, 1998.

Green, Stanley. *The Mexican Republic: The First Decade, 1823–1832.* Pittsburgh: University of Pittsburgh Press, 1987.

Guardino, Peter. "Barbarism or Republican Law: Guerrero's Peasants and National Politics, 1820–1846." *Hispanic American Historical Review* 75 (1995): 185–214.

Hale, Charles A. *Mexican Liberalism in the Age of Mora, 1821–1853.* New Haven, Conn.: Yale University Press, 1968.

Lamar, Quinton Curtis. "A Diplomatic Disaster: The Mexican Mission of Anthony Butler, 1829–1834." *The Americas* 45 (1988): 1–18.

Macune, Charles W. "The Impact of Federalism on Mexican Church–State Relations, 1824–1835: The Case of the State of Mexico." *The Americas* 40 (1984): 177–90.

Rippy, J. Fred. *Joel R. Poinsett, Versatile American.* Durham, N.C.: Duke University Press, 1935.

Rodríguez O., Jaime. "The Conflict between Church and State in Early Republican Mexico." *New World* 2 (1987): 93–112.

Sims, Harold Dana. *The Expulsion of Mexico's Spaniards, 1821–1836.* Pittsburgh: University of Pittsburgh Press, 1990.

Weber, David J. *The Mexican Frontier, 1821–1846: The American Southwest under Mexico.* Albuquerque: University of New Mexico Press, 1982.

18

Santa Anna, the Centralized State, and the War with the United States

Santa Anna is the first of three towering Mexican political figures who would leave a preponderant imprint on their country's nineteenth-century historical experience. His contributions, corrosive perhaps, were quite at variance with those of his successors, Benito Juárez and Porfirio Díaz, but they were no less pronounced for he, too, was an event-making man. His intelligence, resolution, and temperament, his sins and ambitions, charted the course Mexico was to follow from the early 1830s to the middle 1850s. Mexican history from 1833 to 1855 constantly teetered between simple chaos and unmitigated anarchy. The country entered a phase of intense mutual recrimination. Nobody seemed willing to compromise. Between May 1833 and August 1855 the presidency changed hands thirty-six times, the average term being about seven and a half months. Santa Anna occupied the presidential chair on eleven different occasions, and his whim was Mexico's imperative. Even when he was out of office he was a powerful force to be reckoned with and a constant danger to the incumbent regime and to anyone aspiring to the succession.

SANTA ANNA: THE EXPEDIENCY OF POLITICAL PRINCIPLES

Antonio López de Santa Anna Pérez de Lebrón was born on February 21, 1794. His schooling in Veracruz left much to be desired, but the criollo youth showed no real flair for books anyway. Shortly after his sixteenth birthday he joined the army and within a year received his baptism of fire in a small engagement against a band of pro-Hidalgo rebels. For the next decade the young royalist cavalry officer staunchly supported the crown's efforts in New Spain and won special commendation for his heroics. But in 1821 Santa Anna, like many of his criollo comrades, followed Iturbide's lead and switched allegiance; in the process they sealed Spain's fate.

The highlights of Santa Anna's career in the period immediately following Independence have already been touched upon. In 1823, under the banner of the Plan de Casa Mata, he led the republican forces against the empire and contributed in no small way to the overthrow of Iturbide. When Mexico's first vice-president, conservative Nicolás Bravo, proclaimed a revolt against President Victoria, Santa Anna took the lead in suppressing the movement and, following the next presidential election, saw to it that the defeated liberal candidate, Vicente Guerrero, was installed in office. In 1829, when Spain tried to bring its former colony back into the fold, it was Santa Anna again who defeated the Spanish forces at Tampico to save the infant republic, and, in 1832, when the Bustamante dictatorship became intolerable, he overthrew it. On the surface, at least, his entire career seemed to constitute an unbroken chain of victories in the defense of Mexican liberalism. As the accolades mounted, Santa Anna fell victim to the greatest temptation of the wartime hero. He would change the field of battle from the military to the political front.

When the state legislatures cast their presidential votes in 1833, no one was surprised at the outcome. Santa Anna won by the largest majority in Mexican history. The vice-presidency went to Valentín Gómez Farías, a man of intellectual distinction and a politician whose liberal credentials were impeccable. Santa Anna had coveted the presidency for a decade, but once he achieved the goal he quickly wearied of the daily routine, long hours, and general tedium of presidential business. Moreover, as the champion of liberalism, he was expected to embark upon a series of far-reaching reforms long called for by his liberal cohorts. Such reforms were bound to prompt controversy, divide the society once again, and erode his tremendous popularity. Santa Anna's response was unique but not entirely out of character. He decided to return to his magnificent estate, Manga de Clavo, in Veracruz, leaving the office in the hands of Vice-President Gómez Farías.

The vice-president, in good nineteenth-century liberal fashion, immediately began to sponsor a number of reforms aimed at two intrenched institutions: the army and the church. The military reforms were modest. To curtail the inordinate influence of the army, the Gómez Farías administration reduced the size of the military and legislated the abolition of the military fueros; army officers would now have to stand trial in civil courts. The clerical reforms were much more wide-ranging, as the liberals maintained that the Mexican clergy contributed less to the spiritual needs of the community than ever before. The initial step was a hesitant one, designed perhaps to test the wind. Clergymen throughout the country were advised that they should limit their directives and admonitions from the pulpit to matters of religion.

General Antonio López de Santa Anna (1794–1876). The dominant figure of the first half of the nineteenth century, Santa Anna actually served in the presidency on eleven different occasions. A master politician, nobody understood Mexico's political dynamics better.

Emboldened by the lack of a forceful rejoinder, the Congress, under the prodding of Gómez Farías and his liberal theoreticians José María Luis Mora and Lorenzo de Zavala, then voted to secularize education. Not only was the University of Mexico closed down because its faculty was made up primarily of priests, but all future clerical appointments in the republic would be made by the government rather than by the papacy. Then, within the month the government struck out at the church where it really hurt—the ecclesiastical treasury. The mandatory payment of the tithe was declared illegal. In addition, in the name of individual freedom (a concept much in vogue with nineteenth-century liberals) the Congress enacted legislation permitting nuns, priests, and lay brothers, who had taken oaths to spend their entire lives as brides and servants of Christ, to forswear their vows. In one final measure the Franciscan missions in California were secularized and their funds and property sequestered.

The response from the vested interests was almost predictable. To the rallying cry of *Religión y Fueros* the church, the army, and other conservative groupings banded together and called for the overthrow of the government. The conservatives scouted the country for a figure to protect their prerogatives and turned to the maker and unmaker of presidents par excellence—Antonio López de Santa Anna. Again thirsting for public acclaim the retired president jumped at the new opportunity for action. Not embarrassed by lack of consistency, the embattled champion of all liberal causes since 1821 suddenly began denouncing anti-clerical atheists, York Rite Masons, naive federalists, subversive anarchists, Jacobins, Gómez Farías, and his liberal cohorts. The insurrection, although hampered by a cholera epidemic among the troops, succeeded, and within a short time Santa Anna made his second sortie into the presidency and rescinded most of the Gómez Farías reforms.

The new Santa Anna regime was openly conservative, Catholic, and centralist. The president's response to the perplexities of making a more perfect union was to abolish the federalist Constitution of 1824. The new charter, consisting of seven main parts, is remembered in Mexico's constitutional evolution as the *Siete Leyes*, or the Constitution of 1836. To ensure centralist organization, the states of the old federal republic were transformed into military departments governed by political bosses handpicked by the president himself. The presidential term was extended from four years to eight, but no president under the Constitution was to serve so long. The right to hold high political office was extended only to those with a high annual income. The financial qualifications for voting and officeholding gave the Siete Leyes an aristocratic flavor that obviously pleased the regime's conservative backers.

Santa Anna's decision to abolish the federal republic and to replace it with a centralist state precipitated a series of interrelated events that were to dominate his life and his country for the next twelve years. The switch to centralism was well received by some, as the concept of federalism had already lost much of its magic appeal, but several liberal politicians led revolts against him, and in 1847 Maya peasants initiated what came to be known as the Caste War of Yucatán. Calling for tax relief and an end to land encroachments, debt peonage, and administrative abuses by the Yucatecan elites, they controlled half of the Yucatecan peninsula by 1848. But the most serious opposition by far came from the northern province of Texas, which, in turn, provoked a disastrous war with the United States.

DISCONTENT IN TEXAS

Throughout the colonial period Texas was one of the northern provinces of New Spain. It was sparsely populated, and the Franciscan missionaries who penetrated the area found the Indian population intractable. At the beginning of the eighteenth century the Texas territory had fewer than three thousand sedentary colonists and, a hundred years later, only seven thousand. Because the Spanish crown wanted to populate and colonize the territory, in 1821, just prior to the winning of Mexican Independence, the commandant general in Monterrey granted Moses Austin, an American pioneer, permission to settle some three hundred Catholic families in Texas. Austin died and Mexico became independent before the project could be initiated, but Austin's son, Stephen F. Austin, took up the idea, had the concession confirmed by the new Mexican government, and began the colonization at once. Under the terms of the new concession Stephen Austin was authorized to bring in as many as three hundred families the first year provided that they were of good moral character, would profess the Roman Catholic religion, and agreed to abide by Mexican law. No maximum was set on future immigration into Texas, and, in fact, other concessionaires were awarded similar grants.

The influx of Americans into Texas was tremendous. The land was practically free—only ten cents an acre as opposed to $1.25 an acre for inferior land in the United States. Each male colonist over twenty-one years of age was allowed to purchase 640 acres for himself, 320 acres for his wife, 160 acres for each child and, significantly, an additional 80 acres for each slave that he brought with him. As a further enticement the colonists were given a seven-year exemption from the payment of Mexican taxes. By 1827 there were twelve thousand United States citizens living in Texas, outnumbering the Mexican population by some five thousand. By 1835 the immigrant population had reached thirty thousand, while the Mexican population had barely passed 7,800.

The Mexican government originally believed that immigrants from the United States could be integrated into the Mexican community and passed a number of laws to foster this integration. In addition to the requirement that the colonists be Roman Catholic, all official transactions were to be concluded in the Spanish language, no foreigners would be allowed to settle within sixty miles of the national boundary, and foreigners who married Mexican citizens could be eligible for extra land. All governmental efforts to encourage peaceful integration failed, however, as tensions rose between the Mexicans, always more and more in the minority, and the immigrants. The colonists who came were not, by and large, Roman Catholics; furthermore, a number of them were fugitives from U.S. justice. Political, religious, and cultural conflict did not take long to surface.

One major grievance of the Texans was that the province was appended politically to the state of Coahuila, which had nine times its population. Although Texans were easily outvoted by the Coahuilans on issues they considered crucial. In addition, all appellate courts were located far away in Saltillo, and the time and expense involved in carrying out an appeal completely discouraged the use of the judicial machinery.

But the Mexicans had serious grievances as well. A number of fili-
bustering expeditions from the United States, like that of Tennessean
James Long, prompted genuine fear that the United States government was bent on securing the Texas territory for itself. Although
Long's army was subsequently defeated by the Mexicans, clamor in the
U.S. Congress and in the American press for changing the boundary
or for acquiring much or all of Texas through a new treaty or by stealth
excited apprehensions in Mexico City.

As Mexican politicians began to realize that their problems in Texas
were getting out of hand, they passed laws to prevent a further weak-
ening of Mexican control. Because slavery was not important anywhere
else in the republic, President Guerrero's emancipation proclamation
of 1829 was clearly directed at Texas. Although manumission was not
immediately enforced, it was hoped that the decree itself would make
Mexico less attractive to colonists from the U.S. South and would thus
arrest future immigration. More important was the colonization law of
April 6, 1830, which explicitly forbade all future immigration into Texas
from the United States and called for the strengthening of Mexican
garrisons, the improvement of economic ties between Texas and the
remainder of Mexico by the establishment of a new coastal trade, and
the encouragement of increased Mexican colonization.

Texans considered these measures repressive, but the last straw for
them was receipt of the news from Mexico City that Santa Anna had ar-
bitrarily annulled the federal Constitution of 1824. The centralist tendencies of the new regime meant that, instead of having a greater voice
in the management of local affairs, the Texans were to have no voice at
all. As the Texas leaders began to debate their future course of action,
they were urged to separate themselves not only by United States expansionists, who argued theatrically that the Texans should detach themselves from the yoke of dictatorship, but also by a number of Mexican
liberals opposed to everything Santa Anna stood for. Among the latter,
the most active was Lorenzo de Zavala, a leader of the Constitutional
Congress of 1823–24, a founder of the York Rite lodges, and most recently a Mexican minister to France. When Santa Anna took all governmental powers into his own hands, Zavala advised the Texans that the
dictator had forfeited all claims to obedience. The Texans needed little
prompting, however; they declared independence and chose David Burnet as president of the Lone Star Republic and Zavala as vice-president.

THE WAR FOR TEXAS INDEPENDENCE

It was time for Santa Anna to take the field again. In the winter of
1835 he moved north at the head of some six thousand troops. But be-

cause of innumerable difficulties during the long trek it was not until early March 1836 that he reached the outskirts of San Antonio de Béxar (today San Antonio) and found that the Texans, under the command of William Barrett Travis, had taken refuge in the old Franciscan mission of the Alamo. Among them were such Texas patriots as Davy Crockett and Jim Bowie, as well as Mexicans who opted for independence. The essentials of what happened on March 6 are known to every schoolchild both north and south of the Rio Grande (called the Río Bravo in Mexico), though the distortions of nationalism have taken their toll on the history in both countries.

For several days prior to March 6, 1836, Santa Anna had laid siege to the Alamo. The high, stout walls seemed impregnable, and the defenders were not about to surrender to the greatly superior Mexican force. On the late afternoon of March 5 the Texans might have heard a bugle, but most assuredly they did not recognize the sounds coming over the walls as the *degüello*, a battle call used since the time of the Spanish wars against the Moors to signal that the engagement to follow was to be to the death, with no quarter to be shown the enemy. The order had come directly from Santa Anna, and he planned to enforce it.

The next morning the Mexican commander threw waves of soldiers against the adobe fortress. Hundreds were cut down by heavy artillery, but after the first hour the numerical superiority of the attackers began to tell. Several breaches were opened in the wall, and the fighting continued inside. The defenders were killed to the last man, including five who were executed as prisoners after the fighting had ended. The high toll on both sides underscored that a peaceful settlement was impossible.

While the battle of the Alamo is famous in the military annals and folklore of the Texas Revolution, a much more significant episode took place several weeks later. General José Urrea engaged a force of Texans under the command of Colonel James W. Fannin at the small town of Goliad. Surrounded and outnumbered, Fannin surrendered in the belief that he and his men would be afforded the recognized rights of prisoners of war. General Urrea wrote to Santa Anna urging clemency for Fannin and the other prisoners, then moved on to another engagement, leaving the Texas prisoners in the charge of Lieutenant Colonel Nicolás de la Portilla. Using the national law of piracy as his authority, Santa Anna sent his reply to Portilla on March 23, stating that the prisoners were to be treated as pirates and executed. Nicolás de la Portilla found himself in the position of many a military commander from the Peloponnesian War to Vietnam. His military duty conflicted directly with his moral principles. In his diary he recorded his two terrible days. On March 26, conflicting orders from Urrea and

Santa Anna reached him—the latter instructing him to execute all the prisoners immediately.

> What a cruel contrast in these opposite instructions! I spent a restless night.
>   March 27. At daybreak I decided to carry out the orders of the general-in-chief because I considered them superior. I assembled the whole garrison and ordered the prisoners, who were still sleeping, to be awakened. There were [365]. . . . The prisoners were divided into three groups and each was placed in charge of an adequate guard. . . . I gave instructions to these officers to carry out the orders of the supreme government and the general-in-chief. This was immediately done.[1]

The month following the battles of the Alamo and Goliad was one of reorganization for the Texas army. Although Santa Anna could take heart from the early military campaigns, and although he had Sam Houston and the Texans on the run, his victories proved to be costly ones. The excesses committed by his troops in both engagements, but especially the execution of the prisoners at Goliad, crystalized opposition to Mexico in the United States. Supplies and men began to pour into Texas, and by the third week in April Houston caught Santa Anna's troops off guard near the San Jacinto River on April 21. Within half an hour the Mexican army was routed, and Santa Anna himself fled for safety. Two days later he was captured by one of Houston's patrols.

THE LONE STAR REPUBLIC

As a prisoner Santa Anna signed two treaties, one public and one private, with Texas President David Burnet. In the public treaty he agreed that he would not again take up arms against the movement for Texas independence nor would he try to persuade his fellow Mexicans to do so. All hostilities between Mexico and Texas were to cease immediately, and the Mexican army would be withdrawn across the Rio Grande. Prisoners of war in equal numbers would be exchanged. From the Mexican point of view, the secret agreement, later made public, was much more controversial. In return for his own release and transportation to Veracruz, Santa Anna agreed to prepare the Mexican cabinet to receive a peace mission from Texas so that the independence of the Lone Star Republic

---

1. Quoted in Carlos E. Castañeda, ed. and trans., *The Mexican Side of the Texas Revolution* (Dallas, 1928), p. 236n.

could be formally recognized.

When he returned to Mexico, Santa Anna discovered that the treaties had prompted outrage from the intellectual community, the liberals, and many ardent nationalists. His sensitivities dazed, Santa Anna was on the defensive, and from his seclusion at Manga de Clavo he offered the excuse that he had made the promises as an individual and that they were not binding on the government. The legislature responded by enacting a law stipulating that any agreement reached by a Mexican president while held prisoner should be considered null and void. No peace commission from Texas was to be received, and no recognition would be extended.

Texas remained independent as the Lone Star Republic from 1836 to 1845. On the surface it would appear preposterous that without the direct support of the United States, Texas should have been able to retain this independent status in face of greatly superior Mexican resources and manpower. But Mexico was so racked with internal convulsions during these nine years that it was unable to bring Texas back

Santa Anna as a prisoner of Sam Houston. The Mexican victory at the Alamo was offset by Santa Anna's defeat and capture following the battle of San Jacinto.

into the fold. The Texas issue, in fact, served to magnify political tensions in Mexico.

The United States recognized the independence of Texas in March 1837. Although there was a good deal of sympathy for immediate annexation in both Texas and the United States Congress, calmer heads prevailed for eight years. Not only did many congressmen believe that annexation would provoke war with Mexico, but the matter became inexorably entangled in the slavery issue. If Texas entered the Union it would come in as a slave state, and, as a result, annexation was generally opposed by the North. In 1844, however, James K. Polk won the presidency on a platform that included annexation. After the election, but prior to Polk's inauguration, President John Tyler had an annexation measure introduced as a joint resolution of Congress. It passed both houses in early 1845. The stage was set for a major conflict, and Mexico was clearly being swept into the vortex of war.

THE PRELUDE TO WAR

As soon as the joint resolution annexing Texas passed the U.S. Congress, the Mexican minister in Washington lodged a formal protest and asked for his passport. Within a month his counterpart in Mexico City had received his passport as well. As diplomatic relations were ruptured, both countries began preparing for war. The Mexican government sought to negotiate a new loan, the proceeds of which would be directed into the war effort, if, indeed, the conflict occurred. It also authorized the formation of a new voluntary civilian militia to reinforce regular army units. President Polk ordered army troops into the border region and dispatched naval vessels to the Mexican coast. But he asked the Mexican president, José Joaquín Herrera, to receive a special envoy in Mexico City, and Herrera agreed to receive John Slidell.

The specific issue Slidell was asked to negotiate was a boundary dispute in Texas. Throughout the entire colonial period the western boundary of Texas had been the Nueces River. The Austin family's grants also recognized the Nueces as the western boundary of Texas. Yet despite of thousands of Spanish colonial documents, Mexican documents, and all reliable maps, in December 1836 the Congress of the Republic of Texas claimed the Rio Grande as the western boundary. The Texans based their claim on two flimsy grounds. During the period of Texas colonization the Mexican government had allowed some United States immigrants to settle in the territory between the Nueces and the Rio Grande. It was all Mexico, so it really did not matter. Second, and even more important for the Texas argument, when Santa Anna agreed to withdraw his troops following his stunning defeat at San Jacinto, he ordered them back across the Rio Grande, tacit admission, so the Texans cried, that the western boundary was indeed the Rio Grande. At stake were not merely the 150 miles between the Nueces and the Rio Grande where they entered the Gulf of Mexico. The Rio Grande meandered aimlessly not north, but northwest, and the Texans claimed it to its source. Thousands and thousands of square miles of territory, indeed, half of New Mexico and Colorado, fell within the claim. When Texas entered the Union as the twenty-eighth state, the Polk administration decided to support the Texan pretensions. Albuquerque, Santa Fe, and Taos belonged to the United States as well as San Antonio, Nacogdoches, and Galveston.

But the American president wanted still more. Slidell also carried secret instructions to secure California and the rest of New Mexico. Five million dollars was deemed a fair price for the New Mexico territory and $25 million, or even more, for California. But diplomatic secrets had a way of leaking out, even in the middle of the nineteenth century. The Mexican press, learning the true nature of the Slidell mission, appealed to Mexican nationalism; newspapers, circulars, and broadsides threatened rebellion if President Herrera negotiated with

UNITED STATES–TEXAS BORDER DISPUTE

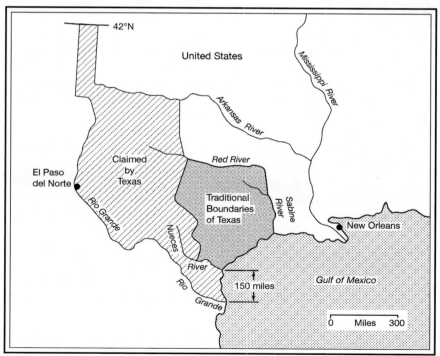

the ignominious Yankee pirates. The insecure Herrera ended discussions with Slidell. Still, Mexico could not present a united front. General Mariano Paredes, dispatched north to reinforce Mexican troops along the border, decided to overthrow the government and had himself installed in the highest office. What an inviting picture northern Mexico presented to the expansionists of the United States!

When Slidell returned to Washington, President Polk held a special cabinet meeting to weigh war feeling. Influential voices cautioned against precipitate action, but the president had already made up his mind. Nonetheless, Secretary of the Navy George Bancroft and Secretary of State James Buchanan would not vote for a declaration of war unless the United States was attacked by Mexico. By a strange quirk of history, hostilities began that very day. Polk had already ordered General Zachary Taylor into the disputed territory between the Nueces and the Rio Grande. The Mexican commander ordered him to withdraw, but instead Taylor penetrated all the way to the Rio Grande. While the cabinet was meeting, a skirmish broke out between Taylor's dragoons and General Mariano Arista's cavalry. On the evening of May 9 Taylor reported to Washington that sixteen of his men had been killed or wounded. Polk now had the perfect excuse. He went before the Congress and delivered a provocative war message that bore little resemblance to the truth.

> We have tried every effort at reconciliation. The cup of forbearance had been exhausted even before the recent information from the frontier of the Del Norte. But now, after reiterated menaces, Mexico has passed the boundary of the United States, has invaded our territory, and shed American blood on American soil. She has proclaimed that hostilities exist, and that the two nations are now at war.[2]

With a provision limiting debate to two hours, the declaration of war was stampeded through Congress. How different things looked from Mexico City: not only had the Americans taken Texas, but they had changed the traditional boundary to double its size! When the Mexicans sought to defend themselves against the additional encroachment, the Yankees cried that Mexico had invaded the United States! But there was little time for contemplation of moral issues, and the Mexican nation was as divided as ever. In the still factionalized political milieu, the army overthrew President Paredes and invited Santa Anna back from his most recent exile. The general who had fought the

---

2. Quoted in Armin Rappaport, ed., *The War with Mexico: Why Did It Happen?* (New York, 1964), p. 6.

Spanish in 1829, the Texans in 1836, and the French in 1838 would lead his fellow countrymen against the Americans in 1846.

THE COURSE OF THE WAR

Because President Polk, despite a good deal of opposition, was able to move more decisively than the ephemeral governments in Mexico City, Mexico from the outset was on the defensive. The American strategy called for a three-pronged offensive. The Army of the West would occupy New Mexico and California; the Army of the Center would be sent into northern Mexico; and the Army of Occupation would carry the battle to Mexico City. General Stephen W. Kearny, commanding the Army of the West, got under way first. Leaving Fort Leavenworth, Kansas, with some fifteen hundred men in June of 1846, he began the nine-hundred-mile trek toward Santa Fe. Governor Manuel Armijo, not a favorite in the Mexican history textbooks, either accepted a bribe or was afraid to make a stand. He ordered his three thousand troops to evacuate the town shortly before the Americans arrived on August 19. New Mexico had fallen without the firing of a single shot.

Kearny then divided his Army of the West into three. One contingent, under Colonel Sterling Price, continued the occupation of Santa Fe; a second, under Alexander Doniphan, was dispatched directly south to Chihuahua; Kearny himself led the third west to California. California was almost a repeat of New Mexico. By the time Kearny arrived it was already in American hands, having fallen to Naval Commodore John D. Sloat and Colonel John C. Frémont with little opposition. Doniphan, on the other hand, had to engage the enemy in Chihuahua. The major battle, fought on the Sacramento River on the outskirts of Chihuahua City, was an artillery duel. Doniphan won the battle, and by February 1847 Chihuahua was under American control. Chihuahuenses were treated to the spectacle of American troops bathing in public fountains, cutting down boulevard shade trees for firewood, and singing "Yankee Doodle" in the main plaza.

The successes of Zachary Taylor's Army of the Center were not so easily won. Taylor's force, some six thousand strong, moved on Monterrey in August 1846. By September they were in sight of the city but were blocked off by the seven thousand Mexicans under General Pedro de Ampudia guarding the entrance. Three days of fierce battle were recorded in the middle of the month. Heavy losses were sustained on both sides before Ampudia sent up the white flag and surrendered the city. By this time Santa Anna had raised an army of about twenty thousand men and was training them in San Luis Potosí. The

UNITED STATES INVASION, 1846–48

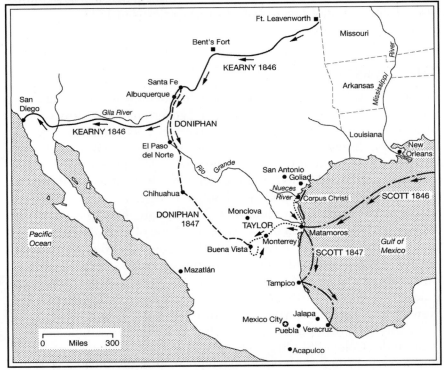

hard march to Saltillo was disastrous. Insufficient food and water supplies and an unusually harsh winter not only weakened the men but prompted thousands of desertions along the way. Preliminary fighting on February 21 saw Santa Anna force Taylor to pull in his perimeters. The following morning Santa Anna brazenly demanded that Taylor surrender. "Tell Santa Anna to go to Hell," Taylor barked to an aide, but the message actually sent observed proper military niceties and read, "In reply to your note of this date summoning me to surrender my forces at discretion, I beg leave to say that I decline acceding to your request."[3]

The battle of Buena Vista began in earnest later in the day. Santa Anna's assaults on Taylor's well-fortified positions did a good deal of damage, but all were repulsed. Evening found a stalemate. Santa Anna could have attacked again the following morning but instead decided to gather up a few war trophies—a few flags and three cannon—and

3. Quoted in Charles L. Dufour, *The Mexican War: A Compact History* (New York, 1968), p. 172.

carry them back to Mexico City as proof of his smashing victory. In reality, northeast Mexico had been lost to the invaders.

The major United States offensive, however, was waged by General Winfield Scott's Army of Occupation. As Mexico refused to abandon the fight, the United States resolved to carry the battle to Mexico's heartland and to the capital itself. Making his amphibious landing on March 9, 1847, slightly to the south of the harbor of Veracruz, General Scott and his ten thousand men were not opposed as they established their beachhead. Veracruz, for centuries an object of foreign invasion and attack, was a walled city currently garrisoned by four thousand troops. Scott decided to avoid the fortress of San Juan de Ulloa with its twelve hundred troops. By ordering his troops to surround the city and attack from the rear, he not only neutralized the harbor fortress but also cut off the city's source of land supplies and all avenues of exit. Militarily sound, but morally questionable, the plan of attack called for a heavy mortar bombardment of the city that resulted in the deaths of hundreds of innocent civilians. For the next forty-eight hours Scott devastated the city and refused all entreaties of foreign consuls to allow women, children, and other noncombatants to evacuate. He would countenance no manner of truce not accompanied by unconditional surrender.

With military and medical supplies diminished, hundreds of civilian corpses building up in the streets, fires gutting buildings, hospitals de-

The U.S. Navy's bombardment of Veracruz resulted in extremely high civilian casualties.

stroyed, and the frightening specter of a yellow-fever epidemic mounting, Veracruz surrendered on March 27. Sixty-seven Americans had
been killed or wounded, while the toll of Mexican dead within the city
was between one thousand and fifteen hundred. Civilian casualties outnumbered military casualties almost two to one.

Santa Anna had reached Mexico City when news of the loss of Veracruz arrived. He set out to block General Scott's expected advance
on the capital. His troops engaged Scott's force in mid-April and were
routed at the mountain pass of Cerro Gordo, some twenty miles east
of Jalapa. Santa Anna himself barely escaped capture. He wanted to
make one more stand, at Puebla, but the citizenry there refused to cooperate. Scott took the city unopposed.

As Scott rested in Puebla the citizens of Mexico City began brac-
ing themselves for the imminent attack. The destruction of Veracruz
was well known, and apprehension set in. But not even in the light of
this crisis did the politicos in Mexico City join forces. The states would
not provide money and men for a national government they distrusted.
The city council in the capital originally pledged the support of all municipal employees in the work of constructing fortifications but then
withdrew the pledge, arguing to the federal government that there was
no way to defend Mexico City. The government simply placed the Federal District under martial law and began conscripting a civilian work
force to help in the defense preparations.

As might be expected, the battles for control of Mexico City were
the most monumental of the war. The major preliminary engagements
were fought on the outskirts where the Americans proved superior in
leadership, armament, and tactics. At Churubusco, however, the Mexicans had their finest hour. Fighting bravely, they refused to yield
ground to the larger and better-equipped fighting force. The issue was
finally resolved by intense hand-to-hand combat in which the Mexicans were at last worn down. On August 20, Scott asked for a surrender. Santa Anna agreed to negotiate and used the respite to shore up
his defenses within the city itself. When the armistice expired without
positive result, Santa Anna was in a position to do battle again.

On the morning of September 7, Scott's cavalry charged Mexican
positions at Molina del Rey, and the infantry moved in behind. It was
the bloodiest single encounter of the war, as the Mexicans suffered
over two thousand casualties and the Americans over seven hundred.
When the position fell there was only one fortified position left in the
city—Chapultepec Castle. Located at the crest of a two-hundred-foot
hill and surrounded by a thick stone wall, the castle was defended by
some one thousand troops and the cadets of the Military Academy. After a furious artillery barrage failed to dislodge the defenders, Scott

ordered that the castle be stormed on the morning of September 13. The Mexican land mines failed to explode, and the attackers were able to breach the walls with pickaxes and crowbars. The scaling ladders arrived, and the Americans poured over the top and initiated the bitter hand-to-hand combat. The last defenders were the cadets—the *Niños Héroes*—and because dignity proscribed surrender, many died. The battle of Chapultepec ended the war, and the United States government prepared to negotiate a tough peace.

THE TREATY OF GUADALUPE HIDALGO AND THE AFTERMATH OF WAR

After a series of difficult negotiations, the treaty ending the war was signed on February 2, 1848, at the village of Guadalupe Hidalgo, just outside of Mexico City. The treaty confirmed United States title to Texas and ceded the huge California and New Mexico territories as well. In return Mexico was to retain everything south of the Rio Grande. The United States agreed to make a cash payment of $15,000,000 to the Mexican government and to assume $3,250,000 in claims that United States citizens had against that government. For a total of $18,250,000—less than one year's budget—Mexico's territory was reduced by half. Because of Mexican insistence the United States did obligate itself to protect the property of Mexican citizens who, through no fault of their own, suddenly found themselves residing in the United States. During the next fifty years they would learn that United States courts were not always interested in enforcing the solemn protections promised by the treaty.

When the United States signed the Treaty of Guadalupe Hidalgo it did more than annex half of Mexico. The war and its treaty left a legacy of hostility that would not be easily overcome. While many Mexican intellectuals had not been hesitant to praise the United States, its culture, and its institutions prior to 1846, such commendations were increasingly infrequent in the second half of the nineteenth century. Ironically, from the middle of the sixteenth century, Mexican expeditions had been seeking the Gran Quivira in the north, and finally it was found, at Sutter's Fort, but a few months too late. The gold of California would not make Mexican fortunes or pay its share of Mexico's industrial revolution.

The war reinforced the worst stereotypes that each country held about the other, and these stereotypes in turn contributed to the development of deep-seated prejudices. United States historians rationalized, justified, and even commended the decision to wage the war as well as the prosecution of it. On grounds ranging from regenerating a backward people to fulfilling a preordained destiny, they went so far as to use this war of aggression for the purpose of instilling historical pride in generations of American children. Mexican historians, too, stereotyped and distorted. Not content with an understandably vigorous condemnation of the United States government, they pinned responsibility on the American people and the congenital defects of their Anglo-Saxon heritage.

The U.S. war with Mexico yielded a virulent, almost pathological, Yankeephobia. The fears and hatred of the United States ran deep, and nationalist sentiments were disseminated and popularized in the traditional Mexican *corrido*, the folk song of the common people, as well as in intellectual condemmations of Yankee imperialism. The Niños Héroes came to symbolize all that was best in the Mexican people, especially the young cadet Juan Escutia, who reputedly wrapped himself in the Mexican flag and threw himself over the battlements rather than surrender to the enemy. Every September 13 pilgrimages are made to the monument erected in honor of the boy cadets at the entrance to Chapultepec Park.

The treaty signed at Guadalupe Hidalgo left a stunned and despondent Mexico, but the national humiliation brought no more unity than had the war itself. In 1853 the Santanistas rallied for what turned out to be the last hurrah. With the $15 million from the United States already spent, President Santa Anna, not yet humbled by the defeats of his armies, decided that the treasury (and his own office) could be saved only by selling some more of Mexico to the United States. The United States wanted the Mesilla Valley (today southern New Mexico and Arizona) as it offered the best location for building a railroad to newly acquired California. Santa Anna agreed to sell and negotiated what is known in United States history as the Gadsden Purchase. For $10 million he alienated thirty thousand square miles of territory, but, more importantly, he alienated the liberal opposition so thoroughly that they would be rid of him for the eleventh and last time. The revolution the liberals proclaimed, the Revolution of Ayutla, was a new kind of movement, one in which for the first time ideology was clearly more important than personalities. It would usher in a new breed of Mexican politician who would try to set the country on a new course.

FURTHER TROUBLES

The United States was not Mexico's only foreign problem, for between the Texas secession and the war with the United States, Mexico became involved in a war with France. During the unremitting series of revolts and counterrevolts since Independence, the property of foreign nationals was often damaged. Foreign governments then submitted claims in behalf of their own citizens. Among the numerous French claims were those of a French pastry cook whose delicacies were appropriated and consumed by a group of hungry Mexican soldiers in 1828. In ridicule of the event that followed, Mexican journalists immediately dubbed the episode the Pastry War.

Conflicting property evaluations, rapid changes in the Mexican government, and the always near-bankrupt state of the Mexican treasury prevented resolution of the French claims for years. In early 1838 the French king, Louis Philippe, demanded payment of $600,000. When Mexico did not comply, French King Louis Philippe ordered a blockade of the port of Veracruz with a French fleet of twenty-six vessels and over four thousand men. Mexican attempts to negotiate what they believed to be fair compensation ultimately failed, and the government dispatched a thousand men to reinforce the twelve hundred stationed at the venerable, moss-mottled fortress of San Juan de Ulloa in the harbor of Veracruz.

The French initiated their bombardment on the afternoon of November 27, rending a portion of the fortress walls, exploding supplies of ammunition inside, and forcing the Mexican troops to abandon their first line of defense. It was time for Santa Anna, temporarily out of the presidency, to exert himself once again. Proclaiming that God and justice were on the side of Mexico and that honor demanded he take up the challenge, he offered his services to the fatherland, and the Mexican Congress declared war on France.

Santa Anna arrived at Veracruz on December 4; the following morning some three thousand French troops made a landing. In the street fighting that ensued Santa Anna led his troops personally and drove the French back toward the coast. In one of the assaults the Mexican commander had his horse shot out from under him and, in the process, was severely wounded in the left leg. A few days later it was amputated below the knee. The French, however, had been driven back to their ships and, rather than prolong the venture, they agreed to accept the amount of $600,000, earlier offered by the Mexican government.

The Mexicans could take some heart from having defeated the legions of King Louis Philippe, but there was little time for rejoicing. The liberal-conservative struggle continued unabated. Larger and larger armies (a standing army of ninety thousand by 1855) and a huge civilian bureaucracy drained the treasury, while industry and commerce stagnated. Successive governments tried every imaginable expedient to replenish the coffers. Old currencies were recalled and new

INCOME AND EXPENDITURES, 1839–46

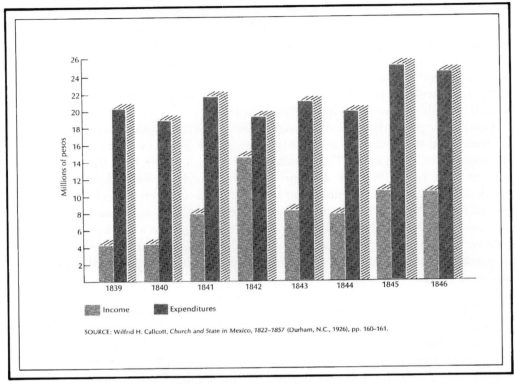

SOURCE: Wilfrid H. Callcott, *Church and State in Mexico, 1822–1857* (Durham, N.C., 1926), pp. 160–161.

ones issued; forced loans were made on businesses and on nunneries and other ecclesiastical corporations; voluntary loans were obtained from private money lenders called *agiotistas*; properties were confiscated; new taxes were levied on carriages, coach wheels, all internal trade, and even on dogs, pulque shops, and the gutters of houses; old taxes on real estate and imports were raised; lucrative mining concessions were sold to the British. In addition, the government declared a head tax of one and one-half pesos annually on all males between the ages of sixteen and sixty. But while Santa Anna raised more money than his predecessors, he also spent more. The average government deficit between 1839 and 1846 was 12.7 million pesos annually.

THE LEGACY OF SANTA ANNA

It is fair to ask if Santa Anna was the cause of Mexico's problems or if Mexico was the cause of Santa Anna's problems. He presided over a brazenly corrupt regime. Bribery was the calling card of those seeking concessions. Santa Anna quickly became a millionaire as he accumulated riches including some 483,000 acres of land. Because local officials studied well the lessons of their superiors, graft and corruption soon penetrated all levels of government. Contraband was rampant, indeed, was encouraged by venal port officials.

Even allowing for the exaggerations of his critics, one must conclude that Santa Anna's lust for power and quest for glory knew no bounds. Until the middle of the nineteenth century, Mexican presidents had been called simply "His Excellency." But Santa Anna had his official designation changed to "His Most Serene Highness." He arranged for gala balls and banquets to be staged in his honor. When a sumptuous new theater was constructed in Mexico City at a cost of 350,000 pesos, it was named the Gran Teatro de Santa Anna. His busts and statues adorned public parks and streets. The presidential home in Tacubaya became a palace.

Salvos of artillery fire and twenty-one-gun salutes preceded the dictator and announced his presence everywhere he went. Congress declared that the small presidential bodyguard was insufficient for a man of his stature and authorized a new guard of twelve hundred men, styled the Lancers of the Supreme Power. Santa Anna's saint's day became a national holiday; friends and favor seekers brought him gifts, totaling several tens of thousands of pesos on a good year. Favorite journalists grasped the occasions to lavish eulogistic editorials, while sycophants in the government delivered orations in honor of His Most Serene Highness. When Santa Anna made awards to others he signed them with an ostentatious display of titles.

But the most bizarre episode of all occurred in the fall of 1842. Santa Anna ordered the disinterment of his amputated leg from its quiet repose on his hacienda of Manga de Clavo. The mummified member was transported to Mexico City and, after an impressive procession through the streets of the capital in which the presidential bodyguard, the army, and the cadets from the Chapultepec Military Academy all participated, it was taken to the cemetery of Santa Fe where it was placed in a specially designed urn and set atop a huge stone pillar. The ceremony was typically Santanesque. Conducted at the site of the shrine, it was attended by the entire cabinet, the diplomatic corps, and the Congress. The speeches, songs, and poems offered in Santa Anna's honor paled all previous efforts at sanctification as the leg shattered by the French cannonball was now being offered to the fatherland.

The Santa Anna dictatorship exacted a heavy price. The only immutable law of the period was that the liberals and conservatives would never agree or compromise on matters of substance. A series of gov-

An 1845 lithograph depicting a one-legged Santa Anna standing on a Manga de Clavo built on extortions of various kinds.

ernments concerned more with show than with development, officials pilfering the treasury with impunity, political factions rife with internal dissension, an economy mired in its own inertia, all militated against progress. Santa Anna himself must bear much of the responsibility. Often clever but never wise, he set an example of dishonesty, deception, and complete failure to adhere to any set of principles. All of his loyalties were mercurial, and the tone he established for the age proved contagious. He was always able to muster sufficient military support to seize the moment but never sufficient political support to seize the hour. The intelligentsia cried out for constructive leadership but did not receive it.

The political atmosphere was still charged with mistrust. Revolts and counterrevolts were accepted as inevitable concomitants of the social order. In Yucatán's Caste War elites drove Maya rebels into remote areas. Although not all Mayas supported the Caste War while some non-Mayas did, the conflict took on a racial character as Mayas called for an end to ethnic discrimination. Maya leaders historically had made alliances with whites, but when these ellites refused, a tenacious group of Maya warriors established a stronghold in today's Quintana Roo. There, they maintained an independent Mayan state until the end of the nineteenth century. Drawing on vibrant Maya cultural traditions and a millenarian cult of the Talking Cross, they established a viable agricultural economy and carried on trade with neighboring British Honduras.

Elsewhere in Mexico some material improvements had been recorded, at least in the larger cities. The textile industry had developed rapidly during the 1840s and 1850s but the retrogressions in the political and economic orders were more noteworthy. Roads were in disrepair, mines were still abandoned, fertile agricultural fields lay vacant, industrialization was but a vague hope for the future, foreign trade was notable only for its absence, and the national debt was growing.

In the end, the greatest misfortune of the age of Santa Anna was the loss of Texas and the war with the United States. These catastrophes contributed more to Mexico's impoverishment, its apparent sterility, its xenophobia, its lack of self-esteem, and its general demoralization than any other event of the nineteenth century.

RECOMMENDED FOR FURTHER STUDY

Alonzo, Armando. *Tejano Legacy: Rancheros and Settlers in South Texas, 1734–1900.* Albuquerque: University of New Mexico Press, 1998.

Callcott, Wilfrid H. *Church and State in Mexico, 1822–1857.* Durham, N.C.: Duke University Press, 1926.

Caruso, Brooke A. *The Mexican Spy Company: United States Covert Operations in Mexico, 1845–1848.* Jefferson, N.C.: McFarland & Co., 1991.

Craib, Raymond B. *Cartographic Mexico: A History of State Fixations and Fugitive Landscapes.* Durham, N.C.: Duke University Press, 2004.

DePalo, William A. *The Mexican National Army, 1822–1852.* College Station: Texas A & M University Press, 1997.

Ducey, Michael T. *A Nation of Villages: Riot and Rebellion in the Mexican Huasteca, 1750–1850.* Tucson: University of Arizona Press, 2004.

Dumond, Don E. *The Machete and the Cross: Campesino Rebellion in Yucatán.* Lincoln: University of Nebraska Press, 1997.

Fowler, Will. *Tornel and Santa Anna: The Writer and the Caudillo, Mexico, 1795–1853.* Westport, Conn.: Greenwood Press, 2000.

Griswold del Castillo, Richard. *The Treaty of Guadalupe Hidalgo: A Legacy of Conflict.* Norman: University of Oklahoma Press, 1990.

Guardino, Peter F. *Peasants, Politics, and the Formation of Mexico's National State: Guerrero, 1800–1867.* Stanford, Calif.: Stanford University Press, 1996.

Hale, Charles A. "The War with the United States and the Crisis in Mexican Thought." *The Americas* 14 (1957): 153–73.

Harris, Charles H., III. *The Sánchez Navarros: A Socioeconomic Study of a Coahuilan Latifundio, 1846–1853.* Chicago: Loyola University Press, 1964.

Jones, Oakah L., Jr. *Santa Anna.* New York: Twayne, 1968.

Kendall, George Wilkins. *Dispatches from the Mexican War.* Norman: University of Oklahoma Press, 1999.

Matovina, Timothy M. *The Alamo Remembered: Tejano Accounts and Perspectives.* Austin: University of Texas Press, 1995,

Pletcher, David M. *The Diplomacy of Annexation: Texas, Oregon, and the Mexican War.* Columbia: University of Missouri Press, 1973.

Randall, Robert W. *Real del Monte: A British Mining Venture in Mexico.* Austin: University of Texas Press, 1972.

Reed, Nelson. *The Caste War of Yucatán.* Stanford, Calif.: Stanford University Press, 1964.

Reséndez, Andrés. *Changing National Identities at the Frontier: Texas and New Mexico, 1800–1850.* Cambridge: Cambridge University Press, 2005.

Richmond, Douglas, ed. *Essays on the Mexican War.* College Station: Texas A & M University Press, 1986.

Robinson, Cecil, ed. *The View from Chapultepec: Mexican Writers on the Mexican American War.* Tucson: University of Arizona Press, 1979.

Rugeley, Terry. *Yucatán's Maya Peasantry and the Origins of the Caste War.* Austin: University of Texas Press, 1996.

Ruiz, Ramón Eduardo, ed. *The Mexican War: Was It Manifest Destiny?* New York: Holt, Rinehart & Winston, 1963.

Samponaro, Frank N. "Santa Anna and the Abortive Anti-Federalist Revolt of 1833 in Mexico." *The Americas* 40 (1983): 95–108.

Santa Anna, Antonio López de. *The Eagle: The Autobiography of Santa Anna.* Austin, Tex.: Pemberton Press, 1967.

Santoni, Pedro. *Mexicans at Arms: Puro Federalists and the Politics of War, 1845–1848.* Fort Worth: Texas Christian University Press, 1996.

Smith, Justin H. *The War with Mexico.* 2 vols. Gloucester, Mass.: Peter Smith, 1963.

Steven, Donald F. *Origins of Instability in Early Republican Mexico.* Durham, N.C.: Duke University Press, 1991.

Tenenbaum, Barbara. *The Politics of Penury: Debts and Taxes in Mexico, 1821–1856.* Albuquerque: University of New Mexico Press, 1986.

Tijerina, Andrés. *Tejanos in Texas under the Mexican Flag, 1821–1836.* College Station: Texas A & M University Press, 1994.

Vázquez, Josefina. "War and Peace with the United States," in *The Oxford History of Mexico.* Edited by Michael C. Meyer and William H. Beezley, pp. 339–69. New York: Oxford University Press, 2000.

19

Society and Culture in the First Half of the Nineteenth Century

It is ironic, yet understandable, that historians seeking to understand how a people lived often rely upon the accounts of foreign travelers. That which is commonplace to a local inhabitant is often colorful or unique to a foreigner. The young Frenchman Alexis de Tocqueville related to the citizens of the United States much that they did not know about themselves, and a series of perceptive visitors to Mexico during the first half of the nineteenth century did the same for its people. While their analyses often reflected their own prejudices, their commentaries are invaluable. One has only to disregard their chauvinism and naïvely antiseptic view of the world to read these accounts with pleasure and profit.

POPULATION

The Mexican Wars for Independence, although small in comparison with other world conflicts, nevertheless took their toll. Accurate casualty figures do not exist, but reliable estimates suggest that a half a million deaths, or about one-twelfth of Mexico's population, is not an exaggeration. The battles left tens of thousands of orphans, widows, cripples, and infirm. The dislocations occasioned by war were not quickly overcome. Impending engagements caused civilians to flee, shopkeepers to close their doors, mothers to pull their children out of school, and those who could afford it to hoard supplies. Many who left a town or city did not return, and families were permanently separated. Several years after the wars ended visitors to Veracruz reported desolate, grass-grown streets and a generally ruinous appearance. Mexico's rate of population growth, which was rapid prior to 1810, leveled off dramatically for the next twenty years.

Although recovery was slow, change in the prevailing social structure was even slower. Reading the accounts of travelers from the late

MEXICAN POPULATION GROWTH, 1800–50

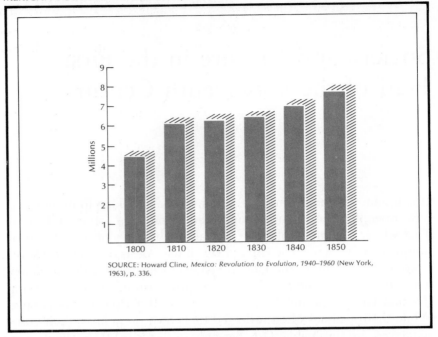

SOURCE: Howard Cline, *Mexico: Revolution to Evolution, 1940–1960* (New York, 1963), p. 336.

colonial period and comparing them to accounts in the nineteenth century, one is struck by how little conditions actually changed. To be sure, the gachupines were eliminated at the top of the social structure, but the criollos simply stepped into the vacuum. The population grew from 4.5 million in 1800 to over 7.5 million fifty years later, but the social categories of that population remained amazingly static.

INDIAN PUEBLOS

Mexico was a rural country in the first half of the nineteenth century. The Indians, making up over a third of the population, lived for the most part in thousands of tiny villages, socially and economically isolated from the remainder of the country. Although these pueblos varied physically from one climate to another, they presented a uniform cultural pattern. Pueblos were the most tradition-bound unit in Mexican society. Each maintained a system of internal government that had changed very little since the early colonial period. With the exception of an occasional parish priest, a white or mestizo rarely lived in the village. In south and central Mexico the huts were made of split reeds covered with thatched roofs. In the north adobe was more common, but in both cases dogs, pigs, and chickens shared the quarters with the family. In 1850 Carl Sartorius, a German natural scientist traveling in Mexico, drew a composite interior from the many Indian dwellings he had seen.

> Inside the hut, upon a floor of earth just as nature formed it, burns day and night the sacred fire of the domestic hearth. Near it, stands the *metate* and *metapile*, a flat and cylindrical stone for crushing the maize, and the earthen pots and dishes, a large water pitcher, a drinking cup and a dipper of gourdshell constitute the whole wealth of the Indian's cottage, a few rude carvings, representing the saints, the decoration. Neither table nor benches cumber the room within, mats of rushes or palm leaves answer for both seat and table. They serve as beds too for their rest at night, and for their final rest in the grave.[1]

Only the larger Indian towns had churches; practically none had schools. Spanish was unknown except to the select few. Medical care, as it existed, was entrusted to the questionable hands of the local *curandero*. The Indian agriculturalist lived outside the monetary economy. His own garden provided his daily needs—corn, beans, chile, and, occasionally, in some areas, squash and a few other vegetables and fruits. The craftsman sometimes had money pass through his hands as he could sell his wares at a neighboring market. But he was scarcely better off than the farmer in the next hut, because, if his money did not vanish in momentary extravagance, he was easy prey to the unscrupulous gambler, pulque vendor, or highwayman as he returned to the pueblo.

The woman in the Indian village was much more than a housekeeper. Even when kept pregnant, she often worked in the field and shared in the physical labor as well as performed all the expected domestic functions. Foreign travelers frequently commented on the heavy loads of firewood the Indian women carried to the hut. Because daily life was difficult, the Indian woman was an integral part of the whole apparatus of survival; nevertheless, rural society was highly patriarchal and the male was the dominant, authoritarian figure in the household as well as in the community. The woman by tradition was expected to be faithful, reverential, and completely obedient in the entire conjugal relationship, and she seldom broke out of this mold, at least in public. She enjoyed a reputation of frugality and from the vil-

---

1. Carl Sartorius, *Mexico about 1850* (Stuttgart, 1961), p. 69.

lage tradition, for practical as well as metaphorical considerations, a phrase was born: *Donde las mujeres comen, las hormigas lloran* (Where women eat, the ants cry).

RURAL TOWNS

The larger rural towns of from a thousand to perhaps thirty-five hundred housed primarily mestizos and Indians who had accommodated themselves to the Hispanic way of life. Spanish was the language of the street and the home. Market day, sometimes weekly and sometimes biweekly, attracted Indians by the hundreds from the surrounding pueblos and provided a festive air. The plaza would be filled with vendors trafficking in cloth, clothing, pottery, cutlery, trinkets, earthenware, and blankets, and with Indian women bent over charcoal fires preparing food for passersby. The day's work finished, the evening hours would be given over to gambling, cards, dancing, and perhaps wagering at the local cockfight. The towns generally had one or two *pulquerías* where hours could be idled away sipping the fermented juice of the century plant, the maguey. For those who found the local shop too depressing or the stench too unbearable, itinerant vendors with full jars on their heads made house calls. Invariably, the church was the most prominent architectural structure in the town. Adorned with a respectable number of saints and a few paintings, the gilded altar stood out in crass contrast to the impoverished surroundings.

If life in the rural towns was somewhat easier than in the Indian pueblo, it still left much to be desired. The streets were dirt, causing dust in the dry season and awful quagmires during the rains. The schools, in those few towns that had them, were equipped with the crudest of facilities, and the teachers were often only slightly more literate than those who sat at their feet. The one-story houses were constructed of adobe or stone and usually left unpainted. Travelers found no hotels, inns, or public restaurants; they were generally put up for the night in the town hall or in the house of a relatively affluent resident who took pity on them. Joel Poinsett, a man who enjoyed his comforts, was not impressed with the facilities he found in a small Veracruz town as he was working his way to Mexico City in 1822.

> We supped on our cold provisions, and stretched ourselves out on the landlady's bed, which did not prove a bed of rest. It consisted only of canes laid lengthways, and covered with a blanket. This, and even the smell of raw meat, might have been endured, but we were visited by

The village of Chalco, southeast of Mexico City, looked much as it had during the colonial period until the railroad passed through during the second half of the nineteenth century.

such swarms of fleas, sancudos, and musquitos [*sic*] that we rejoiced when we saw the light of day beaming through the cane enclosure that constituted the walls of the hut.[2]

The poor males in the towns had one concern that did not trouble those in the Indian village: like their counterparts in the larger cities, they were subject to the dreaded *leva*. A system of forced conscription directed at the uneducated masses (the Indians in the villages were generally excluded simply because they did not speak Spanish), the leva was used by local commanders to fill their military quotas. Troublemakers, vagabonds, and prisoners were taken first, but as the demands of the Wars for Independence, and then the civil wars, continued in the first half of the nineteenth century, tens of thousands of illiterate males were picked up off the streets and pressed into long periods of service without even being allowed to return home to say good-bye to wives, children, and parents.

2. Joel R. Poinsett, *Notes on Mexico Made in the Autumn of 1822, Accompanied by an Historical Sketch of the Revolution* (New York, 1969), pp. 23–24.

Both in the Indian village and the small rural town there was little conception of the larger Mexico. Those loyalties that existed were to the locality—to the patria chica. Contact with the outside world was limited to the occasional traveler passing through or to a body of soldiers on horseback. Mexico was an abstraction not easily fathomed, and even neighbors in the next village were not really trusted.

PROVINCIAL CITIES

One had to visit the larger provincial cities, generally the state capitals, to find any evidence whatsoever of the amenities of wealth and a sense of nationalism. Ranging in population from seven or eight thousand to seventy-one thousand (Puebla in 1852), these cities were well laid out in the classic Spanish pattern. The main streets, paved and well lighted, led into the central plaza surrounded on four sides by the main cathedral, the state or municipal office buildings, and several rows of good shops, generally under a stone arcade. In addition to an impressive selection of native products from many parts of the country, the shops also stocked foreign merchandise; the sizable merchant class thrived. The dreary, repetitive life of the smaller towns was averted by a bullring, a theater, traveling sideshows with tightrope walkers and jugglers, decent book stores, and a wide array of public and religious festivals. Unlike in the pueblo or the rural town, many criollo faces could be picked out of the crowd, and, in fact, if one wandered from the grisly slums to the better residential areas, the complexions of the property owners lightened appreciably. A few provincial aristocrats led lives of primitive plenty, but they were exceptions even among the criollo population. The schools were not bad, but they were only for the wealthy. In 1842, for example, there were only about thirteen hundred schools in all of Mexico. Total enrollment was barely sixty thousand, or less than 1 percent of the population. Only about one-third of the schools were free.

Most of the state capitals grew rapidly in the first half of the nineteenth century. Aguascalientes doubled in population, and Mérida tripled. Veracruz and Guanajuato were almost alone in declining, the former because of constant warfare and heavy bombardments from naval vessels in the harbor and troops on the shore, and the latter because of the generally depressed character of the surrounding mines. By mid-century Puebla and Guadalajara were competing for second place on the nation's population rosters, with Puebla holding a slight lead.

A nineteenth-century woodcut depicting the central plaza of Mérida, Yucatán, about 1850.

MEXICO CITY: THE RICH AND THE POOR

Mexico City was a world unto itself, where all of the richest and many of the poorest in the country seemed to congregate. It was the focal point of the entire nation and exerted an influence on the country quite out of proportion to its size or its political prominence as the national capital. From a population of 137,000 at the turn of the century, it grew to 160,000 at the time of Independence and to 170,000 by 1852. Its wide, clean streets (better lighted than those in New York or Philadelphia) were crowded with expensive imported carriages, a status symbol among the rich. The main cathedral on the central plaza, the zócalo, could certainly rival any in Europe. The very bustle of the city set it apart from any other place in the republic. Street urchins hawked newspapers and pamphlets, scribes sitting on the sidewalks penned out messages for the illiterate, gentlemen on horseback paraded their finest mounts, and foreign artists gathered on park benches to sketch Chapultepec Castle or the snow-covered volcanoes of Popocatépetl and Iztaccíhuatl. In addition to numerous primary and secondary schools (again reserved largely for the affluent), Mexico City housed the venerable University, a school of mines, the Art Academy of San Carlos, a well-endowed botanical garden, libraries, museums, and a surprising number of public parks. By the middle of the century a thriving opera was an integral part of the city's cultural life. The

The urban aristocracy, secular and religious, looked good and lived well despite the political chaos that engulfed Mexico after Independence.

literacy rate, for both men and women, rose modestly during the first half of the nineteenth century.

The Mexico City aristocracy, like their counterparts throughout the world, enjoyed their amenities and were conspicuous in their display of wealth. Many of the homes were truly luxurious. For security and privacy they were generally enclosed by high walls. Interior walls boasted fine imported tapestries. Aristocratic women, whether attending the theater, the opera, or even a high mass, displayed the immodest clothes designed by their favorite French *modiste*, and the men, while not outdoing their wives in fanciful dress, prided themselves on their ability to duplicate the latest fashions from Paris or London. The accumulation of wealth was greatly facilitated by the consistent intermarriage of *la gente decente*.

Describing a ball she attended in 1840, the wife of the Spanish minister to Mexico City noted the female costume:

> One, for example, would have a scarlet satin petticoat, and over it a pink satin robe, trimmed with scarlet ribbons to match. Another, a short rich blue satin dress, beneath which appeared a handsome purple satin petticoat. . . . All had diamonds and pearls . . . I did not see one without earrings, necklace, and broach.[3]

3. Fanny Calderón de la Barca, *Life in Mexico: The Letters of Fanny Calderón de la Barca*, ed. Howard T. Fisher and Marion Hall Fisher (Garden City, N.Y., 1970), pp. 132–33.

The poorest of the poor Indian population was concentrated in the Mexico City districts of Santiago Tlatelolco and San Juan Tenochtitlán, but they spilled over into other areas of the capital. When the upper class filed out of the theater or left the opera they could not fail to see the *léperos*. Described variously in the literature as beggars, vagabonds, panhandlers, riffraff, and outcasts, thousands of them could be seen in the streets of Mexico City every day. Although there were undoubtedly some fakers and reprobates among them, most were genuinely wretched physical specimens: children with bloated bellies, men and women crippled by war or accident or suffering serious genetic deformities, and those of all ages and both sexes in constant drunken stupors. Not unknown in the colonial period, the léperos became institutionally endemic in the first half of the nineteenth century. No foreign traveler to Mexico City failed to notice them. In 1822, for example, Joel Poinsett recorded:

> In front of the churches and in the neighborhood of them we saw an unusual number of beggars, and they openly exposed their disgusting sores and deformities to excite our compassion. I observed one among them wrapped in a large white sheet, who, as soon as he perceived that he had attracted my attention, advanced towards me, and unfolding his covering, disclosed his person perfectly naked and covered from head to heel with ulcers. . . . No city in Italy contains so many miserable beggars, and no town in the world so many blind.[4]

Life for the urban poor who worked rather than begged offered few material rewards. Domestic service, though remuneration was small, was highly sought by both sexes because it generally offered a clean room in which to sleep and food enough to sustain one well. In the streets the most visible employee was the *cargador*, a direct descendant of the tameme of the colonial period and nothing more than a human beast of burden. In the cities, and between the cities, the sight described by Edward Tayloe, Joel Poinsett's private secretary, was common.

> There are no carts or drays for the transportation of goods, so that everything is carried upon the backs of these poor creatures, who are enabled to carry a load of 300 lbs. by means of a leather band or strap, the cargador leaning forward at an angle of about 45°, the burden resting on the back supported by this strap. With so heavy a load they travel great distances, moving in a brisk walk or trot.[5]

---

4. Poinsett, *Notes on Mexico*, p. 73.

5. Edward Thornton Tayloe, *Mexico, 1825–1828: The Journal and Correspondence of Edward Thornton Tayloe*, ed. C. Harvey Gardiner (Chapel Hill, 1959), pp. 50–51.

The cargadores, a legacy of the colonial tamemes, carried everything on their backs.

But the cargador carrying supplies into the city or delivering on his back an imported French piano had little to complain about in comparison to his counterpart who was taken from the city to work in the mines. Employed to bring the ore out of the deep shafts and paid by the pound, the cargadores often carried extremely heavy loads on their backs as they worked their way up ladders. Accidents were frequent; the widows might sometimes be given a small share of the last load.

The Indians and mestizos, whether they lived in a small village or in Mexico City, constituted Mexico's labor force: farmers, servants, day laborers, cargadores, vendors, military recruits, craftsmen, and errand boys. Women worked as domestic servants, spinners in the textile mills, food preparers, waitresses, and as vendors on the streets and in the marketplaces. They suffered a short and tight social leash. If they committed no crime but in some way transgressed anticipated norms of female behavior a magistrate could send them to a *casa de depósito,* a protective institution designed to teach fallen women how to behave. The situation of the male worker was in some ways worse. If accused of a crime, the word of the employer was generally taken and the worker had no recourse. Held in filthy prisons, often without formal charges, the father who stole a loaf of bread was confined in the same common cell with the convicted murderer, the young boy with the hardened criminal, and the physically challenged with the mentally insane. If Mexican politicians in the first half of the nineteenth century did little to change the fabric of society, it was not because the intel-ligentsia failed to urge a new course of action. And it was this very tal-ented group of Mexican writers, musicians, artists, and scholars that made Mexico City so different from the remainder of the republic.

INTELLECTUALS AND ARTISTS

The prime literary current in Mexico, as in all of Latin America, in the period following Independence was romanticism. Intensely concerned with freedom and individualism, the Mexican romantics, in both prose and poetry, set out to explore the meaning of their newly won inde-pendence and to foster a distinctive culture. They turned their backs on Spain and sought to define a new form of national artistic expres-sion. But to understand and convey the nascent nationalism they had to understand their Mexico, and thus they began writing with great emotion and sentimentality about the aboriginal heritage, the physical environment, the wars of Conquest, and, of course, the recent move-ment for Independence.

In 1836 the young novelists, poets, and dramatists began meeting in the newly formed Academia de San Juan de Letrán, and for the next twenty years the academy midwifed the birth of Mexican national lit-erature. Of the early romantic coterie who met there regularly, only two left indelible impressions on the romantic movement itself: Fer-nando Calderón (1809–49) and Ignacio Rodríguez Galván (1816–42). Calderón, a sometime soldier and liberal politician, experimented with lyric poetry, then turned to drama, both comedy and tragedy. His amus-ing satirical plays, some with veiled criticism of the Santa Anna dicta-torship, were performed on the leading stages of Mexico in the 1840s and 1850s and earned him his place among Latin American romantic dramatists. Rodríguez Galván was a better poet than Calderón but less successful as a dramatist. Self-taught and constantly poverty stricken, he penned patriotic verse and described the Mexican landscape, but, most important, lamented the Spanish injustices against the Indian populations. In the process he won his position as Mexico's foremost lyrical poet of the first half of the nineteenth century. His *Profecía de Guatimoc* (1839) has been called the masterpiece of Mexican roman-ticism. The passion, the sentimentality, and the anti-Spanish, pro-Indian orientation are exemplified in the following verse:

> Nada perdona el bárbaro europeo.
> Todo lo rompe, y tala, y aniquila
> Con brazo furibundo.

> Es su placer en fúnebres desiertos
> Las ciudades trocar (¡ Hazaña honrosa!).
> Ve el sueño con desdén, si no reposa
> Sobre insepultos muertos.[6]

Mexican music, like its literature, rejected its Spanish parentage in the early post-Independence years. Nowhere is this more graphically illustrated than in the decision of José Mariano Elízaga (1786–1842), Mexico's most famous composer of the second quarter of the nineteenth century, to drop the title "Don" (signifying the Spanish gentleman) from his name. Once the Spanish army was driven back across the Atlantic, the composer informed the Mexican populace that henceforth he preferred to be called simply Citizen Elízaga.

By sheer chance Elízaga, during the Wars for Independence, was the piano tutor to Anna María Huarte, who subsequently married Agustín de Iturbide. With the defeat of the Spanish and the establishment of the empire, Iturbide brought him to Mexico City and underwrote the preparation of Elízaga's theoretical treatise, *Elementos de música*. But Elízaga is remembered less as a musical theoretician than for his original compositions and great organizing skills. His compositions were all designed for use in the churches, but the liturgy was much too radical for the conservative, Spanish-thinking hierarchy. As a result his masses and lamentations were never performed within the walls of the church. But Citizen Elízaga did encounter success in an important ancillary venture. In 1824 he founded Mexico's first philharmonic society, and the following year this group initiated Mexico's first national conservatory, the Academia de Música.

The Mexican artistic community strove for a type of new nationalistic expression as well. Scarcely had the new republican government of Guadalupe Victoria been established when Pedro Patiño Ixtolinque, the general director of the Art Academy of San Carlos and Mexico's most famous sculptor, set to work on a monument honoring Father Morelos. An early American visitor to the academy was impressed with

---

6.   The barbarous European forgives nothing.
   He breaks and he destroys and he annihilates
   With a frenzied arm.
      He takes pleasure in converting cities
   Into desert wastes (Honorable, indeed!).
   He views sleep with contempt if he cannot rest
   On unburied bodies.

   Quoted in John Lloyd Read, *The Mexican Historical Novel, 1826–1910* (New York, 1939), p. 59.

its facilities but, displaying a common anti-Catholic bias, also found fault: "Connected with this academy is a disgusting sort of work shop, where gods and saints are manufactured in wood and stone for the churches in town and country."[7]

Both in painting and the plastic arts the rejection of Spain and many things Spanish was abundantly evident, much more in the choice of theme, however, than in esthetic innovation. If the emulation of Spanish technique bordered on the abject, the selection of subject matter showed the budding of a Mexican consciousness. Although the young republic housed a few artists of unusual talent, the three decades following Independence were not particularly distinguished years for Mexican art. Within the century, however, the experimentation with native Mexican themes would pay dividends.

Of all the great Mexican historians of the post-Independence years only one—Lucas Alamán (1792–1853)—did not allow an anti-Spanish bias to vitiate his historical scholarship, but he was no less partisan than his ideological foes. A criollo aristocrat, a convinced monarchist, and a firsthand witness to the excesses committed by Hidalgo's Indian army in Guanajuato, he came to the defense of the Spanish officials and, by logical extension, of the Spanish crown. His five-volume *Historia de México* (1849–52) indicates clearly that he considered Cortés the conveyer of civilization and religion and the founder of the Mexican nation. Spain's imperial system in the New World was benevolent and progressive. The Wars for Independence, according to Alamán, had to be viewed in two stages. The early stage, that of Father Hidalgo, he censured as an insane attack on property and civilization itself. But the conservative conclusion of the Independence movement by Iturbide could be rationalized. The mother country, defying all true Hispanic values, had turned disturbingly liberal with King Ferdinand's acceptance of the Constitution of 1812. The leadership of the Independence movement in the colonies was actually defending traditionally Hispanic values but had to sever political ties to do so.

But Lucas Alamán stands almost alone in the historiography of the 1830s and 1840s. His contemporaries, Carlos María de Bustamante, Lorenzo de Zavala, and José María Luis Mora, viewed history quite differently. While they could not agree among themselves on many of the intricacies of the Wars for Independence, they all viewed the movement as a struggle against three centuries of Spanish tyranny. The Black Legend, stressing the avarice, inhumanity, and bigotry of the Spaniards,

---

7. Tayloe, *Mexico, 1825–1828*, p. 58.

is not difficult to spot. The Independence movement was a repudiation of Spain, and the three histories mirroring this repudiation contributed in their own way to the cultural disavowal of the Hispanic part of the Mexican spirit. This pervasive anti-Hispanism was strongly reinforced by Spain's attempted reconquest in 1829.

The greatest weakness of Mexico's post-Independence culture was its essentially negative quality. The new nationalism was defined primarily in terms of what it was not—it was not Spanish. Mexico, the linguistic purist insisted, should be written not with the Spanish *j* but with an *x*, considered more Indian. The cultural nationalism expressed dissatisfaction with the past and, by extension, with much of the present but did not spell out precisely the direction in which Mexico ought to move. It was sufficient for the time being to propose that an anti-Hispanic intellectual emancipation should follow the political emancipation begun by Hidalgo. The more positive approach in defining the cultural essence of the new nationality would have to await another generation of Mexican intellectuals and artists.

RECOMMENDED FOR FURTHER STUDY

Arrom, Silvia Marina. *The Women of Mexico City*. Stanford, Calif.: Stanford University Press, 1985.

Brushwood, John S. *Mexico in Its Novel: A Nation's Search for Identity*. Austin: University of Texas Press, 1966.

Calderón de la Barca, Fanny. *Life in Mexico: The Letters of Fanny Calderón de la Barca*. Edited by Howard T. Fisher and Marion Hall Fisher. Garden City, N.Y.: Doubleday, 1970.

Caponigri, A. Robert, trans. *Major Trends in Mexican Philosophy*. Notre Dame, Ind.: University of Notre Dame Press, 1966.

Fernández, Justino. *Mexican Art*. London: Spring Books, 1965.

Gilmore, N. Ray. "The Condition of the Poor in Mexico, 1834." *Hispanic American Historical Review* 37 (1957): 213–26.

González, Deena. *Refusing the Favor: The Spanish-Mexican Women of Santa Fe, 1820–1880*. New York: Oxford University Press, 1999.

Green, Stanley C. *The Mexican Republic: The First Decade, 1823–1832*. Pittsburgh, Pa.: University of Pittsburgh Press, 1987.

Guardino, Peter. *The Time of Liberty: Popular Political Culture in Oaxaca, 1750–1850*. Durham, N.C.: Duke University Press, 2005.

Hale, Charles A. *Mexican Liberalism in the Age of Mora, 1821–1853*. New Haven, Conn.: Yale University Press, 1968.

Martin, Luis. "Lucas Alamán: Pioneer of Mexican Historiography." *The Americas* 32 (1975): 239–56.

Olivera, Ruth R., and Liliane Crete. *Life in Mexico under Santa Anna, 1822–1855*. Norman: University of Oklahoma Press, 1991.

Penyak, Lee M. "Safe Harbors and Compulsory Custody: *Casas de Depósito* in Mexico, 1750–1865." *Hispanic American Historical Review* 79 (1999): 83–99.

Poinsett, Joel R. *Notes on Mexico Made in the Autumn of 1822, Accompanied by an Historical Sketch of the Revolution.* New York: Praeger, 1969.

Sartorius, Carl. *Mexico about 1850.* Stuttgart: F. A. Brockhaus Komm, 1961.

Shaw, Frederick J. "The Artisan in Mexico City (1824–1853)," in *Labor and Laborers through Mexican History.* Edited by Elsa Cecilia Frost, Michael C. Meyer, and Josefina Zoraida Vásquez, pp. 399–418. Mexico City and Tucson: El Colegio de México and University of Arizona Press, 1979.

Stevenson, Robert. *Music in Mexico: A Historical Survey.* New York: Crowell, 1971.

Tayloe, Edward Thornton. *Mexico, 1825–1828: The Journal and Correspondence of Edward Thornton Tayloe.* Edited by C. Harvey Gardiner. Chapel Hill: University of North Carolina Press, 1959.

Ward, Henry G. *Mexico in 1827.* 2 vols. London: Colburn, 1828.

Warren, Richard A. *Vagrants and Citizens: Politics and the Masses in Mexico City from Colony to Republic.* Wilmington, Del.: Scholarly Resources, 2001.

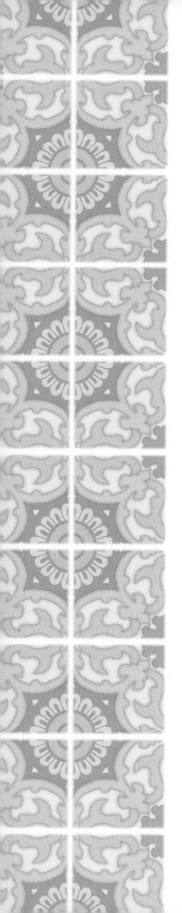

VI

LIBERALS AND CONSERVATIVES SEARCH FOR SOMETHING BETTER, 1855–76

20

The Reform and the French Intervention

THE REVOLUTION OF AYUTLA

The Revolution of Ayutla, the armed movement that ousted Santa Anna from power in 1855, brought together some of the most original and creative minds in Mexico. Far from being ivory tower scholars, they were a group of writers and intellectuals who syncretized their own creative work with a spirit of public service, a sense of social consciousness, and a profound desire to see Mexico emerge at last from its long night of political shame. Humiliated by the war with the United States, they sought to re-evaluate the Mexican national conscience and redefine national goals. Secularly oriented and antimilitarist, they deeply mistrusted the church hierarchy and had little use for the ambitious, self-serving Mexican army.

Influenced by the European Enlightenment and French philosophy, attorney Melchor Ocampo practiced law, began farming scientifically, cataloged flora and fauna, studied Indian languages, and collected one of the best private libraries in Mexico. He also made the decision to enter politics. In the 1840s and 1850s he served as governor of Michoacán and as a congressman in the national legislature. Shortly after the war with the United States he won acclaim when he became involved in a virtual death struggle with the clergy of Michoacán. The issue—the refusal of a local curate to bury the body of a penniless peón because the widow could not pay the sacramental fees—became a *cause célèbre* and was used effectively by Ocampo to demonstrate the ineptitude and decadence of the ecclesiastical effort.

Other liberals took up the cause of denouncing corruption in both church and state. Among them were Santos Degollado, who also served briefly as governor of Michoacán, and Guillermo Prieto, the son of a Mexico City baker, who edited *El Siglo XIX* and popularized the anti-Santa Anna cause. Both were persecuted by the government which forced them into jail or exile.

But the real leader of the young, socially motivated intellectuals, and the personification of Mexican history in the two decades following mid-century, was Benito Juárez, a Zapotec Indian from the state of Oaxaca. Born on March 21, 1806, in the mountain village of San Pablo Guelatao, Juárez was orphaned at the age of three and raised by an uncle. Only a handful of the 150 villagers knew any Spanish, and Juárez had learned but a few words when, at the age of twelve, he left the adobe hut in the Zapotec village and walked forty-one miles to the state capital. An older sister working as a cook in Oaxaca City found employment for the boy in the home of a Franciscan lay brother who was a part-time bookbinder. In return for daily chores in the house and helping in the bindery, the Franciscan paid Juárez's tuition so that the boy could begin his schooling. At his benefactor's insistence he entered the seminary in Oaxaca but quickly realized that the priesthood was not his calling. He opted instead for the law and worked his way through law school, graduating in 1831.

That year he entered political life on the Oaxaca city council and subsequently served in the state legislature. But he did not abandon his career as a barrister and defended, without fee, groups of poor villagers challenging the exorbitant rates charged by the clergy for the sacraments or protesting the arbitrary dictates of the local hacendado class. Not notably successful in his legal campaign to make the lives of the poor easier, the self-effacing attorney now realized that only structural alteration of the system could effect the changes he envisioned, and his liberalism strengthened.

When war broke out between Mexico and the United States, Juárez, a delegate in the national Congress in Mexico City, was recalled to his home state to serve a term as provisional governor. Later the defeated and disgraced Santa Anna sought refuge in Oaxaca, but Governor Juárez let him know he was not welcome there. In 1848 Oaxaqueños elected Juárez to a full term as constitutional governor. The Juárez governorship was far from revolutionary, but he did give the state a genuine lesson in energetic, honest, and sound management. Not only did he preside over the construction of fifty new rural schools and encourage female attendance, but he also sought to open the state up to world trade by rehabilitating the abandoned Pacific port of Huatulco (today Puerto Angel). Even more amazing for mid-nineteenth-century Mexico he cut back markedly on the huge state bureaucracy and was able to accomplish his material advances while making regular payments on the state debt.

When Santa Anna returned to power for the last time, he moved to deal with the liberal threat. Juárez was arrested and then exiled to New Orleans. When he arrived in the Louisiana city he found that other Mexicans of his ilk had already taken refuge there. José María Mata and Ponciano Arriaga were active members of a revolutionary clique that was led by Melchor Ocampo. Juárez joined the exiles in plotting to overthrow the dictatorship when they decided to cast their lot with an old guerrilla chieftain, Juan Alvarez, then leading an antigovernment rebellion in the state of Guerrero. In 1854, the *Plan de Ayutla* put forth a statement of liberal principles and a long list of grievances against Santa Anna. The plan called for the convocation of a liberal junta to designate an interim president to replace the dictator.

The Revolution of Ayutla rapidly gained strength. In Jalisco, Santos Degollado gathered a formidable rebel army around him. In Nuevo León, Santiago Vidaurri and in Guanajuato, Manuel Doblado pronounced against the dictatorship and joined the Ayutla movement. The exiles in New Orleans helped with arms and ammunition, and in the early summer of 1855 they sent Juárez to Acapulco to join Alvarez as a political aide. With a wide base of support, in August 1853 the liberals forced Santa Anna, whose popularity was at its lowest ebb, to resign and go into exile for the last time.

THE REFORM LAWS

The government established in Mexico was composed primarily of luminaries of the Ayutla Revolution. Juan Alvarez became provisional president; Ignacio Comonfort, secretary of war; Melchor Ocampo, secretary of the treasury; Miguel Lerdo de Tejada, secretary of development; and Benito Juárez, secretary of justice. The provisional presidency of Alvarez marks the beginning of a period in Mexican history remembered as the Reform. For the first time since the Gómez Farías administration in 1833 the liberals set themselves in earnest to the task of destroying the sustaining structures of the conservative state.

Ignacio Comonfort (1812–63). A bureaucrat of minor importance for most of his life, and subsequently a colonel in the militia, Comonfort was thrust into the presidency in 1855 and found himself caught in the endless liberal-conservative struggle.

The first significant piece of legislation to emerge from the Reform bore the name of the secretary of justice. *Ley Juárez* abolished the military and ecclesiastical fueros, the special dispensations exempting soldiers and clerics from having to stand trial in civil courts. Ley Juárez did not, as sometimes contended, abolish all military and ecclesiastical courts; rather, it placed stringent restrictions on their jurisdictions. The ecclesiastical and military courts were now competent to sit only on cases involving the alleged transgression of canon or military law. If, on the other hand, a cleric or a soldier were charged with a violation of civil or criminal law, he would be required, like everyone else, to stand trial in a state or federal court. Ley Juárez thus became an important milestone in an ongoing battle to secure the concept of equality before the law.

Ley Juárez invoked the fury of the church and conservatives generally. But it also exposed a schism in the ranks of the liberals. The moderates (*moderados*) favored backing down, while the more staunchly liberals (*puros*) refused. Before the month was out President Alvarez and most of the cabinet had resigned. The presidency devolved on Ignacio Comonfort, who was more of a compromiser than a firebrand.

In June 1856 President Comonfort's secretary of the treasury, Miguel Lerdo de Tejada, drafted an important new law that the radicals hoped would weaken the church and the moderates hoped would increase national revenue. *Ley Lerdo* prohibited ecclesiastical and civil institutions from owning or administering real property not directly used in day-to-day operations. The Roman Catholic Church could retain its church buildings, monasteries, and seminaries and local and state units of government their meeting halls, jails, and schools, but both had to divest themselves of other urban and rural property. The massive holdings the church had gradually acquired through the centuries were to be put up for sale at public auction.

Ley Lerdo indicates that neither the puros nor the moderados of the nineteenth century were thinking in terms of social revolution. The liberals wanted to stimulate the land market to encourage economic development. The properties were not to be distributed to the landless peón but were to be sold. Only the wealthy or at least those in a position secure enough to obtain credit were able to buy. Even if an occasional peón could have obtained financing to purchase a small plot, threats of ecclesiastical penalty from the local priest were enough to dissuade him from pursuing the idea. In practice, the enforcement of Ley Lerdo worked to the detriment of the rural masses because it removed the long-standing legal recognition of the Indian communities' rights to own property. The mandate for individual ownership of land meant that many communities lost their corporate lands (*ejidos*) eventually. Ley Lerdo failed to create a new class of small peasant landowners and ultimately abetted the transfer of land to hacendados and some upwardly mobile *rancheros*. In the chaotic years that followed the implementation of Ley Lerdo, the liberal governments did not profit greatly from the break-up and sale of the corporate civil or ecclesiastical properties.

The reformers were not yet finished. In January 1857 President Comonfort signed into law a statute taking the powers of registry out of the hands of the church and giving them to the state. All births, marriages, adoptions, and deaths were henceforth to be registered by civil functionaries, and cemeteries were placed under the control of a Department of Hygiene. Still another blow at the church was struck a few months later. *Ley Iglesias* prohibited the church from charging high fees for administering the sacraments. The poor were to receive their sacramental blessings at no charge, and those who could afford to pay were to be charged modestly.

THE CONSTITUTION OF 1857

The internal tensions provoked by the Reform Laws were in full evidence when, as provided by the Plan de Ayutla, delegates met to draft a new constitution. Because the conservatives had opposed the Revolution of Ayutla, they were largely unrepresented in the constitutional assembly. The debates would be between moderados and puros.

The federal Constitution of 1857 in many ways was modeled after its ancestor of 1824. The major difference in political structure was provided by an article setting up a unicameral national legislature. For purposes of economy and efficiency the framers of the document believed that a single house was sufficient, but the main reason for switching from two houses to one was neither of these. It would be better, many believed, to have one strong house, instead of two weak ones, as a legislative bulwark against dictatorship. But Mexican history showed as well that a strong national government was mandatory if the country were to escape the perils of exaggerated regionalism. The Reform liberals were not nearly so federalist as some have believed.

The Constitution of 1857 represented much more of a liberal victory than its federal predecessor of 1824. Most of the liberal legislation of the Reform, including Ley Juárez, Ley Lerdo, and Ley Iglesias, was actually incorporated into the Constitution, which also emphasized individual liberty and the inviolability of property rights. The first thirty-four articles of the document spelled out in detail equality before the law and freedom of speech, of the press, of petition, of assembly, of the mails, and of education. They further abolished slavery, other compulsory service, and all titles of nobility and guaranteed the rights to carry arms, to have bail, and of *habeas corpus*.

The articles that prompted the most heated debate were, of course, those which in some way touched upon the religious issue. While the Constitution contained no article specifying freedom of religion, it did not establish Roman Catholicism as the state church and thus, by its silence, provided for the exercise of other religions. The inclusion of Ley Juárez and Ley Lerdo brought the church defenders to their feet again, alleging that religious toleration would destroy the family and eventually provoke rebellion and anarchy. Religious freedom would nullify the abolition of slavery and allow thousands of Muhammadan immigrants to enter the Mexican republic with their concubines! The puros were gradually worn down by the opposition. In the end a vote on religious freedom was never taken, as a majority of the delegates voted to remove the article from debate.

Nonetheless the church hierarchy was not satisfied and issued decree after decree in an attempt to nullify the new Constitution. Those Catholics who took advantage of Ley Lerdo by purchasing church property were threatened with excommunication, as were those who swore allegiance to the objectionable articles of the Constitution. Bishop Clemente de Jesús Munguía of Michoacán and Archbishop Lázaro de la Garza of Mexico City specified that the faithful could not accept, among other articles, those which provided for freedom of education, freedom of speech, freedom of the press, freedom of assembly, and, of course, Ley Juárez and Ley Lerdo. Pope Pius IX actually backed these positions, declaring the Constitution to be null and void.

The strong reaction of the church created a real quandary for Mexicans. If they did not swear allegiance to the Constitution they would be considered traitors to the state, and if they did they would be heretics in the eyes of the church. The quandary was not merely theoretical, however. Civil servants who refused to take the oath of allegiance to the Constitution lost their jobs; soldiers who took it were not treated in Catholic hospitals; if they died they did not receive the last rites nor were they buried in consecrated ground. Priests who offered the sacraments to communicants who had not forsworn the Constitution were suspended. By pitting brother against brother and father against son, the Reform Laws and the Constitution divided Mexican society into two hostile and completely uncompromising camps and led to yet another civil war.

The War of the Reform

The War of the Reform, the civil conflict that engulfed Mexico from 1858 to 1861, was in many ways the culmination of the ideological disputations, the shuffling of constitutions, the church-state controversies, and the minor civil wars that had shattered the peace periodically since Independence. The war began, as most Mexican wars, with a new plan, this time the *Plan de Tacubaya*, proclaimed by conservative general Félix Zuloaga. Emboldened by promises of clerical and military support, Zuloaga promptly dissolved the Congress and arrested Benito Juárez, the chief liberal spokesman within the Comonfort government. Juárez had recently been elected chief justice of the Mexican Supreme Court, a position that, according to the new Constitution, made him next in line for the presidency should a vacancy occur in the top office. Finding himself caught between two extremes and not totally comfortable with some of the constitutional provisions, President Comonfort resigned. When the army declared Zuloaga as the new president, Juárez managed to escape north to Querétaro, where his liberal cohorts proclaimed him president. With two presidents, two governments, and two uncompromising ideologies, Mexico plunged headlong into the most passionate and horrifying civil war to date.

The opposing sides in the three-year war defy the simple classification historians have traditionally given. It was not Indians versus whites and rural versus urban. While it is true that the clergy and the army generally supported the Zuloaga government in Mexico City, the Indian masses were found in both camps. Some Indian communities, convinced correctly that their ejido lands were threatened by the liberals under Ley Lerdo, were persuaded that their future rested with the conservatives. Led by Indian caciques such as Tomás Mejía of Querétaro, they gave the conservatives an important source of strength scarcely counted on. But the conservatives' principal leadership came from the army generals such as Miguel Miramón and Leonardo Márquez. And the liberals certainly were not without Indian support of their own, as many leaders convinced their people that their interests would best be served by casting their lot with their fellow Indian, Benito Juárez. These chieftains placed themselves and their followers under the orders of liberal commanders Santos Degollado, Santiago Vidaurri, and Manuel Doblado.

The liberals eventually succeeded in establishing their capital in Veracruz, where they could control the customs receipts and obtain military supplies from the outside world. From there Juárez and his government issued manifestos damning the enemy, enticing support, seeking the recognition of foreign governments, and outlining military strategy. At the same time in Mexico City the Zuloaga administration declared the Reform Laws null and void, swore allegiance to the Holy See, took communion in public, and planned military campaigns.

For the first two years of the war the liberals had a hard time holding their own. The conservative army, better trained, equipped, and

led, won most of the major engagements and held the most populous
states of central Mexico. But when, in the early spring of 1859, General Miramón attempted to dislodge the liberals from Veracruz, he was
beaten back. The fighting throughout the republic was vicious, and
noncombatants were subjected to wanton depredation by overzealous
commanders of both armies. The conservatives shot captured prisoners in the name of holy religion, and the liberals did the same in defense of freedom and democratic government, sometimes desecrating
churches and executing priests.

The intensity of the military campaigns manifested itself in the political arena as well. The Juárez government issued a series of decrees
from Veracruz that made the earlier Reform Laws seem innocuous by
comparison. The liberals who had felt short-changed by the Constitution would now be satisfied. Births and marriages were made civil ceremonies, all cemeteries were secularized, monastic orders were out-
lawed, no new nuns could be admitted to the nunneries, all church
properties and assets were nationalized, the number of official religious holidays was curtailed, religious processions in the streets were
severely limited, and mean-spirited local ordinances even restricted
the ringing of church bells. For the first time in the country's history
clergymen were made subject to Mexican taxation. They scarcely accepted the change with grace. But most importantly, church and state
were separated. The reforms tried to rivet together a society in which
the church would be indisputably subordinate to the state.

By 1860 the tide of the battle had turned in favor of the liberals.
Juárez found two excellent field commanders in Ignacio Zaragoza and
Jesús González Ortega, while the enemy unwittingly aided the liberal
cause by bickering among themselves. In August, Zaragoza and
González Ortega combined their forces at Silao to hand General Miramón his first serious defeat. The final battle occurred three days before Christmas when González Ortega crushed Miramón's army of
eight thousand at the little town of San Miguel Calpulalpan. The newly
victorious army, some twenty-five thousand strong, entered Mexico
City to a tumultuous welcome on New Year's Day. Juárez arrived ten
days later, but victory was no panacea.

DISCONTENT

The desolation left in the wake of the civil conflict showed on the landscape dotted with burned haciendas and mills, potted roads, unre-
paired bridges, neglected fields, and sacked villages. But more importantly, it was epitomized in the minds and bodies of tens of thousands
of exhausted, crippled, and aggrieved Mexicans. Soldiers slowly drifted

back to their villages to find no work. Bandits continued to infest the highways. Frustration set in quickly. Only the national government could be expected to smooth the transition, but the tired nation was to have no relief. The liberal victory in 1861 proved to be but a brief respite from the ravages of war. The armies would soon begin marching again, but on this occasion one would wear foreign uniforms

Although Juárez won the presidential elections held in March 1861, the liberals were badly split on many issues, especially on what type of punishment should be meted out to their erstwhile enemies. Some

Benito Juárez (1806–72). The presidential terms of Mexico's most noteworthy politician of the mid-nineteenth century were disrupted by civil wars and foreign interventions.

favored harsh retribution to make their enemies pay for the ravages they had propagated, but the president opted instead for a more conciliatory policy. Benito Juárez believed in the chastening impact of open debate. He considered opposition in an open forum a healthy political development in Mexico, and he would not muzzle the barbed criticism in the Congress. But congressional bickering in his own party, coupled with pressure from the opposition, prompted several cabinet resignations and kept the administration in a constant state of turmoil. On one occasion a congressional vote taken to demand Juárez's resignation lost by a single vote.

TROUBLED FINANCES AND FOREIGN INTERVENTION

In the final analysis, however, it was economic rather than political difficulties that precipitated the next war. Juárez inherited a bankrupt treasury and an army, a corps of civil servants, and a police force that had not been paid. The income from the sale of church property had been considerably less than expected. Commerce was stagnant, and most of the customs receipts were already pledged. The nation's transportation system was woefully inadequate, as merchandise was still being conveyed by pack mules, oxen, and human cargadores. Transportation was slow, costly, and inefficient.

In the spring of 1861 the monthly deficit amounted to $400,000, and there was practically no currency in circulation. Worst of all, Mexico's European creditors began clamoring for the repayment of debts, some half a century old. Fully sensitive to the dangers his action might portend, Juárez declared a two-year moratorium on the payment of Mexico's foreign debt. Although he took care to stress that his action was not a repudiation, but simply a suspension in time of stress, the outcry in Europe was predictably anguished. The large majority of the English, French, and Spanish claims were quite legitimate, for foreign citizens had suffered outrages and losses of life and property.

On October 31, 1861, representatives of Queen Isabella II of Spain, Queen Victoria of Great Britain, and Emperor Napoleon III of France affixed their signatures to the Convention of London. The three nations agreed upon a joint occupation of the Mexican coasts to collect their claims. The specific plan they envisioned was to occupy the customshouse at Veracruz and apply all customs receipts on the debt. Although England and Spain were apparently sincere in the pledge not to seek special advantage in Mexico, France had other plans. The enigmatic Louis Napoleon Bonaparte, nephew of Napoleon I, won the presidency of the French republic in 1848 but craved the imperial status of his famous uncle.

Ever since 1852, when a French plebiscite approved the title and dignity that he desired, Emperor Napoleon III had embarked upon an aggressive foreign policy in Algeria, Indochina, and Africa. But, most importantly, the emperor dreamed of planting the Tricouleur in the New World. By coming to the rescue of the church in Mexico he could also hope to curry favor with the strong Catholic element in France. The Mexican imbroglio seemed to present him with a perfect opportunity.

Some six thousand Spanish troops actually landed in Veracruz first. Seven hundred British marines and two thousand French troops arrived early the next month. As soon as it became obvious that the French harbored notions of conquest, the queens of Spain and Great Britain decided to order their respective troops home.

THE FRENCH INTERVENTION

Within a month after the Spanish and British withdrawal the French army, reinforced with an additional forty-five hundred troops, began to march inland on its war of occupation. Arrogant and overconfident, the invading commander General Charles Latrille had already informed his superior in Paris: "We are so superior to the Mexicans in race, organization, morality and devoted sentiments, that I beg your excellency to inform the Emperor that as the head of 6,000 soldiers I am already master of Mexico."[1] But en route to Mexico he discovered that Puebla was not going to be an easy prize. President Juárez had assigned the defense of the city to General Ignacio Zaragoza. Encountering unexpected opposition on the morning of May 5, 1862, Latrille attacked recklessly, and within two hours the French had expended half of their ammunition. The French troops, many weakened by the affliction that sometimes smites the foreign visitor to the Mexican countryside, did not acquit themselves well. General Zaragoza, on the other hand, managed his troops with rare aplomb. The decisive maneuver of the day was carried out by young Brigadier General Porfirio Díaz, commanding the Second Brigade. Late in the afternoon Díaz repelled a determined French assault on Zaragoza's right flank. The dejected invaders retreated to lick their wounds in Orizaba. May 5—*Cinco de Mayo*—would be added to the national calendar of holidays in honor of the Mexican victory.

---

1. Quoted in Paul Vanderwood, "Betterment for Whom? The Reform Period: 1855–1875," in Michael C. Meyer and William H. Beezley, eds., *The Oxford History of Mexico* (New York, 2000]), p. 381.

Porfirio Díaz as a young man. Later to serve as president of Mexico for a third of a century, Díaz was catapulted to national fame because of his role in the victory over the French on May 5, 1862.

Not all Mexicans rejoiced at the news of the French defeat. Many conservative monarchists and just as many church officials not only succored the recuperating French army but priests used their pulpits to urge their communicants to collaborate with the enemy against the godless government. On August 30, 1862, President Juárez ordered that clerics who excited disrespect for the law would be punished by imprisonment or deportation. He also forbade priests from wearing their vestments or any other distinguishing garment outside of the churches.

Upon hearing of the disaster at Puebla, Napoleon, with a sizable reservoir of manpower to draw upon, ordered some thirty thousand reinforcements. It took fully a year before the French army was prepared to march again. Once more they encountered their heaviest resistance at Puebla, but on this occasion the result would be quite different. After a siege of nearly two months, the Mexican defenders under the command of General Jesús González Ortega were forced to turn the city over to the French.

President Juárez realized that the fall of Puebla opened the doors to Mexico City. With the support of Congress at the end of May, Juárez, his cabinet, and what was left of his army withdrew for San Luis Potosí, and the French army entered the Mexican capital unopposed.

THE NEW GOVERNMENT

Much of Mexico's conservative leadership was less concerned with their country's recent loss of sovereignty than with how the conservatives might profit from the demise of Benito Juárez and his liberal government. It did not take them long to learn. On June 16, 1863, the French commander selected a provisional government consisting of thirty-five conservatives. Napoleon III had already made up his mind about the future of Mexico. Having conferred with numerous conservative Mexican émigrés, he had decided that if a monarchy was good for France, it would be good for Mexico as well. The French emperor and his conservative Mexican allies agreed that the Austrian archduke, Ferdinand Maximilian of Hapsburg, would be a perfect emperor. Napoleon had discussed the possibility with Maximilian even before the Convention of London. In October 1863 a delegation of Mexican conservatives visited Maximilian at Miramar, his magnificent palace on a promontory overlooking the Adriatic near Trieste, and offered him the crown. Maximilian accepted only on the condition that his emperorship be approved by the Mexican people themselves. As strange as his stipulation must have sounded to the conservative monarchists, they agreed to indulge Maximilian in this folly. The plebiscite, held under the auspices of the French army, was a farce; when Maximilian was informed that the Mexican people had voted overwhelmingly in his favor, he accepted the throne.

Before leaving for Mexico, Maximilian entered into an agreement with his benefactor, Napoleon III. The Convention of Miramar pledged the new Mexican emperor to pay all expenses incurred by the French troops during their fight for control of the country. Maximilian also agreed to pay the salaries of the French troops, twenty thousand of whom were to remain in Mexico until the end of 1867, and to assume responsibility for payment of all the claims. In return Napoleon gave Maximilian full command over the French expeditionary force in Mexico. The new emperor, by signing the Convention of Miramar, had tripled Mexico's foreign debt before even setting foot on Mexican soil. But Maximilian was eager to begin a new life in a new world. He had his wife Charlotte hire a Spanish tutor; after the first lesson she had mastered a few salutations and had learned that her name henceforth, would be Carlota.

THE ARRIVAL OF THE MONARCHS

Ferdinand Maximilian Joseph and Marie Charlotte Amélie Léopoldine arrived in Veracruz aboard the Austrian frigate *Novara* at the end of

May 1864. He was thirty-two years old and she only twenty-four when they set out to mount the imperial throne. The most distinguished blood of Europe ran through their veins. He was descendant from the Josephs, Leopolds, and Francis of Austrian Hapsburg fame and ultimately from Charles V, and she from Queen Louise of Orléans, Louis Philippe, and the French Bourbons. They were products of European education at its best, schooled in the etiquette of court life, and accustomed to the niceties, proprieties, and extravagances of Viennese aristocratic society. Their first glimpse of Mexico came as a shock as they encountered a sweltering, humid Veracruz where malaria and yellow fever were rampant, and sanitation was nonexistent.

Traditionally liberal, the Veracruzanos refused to come out of their whitewashed adobe houses to greet their new monarchs. By the time the small royal party reached the railroad station to begin the tedious journey, Carlota was in tears. As the train wound its way toward Mexico City, the weather cooled and the scenery improved. But the railroad tracks ended at the little pueblo of Totalco, and the royal party made the rest of the trip by stage. Maximilian had brought his own ornate carriage from Vienna, and, while it would catch many eyes on the good streets of Mexico City, it was scarcely designed for the atrocious tracks that passed for roads in the mountains of rural Mexico. After several breakdowns the imperial party wisely moved from the carriage to the stage for the remainder of the journey. The carriage would be saved for the triumphal entry into the capital. On their way into Mexico City on June 12, they stopped to hear mass at the Basílica de Guadalupe. Maximilian had been advised that it would be wise to curry Indian and church support by paying homage to the Virgin of Guadalupe.

Because the national palace was deemed unsuitable, the royal family established their magnificent imperial court at Chapultepec Castle, built originally for the Spanish viceroys at the end of the eighteenth century. But unlike Agustín I, Mexico's first emperor, Maximilian made himself accessible to the people. Once a week he opened the palace to his subjects, and in many small ways he tried hard for acceptance. To acquaint himself with Mexico's problems he toured the provinces and, on occasion, even donned the regional costume and ate the local food. Upon his return he shocked his conservative friends by suggesting that many priests he had met could profit from some basic lessons in Christian charity. Believing that magnanimity would serve him well and win him converts, Maximilian declared a free press and proclaimed a general amnesty for all political prisoners serving terms of less than ten years.

The emperor was pleased with the first few months of his reign, especially when diplomatic recognition began to come in from Europe. In the summer he wrote his younger brother an enthusiastic letter.

A mass was celebrated for Maximilian and grande dame *Carlota when they reached Mexico City after the difficult journey from Veracruz.*

> I found the country far better than I expected . . . and the people far more advanced than supposed at home. Our reception was cordial and sincere, free from all pretence and from that nauseating official servility which one very often finds in Europe on such occasions. The country is very beautiful, tropically luxuriant in the coast lands. . . . The so-called entertainments of Europe, such as evening receptions, the gossip of teaparties, etc., etc., of hideous memories, are quite unknown here, and we shall take good care not to introduce them.[2]

INTERNAL DIVISIONS AND EXTERNAL INTERFERENCE

But Maximilian's position was scarcely as idyllic as he imagined. His first serious problem, strangely enough, came from his conservative supporters rather than from the liberals who had been driven out of Mexico City to make room for him. The conservatives, led by Juan Almonte and Archbishop Pelagio Antonio de Labastida, naturally expected that

---

2. Quoted in Egon Corti, *Maximilian and Charlotte of Mexico* (New York, 1928), 2: 431–32.

the emperor would immediately set about to suspend the Reform Laws and return the church properties seized by Benito Juárez. But Maximilian's political inclinations tended to the liberal side on the question of the relationship between church and state. Hoping to attract some liberal support to his government he not only refused to return church lands, re-establish Roman Catholicism to the exclusion of all other creeds, and decree education a church monopoly, but, when he found himself in a financial squeeze similar to that of his republican predecessors, he even levied several forced loans against the church.

Nonetheless, very few liberals were persuaded that Maximilian's mildly anticlerical posture and winks at liberalism should occasion a change of attitude on their part. A monarchy, supported by foreign arms and headed by a foreigner, had been established in Mexico, and it was their duty as honorable citizens to overthrow it. By attempting to find a middle ground between the liberals and the conservatives, Maximilian succeeded only in alienating both.

When Juárez withdrew from Mexico City before the French onslaught, he established his government first in San Luis Potosí and then in Chihuahua. But French troops sent by Marshal François Bazaine pushed him and his small loyal army north until they found refuge only in El Paso del Norte (today Ciudad Juárez) on the United States border. But the French hold on the country was tenuous as the Juaristas quickly taught the Europeans the meaning of guerrilla warfare. While the French invariably won the few battles that were fought, they could not completely pacify the country, nor could they hold onto territory once the troops moved on.

In late 1864 and early 1865 the empire was at its strongest. Bazaine defeated Porfirio Díaz in Oaxaca and temporarily secured that pivotal southern state. In October 1865 Maximilian's French advisers informed him, incorrectly, that Juárez had finally given up the fight and had fled the country, seeking refuge in the United States. He was also encouraged to issue a controversial and extremely significant decree. The death penalty was made mandatory for all captured Juaristas still bearing arms, to be carried out without appeal within twenty-four hours of capture. Maximilian had been given and had followed bad advice. In signing the decree he had not only prompted a war of unparalleled ferocity but, in effect, had also signed his own death warrant. Juárez had not abandoned the country and repeatedly promised his supporters that he had no intention of giving up the fight. He realized, however, that he needed substantial help and was gradually convinced by his cabinet and advisers that it could come only from north of the Rio Grande.

The government of Abraham Lincoln had been more than casually interested in France's Mexican venture from the outset. In 1823 President Monroe had intoned his famous doctrine declaring that the American continents were henceforth not to be considered as subjects for future colonization by European powers; any attempt to do so would be viewed as an unfriendly act toward the United States. In the years subsequent to its promulgation the Monroe Doctrine was disregarded incessantly by various countries in western Europe but never so blatantly as in 1862 and 1863 when the French army overran central Mexico, overthrew the Juárez government, and placed Maximilian on the Mexican throne. But Napoleon III had chosen his time well; six months prior to the signing of the Convention of London the shots fired at Fort Sumter had initiated the Civil War in the United States. Convulsed with difficulties far more serious than ever before, the government in Washington was able to do little but issue a few mild protests. The Union hardly wanted to push France into an alliance with the Confederacy. When it came time to consider recognition of the Mexican empire, however, the Lincoln administration refused. Juárez's government in exile was considered by Washington to be the legitimate representative of the Mexican people.

As the fortunes of the North improved and those of the Confederacy declined, Juárez embarked upon an all-out campaign to secure assistance from the United States. He charged the head of the Mexican legation in Washington, Matías Romero, a young but forceful diplomat, with the task of securing some implementation of a resolution, passed in 1864 by the U.S. House of Representatives, that condemned the French intervention. At approximately the same time he dispatched an entire team of secret agents to the United States to secure financial and military aid and to begin recruiting American soldiers of fortune. Romero opened discussions with representatives of the Lincoln administration, but progress was impeded by Lincoln's assassination and the necessity of opening a new round of negotiations with the government of Andrew Johnson.

The end of the Civil War brought about a major change in United States policy. The North had over nine hundred thousand men under arms when Lee surrendered to Grant at Appomattox, a formidable fighting force as the South had discovered. No longer fearful of offending the French, Secretary of State William Seward began applying pressure to Napoleon III. At the same time the government in Washington, prompted by Romero, closed its eyes to violations of neutrality legislation and allowed Juarista agents to purchase arms and ammunition in California for shipment to west coast Mexican ports under republican control. Within a matter of a few months some thirty thousand muskets reached the Juaristas from the Baton Rouge arsenal alone. Juárez's agents were also allowed to pass back and forth across the international line without hindrance from customs officials or border patrols. Some three thousand Union veterans, attracted by good pay and a promised land bonus, joined the Juarista army. Influenced by these developments as well as a new threat to French security in Europe in the form of Otto van Bismarck, Napoleon made his belated decision to begin withdrawing his foreign legion in November 1866.

The gradual withdrawal of the French troops in late 1866 and early 1867 left Maximilian in an impossible position. To no avail he sent a series of envoys to Paris to convince Napoleon that he should honor the commitment he had made in the Convention of Miramar. Maximilian then toyed with the idea of abdicating his throne, but Carlota appealed to his sense of Hapsburg dignity and convinced him that he must stay on. She travelled to Europe herself, but her appeals to Napoleon and the pope were rejected. Pius IX could not have been happy that Maximilian had taken no steps to restore the church lands in Mexico. A distraught Carlota soon lost her mind.

THE REPUBLICAN VICTORY AND THE AFTERMATH

Spurred on by the fortuitous combination of events in Europe and America and recognizing that the underpinnings of the empire were collapsing, Juárez and his republican army assumed the offensive in the spring of 1866. General Luis Terrazas captured Chihuahua City while General Mariano Escobedo shattered a strong French column between Matamoros and Monterrey. Before the end of the year the republicans reoccupied much of Mexico. With the French army pulling out of Mexico, the treasury empty, and Carlota sick in Europe, Maximilian reluctantly decided to make one last stand. Mexico's second empire collapsed in the colonial city of Querétaro while the last installment of French troops was marching toward Veracruz for their European embarkation. Maximilian took command of a few thousand Mexican imperial troops but quickly found himself surrounded by a republican army four times as strong. After nearly a hundred days, Maximilian could no longer withstand the republican seige of Querétaro. Although careful plans had been laid for the emperor's escape, he preferred the solemn dignity of surrender on May 15.

Juárez immediately decided Maximilian's fate; the emperor would be tried by court-martial, and the state would request the death penalty. Despite a rain of pleas for clemency from European monarchs, New World presidents, and delegations of tearful, supplicating women, Juárez remained adamant. Thirteen accusations were leveled against

A contemporary woodcut depicting the execution of Maximilian and two of his Mexican generals, Tomás Mejía and Miguel Miramón, on the Hill of the Bells outside Querétaro.

Maximilian, including violation of Mexico's sovereignty, but the most important was that he had signed the infamous decree of October 1865 resulting in the death of innumerable Mexican citizens. The chief defense attorneys, Mariano Riva Palacio and Rafael Martínez de la Torre, were brilliant advocates; they ardently denied the competence of the court to sit on the case and argued that the leniency shown to Jefferson Davis in the United States after the Civil War should serve as a precedent. The verdict, however, was based more on political considerations than on legal ones. After the War of the Reform Juárez had been magnanimous in his use of executive clemency, and he now believed that Mexico had paid a terrible price as a result. He wanted to demonstrate to the world that Mexico's existence as an independent nation would not be left to chance or to the goodwill of foreign heads of state. By one vote, the court voted for the death penalty. The final appeal to President Juárez was rejected in the interest of assuring public peace.

On the morning of June 19, after having received the last sacrament, Maximilian was led by his executioners to the Hill of the Bells on the outskirts of Querétaro. There he was shot along with several Mexican conservative officers who had been tried with him. As tragic and senseless as the event might have appeared from the calm of abroad, fifty thousand Mexicans had just as surely lost their lives fighting the French.

The price of the French Intervention, however, cannot be assessed solely in terms of the lives lost. The attempt to tamper with Mexico's sovereignty had ended in dismal failure, and, as a result, Mexican nationalism and self-esteem began to grow perceptibly for the first time. The United States had helped in a small way, but it had been Mexicans who drove out the French. The republican victory was, at least in part, a vindication of the Constitution of 1857 and the principles it had espoused. The clerical party had been defeated, and although the country had not seen the last of its major church-state struggles, the church and its defenders in the future would seek more modest goals. The conservatives were discredited, at least for the time, because liberalism in the popular mind became identified with moral authority and independence from foreign aggression.

On the other hand, the Intervention and the empire, despite Maximilian's best efforts, had left Mexican commerce, industry, and agriculture in a quagmire. Education had suffered immeasurably, and the treasury was still empty. The years without a single, central authority reinforced tendencies toward localism and blunted the nationalism that the victory began to abet. Thousands of armed men roamed the countryside. In short, the dramatic events of the years 1861–67 contributed markedly to Mexico's lack of political stability and economic growth in the nineteenth century.

RECOMMENDED FOR FURTHER STUDY

Anderson, William Marshall. *An American in Maximilian's Mexico, 1865–1866: Diaries of William Marshall Anderson.* Edited by Ramón Eduardo Ruiz. San Marino, Calif.: Huntington Library, 1959.

Barker, Nancy Nichols. *The French Experience in Mexico, 1821–1861: A History of Constant Misunderstanding.* Chapel Hill: University of North Carolina Press, 1979.

Bazant, Jan. *Alienation of Church Wealth in Mexico: Social and Economic Aspects of the Liberal Revolution, 1856–1857.* Cambridge: Cambridge University Press, 1971.

Berry, Charles R. *The Reform in Oaxaca, 1856–1876: A Microhistory of the Liberal Revolution.* Lincoln: University of Nebraska Press, 1981.

Broussard, Ray F. "Vidaurri, Juárez and Comonfort's Return from Exile." *Hispanic American Historical Review* 49 (1969): 268–80.

Cadenhead, Ivie E., Jr. *Jesús González Ortega and Mexican National Politics.* Fort Worth: Texas Christian University Press, 1972.

Chowning, Margaret. *Wealth and Power in Provincial Mexico: Michoacán from the Late Colony to the Revolution.* Stanford, Calif.: Stanford University Press, 1999.

Corti, Egon. *Maximilian and Charlotte of Mexico.* 2 vols. New York: Knopf, 1928.

Dabbs, Jack A. *The French Army in Mexico, 1861–1867.* The Hague: Mouton, 1962.

Delaney, Robert W. "Matamoros, Port for Texas during the Civil War." *Southwestern Historical Quarterly* 58 (1955): 473–87.

Duncan, Robert H. "Political Legitimization and Maximilian's Second Empire in Mexico, 1864–1867." *Mexican Studies* 12 (1996): 273–300.

Goldwert, Marvin. "Matías Romero and Congressional Opposition to Seward's Policy toward the French Intervention in Mexico." *The Americas* 22 (1965): 22–40.

Hamnett, Brian. *Juárez.* London: Longman, 1994.

Hanna, Alfred Jackson, and Kathryn Hanna. *Napoleon III and Mexico.* Chapel Hill: University of North Carolina Press, 1971.

Knowlton, Robert J. *Church Property and the Mexican Reform, 1856–1910.* DeKalb: Northern Illinois University Press, 1976.

Miller, Robert R. "Matías Romero: Mexican Minister to the United States during the Juárez–Maximilian Era." *Hispanic American Historical Review* 45 (1965): 228–45.

Olliff, Donathan C. *Reforma Mexico and the United States: A Search for Alternatives to Annexation, 1854–1861.* University: University of Alabama Press, 1983.

Powell, T. G. "Priests and Peasants in Central Mexico: Social Conflict during La Reforma." *Hispanic American Historical Review* 57 (1997): 296–313.

Roeder, Ralph. *Juárez and His Mexico.* 2 vols. New York: Viking Press, 1947.

Scholes, Walter V. *Mexican Politics during the Juárez Regime, 1855–1872.* Columbia: University of Missouri Press, 1957.

Schoonover, Thomas D. *Dollars over Dominion: The Triumph of Liberalism in Mexican–United States Relations, 1861–1867.* Baton Rouge: Louisiana State University Press, 1978.

———. *Mexican Lobby: Matías Romero in Washington, 1861–1867.* Lexington: University Press of Kentucky, 1986.

Sinkin, Richard N. *The Mexican Reform, 1855–1876: A Study in Liberal Nation Building.* Austin: Institute of Latin American Studies, 1979.

Smart, Charles Allen. *Viva Juárez!* London: Eyre and Spottiswoode, 1964.

Tyler, R. Curtis. *Santiago Vidaurri and the Southern Confederacy.* Austin: Texas State Historical Association, 1973.

Vanderwood, Paul. "Betterment for Whom? The Reform Period: 1855–1875," in *The Oxford History of Mexico.* Edited by Michael C. Meyer and William H. Beezley, pp. 371–96. New York: Oxford University Press, 2000.

21

The Restored Republic, 1867–76: Nascent Modernization

Modern Mexican history begins with the liberal victory of 1867.[1] In a very real sense the republic became a nation. Concerned with the growth of political democracy in Mexico, Juárez and his republican cohorts would try for a decade to consolidate their victory by implementing the letter and spirit of the Constitution of 1857 and, at the same time, by setting Mexico on the path of modernization. The sailing was far from smooth, but the political process did show definite signs of maturation. The scars from the recent wars of the Reform and the Intervention were deep, and, while the conservatives endeavored to eliminate the distinctions between victors and vanquished, the liberals set out to inaugurate a new era of peace and material progress. They both had to overcome the deeply engrained suspicion that differences of opinion, ideology, and practical politics should inevitably be settled by force rather than by reason. And while all antagonisms did not dissipate during the Restoration, bellicosity became at least less of a reflex action. But, more important, this nine-year period established the guidelines for the profound changes that would occur in Mexico during the last quarter of the nineteenth century.

JUÁREZ'S THIRD TERM

In marked contrast to Maximilian's entrance into Mexico City in his ornate European carriage in 1864, Juárez entered the capital on July 15, 1867, in a stark black coach. Cheers welled up from the thousands who lined the streets. His reception was triumphant, as it well should have been, but although Juárez enjoyed the display of camaraderie and goodwill, he recognized that it was no time to rest on past laurels. He immediately called for presidential elections, announcing himself as a

---

1. Daniel Cosío Villegas, ed. *Historia moderna de México*, 9 vols. (Mexico City, 1955–72). The first three volumes treat the restored republic.

candidate for a third term. Under the circumstances, few knowledgeable politicians believed that a third term was excessive. Most of the first two had been spent on the run with virtually no chance of implementing a progressive program. While preparing himself for the elections, the president undertook an important political reform. In order to manifest the primacy of civilian over military rule, he reduced the size of the Mexican army from sixty thousand to twenty thousand men.

In October Juárez won the presidential election and late in the year was sworn into office for a third term. In one respect he was faced with a situation not unlike that which he had encountered in 1861 when he returned to office following the liberal victory in the War of the Reform. The administration had to enunciate a policy toward the conservatives who had supported the French-imposed monarchy. During the fight against the empire, the decrees issued from the Juarista headquarters concerning French sympathizers had been harsh indeed. The no-nonsense policy was reaffirmed in Querétaro with the trial and execution of Maximilian. But by late 1867 few liberals were still crying for revenge, and it seemed time to adopt a more conciliatory policy. In a gesture of goodwill Juárez set free many political prisoners and reduced the sentences of others.

ECONOMIC AND EDUCATIONAL REFORMS

The new administration wisely directed its energies into two main fields: a revamping of the economy and a restructuring of the educational foundations of the country. Juárez named Matías Romero, who had served his exiled government so effectively in Washington, as secretary of the treasury. Romero formulated a plan for economic development that called for the improvement of transportation facilities and the fuller exploitation of natural resources through the attraction of foreign capital. He believed that Mexico's economic future rested largely on the revitalization of the mining industry rather than upon industrialization. The key to increased mineral production was a major revision of Mexico's tax and tariff structure. Despite much congressional opposition, through hard work and thrift Secretary Romero succeeded in bringing some order out of the economic chaos by 1872, but the dividends he expected in the form of substantial capital investment would not be noticeable for several years.

While tariff and tax revision were important, other factors still discouraged the potential investor. Mexico had an image to live down. Political instability, minor rebellions, the presence of private armies and groups of bandits for whom lawlessness had become a way of life, all dissuaded foreign capitalists seeking lucrative investment fields. Travel on Mexico's roads and shipment of merchandise were precarious. One of the answers was found in a relatively new concept of public security. Prior to the French Intervention, Benito Juárez had authorized the establishment of a rural police force, the *rurales*, modeled in some ways on the Spanish *guardia civil*. But jurisdiction over the security guard was divided between two government departments: War and Interior. The overlapping and often confusing jurisdictions undermined the effectiveness of the organization, and it did not amount to much. After the overthrow of the empire, however, Juárez's Congress authorized an increased budget for the rurales, and, in 1869, placed them under the sole jurisdiction of the Department of Interior. With more adequate funds and with the organizational problem resolved, the rurales began to play a major peace-keeping role. Patrolling the roads, assisting the army, guarding special shipments of bullion and merchandise, and policing local elections, they contributed toward stabilization of life in the countryside.

Without question the most important economic development to occur during the early years of the Restoration was the completion of the Mexico City–Veracruz railroad. The enterprise had begun in 1837, and short segments of a couple of kilometers had been completed periodically since that time. But in 1860, when the United States had over thirty thousand miles of track in operation, Mexico had barely 150 miles. The stage between Mexico City and Guadalajara (a distance of some 425 miles) often took more than a week even if it was not mired in the mud or assaulted by bandits. To be sure, construction in the rugged terrain between the Mexican capital and Veracruz on the Gulf was an engineering nightmare, for the roadbed had to rise from sea level to over nine thousand feet and had to be built across huge canyons and precipices. But railroad technology was clearly ahead of Mexico's determination to see the project through.

During the period of the empire the concession rights were held by the Imperial Mexican Railway Company, a corporation registered in London. The British engineers who worked for Maximilian made considerable progress in laying portions of the roadbed, but by 1866 the company was almost bankrupt and all work stopped. Upon the restoration of the republic Juárez articulated his profound concern for completion of the line. He exempted the company from the forfeiture legislation that applied to all who had supported Maximilian on the condition that construction be resumed. Realizing that the company was broke, Juárez also agreed to pay it an annual subsidy of 560,000 pesos for twenty-five years. The agreement reached by the government and the company produced considerable bombast in the Mexican Congress.

Among the leading stockholders was Antonio Escandón, a conservative who had been a member of the Mexican delegation that visited Miramar in October 1863. Cries of governmental favoritism to traitors were heard in the Congress, but Juárez believed that the railroad was more important than partisan politics and went ahead with his plans.

In an attempt to soothe passions the company was renamed the Ferrocarril Mexicano (Mexican Railroad Company). The British engineers did a fantastic job of construction, digging endless tunnels and breaching the Barranca de Metlac, a chasm 900 feet across and 375 feet deep. Gradually all the gaps were closed, the rails tied to one another, and the job finished on December 20, 1872. The line was officially inaugurated on January 1 of the following year. Archbishop Pelagio Antonio de Labastida formally blessed the new project at the Buenaventura station in Mexico City, signifying a reduction in tensions between church and state. Church endorsement of a liberal government enterprise a

Spanning the Metlac Ravine was an engineering achievement of major proportions.

decade before would have been unthinkable. The successful completion of the railroad whetted the appetite, encouraging others to begin
thinking of the desirability, indeed the necessity, of constructing other
major lines.

Education, too, began to move in a new direction with the restoration of the republic. In the fall of 1867 Juárez appointed a five-man
commission to reorganize the entire educational structure of the country. The committee was headed by Gabino Barreda, a medical doctor
who had studied in France and become a devotee of the positivist philosophy of Auguste Comte. While positivism would not become the
official state doctrine in Mexico for another fifteen years, its roots most
definitely can be found in Barreda's educational values. The curriculum recommended by the committee and adopted by the Congress in
late 1867 placed heavy emphasis on arithmetic, the rudiments of
physics and chemistry, and practical mechanics in the primary schools
and further emphasis on mathematics and the natural sciences in the
secondary schools. The arts and the humanities, while not entirely ignored, were subordinated to an understanding of the physical world.

More important to Juárez than the curriculum itself was the fact
that primary education in Mexico was made free and obligatory for the
first time. All towns with a population of over five hundred were to
have one school for boys and one for girls. Two more schools were to
be built for every additional two thousand inhabitants. But, as had been
the case in Mexico since the arrival of the Spaniards in 1519, theory
and practice, the law and the reality, seldom merged. Universal primary education remained but a liberal dream.

Juárez and his secretary of foreign relations, Sebastián Lerdo de Tejada, took special care to cultivate friendly diplomatic relations with Mexico's neighbors and with the powers of Europe, most of which had recognized the empire of Maximilian. In his first address to the Congress in
1867 the president acknowledged the sympathy and support the United
States had given him during the recent unpleasantness. The relationship
between the two countries was further cemented when William Seward
visited Mexico in 1869, and the two countries agreed to lay claims, accumulated since the Treaty of Guadalupe Hidalgo, before a mixed claims
commission. Gradually relations with Europe were renewed as well.

DIVISION AMONG THE LIBERALS AND THE
DEATH OF JUÁREZ

Juárez's third term was his best, and in the presidential elections of
1871 he decided, against the advice of many friends, to seek a fourth.
The onetime pillar of constitutional liberalism had become prey to the

A caricature by Santiago Hernández of Juárez and his opposition. Entitled "Little Fingers," it illustrates how the opposition whittled away at Juárez's power.

nineteenth-century Latin American political myth of indispensability; he had allowed his very human desire for power and accomplishment to impugn his earlier ideals. His popularity had been ebbing for at least a year. The election of 1871 was one of the most hotly contested of the nineteenth century as two former supporters ran against him: Porfirio Díaz, who had won his military laurels in the wars against the French; and Sebastián Lerdo de Tejada, the brother of the author of Ley Lerdo. The election thus occasioned a three-way split in the undisciplined liberal party—Juaristas, Porfiristas, and Lerdistas. Juárez still enjoyed a wide base of popular support and, in addition, had most of the federal bureaucracy working in his behalf. Lerdo counted on the strong backing of the professional classes and many of the socially prominent and wealthy, while Díaz was supported by some of the military outcasts from the conservative party and a vast entourage of disappointed office seekers. Both the Lerdistas and the Porfiristas attacked the concept of constant re-election as a violation of the republican principles Juárez had always espoused.

When the ballots were counted after the June election, none of the three candidates received the requisite majority of the votes. The choice, according to the Constitution of 1857, thus fell upon the Congress. The Juaristas had done well in the congressional elections and

dominated that body when it convened in the early fall. After a number of bitter credentials fights the new delegates were seated, and when
the important vote was taken, Juárez was elected. Of the two defeated
candidates, Díaz accepted the decision with less grace. On November 8, 1871, he proclaimed himself in revolt against the Juárez regime.

The *Plan de la Noria* proclaimed that indefinite re-election of the
chief executive repudiated the principles of the Revolution of Ayutla
and endangered the country's national institutions. It was necessary to
overthrow those who considered national office to be their personal
prerogative. No officeholder who exercised national jurisdiction of any
kind in the year preceding presidential elections should be eligible to
run for that high position. Those who accept the plan, Díaz proclaimed,
"will fight for the cause of the people and the people will be the only
victors. The Constitution of 1857 will be our banner and less government and more liberty our program."[2] But Díaz's fellow citizens were
not yet ready for another armed insurrection, and Díaz was disappointed
at the lack of interest his plan generated. While a few local caciques
declared for the movement, Díaz had not struck a responsive chord.
The army he put in the field was quickly defeated by the federals.

The revolt of La Noria was in complete disarray when, on July 19,
1872, Juárez suffered a coronary seizure and died in office. Sebastián
Lerdo de Tejada, the chief justice of the Supreme Court, became acting president and scheduled new elections for October. Lerdo enjoyed a reputation for keen intelligence, great administrative ability,
and unquestionable republican sympathies. In public speeches and
debates he often attained forensic perfection. He decided to run
against Porfirio Díaz in the elections and defeated him easily. Since
Díaz's revolution against Juárez had been predicated almost entirely
on the principle of no-re-election, the caudillo from Oaxaca accepted
the outcome.

LERDO'S PRESIDENCY

President Lerdo believed that the foundation of Mexico's future
progress rested heavily on the establishment of peace. The material
progress he envisioned was impossible without order, and order was
impossible without firm executive control. The national government
had to curb disruptive localism and weaken the army. Mexican liberalism was undergoing a significant change. It was becoming increasingly

---

2. Quoted in Ernesto de la Torre Villar et al., eds. *Historia documental de México*
   (Mexico City, 1964), 2: 361.

Pilgrimages were made to Juárez's tomb in Mexico City long after his death in 1872.

elitist and was no longer antithetical to centralism and dictatorship. When political disputes occurred in the states, Lerdo did not hesitate to intervene with federal forces.

Lerdo wisely retained many Juaristas in his government and, in seeking his goals, followed the same general policies that had been formulated by his famous predecessor. He used the rurales to patrol and protect the Mexico City–Veracruz railroad. To foster communications development he let railroad contracts for the construction of a new line north from Mexico City to the United States border. A company made up of both Mexican and British investors—the Central Railroad of Mexico—obtained the concession. A United States concern, headed by Emile la Sere of New Orleans, received promise of a subsidy of 12,500 pesos for each mile of track it laid down across the Isthmus of Tehuantepec. And, finally, the government encouraged feeder lines to connect with the recently completed Ferrocarril Mexicano and negotiated other contracts for the construction of telegraph lines. Lerdo's goal—to connect all of the state capitals to Mexico City by telegraph— was not reached, but he did add over sixteen hundred miles of telegraph line.

In the field of education Lerdo surpassed the efforts of his predecessor. Augmented federal and local funds resulted in a sharp increase in school construction but only a gradual increase in school enrollment. Between 1870 and 1874 the number of schools in Mexico almost doubled, but even in the latter year the 349,000 students represented only one out of nineteen school-age children. And years of tradition had established another pattern that was difficult to break; of these only seventy-seven thousand were female.

With school construction growing much more rapidly than enrollment, many school seats remained empty. Availability of classroom space was not itself the answer. An available school seat did not mean that a competent teacher would be found or that a poor father would sacrifice the meager supplement to the family income that three or four small children working in the fields, shining shoes, or selling newspapers might provide.

The Lerdo administration made progress in other areas. The government added France to the list of European countries with which diplomatic relations had been restored. Secretary of the Treasury Romero continued his work on tariff revision and was able to codify his efforts. Lerdo also broke ground on one important political reform. The unicameral national legislature provided by the Constitution of 1857 had been under attack for years. The president proposed that a second house be added, and the legislative branch responded to the request in 1875. A Senate was added to the Chamber of Deputies,

SCHOOLS AND STUDENT ENROLLMENT, 1844–74

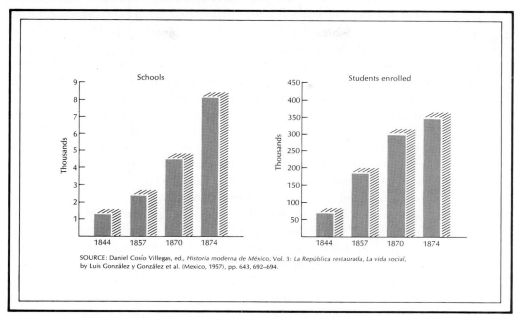

SOURCE: Daniel Cosío Villegas, ed., *Historia moderna de México*, Vol. 3: *La República restaurada, La vida social*, by Luis González y González et al. (Mexico, 1957), pp. 643, 692–694.

bringing the legislature back to the formula that had been first tested in 1824. Lerdo wanted the second, more elite body because he believed that it could be useful to him in his centralization efforts.

Lerdo's administration turned out to be one of the better ones that Mexico had yet experienced. But as any man of action, he could not emerge from the Mexican presidency unscathed. The enemies mounted, the press assailed him mercilessly, and prominent politicians of both parties spoke out strongly against him. The rumors were vicious. He had at one time studied for the priesthood and was even charged with making up for lost time as a celibate. When Lerdo announced that he was planning to seek re-election in 1876, Porfirio Díaz perceived that history was finally on his side. In March 1876, five years after his unsuccessful attempt to overthrow Benito Juárez under the Plan de la Noria, Díaz was ready to try again. He issued the *Plan de Tuxtepec*, charging that Lerdo had repeatedly violated the sovereignty of the states and the municipalities, sacrificed Mexico's best interests in negotiating the railroad contracts, reduced the right of suffrage to a farce, and squandered public funds. But, most importantly, the plan established no-re-election of the president and the governors of the states as the supreme law of the land. Effective suffrage and no-re-election were to be the guiding principles of the Mexican political process.

The Revolution of Tuxtepec was decided in one decisive battle as soldiers in a score of states flocked to the new banner. The opposing forces met on November 16 at Tecoac in the state of Tlaxcala; Díaz, reinforced by cohort Manuel González, carried the day. Recognizing that the path to Mexico City was wide open, the president, with little disposition to carry on, abandoned the struggle and made his way to Acapulco where a steamer was waiting to carry him to the United States. Porfirio Díaz occupied Mexico City on November 21, 1876; he would control the country, directly or indirectly, for the next third of a century.

Careful examination of the restored republic reveals it to be a critical transition between the demise of the empire and the establishment of the Díaz dictatorship. For the first time in Mexican history the administrations in power seemed more to pull the country together than to drive it apart. All of the major changes generally attributed to Díaz and his successive cabinets in the last quarter of the nineteenth century and first decade of the twentieth are firmly rooted in the years 1867 to 1876: tax and tariff reform; increased public security, especially in the rural areas; recognition of the need to attract foreign capital; the improvement of transportation and communication facilities; the cultivation of better relations abroad; a slightly less antagonistic relationship between church and state; and increased centralism disguised as federalism. Juárez and Lerdo, especially the former, laid the foundations, and Porfirio Díaz would construct the edifice. But modern Mexico did begin in 1867. Díaz's subsequent accomplishments were possible because his two predecessors in the presidential chair had paved the way.

RECOMMENDED FOR FURTHER STUDY

Acuña, Rodolfo F. *Sonoran Strongman: Ignacio Pesqueira and His Times.* Tucson: University of Arizona Press, 1974.

Bazant, Jan. *Alienation of Church Wealth in Mexico: Social and Economic Aspects of the Liberal Revolution, 1856–1875.* Cambridge: Cambridge University Press, 1971.

Glick, Edward B. *Straddling the Isthmus of Tehuantepec.* Gainesville: University of Florida Press, 1959.

Knapp, Frank A. *The Life of Sebastián Lerdo de Tejada: A Study of Influence and Obscurity.* Austin: University of Texas Press, 1951.

Mallon, Florencia E. *Peasant and Nation: The Making of Postcolonial Mexico and Peru.* Berkeley: University of California Press, 1995.

Pletcher, David M. "The Building of the Mexican Railway." *Hispanic American Historical Review* 30 (1950): 26–62.

Scholes, Walter V. *Mexican Politics during the Juárez Regime, 1855–1872.* Columbia: University of Missouri Press, 1957.

Sinkin, Richard N. *The Mexican Reform, 1855–1876: A Study in Liberal Nation Building*. Austin: Institute of Latin American Studies, 1979.

Smart, Charles Allen. *Viva Juárez!* London: Eyre and Spottiswoode, 1964.

Thomson, Guy P.C., with David G. LaFrance. *Patriotism, Politics, and Popular Liberalism in Nineteenth-Century Mexico: Juan Francisco Lucas and the Puebla Sierra*. Wilmington, Del.: Scholarly Resources, 1999.

Vanderwood, Paul. "Genesis of the Rurales: Mexico's Early Struggle for Public Security." *Hispanic American Historical Review* 50 (1970): 323–44.

Weeks, Charles A. *The Juárez Myth in Mexico*. University: University of Alabama Press, 1987.

22

Society and Culture in the Middle of the Nineteenth Century

RURAL LIFE

Mexico was still overwhelmingly rural in the 1850s, 1860s, and 1870s, and life for the average citizen changed very little. Those who resided in the Indian pueblo or the mestizo village lived much like their parents or their grandparents. In terms of earning power, standard of living, diet, life expectancy, and education, the life of the rural Mexican during the empire and the restored republic closely mirrored that which two earlier generations of independent Mexicans had experienced. In almost every important respect he remained outside of the mainstream of national society, and his life was one of privation.

The gap separating brown and white Mexico, poor and rich Mexico, was not bridged in the middle of the century. It might even have grown more pronounced. The dichotomy of Mexican worlds in 1865 was described by Francisco Pimentel.

> The white is the proprietor; the Indian the worker. The white is rich; the Indian poor and miserable. The descendants of the Spaniards have within their reach all of the knowledge of the century and all of the scientific discoveries; the Indian is completely unaware of it. The white dresses like a Parisian fashion plate and uses the richest of fabrics; the Indian runs around almost naked. The white lives in the cities in magnificent houses; the Indian is isolated in the country, his house a miserable hut. They are two different peoples in the same land; but worse, to a degree they are enemies.[1]

Foreign travelers to Mexico found the main roads slightly better than they would have a generation earlier, but most others were still

---

1. Quoted in Daniel Cosío Villegas, ed., *Historia moderna de México*, vol. 3: *La república restaurada, La vida social*, by Luis González y González et al. (Mexico City, 1957), p. 151.

an abomination. They were all very dangerous because of the bandits who continued to plague the highways. Scarcely a visitor to the country failed to note this institutionalized ill. The wife of Prince Salm-Salm, one of Maximilian's confidants, described the anxieties of passengers of the stagecoach from Veracruz to Mexico City as follows:

> It occurs very frequently that the diligence is attacked and plundered by robbers, and many horrible adventures of that kind are recorded, furnishing the passengers not very reassuring matter for conversation, and keeping them in a continual excitement. . . . The coachman does not even attempt to escape or resist; it is his policy to remain neutral, for if he acted otherwise it would not only be in vain, but cost him his life—a bullet from behind some bush would end his career on the next journey. . . .[2]

Overnight lodging in the larger towns, while generally not elegant, had improved since the early post-Independence years. But villages and Indian pueblos remained unchanged. William Marshall Anderson, a United States citizen who visited Mexico during the empire, found in one southern village "no shelter nor place to rest but a miserable grass covered shanty, no bigger or better than my sheep pen." As he moved north the architecture changed but not the amenities. "Unplastered stone walls and a dirt floor constitute the comfort and elegance of our accommodation."[3]

By the 1850s and 1860s rural Mexicans were certainly long accustomed to the indignities of an army marching through their village or, if they were unfortunate, stopping for food or supplies. But the Intervention and Restoration periods added several new ingredients. The French troops comported themselves even worse than their American predecessors of 1846–48. They treated the Mexican peasants with utmost disdain and were far from polite in their solicitation of female indulgence. Common sense defies that the generation of blue-eyed, light-skinned babies born in Mexico in the 1860s were all the product of French debauchery, but the not-too-subtle physiognomic changes in those villages hosting a French garrison, or having one nearby, suggest that to the victor belong the spoils.

The social consequences of war did not end with the expulsion of the French. When President Juárez cut back on the size of the Mexican

---

2. Princess Felix Salm-Salm, *Ten Years of My Life* (London, 1876), 1: 183–85.

3. William Marshall Anderson, *An American in Maximilian's Mexico, 1865–1866: The Diaries of William Marshall Anderson*, ed. Ramón Eduardo Ruiz (San Marino, Calif., 1959), pp. 15, 80.

army, tens of thousands of former soldiers were left jobless and hundreds of miles from home. Not a few of them formed bands, and, with a horse, gun, and tattered uniform still bearing military insignia, many took out their frustrations on rural villages or hacienda complexes. The newspapers of the period were filled with stories of brigandage and plunder. Lawlessness became a social cancer reaching epidemic proportions.

POPULATION AND SOCIAL PROBLEMS

As might be expected during a period of foreign war and domestic turmoil, the population of Mexico grew very slowly during the middle of the nineteenth century. Some of the state capitals even lost inhabitants, and northern Mexico still supported only a scanty population. From a figure of 7,860,000 in 1856, the census counters could find only 8,743,000 Mexicans in 1874. The slow rate of growth cannot be attributed to a low birth rate. To the contrary, the birth rate was high, but war casualties and a very high infant mortality rate kept the population down.

Policy makers during both the empire and the restored republic wished to open up new lands, and some even spoke of the need to encourage the development of a new class of independent farmers. Be-

Saltillo, the capital of Coahuila, hardly grew at all in the 1860s and 1870s, but it was one of the more charming provincial capitals of the north.

cause of the slow rate of population growth, however, European immigration was deemed to be the answer. Despite Mexico's one sad experience with foreign immigrants in Texas, laws were put on the books in the 1850s and 1860s to encourage immigration from Europe. But religious intolerance, political instability, and much administrative mismanagement all mitigated against a successful program. When the liberals consolidated their victory after the expulsion of the French, they believed that the basic problems were resolved and that part of the flow of immigrants to Argentina, Chile, Brazil, and the United States would be diverted to Mexico. But their project met with no more success than had earlier ones. Mexico had not yet lived down its reputation, and the three thousand immigrants from western Europe, the United States, and China who began to arrive annually during the Restoration did not even offset the emigration of Mexicans to the United States. In 1876 only about twenty-five thousand people in Mexico were foreign-born, and they almost all resided in the larger cities.

Mexico City's population grew to two hundred thousand during the restored republic, and the capital experienced some remarkable physical transformations. Without question the most notable was the construction of an impressive new thoroughfare that connected Chapultepec Castle to the heart of the city. The project had been initiated under Maximilian, who had named it the Calzada de la Emperatriz in honor of Carlota. The emperor did not live to see the project finished. It would be completed during the restored republic and Benito Juárez changed the name, most appropriately, to the Paseo de la Reforma. It

The turbulence of the French Intervention and the Restoration made it inevitable that soldiers would be found congregating in Mexico City.

would remain Mexico's most imposing boulevard. But with growth and change Mexico City began to experience increased social problems. Prostitution had long been accepted as a necessary evil in Mexico, but when the women of the street began openly soliciting clients at the entrance to the main cathedral and the hundreds of smaller churches, a public uproar followed. Those who called for a crackdown pointed to the burgeoning rate of venereal disease and the perversion of the young and innocent. The defenders argued somewhat theatrically that the institution had to be retained as a safeguard of the chastity of honorable women who would be deflowered on the street if the virile *machos* of the capital had no such release. A sensible compromise was reached. The women of pleasure were pushed into well-defined red-light zones so as not to offend the causal passerby and were made subject to periodic medical inspection to arrest the rate of venereal disease.

The Roman Catholic Church had always made alms giving a virtue, and by the middle of the nineteenth century mendicancy was as institutionalized as prostitution. While léperos could be found in all of the larger towns and cities, they congregated by the thousands in Mexico City. Men and women with one hand extended—cripples, the blind, alcoholics, even abandoned children—were found everywhere in the capital. If unsuccessful on the streets or in the churches, they moved from door to door in both residential and business zones. Government attempts to curb mendicancy included the establishment of new charitable institutions and hospitals for the poor, but such efforts, as well intentioned as they might have been, accomplished little.

THE THREE CLASSES

The lot of the urban working class at mid-century was in some ways even worse than that of the beggars. Workers could not count on private charity, church support, government aid, or welfare institutions. Job security was nonexistent, the worker being completely subject to the whims of his employer. While the industrial revolution had scarcely touched Mexico, the capital did have its share of factories producing textiles, soap, cigarettes, flour, and alcoholic beverages. The thousands working in these small industries enjoyed but few protective laws. Legislation regulating child labor, safety precautions, and other working conditions was scant, and those laws on the books were seldom enforced. Slightly better off were people who worked for themselves, the tens of thousands of street vendors each with a distinctive call hawking tortillas, sweet bread, fruit, flowers, water, ice, candy, pottery, straw baskets, tamales, pulque, roasted corn, milk, ice cream, rosaries, crucifixes, pictures of the Virgin of Guadalupe, and an endless variety of other goods. But their diet was grossly deficient and their life expectancy short; they were all illiterate and lived in shacks on the outskirts of Mexico City.

One of the best jobs the illiterate city dweller could hope for was domestic service. As a generation earlier, the maids, gardeners, doorkeepers, valets, stable masters, chambermaids, and nanas did relatively well. They received up to fourteen or fifteen pesos a month without food, or three or four with. But they were at least assured a clean room in which to live and, despite long hours, tolerable working conditions in one of the nicer residential districts of the capital.

The still tiny middle class—composed of shopkeepers, merchants, small independent entrepreneurs, professional men, government officials, and other white-collar workers—lived comfortably but without amenities. The houses (often rooms above their stores) were small but adequately furnished with locally made products. Tiles or straw mats covered the floor; rugs were unusual. Because of a grossly inadequate water supply system, very few smaller homes had private baths. Public bathing facilities were scarce and inconvenient enough that neither daily nor weekly bathing was common; the trade in cheap perfumes and colognes was good.

The palatial residences of the wealthy families were mainly in the district of Tacubaya, at the western end of the city. It was a genuine showplace, described by an English visitor in the 1860s as a district where "all the men with heavy purses build villas and country houses, to which they retire in the summer months. . . . It is really a very pretty place."[4]

The façades of the houses were often decorated by students or professors from the Art Academy of San Carlos. Elegant patios, marble staircases, carved doors, crystal chandeliers, gold candelabra, imported pianos and carpets, rosewood furniture, and old Spanish paintings were staple items in every aristocratic home. Most also had private chapels with the patron saints of the family's members represented. The real marks of distinction, however, were the resplendent private baths, decorated with imported French fixtures. Many of these aristocratic homes required twenty or twenty-five servants to keep them going. Some of the affluent required fewer but hired more in unabashed ostentation.

Women who visited Mexico in the 1860s and 1870s often commented upon the general ignorance of the ladies of the genteel aristocracy they found there. Princess Salm-Salm dwelled upon the subject in her memoirs, but the best description comes from Countess Paula Kollonitz, a lady-in-waiting to Empress Carlota.

---

4. J. F. Elton, *With the French in Mexico* (London, 1867), pp. 37–38.

Growing from a squalid Indian community to the most fashionable sub-urb of Mexico City, by 1850 Tacubaya often housed Mexican presidents, cabinet ministers, bishops, and all of the wealthiest residents of the capital, both Mexican and foreign. At mid-century its population stood at 5,000, but vacationers swelled the count to 6,500 during the summer months.

> I never saw any book in the hand of a lady, except her prayer book. . . . They write letters, for the most part, with an unpractised hand. Their ignorance is complete; they have not the smallest idea of geography and history. Europe to them consists of Spain, from whence they sprang; Rome, where the Pope rules; and Paris, from whence come their clothes. They have no conception of other countries or other nations, and they could not comprehend that French was not our native tongue.[5]

One wonders just how much the ladies of Europe knew about Mexico, Argentina, or Chile, much less Honduras, Ecuador, or Bolivia, but the point should not be lost. Women, even aristocratic women, had received short shrift in the educational system, and the results were patent.

SOCIAL AMUSEMENTS AND CULTURAL ACHIEVEMENTS

Everyday diversion was one of the few activities that could easily cut across class lines. Members of the lower, middle, and upper strata could be seen enjoying the promenades around the Alameda, the great central park in the downtown business district, which was equipped with

---

5. Countess Paula Kollonitz, *The Court of Mexico* (London, 1868), pp. 160–61.

A Sunday bullfight at the Plaza de Toros de San Pablo, near Mexico City.

hydrogen gas lamps in 1873. Everyone enjoyed the free concerts staged in the bandstands of the public parks, and all partook of secular or religious fiestas. Public fairs and touring circuses from Europe or the United States also attracted all elements of society, as did games of dice played on outdoor tables. But the greatest social leveler of all was the bullfight, a spectacle where the cabinet minister could converse with his shoeshine boy and the aristocrat from Tacubaya could debate the awarding of ears and tails with his gardener.

The bullfight was introduced in Mexico in the early sixteenth century and quickly became a cultural institution. The main ring used in Mexico City in the middle of the century was the Plaza del Paseo Nuevo. Built in 1851 at a cost of almost a hundred thousand pesos, it seated ten thousand and was filled each time a fight was held. To be sure, the more affluent sat in the shade and the masses in the sun, the rich drank cognac and the poor pulque, but they all saw the same show. Toreros Bernardo Gaviño, Pablo Mendoza, and Ignacio Gadea were the rage of the era. But not all of the performances were good, and after one particularly bad fight in 1867, during which several horses were killed and blood filled the ring, the press began a concerted campaign for abolition of the sport. Emphasizing the brutality of the spectacle, the opponents succeeded in having the Congress pass legislation outlawing bullfighting in the Federal District over which it had jurisdiction. But the owners of the bullrings, the raisers of fighting stock, the performers, and the thousands of fans argued for reconsideration. The law remained on the books for twenty years, but, meanwhile, ingenuity accomplished what congressional lobbying could not. In 1874 a new ring was dedicated in Tlalnepantla, just outside the Federal District but not so far as to deter the avid aficionados of Mexico City. The placards announcing the Sunday spectacles were plastered all over the walls of the capital.

If popular culture reached virtually everyone, "high culture" was obviously not directed to the illiterate masses. Yet in many ways the arts of the mid-nineteenth century were socially aware and embodied much more than the rejection of the Spanish past that had typified creative endeavors in the first three decades after Independence. The social awareness of the 1850s, 1860s, and 1870s did not generally manifest itself as a series of pleas for the impoverished masses. Rather it called for the establishment of a new, stronger, secular, more developed, and progressive Mexico. It began to inculcate pride in the concept of mexicanidad and to show what patriotism could mean. Further, it tried to overcome the damage that had been done to Mexico's self-image.

In literature the romantic novel was not superseded but did assume a distinctly new flavor. The new novel, while no less moralistic than the old, was more instructive. To a generation that had witnessed many civil wars and two foreign wars, the cultural orientation was historical, and the historical novel lent itself perfectly to the goals of the new intelligentsia. Armies, and especially foreign ones, marching through poor native villages, raping and looting on their way, provided an abundance of subject matter for historical novelists like Juan A. Mateos, Ireneo Paz, and Vicente Riva Palacio. These writers evoked compassion in the reader not because the Indians and mestizos were poor and subject to abuse but because they were Mexican and subject to abuse.

The literary giant of the period was Ignacio Manuel Altamirano (1834–95). Born to Indian parents in Tixtla, Guerrero, he went to school first in the pueblo and later in Mexico City, but his education was interrupted by the wars of the Reform and the French Intervention. In 1861 he had been elected to the Congress, where he voiced radical opinions. After the expulsion of the French he edited several literary journals and then turned his attention to the novel, a literary form he believed should be didactic. In 1869 and 1871 he published two widely acclaimed short novels, *Clemencia* and *La Navidad en las montañas* (translated as *Christmas in the Mountains*). Set in Guadalajara during the French Intervention, *Clemencia* propounded the ideal of patriotism through the characterization of an officer in the republican army. The social content of *La Navidad en las montañas*, however, is still more apparent. In it the author attacked forced conscription (the leva), urged the development of a new educational system, and denounced the clergy for its failure to meet the real needs of the Mexican community.

The period of Maximilian's empire could have been a productive one for Mexican music and art. The Hapsburg emperor had polished and refined cultural interests and lent his personal support and that of his office to the fine arts. He even underwrote the production costs of an opera by Melesio Morales, Mexico's foremost mid-century composer. But not even the fine arts could escape the intense partiality of the age. The old Art Academy of San Carlos, subsequently changed to the National Academy, was redesignated the Imperial Academy by Maximilian. Dedicated Juarista liberals in the academy could not serve Maximilian in good conscience, and many resigned their posts. When the French were expelled, the academy was reorganized again, this time as the National School of Fine Arts, and many of those artists who had painted for the French found it expedient to step down.

Mexican art in the 1850s, 1860s, and 1870s was dominated by two figures of primary importance: Pelegrín Clavé (1810–80) and Juan Cordero (1824–84). Clavé, a Spaniard by birth, taught at the academy for almost twenty years. He was a portrait painter of the first class; his most famous work was a portrait of Benito Juárez, which today hangs in the Chapultepec Museum. Cordero, much like the historical novelists of the period, was comfortable with historical and philosophical themes that taught a message. In 1874 he completed a mural in the main staircase of the National Preparatory School entitled *Triumph and Study over Ignorance and Sloth*. It depicted Mexican progress in terms of science, industry, and commerce. This trilogy, he believed, would destroy ignorance and greed. The new muses, Electra and Vaporosa, did not toy with harps but rather with a magnetic compass and an apparatus that converted water into steam. A locomotive pulling heavy freight cars depicted the benefits of science. It is not surprising that the positivist creed is clearly present in this work; it was commissioned by Gabino Barreda, the director of the National Preparatory School.

The music of social awareness also followed on the heels of the collapse of Maximilian's empire. Aniceto Ortega's two most famous marches, both completed in 1867, celebrated the defeat of the invader. They were appropriately entitled *Marcha Zaragoza* and *Marcha Republicana*.

Nowhere is the mid-century culture of a new Mexico better illustrated than in the field of philosophy, and seldom can the beginning of a philosophical movement be so accurately pinpointed as Mexican positivism. On September 16, 1867, in an Independence Day cele-

Gabino Barreda (1818–81). Barreda, who founded the National Preparatory School in 1867, also introduced Mexico to the positivism of Auguste Comte and in the process provided the philosophical underpinnings for Mexican cientificismo. In good positivist fashion, the curriculum he introduced at the school subordinated the arts to the sciences.

bration in Guanajuato, Gabino Barreda delivered an eloquent speech subsequently known as the "Civic Oration." As a student of Auguste Comte, Barreda had read and observed widely. He interpreted Mexican history as a struggle between a negative spirit (represented most recently by the alliance of the conservative and the French) and a positivist spirit (embodied by the liberal republican forces). The combative phase of the struggle had ended with the execution of Maximilian, and the country was now prepared to embark upon the constructive phase. Barreda was optimistic. Mexico's material regeneration could be achieved through the most prudent application of scientific knowledge and the scientific method. He ended his speech by coining a new slogan for the new Mexico: "Liberty, Order, and Progress." Within a short time, however, Mexican liberals would sense that Liberty was not an equal partner in the positivist trinity. It would be sacrificed, almost meticulously, to Order and Progress. The liberal party would split asunder over the positivist issue, and the moderates, who placed their faith in Order and Progress, would gain the upper hand. Championing a gradualist approach to positivist dogma they would be the harbingers of Mexican modernity.

RECOMMENDED FOR FURTHER STUDY

Altamirano, Ignacio Manuel. *Christmas in the Mountains*. Translated by Harvey L. Johnson. Gainesville: University of Florida Press, 1961.

Arrom, Silvia M. *Containing the Poor: The Mexico City Poor House, 1774–1881.* Durham, N.C.: Duke University Press, 2001.

Brushwood, John S. *Mexico in Its Novel: A Nation's Search for Identity.* Austin: University of Texas Press, 1966.

Hale, Charles A. *The Transformation of Liberalism in Late Nineteenth-Century Mexico.* Princeton, N.J.: Princeton University Press, 1989.

Pedelty, Mark. *Musical Ritual in Mexico City: From the Aztec to NAFTA.* Austin: University of Texas Press, 2004.

Raat, William D. "The Leopoldo Zea and Mexican Positivism: A Reappraisal." *Hispanic American Historical Review* 48 (1968): 1–18.

Rugeley, Terry. *Of Wonders and Wise Men: Religion and Popular Cultures in Southeast Mexico, 1800–1876.* Austin: University of Texas Press, 2001.

Salm-Salm, Princess Felix. *Ten Years of My Life.* 2 vols. London: Richard Bentley & Son, 1876.

Stevenson, Robert. *Music in Mexico: A Historical Survey.* New York: Thomas Y. Crowell, 1971.

Wasserman, Mark. *Everyday Life and Politics in Nineteenth-Century Mexico.* Albuquerque: University of New Mexico Press, 2000.

Wilson, Robert A. *Mexico: Its Peasants and Its Priests.* New York: Harper and Brothers, 1856.

Zea, Leopoldo. *The Latin American Mind.* Norman: University of Oklahoma Press, 1963.

———. *Positivism in Mexico.* Translated by Josephine H. Schulte. Austin: University of Texas Press, 1974.

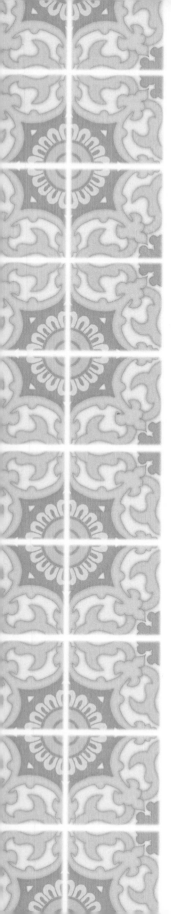

VII

THE MODERNIZATION OF MEXICO, 1876–1910

23

The Porfiriato: Order and Progress

Porfirio Díaz controlled the destiny of the Mexican nation for a third of a century. These were interesting and vital years in the entire western world. Innovation characterized the era—in technology, political and economic systems, social values, and artistic expression. Otto von Bismarck transformed the German states into a nation. William Gladstone introduced England to a new kind of liberalism. The leading powers of Europe partitioned Africa unto themselves. The United States emerged as a world power, and Spain lost Cuba, Puerto Rico, and the Philippines—the last remnants of its once-glorious empire. Russia experienced a revolution that, though abortive, presaged things to come in 1917. Pope Leo XIII enunciated *Rerum Novarum*, proclaiming that employees should be treated more as men than as tools. Thomas Hardy and Thomas Mann revolutionized the world of fiction, while Renoir and Monet did the same for art. But even in a world of profound change, Porfirio Díaz's Mexico must be considered remarkable.

MEXICO IN 1876

When Díaz assumed control of Mexico in 1876, except in a few of the larger cities, the country had scarcely been touched by the scientific, technological, and industrial revolutions or the material conquests of the nineteenth century. While much of western Europe and the United States had been transformed in the last fifty years, Mexico had languished, less out of inertia than because of the intermittent chaos and resultant exhaustion. In the fifty-five years since Independence the presidency had actually changed hands seventy-five times, making continuity of policy impossible.

Although the period of the Restoration had pointed Mexico in a new direction, plans for change had only been partially implemented. In 1876 Díaz inherited an empty treasury, a long list of foreign debts, and a huge bureaucratic corps whose salaries were in arrears. Mexico's credit rating abroad was abominable, and its politics had become somewhat of a joke in Europe. The value of Mexican imports consistently exceeded the value of exports, presenting a serious balance-of-payments problem. It was virtually impossible to secure sorely needed infusions of foreign capital, and the Mexican affluent, knowing the precarious nature of the political process, would not invest their own resources to any large degree. Because of graft, ineptitude, and mismanagement the public services were poorly run. The mail, if it arrived at all, came inexcusably late.

Mining had never really recovered from the chaotic and dour days of the Wars for Independence. A small number of mines operated inefficiently without benefit of technological improvements, and no coordinated efforts at new geological exploration had been undertaken. The economic situation of agriculture was much the same. Modern reapers and threshers and newly developed chemical fertilizers were still oddities. Practically nothing had been done to improve the breeding of stock animals.

When Díaz came to the presidency the iron horse had just started to compete with the oxcart, the mule train, and the coach. Telegraph construction had barely begun. The dock facilities on both coasts were in sad disrepair, and many of the most important harbors were silted with sand. Veracruz was so unsafe for shipping that some favored abandoning it altogether. The rurales had not yet been able to contain banditry and rural violence. A tremendously high infant mortality rate testified to the lack of modern sanitation and health facilities even as the last quarter of the nineteenth century began. Yellow fever plagued the tropical areas of the Gulf coast, particularly in the immediate environs of Veracruz.

Mexico City had a special health problem. Situated in a broad valley, it was surrounded by mountains and a series of lakes, almost all of which were at a higher elevation than the city. Heavy rains invariably brought flooding. In addition to extensive property damage (floods often caused adobe walls to crumble), the waters then stagnated in low-lying areas for weeks and months. Disease, reaching epidemic proportions, frequently followed on the heels of a serious flood. Projects to provide an adequate drainage system for the city had been proposed since the seventeenth century. The height of the surrounding mountains, however, thwarted proposals for a foolproof system of drainage canals and dikes, and the projects initiated from time to time were never fully successful.

ORDER AND PROGRESS UNDER DÍAZ

If progress were to displace stagnation, Díaz believed it would be necessary first to change Mexico's image drastically and to remove the

stigma popularly associated with Mexican politics. Only if the potential investors from the United States and Europe were convinced that
stability was supplanting turbulence could they be expected to offer
their dollars and pounds sterling, for profit, to quickly vitalize the manufacturing, mining, and agricultural sectors of the Mexican economy.
The task, then, as Díaz perceived it, was first to establish the rule of
law. He was fully prepared to accept the positivist dictum of Order
and Progress, in that order.

Díaz's liberal credentials and personal integrity were impeccable. Born
to a family of modest means in the city of Oaxaca in 1830, he tried studying first for the priesthood and then for the law. But he eventually opted
for a career in the army. Joining the Oaxaca National Guard in 1856, he
fought under the liberal banner during the War of the Reform. With the
liberal victory promotions came with startling rapidity, and by the time
of his history-making defeat of the French in Puebla on May 5, 1862, he
was a thirty-two-year-old brigadier general. During the period of the empire he won additional military fame championing the cause of liberal republicanism as a guerrilla fighter against the French army. Not even his
abortive revolt of La Noria against Benito Juárez or his successful revolt
of Tuxtepec against Lerdo de Tejada, both fought in defense of the liberal principle of no re-election, tarnished his liberal reputation.

During his first term, which lasted until 1880, Díaz was faced with
a number of insurrections. Agrarian rebellions protesting seizure of village lands flared in many states, but not all the revolts were of an agrarian nature. Some were prompted by Díaz's failure to reward supporters or by his heavy-handed appointments at the state level. But the
most serious were a number of revolts launched along the United
States border in support of exiled president Lerdo de Tejada. These
military movements not only threatened the success of Díaz's pacification program but also damaged his efforts to cultivate more friendly
relations with his northern neighbor. But Díaz was not hesitant in meeting force with force. Rebel leaders who were not shot down on the
field of battle were disposed of shortly after their capture. Characteristic of Díaz's attitude toward those who would disrupt the national
peace was his reaction to a revolt in Veracruz during his first year in
office. When Governor Luis Mier y Terán asked for instructions concerning captured rebels in that state, Díaz reportedly telegraphed him,
Mátalos en caliente (Kill them on the spot). Such lessons were not lost
on potential revolutionaries elsewhere. Mexico was not as tranquil in
the post-1880 period as often portrayed. Yet the peace was not shattered as often or as violently as in the past. Over eight hundred corpsmen had been added to the rurales to curb brigandage. Order was
gradually coming, and progress would accompany it.

Within a couple of years of his assumption of the presidency Díaz had been recognized by most of western Europe and Latin America, but the United States held out pending the satisfactory resolution of several outstanding problems. One obstacle was overcome when Díaz in 1876 agreed to terms that would satisfy U.S. claimants over damages to their properties in Mexico. The Hayes administration had one further grievance. Groups of Mexican bandits and Indians occasionally crossed the border, attacked settlements in the United States, and drove herds of cattle back into Mexico. The Mexican government, in the name of national sovereignty, refused to grant permission to United States forces to cross over into Mexico in pursuit. In the summer of 1877 border depredations brought the two nations almost to the brink of war. Díaz was at his best at this crucial juncture. While he would not permit American troops to enter Mexican territory, he did dispatch additional troops of his own to the border region to prevent further encroachments. Tensions gradually subsided, and President Hayes authorized recognition of the Díaz regime in the spring of 1877.

During his first administration Díaz also began to put Mexico's economic house in order. As a symbolic gesture he reduced his own salary and then ordered similar reductions for other government employees. Thousands of useless bureaucrats were eliminated from the rolls altogether. In addition, the administration attacked a problem endemic since the colonial period—smuggling. To prevent the annual loss of hundreds of thousands of dollars in import and export duties along the United States border and in Mexico's leading ports, Díaz decreed heavy sentences for individuals and companies trafficking in smuggled goods. To stimulate legal commerce with the United States three new Mexican consulates were opened along the Texas border, at Rio Grande City, Laredo, and Eagle Pass.

As Díaz's first term drew to a close, several of the states urged that the no-re-election law be amended so that Díaz could be eligible to serve another term. But Díaz preferred the law as it was; it provided that neither the president nor the state governors were eligible for immediate re-election but could serve again after the lapse of an intervening term. He dutifully retired from office. By voluntarily stepping aside Díaz could give further substance to the growing conviction abroad that Mexico had begun to mature politically. As the term ended, Díaz threw his support behind forty-seven-year-old Manuel González, an imposing military man who had rendered yeoman service in the fight against Lerdo and who was currently serving as secretary of war. González won the election with a large majority.

THE GONZÁLEZ PRESIDENCY

The González presidency was controversial. The new president wanted to follow the patterns established by Díaz and, in fact, even brought his predecessor into the government for a short time as head of the Department of Development. Revenues increased, but so did expenditures as the administration plunged headlong into further development. Modernization was expensive. Railroad construction continued, but the companies required large subsidies from the government—as high as $9,500 for each kilometer of track laid. The government also fostered new steamship lines and established the first cable service in the country. But González had overextended his regime and found himself without sufficient funds to meet government obligations.

Stories of graft and corruption began filling the press, and political pamphlets denouncing the regime circulated on the streets of Mexico City. The president and his cabinet were charged with a variety of personal and public improprieties, ranging from negotiating illegal contracts and receiving rebates, selling government properties to administration favorites for practically nothing, stealing from the treasury at a fantastic rate, and sexual misconduct. The public turned against the president.

The charges were either fabrications or gross exaggerations. The suggestion that Díaz fabricated the stories to discredit González is more fanciful and cynical than accurate; the best scholarship of the period suggests that Manuel González was not a puppet of Porfirio Díaz. González called his own shots and, in fact, must be given credit for encouraging the developmental process that had begun timidly with the restoration of the republic. But perhaps the most important lesson to be drawn is that the attacks against the president, as intense as they were, did not occasion any serious armed insurrection. The vituperations certainly could have tarnished Mexico's changing image, but when elections, rather than a new revolutionary plan, followed, many were convinced that the country had finally turned the corner.

THE RETURN OF DÍAZ

Díaz used his four years out of office to relax and to build a new political machine. He served for a brief time in the González cabinet and for slightly over a year in the governorship of his native state of Oaxaca. His first wife, Delfina Ortega, had died in 1880, and the following year he married Carmen Romero Rubio, the daughter of Manuel Romero Rubio, a Lerdista statesman and cabinet member. She was eighteen; Díaz had just celebrated his fifty-first birthday. They traveled to the United States on their honeymoon as Mexico's representatives to the New Orleans World's Fair; newspapermen often mistook her for his daughter. But the well-bred, sensitive, and perfectly-prepared-to-be-a-first-lady Señora Díaz began to educate her husband in the social graces. She performed her task admirably, and within a couple of years Díaz was much more the polished gentleman when he ran for the presidency in 1884. In September Díaz swept to victory. From this time forward he would not feel the need to step out of office after completing each term and would remain in the presidency continually until 1911. The conditions that greeted him in 1884 were a far cry from those of 1876.

FOUNDATIONS OF MODERNIZATION

Returning with renewed vigor, Porfirio Díaz had a plan for consolidating his political position and stabilizing the country. Mexico entered a period of sustained economic growth the likes of which it had never before experienced. As Mexico entered the modern age, steam, water, and electric power began to replace animal and human muscle. A number of new hydraulic- and hydroelectric-generating stations were built as the modernization process tied itself to the new machines it supported. The telephone arrived amid amazement and wonder in the 1880s. The Department of Communications and Public Works supervised and coordinated the installation of the wireless telegraph and submarine cables. A hundred miles of electric tramway connected the heart of Mexico City to the suburbs.

A major breakthrough in health and sanitation occurred when Díaz hired the British firm of S. Pearson and Son, Ltd., to bring modern technology to the drainage problem of Mexico City. For sixteen million pesos the English engineers and contractors, with the experience of the Blackwell Tunnel under the Thames and the East River Tunnel in New York behind them, successfully completed a thirty-mile canal and a six-mile tunnel that relieved the Mexican capital of the threat of constant flooding and resultant property damage and disease. At approximately the same time the face of the country was scoured to bolster the country's own self-respect and its image abroad. A public building spree changed the contours of boulevards, parks, and public buildings. Monuments and statues were dedicated to the world's leading statesmen, intellectuals, and military figures. A new penitentiary costing 2.5 million pesos opened in 1900, and a 3-million-peso post office in 1907. A new asylum for the insane, a new municipal palace, and a new Department of Foreign Relations were dedicated prior to the centennial celebrations of 1910. The white marble National Theater, however, missed the centennial target date, and the heavy structure began to sink into the spongy subsoil of Mexico City before it could be finished. Each time a new project was completed, it was formally dedicated in an elaborate and well-planned ceremony to which foreign diplomats, dignitaries, and businessmen received special presidential invitations. Their impressions of Mexico, relayed to colleagues back home, would help effect the change of image.

Mexico's own adaptation of positivism provided the philosophical underpinning of the regime. The *científicos*, as those who followed in the footsteps of Gabino Barreda came to be known, were not all orthodox Comteans. Some blended Comte with John Stuart Mill, and others added a large dose of Herbert Spencer. A few of the científicos called for modest programs ushering the Indian masses into a rapidly modernizing world, but many were paternalistic toward the Indian at best and elitist at worst, believing that Mexico's future lay solely with the criollo class. According to Justo Sierra, a científico spokesman, Mexico had to pass through a period of "administrative power" (a euphemism for dictatorship) before it could attain nationhood. Then the time would be ripe to discuss the broadening of the participatory base.

The president and his científico advisers realized first of all that a series of structural reforms were needed to place Mexico's economic house in order, and they were fortunate to find an economic genius in their midst. José Ives Limantour, soon renowned in European financial circles, was the son of a French émigré. A man of many talents, he was a scholar, an accomplished jurist, and a dedicated linguist. First as subsecretary and then secretary of the treasury, he applied the best positivist thought of the day to the reorganization of the country's finances, which offered a fertile field for his talents. For Limantour, Mexico's future was fully dependent upon its economic regeneration. To be sure, Matías Romero, during the Restoration, had begun work on a revision of the tariff, but much remained to be done. Gradually, during the 1880s and 1890s Secretary Limantour lowered or eliminated the duties on many imports and permitted special tariff exemptions for economically depressed areas of the country. He also negotiated a series of loans at favorable rates of interest and, most important for the economic well-being of the country, shifted Mexico from the silver to the gold standard.

As significant as any of the individual reforms was Limantour's decision to overhaul the nation's administrative machinery so that the reforms could be properly implemented. While it would be foolhardy to suggest that all graft and corruption were eliminated, Limantour did improve the situation markedly, at least at the lower echelons of

José Limantour (1854–1935). An advocate of positivism, Limantour, as secretary of the treasury, brought order and reason to Porfirian finances. Able and attentive to detail, he was the epitome of the Porfirian statesman who would reinvent Mexican society.

government. The dividends were startling. In 1890 the last installment of the debt to the United States, growing out of the mixed claims settlement, was paid, and four years later Mexico had not only balanced its budget for the first time in history but actually showed that revenues were running slightly ahead of expenditures. When Díaz left office in 1911 the treasury had about seventy million pesos in cash reserves. Beyond all expectations he had succeeded in reassuring the outside world that Mexico had not only turned the corner but also deserved international dignity and respect.

The image abroad did change. As Limantour applied his skills to the reorganization of the treasury and Mexico met its foreign obligations on a regular basis, diplomatic relations were opened with all of Europe, and new treaties of friendship, commerce, and navigation were signed with Great Britain, France, Norway, Ecuador, and Japan. For the first time Mexico began to participate actively in international conferences. Foreign heads of state were lavish in their praise of the Díaz regime. By the late 1880s and early 1890s Díaz had begun to receive medals and decorations from foreign governments.

THE RAILROAD BOOM

Díaz was fully prepared to take advantage of the good economic indicators and the new reputation he had so assiduously cultivated. His government embarked upon a multifaceted program to modernize the transportation and mining sectors of the economy. To accomplish this he turned to foreign investment and technology in the 1880s. The Mexican Central Railroad Company, backed by a group of Boston investors, received the concession to construct the major line north from Mexico City to El Paso, Texas. Work began from both terminal points, and the 1,224-mile project was completed in an amazingly short four-year period. The Central was soon flanked by two other new lines to its east and west. In 1888 the Mexican National Railroad Company, originally chartered under the laws of Colorado but subsequently purchased by a group of French and English entrepreneurs, successfully completed a new narrow-gauge line between Mexico City and Laredo, Texas, a distance of eight hundred miles and the shortest route from the Mexican capital to the United States border. Shortly after the turn of the century it was converted to standard gauge. Finally the Sonora Railroad Company, headed by Thomas Nickerson, built the line between Guaymas, on the Pacific Ocean, and Nogales, Arizona. By 1890 the total trackage of these three major companies approached two thousand miles.

Efforts to connect the country from east to west did not proceed so smoothly. After earlier attempts to build a line across the Isthmus of Tehuantepec languished, in 1894 Chandos S. Stanhope completed a

Porfirio Díaz (1830–1915). As soldier, rebel, statesman, and president, Diaz compelled respect and dominated his country as no previous figure in the nineteenth century.

line, but the construction work and terminal facilities were grossly inadequate. Díaz was forced to grant a new concession to S. Pearson and Son, Ltd., the famous British concern. Sir Weetman Dickinson Pearson drove an especially hard bargain, and the completed line proved to be one of the most costly in Mexican history. In 1907 the trains were running regularly between Puerto México on the Gulf coast and Salina Cruz on the Pacific. With the Panama Canal already under construction, the Tehuantepec Railroad would soon be rendered obsolete.

Numerous lesser lines were undertaken in the 1880s and 1890s. A line in the south connected Mexico City with Guatemala, and short feeder lines connected most of the state capitals with the major trunks running between Mexico City and the United States border. By the end of the Díaz regime railroads interlaced the entire country; from about four hundred miles of track in 1876, Mexico in 1911 could boast fifteen thousand. Approximately 80 percent of the capital outlay came from the United States. In 1908, however, under the constant prodding of Limantour, the Díaz government purchased the controlling interest in the major lines.

These achievements did not come easily. Mexico's lack of requisite managerial skills and, more generally, a prevailing development cul-

The arrival of the daily train triggered a burst of activity in hundreds of Mexican towns. This station scene was captured by American photographer Sumner W. Matteson in the station of Amecameca in 1907.

ture meant that years passed before the railroads were smooth-running operations, but ultimately they would contribute to the tremendous economic transformation of the country. As the cities were linked to the outlying areas, raw materials could be shipped to industries and finished goods distributed to a greatly expanded domestic market. As products could be quickly transported to population centers and the leading ports, new agricultural lands, specializing in commercial agriculture, were opened, and land values increased as peasants were dispossessed of their lands.[1] Mexico's textile industry, for example, relied primarily upon imported cotton at the beginning of the Díaz period, but with the opening of new lands in the north, near the railroad lines, cotton production by 1910 not only doubled but made the country almost self-sufficient. When the railroad arrived in Morelos the sugar planters began importing new machinery and setting up new mills to expand production. The larger market for locally produced products drove the costs down and, at least theoretically, widened the base of consumer use. Communities isolated by geography and centuries of tradition were gradually brought into greater contact with one another, and, as a result, the phenomenon of patria chica was challenged seriously for the first time.

THE REVIVAL OF MINING

The railroads were a means to many ends, and not least among these was the revival of Mexico's potentially wealthy mining industry. The railroads, of course, offered the only practical and economical means of transporting massive shipments of ore. But, equally important, the Díaz-controlled legislature passed a new mining code in 1884. In order to appeal to the foreign investor the code made no mention of traditional Hispanic jurisprudence reserving ownership of the subsoil for the nation. Further, the proprietor of the surface was explicitly granted ownership of all bituminous and other mineral fuels. Several years after the mining code was enacted, the mining tax laws were revised, exempting certain minerals altogether and lowering the tax rates on others. United States and European investors recognized that the potential profits were great and entered Mexico in increasing numbers in the

---

1. One perceptive analysis of some fifty-five agrarian protests during the early Porfiriato indicates that over 90 percent occurred at a distance of less than forty kilometers from a new or projected railroad line. See John Coatsworth, "Railroads, Landholding, and Agrarian Protest in the Early Porfiriato," *Hispanic American Historical Review* 54 (1974): 55–57.

1880s and 1890s. The new miners introduced modern machinery and new processes of extracting the metal from the ore, producing a radical transformation of the entire industry.

Between 1880 and 1890 three large mining developments were initiated by foreigners in Mexico: Sierra Mojada in Coahuila; Batopilas in Chihuahua; and El Boleo in Santa Rosalía, Baja California. Within a few years the Sierra Mojada region was yielding a thousand tons of silver and lead per week, and Batopilas had made a fortune for its owners. El Boleo, under French and German ownership, proved to be one of the richest copper mining areas in North America.

The introduction of the cyanide process, which made it profitable to extract metal from ores containing only a few ounces of metal to the ton, revolutionized the mining of gold and silver. Largely because of new explorations and the adoption of modern mining techniques, the value of gold production rose from about 1.5 million pesos in 1877

Colonel William Greene's town of Cananea, Sonora, was the hub of Mexico's copper production and a symbol of the foreign domination of the country's natural resources.

to over 40 million pesos in 1908. Silver production followed a similar pattern, rising from 24.8 million pesos in 1877, to over 85 million pesos worth of silver was being mined in 1908.

Some of the foreign investment came in the form of huge conglomerates. The Guggenheim interests, for example, spread out over much of Mexico and entered numerous interrelated mining activities. They owned the American Smelting and Refining Company, based in Monterrey but with large plants in Chihuahua. Durango, and San Luis Potosí as well. The Aguascalientes Metal Company, the Guggenheim Exploration Company, and the Mexican Exploration Company were either partially or totally owned and controlled by Daniel Guggenheim and his six brothers. In addition, the Guggenheims acquired many already proven mines, such as the Tecolote silver mines and the Esperanza gold mine, as well as new mines in Durango, Chihuahua, Coahuila, and Zacatecas. By 1902 Guggenheim investments in northern Mexico totaled some $12 million.

Other foreign investors came to Mexico with practically nothing and built multi-million-dollar businesses. Perhaps the best example is Colonel William Greene, the copper king of Sonora. In 1898 Greene obtained an option on a Sonora copper mine for forty-seven thousand pesos from the widow of Ignacio Pesqueira, a former governor of the state. Greene sold stocks for his mining venture on Wall Street, and within a few years his Cananea Consolidated Copper Company was one of the largest copper companies in the world, operating eight large smelting furnaces and employing thirty-five hundred men. With some of the profits Greene became a lumber factor and a rancher as well; one of his ranches grazed some forty thousand head of cattle.

OIL FIELDS AND OTHER INDUSTRIAL ENTERPRISES

American and British investors engaged in a spirited competition for the exploitation of Mexico's oil. The first wells were sunk in areas where surface seepages clearly indicated the presence of petroleum reserves, but after the turn of the century systematic geological exploration began in earnest. The American interests were led by Edward L. Doheny, an American who had successfully developed oil fields in California; he now purchased over six hundred thousand acres of potentially rich oil lands around Tampico and Tuxpan. Within a short time his Mexican Petroleum Company brought forth Mexico's first commercially feasible gusher, El Ebano.

The British answer to Doheny was Sir Weetman Dickinson Pearson, who had worked on the drainage of Mexico City, the modernization of the Veracruz harbor, the reconstruction of the Tehuantepec Railroad, and the building of the terminal facilities at Puerto México and Salina Cruz. Enjoying cordial relations with Díaz, Pearson eventually obtained drilling concessions in Veracruz, San Luis Potosí, Tamaulipas, and Tabasco. Progress came slowly at first to Pearson's El Aguila Company, but a dramatic hit brought forth the Potrero del Llano, Number 4, a gusher that, when successfully capped, produced more than a hundred million barrels in eight years. Doheny's Mexican Petroleum Company and Pearson's El Aguila Company, whose board of directors included Porfirio Díaz, Jr., dominated the petroleum industry in the early twentieth century and within a few years made Mexico one of the largest petroleum producers in the world.

It would be an exaggeration to suggest that Mexico experienced a profound industrial revolution during the Díaz years, but the industrial process did make itself felt. In 1902 the industrial census listed fifty-five hundred manufacturing industries. The volume of manufactured goods doubled during the Porfiriato. The process began in Monterrey, Nuevo León, where, in addition to the huge Guggenheim interests, other American, French, German, and British investors backed industrial enterprises. Attracted by excellent transportation facilities and by the progressive policies of Governor Bernardo Reyes, which included tax exemptions for industries, foreign and domestic capital was directed into Mexico's first important steel firm, the Compañía Fundidora de Fierro y Acero de Monterrey. Within a few years the company was producing pig iron, steel rails, beams, and bars, and by 1911 it was making over sixty thousand tons of steel annually. Monterrey was soon dubbed the Pittsburgh of Mexico.

In 1890 José Schneider, a Mexican of German extraction, founded the Cervecería Cuauhtémoc, which quickly became the largest and most important brewery in the country. Among its products was Carta Blanca, the number-one selling beer in Mexico. By 1900 it was also producing bottles for its products, other kinds of glassware, bottle caps, and packing cartons for both local use and national consumption.

Other industrial concerns based in Monterrey constructed new cement, textile, cigarette, cigar, soap, brick, and furniture factories, as well as flour mills and a large bottled-water plant. Capital investment in the city grew steadily throughout the Díaz regime but most dramatically during the first decade of the new century, when it rose from under thirty million to over fifty-five million pesos. Smaller fledgling textile and paper mills, cement factories, leather works, and soap, shoe, explosives, and tile manufacturers located themselves in other areas of the country, but by 1910 Monterrey was without question the industrial capital of Mexico.

GROWTH OF FOREIGN TRADE, 1877–1910

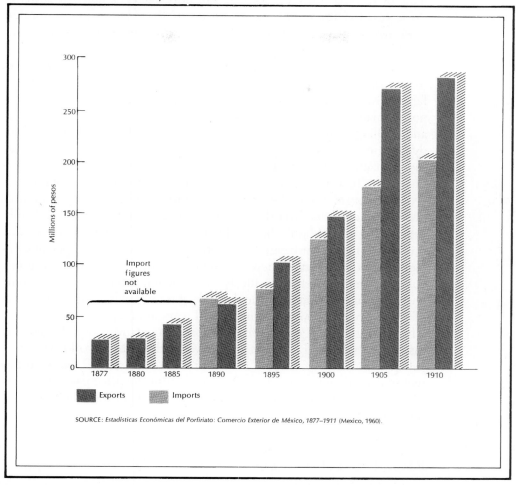

SOURCE: *Estadísticas Económicas del Porfiriato: Comercio Exterior de México, 1877–1911* (Mexico, 1960).

The improvement of harbor and dock facilities during the Porfiriato opened Mexico up to world commerce on a grander scale than ever before. Millions of pesos spent on Veracruz transformed it markedly, although its status as chief port was seriously challenged by Tampico, located at the mouth of the Panuco River. After U.S. engineers supervised the dredging of the harbor and the modernizing of dock facilities, this northern city grew rapidly as a business and commercial center and challenged Veracruz in volume handled. Similar improvements were made in the harbors of Mazatlán, Manzanillo, Puerto México, and Salina Cruz. By the turn of the century the number of serviceable ports had increased to ten on the Gulf coast and fourteen on the Pacific side. Partially because of the improvements in port facilities, and partially because of Limantour's reforms in the tariff structure, Mexico's foreign trade (exports and imports) increased from about 50 million pesos in 1876 to about 488 million pesos in 1910.

Although many of the trappings of traditional society were still to be found, the Mexico of the first decade of the twentieth century was a far cry from that of 1876. Improved public services and modern transportation and communication facilities opened the country to new ideas and challenged the concept of patria chica. The economy boomed, and dynamism permeated the atmosphere. Technology in general and mechanization in particular made tremendous strides. Foreign travelers for the first time marveled more than they criticized, for peace and growth allowed them the luxury of contemplating the many natural beauties Mexico had to offer. Mexico's foreign credit rating was firmly established throughout the world. But perhaps the most important product of the modernization process was that Mexicans, especially urban Mexicans, began to view themselves differently. A new consumer culture began to alter urban lifestyles. Self-confidence replaced the embarrassment occasioned by the decades of internecine strife. For a third of a century there were no major civil wars, no major liberal-conservative struggles, and no major church-state controversies. Mexico was assuming its rightful position in the twentieth-century world. Very few yet questioned the costs the transformation had exacted, because the material dividends seemed so self-evident. But the price paid was great, and the rapid modernization contained seeds of self-destruction.

RECOMMENDED FOR FURTHER STUDY

Beatty, Edward. *Institutions and Investment: The Political Basis of Industrialization in Mexico before 1911.* Stanford, Calif.: Stanford University Press, 2001.

Benjamin, Thomas, and William McNellie, eds. *Other Mexicos: Essays on Regional Mexican History, 1876–1911.* Albuquerque: University of New Mexico Press, 1984.

Bernstein, Marvin D. *The Mexican Mining Industry, 1890–1950: A Study of the Interaction of Politics, Economics, and Technology.* Albany: State University of New York Press, 1964.

Boortz, Jeffrey L., and Stephen Haber, eds. *The Mexican Economy, 1870–1930: Essays in the Economic History of Institutions, Revolution, and Growth.* Stanford, Calif.: Stanford University Press, 2002.

Buchenau, Jurgen. *Tools of Progress: A German Merchant Family in Mexico City, 1865–Present.* Albuquerque: University of New Mexico Press, 2004.

Buffington, Robert M., and William E. French. "The Culture of Modernity," in *The Oxford History of Mexico.* Edited by Michael C. Meyer and William H. Beezley, pp. 397–432. New York: Oxford University Press, 2000.

Coatsworth, John. "Railroads, Landholding, and Agrarian Protest in the Early Porfiriato." *Hispanic American Historical Review* 54 (1974): 48–71.

Coerver, Donald. *The Porfirian Interregnum: The Presidency of Manuel González of Mexico, 1880–1884.* Fort Worth: Texas Christian University Press, 1979.

Ficker, Sandra Kuntz. "Economic Backwardness and Firm Strategy: An American Railroad Corporation in Nineteenth Century Mexico." *Hispanic American Historical Review* 80 (2000): 267–98.

Hart, John Mason. *Empire and Revolution: The Americans in Mexico since the Civil War.* Berkeley: University of California Press, 2002.

Hibeno, Barbara. "Cervecería Cuauhtémoc: A Case Study of Technological and Industrial Development." *Mexican Studies* 8 (1992): 123–43.

Kroeber, Clifton, B. *Man, Land and Water: Mexico's Farmland Irrigation Policies, 1885–1911.* Berkeley: University of California Press, 1984.

Meyers, William K. "Politics, Vested Rights, and Economic Growth in Porfirian Mexico." *Hispanic American Historical Review* 57 (1977): 425–54.

Mora-Torres, Juan. *The Making of the Mexican Border: The State, Capitalism, and Society in Nuevo León, 1848–1911.* Austin: University of Texas Press, 2001.

Pletcher, David M. *Rails, Mines, and Progress: Seven American Promoters in Mexico, 1867–1911.* Ithaca, N.Y.: Cornell University Press, 1958.

Raat, William D. "Leopoldo Zea and Mexican Positivism: A Reappraisal." *Hispanic American Historical Review* 48 (1968): 1–18.

Schell, William Jr. *Integral Outsiders: The American Colony in Mexico City, 1876–1911.* Wilmington, Del.: Scholarly Resources, 2001.

Tinker Salas, Miguel. "Sonora: The Making of a Border Society, 1880–1910." *Journal of the Southwest* 34 (1992): 429–56.

Tischendorf, Alfred. *Great Britain and Mexico in the Era of Porfirio Díaz.* Durham, N.C.: Duke University Press, 1961.

Topik, Steven C. "The Emergence of Finance Capital in Mexico," in *Five Centuries of Mexican History.* Edited by Virginia Guedea and Jaime E. Rodríguez, Vol. II, pp. 227–42. Mexico City and Irvine: Instituto Mora and University of California Irvine, 1992.

Trillo, Mauricio Tenorio. "1910 Mexico City: Space and Nation in the City of the Centenario." *Journal of Latin American Studies* 28 (1996): 75–105.

Wasserman, Mark. *Capitalists, Caciques and Revolution: The Native Elite and Foreign Enterprises in Chihuahua Mexico, 1854–1911.* Chapel Hill: University of North Carolina Press, 1984.

Wells, Allen. *Yucatan's Gilded Age: Haciendas, Henequen and International Harvester.* Albuquerque: University of New Mexico Press, 1985.

Weiner, Richard. *Race, Nation, and Market: Economic Changes in Porfirian Mexico.* Tucson: University of Arizona Press, 2004.

24

The Costs of Modernization

DICTATORSHIP BY FORCE

Modernization came to Mexico during the Díaz regime not simply as the result of positivist theory and careful economic planning. The peace that made it all possible was in part attributable to brute force. Díaz maintained himself in power from 1876 to 1911 by a combination of adroit political maneuvering, intimidation, and, whenever necessary, callous use of the federal army and the rurales. He was the consummate bully.

Throughout the thirty-four years the dictator maintained the sham of democracy. Elections were held periodically at the local, state, and national levels, but they were invariably manipulated in favor of those candidates who held official favor. The press throughout the epoch was tightly censored; journalists who dared to oppose the regime on any substantive matter found themselves in jail or exile, while recalcitrant editors found their newspapers closed down. Filomeno Mata, the editor of the *Diario del Hogar*, suffered imprisonment over thirty times for his anti-re-electionist campaigns. While a few persistent critics were killed, the large majority of the journalists were bludgeoned into submission and ceased to constitute a problem.

The dictator played off political opponents against one another, or bought them off. Potentially ambitious generals or regimental commanders were shifted regularly from one military zone to another to assure that they would be unable to cultivate a power base. State governors were invited to assume the same position in other states or to become congressmen, cabinet secretaries, or diplomats to remove their influence at home. Not even members of the Díaz family were immune. When the dictator's nephew, Félix Díaz, decided to run for the governorship of Oaxaca against Don Porfirio's wishes, he shortly found himself on a ship bound for Chile, where he was given a diplomatic post and allowed to cool off. Most influential Mexicans cooperated with the regime and were rewarded with political favors and lucrative economic concessions. Díaz himself never accumulated a personal fortune, but many of his civilian and military supporters in high positions had ample opportunity for graft. The científico advisers, for example, always seemed to know in advance the route of a new boulevard or railroad line, the property could thus be bought up at a low price and sold back to the government for a profit.

When Díaz needed to use force it was provided by the army and the rurales. He recognized the need for professionalizing the army, and, although he did not invite foreign military missions into the country, he did send military observers to West Point and to the French officer's school at St. Cyr. The recently reorganized Colegio Militar de Chapultepec provided formal instruction for the officer corps and made use of the most current European training manuals. By the turn of the century about half of the active officers (but very few of the generals) were graduates of the Chapultepec academy. The cadets, resplendent in snappy uniforms, were highlighted at the frequent military parades during which Díaz took the opportunity to display the latest armament obtained from France or Germany.

The rurales, Díaz's praetorian guard, also constituted an important enforcement tool for the *Pax Porfiriana*. The dictator strengthened the corps considerably, not simply to curtail brigandage in the rural

To reinforce the desired image, the rurales were always featured during military parades. Sumner Matteson photographed this salute to President Díaz on May 5, 1907.

areas but to serve as a counterpoise to the army itself. By the end of the regime the strength of the rurales had been increased to over twenty-seven hundred men. While the force was not large, it was used to good advantage by the dictator. In addition to its original patrolling functions, Díaz had rural corpsmen guard ore shipments from the mines, support local police forces, escort prisoners, enforce unpopular court decisions, and guard public payrolls and buildings. We are now quite certain that the rurales were neither as harsh nor as efficient as generally thought. While Díaz did not, as commonly understood, deliberately induct known bandits into the corps, neither did he try to set straight their image for cruelty and excess. The myth served his purposes well, for the rurales were feared by brigands, marauders, political opponents, and recalcitrant villagers. When trouble flared it was often more prudent to send in the nearest corps than to allow a distinguished federal general the chance to enhance his reputation.

Díaz used the military not only to force compliance with the dictates of Mexico City but to administer the country as well. By the mid-1880s it was not unusual for military officers, most often generals of unquestionable loyalty, to dominate the state governorships and to be well represented among the three hundred *jefes políticos* (local political bosses). In 1900, although relative peace had already been achieved, Díaz was still spending almost one-fourth of the total budget on the military establishment. He believed it was worth it because the modernization process was so intertwined with his concept of enforced peace.

Díaz's científico advisers have been labeled racist for their conscientious denigration of the Indian population. But the generalization has certain flaws, for it presupposes a monolithic philosophical framework within the científico community. José Limantour was less a follower of Comte than of Darwin. He adapted notions of natural selection and survival of the fittest to Mexican reality as he understood it and emerged from his introspection calling for an aristocratic elite to reorder society. Little or no help could be expected from the Indian population. Francisco Bulnes, a prolific historian and apologist for científico rule, was more openly racist. Five million (white) Argentines, he argued, were worth more than fourteen million Mexicans. The Mexican Indian was sullenly intractable and hopelessly inferior, not because of innate corruption of his genes but because his grossly deficient diet sapped his mental, moral, and physical vitality. He responded more to the logic of force than to the art of persuasion. Less biologically oriented was Justo Sierra, the most famous científico of them all. Cofounder of the conservative newspaper *La Libertad*, author of *Evolución política del pueblo mexicano*, secretary of education during part

The federal artillery corps, well trained and well equipped, was the pride of the Díaz army.

of the Porfiriato, and first rector of the national university, Sierra argued forcefully that social and cultural forces, not biological ones, had shaped the Indian's inferior position. And unlike Limantour and Bulnes, Sierra asserted the Indian's educability.

In the political sense the científicos may have had a point. Perhaps Mexico was not yet ready for democracy, and perhaps it was too early to broaden the participatory base. But their impassioned defense of the need for "administrative power" implied at best self-deception and at worst blatant hypocrisy. If they truly believed that the Indian masses could be prepared for a more active role in the political life of the Mexican nation, the logical place to begin the preparation process was an educational system that reached the people. But the schools built during the Porfiriato, even when the Department of Education was in Justo Sierra's hands, were almost all located in the cities where the criollos lived, not in the rural areas where they might serve the Indian and mestizo population. At the end of the Porfiriato Mexico still had two million Indians not speaking Spanish. They had been left aside.

THE HACENDADOS

Mexico greeted the twentieth century still a predominantly rural country, and the rural peasantry bore most of the costs of modernization.

The payment was exacted in fear of the rurales, intimidation by local hacendados, constant badgering by jefes políticos and municipal officials, exploitation by foreign entrepreneurs, and, most important, seizure of private and communal lands by government-supported land sharks.

Life in rural Mexico had been dominated by the hacienda complex since the colonial period, but the abuses of the system were exacerbated markedly during the Díaz regime as railroad construction pushed land values up. The problem of exaggerated land concentration was directly attributable to a new land law enacted in 1883. This law, designed to encourage foreign colonization of rural Mexico, authorized land companies to survey public lands for the purpose of subdivision and settlement. For their efforts the companies received up to one-third of the land surveyed and the privilege of purchasing the remaining two-thirds at bargain prices. If the private owners or traditional ejidos could not prove ownership through legal title, their land was considered public and subject to denunciation by the companies.

The process that ensued was predictable. Very few rural Mexicans could prove legal title. All they knew for sure was that they had lived and worked the same plot for their entire lives, and their parents and grandparents had done the same. Their boundary line ran from a certain tree to a certain stream to the crest of a hill. The few who could produce documents, some dating back to the colonial period, were convinced by the speculators and their lawyers that the papers had not been properly signed, or notarized, or stamped, or registered. But not even those communal ejidos that could produce titles of indisputable legality were immune. The Constitution of 1857 with its Reform laws was once again applied to the detriment of the ejidos, and with greater vigor than ever before.

Within five years after the land law became operative, land companies had obtained possession of over sixty-eight million acres of rural land and by 1894 one-fifth of the total land mass of Mexico. Not yet completely satisfied, the companies received a favorable modification of the law in 1894, and by the early twentieth century most of the villages in rural Mexico had lost their ejidos and some 134 million acres of the best land had passed into the hands of a few hundred fantastically wealthy families. Over one-half of all rural Mexicans lived and worked on the haciendas by 1910.

The Mexican census of 1910 listed 8,245 haciendas in the republic, but a few wealthy individuals, often tied together by a marriage network of family elites, owned ten, fifteen, or even twenty of them. Though varied in size, haciendas of forty or fifty thousand acres were not at all uncommon. Fifteen of the richest Mexican hacendados owned haciendas totaling more than three hundred thousand acres each. The state of Chihuahua affords a classic example of how the hacienda system operated and brought wealth and prestige to one extended family. Throughout the Díaz regime the fortunes of that north central Mexican state were guided by the Terrazas-Creel clan. Don Luis Terrazas, the founder of the dynasty, had served as governor prior to the French Intervention and fought with Juárez against the French in the 1860s. His land acquisitions began shortly thereafter, when he obtained the estate of Don Pablo Martínez del Río, a French sympathizer. In the 1870s, 1880s, and 1890s, in and out of the gubernatorial chair, he acquired additional haciendas, profiting immensely from the land laws of the Díaz government. By the early twentieth century Terrazas owned some fifty haciendas and smaller ranches totaling a fantastic seven million acres. Don Luis was the largest hacendado in Mexico and perhaps in all of Latin America; his holdings were eight times the size of the legendary King Ranch in Texas. He owned 500,000 head of cattle, 225,000 sheep, 25,000 horses, 5,000 mules, and some of the best fighting bulls in the western hemisphere. Encinillas, northwest of Chihuahua City, was the largest of his haciendas, extending to some 1,300,000 acres and employing some 2,000 peones. San Miguel de Babícora was over 850,000 acres, while San Luis and Hormigas were over 700,000 acres each.

But the wealth and power of the Terrazas family cannot be judged in terms of landholding and its related activities alone. Don Luis also owned textile mills, granaries, railroads, telephone companies, candle factories, sugar mills, meat packing plants, and several Chihuahua mines. Each of his twelve children was married with the care characteristic of Renaissance nobility. Daughter Angela Terrazas married her first cousin, Enrique Creel, the son of an American consul in Chihuahua and a man of wealth, erudition, and prestige. Enrique Creel also served several times in the state governorship and, in addition, was Mexico's secretary of foreign relations in 1910–11. Creel's own haciendas totaled more than 1,700,000 acres. He was also one of the founders and directors of the Banco Minero de Chihuahua, which gradually absorbed many of the other banks in the state. He was a partner, furthermore, in many of his father-in-law's enterprises and directed or owned iron and steel mills, breweries, granaries, and a coal company. Other daughters and sons also married well. The sons, as to be expected, became hacendados and entrepreneurs. Sons Alberto and Juan each had haciendas totaling over 600,000 acres, and son-in-law Federico Sisniega held some 260,000 acres and was a director of the Banco Nacional de Chihuahua. To strengthen the already strong Terrazas-Creel ties, son Alberto married his niece, Emilia Creel, the daughter of his sister Angela and Enrique Creel. Son Federico Terrazas married into the Falomir family and daughter Adela into the Muñoz family, two of the other most wealthy and prestigious families in the state.

It is virtually impossible to calculate the extent of either the fortune or the power wielded by the Terrazas-Creel clan. Luis Terrazas himself probably did not know how much he owned. He surely did know, however, that the value of rural land in Chihuahua rose from about \$.30 per acre in 1879 to about \$9.88 per acre in 1908. Had he been able to liquidate only his personal, nonurban landholdings on the eve of the Mexican Revolution, he would have carried over \$69 million to the bank.

One can be certain that little of major importance occurred in Chihuahua without the approval of patriarch Don Luis Terrazas. During the Díaz regime members of the extended family sat for a total of sixty-six terms in the state legislature and twenty-two terms in the national legislature. Because residency requirements were loosely defined, Enrique Creel and Juan Terrazas became national senators from other Mexican states. Municipal and regional officialdom bore either the Terrazas-Creel names or their stamp of approval. The immense power was built upon a foundation of land, and the state of Chihuahua was a microcosm of what was happening throughout the Mexican republic.

The state of Morelos was dominated not by one extended family but rather by a handful of powerful sugar families: the García Pimentels, the Amors, the Torre y Miers, and a few others. To fund the purchase of expensive new machinery these families had to increase production and so began expanding into new lands. As no public lands were available, they completely encircled small ranches and even villages, thereby choking off all infusions of economic lifeblood. Some towns stagnated, while others vanished from the map altogether. The town fathers of Cuautla could not even find sufficient land for a new cemetery and were reduced to burying children in a neighboring village.

THE PEONES

The millions of rural Mexicans who found themselves in dying villages or subsisting as peones on the nation's haciendas were worse off financially than their rural ancestors a century before. The average daily wage for an agricultural worker remained almost steady throughout the nineteenth century—about thirty-five centavos. But in the same hundred-year period the price of corn and chile more than doubled, and beans cost six times more in 1910 than in 1800. In terms of purchasing power correlated with the price of corn or cheap cloth, the

Mexican peón during the Díaz regime was twelve times poorer than the United States farm laborer.

Working conditions varied considerably from region to region and even from hacienda to hacienda, but they were generally poor. Peones often availed themselves of the talents of a scribe to spell out their gamut of complaints. While it was not uncommon for the peón to be allotted a couple of furrows to plant a little corn and chile and on occasion he might receive a small ration of food from the hacienda, he worked from sunrise to sunset, often seven days a week, raising crops or tending cattle. Sometimes he was allowed to cut firewood free; on other occasions he paid for the right. The scant wages he received most often were not paid in currency but in certificates or metal discs redeemable only at the local *tienda de raya*, an all-purpose company store located on the hacienda complex. Credit was extended liberally, but the prices, set by the hacendado or the mayordomo, were invariably several times higher than those in a nearby village. For the hacendado the situation was perfect. The taxes on his land were negligible; his labor was, in effect, free, for all the wages that went out came back to him through the tienda de raya with a handsome profit. The peón found himself in a state of perpetual debt, and by law he was bound to remain on the hacienda so long as he owed a single centavo. Debts were not eradicated at the time of death but passed on to the children. Should an occasional obdurate peón escape, there was scarcely any place for him to go. Many states had laws making it illegal to hire an indebted peón.

The bookkeeping procedures in the tienda de raya always seemed to work to the disadvantage of the illiterate peón. Goods charged against his account were more expensive than they would have been had he been able to pay cash. And other items were often debited to his account. Charges for a marriage ceremony or a funeral often exceeded the monthly wage. Fines for real or imagined crimes on the hacienda were added; forced contributions for fiestas and interest on previous debts were tallied. And, in the most ignominious charge of all, some hacendados even added a monthly fee for the privilege of shopping at the tienda de raya.

Stories of corporal punishment of the peón (petty theft could bring two hundred lashes) and sexual violation of the young women on the haciendas are commonplace, but they are virtually impossible to prove or disprove. It is certain that conditions on the henequen haciendas of Yucatán were the worst in the republic. While the rebellious Mayas of the Cross in the eastern Yucatán peninsula maintained a more autonomous but politically fragmented existence, the henequen hacendados worked their Maya peons like slaves. Because many of the pe-

For a couple of centavos the rural, illiterate Mexicans could hire a scribe to scratch out a few lines to a relative or friend.

ones in Yucatán were deportees from other parts of Mexico (some were recalcitrant Yaqui Indians from Sonora, and others were convicted criminals), they were forced to work in chains, and flogging was not uncommon. There is little evidence, however, that this type of physical maltreatment was widespread throughout Mexico. Surely the peón and his family were everywhere subject to the personal whims of the hacendado or the mayordomo, but hacienda records and correspondence to local, state, and even national officials reveal that complaints, while frequent, rarely contained charges of physical abuse. More common are complaints of intolerable working conditions, violence in the peón community itself, and dishonest record keeping in the tienda de raya—and always the sense of poverty, powerlessness, and hopelessness. During especially busy times like planting or harvesting, the permanent work force was augmented by temporary workers, often from surrounding villages. New arrivals, frequently earning a slightly higher wage than the resident peones seemed to break the socioeconomic equilibrium, and violence between the two groups of workers was a constant threat.

The dichotomies of nineteenth-century Mexican life, especially those of wealth and poverty, are almost all to be found on the hacienda.

The main hacienda house was sumptuous, externally and internally. But the hacendado would seldom spend more than a few months a year there. Most often he had other haciendas to attend, inevitably businesses to manage in the cities, and then he had to visit his children in their fine European or United States boarding schools. The hacienda provided, in addition to its income, a summer vacation home, a change of pace, and social status. The hacendado's teen-age children, remarkable for their conspicuous consumption, used trips to the hacienda to impress their friends. The extended families could be comfortably accommodated, and young boys, donned in charro costume and mounted on carefully bred and well-groomed horses, could fancy themselves country squires. Birthdays, saints' days, and feast days were reason enough to move the family from the state capital to the hacienda for an outing, and on special occasions, like an eighteenth birthday or a wedding, entire train cars could be reserved to carry guests, musicians, local dignitaries, and domestics.

The contrast between the hacendado and those who worked the hacienda and made it live is so stark as to be absurd. Because all "justice" on the hacienda was administered by the mayordomo, the peón had no genuine judicial rights or legal recourse. If a mayordomo over-

In 1907, photographer Sumner Matteson was surprised to find burros, horses, mules, and people sharing quarters in this pulque hacienda, where the stench of animals was rivaled only by the stench of fermenting pulque.

reacted in punishment of some real or imagined offense, he was accountable to nobody. Within a mile of the grand hacienda house were miserable, one-room, floorless, windowless adobe shacks. Water had to be carried in daily, often from long distances. The individual plots allotted to the peón were worked often after sunset, when the important work of the day had been completed. Twice a day a few minutes would be set aside to consume some tortillas wrapped around beans and chile, washed down with a few gulps of black coffee or pulque. Protein in the form of meat, fish, or fowl, even on the cattle haciendas, was a luxury reserved for a few special occasions during the year. Infant mortality on many haciendas exceeded 25 percent.

Diversion in the form of a local fiesta might occur once a year. An amateur bullfight could be staged in the hacienda corral, and resident aficionados would try their hand with a half-grown fighting bull that somehow looked bigger as it got closer. The peones, fortified with pulque or mescal, who found momentary escape entertaining their friends often paid dearly for their bravado, but a broken arm or a punctured thigh was a small matter when one had nothing to look forward to but the drab existence and appalling squalor of the next twelve months.

Porfirio Díaz had developed his country at the expense of his countrymen. He hermetically sealed himself off from the stark realities of Mexican masses. The great material benefits of the age of modernization in no way filtered down to the people. They were still an amorphous mass destitute of hope. Their lives were not in the least changed because the new National Theater was built in Mexico City or because José Limantour was able to borrow money in London or Paris at 4 percent. In fact, for them the cost of modernization had been too great.

RECOMMENDED FOR FURTHER STUDY

Anderson, Rodney D. *Outcasts in Their Own Land: Mexican Industrial Workers, 1906–1911.* DeKalb: National Illinois University Press, 1976.

Beezley, William H. "Opportunity in Porfirian Mexico." *North Dakota Quarterly* 40 (1972): 30–40.

Flandrau, Charles M. *Viva Mexico.* Urbana: University of Illinois Press, 1964.

Holden, Robert H. *Mexico and the Survey of Public Lands: The Management of Modernization, 1876–1911.* Dekalb: Northern Illinois University Press, 1994.

Hu-Dehart, Evelyn. *Yaqui Resistance and Survival: The Struggle for Land and Autonomy, 1821–1910.* Madison: University of Wisconsin Press, 1984.

Katz, Friedrich. "Labor Conditions on Haciendas in Porfirian Mexico: Some Trends and Tendencies." *Hispanic American Historical Review* 54 (1974): 1–47.

Meyers, William K. *Forge of Progress, Crucible of Revolt: The Origins of the Mexican Revolution in La Comarca Lagunera, 1880–1911.* Albuquerque: University of New Mexico Press, 1994.

Raat, William D. "Ideas and Society in Don Porfirio's Mexico." *The Americas* 30 (1973): 32–53.

Ruiz, Ramón. *The People of Sonora and the Yankee Capitalists.* Tucson: University of Arizona Press, 1988.

Sandels, Robert. "Silvestre Terrazas and the Old Regime in Chihuahua." *The Americas* 28 (1971): 192–205.

Snodgrass, Michael. *Deference and Defiance in Monterrey: Workers, Paternalism, and Revolution in Mexico, 1890–1950.* Cambridge: Cambridge University Press, 2003.

Vanderwood, Paul. *Disorder and Progress: Bandits, Police and Mexican Development.* Rev. ed. Wilmington, Del.: Scholarly Resources, 1992.

———. *The Power of God Against the Guns of Government: Religious Upheaval in Mexico at the Turn of the Nineteenth Century.* Stanford, Calif.: Stanford University Press, 1998.

Walker, David W. "Homegrown Revolution: The Hacienda Santa Catalina del Alamo y Anexas and Agrarian Protest in Eastern Durango, Mexico, 1897–1913." *Hispanic American Historical Review* 72 (1992): 239–73.

———. "Porfirian Labor Politics: Working Class Organizations in Mexico City and Porfirio Díaz." *The Americas* 37 (1981): 257–90.

Wasserman, Mark. "The Social Origins of the 1910 Revolution in Chihuahua." *Latin American Research Review* 15 (1980): 15–38.

Wells, Allen. "Family Elites in a Boom-and-Bust Economy: The Molinas and Peóns of Porfirian Yucatán." *Hispanic American Historical Review* 62 (1982): 224–53.

Wells, Allen, and Gilbert M. Joseph. *Summer of Discontent, Seasons of Upheaval: Elite Politics and Rural Insurgency in Yucatán, 1876–1915.* Stanford, Calif.: Stanford University Press, 1997.

Womack, John, Jr. *Zapata and the Mexican Revolution.* New York: Knopf, 1968.

Young, Elliott. *Catarino Garza's Revolution on the Texas-Mexico Border.* Durham, N.C.: Duke University Press, 2004.

25

Society and Culture
during the Porfiriato

The changes in Mexican society and culture during the Porfiriato were every bit as profound as those in the political and economic realms. Most noteworthy perhaps was the fact that Mexicans began to view themselves differently. Self-esteem replaced the sense of shame that had characterized the introspective diagnoses of the past. For the first time Mexico had shown its potential and had began to catch up with a rapidly changing world. Optimism had replaced pessimism, and xenophilia at least challenged xenophobia.

POPULATION

The stability of the Porfiriato resulted in Mexico's first period of prolonged population growth. In the absence of war and its social dislocations and with modest gains recorded in health and sanitation, the population grew from 8,743,000 in 1874 to 15,160,000 in 1910. From 1810 to 1874 the average annual population growth had been about 43,000, but during the Díaz era population increased at an average of 180,000 per year. Mexico City and the state capitals grew even more rapidly than the population at large, increasing some 88.5 percent during the epoch. From a population of 200,000 in 1874, Mexico City in 1910 was the home of 471,066 Mexicans.

Railroad development, mining activities, and port improvements caused a number of tiny villages to burgeon into towns and cities. Torreón, at the intersection of the Mexican Central Railroad and the International Railroad (running from Eagle Pass, Texas, to Durango), jumped from fewer than 2,000 inhabitants in 1876 to over 43,000 in 1910; Sabinas, Coahuila, from 788 to 14,555; and Nuevo Laredo from 1,283 to almost 9,000. The two port terminuses of the Tehuantepec Railroad recorded similar gains. Puerto México had only 267 inhabitants in 1884 but reached 6,616 by 1910, while Salina Cruz grew from 738 in 1900 to almost 6,000 ten years later. Colonel Greene's copper town of Cananea hardly existed at the beginning of the Porfiriato. From

POPULATION OF SELECTED MEXICAN CITIES DURING THE PORFIRIATO

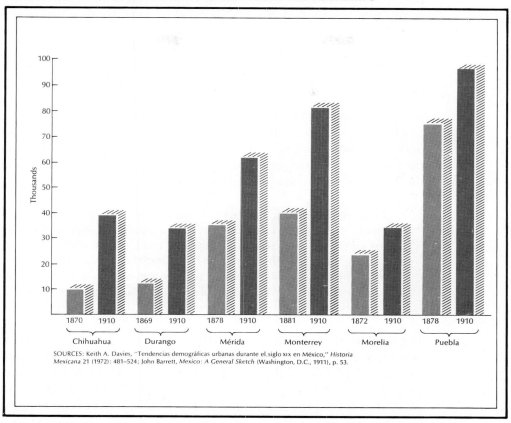

SOURCES: Keith A. Davies, "Tendencias demográficas urbanas durante el siglo xix en México," *Historia Mexicana* 21 (1972): 481–524; John Barrett, *Mexico: A General Sketch* (Washington, D.C., 1911), p. 53.

a population of about 100 in 1876, it catapulted to almost 15,000 in 1910.

Urban Improvements

The rapid growth of towns and cities throughout the republic was accompanied by an obvious dynamism in society. The sleepy Mexico that caught the visitor's eyes earlier in the century had awakened from its slumber. Travelers were astonished by the amount of construction going on everywhere. By 1910 all the state capitals had electricity, and most had tramways. Weekly newspapers became dailies, potable water systems and sewage systems were extended, hospitals were constructed, and new hotels sprang up to cater to the greatly increasing tourist trade. Even small, out-of-the-way towns improved their facilities. Whereas travelers during the first fifty years after Independence were often horrified at Mexico's hotels and inns, tourists late in the Díaz regime were pleasantly surprised.

On occasion growth got out of hand. When Mexico City held its Independence Day celebrations in September 1882, the forty thousand tourists who descended on the capital simply could not all be accommodated. But the lesson was not lost. In 1910, during the more elaborate centennial celebrations, there were rooms for everyone.

The transportation system in the capital was excellent, with first-, second-, and third-class streetcars and cabs carrying passengers throughout the city. The streetcars were sometimes put to strange uses. One caught the eye of an Irish visitor during the late Porfiriato.

> A curious feature of the streets is the electric tramway hearse. Frequently one sees a funeral consisting of a number of cars on the rails; first comes an open one like a long low truck with a black catafalque covering, under which reposes the coffin and the wreaths; the next may be another piled up with wreaths and crosses, and then follows car after car with the mourners. This of course stops all the tramway traffic for the time being.[1]

But to many the most dramatic change was in the field of law and order. Scarcely a traveler in the late nineteenth century failed to comment upon the relative absence of obvious crime and political upheaval. Most were astute enough to realize that payment for law and order was exacted in fear of the army, rurales, and local law-enforcement agencies; they considered the result worth the price. Perhaps once Mexico had passed through the difficult transition from a law-breaking to a law-respecting society, the intimidating atmosphere could be relaxed.

The changing face of urban Mexico was accompanied by a not-too-subtle modification of the value structure. Porfirio Díaz recoiled at English and United States suggestions that the time-honored tradition of the Mexican bullfight was nothing more than a cruel and barbarous spectacle. It was the epitome of a clash of values. The phenomenon has been perfectly captured by historian William Beezley, who wrote that while most Mexicans saw "the ballet of cape and animal," foreigners "saw only blood and sand." Díaz ultimately placed a higher premium on international respect than on preserving this part of Mexico's Hispanic heritage and, although he later reversed himself, during his first administration prohibited bullfighting in the Federal District,

---

1. Mary Barton, *Impressions of Mexico with Brush and Pen* (London, 1911), pp. 45–46.

Zacatecas, and Veracruz, areas where tourists would be most likely to witness the Sunday event. An American import soon offered itself as a substitute. Abner Doubleday's baseball made its Mexican debut in the 1880s and had caught on beyond anyone's expectations by the turn of the century. Not a few Mexican traditionalists lamented the exchange of the bat, the ball, and the baggy pants for the cape, the sword, and the suit of lights.[2]

SOCIAL CLASSES

The Porfiriato also witnessed some improvement in the lot of women as a select few began to enter professions hitherto regarded as the sole preserve of men. The medical school in Mexico City graduated its first woman doctor in 1887, and by the turn of the century others had followed. In the 1890s and early 1900s women began to make significant inroads into dentistry, law, pharmacy, higher education, and journalism. A new commercial school for women was inaugurated in 1903, and shortly thereafter its classes were filled. But Mexico was not yet quite ready for an active feminist movement designed to challenge in depth the traditional roles of the sexes. The prerogatives of the males were not to be questioned. The Admiradoras de Juárez, a militant feminist organization founded in 1904 by Laura Torres, was attacked by Justo Sierra as a refuge for old and ugly women whose only recourse was to try to become men. His advice to the women was to leave politics and law to the opposite sex and to concentrate instead on creating a better social atmosphere in which Mexicans could live more happily. Despite Sierra, however, many talented Mexican women no longer felt the need to confine themselves exclusively to the home.

Of course, not everything changed from 1876 to 1910. There was certainly more crime and alcoholism than the foreign visitors saw in the tourist zones of the cities. The léperos and cargadores continued to attract their attention. Although most visitors were not aware of the working conditions in the factories throughout the republic, the plight of the urban laborer had changed little, but there were many more of them. A few employers initiated modest reform early in the twentieth century. The Cervecería Cuauhtémoc in Monterrey, a Mexican-owned and Mexican-managed enterprise, was the first major industrial concern to adopt the nine-hour day. Few other Mexican industries, however,

2. These themes are developed in William H. Beezley, *Judas at the Jockey Club and Other Episodes of Porfirian Mexico* (Lincoln, 1987), pp. 13–25.

Life for the peón on the hacienda was bad; living in a city slum was even worse. But nowhere was it more difficult than in the mines.

and practically none owned by foreigners, followed suit. Even at the end of the Porfiriato the workweek for the large majority of urban laborers was seven days and the workday eleven or even twelve hours. Pensions were almost unknown, as was compensation for accidents suffered on the job.

The diet of the lower classes—day laborers, rank-and-file soldiers, beggars, domestics, street vendors, and the unemployed—remained monotonous and constantly inadequate. Corn, beans, chile, and pulque still constituted the staples; meat was almost totally absent. The grossly deficient diet and unsanitary living conditions made the masses susceptible to a wide array of debilitating diseases, and the large majority passed their entire lives without a single visit to a qualified doctor. Life expectancy remained constant—about thirty years. Infant mortality remained unacceptably high, averaging 30 percent for most of the Porfiriato. A Protestant missionary in Díaz's Mexico recalled his impressions.

> I used to ask, "How many of you, fathers and mothers, have children in heaven?" Usually all hands would promptly go up, while the replies came, *"Tengo cinco." "Tengo ocho."* . . . Deplorable ignorance as to proper sanitary conditions in the home and the care of children is re-

Modernization occurred at the expense of the poor, in both urban and rural settings.

sponsible for a large proportion of this death harvest among the little ones. Children's diseases, as measles and scarlet fever, carry multitudes away.[3]

The lower-class barrios of Mexico City—La Merced, La Palma, and Nonoalco—were so bad that some suggested they be burned to the ground. There was no indoor plumbing in these districts, and only one public bathhouse per fifteen thousand people. Garbage collection was sporadic at best. Only the completion of Mexico City's drainage canal registered a positive impact on the lower-class neighborhoods, as the masses at least were able to escape the ravages of seasonal flooding.

---

3. Alden Buell Case, *Thirty Years with the Mexicans: In Peace and Revolution* (New York, 1917), pp. 61–62.

Consumption of pulque and other alcoholic beverages among the lower classes did not increase during the Porfiriato, but the public and private outcry against alcohol did. Because alcoholism was unempirically linked to robberies, sex crimes, child abandonment, and mendicancy, temperance societies sprang up throughout the country. The Catholic press initiated a journalistic campaign, and state and local governments enacted legislation to curtail the use of alcoholic beverages. But limiting the hours of pulquerías and restricting new openings seemed to do little good, so the establishments were made as uncomfortable as possible. To discourage the patron from squandering away too much time and money, pulquerías were to have no windows, no chairs, no music, and, most important, no women. But profuse legislation did not accomplish its goal. Both alcoholism and toxemia from the high bacterial content of the pulque were widespread as the nineteenth century gave way to the twentieth.

The most dramatic change in the social structure was the expansion of the middle class. The earning power of skilled artisans, government bureaucrats, scribes, clergymen, low-ranking army officers, and professional men had increased. They demonstrated no class solidarity, but their lives were perceptibly different from the lower classes whence they had sprung. The booming economy made it possible for many a small businessman and neighborhood merchant to move his family from the drab room above the store or from his parents' residence into a larger and more comfortable apartment or house. The extension of water and sewage facilities provided many the luxury of indoor plumbing for the first time in their lives. The middle-class diet included meat and soup several times a week.

With middle-class status, creating the proper impression became important. It was not unusual for the monthly wage or monthly profit to be idled away on a single night of entertainment for friends. While the middle-class wife was beginning to break out of the home, she generally resigned herself to her husband's marital infidelity and to having but a small voice in the family's decision-making process. Seemingly possessed of infinite patience, she found some solace in the church and endured her submissive role with remarkable stoicism.

Middle-class children were taught to make class distinctions based upon outward appearances. If a well-dressed person appeared at the door they were expected to report to their parents *Allí está un señor*, but if the caller was dressed poorly the proper announcement was *Allí está un hombre*.[4] Although only recently sprung from the lower class

---

4. Jesús Silva Herzog, *Una vida en la vida de México* (Mexico City, 1972), p. 9.

José Guadalupe Posada (1852–1913), Mexico's most famous printmaker, parodies a fashionable lady during the Porfiriato.

themselves, many members of the middle class could be callous in their appreciation of the problems of the downtrodden.

While the poor continued to live in misery and a new, small middle class emerged in the cities, the rich became more convinced than ever that upon the pillar of private property civilization itself was braced. The pinnacle of social acceptance during the Porfiriato was to be invited, for a monthly dues of seven hundred pesos, to enjoy the amenities of the Jockey Club in Mexico City. The club was located in the Casa de Azulejos, the most opulent mansion in the capital. One could enjoy a sumptuous dinner there, spend an hour at the baccarat table, and hope to see cabinet ministers, governors, military zone commanders, or perhaps even Don Porfirio and Doña Carmen themselves.

The true measure of aristocratic success was to see how French one could become in taste and manners. The advantages of a French education and a French governess for aristocratic children were beyond debate. Beautiful Spanish colonial furniture was stored away, and modern French furniture adorned the houses. When Mexican composer Gustavo E. Campa wrote an opera based on the life of Nezahualcoyótl, "the Poet King of Texcoco," he entitled it not *El Rey Poeta* but *Le Roi Pòete* and prepared the libretto in French. Membership in the Sociedad Filarmónica y Dramática Francesa assured one of brushing elbows with the most Frenchified members of Mexican society at a concert or a ball and might even garner one an invitation to attend one of the famous soirées at the Lyre Gauloise. The Paseo de la Reforma was redecorated to look like the Champs Elysées, while architectural design aped *fin-de-siècle* Paris. When Mexican millionaire Antonio Escandón donated a statue of Columbus to adorn the fashionable avenue, he commissioned the Parisian sculptor Charles Cordier to do the work. Having no notion of the revolution that would soon engulf Mexico, the aristocracy blissfully celebrated Bastille Day, July 14, with almost as much enthusiasm as their own Independence Day.

French cuisine reigned supreme in the capital. The best and most expensive restaurants were the Fonda de Recamier and the Maison Doreé. Between the Consommé Brunoise Royale and the Tournedos au Cèpes, one could sip imported French wine and listen to the orchestra play "Bon Aimée," "Amoureuse," "Rendezvous," or some other tune everyone knew to be *à la mode*. For the athletic there was also membership in the French Polo Club and for the more sedate a season ticket to the French comic opera to partake of such quickly forgettable productions as *Les cloches de Corneville* or *La Fille de madame Angot*. Those who had pretensions to both music and athletics adopted the cancan, a French import that took Mexico by storm in the 1880s.

CULTURAL AND INTELLECTUAL LIFE

Literary expression during the Porfiriato found nineteenth-century romanticism yielding first to realism and almost simultaneously to modernism. The realists of the period, unlike their romantic predecessors, were not interested in instruction or moralizing. Hoping that the enforced stability of the Porfiriato would encourage the development of the arts, they early made their peace with the regime. Not a socially conscious group, the realists viewed the poor not as oppressed but rather as lazy and shiftless. On occasion a crusader emerged from the realist ranks, such as Arcadio Zentella, who decried the evils of the hacienda system in his novel *Perico* (1885). But Zentella was the exception.

More typical was José López Portillo y Rojas (1850–1923), perhaps Mexico's best realist novelist of the nineteenth century. Born to a prominent Guadalajara family, he studied law and traveled widely in Europe, imbibing the French spirit, before dedicating himself to literature. In his novel *Nieves* (1887) López Portillo did recognize that an occasional hacendado might brutalize a peón, but he found no fault with the system that conditioned the relationship or anything reprehensible in a society that tolerated it. His solution was a simplistic one. It was all a matter of volition. The poor of Mexico simply had no desire to improve themselves. "Our workers will come out of their abject condition," he wrote in *Nieves*, "when they aspire to eat well, to dress decently, and to acquire the comforts of life."[5]

The realistic period in Mexican literature was briefly prolific but not very distinguished. Much more important were the modernists of the Porfiriato. Culturally mature, stylistically innovative, and concerned with refinements in the language and a new kind of imagery, the modernists stood in favor of a symbolic revolt not against Porfirian society but against nineteenth-century culture. While the modernists generally also turned their backs on political, economic, and social problems as they sought refuge in the world of imagination, they succeeded in transforming Mexican literature into an art. Modernist literature was elitist—it was designed for the upper class—but without question it was literature of vitality, perception, and grace. Just as Limantour's balancing of the budget had yielded economic confidence, just as Díaz's quelling of rebellion had yielded political confidence, the modernist movement brought forth genuine cultural confidence.

The best and most versatile of the modernist fiction writers was Amado Nervo (1870–1919). After studying briefly for the priesthood, Nervo left the seminary and became a journalist in Mazatlán. At the turn of the century he moved to Paris—for Mexicans a cultural mecca—where he met the founder of the Latin American modernist movement, the Nicaraguan poet Rubén Darío. Before his literary career had ended, Nervo had to his credit more than thirty volumes—novels, poetry, short stories, plays, essays, and criticism.

The theme of Nervo's first novel, *El bachiller* (1895), was sensational and even horrifying. A young priest, tempted by physical love, castrates himself to avoid seduction. But the theme was developed with such skill and grace that few took umbrage or reproved the licentious plot. If Mexicans really wanted to be wordly they had to understand that the French were not offended by Gustav Flaubert's even more salacious *Madame Bovary*. In much of his work Nervo showed himself a perceptive amateur psychologist. His insight into the motivations of the protagonists he created and his appreciation of the conflicts between the material and the spiritual captivated his readers. Like most

---

5. José López Portillo y Rojas, *Cuentos completos*, vol. 1: *Nieves, El primer amor* (Guadalajara, 1952), p. 41.

of his contemporaries, he was not interested in analyzing broad social problems but rather in probing personal problems of both a psychological and a philosophical nature.

Mexican artists during the Porfiriato, unlike their literary colleagues, did not make their peace with the regime. The Art Academy of San Carlos continued to dominate the artistic community, but it was poorly supported by the government. The future giants of Mexican art— Diego Rivera and José Clemente Orozco—were students at the academy and began perfecting the techniques that would win them world acclaim two decades hence. While heavy emphasis was placed upon copying European models, a few of the students began to break with tradition and experiment with Mexican themes.

Díaz and his científico advisers, in art as in so many other areas, continued to show preference for all things foreign. To celebrate the centennial of Mexico's Independence, the government constructed a new building to house a Spanish art display and provided a subvention of thirty-five thousand pesos for the Spanish show. When the Mexican artists at the academy protested that they wanted to put on a national art show to coincide with the celebrations, they were forced to limp along with their old building and a paltry three thousand pesos to realize their efforts. Those who saw the Mexican exhibition probably understood why the regime chose not to support it. It was youthful, exuberant, and iconoclastic in both technique and theme. Gerardo Murillo, who changed his name to Dr. Atl, a Náhuatl word meaning *water*, had experimented with wax, resin, and oil in several scandalous bacchanals, while other young artists developed Indianist themes. Many of Mexico's most promising artists exhibited there for the first time and seemed to take special pride in their bold departures from staid European models. Slums and brothels decorated canvases, and somber Indian faces depicted the stark reality of Mexican life. This was not the impression of the stable, conservative, white, progressive Mexico that Díaz wanted portrayed.

The Porfiriato also distinguished itself as a productive period in Mexican historical scholarship. The best of the historians put polemic behind them and moved into the archives for painstaking research. Manuel Orozco y Berra and Luis González Obregón interested themselves primarily in the colonial period and produced seminal works on the society and culture of New Spain. Perhaps the greatest historian of the epoch was Joaquín García Icazbalceta (1825–94), who collected and edited several monumental series of colonial documents and prepared a bibliography of the sixteenth century—*Bibliografía mexicana del siglo xvi*—listing and annotating all of the books published in Mexico between 1539 and 1600. But his most distinguished work was a four-volume biography of the first bishop and archbishop of Mexico, Fray Juan de Zumárraga.

Of those historians not concerned with the colonial period, one name stands out far above the rest. Justo Sierra (1848–1912) set himself to the task of attempting a new interpretive synthesis of Mexican history. The result would occupy a unique niche in Mexican historiography. *México: Su evolución social* was published at the turn of the century and shows Sierra as an eclectic. Though the book was written during the period of positivist domination of Mexican intellectual thought, one can still detect the impact of historical romanticism on the author. Unlike the historians who preceded him, Sierra, from a new perspective, could view Mexican history with optimism. The chaotic and unseemly events of the early nineteenth century were, for him, necessary steps in the progress of mankind. Criticism of past Mexican politicians and institutions was abundant but never indulged. Sierra's analysis of his contemporary Mexico was especially brilliant: even Díaz did not emerge completely unscathed. Sierra trod a path between a tolerably mild censure and the apologia that Díaz undoubtedly would have preferred. While Sierra could not overlook the authoritarianism of the regime, on balance he found it worthwhile. For Justo Sierra the Díaz regime, much like the early nineteenth century, was simply a step in Mexico's evolutionary process. It, too, had to yield to something else. And in the best nineteenth-century liberal tradition, the ultimate goal was not a more equitable distribution of wealth but rather liberty.

Mexico's cultural and intellectual life flourished from 1876 to 1910. When it did not come into direct conflict with the goals of the dictatorship, it received encouragement and even direct support. The novelist could concern himself with refining the language, the artist with painting a landscape, and the historian with probing Mexico's colonial heritage, all with little to fear. But artistic and intellectual expression that ran contrary to the all-important image so assiduously cultivated by the regime did not fare so well. Freedom of expression existed for those who accepted the dictatorship for what it was and who, because of personal interests, rejected the sound instinct that makes the independent intellectual suspicious of government. Only they could continue to pursue their individual tasks.

During the three and one-half decades of peace and economic growth a younger generation of liberal intellectuals gradually emerged. As they began to test the cultural atmosphere with matters of honest concern, and as they began to expose some of the obvious shortcomings of the regime, they encountered no benevolent patronage or passive resignation. The more passionate and direct their indictments, the more likely they were to experience harsh retribution. Despite harassment, intimidation, and incarceration, these young intellectuals were not easily dissuaded from their goals and contributed in no small way to the outbreak of revolutionary activity in Mexico in 1910.

RECOMMENDED FOR FURTHER STUDY

Agostini, Claudia. *Monuments of Progress: Modernization and Public Health in Mexico City, 1876–1910.* Calgary: University of Calgary Press, 2003.

Barton, Mary. *Impressions of Mexico with Brush and Pen.* London: Methuen, 1911.

Beezley, William H. *Judas at the Jockey Club and Other Episodes of Porfirian Mexico.* Lincoln: University of Nebraska Press, 1987.

Brushwood, John S. *Mexico in Its Novel: A Nation's Search for Identity.* Austin: University of Texas Press, 1966.

Charlot, Jean. *The Mexican Mural Renaissance, 1920–1925.* New Haven, Conn.: Yale University Press, 1967.

Díaz, María Elena. "The Satiric Penny Press for Workers in Mexico, 1900–1910: A Case Study in the Politicisation of Popular Culture." *Journal of Latin American Studies* 22 (1990): 497–526.

Fowler-Salamini, Heather, and Mary Kay Vaughan, eds. *Women of the Mexican Countryside, 1850–1990: Creating Spaces, Shaping Transition.* Tucson: University of Arizona Press, 1994.

French, William E. *A Peaceful and Working People: Manners, Morals, and Class Formation in Northern Mexico.* Albuquerque: University of New Mexico Press, 1996.

Hale, Charles A. *The Transformation of Liberalism in Late Nineteenth-Century Mexico.* Princeton, N.J.: Princeton University Press, 1989.

Piccato, Pablo. *City of Suspects: Crime in Mexico City, 1900–1931.* Durham, N.C.: Duke University Press, 2001.

Pilcher, Jeffrey M. "Tamales or Timbales: Cuisine and the Formation of Mexican National Identity." *The Americas* 53 (October, 1996): 193–216.

Porter, Susie S. *Working Women in Mexico City: Public Discourse and Material Conditions, 1879–1931.* Tucson: University of Arizona Press, 2003.

Sierra, Justo. *The Political Evolution of the Mexican People.* Translated by Charles Ramsdell. Austin: University of Texas Press, 1969.

Tenorio Trillo, Mauricio. *Mexico at the World's Fairs: Crafting a Modern Nation.* Berkeley: University of California Press, 1996.

Tyler, Ron, ed. *Posada's Mexico.* Washington, D.C.: Library of Congress, 1979.

Vaughan, Mary Kay. *The State, Education and Social Class in Mexico, 1880–1928.* DeKalb: Northern Illinois University Press, 1982.

Wasserman, Mark. *Everyday Life and Politics in Nineteenth-Century Mexico: Men, Women and War.* Albuquerque: University of New Mexico Press, 2000.

Widdifield, Stacie G. *The Embodiment of the National in Late Nineteenth Century Mexican Painting.* Tucson: University of Arizona Press, 1995.

Wood, Andrew G. *Revolution in the Street: Women, Workers, and Urban Protest in Veracruz, 1870–1927.* Wilmington, Del.: Scholarly Resources, 2001.

VIII

THE REVOLUTION

The Military Phase, 1910–20

The Liberal Indictment
and the Overthrow of Díaz

THE LIBERAL LEADERSHIP

The opening of the twentieth century found Mexico a far different place than it had been only twenty-five years earlier. It would be sheer folly to gainsay the tremendous material benefits that had accrued in the industrial, commercial, and mining fields. But there is no Ciudad Porfirio Díaz in Mexico today, no public school or street bears his name, and it is hard to find a public statue or monument erected in his honor. Porfirian capitalism shunned the masses; the economic surplus generated by the dynamic economy had been appropriated by the few. A system that perpetuated itself for the sake of order and economic progress, and atrophied in the process, became less and less palatable to an increasing number of young, socially aware Mexicans. The federal Constitution of 1857, with its theoretical guarantees, had been violated incessantly. Elections at all levels of government were a farce. The administration of justice in rural Mexico was a euphemism for the capricious whims of the local jefe político. Freedom of the press did not exist, and the restrictions of the Reform limiting the participatory role of the clergy were not enforced. To those who were concerned with the longevity of the regime, Don Porfirio became "Don Perpetuo," while those more concerned with the brutality dubbed him "Porfiriopoxtli." The científicos continued to be loyal apologists for the dictatorship, but a younger generation of intellectual activists, embracing a new faith and unwilling to be intimidated by the arrogance of the científicos, began to question the effete dictatorship.

One of the first to speak out for reform was Wistano Luis Orozco, a jurist from Guadalajara. Unlike the majority of liberal malcontents, he was concerned with social, not political, issues. As early as 1895 he had written a volume criticizing the Díaz land laws and the land companies that profited from them. Arguing that the concentration of landownership was detrimental to both the rural peasantry and the

...culture, he called for the government to break up and
...ds and begin buying up some of the huge haciendas
...pose. But Orozco was not propagandizing for revolu-
...l the reforms he envisioned could be effected from
...istration.

...ptosí, Camilo Arriaga, a mining engineer by profes-
...positivist doctrine he had learned in the schools and
...entury counted himself in the small anti-Díaz camp.
...th-century liberal, Arriaga moved into the opposition
told because of Díaz's *modus vivendi* with the Roman Catholic Church.
In late 1900 he called for the organization of liberal clubs throughout
Mexico and summoned a national liberal convention to meet in San
Luis Potosí. Although the resolutions adopted at the 1901 convention
were narrowly conceived and primarily anticlerical, the malcontents
would gradually broaden the base of their antigovernment attack.

The least timid members of the liberal movement in the early twentieth century were the Flores Magón brothers—Jesús, Ricardo, and
Enrique. In August of 1900 the brothers began publication of *Regeneración*, a Mexico City weekly. Not yet ready to preach the injustice
of private land ownership, through its columns they supported the
nascent liberal movement in San Luis Potosí and decried the excesses
of Porfirismo. But when they attacked a local jefe político in Oaxaca
in the columns of *Regeneración*, the brothers were arrested in the late
spring of 1901 and confined to Belén prison for a year. Their arrest
served to invigorate the liberal movement as freedom of the press and
suppression of the jefes políticos became new causes the liberals could
add to their militant anticlericalism. By the time the Flores Magón
brothers were released Camilo Arriaga had been arrested, as had other
leaders of the liberal cause. The brothers renewed their attacks, this
time in the columns of *El Hijo de Ahuizote*; six months later they were
in prison once again. A release and a third brief arrest convinced them
of the futility of trying to conduct their campaign from Mexican soil;
in January 1904, broke and disheartened, they crossed over into the
United States to attack the Díaz regime from exile.

From San Antonio, Texas, the Flores Magón brothers and Arriaga,
who joined them shortly, began soliciting funds from liberals to rein-
stitute *Regeneración*. Former subscribers and liberal clubs throughout
Mexico made small contributions, and an unexpected benefactor was
found in Francisco I. Madero, son of a wealthy Coahuila hacendado.
The first issue of the newly revived tabloid came off the press in the
fall of 1904. The *Regeneración* published from San Antonio was much
more militant and belligerent; attacks against Díaz were more cate-
gorical and vicious and the remedies more radical.

Cartoon from El Hijo de Ahuizote *titled "The Governors Praying for Díaz Support."*

In reaction, Díaz dispatched a would-be assassin to the Texas city to end once and for all his problem with the Flores Magón brothers. The assassination attempt failed, but the liberals in exile decided it would be wiser to move deeper into the heartland of the United States. The exiles chose St. Louis, Missouri, and in 1905 not only again began publishing *Regeneración* but also organized a revolutionary junta for the expressed purpose of overthrowing the Díaz dictatorship. But the local St. Louis authorities were no more friendly than those in San Antonio; they arrested the Flores Magón brothers, charging them with violating United States neutrality laws. Although they were released, Ricardo's subsequent activities in other parts of the United States landed him in jail several times, and he died in Fort Leavenworth, Kansas, in 1922.

In the summer of 1906 the junta in St. Louis published its Liberal Plan. Part of it was a simple rehash of nineteenth-century liberal concerns. It called for freedom of speech, freedom of the press, suppression of the jefes políticos, the complete secularization of education, and the nationalization of all church property. But the Liberal Plan of 1906 added a series of new concepts manifesting graphically that a new age of liberalism had finally dawned. Socially oriented measures included the abolition of the death penalty (except for treason), educational reform in favor of the poor, and prison reform emphasizing rehabilitation rather than punishment. More revolutionary yet was the call for

Treatment of the Mexican Liberal party. A print by José Guadalupe Posada.

a nationwide eight-hour workday and a six-day workweek, the abolition of the tienda de raya, the payment of all workers in legal tender, and the prohibition of child labor. The rural areas of Mexico were not overlooked as they had been so often in the past. All uncultivated lands were to be taken over by the state and redistributed to those who would work them. To enable the small farmer to take advantage of the new law, an agricultural credit bank would be established to provide low-interest loans. And, finally, special emphasis would be placed on restoring the ejido lands seized illegally from the Indian communities.

The discontent over the political abuses of the Díaz dictatorship had been gradually transmuted into a new gospel of social reform. For the first time in Mexican history an articulate and organized minority, albeit a small one, had displayed genuine concern for the plight of the masses. The liberal leaders in exile had immersed themselves in European social thought and had begun to apply the lessons to Mexican reality as they understood it. In the thousands of copies of *Regeneración* smuggled into Mexico monthly, the Flores Magón brothers and their liberal compatriots in exile exposed the regime as intellectually impoverished and socially bankrupt. They received their first promising news from the fatherland in the summer of 1906. It came from Cananea, Sonora.

LABOR UNREST

On June 1, 1906, the Mexican workers at Colonel William Greene's Cananea Consolidated Copper Company went out on strike. The liberal junta had not planned the strike, but young socialist activists in Cananea—Manuel Diéguez, Estéban Calderón, and Francisco Ibarra—had been in correspondence with the exiles, had formed an affiliate liberal club in Cananea, and had agitated the workers, distributing copies of *Regeneración*.

The grievances of the miners at Cananea were manifold. Mexicans were paid less than their United States counterparts for performing the same jobs. Qualified Mexican laborers were consigned to undesirable posts, while the technical and managerial positions were staffed entirely by United States personnel. The workers elected a delegation, including Diéguez and Calderón, to negotiate these matters, and salary and hours, with the management. When Colonel Greene refused to arbitrate, the activists decided to stop all company operations.

The violence began in the company lumberyard. Disgruntled but unarmed workers attempted to force their way through a locked gate, and the resident manager ordered high-pressure water hoses to be turned on them. When the gate finally buckled and the workers swarmed into the yard, they were greeted with several volleys of rifle fire. During the chaos of the next hour several dozen Mexicans and two United States managers were slain. The remaining workers retired, leaving the lumberyard in flames. The atmosphere was explosive as the workers marched into Cananea. Colonel Greene informed Governor Rafael Izábal of the danger and telephoned friends across the border in Arizona to raise a volunteer force in his behalf. When the governor was apprised that the rurales could not arrive until late the next day, he gave permission for 275 Arizona Rangers to cross the border to patrol the streets of Cananea. To veil the violation of Mexico's neutrality, Izábal did not allow the Rangers to enter the country as a force. They crossed over individually and were subsequently sworn in as Mexican volunteers.

The situation in Cananea was still tense when the American force arrived, together with Governor Izábal. While no major military engagements ensued, the Rangers and the workers did exchange fire on several occasions, and deaths resulted on both sides. Late in the day a detachment of rurales arrived under the command of Colonel Emilio Kosterlitzky. "Justice" was quick for those workers Kosterlitzky considered ringleaders: they were rounded up, escorted out of town, and hanged from trees. The strike was broken, and the workers, threatened with induction into the army, returned to their jobs. Nonetheless, it

Mothers, wives, sisters, and daughters supported the miners' demands by demonstrating in Cananea.

focused attention on the Díaz policy of protecting foreigners at the expense of Mexicans. United States troops had been allowed to cross into Mexican territory and kill Mexicans to guard the interests of an American mining magnate.

The discontent of the miners at Cananea proved not to be an isolated phenomenon. Even as the strike in Sonora was being suppressed, liberal leaders among the textile workers in Veracruz organized the Gran Círculo de Obreros Libres and began seeking affiliate clubs in neighboring states. The last six months of 1906, with the echos of Cananea still fresh, witnessed the most intense labor conflict of the entire Porfiriato. Late in the year textile strikes supported by the Gran Círculo occurred in Puebla, Orizaba, and Tlaxcala, but the major showdown was postponed until January 1907.

Working conditions in the Río Blanco textile mills were nothing short of horrible. The common workday was twelve hours, the wages were grossly inadequate, and, on top of everything else, the workers were required to pay for the normal depreciation of the machinery they used. Children of eight and nine years of age performed physically demanding work. All strikes were illegal, and workers whose affiliation with the Gran Círculo became known were subject to immediate dismissal. The abuses seemed so patent that the workers agreed to lay their complaints directly before President Díaz for his arbitration. The dictator agreed to hear the complaints, but when he issued his decision he supported the textile owners on almost every count. On Sunday, January 6, the workers held a mass meeting and decided to strike the following day.

The trouble set in at the grocery counter of the tienda de raya. Several of the wives of the striking workers were refused credit for food. Insults led to pushing and shoving, then fisticuffs, and finally shooting. The enraged strikers put the tienda de raya to flame, and the local jefe político ordered in the rurales and the federal troops. When the troops arrived they fired point-blank into the crowd and killed several women and children along with numerous workers. The crowd dispersed, but when some of the workers returned later to collect the bodies of the dead they were again assaulted by the troops and even more were killed, the dead numbering over a hundred.

The government reaction to the textile strike at Río Blanco was the grossest evidence of mass suppression yet. It was easy—too easy—to blame labor unrest entirely on liberal agitators in the United States without questioning seriously whether the grievances had any basis in fact. Again law and order were assured at the expense of personal liberty and social justice.

HEIGHTENED POLITICAL ACTIVITY

Despite the liberal indictment and despite the suppression of the nascent labor movement, most Mexican politicians believed that a revolution could be avoided and that change could be effected through the political process. The moderates were encouraged when in early 1908 the dictator granted an interview to the United States journalist James Creelman.

> No matter what my friends and supporters say, I retire when my presidential term of office ends, and I shall not serve again. I shall be eighty years old then. I have waited patiently for the day when the people of the Mexican Republic should be prepared to choose and change their government at every election without danger of armed revolution and without injury to the national credit or interference with the national progress. I believe that day has come. I welcome an opposition party in the Mexican Republic.[1]

---

1. Quoted in Frederick Starr, *Mexico and the United States* (Chicago, 1914), p. 253.

Díaz's bombshell that he did not plan to seek re-election in the up-coming presidential elections of 1910 ushered in a rash of political activity and intellectual ferment. Shortly after this interview the Mexican literati went to work. The Yucatecan sociologist Andrés Molina Enríquez, a positivist but not a Porfirista, published an important volume entitled *Los grandes problemas nacionales* (translated as *The Great National Problems*). A brilliant analysis of contemporary Mexican society, the work called for a penetrating program of reform, especially in the rural areas. Molina Enríquez knew that agrarian discontent had already manifested itself in sporadic outbreaks of violence, and he feared that if positive steps were not taken the movement might fall into radical or anarchist hands.

A still more influential book, *La sucesión presidencial en 1910* (translated as *The Presidential Succession in 1910*), came from the pen of Francisco I. Madero. Unlike Molina Enríquez, Madero held that Mexico's problems were primarily political in nature. The greatest danger to Mexico, as Madero perceived it, was continued military dictatorship. Although Madero himself did not believe that Díaz was going to step down voluntarily, he urged Mexicans to take the dictator at his word and to begin forming an opposition party, an anti-reelectionist party dedicated to the principles of effective suffrage and no re-election. Madero's book affirmed that the desired change could be effected through the ballot box, and, together with the Creelman interview, it set into motion the political forces that would ultimately lead to the conflagration in the fall of 1910.

Within the administration itself various factions began to vie for the mantle of succession. The followers of General Bernardo Reyes, the capable and energetic former governor of Nuevo León and secretary of war, pushed their hero as a logical successor to Díaz, or at least his vice-presidential running mate. Other científicos, led by José Limantour, supported the slate of Díaz and Ramón Corral, a former governor of Sonora and currently vice-president. They accepted and for good measure sent Reyes to undertake a military study mission in Europe. The general's acceptance of the contrived assignment in November 1909 was tantamount to political exile.

MADERO AND THE ANTI-RE-ELECTIONIST CAUSE

The political opposition to Díaz in the 1910 presidential elections would come, at any rate, from outside the official party, as Francisco I. Madero dedicated himself to the Anti-Re-electionist cause. Born in Coahuila in 1873 to a family of wealth and prestige, young Madero received the best education that money could provide. The family had garnered a fortune in mining, land speculation, cattle, and banking;

Madero's father was happy to send his teenage son to Paris and then to Berkeley, California, for proper grooming. Upon his return to Coahuila, Madero was placed in charge of some of the family haciendas and quickly developed an unusual interest in the welfare of the peones who worked them. He not only observed the gross social inequities firsthand but took time to ponder the pathetic written complaints that crossed his desk daily. Stories of physical abuse at the hands of the mayordomos were not as frequent as tales of poverty that left children without shelter or food, of sickness without the possibility of medical care, of military conscription as a means of punishment, and of incarceration without the formalities of law. He did what he could on the family properties, but he realized fully that the Madero haciendas were simply a microcosm of rural Mexico. For Madero nothing could change until democratic processes had a chance to work their miraculous cures. Though Madero had initially contributed to the cause of the Flores Magón brothers, he became estranged from them as they grew more radical. In the spring of 1908 he set to work on his manuscript, *La sucesión presidencial en 1910.*

To foment anti-re-electionism and to test the political winds, Madero toured Mexico in the last half of 1909. During the summer and early fall he made public appearances in Orizaba, Veracruz, Progreso, Mérida, Campeche, Tampico, Monterrey, and Torreón. If the receptions were not always as enthusiastic as he would have liked, he was building a revolutionary network to which he would later appeal. The winter months were no less hectic as Madero, his close confidants, and his wife continued their political tours to Querétaro, Guadalajara, Manzanillo, Mazatlán, and into the northern states of Sonora and Chihuahua. Gaining confidence and stature along the way, Madero offered himself as an energetic, capable, and articulate young leader in stark contrast to a tiring and decrepit regime—not a member of Díaz's cabinet was under sixty; many of the state governors were in their seventies. Especially well received in Chihuahua, Madero held several meetings with Abraham González, an ardent foe of the dictatorship and president of the Centro Anti-Re-eleccionista Benito Juárez.

The convention met in April 1910 with broad geographical representation. The 120 delegates in attendance, following the lead of Abraham González and his Chihuahua colleagues, officially nominated Madero for the presidency. The following afternoon the vice-presidential nomination was given to Dr. Francisco Vásquez Gómez, a distinguished physician but a lukewarm liberal at best.

The philosophy of the Anti-Re-electionist party came out gradually during the campaign that carried the candidate to twenty-two of the twenty-seven Mexican states. Madero simply expanded upon the ideas contained in his book. Mexican presidents, he argued, should serve only a single term because they should be focused not on the next election but on the next generation. Political reform, predicated upon free and honest elections, was basic to the entire program. Social benefits might then accrue, but democracy was the one imperative. During a campaign speech in San Luis Potosí, Madero was interrupted by a question voiced from the audience asking why he did not break up his own haciendas. Madero's answer epitomized his philosophy. The Mexican people, he responded, did not want bread; they wanted liberty. Not long thereafter, the Díaz administration began arresting Anti-Reelectionist leaders, including Madero himself.

Election day, June 21, 1910, found Madero in prison in San Luis Potosí and thousands of his Anti-Re-electionist colleagues in jails throughout the republic. Nobody was surprised when the government announced that Díaz and Ramón Corral had been overwhelmingly re-elected for still another term. The Madero family was able to arrange for Madero's release on bail with the proviso that he confine himself to the city of San Luis Potosí. He did remain in the city for several months, but in early October, when the rigor of his confinement was relaxed, he boarded a northbound train in disguise and escaped to the United States.

THE LAST HURRAH

Soon after the election Díaz began preparations for his final extravaganza. In September he would celebrate his eightieth birthday and Mexico the hundredth anniversary of its Declaration of Independence. The entire month was given over to pageants, celebration, and commemoration. Civic ritual competed mightily with self-congratulation to dominate the public's sensibility. A soaring column capped by a gold angel was unveiled on the Paseo de la Reforma in honor of the Independence movement. An equally impressive monument to the Niños Héroes was dedicated at the entrance to Chapultepec Park. Distinguished guests from abroad had their expenses paid to partake of the festivities. Gala balls were held in their honor, and imported French champagne flowed like water. Flags were displayed everywhere, banquets followed banquets, parades crowded the streets, fireworks lit up the night skies, and *mariachis* (folk musicians) strolled the downtown avenues. Foreign governments took part as well. The American colony, thinking of no better way of commemorating the heroic deeds of Father Hidalgo, sent Díaz and the Mexican people a statue of George Washington, and the Italians—not to be outdone—sent one of Giuseppe Garibaldi. In a rare display of *entente cordiale* the Third French Republic returned the keys to the city of Mexico that had been ingloriously sequestered by the army of Napoleon III a half-century before. King Alfonso XIII demonstrated the lasting confraternity of the Spanish people by returning the uniforms of José María Morelos.

The centennial celebrations epitomized everything that was right and everything that was wrong with the Díaz regime. Beggars were pushed off of the streets of the capital city for the duration so that the guests would receive the proper impressions of a prosperous Mexico. The cost of the celebrations exceeded the entire educational budget for the year 1910. Mexico was at last enjoying its place in the international sun—respect was no longer lacking. But while the champagne was flowing for a few, tens of thousands were suffering from malnutrition. While guests were treated to young female companions, Indian women in Yucatán were dying in childbirth. While European waiters served at the banquets, urban Mexicans were unemployed. While letters of congratulation arrived on time, 85 percent of the population was still illiterate. While visitors rode in shiny new motorcars on well-paved streets in the center of the city, mud and filth engulfed the workers' barrios in the suburbs. In September 1910 Mexico appeared to many to be enjoying its finest hour. But with social reform still alien to the Porfirian mentality, the peace would soon prove to be fragile and the showy façade would collapse with it.

THE PLAN DE SAN LUIS POTOSÍ

For years Francisco Madero had resisted the prodding of liberals who exhorted that Díaz must be overthrown by force. But when he escaped from San Luis Potosí and made his way north to the sanctuary of the United States border, he realized that it was no longer possible to unseat the dictator by constitutional means. Now he would call his fellow Mexicans to arms in the task of national redemption.

In the middle of October 1910, as supporters gathered around him in San Antonio, Texas, he began drafting a revolutionary plan. To avoid any possible international complications with the United States, he dated the plan October 5, the last day he had been in San Luis Potosí, and, in fact, called it the *Plan de San Luis Potosí*. He made his appeal emotionally.

> Peoples, in their constant efforts for the triumph of the ideals of liberty and justice, find it necessary at certain historical moments to make the greatest sacrifices. Our beloved fatherland has reached one of those

moments. A tyranny that we Mexicans have not been accustomed to suffer since we won our independence oppresses us in such a manner that it has become intolerable.

But this violent and illegal system can no longer exist. . . . [As] a patriot . . . [I am] ready to sacrifice himself, if necessary, to obtain liberty and to help the people free themselves from the odious tyranny that oppresses them. . . .

I declare the last election illegal and accordingly the republic, being without rulers, I assume the provisional presidency of the republic until the people designate their rulers pursuant to the law. . . .

I have designated Sunday, the 20th day of next November, for all the towns in the republic to rise in arms after 6 o'clock P.M.[2]

The Plan de San Luis Potosí, like *La sucesión presidencial en 1910* before it, demonstrates amply that Madero's concerns were primarily political. The few references to Mexico's social maladies were vague and ill conceived. Yet the boldness of the statement and the self-confidence it reflected struck a responsive chord. The leaders who had previously worked for the Anti-Re-electionist party began preparing

Aquiles Serdán and his family in Puebla. A print by Fernando Castro Pacheco.

---

2. The text of the plan can be found in Isidro Fabela, ed., *Documentos históricos de la revolución mexicana* (Mexico City, 1960–73), 6: 69–76.

themselves for November 20. The revolution actually began two days prematurely in the town of Puebla. There the local liberal leader, Aquiles Serdán, had stored arms and ammunition in his home. An informant notified the police, and the fight was on. Serdán and his family became the first martyrs of the new cause. Madero himself crossed over into Mexico on the evening of November 19, but, when his expected rebel army failed to rendezvous, he crossed back into the United States without firing a shot. It was not yet clear that the masses would rally to the cry of *¡Viva la Revolución!*

THE RISE OF REBEL ARMIES AND THE RESIGNATION OF DÍAZ

Local corridos record the names of the many who took up arms everywhere on the stipulated day. But nowhere did the sparks fly as in Chihuahua. Town after town responded on November 20 and 21. Toribio Ortega marched on Cuchillo Parado, Gaspar Durán on Calabacillas, José de la Luz Blanco on Santo Tomás, Guadalupe Gardea on Chuviscar, Feliciano Díaz on Témoris, Cástulo Herrera on Temósachic, Guillermo Baca on Hidalgo del Parral, Pancho Villa on San Andrés, and Pascual Orozco on San Isidro and Miñaca.

The rebel forces were not armies, but neither were they merely peasant mobs. There were peones, to be sure, but in addition servants, shopkeepers, mechanics, beggars, miners, federal army deserters, lawyers, United States soldiers of fortune, young and old, bandits and idealists, students and teachers, engineers and day laborers, the bored and the overworked, the aggrieved and the adventuresome, all constituted the rank and file. Some were attracted by commitment to the cause and some by the promise of spoils; some joined impulsively and others with careful forethought. Some preferred Flores Magón radicalism and some Madero liberalism; many had heard of neither. Even among the politically astute some viewed the November movement as a fight against hacendados, others decided to offer their lives to oppose local jefes políticos, while still others saw the Revolution as a chance to recapture Mexico from the foreign capitalists. But they all had one thought in common: Díaz was the symbol of all Mexico's ills, and they were convinced that almost any change would be a change for the better. Thus they were willing to strap cartridge belts on their chests; find, buy, or steal rifles somewhere; and become *guerrilleros*. Indifferently armed, without uniforms, with no notion of military discipline, the disparate rebel bands lived off the land and attacked local authorities and small federal outposts in tiny pueblos. It did not take them long to realize that they enjoyed a dormant but fortuitous

The Mexican guerrilla at the beginning of the Revolution would soon be immortalized in legend and song.

asset—the cooperation of much of rural Mexico. Madero's communications network began to inform him that his recent efforts had not been in vain.

The Díaz regime was by no means prepared to lay down and roll over. With more frenzy than care, army units and corps of rurales were dispatched on scattered missions in Mexico's ten military zones, and slowly they began to curtail the spread of the rebellion. Only in Chihuahua did the rebel movement continue to grow. The military leadership there had devolved upon Pascual Orozco, Jr., a tall, gaunt mule skinner whose business had suffered because he did not enjoy the favor of the Terrazas-Creel machine. When Orozco was contacted by Abraham González, the leader of the Anti-Re-electionists in the state, he had already been reading copies of *Regeneración* and did not have to be convinced that he should begin recruitment in Guerrero District. González supplied some modest funds and a few weapons. By November 20, Orozco had attracted about forty men to the cause. During the next two weeks, striking rapidly from the almost inaccessible *sierras* of western Chihuahua, he garnered four victories. Pancho Villa, José de la Luz Blanco, Cástulo Herrera, and other local leaders placed themselves under his command, and the Orozco army increased by twentyfold. On January 2, 1911, the Chihuahua rebels ambushed and almost totally destroyed a large federal convoy sent to pursue them. Now cocksure, Orozco stripped the dead soldiers of their uniforms, wrapped up the articles of clothing, and sent them to Don Porfirio with a graphically descriptive taunt: *Ahí te van las hojas; mándame más tamales* (Here are the wrappers; send me some more tamales).

In February Madero decided to cross over into Mexico for the second time and, although he had no special military talent, to assume military as well as political command. After a punishing defeat at Casas Grandes, Madero realized that he had better leave the day-to-day fighting to Orozco, Villa, and the other guerrilla leaders who had already proved themselves on the field of battle.

Soon the insurrection began to bear fruit in Sonora, Coahuila, Sinaloa, Veracruz, Zacatecas, Puebla, Guerrero, and Morelos. In Baja California the Flores Magón brothers and their followers had the government on the run. Picking their own ground and their own time of battle, the small rebel contingents throughout the country kept the federals constantly off balance. The military bureaucracy was inflexible, the government campaigns uncoordinated, the communications network tenuous, and the supply system inadequate. The rebels, on the other hand, moved in smaller units, lived off the land, and generally enjoyed the sympathy and cooperation of the local populace. They found it easier to smuggle in ammunition from the United States than federal commanders did to requisition it from Mexico City.

In the late spring of 1911 Orozco and Villa convinced Madero that the northern rebels should expend all their energy on capturing Ciudad Juárez, the border city across the Rio Grande from El Paso, Texas. By early May the most seasoned rebel troops had congregated on the outskirts of the city and were ready to attack. Suddenly, however, Madero changed his mind. Fearing that stray rebel shells might fall on El Paso and thus occasion United States intervention, he ordered a retreat. In direct violation of his commander's order, Orozco ordered the attack. Although the advantage of manpower and firepower lay with the rebels, the federal defense of the city, entrusted to General Juan Navarro, was stubborn. Thousands of El Paso residents climbed to their rooftops to watch the proceedings and cheer on their favorites. On the morning of May 10 the tide turned in favor of the rebels. Low on ammunition and completely encircled by the enemy, General Navarro decided to surrender and in the early afternoon hoisted a white flag over the federal barracks.

Madero did not know whether to be grateful, angry, or embarrassed. Against his order Orozco had handed him an important city, an official port of entry from the United States, and a provisional capital. When a few days later the provisional president named his cabinet, Orozco's name was curiously absent. The showdown took place on May 13 during a meeting of the new provisional government. Revolvers in hand to emphasize their point, Orozco and Villa burst into the room with a series of demands that highlighted their frustrations with Maderós failure to reward his rebel followers and appoint men who would more forcefully advance their goals.

The confrontation was momentarily defused, but it had significance that no one present could have foreseen. Though only five months old, the revolutionary coalition was already falling apart. The military's challenge to the civilian leadership would be repeated regularly for the next chaotic decade. But more important yet, the affair portended an age of bitter factionalism that exacerbated personal rivalries, turned Mexican against Mexican, extended the war, exacted a tremendously high toll of life, and increased the pain and anguish for hundreds of thousands.

Meanwhile, rebels throughout the country took heart and redoubled their efforts. Tehuacán, Durango, Hermosillo, Cananea, Torreón, and Cuautla fell into revolutionary hands. Business fell victim to the

The battle of Ciudad Juárez (May 1911) proved to be the decisive engagement for control of the north.

The revolutionary leadership following the capture of Ciudad Juárez.
The coalition would soon fall apart.

trauma of uncertainty, and merchants bemoaned the lack of trade. The
press became increasingly outspoken in criticism of the regime. Federal troops, who had not acquitted themselves too badly to this point,
began deserting to the Revolution *en masse*. Díaz reluctantly agreed
to dispatch a team of negotiators to meet with Madero and his staff.
The Treaty of Ciudad Juárez provided that Díaz and Vice-President
Corral would resign before the month was out. Francisco León de la
Barra, the secretary of foreign relations and an experienced diplomat,
would assume the interim presidency until new elections could be held.
Don Porfirio signed his resignation and submitted it to the Congress
on May 25.

Díaz had indeed been overthrown, but the Revolution had scarcely
triumphed. It had barely yet begun. The conviviality and jubilee of the
next few days soon gave way to acrimonious debate as Mexicans began to ask themselves, what, exactly, they had won. Their answers, of
course, were predicated upon what had motivated them to join the
movement at the outset. As the dictator sailed away into European exile the one bond that had held them together vanished from sight. An
old age had ended without a new age beginning.

THE INTERIM PRESIDENCY AND DIVISION WITHIN
THE REBEL RANKS

The interim presidency of León de la Barra (May to November 1911)
turned out to be a crucial period. Madero's radical supporters, including the Flores Magón brothers, were unhappy enough with the

choice of the interim president, but they were even more displeased when the provisional cabinet named by León de la Barra included a majority of Porfiristas. Emiliano Zapata in Morelos adopted a cautious wait-and-see attitude. Orozco in Chihuahua was still bristling from his recent encounter with Madero following the battle of Ciudad Juárez.

Unaware that the rumblings within his ranks were serious, in early June, Madero left the north for Mexico City. His seven-hundred-mile journey by train was truly triumphant, as thousands of enthusiastic admirers greeted him at large and small stations along the way. His reception in the capital was no less spectacular, as recorded by Edith O'Shaughnessy, the wife of the United States chargé d'affaires in the Mexico City embassy.

> There was a great noise of *vivas*, mingling with shouts of all kinds, tramping of feet, and blowing of motor horns. I could just get a glimpse of a pale, dark-bearded man bowing to the right and left. I kept repeating to myself: *"Qui l'a fait roi? qui l'a couronné?—la victoire."* . . . There were three days of continual plaudits and adoration, such as only the Roman emperors knew. . . . People came from far and near, in all sorts of conveyances or on foot, just to see him, to hear his voice, even to touch his garments for help and healing. . . .[3]

Among those there to greet Madero and talk to him was the most famous revolutionary of all—Emiliano Zapata. Like Orozco in the north, Zapata had never been a peón. His family had passed on a little land to him, and he supplemented his modest income as a muleteer, a horse trainer, and a stable master. Elected in 1909 to local office by the villagers of Anenecuilco, Morelos, he was regularly exposed to the full array of tragedies that had beset rural Mexico during the late Díaz regime. More concerned with local land problems than with the national movement to unseat the dictator, he did not call his villagers to support the Plan de San Luis Potosí on November 20, 1910. But within a few months he had linked the future of his own people with that of the Maderista cause and began recruiting an insurgent army. When appropriate, he made his appeal to local inhabitants in Nahuatl rather than in Spanish. A teenage girl in Milpa Alta remembered when Zapata addressed the villagers.

> Notlac ximomanaca! Nehuatl onacoc; oncuan on ica tepoztli ihuan nochantlaca niquinhuicatz. Ipampa in Totazin Díaz aihmo ticnequi

---

3. Edith O'Shaughnessy, *Diplomatic Days* (New York, 1917), p. 53.

Emiliano Zapata (1879–1919). Although Zapata played only a minor role in the fight again Díaz, his stature as a revolutionary grew steadily until his assassination in 1919.

yehuatl techixotiz. Ticnequi occe altepetl achi cuali. Ilhuan totlac ximomanaca ipampa amo nechpactia tlen tetlaxtlahuia. Amo conehui ica tlacualo ica netzotzomatiloz. Noihqui nicnequi nochtlacatl quipiaz itlal: oncuan on quitocaz ihuan quipixcaz tlaoli, yetzintli ihuan occequi xinachtli. Tlen nanquitoa? Namehuan totlac namomanazque?[4]

Zapata's military contributions to the overthrow of the Díaz dictatorship were not great, but he had scored a couple of victories over the federal forces by the time Díaz submitted his resignation in May

4. "Join me. I rose up. I rose up in arms and I bring my countrymen. We no longer wish that our Father Díaz watch over us. We want a much better president. Rise up with us because we don't like what the rich men pay us. It is not enough for us to eat and dress ourselves. I also want for everyone to have his piece of land so that he can plant and harvest corn, beans, and other crops. What do you say? Are you going to join us?"

The Spanish and Nahuatl texts are found in Fernando Horcasitas, *De Porfirio Díaz a Zapata: Memoria Náhuatl de Milpa Alta* (Mexico City, 1968), p. 105. Whether Zapata actually used Nahuatl has been the subject of recent scholarly debate.

1911. With the new day now supposedly arrived, Zapata wanted to talk to Madero about the one matter that concerned him most—the land problem in Morelos. To Zapata the overthrow of Díaz had genuine meaning only if land were immediately restored to the pueblos. The encounter between the two men was dramatic. Zapata, with a large sombrero on his head and his carbine in his hand, gestured to the gold watch Madero sported on his vest and then made his point.

> Look, Señor Madero, if I, taking advantage of being armed, steal your watch and keep it, and then we meet again sometime and you are armed, wouldn't you have the right to demand that I return it?
>
> Of course, General, and you would also have the right to ask that I pay you for the use I had of it.
>
> Well, this is exactly what has happened to us in Morelos where some of the hacendados have forcibly taken over the village lands. My soldiers, the armed peasants, demand that I tell you respectfully that they want their lands returned immediately.[5]

With characteristic caution Madero would make no immediate commitment, but when he traveled to Morelos shortly thereafter, he insisted that Zapata demobilize his army as a prerequisite to reducing tensions in the state. Zapata detected something absurd in the request. The revolutionaries had won; yet while the federal army remained intact, the victorious rebels were asked to disband. To show good faith the southern rebel reluctantly agreed. His acquiescence was for naught as interim President León de la Barra decided to send federal troops into the state to enforce the demobilization order. Madero was furious when he learned that federal General Victoriano Huerta had exchanged fire with a band of Zapatistas north of Cuernavaca. He pleaded with the interim president to withdraw the troops, but the tenuous peace had already been shattered. By August the state of Morelos was again in angry revolt, and Madero, perhaps through no fault of his own, could add Zapata's name to his growing list of enemies.

When the campaign for the 1911 presidential elections got under way, the political atmosphere was already tense. Madero's party met in Mexico City in August and gave him the nomination by acclamation. But the vice-presidential nomination divided the convention. Madero decided to dump his 1910 running mate, Francisco Vásquez Gómez, in favor of a Yucatecan lawyer and a journalist, José María Pino Suárez. The convention gave Madero his choice, but Vásquez

---

5. Quoted in Gildardo Magaña, *Emiliano Zapata y el agrarismo en México* (Mexico City, 1934–52), 1: 160.

Gómez and his followers would never reconcile themselves to their sudden political demise.

The opposition candidate around whom many of the old regime could rally, albeit without enthusiasm, was General Bernardo Reyes. By early fall the election was in full swing and the debate heated. In September a group of Madero's supporters, without their leader's knowledge or approval, physically attacked Reyes at a Mexico City rally. The Reyista party protested vigorously and petitioned the Congress to postpone the elections because of the unfair treatment afforded their candidate. But the Congress turned down the request, and Reyes, perhaps realizing that his campaign stood little chance of victory anyway, withdrew from the race and went into a self-imposed exile in San Antonio, Texas. Another powerful enemy was on the list.

The election was held without further incident on October 1, 1911. Only minor candidates opposed Madero, and he swept to an overwhelming victory. Madero's faith in democracy would soon be put to the test, and, while his faith would remain unshaken, democracy would fall victim to the rancor and passion of the day.

RECOMMENDED FOR FURTHER STUDY

Albro, Ward S. *To Die on Your Feet: The Life, Times and Writings of Práxedis G. Guerrero.* Fort Worth: Texas Christian University Press, 1996.

Beezley, William H. *Insurgent Governor: Abraham González and the Mexican Revolution in Chihuahua.* Lincoln: University of Nebraska Press, 1973.

Bell, Edward I. *The Political Shame of Mexico.* New York: McBride, Nast, 1914.

Blaisdell, Lowell L. *The Desert Revolution: Baja California, 1911.* Madison: University of Wisconsin Press, 1962.

Cockcroft, James D. *Intellectual Precursors of the Mexican Revolution, 1900–1913.* Austin: University of Texas Press, 1968.

Creelman, James. *Díaz: Master of Mexico.* New York: Appleton, 1916.

Cumberland, Charles C. *Mexican Revolution: Genesis under Madero.* Austin: University of Texas Press, 1952.

Guzmán, Martín Luis, *Memoirs of Pancho Villa.* Translated by Virgina H. Taylor. Austin: University of Texas Press, 1965.

Hart, John M. *Revolutionary Mexico: The Coming and Process of the Mexican Revolution.* Berkeley: University of California Press, 1987.

Henderson, Peter V. N. *In the Absence of Don Porfirio. Francisco León de la Barra and the Mexican Revolution.* Wilmington, Del.: 1999.

Joseph, Gilbert, and Daniel Nugent, eds. *Everyday Forms of State Formation and Negotiations of Rule in Modern Mexico.* Durham, N.C.: Duke University Press, 1994.

Knight, Alan. *The Mexican Revolution.* Vol. 1: *Porfirians, Liberals and Peasants.* New York: Cambridge University Press, 1986.

MacLachlan, Colin M. *Anarchism and the Mexican Revolution.* Berkeley: University of California Press, 1991.

Meyer, Michael C. *Huerta: A Political Portrait*. Lincoln: University of Nebraska Press, 1972.

———. *Mexican Rebel: Pascual Orozco and the Mexican Revolution, 1910–1915*. Lincoln: University of Nebraska Press, 1967.

Raat, William D. "The Diplomacy of Suppression: *Los Revoltosos,* Mexico and the United States, 1906–1911." *Hispanic American Historical Review* 56 (1976): 529–60.

Ross, Stanley R. *Francisco I. Madero, Apostle of Mexican Democracy*. New York: Columbia University Press, 1955.

Shadle, Stanley F. *Andrés Molina Enríquez: Mexican Land Reformer of the Revolutionary Era*. Tucson: University of Arizona Press, 1994.

Sherman, John W. "Revolution on Trial: The 1909 Tombstone Proceedings against Ricardo Flores Magón, Antonio Villarreal and Librado Rivera." *The Journal of Arizona History* 32 (1991): 173–94.

Truett, Samuel. *Fugitive Landscapes: The Forgotten History of the U.S.-Mexico Borderlands*. New Haven, Conn.: Yale University Press, 2006.

Turner, John Kenneth. *Barbarous Mexico*. Austin: University of Texas Press, 1969.

Womack, John, Jr. *Zapata and the Mexican Revolution*. New York: Knopf, 1968.

27

Madero and the Failure
of Democracy

In late May 1911, on his way to Veracruz and ultimate exile, Porfirio Díaz reputedly told Victoriano Huerta, the commander of his military escort, "Madero has unleashed a tiger. Now let's see if he can control it." The remark, both prophetic and reflective of Díaz's keen perception of his fellow countrymen, augured ominous consequences. For the next decade Mexico would be torn apart, and the catharsis would be slow in coming. There would be little time to repair the devastation of war or to refashion the contours of society. Politics would undermine altruism.

DISAPPOINTING REFORMS

Bursting with optimistic idealism, Madero approached his presidential challenge with all the fresh enthusiasm of the novice. Mexico was embarking upon a democratic era, and democracy, Madero contended, would be equal to the task. But Madero the president, unlike Madero the revolutionary, found himself quickly besieged with demands from all sides. Only when established in the presidential office did he begin to realize fully that the Revolution had profoundly different meanings to different groups of Mexicans. The spurious alliance began to break up irretrievably. Of the disparate elements he had previously counted in his ranks, those of nineteenth-century liberal persuasion, interested in political reform and the growth of democracy, supported him with unabashed devotion. But both the aristocratic elite he displaced and the social revolutionaries he embraced were increasingly displeased with the modest steps he undertook. The press began to assail him mercilessly, but, in the best democratic tradition, he gave it full rein and stoically accepted the barbed criticism and cruel satires.

It was only natural that Madero should be more responsive to the prodding of his former supporters. Although he could defy anyone to

Francisco I. Madero (1873–1913). President of Mexico in the crucial period following the overthrow of Díaz, Madero had a faith in democracy that proved ill suited to the political realities of the day.

show him where he had ever promised sweeping reform, he did, nevertheless, embark upon a meager and imperfect program to restructure the prevailing social order. Though unwilling to accede to Zapata's urgent demand that land be immediately restored to the villages, the president appointed a National Agrarian Commission, under the chairmanship of his conservative cousin Rafael Hernández, to study the land question. Hernández urged that the government begin purchasing a few private estates for subdivision and sale to the small farmer. But only ten million pesos were allocated to the project, and the hacendados demanded such high prices for the land that even this modest plan was soon abandoned in favor of restoring some of the ejido lands that had been seized illegally during the late Porfiriato. The burden of proof, however, fell on the villages, and few village leaders were able to cope with the bewildering legal arguments thrown in their faces by the hacendados' lawyers. A handful of cases were settled in favor of the villages, but progress on the agrarian question was meager.

The story was much the same in the field of labor reform. Late in 1912 the Congress authorized the formation of a Department of Labor but placed it, too, under the jurisdiction of conservative Hernández, a man whose quixotic faith in the law of supply and demand was never shaken. The budget for the Department of Labor was a paltry forty-six thousand pesos. After a convention with government officials in Mexico City, a group of textile factory owners promised to initiate a ten-hour day, but in practice the working schedules did not change.

Perhaps the greatest benefit accruing to labor during the Madero presidency was that labor organizers no longer felt so intimidated as they had in the past. Encouraged by the possibilities of revolutionary change, a group of radicals under the leadership of Juan Francisco Moncaleano, a Spanish anarchist, founded the Casa del Obrero Mundial. Not properly a union, the Casa served as a place where labor leaders could meet, exchange views, and, through their official newspaper, *Luz*, disseminate propaganda favorable to the cause. But the government, caught between business interests and labor demands, was jittery. Madero feared labor strikes, and, although no labor massacres on the scale of Cananea and Río Blanco were recorded, government troops and local police authorities were used to disperse striking workers on a number of occasions. Hernández interpreted the strikes as inspired by agitators rather than resulting from intolerable conditions and finally had Moncaleano expelled from the country. But the strikes continued, and labor unrest began to disrupt the Mexican economy, growing shaky once again. The gains by labor as a result of these strikes were negligible.

In the field of education the social reformers were again disappointed. Although Madero had promised to broaden the educational base during the presidential campaign, the annual budget for 1911 to 1912 allocated only 7.8 percent for educational programs, as opposed to 7.2 percent during the last year of the Porfiriato. The new president did manage to build some fifty new schools and to initiate a modest program of school lunches for the underprivileged. But his education program is really more notable for what it did not do. No dramatic increase in expenditures was requested, nor was any project for revising the científico curriculum advanced.

In sum, the liberals of the twentieth-century stripe felt swindled by Madero as the administration failed at both the national and state levels. As the disappointed asked themselves why the president did not do more, some most assuredly must have realized that he believed that reform should proceed at a slow and gradual pace so as not to disrupt the fragile economy. But another factor was involved as well. Madero's hands were tied and his energies diverted by a series of revolts that broke out against him before he even had a chance to make himself comfortable in the presidential chair. The Revolution's lack of ideological cohesion had begun to exact a terrible toll and in the process imperiled the administration itself.

REVOLTS AGAINST THE NEW GOVERNMENT

Emiliano Zapata was the first to pronounce against the new regime. In November 1911 the Zapatistas promulgated their famous *Plan de Ayala*. The general principles were those of Zapata himself, but the development and articulation were the work of Otilio Montaño, a schoolteacher from Ayala. After withdrawing recognition of Madero and recognizing Chihuahuan Pascual Orozco as titular head of the rebellion, the plan spelled out its program of agrarian reform.

> The lands, woods, and water that the landlords, científicos, or bosses have usurped . . . will be immediately restored to the villages or citizens who hold the corresponding titles to them. . . . The usurpers who believe they have a right to those properties may present their claims to special courts that will be established on the triumph of the Revolution. Because the great majority of Mexicans own nothing more than the land they walk on, and are unable to improve their social condition in any way . . . because lands, woods, and water are monopolized in a few hands . . . one-third of these properties will be expropriated, with prior indemnification, so that the villages and citizens of Mexico may obtain ejidos, townsites, and fields.[1]

The armed conflict began immediately and quickly spread from Morelos to the neighboring states of Guerrero, Tlaxcala, Puebla, Mexico, and even into the Federal District. When Madero's federal commanders were unable to contain the spread of the rebellion, they were replaced by others who promised to conduct a more vigorous campaign. But the Zapatista army continued to grow, and Madero was unable to thwart it. By early 1912 Zapata had disrupted railroad and telegraph service and taken over a number of towns; he had repeatedly defeated the federals and had the government on the run.

At approximately the same time General Bernardo Reyes launched a second movement in the north. In some ways Madero was more con-

---

1. The entire plan is quoted in Jesús Silva Herzog, *Breve historia de la revolución mexicana* (Mexico City, 1962), 1: 240–46.

cerned with the Reyistas than with the Zapatistas. He feared that General Reyes still enjoyed a wide base of support among the army. Reyes crossed over into Mexico from the United States in the middle of December 1911 but found few Mexicans willing to rally to his banner. Unlike Zapata, Reyes was associated in the public mind with the old regime, and the northern Mexicans were not prepared to embrace his movement, even if many believed that Reyes had been treated unfairly in the recent presidential elections. Realizing that his sluggish revolution was not garnering sufficient support, on Christmas Day Reyes surrendered to a detachment of rurales. The commander of Mexico's third military zone, General Jerónimo Treviño, sent him first to prison in Monterrey and then had him transferred to the Prisión Militar de Santiago Tlaltelolco in Mexico City to await trial for treason.

At the end of the year a third revolt broke out against Madero in Chihuahua. Emilio Vásquez Gómez, believing that he and his brother Francisco had been unfairly treated in the last elections, launched his movement calling for Madero's ouster from office. At the end of January Madero was shocked to learn that the Vasquistas had captured Ciudad Juárez. The president knew full well the significance of this border city—he had seen his own revolt triumph there. Realizing the popularity that Pascual Orozco enjoyed in the north, Madero commissioned the Chihuahua commander to take charge of the government campaigns. For the rank and file of the Vásquez Gómez army Orozco—not Madero—had been responsible for the overthrow of Díaz. Orozco had recruited the troops and led them in battle. He was the symbol of Chihuahua manhood and living proof that a poor, indifferently educated northerner could humble a professional army trained in the big city. The Vasquistas did not want to fight Orozco, so they agreed to meet with him. In the simple, folksy idiom of the north, Orozco made an impassioned speech calling for national unity in an hour of crisis, and he persuaded the rebel army to lay down arms without firing another shot.

But a few months later the most serious antigovernment movement broke out in the north. Its leader was the same man who had just called for national unity and saved Madero from the Vasquista offensive—Pascual Orozco. The Orozco rebellion was complex. While it combined nineteenth- and twentieth-century liberalism, it enjoyed the conservative financial support of the Terrazas clique in Chihuahua, who believed they could control the movement once it triumphed.

The *Plan Orozquista*, dated March 25, 1912, was the most comprehensive call for reform yet voiced from Mexican soil. It caustically attacked Madero for failing to abide by his own principles as set forth to the Mexican nation in the Plan de San Luis Potosí. Government corruption was still in evidence at the state and local levels, and nepotism and favoritism were more exaggerated in 1912 than they had been at any time during the Porfiriato. Not only had Madero's cousin, Rafael Hernández, been awarded the critical cabinet position of secretary of development, but his uncle, Ernesto Madero, had been made secretary of the treasury; a relative by marriage, José González Salas, was secretary of war; brother Gustavo Madero and four other members of the family were in the Congress; brother Raúl Madero was given a series of government-supported military assignments; another relative was on the Supreme Court, two were in the postal service, and yet another was an undersecretary in the cabinet. Government army uniforms came from cotton cloth manufactured in Madero mills, while ammunition was purchased from cousin José Aguilar's munitions plant in Monterrey.

The Plan Orozquista, however, was more concerned with social than political reform. Drawing its inspiration from the Liberal Plan of 1906, it called for a ten-hour workday, restrictions on child labor, improved working conditions, higher wages, and the immediate suppression of the tiendas de raya. Anticipating the surge of economic nationalism that would sweep over Mexico in the next two decades, it called for the immediate nationalization of the railroads and the utilization of Mexican nationals in their operation. Agrarian reform also figured prominently. Persons who had resided on their land for twenty years were to be given title to it, while all lands illegally seized from the peasantry were to be returned. All lands owned by the government were to be distributed, and, most important, land owned by the hacendados, but not regularly cultivated, would be expropriated.

With alarming speed Orozco amassed a large army—some eight thousand strong—and began marching south to Mexico City. Capturing federally held towns along the way the rebels prepared themselves for a major showdown. The anticipated battle occurred at Rellano, close to the Chihuahua-Durango border. Madero's secretary of war, José González Salas, opted to command the government forces personally, and the army career officer was humiliated by Orozco's untrained rebels. As the federals retreated in disarray, González Salas, fearful of public rebuke, committed suicide. With panic growing in Mexico City, Madero named Victoriano Huerta to head a new government offensive. Huerta planned his campaigns with much deliberation, and by late May 1912 felt strong enough to meet the rebels face to face. By sheer chance the artillery duel once again occurred on the fields of Rellano, but on this occasion the results were different. Not only was Huerta a better field commander than his predecessor, but the Orozquistas were handicapped by lack of ammunition. Huerta pushed them back to the north and in the process temporarily saved the teetering Madero government.

Madero had no time for rejoicing, for his woes were not yet over. In early October 1912 a fifth serious rebellion broke out against him. This time it was Félix Díaz, the nephew of Don Porfirio, who called an army together in Veracruz. The Felicista movement was clearly counterrevolutionary in orientation and comprised many disgruntled supporters of the former dictator. Félix Díaz appealed to the army and suggested that Madero had trampled on its honor by passing over many competent career officers and placing self-made revolutionary generals in charge of key garrisons. The troops stationed in Veracruz came to Díaz's support, but his appeal to other army units throughout the republic went unheeded. Late in October loyal army troops isolated the rebels in Veracruz and forced their surrender. A hastily conceived court-martial found Díaz guilty of treason and sentenced him to death. But Madero reviewed the sentence and, believing his enemies to be pitied rather than executed, commuted it to imprisonment. Díaz was taken under arms to the capital and placed in the Federal District penitentiary. Madero's generosity was in no way reciprocated. Within two months Félix Díaz in one Mexico City prison had established contact with Bernardo Reyes in another, and the two were plotting to overthrow the government. This sixth rebellion would succeed, and Madero would lose not only his office but, a victim of his own ideals, his life as well.

THE OVERTHROW OF MADERO

Planned for several months, the military coup that began in Mexico City on February 9, 1913, drastically altered the course of the Mexican Revolution. The capital had thus far been spared the ravages of the war that had engulfed much of the nation since November 1910. Now Mexico City residents would be given practical instruction in the full destructive significance of civil war. Early in the morning of February 9, General Manuel Mondragón, supported by several artillery regiments and military cadets, released Bernardo Reyes and Félix Díaz from their respective prisons and marched on the National Palace. Reyes, sporting a fancy military uniform and mounted on a white horse, led the charge and was felled by one of the first machine gun blasts. The rebel leadership then devolved on Félix Díaz. When loyal government troops repulsed the assault on the National Palace, Díaz led his troops westward across the city and installed his army in the Ciudadela, an old and well-fortified army arsenal. Madero, disregarding the advice of several confidants, named General Victoriano Huerta to command his troops. It proved to be a momentous decision.

A federal machine gun nest awaits the rebel advance.

For the next ten days—the *Decena Trágica*—Mexico City became a labyrinth of barricades, improvised fortifications, and trenches. Artillery fire exchanged between the rebels in the Ciudadela and the government troops in the National Palace destroyed buildings and set fires. As commercial establishments were forced to close their doors for the duration, consumer goods became scarce and people panicked. Downtown streets were strewn with burning cars, runaway horses, and abandoned artillery pieces. Live electric wires dangled precariously from their poles. Looters broke store windows and carried off wares with complete impunity. On one occasion an artillery barrage opened a breach in the wall of the Belén prison and hundreds of inmates scurried through the opening to freedom. A few surveyed the chaos outside and decided to remain.

With neither side able to gain a clear military advantage, civilian casualties mounted into the thousands and bodies began to bloat in the streets. Foreign residents sought the sanctuary of embassies, but not all made it in time. Most traffic came to a halt as only ambulances, military vehicles, and diplomatic automobiles, identified by special flags, moved on the streets. On February 17, after nine days of constant fighting, Madero summoned Huerta and asked when the fighting could be expected to cease. Huerta assured him that peace would be restored to the beleaguered city the following day. The residents of the capital were awakened early on the morning of February 18 by the sounds of artillery and machine gun fire, just as they had been for the previous nine days. But in the afternoon the clamor of war stopped. Huerta had decided to change sides. He withdrew recognition of the federal government and dispatched General Aureliano Blanquet to the National Palace to arrest the president. Blanquet encountered Madero in one of the patios and, with revolver in hand, proclaimed, "You are my prisoner, Mr. President." Madero retorted, "You are a traitor." But Blanquet simply reaffirmed, "You are my prisoner."[2] Within a half hour Vice-President Pino Suárez, Madero's brother Gustavo, and most of the cabinet had been arrested as well.

The agreement according to which Huerta joined the rebels is known as the Pact of the Embassy because the final negotiations were conducted under the aegis of the American ambassador in Mexico City, Henry Lane Wilson. A typical diplomat of the age of dollar diplomacy, Wilson saw his role as protector of United States business interests. Throughout the Madero presidency he had meddled shamelessly in Mexico's internal affairs, and during the Decena Trágica he played an active part in charting the course of events. On one occasion, in concert with the British, German, and Spanish ministers, he even demanded Madero's resignation, alleging as his reason the tremendous damage to foreign property in Mexico City. After being rebuffed by the Mexican president, Wilson changed his tactics and worked actively to bring Huerta and Díaz to an accord. On the evening of February 18 the two generals met with Wilson at the American embassy and hammered out the pact that was made public the following day.

> In the city of Mexico, at nine-thirty in the evening on February 18, 1913, General Félix Díaz and Victoriano Huerta met in conference. . . . General Huerta stated that because of the unbearable situation created by the government of Mr. Madero, he had, in order to prevent the further shedding of blood and to safeguard national unity, placed the said Madero, several members of his cabinet, and various other persons under arrest. . . . General Díaz stated that his only reason for raising the standard of revolt was a desire on his part to protect the national welfare, and in that light he was ready to make any sacrifice that would prove beneficial to the country. . . . From this time forward the former chief executive is not to be recognized. The elements represented by Generals Díaz and Huerta are united in opposing all efforts to restore him to power. . . . Generals Díaz and Huerta will do all in their power to enable the latter to assume . . . the provisional presidency.[3]

2. Quoted in Michael C. Meyer, *Huerta: A Political Portrait* (Lincoln, 1972), p. 57.

3. The Pact of the Embassy has been translated and included in its entirety in ibid., pp. 235–36.

Wishing to cloak his assumption of power in some semblance of legality, Huerta first secured the official resignations of Madero and Pino Suárez and then convened a special evening session of the Congress. The resignations were accepted by the legislative body with only five dissenting votes, and the presidency legally passed to the next in line, Secretary of Foreign Relations Pedro Lascuráin. Sworn into office at 10:24 P.M., Lascuráin immediately appointed General Huerta as secretary of interior and at 11:20 P.M. submitted his own resignation. The Constitution of 1857 provided that in the absence of a president, a vice-president, and a secretary of foreign relations, the office passed to the secretary of interior. Huerta, clad in a formal black tuxedo, was sworn into office shortly before midnight. Madero-style democracy had ended in derision as Mexico had its third president in one day.

The political charade perpetrated before the Congress was not the greatest indignity Mexicans were called upon to suffer in February 1913. On the evening of February 21, Francisco Madero and José María Pino Suárez were transferred from the National Palace, where they had been held prisoners since the day of their arrest, to the Federal District penitentiary. The capital city newspapers the following day blared an improbable tale. A group of Madero's supporters attacked the convoy escorting the prisoners, attempted to free them, and during the ensuing melee both the former president and vice-president were killed.

Virtually no one believed this official version, but few Mexicans knew what really happened. Madero and Pino Suárez had been taken to the penitentiary under the guard of Francisco Cárdenas, a major in the rurales. When the convoy reached the prison, Cárdenas ordered the captives out of the cars and, by prearranged signal, the spotlights high on the wall were turned off. The hapless men were then shot point-blank. Perhaps Victoriano Huerta ordered the assassinations, or perhaps it was Félix Díaz, or even Aureliano Blanquet. The nature of the available evidence simply precludes positive determination. But what cannot be doubted is that the senseless murders of Madero and Pino Suárez set the tone of the Revolution for at least the next five years.

RECOMMENDED FOR FURTHER STUDY

Beezley, William H. *Insurgent Governor: Abraham González and the Mexican Revolution in Chihuahua*. Lincoln: University of Nebraska Press, 1973.

Calvert, Peter. *The Mexican Revolution, 1910–1914: The Diplomacy of the Anglo-American Conflict*. Cambridge: Cambridge University Press, 1968.

Cumberland, Charles C. *Mexican Revolution: Genesis under Madero*. Austin: University of Texas Press, 1952.

Gonzales, Michael J. *The Mexican Revolution, 1910–1940*. Albuquerque: University of New Mexico Press, 2002.

Harris, Charles H., and Louis R. Sadler. "The Underside of the Mexican Revolution: El Paso, 1912." *The Americas* 39 (1982): 69–84.

———. "The 1911 Reyes Conspiracy: The Texas Side." *Southwestern Historical Quarterly* 82 (1980): 325–48.

Hart, John Mason. "The Mexican Revolution 1910–1920," in *The Oxford History of Mexico*. Edited by Michael C. Meyer and William H. Beezley, pp. 435–65. New York: Oxford University Press, 2000.

Henderson, Peter V. N. *Félix Díaz, the Porfirians and the Mexican Revolution*. Lincoln: University of Nebraska Press, 1981.

LaFrance, David G. *Revolution in Mexico's Heartland: Politics, War, and State Building in Puebla, 1913–1920*. Wilmington, Del.: Scholarly Resources, 2003.

Meyer, Michael C. *Huerta: A Political Portrait*. Lincoln: University of Nebraska Press, 1972.

———. *Mexican Rebel: Pascual Orozco and the Mexican Revolution, 1910–1915*. Lincoln: University of Nebraska Press, 1967.

Ross, Stanley R. *Francisco I. Madero, Apostle of Mexican Democracy*. New York: Columbia University Press, 1955.

Turner, Frederick C. "Anti-Americanism in Mexico, 1910–1913." *Hispanic American Historical Review* 47 (1967): 502–18.

Wilson, Henry Lane. *Diplomatic Episodes in Mexico, Belgium and Chile*. Garden City, N.Y.: Doubleday, Page, 1927.

Wolfskill, George, and Douglas W. Richmond, eds. *Essays on the Mexican Revolution: Revisionist Views of the Leaders*. Austin: University of Texas Press, 1979.

Womack, John, Jr. *Zapata and the Mexican Revolution*. New York: Knopf, 1968.

28

Huerta and the Failure
of Dictatorship

HUERTA

Victoriano Huerta was born of a Huichol Indian mother and a mestizo father in a small Jalisco village. Attending a poor local school run by the parish priest, he learned to read and write and showed some natural talent for science and mathematics. As a teenager he was taken on as an aide by General Donato Guerra, a career officer who had fought against the French. Guerra used his influence in Mexico City to have Huerta accepted at the National Military Academy. Despite his mediocre educational background, he did well as a cadet and received his commission in 1876 as a second lieutenant assigned to the army corps of engineers.

Huerta's prerevolutionary career coincided almost exactly with the Díaz dictatorship, and he became an effective agent of Don Porfirio's system of enforced peace. During the thirty-four-year Porfiriato, Huerta fought in the north against the Yaqui, in the south against the Maya, and in the central part of the country against other Mexicans unhappy with the autocratic regime. Encountering much success on the field of battle, he rose rapidly in the ranks and by the turn of the century had been awarded his brigadier-general stars. National prominence and some notoriety engulfed him for the first time in the summer of 1911 when interim President León de la Barra dispatched him to Morelos to enforce the demobilization of the Zapatista troops. His relationship with Madero was never good again.

When Bernardo Reyes and Félix Díaz planned the military coup of February 1913, their emissaries approached Huerta and solicited his support. He refused the invitation, however, not out of loyalty to the Madero administration but rather because he wanted the leadership for himself. When Bernardo Reyes was killed during the first major encounter, the situation changed. Huerta dallied for a week and, having determined that he would be able to control Félix Díaz, made his decision to change sides. Sworn into the presidential office a few days later, Huerta was sure he had made the proper choice.

Within a few days federal generals and state governors began to pledge support of the new regime. A group of talented statesmen and intellectuals accepted cabinet portfolios. Sanitation workers started to scour the bloodstained streets of the capital and to attack a ten-day backlog of garbage. Red Cross units tried to identify hundreds of decaying corpses, and electricians repaired wires dangling dangerously from their poles.

REBELLION AND MILITARIZATION

The first genuinely ominous sign came from the northeast where Coahuila Governor Venustiano Carranza, an ardent Madero supporter, announced his decision not to recognize the new regime. Carranza issued a circular telegram to other state governors exhorting them to follow his good example. Within a few weeks he found support in Chihuahua and Sonora. Pancho Villa assumed military leadership of the anti-Huerta movement in Chihuahua, while Alvaro Obregón, a man of considerable military talent, took charge of the antigovernment operations in neighboring Sonora. The alliance of the northern revolutionaries, and their formal pronouncement of defection, was sealed in late March when representatives from the three states affixed their signatures to the *Plan de Guadalupe*. After withdrawing recognition of the Huerta government, the plan named Venustiano Carranza as "First Chief" of the Constitutionalist Army and provided that he, or someone designated by him, would occupy the interim presidency upon Huerta's defeat. An exclusively political document, the plan embodied no program of social reform.

In southern Mexico Huerta encountered an implacable enemy of a different sort. Emiliano Zapata angrily rejected Huerta's invitation to pledge support of the government. In fact, the southern rebel arrested and subsequently executed the federal peace commissioners sent to garner his allegiance. Zapata, unlike the Constitutionalists in the north, did not denounce Huerta for having overthrown Madero. While he found treason in Huerta's sudden shift of sides during the Decena Trágica, he declared himself in rebellion because he saw no hope that the federal government under Huerta would begin to restore the village lands in Morelos. Not trusting the Constitutionalist dedication to agrarian reform either, Zapata never allied himself with the anti-Huerta movement in the north. But by forcing the government to divert some of its war effort from the north to the south, Zapata placed additional military pressure on the new regime.

Modern technology is brought to warfare. In one of the first military uses of aircraft, Huerta employed 80-horsepower planes similar to these in reconnaissance and bombing raids against the Villistas in the north.

Facing rebellion in the north and in Morelos, Huerta's first priority was pacification. With a federal army numbering about fifty thousand, the president announced brazenly to the Congress that he would re-establish peace, "cost what it may." But pacification proved elusive on the field of battle. In March and April the Constitutionalists scored impressive victories in Sonora and Chihuahua, while in the south Emiliano Zapata had done the same. The psychology of the civil war changed drastically in May when First Chief Carranza, in a singularly intemperate decree, announced that federal soldiers who fell into rebel hands would be executed summarily. The Constitutionalists thus declared that they intended to give no quarter, and by the summer of 1913 Huerta had concluded that pacification would come only if he militarized Mexico to the teeth.

Factories and stores not related to the war effort were required to close on Sundays so that civilian employees could be given military training. Railroads left civilian passengers and freight standing in the stations so that military personnel and hardware could be shipped to where it was needed. The National Arms Factory, the National Artillery Workshops, and the National Power Factory received new equipment to increase their productive capacities. Scarcely a week passed without a showy military parade or public display of the latest military equipment. The president himself enjoyed participating in these graphic exhibits of military culture and used the occasions to sport his favorite dress uniforms replete with ribbons covering the left side of his jacket and medals draped from his neck. The Mexican school system felt the impact of the militarization in the late summer of 1913 when school after school found its governing regulations changed to provide for the mandatory wearing of military uniforms. Training in the military arts and sciences was added to the curricula. Military decorations were passed out in wholesale lot to the president's cronies, and new military awards were authorized to compensate favorites or to win over those of doubtful loyalty. Most importantly, the president decreed constant increases in the size of the federal army—from fifty thousand to one hundred thousand to two hundred thousand and finally to a quarter of a million, or about twelve times the number of troops available to Porfirio Díaz when the Revolution broke out.

When small pay increases failed to attract enlistees in large numbers, Huerta fell back on a time-honored tradition—the leva, a system of forced conscription directed exclusively at the indigent masses. Tens of thousands of illiterate men were picked up off the streets of the barrios in the large cities and from the surrounding countryside and sent into the field. The crowds emerging from a bullfight or staggering out of a cantina closing its doors for the night were favorite targets, as were criminals in jail for minor offenses. But the effects of the leva were disastrous. The quality of the federal army declined steadily. The lack of adequate training meant no *esprit de corps*, no discipline, and tremendously high desertion rates. In the fall of 1913 it was not unheard of for entire units of new recruits to turn themselves and their equipment over to the enemy without firing a single shot.

The toll of the civil war in 1913 and 1914 was tremendous. The military presence was obvious everywhere. The population of a village could double to triple overnight as a large unit moved in to camp. Because there was no advance notice, a week's stay could deplete stores of food, supplies, and other basic necessities, thus aggravating the obscenities of war. When the troops withdrew, villages were often on the verge of starvation. The receipts a local merchant might receive as the troops emptied his store were scarcely worth the paper they were hastily scrawled on.

With his military position deteriorating, Huerta became increasingly impetuous, egotistical, and dictatorial. Cabinet secretaries could not work with him for very long, and turnovers followed one another in rapid succession. Recognizing the potential value of a controlled press, Huerta initiated an extensive policy of censorship. Editors who adopted hostile attitudes were removed from their positions, sent into exile, or jailed. A vast network of secret agents and spies reported on the activities of real and potential enemies, and by the fall of 1913 the jail cells in Mexico City and many of the state capitals were crowded with political prisoners.

Without question the most reprehensible facet of the Huerta dictatorship was its unbridled use of political assassination. After the senseless slaying of Madero and Pino Suárez, Maderista Governor Abraham González was the next to be killed. Army officers, congressmen, professional men, and even petty bureaucrats who manifested their discontent were sacrificed to the ill-conceived exigencies of the day. The most celebrated case of all was that of Senator Belisario Domínguez from Chiapas, an outspoken critic of the regime. In late September 1913, against the good counsel of friends in the Senate, Domínguez asked for the floor to read a prepared statement.

> Peace, cost what it may, Mr. Victoriano Huerta had said. Fellow Senators, have you studied the terrible meaning of those words . . . ? The national assembly has the duty of deposing Mr. Victoriano Huerta from the presidency. He is the one against whom our brothers in the north protest with so much reason. . . . You will tell me, gentlemen, that the attempt is dangerous; for Mr. Victoriano Huerta is a bloody and ferocious soldier who assassinates without hesitation anyone who is an obstacle to his wishes; this does not matter gentlemen! The country exacts from you the fulfillment of a duty, even with risk, indeed the assurance, that you are to lose your lives.[1]

Two weeks later Belisario Domínguez was dead from an assassin's bullet. The morally outraged Senate passed a resolution requesting full information from the president and resolving to remain in permanent session until the case be closed. Two days later Huerta responded by dissolving both houses of the legislature and arresting the majority of the congressmen.

ECONOMIC PROBLEMS AND FOREIGN RELATIONS

The war Huerta was fighting against the Constitutionalists in the north and the Zapatistas in the south was costly, and the regime had inherited an empty treasury. By relying on the leva to fill the ranks of the federal army, Huerta depleted the work force in both the cities and the countryside. With no pickers, cotton rotted in the fields, coffee beans fell off the trees, and sugarcane remained unharvested on the large plantations. Mines closed operations; cattlemen in the north lost thousands of head to the rebels; and fruit growers, realizing their perishable products were extremely vulnerable to transportation delays, cut back production. As food and manufactured goods became scarce, a black market began to flourish in the larger cities, and the entire economic structure of the country was severely tested.

The first government expedient was to issue paper money without adequate hard reserves to back it up. The new paper issue depreciated almost as soon as it rolled off the press. Not to be outdone, the

---

1. Quoted in Michael C. Meyer, *Huerta: A Political Portrait* (Lincoln, 1972), pp. 137–38.

Together with several other kinds of scrip, this 20-peso note from Chihuahua state was used by the Constitutionalists in late 1913 and early 1914.

Constitutionalists and the Zapatistas issued their own currency, as did a number of states and large mining and industrial concerns. Late in 1913 there were at least twenty-five different kinds of paper currency in circulation, and nobody was able to ascertain accurately the fluctuating exchange rates. Counterfeiters, of course, had a field day, while bankers and tax collectors were driven almost to insanity.

In addition to his military and economic problems, Huerta faced one other dilemma as well. The United States not only refused to recognize his regime but adopted a frankly hostile attitude toward him. Woodrow Wilson came to the United States presidency almost simultaneously with Victoriano Huerta's rise to power. While the American ambassador to Mexico, Henry Lane Wilson, urged recognition, President Wilson and his newly appointed secretary of state, William Jennings Bryan, both with an abiding faith in the concept of the democratic state, refused. To the White House, Huerta, who came to power by forcefully ejecting the previous regime, was a symbol of all that was wrong with Latin America. Unprepared by temperament or training to understand the complexities of the Mexican Revolution, President Wilson decided to apply his own standards of political ethics to the situation. The moral judgment, as abstractly admirable as it was diplomatically impractical, once made proved unshakable.

Demonstrating little faith in the reports received from Ambassador Wilson, the president and the secretary of state decided to dispatch special agents to Mexico to report on the nature of the growing conflict. The first chosen for the special assignment was William Bayard Hale. Speaking no Spanish, Hale relied heavily on the United States business community for his information, but he managed interviews with several high-level Mexican officials as well. As his reports to the White House began, he noted that the businessmen in Mexico favored early recognition of the regime, but, sensing what the American president wanted to hear, he indicated that he himself did not. Appealing to President Wilson's sense of moral rectitude, Hale characterized Huerta as "an ape-like man, of almost pure Indian blood. He may be said to subsist on alcohol. Drunk or only half drunk (he is never sober) he never loses a certain shrewdness."[2] The American president was impressed with Hale's findings; he would not have written the report any differently, he claimed, had he gone to Mexico City himself. By summer Ambassador Wilson had been recalled and the White House had another special emissary in Mexico—John Lind, a former governor of Minnesota and a longtime friend of Secretary Bryan.

If there was ever any hope for a reconciliation between the United States and Mexico in the late summer and fall of 1913, Lind's reports to Washington eliminated it. Speaking no more Spanish than Hale and being even less conversant with Mexican politics, his dispatches were haughty, bellicose, inaccurate, and often laden with anti-Catholic and anti-Indian slurs. His characterization of the Mexican cabinet ("a worse pack of wolves never infested any community") reveals more about Lind than about Huerta's advisers. Given President Wilson's insistence that Huerta had to go, there were only two genuine avenues open: Wilson could intervene militarily in Mexico, or he could intervene indirectly by channeling United States aid to the Constitutionalists in the north. He chose the second alternative first, and, when that did not work, he opted for military intervention.

DOMESTIC REFORMS

Amazingly, despite the military, economic, and diplomatic pressures the regime faced, Huerta and his advisers found some time for domestic programs. The enemies of the dictatorship labeled them counterrevolutionary, an attempt to reincarnate the age of Díaz. But examination of the regime's social programs reveals that they were anything but that. While Porfirio Díaz had never allocated over 7.2 percent of his budget for education, and Madero had raised the percentage slightly to 7.8 percent, Huerta projected a 9.9 percent allocation for educational services. The funds were still inadequate, but

---

2. Quoted in Larry D. Hill, *Emissaries to a Revolution: Woodrow Wilson's Executive Agents in Mexico* (Baton Rouge, 1973), p. 31.

Huerta did manage the construction of 131 new rural schools with seats for some ten thousand new students. Secretary of Education Nemesio García Naranjo, impressed with Henri Bergson's philosophical assault on positivism, decided to initiate a new curriculum at the National Preparatory School. Breaking sharply with the positivist tradition of Gabino Barreda, García Naranjo made more room for the study of literature, history, and philosophy. He did not abandon the sciences but argued persuasively that the other branches of learning should not be sacrificed to them. By creating a reasonable balance between the arts and the sciences, the secretary struck an important first blow at the científico philosophy of education.

The anticientífico posture of the regime manifested itself in Indian policy as well. Administration spokesman Jorge Vera Estañol was an early champion of *indigenismo*. National unity, he argued, was impossible when millions of Indians were estranged from the rest of the population by language, customs, diet, and life expectancy. The rural education program was well intended but was not sufficiently expansive to bring the Indian into the mainstream of national life. Huerta's secretary of interior, Aureliano Urrutia, a full-blooded Indian, began dispatching teams of government consultants into the pueblos to organize community projects that could make small but meaningful changes in the patterns of daily life. But again the program was so small as to make scarcely a dent in the prevailing structure.

It is in the matter of agrarian reform that the Huerta dictatorship has been most widely misrepresented. The regime initiated its program modestly by distributing free seed to anyone who asked for it and by expanding the activities of the agricultural school in Mexico City. Of greater practical significance Huerta authorized the restoration of seventy-eight ejidos to the Yaqui and Mayo Indians of Sonora. In the late spring of 1913 the president upgraded Madero's National Agrarian Commission to a cabinet department and instructed Eduardo Tamariz, Mexico's secretary of agriculture, to begin studying the problem of land redistribution. Tamariz could find nothing in the Constitution of 1857 that even faintly authorized the expropriation of land, so he had to devise another scheme. He found his solution in the taxation provisions of the Constitution. If taxes were increased on the large haciendas, the land would be less valuable for speculative purposes and hacendados would have to consider sale. Congressional authorization was not forthcoming, but Huerta went ahead on his own and decreed an increase in land taxes.

In the areas of labor, church policy, and foreign relations the Huerta regime also departed drastically from the models of the Porfiriato. The programs the administration sponsored did not add up to a social revolution. The reforms bore little demonstrable relationship to one another, no attempt at syncretization was made, and social mobility for the masses did not, as a result, increase. But the regime was no counterrevolution; it was in many ways more farsighted than that of Madero. Huerta and his advisers allowed themselves to be tossed around by the winds of twentieth-century change and harbored no notions of pegging themselves to a Porfirian status quo. While it is true that Huerta's abuse of political power can justifiably be likened to Don Porfirio's authoritarianism, nevertheless, in the larger social sense both Huerta and his advisers recognized that the days of Díaz were gone forever.

UNITED STATES INTERVENTION AND THE FALL OF HUERTA

By the spring of 1914 Huerta was losing his wars on both the military and the economic fronts. But the final blow was precipitated by his steadily deteriorating relationship with the White House. Early in 1914 President Wilson beefed up the American fleet stationed off Mexican waters. In April a seemingly insignificant event augured the most serious United States–Mexico dispute since the war of the middle of the nineteenth century. Captain Ralph T. Earle of the USS *Dolphin*, stationed off the coast of Tampico, ordered a small landing party to go ashore to secure some badly needed gasoline. Tampico was still in government hands, but the Constitutionalists had attacked several days before and the federal forces were awaiting a more concerted assault. The United States sailors wandered into a restricted dock area and were arrested on the spot.

Within an hour orders came for the sailors' release, accompanied by an official apology. But Rear Admiral Henry T. Mayo, commander of the naval forces off Tampico, considered the apology insufficient and demanded something more elaborate. Since the boat carrying the sailors to shore allegedly flew the American flag, Mayo demanded, among other things, that the Mexican government hoist the American flag at some prominent place on shore and present a twenty-one gun salute to it. President Wilson considered the demands reasonable and prepared himself to make the incident a *casus belli* should Huerta not publicly recant in exactly the manner prescribed. Huerta's secretary of foreign relations insisted that the small landing craft had not carried the flag but agreed to the salute on the condition that the United States return the salute to the Mexican flag. The White House considered the rejoinder impertinent, for both President Wilson and Secretary of State Bryan realized that a United States salute to the Mexican flag could be considered tantamount to recognizing the Huerta regime.

With neither side knowing exactly what to do next, the stalemate was broken when the United States consul in Veracruz wired Washington that a German ship, the *Ypiranga*, was scheduled to arrive in that port on April 21 with a large shipment of arms for Huerta. President Wilson gave immediate orders for a naval occupation of Veracruz. The marines took the city but Mexican casualties mounted into the hundreds, including many noncombatants of both sexes. The public outcry in Mexico City was understandably indignant. Congressmen denounced the United States, and mobs looted American-owned businesses, tore down the statue of George Washington, and threatened tourists. Mexican newspapers urged retaliation against the "Pigs of Yanquilandia." In Monterrey the United States flag was ripped from the consulate and burned on the spot. But the Stars and Stripes, which had precipitated the furor in the first place, was subjected to even greater indignities in the capital. Tied to the tail of a donkey, it was used to sweep clean the streets of the central plaza.

President Wilson's attempt to rid Mexico of a dictator and himself of a self-made enemy almost backfired. Venustiano Carranza and the majority of his Constitutionalists, the supposed beneficiaries of the Veracruz intervention, expressed their strong disapproval of the blatant violation of Mexican sovereignty. Huerta, however, was unable to capitalize upon their displeasure, and his call for all Mexicans to lay aside internal differences and present a united front went unheeded. Even the initial indignation expressed in Mexico City soon dissipated as the United States troops, despite rumors to the contrary, did not march on Mexico City as they had in 1847.

As Huerta called in his troops to make a show of force against the Americans, the Constitutionalists in the north and the Zapatistas in the south quickly moved into the military vacuums. By the early summer, with Pancho Villa's capture of Zacatecas, Huerta's military position had become completely untenable. The continued occupation of Veracruz meant that revenues from the customhouse were stopped before they reached the federal treasury. Recognizing that the diplomatic, economic, and military pressures had all conspired to his disadvantage, Huerta made his decision to resign on July 8, 1914. In his statement of resignation he placed the prime responsibility for what had happened to Mexico on the Puritan who resided in the White House.

It is true that Woodrow Wilson was in large measure responsible for Huerta's overthrow. He had meddled shamelessly in Mexico's internal affairs and, without the semblance of a threat to United States security, had shed innocent Mexican blood to effectuate the foreign policy objectives he deemed opportune. But Wilson cannot be held accountable for the larger calamity that had struck the Mexican na-

U.S. Navy "bluejackets" engage Mexican defenders at Veracruz in April 1914.

tion. Not all Mexico's domestic ills were orphans of United States bullets. Mexicans had not yet agreed on the meaning of their Revolution. Francisco Madero's well-meaning but ineffectual experiment with democracy had failed when he had urged caution and moderation on the burning social issues of the day. But Huerta's dictatorship failed as well. While he was not unwilling to give the social reformers the chance to institute change, many Mexicans could no longer bring themselves to accommodate another brutal dictatorship that exalted order at the expense of liberty. The number of options still open were gradually being reduced, but the better day had not yet dawned.

RECOMMENDED FOR FURTHER STUDY

Blaisdell, Lowell L. "Henry Lane Wilson and the Overthrow of Madero." *Southwestern Social Science Quarterly* 43 (1962): 126–35.

Calvert, Peter. *The Mexican Revolution, 1910–1914: The Diplomacy of the Anglo-American Conflict*. Cambridge: Cambridge University Press, 1968.

Cumberland, Charles C. *Mexican Revolution: The Constitutionalist Years*. Austin: University of Texas Press, 1972.

Grieb, Kenneth J. *The United States and Huerta*. Lincoln: University of Nebraska Press, 1969.

Harris, Charles H., III, and Louis R. Sadler. *The Texas Rangers and the Mexican Revolution*. Albuquerque: University of New Mexico Press, 2004.

Hill, Larry D. *Emissaries to a Revolution: Woodrow Wilson's Executive Agents in Mexico*. Baton Rouge: Louisiana State University Press, 1973.

Katz, Friedrich. *The Life and Times of Pancho Villa*. Stanford, Calif.: Stanford University Press, 1998.

Knight, Alan. *The Mexican Revolution*. Vol. 2: *Counter Revolution and Reconstruction*. New York: Cambridge University Press, 1986.

Meyer, Michael C. "The Arms of the *Ypiranga*." *Hispanic American Historical Review* 50 (1970): 543–56.

———. *Huerta: A Political Portrait*. Lincoln: University of Nebraska Press, 1972.

———. "The Militarization of Mexico, 1913–1914." *The Americas* 27 (1971): 293–306.

Quirk, Robert E. *An Affair of Honor: Woodrow Wilson and the Occupation of Veracruz*. New York: Norton, 1967.

Vanderwood, Paul J. "The Picture Postcard as Historical Evidence: Veracruz: 1914." *The Americas* 45 (1988): 201–26.

29

The Illusory Quest
for a Better Way

THE CONVENTION OF AGUASCALIENTES
AND NEAR ANARCHY

The years following Victoriano Huerta's ouster are the most chaotic in Mexican revolutionary history as the quarrels among erstwhile allies began. In 1914 First Chief Venustiano Carranza allowed that a convention should be held to determine, among other questions, who should be the provisional president of Mexico until such time as national elections could be scheduled. A proper choice, he believed, could finally put an end to the fragmentation that had characterized the Revolution almost from the beginning. The town of Aguascalientes, in neutral territory, was selected to host the convention, and invitations were extended to all the important revolutionary factions, the number of delegates being apportioned according to how many troops had been deployed in the recent anti-Huerta campaigns.

The military delegates, in a wide array of uniforms and most carrying rifles with full cartridge belts, began to arrive in Aguascalientes in early October. At one of the early sessions Alvaro Obregón, the First Chief's official spokesman, presented the Convention with a Mexican flag inscribed with the words, "Military Convention of Aguascalientes." Each of the delegates then went to the podium, placed his signature on the flag, and swore allegiance to the Convention, some offering a few garrulous remarks. The impressive display of confraternity was not destined to last for long, however. When the Zapatista delegation arrived, a few days late, its leader Paulino Martínez asked to speak. In a deliberate affront to Carranza and Obregón he recognized Villa and Zapata as the genuine leaders of the Revolution. Manifesting the typical Zapatista aversion to gradualism, he argued that "effective suffrage and no-re-election" had no meaning for the vast majority of Mexicans. The Revolution had been fought for land and liberty. The speech presaged a serious schism in the Convention between Villistas and Zapatistas on the one hand and Carrancistas and Obregonistas on the other. The debates were not sectarian squabbles; rather they reflected fundamental differences of opinion on the direction the Revolution should take.

Martínez was followed to the rostrum by the vice-chairman of the Zapatista delegation, Antonio Díaz Soto y Gama. A thirty-year-old socialist and a polished orator, he delineated future lines of combat.

> I come here not to attack anyone but to evoke patriotism and to stimulate shame. I come to excite the honor of all of the delegates to this assembly. . . . Perhaps it is necessary to invoke respectable symbols [gesturing to the Convention flag], but I fear that the essence of patriotism does not lie in the symbols, which are, after all, quite similar to the farces of the church. . . . I believe that our word of honor is more valuable than all of the signatures stamped on this flag. In the last analysis this flag represents nothing more than the triumph of the clerical reaction championed by Iturbide. I will never sign this flag. . . . That which we called Independence was not independence for the Indian, but independence for the criollo, for the heirs of the conquerors who continue infamously to abuse and cheat the oppressed Indian.[1]

Soto y Gama's speech was continuously interrupted from the floor both by those who cheered him and by those who were livid at his ridicule of Mexican history and defamation of the flag. Not yet ready to embrace the chastening influence of open debate, some of the delegates even pointed pistols in his direction. The acrimony occasioned by the impassioned speech was not easily abated, and as the Convention set to work on naming a provisional president the underlying issue was whether the Revolution was going to follow the politically oriented plans of San Luis Potosí and Guadalupe or the agrarian Plan de Ayala.

When, against Carranza's wishes, the Convention chose Eulalio Gutiérrez as provisional president of Mexico, the First Chief, haughty as ever, disavowed the action and, from Mexico City, ordered his followers to withdraw. Some, including Alvaro Obregón, obeyed, while others made common cause with the Zapatistas and Villistas. As Villa's troops marched on the capital to install Gutiérrez in the presidency, it was obvious to all that Mexico was on the verge of still another civil war. Carranza believed it was better not to make a stand in Mexico City and withdrew his Constitutionalist government to Veracruz. The

---

1. Quoted in Isidro Fabela, ed., *Documentos históricos de la revolución mexicana* (Mexico City, 1960–73), 23: 181–82.

United States government had agreed to pull out its troops just in time
for Carranza to make the gulf port his provisional capital.

MULTIPLE CIVIL WARS

In early December 1914 Carranza's two principal antagonists, Pancho
Villa, "the Centaur of the North," and Emiliano Zapata, "the Attila of
the South," staged a dramatic meeting at Xochimilco on the outskirts
of Mexico City. While their followers had knotted the bonds of intellectual camaraderie at the Convention, the two leaders had never before met. The historian Robert Quirk has recreated the encounter from
eyewitness accounts.

> Villa and Zapata were a study in contrasts. Villa was tall and robust,
> weighing at least 180 pounds, with a florid complexion. He wore a trop-
> ical helmet after the English style. . . . Zapata, in his physiognomy, was
> much more the Indian of the two. His skin was very dark, and in com-
> parison with Villa's his face was thin with high cheek bones. He wore
> an immense sombrero, which at times hid his eyes. . . .
>   The conference began haltingly . . . both were men of action and
> verbal intercourse left them uneasy. . . . But then the conversation
> touched on Venustiano Carranza and suddenly, like tinder, burst aflame.
> They poured out in a torrent of volubility their mutual hatred for the
> First Chief. Villa pronounced his opinion of the middle class revolu-
> tionaries who followed Carranza: "Those are men who have always slept
> on soft pillows. How could they ever be friends of the people, who have
> spent their whole lives in nothing but suffering?" Zapata concurred: "On
> the contrary, they have always been the scourge of the people. . . . Those
> *cabrones!* As soon as they see a little chance, well, they want to take ad-
> vantage of it and line their own pockets! Well, to hell with them!"[2]

But while Villa and Zapata could agree enthusiastically about their
profound disdain for Carranza, their alliance was short lived. Although
each had promised to support the military engagements of the other,
cooperation against Carranza was noticeable only by its absence. The
early months of 1915 saw the Mexican Revolution degenerating into
unmitigated anarchy. Civil wars ravaged many states. Civilian casualties mounted as atrocities were committed on all sides. While it is not
difficult to find things noble in Hidalgo's revolution of 1810 and
Madero's revolution of 1910, it is difficult to find nobility in the Mex-

---

2. Robert E. Quirk, *The Mexican Revolution, 1914–1915: The Convention of Aguascalientes* (New York, 1963), pp. 135–38.

Pancho Villa (left) and Emiliano Zapata (right) meet in Mexico City. The camaraderie was more apparent than real.

ican chaos of 1915. Hidalgo, and Madero a century later, had exhibited a reasonable measure of tolerance and patience before their forbearance ultimately was exhausted. Many of the regional warlords of this period employed military force for reasons no more profound than instant political self-gratification.

With his own Conventionist coalition falling apart as well, provisional President Gutiérrez abandoned Mexico City and Obregón took the capital unopposed. But nothing was thereby settled. Gutiérrez, still claiming to be president, established a new government in Nuevo León; Carranza, claiming national executive control as first chief, continued to govern from Veracruz; the Zapatistas supported Roque González Garza as president; while Pancho Villa, pretending to speak for the entire nation, ruled from Chihuahua. None of the governments recognized the paper money, coinage, or legal contracts of the others.

The muddied political waters were cleared somewhat in the most famous military engagement of the Revolution—the battle of Celaya—in April 1915. While Pancho Villa prepared to put his slightly tarnished record of military victories on the line, Alvaro Obregón had immersed himself in the battle reports from war-torn Europe. He had learned, among other things, that one of the best ways to blunt a concerted cavalry charge was to encircle carefully laid out defensive positions with rolls of barbed wire. In early April, when Villa attacked with a force estimated at twenty-five thousand men, Obregón was ready. He had planned his defenses with consummate skill, and, when Villa launched a furious cavalry charge, Obregón's well-placed artillery and machine guns began cutting the attackers to pieces. Villa was forced to retreat, but in the middle of the month tried again to dislodge Obregón's forces. The second Villista offensive was even less successful than the first; in fact, it was a disaster. Bent upon victory even at exorbitant costs, Villa threw his cavalry against the barbed-wire entrenchments only to see wave after wave massacred. When it all ended, thousands of bodies were strewn across the fields of Celaya and impaled on the barbed wire. Obregón's official report listed over four thousand Villistas dead, five thousand wounded, and six thousand taken prisoner. He calculated his own losses at only 138 dead and 227 wounded.

The battle of Celaya did not immediately destroy Villa's capacity to make war, but it did presage his ultimate defeat. By the summer and fall of 1915 First Chief Carranza was clearly gaining the upper hand as both the Villistas in the north and the Zapatistas in the south found themselves increasingly isolated and without national support. In the White House President Wilson decided to throw the official support of the United States behind the Constitutionalists. He extended diplomatic recognition to the Carranza regime in October. Pancho Villa, who had courted the United States for years and who had not even criticized the invasion at Veracruz, was incensed. Determined not to turn the other cheek, he began to take his vengeance on private United States civilians.

The first serious incident occurred at Santa Isabel (today General Trías), Chihuahua. The strange scenario began on January 9, 1916, at El Paso, Texas, where a group of United States mining engineers and technicians from the Cusi Mining Company boarded a train for Mexico. Assured of a safe conduct and Mexican government protection, they set out to reopen the Cusihuiriachic mine. At the hamlet of Santa Isabel the train was stopped by a barrier laid across the tracks. A band of Villistas boarded the car carrying the Americans, dragged them off, and murdered fifteen of them on the spot.

But an even more outrageous incident occurred exactly two months later. Early in the morning of March 9, 1916, Villa dispatched 485 men across the border from Palomas, Chihuahua, and attacked the dreary, sun-baked adobe town of Columbus, New Mexico. One of the first shots stopped the large clock in the railroad station at 4:11 A.M. For the next two hours the Villistas terrorized the town's four hundred in-

Pancho Villa (1878–1923). Never an "armchair general," Villa often led his troops into battle. His famous Division of the North, numbering some fifty thousand men, was the largest revolutionary force ever amassed in America.

habitants. Shouting *¡Viva Villa!* and *¡Muerte a los Gringos!* they shot and burned and looted. Troopers from the Thirteenth Cavalry succeeded in driving them off by daybreak, but eighteen Americans had been killed, many were wounded, and the town was burned beyond recognition.

The clamor for United States intervention was immediate and predictable. Senator Albert Bacon Fall of New Mexico called for a half-million men to occupy all of Mexico. President Wilson was not willing to go that far, but he did agree to dispatch a small punitive expedition under the command of General John J. Pershing, an army man who years before had chased the Apache chief, Geronimo, through the same northern Mexican desert. It took a week for Pershing to organize his expedition, and that was more than enough time for Villa to cover his tracks. Approximately six thousand United States army troops wandered hot and thirsty through the rough terrain in a futile effort to locate their prey. Little if any help could be expected from the rural Mexicans, and as the Americans entered small pueblos they were often greeted with shouts of *¡Viva Mexico, Viva Villa!* As the expedition

General Pershing's cavalry expedition into northern Mexico may have hardened his troops for the upcoming war in Europe, but his effort to capture Pancho Villa was in vain.

cut south into Mexico, First Chief Carranza began to get nervous and ordered Pershing to withdraw. Not yet ready to admit defeat, Pershing engaged a group of Carrancista troops ordered to forestall his southward thrust. When hostilities began he received orders to withdraw gradually to the north, but the expedition was not pulled out of Mexico until January 1917. By that time the United States had spent $130 million in its unsuccessful attempt to catch and punish the Columbus raiders.

THE CONSTITUTION OF 1917

The failure of the Pershing punitive expedition notwithstanding, Villa got progressively weaker and Carranza gradually consolidated his position in Mexico City. The First Chief's advisers convinced him that the time had come to give some institutional basis to the Revolution that had engulfed the nation for almost six years. In an attempt to legitimize the Revolution he reluctantly agreed to convoke a congress to meet in Querétaro for the purpose of drawing up a new constitution. Remembering how he had lost control of the Convention of Aguascalientes, he vowed not to repeat the error in Querétaro. No individual or group who had opposed the Constitutionalist movement would be eligible to participate; thus no Huertistas, Villistas, or Zapatistas were included among the delegates when the first session convened in November 1916. But First Chief Carranza quickly learned what he should have already known; the Constitutionalists themselves were scarcely in ideologic agreement.

The delegates at Querétaro represented a new breed of Mexican politician and, in a sense, constituted a new social elite. Unlike the Convention of Aguascalientes, military men constituted only 30 percent of the delegates. Over half had university educations and professional titles. The large majority were young and middle class; because they had been denied meaningful participation during the Porfiriato, many were politically ambitious.

With every intention of controlling the proceedings, Carranza submitted to the Querétaro Congress a draft of a new constitution he himself preferred. It showed him to be a liberal in the best nineteenth-century tradition. His draft differed little from the Constitution of 1857, although it contained a series of sections strengthening executive control. It occasioned an inevitable split in the Congress between those moderates who supported Carranza and the radicals (called Jacobins by their opponents) who desired something more likely to harbinger rapid social reform.

The debates in Querétaro, focusing on everything from temperance to prison reform, were acrimonious. After the first few votes had been taken, it was clear that the radicals held the majority. Led by thirty-two-year-old Francisco Múgica, they succeeded in pushing through a number of anticlerical provisions and three extremely significant articles that came to embody the fundamental orientation the Revolution was to assume in the 1920s and 1930s.

The anticlericalism of the Congress was even more intense than it had been during the height of the liberal-conservative struggle during the nineteenth century. All of the old arguments were heard, but, in addition, the church was now seen to be blocking the path of the social revolution. Article after article limited the powers of the church. Marriage was declared a civil ceremony; religious organizations would enjoy no special legal status, and, as a result, priests were considered ordinary citizens; public worship outside the confines of the church was banned; state legislatures could determine the maximum number of priests to be allowed within state boundaries; all priests in Mexico had to be native born; clergymen were prohibited from forming political parties; priests had to register with civil authorities; and new church buildings had to be approved by the government. The anticlerical tenor of the Querétaro Congress also surfaced in one of the three most important articles.

The drafting of Article 3 was assigned to Múgica's committee on education, and his proposal touched off passionate exchanges on the floor of the Congress. Few took umbrage at the principle that primary education should be free and obligatory in the Mexican republic, but Múgica and his radical cohorts had one additional criterion to add. Education should be secular. The lessons of history convinced Múgica that the clergy had sacrificed all claim to obedience. He saw the church as the implacable enemy of the Mexican people and an unrepentantly anti-democratic institution.

The responses of Félix Palavicini and other Carranza supporters in the Congress were just as terse, personal, and caustic. But when the final vote was taken, Francisco Múgica's Article 3 passed by a margin of almost two to one. With the radicals' dominance well established, two other major issues were resolved in their favor. And if the debates on education reminded many of the anticlerical rhetoric of the Reform, the ensuing disputation on land and labor left no doubt that a new age of liberalism had dawned.

Article 27 addressed itself to Mexico's endemic land problem and can be considered a direct outgrowth of Díaz's alienation of Mexico's subsoil rights and his policy of allowing the land companies to appropriate the old communal lands. While the Zapatistas were not present in Querétaro, the issue that had made them a potent force had to be squarely faced. Article 27 required that lands seized illegally from the peasantry during the Porfiriato be restored and provision be made for those communities that could not prove legal title. Equally as important, the private ownership of land was no longer considered to be an absolute right but rather something of a privilege. If land did not serve a useful social function, it could be appropriated by the state: "The nation shall at all times have the right to impose on private property such limitations as the public interest may demand, as well as the right to regulate the utilization of natural resources . . . in order to conserve them and to ensure a more equitable distribution of public wealth." A special section of Article 27 deeply disturbed foreign nationals who owned property in Mexico.

> Only Mexicans by birth or naturalization have the right to acquire ownership of lands, waters, . . . or to obtain concessions for the exploitation of mines or waters. The state may grant the same right to foreigners,

provided that they agree before the Department of Foreign Relations to consider themselves as nationals in respect to such property, and bind themselves not to invoke the protection of their government.[3]

The last, precedent-breaking article treated the labor question and sought to provide a reasonable balance between labor and management. Article 123 provided for an eight-hour workday, a six-day workweek, a minimum wage, and equal pay for equal work regardless of sex or nationality. Most importantly, it gave both labor and capital the right to organize for the defense of their respective interests and allowed that the workers had the right to bargain collectively and go on strike.

The Constitution of 1917 was not nearly as radical as many contemporary observers found it, but it did coagulate into a repudiation of nineteenth-century laissez-faire liberalism. Although ideologically indebted to the Liberal Plan of 1906, the Plan Orozquista, and the Plan de Ayala, it was more reformist than revolutionary. Carranza accepted it with great reluctance. It bore scant resemblance to the draft he had proposed, but he had set the requirements for delegates himself and, more importantly, wanted to become constitutional president after having served as First Chief for four years.

THE CARRANZA PRESIDENCY

Carranza handily won the special elections that were held in March 1917 and took the oath of office on May 1. Not only was the country far from pacified, but the economy was in a state of acute distress. The banking structure had been shattered, in part because of the general chaos but also as a direct result of the worthless paper money that had inundated the commercial markets. Mining suffered enormous losses, with gold production declining some 80 percent between 1910 and 1916 and silver and copper production falling off 65 percent during the same period. Industrial production fell off as well, and wages were depressed. The communication and transportation networks in which Díaz had taken so much pride were in shambles. Agricultural shortages pushed food prices up, and the inflation took a terrible toll on poor urbanites trying to live on a monetary economy.

Carranza quickly let it be known that, although he had accepted the Constitution of 1917, he had no idea of enforcing it. Confusing change in government with change in society, he believed the Revolution to

---

3. Quoted in *Diario de los debates del Congreso Constituyente, 1916–1917* (Mexico City, 1960).

be over. In fact, it had scarcely begun. Still prompted by the inviolability of private property, under Article 27 Carranza distributed only
450,000 acres of land, a paltry sum when one considers that many hacendados had more than this and Luis Terrazas alone owned in excess
of seven million acres. In addition, the land Carranza did distribute
had been taken away from his political enemies. This was neither the
spirit nor the intent of Article 27.

The record of the administration on labor was no better. Even before the new Constitution was enacted, Carranza's labor policy was
known. In the fall of 1915, when workers in Veracruz struck protesting payment of wages in worthless paper currency, Carranza used his
army to put down the strike. A year later, when railroad workers declared a strike, Carranza found it treasonous and arrested the leaders.
Mexican labor leaders, hoping for a better day with the adoption of
Article 123, were disappointed as well. On a few occasions innocuous
concessions were granted to labor, but the labor movement did not
have an advocate in the presidential chair.

Though without his blessings or support, an event did occur during
Carranza's presidency that was a landmark in the Mexican labor movement. In 1918 the labor leader Luis Morones founded Mexico's first
nationwide union, the Confederación Regional Obrera Mexicana
(CROM). The gains made by the labor movement in the next two years
were marginal, but the establishment of the confederation did lay the
foundation for future progress.

There can be no doubt that Carranza's presidency was complicated
by World War I. The eventual entrance of the United States into the
European conflagration was a foregone conclusion, and the Mexican
government was anxious that it be sooner rather than later. Perhaps
Washington would then be too concerned with trans-Atlantic matters to
intervene again in Mexican affairs. But Mexico's own position had to be
carefully defined. Many Latin American nations were prepared to follow the lead of the United States and break diplomatic relations with
Germany. Should not Mexico also align itself with its Western Hemisphere counterparts? While many prominent Mexicans urged this course
of action, others argued with understandable passion that, unlike France,
England, and the United States, Germany had never landed troops on
Mexican soil; Germany had not stolen half of the national territory or
presumed to dictate how Mexico should manage its own affairs.

As Carranza himself weighed the alternatives, he received a strange
proposal from the German foreign secretary, Arthur Zimmermann. In
return for a formal alliance with Germany, on the successful conclusion
of the war Mexico would receive back the lands it had lost to the United
States in the middle of the nineteenth century. However tempting the

offer sounded, Carranza had to turn it down. Germany, he realized, was much too bogged down in Europe to come to Mexico's assistance in a war with the United States. The best course for Mexico to follow, Carranza determined, was to maintain strict neutrality during the war.

Although the European conflict was disquieting to Mexico and resulted in some economic dislocation, the slow pace of the reform program cannot properly be attributed to it. Carranza did not want to accelerate the pace of the Revolution. Of all the disillusioned groups of revolutionaries in Mexico, the Zapatistas were most dismayed. The president sent thousands of federal troops into Morelos under trusted General Pablo González. Conducting a very competent campaign, González took a number of Zapatista towns, but the guerrilla chieftain himself eluded capture. The fighting in Morelos was relentless— perhaps the most terrible of the entire Revolution. Thousands of innocent civilians were charged with succoring Zapatistas and executed. Entire towns were burned, crops methodically destroyed, and cattle stolen. The Zapatistas responded in kind and on one occasion blew up a Mexico City–Cuernavaca train, killing some four hundred passengers, mostly civilians.

In March 1919 Zapata directed an open letter to Carranza. It was a passionate statement but one that helps to explain why Zapata had fought every Mexican head of state for a full decade. It was not written to the president whom he did not recognize, nor to the politician whom he did not trust, but to Citizen Carranza.

Venustiano Carranza (1859–1920). The First Chief of the Constitutionalist Army assumed the presidency in 1917 but, despite revolutionary rhetoric, moved slowly on the issues of social reform. His timidity on these central issues ultimately cost him popular support.

As the citizen I am, as a man with a right to think and speak aloud, as a peasant fully aware of the needs of the humble people, as a revolutionary and a leader of great numbers, . . . I address myself to you Citizen Carranza. . . . From the time your mind first generated the idea of revolution . . . and you conceived the idea of naming yourself Chief . . . you turned the struggle to your own advantage and that of your friends who helped you rise and then shared the booty—riches, honors, businesses, banquets, sumptuous feasts, bacchanals, orgies. . . .

It never occurred to you that the Revolution was fought for the benefit of the great masses, for the legions of the oppressed whom you motivated by your harangues. It was a magnificent pretext and a brilliant recourse for you to oppress and deceive. . . .

In the agrarian matter you have given or rented our haciendas to your favorites. The old landholdings . . . have been taken over by new landlords . . . and the people mocked in their hopes.

EMILIANO ZAPATA[4]

Carranza was not about to retire in the face of polemical thunder. He had one more plan for ending his problem with Zapata. The president discussed with General Pablo González a daring plot to deceive Zapata and then to kill him. The scheme was put into operation at once. Colonel Jesús Guajardo, one of González's subordinates in the Morelos campaigns, wrote to Zapata that he wanted to mutiny and to turn himself, some five hundred men, and all of their arms and ammunition over to the Zapatistas. Zapata demanded proof of Guarjardo's sincerity, for tricks had been played in the past, and asked that several former Zapatistas, who had previously defected to the federal cause, be tried by court-martial and executed. Colonel Guajardo agreed and carried out the order. Zapata was still not fully convinced when news reached him from his own network of spies that Guajardo had captured the town of Jonacatepec in the name of the Zapatistas. Zapata at this juncture agreed to meet the defecting federal officer. A conference was set for April 10, 1919, at the Hacienda de Chinameca in Zapata's home territory. With only a few men accompanying him, Zapata rode into the hacienda in the early afternoon. A young eyewitness later described what happened.

Ten of us followed him just as he ordered. The rest of the people stayed [outside the walls] under the trees, confidently resting in the shade with their carbines stacked. Having formed ranks, [Guajardo's] guard looked ready to do him honors. Three times the bugle sounded the honor call;

---

4. Quoted in Fabela, ed., *Documentos históricos de la revolución mexicana*, 21: 305–10.

and as the last note died away, as the General in Chief reached the threshold of the door . . . at point blank, without giving him time even to draw his pistols, the soldiers who were presenting arms fired two volleys, and our unforgettable General Zapata fell never to rise again.[5]

While Carranza had thus ridded himself of his most implacable adversary, he did not have much time left himself, as he would also die by the bullet. In 1920, when the president attempted to name his successor in the high office, Alvaro Obregón allied himself with fellow Sonorans Adolfo de la Huerta and Plutarco Elías Calles and declared himself in revolt. Under a new revolutionary banner, the *Plan de Agua Prieta*, a new army of northerners began marching on Mexico City. In May, Carranza was forced to flee the capital and, on his way into exile, was assassinated by one of his own guards in the squalid village of Tlaxcalantongo. The assassin was a loyal Obregonista, but evidence directly linking Obregón to the murder is scanty.

The Carranza regime has not yet received the type of careful historical evaluation it merits. When it is subjected to the tests of archival research it might very well prove to be the period of counterrevolution in the Mexican social upheaval. Carranza was so imbued with hatred for Victoriano Huerta, his predecessor, that he not only repudiated everything Huerta did but, in fact, nullified in the name of the Constitutionalist Revolution many of the more progressive measures undertaken by that dictatorship in the period 1913–14. Having determined that Huerta had raised teachers' salaries, Carranza reduced them to their former levels at the very time that inflation had pushed consumer prices up. Land that Huerta had begun to redistribute to the communal ejidos was restored to its Porfirian proprietors. While Francisco Madero had projected 7.8 percent of his total budget for education, and Huerta 9.9 percent, the figure under Carranza had slipped, by 1919, to an appalling .09 percent. Expenditures for all social programs dropped from 11.6 percent in 1913 to 1.9 percent in 1919.

While the counterrevolutionary thesis must remain a thesis pending further investigation, what is certain is that the social revolution did not find a protagonist in the First Chief. Carranza would never have admitted that laissez faire could conflict with social welfare. One should not be misled by the fact that the socially oriented Constitution of 1917 was enacted during the Carranza years. Carranza was unhappy with its progressive articles and reacted to them by applying the

---

5. Quoted in John Womack, Jr., *Zapata and the Mexican Revolution* (New York, 1968), p. 326.

old colonial maxim, *Obedezco pero no cumplo*. He simply failed to take into account the aspirations of the social reformers.

Mexico had finally rounded the corner by 1920. The violence was not yet completely spent, but generally the struggles in the post-1920 period became less chaotic and more deliberative as national politicians found more constructive releases for their energy and fervor. A gradual stabilization of the political order, coupled with a modest implementation of the new Constitution, would begin to change the contours of society in the 1920s. As the shock of carnage receded into the past, the goals of a better life began to be realized, but progress was slow and arduous. Not until the 1930s would Mexico inaugurate a president undeterred by centuries of tradition or by the vested interests.

RECOMMENDED FOR FURTHER STUDY

Bailey, David C. "Alvaro Obregón and Anti-clericalism in the 1910 Revolution." *The Americas* 26 (1969): 183–98.

Braddy, Haldeen. *Pershing's Mission in Mexico*. El Paso: Texas Western College Press, 1966.

Brunk, Samuel. *Emiliano Zapata: Revolution and Betrayal in Mexico*. Albuquerque: University of New Mexico Press, 1995.

Buffington, Robert. "Revolutionary Reform: The Mexican Revolution and the Discourse on Prison Reform." *Mexican Studies* 9 (1993): 71–93.

Chacón, Ramón D. "Salvador Alvarado and the Roman Catholic Church: Church-State Relations in Revolutionary Yucatán, 1914–1918." *Journal of Church and State* 27 (1985): 245–66.

Clendenen, Clarence C. *The United States and Pancho Villa: A Study in Unconventional Diplomacy*. Ithaca, N.Y.: Cornell University Press, 1961.

Coerver, Don M., and Linda B. Hall. *Texas and the Mexican Revolution: A Study in State and National Border Policy, 1910–1920*. San Antonio, Tex.: Trinity University Press, 1984.

Garner, Paul. "Federalism and Caudillismo in the Mexican Revolution. The Genesis of the Oaxaca Sovereignty Movement (1915–20)." *Journal of Latin American Studies* 17 (1985): 111–33.

Gerlach, Allen. "Conditions along the Border—1915: The Plan de San Diego." *New Mexico Historical Review* 43 (1968): 195–212.

Gilderhus, Mark T. *Diplomacy and Revolution: U.S.–Mexican Relations under Wilson and Carranza*. Tucson: University of Arizona Press, 1977.

Gonzales, Michael J. "U.S. Copper Companies, the Mine Workers' Movement, and the Mexican Revolution, 1910–1920." *Hispanic American Historical Review* 76 (1996): 503–34.

Hall, Linda B. *Alvaro Obregón: Power and Revolution in Mexico, 1911–1920*. College Station: Texas A&M University Press, 1981.

Harris, Charles H., and Louis R. Sadler. "The Plan of San Diego and the Mexican–United States War Crisis of 1916: A Reexamination." *Hispanic American Historical Review* 58 (1978): 381–408.

Hart, John M. *Revolutionary Mexico: The Coming and Process of the Mexican Revolution*. Berkeley: University of California Press, 1987.

Henderson, Timothy J. *The Worm in the Wheat: Rosalie Evans and Agrarian Struggle in the Puebla-Tlaxcala Valley of Mexico, 1906–1927*. Durham, N.C.: Duke University Press, 1998.

Katz, Friedrich. *The Life and Times of Pancho Villa*. Stanford, Calif.: Stanford University Press, 1998.

———. *The Secret War in Mexico: Europe, the United States and the Mexican Revolution*. Chicago: University of Chicago Press, 1981.

Martínez, Oscar J. *Fragments of the Mexican Revolution: Personal Accounts from the Border*. Albuquerque: University of New Mexico Press, 1983.

Meyer, Michael C. "The Mexican-German Conspiracy of 1915." *The Americas* 23 (1966): 76–89.

Niemeyer, E. V., Jr. *Revolution at Querétaro: The Mexican Constitutional Convention of 1916–1917*. Austin: University of Texas Press, 1974.

Pasztor, Suzanne B. *The Spirit of Hidalgo: The Mexican Revolution in Coahuila*. Calgary: University of Calgary Press, 2002.

Quirk, Robert E. *The Mexican Revolution, 1914–1915: The Convention of Aguascalientes*. New York: Citadel Press, 1963.

Richmond, Douglas W. *Venustiano Carranza's Nationalist Struggle, 1893–1920*. Lincoln: University of Nebraska Press, 1984.

Sandos, James. "German Involvement in Northern Mexico, 1915–1916: A New Look at the Columbus Raid." *Hispanic American Historical Review* 50 (1970): 70–88.

Womack, John, Jr. *Zapata and the Mexican Revolution*. New York: Knopf, 1968.

30

Society and Culture
during the Age of Violence

THE IMPACT OF THE REVOLUTION
ON THE MASSES

The rapid changes in the presidential chair, the heated debates in Aguascalientes and Querétaro, and the redounding phrases of the Constitution of 1917 surely had little immediate meaning to the Mexican masses.
It was the violence of that first revolutionary decade that most dominated their lives and left Mexico a country without charm or gaiety. For
every prominent death—Francisco Madero, José María Pino Suárez,
Pascual Orozco, Emiliano Zapata, or Venustiano Carranza—a hundred
thousand nameless Mexicans also died. By any standard the loss of life
was tremendous. Although accurate statistics were not recorded, moderate estimates calculate that between 1.5 and 2 million lost their lives
in those terrible ten years. In a country with a population of roughly 15
million in 1910, few families did not directly feel the pain as one in every
eight Mexicans was killed. Even Mexico's high birthrate could not offset the carnage of war. The census takers in 1920 counted almost a million fewer Mexicans than they had found only a decade before.

Some of the marching armies were equipped with small medical
teams, and Pancho Villa even fitted out a medical train on which battlefield operations could be performed. But medical care was generally so primitive that within a week after a major engagement deaths
of wounded often doubled or tripled losses sustained immediately on
the battlefield. And in more cases than one likes to recount captured
enemy prisoners, both federals and rebels, were executed rather than
cared for and fed. Civilian deaths rose into the hundreds of thousands
as a result of indiscriminate artillery bombardments and, in some cases,
the macabre policy of placing noncombatants before firing squads in
pursuit of some imperfectly conceived political or military goal.

It is axiomatic that war elicits not only the worst in man but often
psychotic behavior in otherwise normal human beings. While Mexican

*Execution without benefit of trial was common
during the violent decade of 1910–20. Bodies
were left hanging for weeks as object lessons.*

history does not have names such as Andersonville, Dachau, Auschwitz,
or My Lai to connote atrocity, the cumulative stress of exhaustion and
constant exposure to death did produce its psychiatric casualties during the first decade of the Revolution and, on occasion, led to behavior that can only be termed sadistic. The inhumanity visited upon civilians by soldiers became legendary in the folklore of the Revolution.
One could pass off stories of mutilated prisoners hanged from trees or
telephone posts as exaggerations had not scores of eager photographers
captured hundreds of horrifying scenes for posterity. Bodies with hands
or legs or genitals cut off were a grotesque caricature of a movement
originally motivated by the highest ideals.

Fratricidal horrors so outrageous and so cataclysmic exacted burning resentment and fear in the civilian population. An approaching unit
invariably meant trouble for poor, rural Mexicans. The best that could
be hoped for was a small band demanding a meal. But often the demands were more outrageous as the war could not lend itself to de-
cency or compassion. In northern Mexico tens of thousands of rural
Mexicans joined their middle class and wealthy counterparts in seeking the security of the United States. On a single day in October 1913
some eight thousand refugees crossed the border from Piedras Ne-

gras, Coahuila, to Eagle Pass, Texas. While the vast majority left the country with the idea of returning once the situation stabilized, most remained in the United States. But in central and southern Mexico there was virtually no place to run, and the civilian population had no choice but to keep their heads low and resign themselves to the worst. The documentary evidence from the period suggests forcefully that the excesses of war cannot be attributed simply to one side or another. Both federals and rebels were guilty. An excellent community study of a village in Morelos corroborates the contemporary sources. Informants who had lived through the revolutionary period declared that both sides posed an equal threat in this war without scruple.[1]

Fear in the rural areas was challenged only by frustration. Two months spent clearing a field and planting crops under a burning sun could be wiped out in five minutes as an army of five hundred horsemen galloped through the carefully tilled rows of corn and beans. Then they might stop at the one-room hut and confiscate the one milch cow and four turkeys that held out some promise for a slightly less redundant diet in the six months to follow.

There is precious little published evidence upon which to assess the impact of the early Revolution on life in rural Mexico. But the findings of Professor Luis González, in his perceptive and beautifully written account of the Michoacán village of San José de Gracia (population about 1,200 in 1910) are probably not atypical. By 1913, when violence engulfed the region for the first time,

> Don Gregorio Pulido had given up taking local products to Mexico City, for bands of revolutionaries made the roads unsafe for travel. The San José area began to return to the old practice of consuming its own products. Trade declined. Padre Juan's goal of increasing prosperity receded in the distance. From 1913 on, increased poverty was the rule. . . . Everything in San José shifted into reverse. The revolution did no favors for the town or the surrounding *rancherías*. . . . Parties of rebels often came to visit their friends in San José, either to rescue the girls from virginity, or to feast happily on the delicious local cheeses and meats, or to add the fine horses of the region to their own. . . . They summoned all the rich residents and told them how much money in gold coin each was to contribute to the cause. In view of the rifles, no one protested.[2]

---

1. Lola Romanucci-Ross, *Conflict, Violence and Morality in a Mexican Village* (Palo Alto, Calif., 1973), pp. 15–16.

2. Luis González, *San José de Gracia: Mexican Village in Transition* (Austin, 1974), pp. 124–25.

The "armies" the peones of rural Mexico saw and feared did not look much like armies. Standard uniforms were unheard of among the rebels, and weapons consisted of whatever could be found or appropriated. Sometimes makeshift insignias identified rank but gave slight clue as to group affiliation. Anonymity served rebel commanders well as it left them unconcerned with the niceties of accountability, but it caused problems for the rural *pacífico* wanting to respond correctly to the question, "Are you a Huertista, a Villista or a Carrancista?"

For Mexican women the Revolution often had a degrading personal meaning. With husbands, fathers, and sons serving somewhere in the ranks, they were subjected to the terror and indignity of wanton assault. But many did not mope or simply stay home to become the target of rape. Freeing themselves from the eternal task of grinding corn, thousands joined the Revolution and served the rebel armies in the capacity of spies and arms smugglers. So active were the women in smuggling ammunition across the border in Ciudad Juárez that the United States Customs Bureau was forced to employ teams of female agents to search the undergarments of suspicious, heavy-looking ladies returning from shopping sprees in El Paso.

Perhaps the most noteworthy role assumed by women was that of *soldadera*. The soldaderas were more than camp followers. They provided feminine companionship, to be sure, but because neither the federal army nor the rebel armies provided commissary service, they foraged for food, cooked, washed, and, in the absence of more competent medical service, nursed the wounded and buried the dead. Both sides were dependent upon them, and in 1912 a federal battalion actually threatened mutiny when the secretary of war ordered that the women could not be taken along on a certain maneuver. The order was rescinded. Not infrequently, the soldaderas actually served in the ranks, sometimes with a baby slung in a *rebozo* or a young child clinging to their skirts. Women holding officer ranks were not uncommon in the rebel armies.

The soldadera endured the hardships of the campaign without special consideration. While the men were generally mounted, the women most often walked, carrying bedding, pots and pans, food, firearms, ammunition, and children. Often the men would gallop on ahead, engage the enemy in battle, and then rest. By the time the women caught up, they were ready to move again, and the soldadera would simply trudge on. Losing her special "Juan" in battle, she would wait an appropriately decent period and then take on another, to prepare his favorite meal and share his bed. Not a few gave birth in makeshift military camps, and some even on the field of battle.

*Among the disparate revolutionary contingents in Mexico, the Yaqui In-
dians of Sonora figured prominently in the campaigns of the northwest.*

The hard life of the soldadera was a relative thing. A fascinating oral
history of a Yaqui woman from Sonora who was deported to Yucatán,
cut her hands raw on the henequen plants, and saw her babies die
from lack of adequate care, reveals that she was thrilled to become a
soldadera. She later recalled that "her personal misery decreased by
impressive leaps and bounds. . . . At no point during the next several

years did she view her life as anything but a tremendous improvement after Yucatán."[3]

While, with the protection of anonymity, men could treat women as virtual slaves, public displays were more often marked by the type of chivalric indulgence so long identified with the Hispanic tradition. One traveler to Mexico City in 1918 was especially amused by the sign he found posted in the streetcar:

> GENTLEMEN: When you see a lady standing on her feet you will not find it possible to remain sitting with tranquility. Your education will forbid you to do so.
>
>   GENERAL MANAGER OF THE RAILWAYS[4]

In an oblique and unintended sort of way the Revolution contributed to the emancipation of the Mexican woman. As the shortage of adult males in the cities contracted the labor supply, women began to make some inroads into the business world. At first their contributions consisted of the simplest type of work in the stores, but once escaped from the confines of the house they would not be persuaded easily to return. In Yucatán, at least, a concerted policy of women's liberation was initiated by Governor Salvador Alvarado. A farsighted revolutionary, Alvarado declared: "I have always believed that if we do not elevate the role of women we will find it impossible to build a country."[5] Not only did he lower the age of majority of women from age thirty-one to twenty-one, but he actively began placing women in open positions in state government. In 1916 he sponsored a Congreso Femenino in Mérida, Yucatán. Four major themes were discussed: the social means to be employed to remove the yoke of tradition; the role of primary education in women's liberation; the arts and occupations the state should support to prepare the women for a fuller life; and the social functions women should employ to contribute toward a better society.

The Revolution, to be sure, had different meanings to different Mexicans during those years of greatest violence. But a most recurrent theme is the fear of the leva, the institution that snatched away the male population for service in the military. One corrido, popular in 1914, capsulized the problem in the doggerel of the masses.

---

3. Jane H. Kelly, "Preliminary Life History of Josefa (Chepa) Alvarez" (mimeographed, 1970), p. 16.

4. Quoted in P. Harvey Middleton, *Industrial Mexico: 1919 Facts and Figures* (New York, 1919), p. 6.

5. Salvador Alvarado, *Actuación revolucionaria del General Salvador Alvarado en Yucatán* (Mexico City, 1965), p. 49.

Armies had to be fed, and the task of grinding corn for the daily supply of tortillas continued as it had for centuries.

A familiar sight between 1910 and 1920, the soldaderas experienced both the excitement and privations of life on the military campaign.

> La leva, la odiosa leva
> que sembró desolación
> en todo el suelo querido
> de nuestra noble nación.
>   Al obrero, al artesano
> al comerciante y al peón,
> los llevaban a las filas
> sin tenerles compasión.[6]

Edith O'Shaughnessy, the wife of the United States chargé in Mexico City, described the leva in her memoirs.

> I was startled as I watched the faces of some conscripts marching to the station today. On so many was impressed something desperate and despairing. They have a fear of . . . eternal separation from their loved ones. They often have to be tied in the transport wagons. There is no system about conscription here—the press gang takes any likely looking person. Fathers of families, only sons of widows, as well as the unattached, are enrolled, besides women to cook and grind in the powder mills.[7]

Among those who suffered most were foreign residents of Mexico. Because the Revolution was in part a reaction against Díaz's coddling of foreign interests, not a few revolutionaries took out their wrath on the foreign community. Cast in the role of exploiters, foreign oilmen and miners were forced to pay not only taxes to the government but tribute to various groups of rebels and bribes to local bandits. But other frugal and industrious foreigners, without the slightest claim to exploitation, suffered worse. After a battle for control of Torreón in 1911 over two hundred peaceful Chinese residents were murdered simply because they were Chinese. A few years later Spanish citizens in Torreón were expelled from the country and their property confiscated by Pancho Villa. Colonies of United States Mormons in Chihuahua and Sonora were terrorized to such an extent that they finally packed up those belongings they could carry and left their adopted home.

City dwellers, too, were subject to the ravishments of war. Almost all of the larger cities in the country hosted battles at some time between 1910 and 1920, and some witnessed three or four major en-

---

6. Quoted in Merle E. Simmons, *The Mexican Corrido as a Source for Interpretive Study of Modern Mexico (1870–1950)* (Bloomington, 1957), p. 121.

7. Edith O'Shaughnessy, *A Diplomat's Wife in Mexico* (New York, 1916), p. 58.

THE VIOLENCE TAKES A TOLL

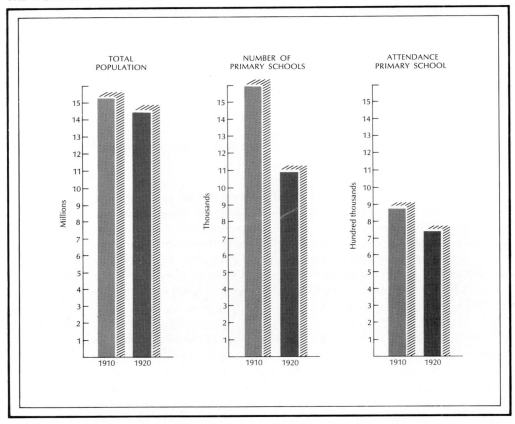

gagements and were turned into debris before the decade ran its course. The sight of burning buildings, the sound of wailing ambulances, and the nausea of mass burials brought home in tangible terms and most immediate meaning of the Revolution. Starvation reached major proportions in Mexico City, Guadalajara, and Puebla.

The construction boom of the Porfiriato ended shortly after the outbreak of hostilities. While a few unfinished public projects were completed, for the most part those workmen who could be spared from the ranks were kept busy clearing debris, repairing damaged structures, knocking down gutted buildings, and trying to put the railroad lines back in operation.

The early Revolution took a terrible toll in education. Hundreds of schools were destroyed and hundreds of others abandoned. In the Federal District alone the number of primary schools in operation declined from 332 in 1910 to 270 ten years later. The story repeated itself in city after city, town after town. Total primary school attendance in the country declined from 880,000 to 740,000 in the same ten-year period.

INTELLECTUALS AND ARTISTS

The first decade of the Revolution, as violent as it was, nevertheless spawned a new generation of Mexican intellectuals and artists. During the last year of the Porfiriato a group of young thinkers had banded together to form the Ateneo de la Juventud. Among its charter members was a small group that would come to dominate early revolutionary thought: Antonio Caso, Alfonso Reyes, José Vasconcelos, and Martín Luis Guzmán. Meeting fortnightly, the members of the Ateneo began to formulate a philosophical assault on materialism in general and on positivism in particular. Impressed with Immanuel Kant and Arthur Schopenhauer, but most especially with Henri Bergson's masterpiece *L'Evolution créatrice* (1907), they lashed out against the científicos and launched a movement for ideological and educational reform based on a healthy respect for the humanities.

By 1912 the members of the Ateneo were ready to give some practical application to their antipositivist posture. Interested in moving into areas that Díaz had ignored, in December 1912 they founded a "people's university," the Universidad Popular Mexicana, and took their message to the factories and shops in Mexico's leading population centers. Mexico's future happiness, they preached, was not dependent upon commercial or industrial growth but rather upon social progress. The Universidad Popular Mexicana did not offer degrees; rather it tried to bring humanistic knowledge to those who would not otherwise receive it. Stressing lessons in citizenship and patriotism as well as practical instruction in hygiene and stenography, the *ateneístas* who constituted the faculty not only lectured but sponsored weekend tours to art galleries, museums, and historical and archaeological sites. They all served without pay.

The winds of change shook the literary and artistic communities as well. A new age in the Mexican novel was born in 1915 when Mariano Azuela (1873–1952) wrote *Los de abajo* (translated as *The Underdogs*). A classic in twentieth-century Mexican literature, *Los de abajo* is a social novel and marked the beginning of a trend that would last for thirty years. Azuela was deeply concerned with the progress of the Revolution and through the character of Demetrio Macías probed its meaning. Historical novels were not new in Mexico, but Azuela added new ingredients. The story is related not in the sophisticated dialogue of the French school but in the coloquial language of the Mexican masses. Avoiding the intrusion of secondary plots, Azuela tells the story of real revolutionaries, not those who intellectualized the movement and coined its resounding phrases. Demetrio Macías is caught up in the struggle without really knowing why, yet when confronted with complex decisions is able to make proper choices with amazing spontaneity. Luis Cervantes, a middle-class federal deserter, joins Macías's guerrilla band and tries to articulate the revolutionary goals for him, but the uneducated Macías recognizes the shallowness and hypocrisy of Cervantes's explanations and the inherent opportunism in his actions.

The day-to-day dehumanizing realities of the Revolution are all there—pillage, looting, burning, destruction, theft, and general debauchery. Illustrative of the passion the Revolution evoked is Azuela's description of the battlefield after a struggle for control of Zacatecas: "The three-hundred-foot slope was literally covered with dead, their hair matted, their clothes clotted with grime and blood. A host of ragged women, vultures of prey, ranged over the tepid bodies of the dead, stripping one man bare, despoiling another, robbing from a third his dearest possessions."[8] The novel ends where it began—at the Canyon of Juchilpa. Demetrio Macías, by this time a general, is killed where he first ambushed a federal convoy. The circle has been completed, and nothing has really changed. After all the suffering and killing, the Revolution seems to be back where it began. While social programs have been shunted aside and forgotten, the Revolution has become almost self-perpetuating—it just goes on and on. Shortly before he dies Demetrio's wife asks him why he must continue fighting. He answers by tossing a rock over a precipice and responding with a beautifully appropriate metaphor: *Mira esa piedra cómo ya no se para* (Look at that rock—it just keeps rolling).

Mexican music, too, changed its tone as a new nativist movement was introduced by Manuel Ponce (1882–1948), a talented young pianist and composer from Zacatecas. Ponce decried that Mexican salons in 1910 should welcome only foreign music. He urged the acceptance of the native folk tradition and believed that the Revolution was already beginning to usher it in. In an essay he attacked the stodgy salons.

> Their doors remained resolutely closed to the *canción mexicana* until at last revolutionary cannon in the north announced the imminent destruction of the old order. . . . Amid the smoke and blood of battle were born the stirring revolutionary songs soon to be carried throughout the

---

8. Mariano Azuela, *The Underdogs*, trans. E. Munguía (New York, 1963), pp. 80–81.

length and breadth of the land. *Adelita, Valentina*, and *La Cucaracha*, were typical revolutionary songs soon popularized throughout the republic. Nationalism captured music at last. Old songs, almost forgotten, but truly reflecting the national spirit, were revived, and new melodies for new corridos were composed. Singers traveling about through the republic spread far and wide the new nationalistic song; everywhere the idea gained impetus that the republic should have its own musical art faithfully mirroring its own soul.[9]

Ponce was a major contributor to the movement he described. In 1912 and 1913 he composed his *canciones mexicanas*, including the famous *Estrellita*. And at approximately the same time he was training the individual destined to become the most illustrious name in twentieth century Mexican music—Carlos Chávez.

Of all the intellectual and artistic groups in the country, Mexican painters showed themselves to be most restless. Having already embarrassed the Díaz regime at the centennial celebrations of 1910, these recalcitrant artists continued to scandalize staid society during the first decade of the Revolution. When neither interim President León de la Barra nor Francisco Madero was willing to remove the Porfirian director of the Art Academy of San Carlos, the artists took matters into their own hands. Not only did they go out on strike demanding the resignation of the director but on one occasion pelted the poor soul with rotten tomatoes. The desired change came with Victoriano Huerta, who named Alfredo Ramos Martínez, an impressionist, as director. Ramos Martínez reformed the curriculum, de-emphasizing the stifling classroom training in copying and formal portrait work that strived for photographic precision. Instead he encouraged the students to venture out into their Mexican world and paint what they saw and what they felt.

When the Constitutionalists came in, Ramos Martínez went out but his innovative ideas were not to be overturned. The new director, Dr. Atl (Gerardo Murillo), was even less conventional than his predecessor. Politically a loyal Carrancista but artistically a free spirit, Dr. Atl wanted to convert the academy into a popular workshop for the development of the arts and crafts. But when Pancho Villa marched his army into Mexico City following the Convention of Aguascalientes, the director and his loyal students, including José Clemente Orozco and David Alfaro Siqueiros, fled to Orizaba. The days of Mexican academic art were over.

---

9. Quoted in Robert Stevenson, *Music in Mexico: A Historical Survey* (New York, 1971), pp. 233–34.

The second decade of the twentieth century was still an experimental period for the Mexican artist. Diego Rivera spent most of his time in France and Spain, dabbling with some success in cubism. Siqueiros abandoned the brush for the gun and served in the Carrancista army for several years, storing up penetrating impressions of camp life, battles, and death, all of which he would later re-create. Orozco spent much of his time painting posters and sketching biting political cartoons and caricatures for Carrancista newspapers. In different ways these three giants of twentieth century Mexican art were preparing themselves for an artistic renaissance and the most important development in Latin American painting—the muralist movement of the 1920s and 1930s.

SOCIAL CHANGE

Even during the chaos of violence certain unstructured social change was occurring in Mexico. Internal migrations took place, northerners and southerners came into more frequent contact with one another, and distinct regional language patterns began to yield to a more homogeneous national tongue. Increased travel, even that occasioned by the leva, provided a broader conception and a deeper appreciation of Mexico. Greater physical mobility brought about by the war tended to increase miscegenation and began to homogenize previously isolated zones. Thousands of Mexicans escaped obscurity and rose to positions of tremendous power in the various armies. Even though they did not always exercise their newfound influence with moderation, for them the Revolution was an agent of social change.

By 1920 a new kind of revolutionary nationalism had begun to emerge. The dead heroes had become martyrs to a young generation of Mexicans who did not always realize that their favorite protagonists had been killed fighting one another. The heroes loomed larger in death than in life, and their errors of judgment and human frailties could be overlooked. Madero became a symbol of democracy, Orozco of Mexican manhood, Carranza of law and justice, and Zapata of land for the humble. The newly developing revolutionary nationalism had its antiheroes as well: Porfirio Díaz, who had caused the holocaust; and Victoriano Huerta, the very incarnation of treachery and deceit.

In concrete terms, life for the great majority did not improve in the decade 1910 to 1920. In fact, because of the violence, it deteriorated in many ways. But the base of power in the republic had shifted into new hands, and the country was finally on the threshold of better times.

RECOMMENDED FOR FURTHER STUDY

Alonso, Ana María. *Thread of Blood: Colonialism, Revolution, and Gender on Mexico's Northern Frontier*. Tucson: University of Arizona Press, 1995.

Azuela, Mariano. *The Underdogs*. Translated by E. Munguía. New York: New American Library, 1963.

Baldwin, Deborah J. *Protestants and the Mexican Revolution: Missionaries, Ministers and Social Change*. Champaign: University of Illinois Press, 1990.

Brushwood, John S. *Mexico in Its Novel: A Nation's Search for Identity*. Austin: University of Texas Press, 1966.

Buffington, Robert M. *Criminal and Citizen in Modern Mexico*. Lincoln: University of Nebraska Press, 2000.

Charlot, Jean. *The Mexican Mural Renaissance, 1920–1925*. New Haven, Conn.: Yale University Press, 1967.

González, Luis. *San José de Gracia: Mexican Village in Transition*. Austin: University of Texas Press, 1974.

Guzmán, Martín Luis. *The Eagle and the Serpent*. Translated by Harriet de Onís. Gloucester: Peter Smith, 1969.

Innes, John S. "The Universidad Popular Mexicana." *The Americas* 30 (1973): 110–22.

Macías, Anna. "Women and the Mexican Revolution, 1910–1920." *The Americas* 37 (1980): 53–82.

O'Shaughnessy, Edith. *A Diplomat's Wife in Mexico*. New York: Harper and Brothers, 1916.

Robe, Stanley L. *Azuela and the Mexican Underdogs*. Berkeley: University of California Press, 1979.

Romanell, Patrick. *Making of the Mexican Mind*. Lincoln: University of Nebraska Press, 1952.

Rutherford, John. *Mexican Society during the Revolution: A Literary Approach*. New York: Clarendon Press, 1971.

Salas, Elizabeth. *Soldaderas in the Mexican Military: Myth and History*. Austin: University of Texas Press, 1990.

Simmons, Merle E. *The Mexican Corrido as a Source for Interpretive Study of Modern Mexico (1870–1950)*. Bloomington: Indiana University Press, 1957.

Sommers, Joseph. *After the Storm: Landmarks of the Modern Mexican Novel*. Albuquerque: University of New Mexico Press, 1968.

Stevenson, Robert. *Music in Mexico: A Historical Survey*. New York: Thomas Y. Crowell, 1971.

1,500 Years of Mexican Art History

A Concise Visual Tour

Distinguished for its strength, dynamism, and creativity, the Mexican art endeavor has long commanded world attention and acclaim. Centuries before that first colossal encounter between the European and American worlds, ancient Mexican architects were designing massive pyramids and laying out imposing cities, replete with temples, palaces, plazas, and ball courts. As these structures integrated the supernatural, transformed the physical landscape, and altered the surrounding skyline, talented artists and master sculptors were summoned to decorate the walls with paintings, fill the niches with statues, and inspire the masses. In the process they left their indelible aesthetic touch in the form of murals and sculptured figures fashioned with equal skill from materials as dissimilar as soft clay and hard stone.

The sixteenth century witnessed not only Spain's physical conquest but an artistic invasion as well. New forms and new styles resting on an absolutely different ethic came to dominate creative output. For three full centuries Spanish colonial art and architecture proved a faithful handmaiden to a distinctive Hispanic culture. Just as in the mother country, colonial art and architecture came to the service of the Roman Catholic religion. The most extravagant exemplars of colonial architecture are found in the countless churches and cathedrals that adorned city plazas and dotted the Mexican countryside from the rain forests of the south to the deserts of the far north. Few colonial structures could compete with them in either quality or scale. In the sixteenth and early seventeenth centuries, it was the awe-inspiring but austere classic style that dominated church architecture, giving way in the later seventeenth century to the Baroque with its easily recognizable sculptured facades and proliferation of ornamentation, and ultimately yielding to an elaborate extension of the baroque known as Churrigueresque.

Similarly, the best colonial easel art was religious in both subject and tone and followed the strict directives of the Council of Trent (1563). To be sure most viceroys took time to sit for the mandatory portrait, but the most gifted artists of the colonial period were also summoned to do the portraits of bishops, archbishops, and inquisitors or to capture the Christening of indigenous nobility, the crucifixion, the coronation of the virgin, the miracles of the saints, and other scenes of piety and devotion. Colonial sculpture differed from its pre-Columbian predecessor as it was regularly carved from wood embellished with polychrome. The devotional statuary (called *santos* or *bultos*), in concert with the religious paintings, clearly served the purposes of Spain's evangelical mission and most often found its permanent home in the magnificent churches and convents of the viceroyalty. Another expression, unique to Mexico, is the category of *casta* paintings that depicted the offspring of a multitude of racial mixtures.

With Mexico's independence from Spain at the beginning of the nineteenth century, art assumed a distinctly secular tone for the first time. Although a number of independence heroes were captured with oil on canvas, a changing nineteenth-century artistic imagination gradually expanded to embrace a much larger and diverse Mexican universe. No longer preoccupied with religious expression, a new genre known as *costumbrista* interpreted everyday life and customs, documenting the intrinsic vitality of an urban street scene or the elation of a local fiesta. The *costumbristas* shared the stage with Mexico's nineteenth-century landscape artists, best exemplified by José María Velasco. These painters found their inspiration in the majesty of a towering volcano, or the freshness of a river flowing bank to bank. José María Ibarrarán y Ponce painted the Canal de la Viga, an important pre-Columbian trading route connecting Lake Chalco and Lake Xochimilco. Seen on the cover of this book, the painting shows how the waterway became a favorite weekend recreation area for the *gente decente* (upper classes) in the Porfirian era, here portrayed in their finery and flanked by the common folk. Attentive always to the subtleties of light and color, the landscape painters detailed panoramic images of Mexico's incredibly rich and varied topography. As the country moved hesitantly from the incessant chaos of the early nineteenth century to become a more stable and modern polity, the artistic community participated in the important transition to modernity. The artists of the late nineteenth century made it their task to reach an international audience in the effort to offset the negative Mexican image too often held by influential foreign nationals.

It was with Mexico's twentieth-century social revolution that that the rich artistic heritage of the centuries culminated in a muralist renaissance. Beginning in the 1920s and 1930s the revolutionary muralists, enjoying generous government patronage, brought their genius to the walls of public buildings where they could interpret and disseminate the lessons of Mexico's revolutionary ideal. Flanked by a coterie of gifted artistic compatriots, the three giants of the movement were Diego Rivera, José Clemente Orozco, and David Alfaro Siqueiros. While Orozco attended Mexico's well-known San Carlos Academy, Rivera and Siqueiros studied painting in Europe.

A quintessential expression of the art of social protest, the Mexican muralists accentuated the grandeur of Mexico's Indian past, criticized the excesses of the conquest, and found ample opportunity to censure corruption or betrayal of revolutionary ideals. While emphasizing content over form, their technique was superb. Even today art critics look in vain to find a more momentous example of public art in the twentieth century, for it changed the way Mexicans looked at themselves and how the outside world viewed Mexico. Yet other Mexican artists like Rufino Tamayo, who earned international acclaim, broke tradition with the muralists and turned to more universal representations.

Pre-Columbian Classic Period

The north courtyard of the palace in the magnificent city of Palenque dates from the 7th century A.D. Maya architects designed it not only to be aesthetically pleasing but to withstand the ravages of time.

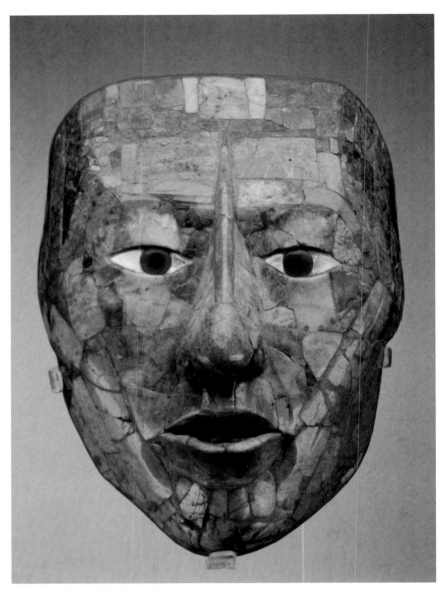

The Death Mask of Pacal. Hanab Pacal ruled at Palenque from 615 to 683 A.D. His death mask, fashioned improbably of jade mosaic was found in Palenque's Temple of Inscriptions and today is included in the rich collection of the National Museum of Anthropology.

Anthropomorphic Female Figurine from Nayarit, Classic Period. Prior to the conquest many indigenous peoples of western Mexico buried the dead, accompanied by decorative offerings, in underground tombs. Finely polished and then protected with lacquer, this beautiful ceramic work of a female giving birth was uncovered in one of these tumbas de tiro *in central western Mexico.*

Cacaxtla Mural. Flourishing from around 700 A.D. to 950 A.D., the fortified city of Cacaxtla in what is now Tlaxcala encapsulates much of the depth and diversity of pre-Columbian architecture, painting, and statuary. The mural pictured here portrays a figure adorned in eagle regalia and standing on the omnipresent religious symbol of ancient Mexico, the feathered serpent.

COLONIAL

Cathedral of Oaxaca. Located on the Oaxaca City's main plaza (the zócalo) the Cathedral's massive fortified walls and twin bell towers are reminiscent of sixteenth-century churches but the facade with its exquisitely carved figures and bas-relief columns clearly identify it as Baroque. Utilizing local limestone of a greenish-yellow tone, construction began in the sixteenth century but took over a century to complete.

One of Mexico's most unique churches, Santa María de Tonantzintla in the state of Puebla, features the extensive use of ceramic tile. Completed in the eighteenth century, the simple beauty and symmetry of the tiled exterior stands in stark contrast to the interior which encompasses a veritable explosion of the Mexican Churrigueresque.

Portrait of Sor Juana Inés de la Cruz. Miguel Cabrera (1695–1768),
the most prolific and distinguished Mexican artist of the colonial period,
devoted much of his distinguished career to producing works to adorn
church altars and sacristies, but he also left this stunning portrait of
the most renowned lady of the colonial church, Sor Juana Inés
de la Cruz.

Casta Painting by Miguel Cabrera, 1763. Late in his career Cabrera moved beyond religious art to test his considerable talent in casta painting. This unique genre, with no European model upon which to build, captured the centrality of mestizaje to Mexican colonial life by depicting parents of different races with beautiful children showing unmistakable indebtedness to both.

Nineteenth Century

José Agustín Arrieta, La Sorpresa, *1850. Born in Puebla and trained in Mexico City, Arrieta delighted in street and market scenes. This oil on canvas open air market is one of his most famous and now has its home in the National Museum of History.*

Salvador Murillo, El Puente de Chiquihuite, 1875. In an area of Mexico long remembered for its oxcarts and mule trains, landscape painter Murillo found the modernization symbolism of a long bridge and steam engine pulling a train too much to resist in this oil on canvas painted at the end of the Restored Republic.

Luis Coto, La Colegiata de Guadalupe, 1859. Landscape painter Luis Coto found a way to contrast the old traditional Mexico and the new modern Mexico. On the northern edge of Mexico City at Tepeyac Hill where the Virgin appeared to Juan Diego in 1531, he painted the seventeenth-century Guadalupe Collegiate Church behind a new locomotive pulling carriages.

José María Velasco, The Valley of Mexico from the Cerro de Tepeyac, 1894. Combining minute foreground detail and a broad panoramic vision, Velasco was Mexico's master nineteenth-century landscape artist. Here the towering twin volcanoes of Popocatépetl and Iztaccíhuatl dominate the skyline of the high valley of Mexico.

Diego Rivera from Día de los Muertos, *1923–24. Decorating the Court of the Fiestas at Mexico's Ministry of Education, Rivera's Day of the Dead mural celebrates the unique festival with raucous music and drinking. No kings, no viceroys, no bishops, no presidents or generals are to be found, but rather a coterie of everyday Mexicans of different colors, different social classes, dead and alive, brought together by culture and tradition and joined in solidarity.*

José Clemente Orozco, Zapata, 1930. Orozco's Zapata, arguably his most celebrated work, was painted eleven years after the assassination of the famous Mexican revolutionary. Silhouetted in a doorway, a pensive and charismatic Zapata and two of his soldiers witness the utter despair of two peones.

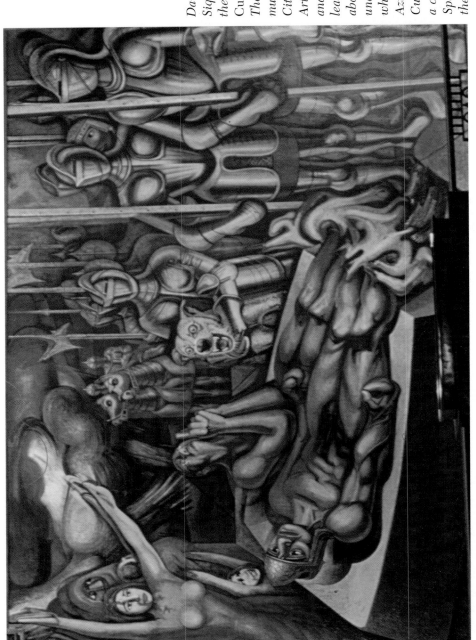

David Alfaro Siqueiros from the Tormento de Cuauhtémoc, 1951. The imagery of this mural in Mexico City's Place of Fine Arts is so powerful and intense that it leaves little doubt about Siqueiros' understanding of what happened to Aztec chieftain Cuauhtémoc while a captive of the Spaniards during the conquest.

Diego Rivera, Paisaje Zapatista, *1915. Rivera symbolically evoked the power of the peasant revolution in this painting that predated Orozco's rendering of Zapata. The abstract landscape illustrates the influence of Cubism as Rivera applied it to unmistakably Mexican material culture.*

Rufino Tamayo, Dos Figuras en Rojo, 1973. Distancing himself from the muralists, the Oaxacan painter Tamayo abstained from using art as a political statement and drew on Mexican folk art and pre-Columbian motifs to produce works rich in color and texture that became more abstract over time. Here we see a man and a woman rendered ambiguously in both their interior and exterior forms.

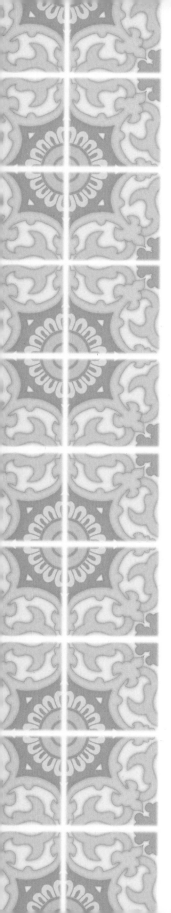

IX

THE REVOLUTION
The Constructive Phase, 1920–40

31

Alvaro Obregón Cautiously Implements the Constitution

DOMESTIC REFORMS

With the election of Alvaro Obregón to a four-year presidential term in 1920, Mexican politicians set to work on implementing the Constitution that had been drafted and promulgated at Querétaro in 1917. The war-torn country was closer to peace than it had been for a decade. Zapata had been killed, and, just a few weeks before Obregón assumed the high office, even the indomitable Pancho Villa had accepted a peace offering from the federal government. A good-sized hacienda, Canutillo, was given to him as an assurance that he would not again break the peace. The rigorous defender of the poor had grown tired, and he swallowed his pride to settle down in the comfortable role of an hacendado.

Obregón immediately turned his attention to the pressing problems of national reconstruction. A powerful and persuasive orator, he enjoyed a wide base of popular support. He was far from being a radical, but, unlike the nineteenth-century liberals, he was concerned with more than political reform. Unfortunately, the beginning of his administration coincided with the post–World War I economic slump. Prices of gold, silver, copper, zinc, henequen, and cattle were depressed. Unemployment was rampant in these industries, and the government's foreign exchange from these products fell off drastically. Hunger and general privation were more evident than they had been during the late Porfiriato. Only the price and demand for oil remained stable, and by 1921 Mexico was producing 193 million barrels, making it the world's third largest producer of petroleum. Oil reserves, even with an inadequate taxation structure, sustained the administration and enabled the president to embark upon a modest implementation of the Constitution of 1917.

To implement Article 3 Obregón named José Vasconcelos, one of Mexico's most illustrious men of letters, to be secretary of education.

MEXICO

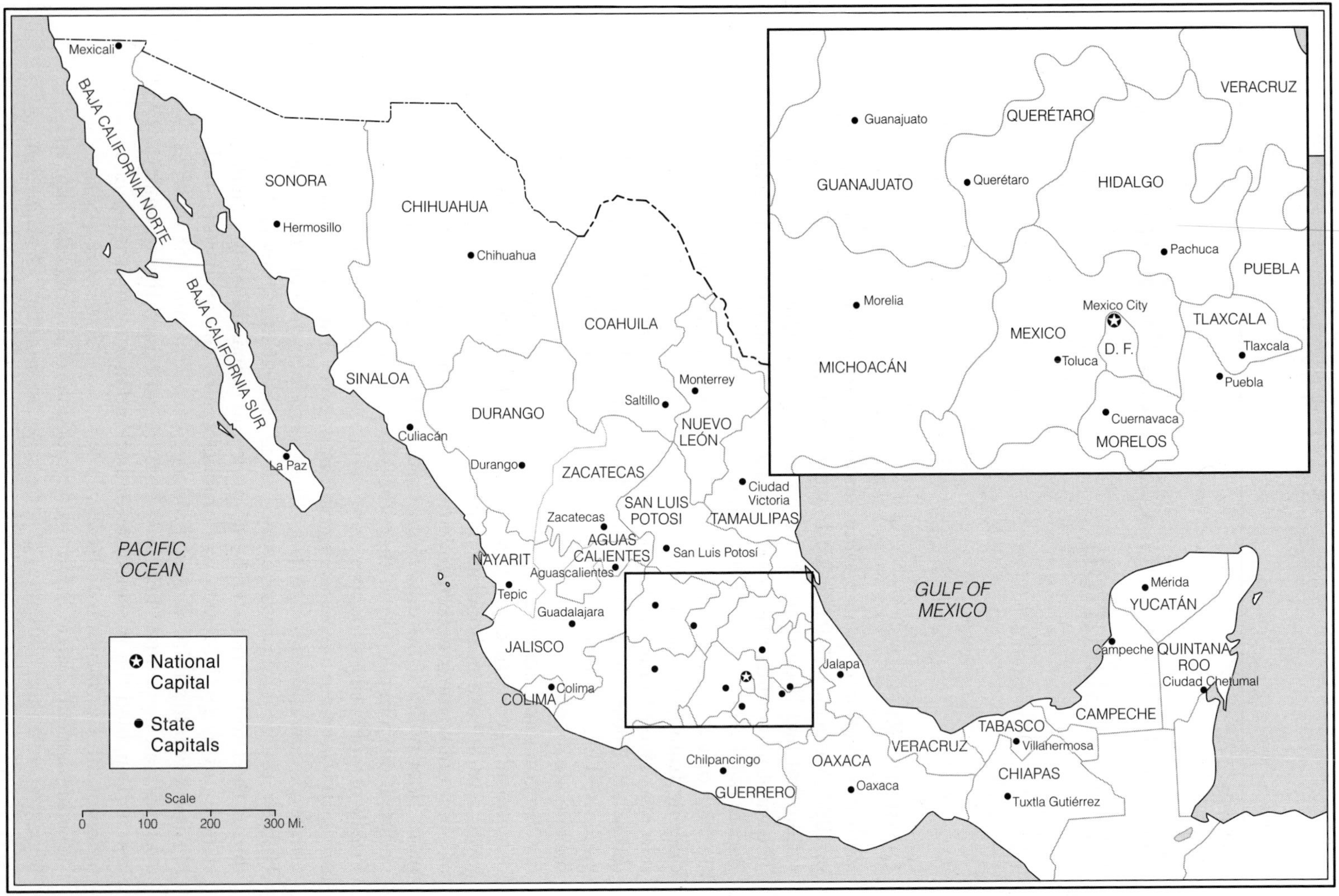
Mexicali
BAJA CALIFORNIA NORTE
BAJA CALIFORNIA SUR
La Paz
SONORA
Hermosillo
CHIHUAHUA
Chihuahua
COAHUILA
Saltillo
Monterrey
NUEVO LEÓN
SINALOA
Culiacán
DURANGO
Durango
ZACATECAS
Zacatecas
SAN LUIS POTOSI
San Luis Potosí
Ciudad Victoria
TAMAULIPAS
AGUAS CALIENTES
Aguascalientes
NAYARIT
Tepic
Guadalajara
JALISCO
Colima
COLIMA
PACIFIC OCEAN
GULF OF MEXICO
Mérida
YUCATÁN
Campeche
QUINTANA ROO
Ciudad Chetumal
CAMPECHE
TABASCO
Villahermosa
CHIAPAS
Tuxtla Gutiérrez
VERACRUZ
Jalapa
OAXACA
Oaxaca
Chilpancingo
GUERRERO
National Capital
State Capitals
Scale
0
100
200
300 Mi.
Guanajuato
GUANAJUATO
QUERÉTARO
Querétaro
HIDALGO
VERACRUZ
Pachuca
PUEBLA
Morelia
MICHOACÁN
Mexico City
MEXICO
D. F.
Toluca
TLAXCALA
Tlaxcala
Puebla
Cuernavaca
MORELOS

Vasconcelos had been educated in Mexico City and received his law degree at the age of twenty-three. Late in the Porfiriato his antipositivist rebellion led him to join the Ateneo de la Juventud, and he shortly distinguished himself as one of the most brilliant minds in Mexico. An enthusiastic supporter of Francisco Madero, he became a Constitutionalist at the time of Huerta's coup and subsequently served in Eulalio Gutiérrez's Convention government. With the flight of Carranza from Mexico City in 1920, Vasconcelos briefly served as rector of the National University, but Obregón wanted him in the cabinet and he accepted the portfolio of education shortly after Obregón's inauguration.

If Nemesio García Naranjo, Huerta's secretary of education, had provided the initial impetus for the anticientífico revision of the curriculum, Vasconcelos was the patron of the rural school. With dramatically increased federal funds placed at his disposal, he sent dedicated teachers into hundreds of hamlets with a basic curriculum: reading, writing, arithmetic, geography, and Mexican history. Because the economic realities of rural Mexico dictated that children would attend only a few years of school, there simply was not much time for frills.

Vasconcelos had to inspire the teachers with a deep sense of national mission, because life in rural Mexico, for many of them, was a type of cultural exile. Some of the villages were a two- or three-days' ride by horseback from the nearest railroad station, most lacked electricity, and few amenities of the comfortable life were to be found. In addition, the new teachers were not always welcomed with open arms. They often encountered deep hostility from villagers who did not want to change their traditional ways and from local priests who resented government encroachments into what they considered a church preserve. But the teachers did go into the hamlets and labored with dedication. Children attended during the day, while many adults consented to attend classes at night.

Vasconcelos's plan was designed not to segregate the Indian but through education to incorporate him into the mainstream of mestizo society. Vasconcelos would subsequently undergo a tremendous intellectual *volte-face*, but at this time he called for the incorporation of the Indians into a raza cósmica. In his memoirs he described the process as follows:

> I also set up auxiliary and provisional departments, to supervise teachers who would follow closely the methods of the Catholic missionaries of the Colony among Indians who still do not know Spanish. . . . Deliberately, I insisted that the Indian Department should have no other purpose than to prepare the native to enter the common school by giv-

FEDERAL EXPENDITURES FOR EDUCATION

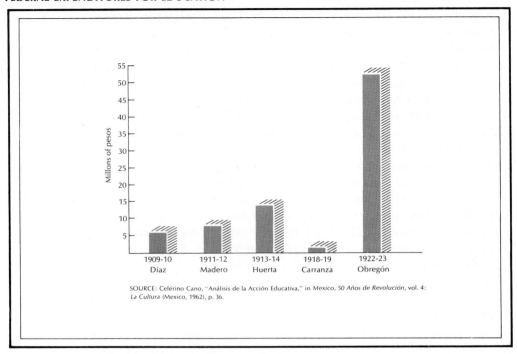

SOURCE: Celerino Cano, "Análisis de la Acción Educativa," in *Mexico, 50 Años de Revolución*, vol. 4: *La Cultura* (Mexico, 1962), p. 36.

ing him the fundamental tools in Spanish, since I proposed to go contrary to the North American Protestant practice of approaching the problem of teaching the native as something special and separate from the rest of the population.[1]

Over a thousand rural schools were built in Mexico between 1920 and 1924, more than had been constructed during the previous fifty years. To support the new endeavor, the secretary of education began a program of public libraries. Almost two thousand libraries had been established by 1924, most of them stocked with books designed to reinforce the humanist tradition of Mexico's new intelligentsia. Government presses printed millions of primary readers for both the schools and the libraries. A library set for a typical rural school consisted of about fifty books packed in special crates that could be transported on muleback.

Vasconcelos believed in the utility of informal education as well and employed some of Mexico's leading artists—Diego Rivera, José

---

1. José Vasconcelos, *A Mexican Ulysses: An Autobiography*, trans. William Rex Crawford (Bloomington, 1963), p. 152.

Clemente Orozco, and David Alfaro Siqueiros—to begin ornamenting the walls of public buildings with murals. The murals were designed for the people rather than for the art critics, but they received world acclaim as well. The themes were anthropological and historical for the most part and, with no shortage of polemicism, sought to instruct the literate and illiterate alike in the truths that the Revolution had come to hold dear.

Article 3 of the Constitution had stipulated, of course, that education should be secular and free, but President Obregón found this provision impossible to implement in full. The church was not removed entirely from the educational field because the state had neither the funds nor the teachers to educate all the children in Mexico. Both the president and the secretary of education opposed church education strongly, but, when confronted with an apparent impasse, they allowed that under guarded conditions it was preferable to no education at all. To assure that the church would not misconstrue the government's tolerant attitude toward Catholic education, however, Obregón encouraged the work of Protestant missionaries in Mexico. He openly endorsed the work of the YMCA (Asociación Cristiana de Jóvenes) and even supported its activities with state funds. The church naturally opposed this new development, but, with a few exceptions, open hostilities were avoided. Few realized in the early 1920s that church-state relations were undergoing a lull before a terrible storm.

Obregón's labor policy favored Luis Morones and the newly formed CROM. Because labor development had been so long stifled, Obregón leaned in the opposite direction, at least as far as the CROM was concerned. Nor did Luis Morones view the CROM as a government adversary. Realizing that Obregón had the power to crush the nascent labor movement if he wished, Morones worked to establish a balance between labor and capital rather than to attack the structure of the capitalist system. These modest goals were fully consonant with governmental policy, and, as a result, Morones and Obregón worked hand in hand and the union offered the government stellar support. In turn, the administration financed the CROM's national labor conventions and provided free railroad passes for anyone who wished to attend. Blessed with government benevolence, membership in the union rose steadily from fifty thousand in 1920 to an estimated 1.2 million in 1924.

Other developing unions did not fare so well, however. Two radical labor groups, the Communist Federation of the Mexican Proletariat and the anarchist-led Industrial Workers of the World, tried unsuccessfully to gain a foothold in the labor movement. In addition to the burdens of foreign leadership, which ran counter to the newly developing revolutionary nationalism, they both quickly incurred the strident opposition of the administration. Obregón expelled a number of foreign labor leaders from the country and declared strikes of the radical unions illegal. But it was not simply the radicalism of these unions that bothered the president; he was equally obdurate with the conservative Roman Catholic union movement.

Many Mexican labor leaders, however, had expected more because Obregón's followers had helped draft Article 123 and because the president had been sympathetic to labor's interests during his military career. But in Obregón's attempt to placate diverse interests in the country, labor often found itself shunted to one side. When asked to intervene in labor's behalf, the president time after time responded that the issue in dispute should be resolved at the state or local level. In states with progressive governors labor did not fare too badly, but in those with conservative administrations it languished. Obregón had decided that Article 123 of the Constitution would be implemented according to his understanding of Mexican reality, and he had decided that only the CROM represented legitimate workers' goals.

On the matter of agrarian reform Obregón again showed himself as a compromiser. He was aware that the Mexican economy, for better or for worse, was still tied to the hacienda system and that a rapid redistribution of land would result in reduced agricultural productivity.

Alvaro Obregón (1880–1928). President of Mexico from 1920 to 1924, Obregón is shown here recovering from the amputation of his right arm following the battle of Santa Rosa (1915).

The rural population would produce enough to feed itself but not enough to feed the nonagrarian sector of the society. On the other hand, Obregón had traveled in rural Mexico and had been touched by the abject poverty he had encountered there.

He decided not to declare all-out war on the hacendados of the republic. Rather, he moved with caution and deliberation, hoping that the modest redistribution he did sponsor would not be too disruptive. By the time his term expired, in 1924, he had distributed some three million acres to 624 villages. The land went to the communal ejidos rather than outright to individuals, but the number of villagers directly benefiting was calculated at 140,000. The radical agrarianists, such as Antonio Díaz Soto y Gama, were understandably disappointed. They believed that the president's agrarian logic was specious. Luis Terrazas alone still owned as much land as the total distributed by the administration. Obregón had failed to strike while the agrarian iron was hot. It was true that he had multiplied by nine times the amount distributed by Carranza, but in 1924, seven years after the adoption of the Constitution, Article 27 had not yet benefited the overwhelming majority of rural Mexicans.

Why had Obregón not moved faster in the agrarian field? Without question he himself believed in the wisdom of a moderate course. In a speech made before the Congress he declared:

> We must act so carefully as to solve the problem without endangering our welfare and our economical interests. If we begin by destroying the big estates in order to create afterwards the small property, I sincerely believe we have made a blunder. . . . We must not destroy the big estates before creating the small one, as an unbalanced state might follow leading us to dearth. I am of the opinion that we must act cautiously.[2]

Obregón was a cautious man but not simply as a matter of personal predilection. He felt it necessary to re-establish the political stability absent since the overthrow of Díaz. In addition, overshadowing many of his policy decisions was the specter of possible United States intervention to protect the interests of its citizens owning property in Mexico. The fears were not idle ones, as United States troops had been in Mexico twice since the Revolution began, once in Veracruz and two years later in the north in the futile attempt to capture Pancho Villa.

---

2. Quoted in Eyler N. Simpson, *The Ejido: Mexico's Way Out* (Chapel Hill, N.C., 1937), pp. 87–88.

RELATIONS WITH THE UNITED STATES

Obregón's presidential term coincided with the Republican administration of Warren G. Harding in the United States. Supported by big business, Harding had won the presidency by a landslide and believed that his government's prime responsibility was the encouragement of private enterprise, both at home and abroad. Of all the corporate enterprises that dominated the Republican convention of 1920, none rivaled the oil interests of Harry F. Sinclair, Edward L. Doheny, and Jake Hammon. Within a couple of years the extent of petroleum influence in the administration would be exposed to the world in the scandal of Teapot Dome. But the petroleum interests were at work from the beginning.

For several years, through powerful lobby groups such as the National Association for the Protection of American Rights in Mexico and the Oil Producer's Association, under the chairmanship of Edward Doheny, American businessmen had been urging the United States government to become more active in the defense of their Mexican interests. Not encountering much success during the Wilson presidency, they found a much more receptive audience in President Harding and Secretary of State Charles Evans Hughes. Often working through Secretary of Interior Albert Bacon Fall (later arrested in the Teapot Dome scandal), they presented their case to the American president. Their Mexican oil properties, they contended, were about to be seized out from under them by Article 27, and, accordingly, the United States should not recognize the Obregón regime. Secretary Fall had long considered Americans living in Mexico as his special constituency and had won for himself, over the years, a reputation of being extremely well versed in Mexican affairs. When he wrote, "So long as I have anything to do with the Mexican question, no government of Mexico will be recognized, with my consent, which does not first enter into a written agreement promising to protect American citizens and their property rights in Mexico,"[3] President Harding was willing to be persuaded. From 1920 to 1923 Obregón was not recognized by the United States.

The United States oil interests, supported by the Harding administration and fully aware that any oil stoppage would cripple Obregón, argued that Article 27, if applied retroactively, would constitute an international wrong of the gravest proportions. Although Obregón needed the oil revenues, he could not buckle under to United States pressure; it would have been political suicide. The apparent impasse

---

3. Quoted in John W. F. Dulles, *Yesterday in Mexico: A Chronicle of the Revolution, 1919–1936* (Austin, 1961), p. 159.

was averted by the Mexican Supreme Court. When, in September 1921, the Texas Company challenged the retroactive application of Article 27 in the Mexican courts, the Supreme Court handed down a decision propounding the doctrine of "positive acts." The oil lands could not be seized under Article 27 if the company in question had performed some "positive act" (such as erecting drilling equipment) to remove oil from the soil prior to May 1, 1917, the date on which the Constitution went into effect. If the company had not engaged in such a "positive act" prior to May 1, 1917, or if the concession had been granted after that date, Article 27 could be invoked at the pleasure of the state. This decision greatly relieved American oil interests, but, according to Mexican legal practice, five consecutive concurring decisions were necessary to establish a binding precedent. By the following year the four additional decisions had been rendered, and President Obregón then believed that he could enter into negotiations with the United States without being accused of treason.

In the spring of 1923 both countries named commissioners who agreed to meet on Bucareli Street in Mexico City during the summer. Under the terms of the agreements they reached, the Mexican government in essence agreed to uphold the doctrine of "positive acts" in its future relations with all the oil companies, and the Harding administration promised, in return, to extend diplomatic recognition. In addition, both countries agreed to establish a mixed claims commission to adjudicate the claims United States citizens had brought against Mexico for damages suffered during the Revolution

POLITICAL TENSIONS AND REBELLION

At about the same time that the commissioners of the two countries were meeting on Bucareli Street in the capital, an extraordinary event occurred on Gabino Barreda Street in Parral, Chihuahua. The retired General Pancho Villa had just traveled from Canutillo to the little village of Río Florido to participate in the christening of an old comrade's baby son. After the ceremony Villa went on to Parral, where he decided to spend the night with a lady friend before returning to his famous hacienda. Early the following morning, surrounded by his bodyguards, he began the return trip to Canutillo. As his Dodge touring car turned onto Calle Gabino Barreda, eight men armed with repeating rifles burst out of a corner house and peppered the automobile. Within seconds Villa and several of his companions were dead.

Responsibility for the assassinations was not easy to fix; in fact, historians are not yet in complete agreement. Some contemporaries considered the murder to have been a personal affair in which a group of aggrieved citizens took vengeance for prior Villista depredations. But most believed that the murder was politically motivated, as Mexican politics had begun to heat up once again during the summer of 1923 and Villa had threatened to come out of retirement.

The assassination of Villa tended to exacerbate an already tense political atmosphere. The nationalists were unhappy with the Bucareli Agreements. Obregón, they contended, had truckled to the American oil men and their White House representatives. Their dissatisfaction was kept in check for a few months, however, until it merged with other disaffections in the Mexican community. The time was approaching when a decision had to be made concerning the presidential succession of 1924, and Obregón chose to support his fellow Sonoran and secretary of interior, Plutarco Elías Calles. This choice touched off political violence.

The revolution that began in Mexico in late 1923 combined the antagonisms of various interest groups. Many conservatives, including a number of wealthy hacendados and Catholic leaders, feared that Plutarco Calles was a genuine radical and sought to head him off before the upcoming elections. They were joined by military men, disgruntled at Obregón's reduction of the federal army for purposes of economy. Each carried important federal garrisons into the rebel ranks. But the rebellion was not simply an alliance of conservatives, as many ardent nationalists, unhappy with the Bucareli Agreements, pledged their support of the new movement, as did a number of labor leaders who had not been included within the ranks of the CROM. The opposition coalesced around still another leading figure from Sonora, Adolfo de la Huerta. De la Huerta was an experienced politician; he had served as interim president a few years earlier and had been Obregón's secretary of the treasury, a position he had managed—later charges notwithstanding—with rare aplomb.

Despite the wide base of opposition, Obregón was not without his own sources of strength. Those unions under CROM control supported him unabashedly, as did a number of peasant organizations. Although some key army garrisons went over to the rebel side, many significant ones remained loyal to the government. But, most importantly, the recent diplomatic recognition by the United States provided Obregón's government not only with the moral support of Washington but also with an ample supply of war matériel. The war itself lasted only a few months, but it was a grueling episode for those who thought the days of violence had passed, and the toll of lives was tremendous. Some seven thousand Mexicans were killed before the rebels of de la Huerta admitted their defeat.

Obregón had been able to assert the dominance of the national government in the face of tremendous odds. Inheriting a country in financial peril and a citizenry with now-whetted aspirations, he emerged, if not unscathed by the political antagonisms of the day, at least with a good measure of dignity and respect, and his administration could take some pride in having put down a major antigovernment uprising. But, as the president neared the end of his term, some of the Mexican intelligentsia, indulging in self-criticism, realized that he had been slow to implement the reforms promised by the Constitution. They knew that through shrewd pragmatism he had co-opted the radical thrust of the Revolution, and, while occasionally yielding to the rhetoric of reform, he had not done much to alter the sustaining structure of society. On the other hand, many Mexican intellectuals, politicians, and journalists were willing to rationalize that in the early 1920s Mexican progress should be measured by Mexican standards. Since 1884 every Mexican president had been assassinated or driven from office by revolution. When Plutarco Calles won the presidential elections in 1924 and was inaugurated later that year, the ceremony marked the first time in forty years that the office was handed over peacefully from one chief executive to the next. Mexicans in their early sixties could perhaps remember that Manuel González had yielded peacefully to Díaz, but not a living soul could recall another instance. Political stability was returning to revolutionary Mexico, and with it Mexicans could not only afford the luxury of greater social experimentation but could begin to demand more from their leadership.

RECOMMENDED FOR FURTHER STUDY

Clark, Marjorie. *Organized Labor in Mexico*. Chapel Hill: University of North Carolina Press, 1934.

Dulles, John W. F. *Yesterday in Mexico: A Chronicle of the Revolution, 1919–1936*. Austin: University of Texas Press, 1961.

Gilderhus, Mark T. "Senator Albert Bacon Fall and 'The Plot against Mexico.'" *New Mexico Historical Review* 48 (1973): 299–311.

Haddox, John H. *Vasconcelos of Mexico*. Austin: University of Texas Press, 1967.

Hall, Linda B. *Oil, Banks, and Politics: The United States and Postrevolutionary Mexico, 1917–1924*. Austin: University of Texas Press, 1995.

Hansis, Randall. "The Political Strategy of Military Reform: Alvaro Obregón and Revolutionary Mexico, 1920–1924." *The Americas* 36 (1979): 197–232.

Lear, John. *Workers, Neighbors, and Citizens: The Revolution in Mexico City*. Lincoln: University of Nebraska Press, 2001.

Lieuwen, Edwin. *Mexican Militarism: The Political Rise and Fall of the Revolutionary Army*. Albuquerque: University of New Mexico Press, 1968.

Ruiz, Ramón Eduardo. *Mexico: The Challenge of Poverty and Illiteracy*. San Marino, Calif.: Huntington Library, 1963.

Schell, Patience A. *Church and State Education in Revolutionary Mexico City.* Tucson: University of Arizona Press, 2003.

Vasconcelos, José. *A Mexican Ulysses: An Autobiography.* Translated by William Rex Crawford. Bloomington: Indiana University Press, 1963.

Wilkie, James W. *The Mexican Revolution: Federal Expenditure and Social Change since 1910.* Berkeley: University of California Press, 1967.

32

Mexico under Plutarco Calles, 1924–34

For a full decade beginning in 1924 Mexico found itself in the firm grip of General Plutarco Elías Calles. Though more popular among reformist groups in 1924 than Alvaro Obregón, ten years later his name was anathema to Mexican liberals. Born in Guaymas, Sonora, in 1877 to a poor family, Calles attended normal school in Hermosillo, did quite well in the classroom, and upon graduation, became a primary school teacher in the public school system. His political career began with the Revolution, and he served in a number of minor political and military capacities before becoming provisional governor of his home state in 1917. His loyal support of Obregón over a ten-year period won for him official endorsement for the presidency in 1924, and, with labor and agrarian support, he carried the election easily.

CALLES'S DOMESTIC PROGRAM

Conservative elements in Mexico were far from elated by the election that year, for Calles enjoyed a liberal, even a radical, reputation. Landowners, both domestic and foreign, feared loss of property; industrialists anticipated higher wages for their workers; and church leaders recognized the new president as a confirmed anticleric. Each fear, it appeared, was grounded in understandable fact, and Calles soon let it be known that his domestic policy would not be characterized by the compromise and caution so typical of his predecessor. He was not only willing to ride the swelling tide of social revolution but sincerely believed, at least at the outset, that its course was inevitable. Better to be out in front, he conjectured, than to be dragged along.

Calles was the most strong-willed president since Díaz. He had an abiding faith in his own political instinct and, over his years in office, became increasingly domineering. Outspoken but often eloquent in public oratory, Calles was untormented by scruple when treating with his enemies. As the years passed he became less and less tolerant, more openly dictatorial, and relied heavily on the army to dispatch government foes. Deviation from presidential fiat was not tolerated during the Calles years. Political prisoners began filling the jails, and an alarming number "committed suicide." That the excesses were gross cannot be denied, but they were not, as enemies of the regime later charged, comparable to Jacobin or Stalinist purges following the French and Russian revolutions.

Calles inherited a more prosperous Mexico than had Obregón. The postwar economic slump was over and had given way to a sustained economic growth. Mexican raw materials were again in much demand from a recovered world economy. With a solid public treasury, Calles stepped up land distribution, just as the hacendados feared that he would do. Where Obregón had distributed some 3 million acres, Calles distributed 8 million between 1924 and 1928. The vast majority of the land was granted to the communal ejidos rather than outright to individual heads of families. Because the uneducated peasant could not alienate his land through cheap sale, he was not subject to the machinations of the local land speculators. To try to stem a decline in agricultural productivity, the administration initiated a series of irrigation projects, established a number of new agricultural schools, and began to extend agricultural credit to the small farmer. While the radical agrarians had hoped that Calles would do still more, the pace of agrarian reform had accelerated demonstrably. And even the Maya peasants of the Caste War were finally lured into the national family as the last of the rebellious villages accepted land titles from the government.

Calles's labor policy continued to favor Luis Morones and the CROM; in fact, Morones was brought into the cabinet as secretary of labor and quickly became the president's most intimate confidant. Other highly placed CROM officials served in the Congress, in the state legislatures, and even held state governorships. Hundreds of independent unions were brought into the CROM, and hundreds of new unions were organized. By 1928 CROM membership had reached 1.8 million, and the parent organization had affiliates in most of the states. The influence of the CROM became pervasive and its support of the government unabashed. The confederation even prevented printers from type-setting anti-Calles publications. The president returned the favors by supporting the CROM against employers and, more important, against other unions. Wages rose gradually, though never enough to constitute a serious burden to management. But by 1928 many sincere labor leaders had began to worry about Morones. He was becoming a very wealthy man, and most believed that his diamond rings, new automobiles, and vast holdings in urban real estate had been acquired with union funds and through various extortion schemes.

A prosperous Luis Morones came to dominate the Mexican labor movement under President Calles. At one time considered a possible successor to Calles, charges of corruption put an end to his political ambitions.

In the area of education Calles had inherited a new, well-constructed foundation from Obregón and Vasconcelos. In 1924 there were approximately one thousand federally supported rural schools in operation. Calles and his able secretaries of education, José Manuel Puig Casauranc and Moisés Sáenz, continued the emphasis of rural education. Before the presidential term expired in 1928 they had added two thousand additional rural schools. To facilitate the acculturation of the Indian, heavy emphasis was placed on the teaching of Spanish. Only if Spanish became the language of the village, they believed, could the Indian be made a part of the national culture.

The government's health and sanitation program was built almost from scratch. When the Revolution broke out in 1910, sanitation conditions in Mexico were hardly better than they had been during the colonial period. Calles was appalled and gave his support to a newly organized Department of Public Health. The department superintended the establishment of a new sanitary code designed to ensure cleaner markets and purer public milk supplies. For the first time in Mexican history major vaccination campaigns were undertaken. In 1926 alone over five million Mexicans were inoculated against smallpox. The government also began regular inspections of bakeries, butcher shops, dairies, cantinas, and barber shops. Those establishments that did not meet prescribed sanitary standards were closed down and their owners fined.

RELATIONS WITH THE UNITED STATES

Relations with the United States still centered around oil. The Bucareli Agreements notwithstanding, United States Ambassador James

Sheffield sought further assurances that foreign property interests would be protected. When Calles refused to go beyond the promises made on Bucareli Street, Sheffield started to bombard the U.S. State Department with Red scare dispatches. The coincidence of the Mexican and Bolshevik revolutions troubled U.S. observers who tended to equate them. Although the Mexican governments of the 1920s were adept at playing upon U.S. fears concerning Mexico's relations with the Soviets, there was in fact no direct connection between the revolutions. Nonetheless, Sheffield gradually convinced his superior, Secretary of State Frank B. Kellogg, that a Bolshevik plot was about to divest United States citizens of their just property rights. In the summer of 1925 Secretary Kellogg made a remarkable statement to the press. After reporting that an anti-Calles revolution was pending in Mexico, he continued:

> It should be made clear that this Government will continue to support the Government in Mexico only so long as it protects American lives and American rights and complies with its international obligations.
>
> The Government of Mexico is now on trial before the world. We have the greatest interest in the stability, prosperity, and independence of Mexico. . . . But we cannot countenance violation of her obligations and failure to protect American citizens.[1]

Calles expressed his strong displeasure with Kellogg's statement, for it appeared that the United States was once again nourishing aggressive designs. In a terse rejoinder the Mexican president declared that his government was well aware of its international obligations, but he rejected outright the inherent threat to Mexico's sovereignty in the secretary's pronouncement. He would never allow that any nation should create in Mexico a privileged position for its nationals.

To indicate that he would countenance no tampering with Mexico's sovereignty, Calles had his legislature enact a new petroleum law in December 1925. The legislation required all oil companies to apply to the government for a confirmation of their concessions. To determine whether or not to grant the confirmations, Mexico would apply the doctrine of "positive acts," as had been provided under the terms of the Bucareli Agreements, but the concessions would be granted only for a period of fifty years. As Calles began to enforce the new petroleum law, relations between Mexico City and Washington almost reached the breaking point.

---

1. Quoted in David Bryn-Jones, *Frank B. Kellogg: A Biography* (New York, 1937), p. 176.

In 1927 President Calvin Coolidge replaced Ambassador Sheffield in Mexico City with an old friend from Amherst College, Dwight Morrow, a partner in the famous financial firm of J. P. Morgan. Mexicans were, of course, convinced that the United States had sent yet another representative of Wall Street to press the case for the oil companies. But Morrow turned out to be a pleasant surprise. He did not make the Mexicans suspect that he was actually receiving his paychecks from Standard Oil. His first formal address in Mexico City presaged a more harmonious diplomatic atmosphere: "It is my earnest hope," he advised his Mexican audience, "that we shall not fail to adjust outstanding questions with that dignity and mutual respect which should mark the international relations of two sovereign and independent states."[2]

From the outset Morrow demonstrated a genuine interest in everything Mexican. He and his family lived in a Mexican-style house and shopped in the open marketplaces, marveling at native pottery and textiles. The ambassador visited the rural areas, taking special interest in new schools and irrigation projects and inquiring generally about the progress of the social revolution. He even began to study Spanish—not common for United States ambassadors in the 1920s—and invited Charles Lindbergh to Mexico on a goodwill tour. Morrow's relationship with Calles was unusually informal. The president and the ambassador began having breakfast together, and in this relaxed atmosphere, unencumbered by the bevy of official aides, they set to work on the sticky diplomatic problems besetting the two countries.

When the oil controversy first came up, Morrow did not warn that Mexico was on trial before the world; rather, in soft, diplomatic language he told Calles that he believed the issue should be settled in the Mexican courts and expected no special consideration for United States citizens. Calles was impressed and quite possibly used his influence to see that the courts rendered a compromise decision. The Supreme Court ultimately held that the oil companies did have to apply for new concessions from the government, that the doctrine of "positive acts" would apply, but that the new permits would not expire at the end of fifty years. Both sides had given a little, but the genuine significance lay in the response of the U.S. Department of State. Remembering Calles's sensitivity to the question of sovereignty, an official release noted that the petroleum controversy had been resolved by the Mexican government and that any future controversies would also be resolved by the Mexican government without any interposition from the

---

2. Quoted in David C. Bailey, *Viva Cristo Rey: The Cristero Rebellion and the Church-State Conflict in Mexico* (Austin, 1974), p. 176.

United States. For the first time Washington had formally recognized Mexico's full legal sovereignty, even when the interests of United States citizens were involved.

THE CRISTERO REBELLION AND THE ASSASSINATION OF OBREGÓN

Calles's most serious problem turned out to be not with the United States but rather with the Roman Catholic Church. Whereas Obregón had turned his back on the anticlerical articles of the Constitution, Calles decided to enforce them. Although tensions had been building up gradually throughout the early 1920s, the event that triggered new hostilities was an interview José Mora y del Río, the archbishop of Mexico, gave to the press in February 1926. Reacting to the implementation of anticlerical provisions in a number of states, the archbishop argued that Roman Catholics could not in conscience accept the Constitution. Their opposition to it was stronger than ever, and their position was unshakable. The recalcitrant declaration served no purpose. Calles used the excuse to strike with both fists. He first disbanded religious processions, then began deporting foreign priests and nuns and closing church schools, monasteries, and convents. He also decreed that all Mexican priests had to register with civil authorities. The response of the church was both unique and unexpected. On July 31, 1926, the archbishop declared a strike, and on the following day, for the first time since the arrival of the Spaniards four centuries earlier, no masses were celebrated in Mexico.

The strike lasted for three full years; babies went unbaptized and the old died without receiving the last rites. It was not a peaceful strike. As Calles became more intemperate, gross, and even obscene in his denunciations of the clergy and the pope, Catholic leaders in Michoacán, Puebla, Oaxaca, Zacatecas, Nayarit, and especially in the backcountry of Jalisco began organizing the masses to resist the godless government in Mexico City. To the cry of *¡Viva Cristo Rey!* Anacleto González Flores, René Capistrán Garza, and Enrique Gorostieta led bands of Cristeros against government outposts. There were sordid excesses on both sides. The Catholic guerrillas burned down the new government schools, murdered teachers, and covered their bodies with crude banners marked *VCR*. In April 1927 the Cristeros dynamited a Mexico City–Guadalajara train, killing over a hundred innocent civilians. Not to be outdone, the government troops tried to kill a priest for every dead teacher, encouraged children to throw rocks through stained glass windows, looted churches, and took great pleasure in converting them into stables. Cristeros, or suspected Cristeros, were shot perversely without benefit of trial, some swearing to the last moment that an enemy had painted *¡Viva Cristo Rey!* on their houses. The Cristeros could not withstand the military superiority of the federal army and gradually were worn down. But when Calles's presidential term expired in 1928, the rebellion was not yet completely suffocated.

The presidential election of 1928 and its immediate aftermath were shocking. The Constitution of 1917 had recently been amended to provide for a six-year presidential term and, with Alvaro Obregón specifically in mind, the possibility of re-election if it were not immediate. As the electoral process began to unfold, Calles threw his support behind the former president, no doubt thinking that Obregón would return the favor in 1934. Two opposition candidates also entered the fray: General Francisco Serrano, a former secretary of war, and General Arnulfo Gómez, a capable military man who had performed yeoman service in quelling the de la Huerta rebellion of 1923. Serrano and Gómez did not expend much energy attacking one another, they both concentrated their efforts on Obregón and attacked the principle of re-electionism. When Serrano and Gómez convinced themselves that the election of 1928 was not going to be fair, they rebelled against the government and the contemplated succession of Obregón. But within two months both of the opposition candidates had been captured and executed.

Obregón's victory brought no relief, however, for he never assumed office. On the afternoon of July 17, 1928, he attended a garden banquet in Mexico City's plush district of San Angel. Many dignitaries whom he wanted to join the new administration were in attendance. While the guests were dining, a twenty-six-year-old artist, José de León Toral, sketched caricatures of those sitting at the head table. After showing some of his better drawings to several guests, he moved toward the head table to show the president his work. As soon as Obregón nodded his approval, Toral took a pistol from his pocket and fired five shots into the president-elect's head.

Some of the irate guests beat young Toral almost beyond recognition. That he was not killed on the spot by the hysterical mob reflected the good sense of several officials who immediately realized that the full circumstances behind the assassination had to be determined. At the police station following the assassination, Toral refused to answer any questions. Torture did not suffice to loosen his tongue, and only the threat of torture to his family elicited the desired information. In subsequent weeks, as the story began to unfold, it became increasingly apparent that this senseless act of violence was also an offshoot of Mexico's never-ending conflict between church and state.

Toral was a deeply religious man who lost touch with reality and became a mystic when the Cristero Rebellion broke out. A few months

With historical roots going back centuries, anticlericalism assumed gigantic proportions in the late 1920s and 1930s. Among the ardent advocates were women, long thought to be the "pious" gender.

prior to the assassination he had been introduced to a nun, Sister Concepción Acevedo de la Llata, remembered in Mexican history simply as Madre Conchita. When the church declared its strike she offered spiritual consolation to the faithful in her own home, and it was in this capacity that her path crossed that of Toral. The young zealots who met regularly at Madre Conchita's house became increasingly militant as the rebellion grew more outrageous. They began manufacturing bombs and even discussed plans for killing Obregón. Finally Toral was chosen, or assumed responsibility, for implementing a mission they all considered to be divinely inspired. But just to make sure everything went as planned Toral began target practice in early July with a pistol borrowed from one of Madre Conchita's friends. Shortly after his confession, Madre Conchita and a number of others were arrested as well.

The trial, conducted in November, was a great public spectacle and undoubtedly the most sensational judicial inquiry since the trial of Maximilian. In a gesture of unparalleled magnanimity Obregón's widow asked the court to show Toral mercy, but the state was in no mood to turn the other cheek. The prosecuting attorney and the attorney general who testified in behalf of the state were warmly applauded by the gallery. On the other hand, the defense attorney, Demetrio Sodi, was heckled, disparaged, and shouted down with cries of "Death to the Assassin!" and "Death to the Prostitute Concha!" Jurors, fearful for their lives, came to the courtroom armed with pistols. Taunts of mockery and threats of lynching interrupted the proceedings, as did promises of reprisals to the jurors should they vote to acquit. The crowd became so agitated during the summation of Attorney Sodi that he was unable to conclude his defense. The court would not be used as a platform for Catholic views. The jury did not remain long in consultation. Toral's act, after all, had been witnessed by many; he implicated Madre Conchita during his testimony, and her denials were unconvincing. Toral received the death sentence, and Madre Conchita, because Mexican law forbade the execution of women, was given a prison sentence of twenty years.

THE MAXIMATO AND THE SHIFT TO THE RIGHT

Obregón's assassination created a political vacuum, and only Calles commanded sufficient respect to fill it. He decided not to assume the presidential office himself but would control the nation's destiny as the power behind the scenes. The Congress, charged with choosing an interim president until new elections could be held, selected Calles's man, Emilio Portes Gil, a lawyer and former governor of Tamaulipas. Portes Gil proved to be the first of three puppets to fill out Obregón's term, but Calles, as "the Supreme Chief" (*Jefe Máximo*), clearly called the shots. By the time the election of 1929 occurred, Calles had organized a new, widely based political party, the Partido Nacional Revolucionario (PNR). Mexican presidents never again would be elected by temporary coalitions that would splinter soon after tasting the fruits of victory. The official party would change its name on several occasions, but its control over the Mexican political process would remain intact for the next seventy years.

When the special election occurred, Calles and his newly organized PNR ran Pascual Ortiz Rubio for the presidency. The opposition candidate, running under the rubric of the National Anti-Re-electionist party, was the more experienced and much better known José Vasconcelos. Vasconcelos directed his campaign against the Jefe Máximo rather than against Ortiz Rubio and argued that a vote for Ortiz Rubio was a vote for Calles. But the strategy was useless. When the government announced the results, Ortiz Rubio was declared the winner by the unbelievable margin of 1,948,848 to 110,979. He served only two years. Shortly after he attempted to oppose Calles on several policy decisions, he picked up a morning newspaper to read that he had resigned. On this occasion the Jefe Máximo picked General Abelardo Rodríguez, a man with less administrative talent than relish for power, as puppet number three of the *Maximato*.

Despite the musical chairs played in the presidential office, the years 1928 to 1934 were not barren of accomplishment. An important step forward was made in professionalizing and depoliticizing the Mexican army. Calles had actually initiated the process during his own term in office, but the job was completed under the puppets. By giving the military a major voice within the PNR there was less reason for revolt in support of some disgruntled politician. While the army was by no means taken out of politics, it was co-opted by being brought into the political process. Military expenditures were curtailed during the six-year Maximato, but, since military men themselves participated in the decisions, they accepted the budgetary belt-tightening with admirable restraint.

Equally important to the political well-being of the nation was the resolution of the Cristero Rebellion. Ambassador Morrow played a major but unofficial role in the reconciliation as he arranged a series of meetings between Calles, Portes Gil, and Father John Burke, a prominent Catholic leader in the United States. In early June 1929 Father Burke convinced the Mexican leaders that they should allow several exiled bishops to return to the country so that they, too, could participate in the negotiations. By late June a compromise had been hammered out. The church agreed that priests would have to register with the government and that religious instruction would not be offered in the schools. The government declared publicly that it had no intention of destroying the integrity of the church and even allowed that religious instruction would not be prohibited within the confines of the churches themselves. As a result, the hierarchy ordered the Cristeros to lay down their arms and the priests to resume religious services. Mexico's long-standing church-state controversy was not yet completely over, but it would never again reach the grotesque proportions of the Cristero Rebellion.

The Calles puppetship witnessed a dramatic shift of the Revolution to the right. The social reform programs that were conceived in the early Revolution, formalized in the Constitution of 1917, and gradually implemented during the years 1920 to 1928, were all but abandoned shortly after the assassination of Obregón. Land redistribution after 1928 slowed to a snail's pace. The state of Chihuahua affords a good example. The Terrazas family had been forced to sell most of its huge land holdings during the Obregón presidency but now was allowed to buy them back. Although the Terrazases paid a somewhat higher price than they had received earlier, they bought back only the best lands that they previously owned. The rural education program suffered, and the labor movement was abandoned as the government withdrew its support of the CROM. Luis Morones surely had profited at the public trough. While he might have been beneath contempt and above the law, his personal peculation scarcely justified the all-out attack on the labor movement itself. Other highly placed officials also dipped into the treasury with impunity. With handsome sinecures many bought luxurious homes in Cuernavaca on what the contemporary pundits labeled "the Street of the Forty Thieves." The honest revolutionaries were aghast at this new clique of "millionaire socialists," and the raconteurs celebrated their corruption with hundreds of sardonic anecdotes.

As the Revolution shifted to the right, the regime and its supporters grew more and more sensitive to any form of radicalism. Virtual war was declared on the small, inconsequential Mexican Communist party. The leaders were unceremoniously deported to the penal colony on Isla Tres Marías. The anti-Communist hysteria reached its apex in 1930 and 1931, years that witnessed the appearance of the Gold Shirts, a fascist-inspired organization of thugs whose self-appointed task was to terrorize all Communists and Jews.

THE REVOLUTION: AN ASSESSMENT IN THE 1930s

Something drastic had happened to the Revolution and its leadership. Honest, idealistic men, dedicated to principles of social reform, had been not only diverted from tasks of high priority but corrupted as well. The phenomenon has never been adequately studied, but a provocative sociological hypothesis was posited by Professor Frank Tannenbaum.

> This period [1928–34] . . . is most perplexing. If it were possible to discover what had taken hold of the leadership of Mexico in those debased and clouded years, it would illumine much of Mexican history. Here was a group of new men, most of whom had come from the ranks of the Revolution and had risked their lives in a hundred battles for the redemption of the people from poverty and serfdom. . . . and yet, at the first opportunity, each fell an easy victim to pelf and power. . . .
>
> Their difficulty lay in the fact that they had come to power suddenly and without preparation, either morally, psychologically, politically, or even administratively. They were taken from their villages as barefooted youngsters who had slept on the floor and could barely read, and after a few years spent on the battlefields found themselves tossed into high office and great responsibility. This new world was filled with a thou-

sand temptations they had not dreamed of. . . . Here, at no price at all, just for a nod, all their hearts desired was offered them in return for a favor, a signature, a gesture, a word.[3]

There is much to be said for Professor Tannenbaum's understanding of those perplexing years. While the hypothesis must remain tentative, it does have the ring of reality. At the same time, however, something more tangible was also involved—the Great Depression of 1929–32.

Mexico weathered the depression better than most Latin American countries, as the treasury had about thirty million pesos ($15 million) in cash reserves in 1930. But no country in the world emerged from the great crash unscathed. Important Mexican exports, especially oil and metals, reflected the structural weaknesses of the world market, and, as a result, national income from taxes declined and the value of the peso began to fall. While in 1930 two pesos bought a dollar, by 1932 the cost of the dollar was 3.50 pesos. The entire treasury surplus, and more, was used up in 1931, as government revenues fell eighty million pesos short of expenditures. As a result of the unhealthy economic atmosphere, capital began to flee the country in search of more secure investment fields elsewhere. Many industries were paralyzed because of monetary deflation and tight credit. Emergency tax measures helped the government a little, but programs had to be cut back in many areas. Government workers were fired, wage reductions averaged over 10 percent, and departments were ordered to reduce their expenditures. Given this dreary set of circumstances, the social revolution simply could not progress.

In a more general sense the depression discredited the set of revolutionary principles that had become sacrosanct to many. Poverty cut deeply, and government leaders decided to experiment with new, shortsighted approaches. But the leadership had misread the economic indicators and gave up too easily to a slothful defeatism. The depression had not singled out Mexico; it was not partial to one or another ideology or economic system. The principles upon which the Revolution had been founded were still sound, and in 1934 a new, dynamic leader would give them the opportunity to run their course.

The Mexican revolutionary generation had not yet demonstrated any real political genius. In the Calles decade the question of presidential succession had continued to provoke violence, a president-elect had been assassinated, and the presidential chair had had three occupants

---

3. Frank Tannenbaum, *Mexico: The Struggle for Peace and Bread* (New York, 1956), pp. 69–70.

in a single term. But by 1934 the worst was over. While day-to-day political conduct would not always be exemplary, Mexico had witnessed its last successful revolt. Mexican presidents would never again leave office without finishing their terms. There would be no more interim or provisional presidents. Presidents would never again try to succeed themselves in office, and presidential succession would no longer occasion armed insurrection. In 1934 the political process would stabilize itself, and the social revolution would find a new protagonist.

RECOMMENDED FOR FURTHER STUDY

Bailey, David C. *Viva Cristo Rey: The Cristero Rebellion and the Church–State Conflict in Mexico*. Austin: University of Texas Press, 1974.

Bernstein, Marvin D. *The Mexican Mining Industry, 1890–1950: A Study of the Interaction of Politics, Economics, and Technology*. Albany: State University of New York Press, 1964.

Bortz, Jeffrey. "The Genesis of the Mexican Labor Relations System: Federal Labor Policy and the Textile Industry, 1925–1940." *The Americas* 52 (1995): 43–70.

Brewster, Keith. *Militarism, Ethnicity, and Politics in the Sierra Norte de Puebla, 1917–1930*. Tucson: University of Arizona Press, 2003.

Butler, Matthew. *Popular Piety and Political Identity in Mexico's Cristero Rebellion, 1927–1929*. New York: Oxford University Press, 2004.

Carr, Barry. "The Mexican Communist Party and Agrarian Mobilization in the Laguna, 1920–1945: A Worker-Peasant Alliance?" *Hispanic American Historical Review* 67 (1987): 371–404.

Dawson, Alexander S. *Indian and Nation in Revolutionary Mexico*. Tucson: University of Arizona Press, 2004.

Dulles, John W. F. *Yesterday in Mexico: A Chronicle of the Revolution, 1919–1936*. Austin: University of Texas Press, 1961.

Levenstein, Harvey A. "The AFL and Mexican Immigration in the 1920's: An Experiment in Labor Diplomacy." *Hispanic American Historical Review* 48 (1968): 206–19.

Lieuwen, Edwin. *Mexican Militarism: The Political Rise and Fall of the Revolutionary Army*. Albuquerque: University of New Mexico Press, 1968.

Mabry, Donald J. "Mexican Anticlerics, Bishops, *Cristeros* and the Devout during the 1920s: A Scholarly Debate." *Journal of Church and State* 20 (1978): 81–92.

Miller, Barbara. "The Role of Women in the Mexican Cristero Rebellion: *Las Señoras y las Religiosas*." *The Americas* 40 (1984): 303–24.

Purnell, Jennie. *Popular Movements and State Formation: The Agraristas and Cristeros of Michoacán*. Durham, N.C.: Duke University Press, 1999.

Quirk, Robert E. *The Mexican Revolution and the Catholic Church, 1910–1929*. Bloomington: Indiana University Press, 1973.

Ross, Stanley R. "Dwight Morrow and the Mexican Revolution." *Hispanic American Historical Review* 38 (1958): 506–28.

Simpson, Eyler N. *The Ejido: Mexico's Way Out*. Chapel Hill: University of North Carolina Press, 1937.

Spenser, Daniela. *The Impossible Triangle: Mexico, Soviet Russia, and the United States in the 1920s*. Durham, N.C.: Duke University Press, 1999.

Tannenbaum, Frank. *Mexico: The Struggle for Peace and Bread*. New York: Knopf, 1956.

Tuck, Jim. *The Holy War in Los Altos: A Regional Analysis of Mexico's Cristero Rebellion*. Tucson: University of Arizona Press, 1982.

Wasserman, Mark. "Strategies for Survival of the Porfirian Elite in Revolutionary Mexico: Chihuahua during the 1920s." *Hispanic American Historical Review* 67 (1987): 87–107.

Wilkie, James W. "The Meaning of the Cristero Religious War against the Mexican Revolution." *Journal of Church and State* 8 (1966): 214–33.

33

Cárdenas Carries the Revolution to the Left

Cárdenas

The many Mexicans impatient with the progress of the Revolution in 1934 were delighted with the election of Lázaro Cárdenas to the presidency in that year. His revolutionary career was typical of many who worked their way rapidly through the military ranks, ultimately reaching the grade of brigadier general by the end of the first violent decade. But Cárdenas was a civilian at heart. Not an imposing figure physically, he was attractive as a pensive, methodical man of principle and deep conviction. An avid reader, he was intensely interested in social reform and had that special charismatic quality of evoking passionate enthusiasm among many and strong dislike among some. And he was no run-of-the-mill politician. Supporting first Obregón and then Calles, be became, in the 1920s, a dominant force in his home state of Michoacán.

Cárdenas's governorship in Michoacán from 1928 to 1932 offered Mexicans a preview of what they might expect. The governor allowed himself to be confronted by the people and listened more than he spoke. He actually made important policy decisions, not on the advice of his confidants, but on the direct information received from the public. During years when the national government was shirking its educational responsibilities, Cárdenas opened a hundred new rural schools in Michoacán, inspected many classrooms personally, and made sure that the teachers received their salaries on time. He also encouraged the growth of labor and peasant organizations and even managed a modest redistribution of land at the state level. Throughout it all he continued to live modestly.

As the presidential elections of 1934 approached, Calles decided to throw his support behind Cárdenas, fully believing that the forty-year-old governor would be puppet number four. With the official endorsement of the Jefe Máximo, Cárdenas carried the 1933 PNR convention easily and was elected to the presidency in July of the following year. Immediately he broke with tradition as he cut his own salary in half and refused to move into the presidential mansion in Chapultepec. Instead, he kept his own modest home. Cárdenas had observed the six-year Maximato with some discomfort and once in office determined that he was going to free himself of Calles's domination, revitalize the Revolution, and carry it back to the left. Aware that Calles's control over Portes Gil, Ortiz Rubio, and Rodríguez had rested heavily on army support, the new chief executive assiduously began to cultivate promising junior officers. Not only did he raise salaries and benefits, but he also supported an improved system of education within the army and, in addition, sponsored a far-reaching internal reform of the entire military structure. Confident of the army by 1935, Cárdenas began to remove Calles supporters from the cabinet and other high governmental posts and even relieved Callista generals from their commands. When Calles discovered that he could not manipulate this president as he had the previous three, he began to speak out vociferously against the administration. By the spring of 1936 Cárdenas had had enough. He ordered that Calles and a few of his close supporters be arrested. They were placed aboard a special plane bound for the United States and informed that they should not return to Mexico.

Only once during his term was Cárdenas threatened with a serious internal revolt. Saturnino Cedillo, the conservative political boss of San Luis Potosí, withdrew recognition of the government and declared himself in open rebellion. Although Cedillo had the strong backing and financial support of conservative interests, both domestic and foreign, Cárdenas's army remained loyal and quelled the rebellion within a matter of weeks. The president would not be faced with similar problems again.

Once installed in the presidency Cárdenas did his utmost to keep close contact with the public. While cabinet secretaries and foreign dignitaries fidgeted fretfully in the presidential waiting room, Cárdenas would receive delegates of workers or peasants and patiently listen to their problems. A contemporary observer recounted that one morning the president's secretary laid before him a list of urgent matters and a telegram.

> The list said: Bank reserves dangerously low. "Tell the Treasurer," said Cárdenas. Agricultural production falling. "Tell the Minister of Agriculture." Railroads bankrupt. "Tell the Minister of Communications." Serious message from Washington. "Tell Foreign Affairs." Then he opened the telegram which read: My corn dried, my burro died, my sow was stolen, my baby is sick. Signed, Pedro Juan, village of Huit-

zlipituzco. "Order the presidential train at once," said Cárdenas. "I am leaving for Huitzlipituzco."[1]

The story is undoubtedly apocryphal; yet that it circulated in a so-phisticated capital indicates the reputation the president enjoyed. More deeply committed to social reform than any previous Mexican head of state, Cárdenas came to the presidency at a time when a new, young generation of revolutionaries was beginning to displace the old veterans of the days of violence. Some of the familiar figures contin-ued to serve in the national and state governments, but many names were heard for the first time. The younger generation had kept faith with the revolutionary principles enunciated in the years following the overthrow of the Díaz dictatorship but believed that it was finally time for a statist revolution to give them full rein.

DOMESTIC REFORMS

Agrarian reform more than anything else dominated the adminis-tration's concern during the first few years. Since the initiation of the land redistribution program some twenty-six million acres of land had been parceled out, but the figure appeared more impressive on paper than in Mexico's rural zones. Millions of Mexican peasants still owned no land at all and felt cheated by two decades of revolutionary rhetoric. Cárdenas early made up his mind to fulfill twenty years of promises. Unprepared to tarry leisurely, by the time his term ex-pired he had distributed forty-nine million acres, about twice as much as all his predecessors combined. By 1940 approximately one-third of the Mexican population had received land under the agrar-ian reform program. In fact, most of Mexico's arable land had been redistributed. Only the large cattle haciendas on arid or semiarid land remained untouched.

The vast majority of the land distributed did not go to individuals or even heads of households but rather to the communal ejidos. The land was held in common by the communities, sometimes to be reap-portioned to individuals for their use and sometimes to be worked by the community as a whole. The largest and most important of the eji-dos dating from the Cárdenas redistribution was the huge Laguna cot-ton ejido, some eight million acres on the Coahuila-Durango border. The thirty thousand families that worked the Laguna ejido cooperatively

---

1. Quoted in Anita Brenner, *The Wind That Swept Mexico: The History of the Mex-ican Revolution, 1910–1942* (Austin, 1971), p. 91.

PERCENTAGE OF LAND DISTRIBUTION BY ADMINISTRATION, 1915–40

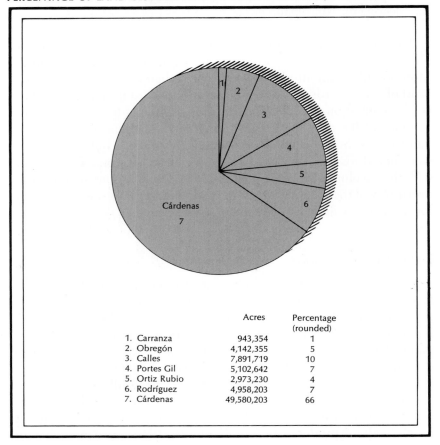

		Acres	Percentage (rounded)
1.	Carranza	943,354	1
2.	Obregón	4,142,355	5
3.	Calles	7,891,719	10
4.	Portes Gil	5,102,642	7
5.	Ortiz Rubio	2,973,230	4
6.	Rodríguez	4,958,203	7
7.	Cárdenas	49,580,203	66

engaged primarily in the cultivation of long-staple cotton but also grew large amounts of wheat, alfalfa, and maize for commercial sale. Most of the families also held small individual plots on which they grew their own subsistence crops. But the Laguna experiment consisted of much more than the mere redistribution of land. Government-supported schools were established, social services in the area were extended, and a modern ejido hospital was built in Torreón, in the center of the Laguna operation. Although the Laguna ejido was the biggest single cooperative land venture initiated by Cárdenas, other large ejidos were established as well. These ventures required large-scale financing, and for this reason the administration founded the Banco de Crédito Ejidal. During the Cárdenas years this agrarian bank made loans available to some thirty-five hundred ejidos.

The ejido was no economic or social panacea, however. A rapid population growth in rural Mexico tended to offset many of the gains, and the Banco de Crédito Ejidal did not possess sufficient capital to meet the continually growing demands. In addition, much favoritism and some corruption circumscribed the distribution of ejido loans. But more important yet, production of many ejidos, even the Laguna ejido, which received adequate loans from the agrarian bank, declined. Cotton production fell by almost nine thousand tons from 1936 to 1938, and henequen production on the new Yucatecan ejidos dropped by forty-five thousand tons during the same period.

Was the ejido program then a failure? The economists answered yes, but the administration was well aware that the redistribution of land would cause an initial decline in productivity. Cárdenas embarked upon the ejido program to meet a social, not an economic, need. The critics were harsh in their denunciation of cooperative agriculture, but what they could not deny was the unalterable fact that Cárdenas's dedication to agrarian reform spelled the demise of the traditional hacienda complex in Mexico. Millions of peasants were given a new faith in the revolutionary concept. While some argued with understandable conviction that the amount of land apportioned to each family under the ejido program was insufficient, and others suggested more theatrically that one form of peonage had simply replaced another, the fact remains that the type of servitude that had bound hacendado and peón for centuries was broken by 1940. Life in rural Mexico scarcely became idyllic as a result. Per capita income, infant mortality, and indeed life expectancy lagged behind that of the cities, but the gap in the quality of life between rural and urban Mexico began to be closed for the first time. If the ejido system was an economic failure, it was a political and social success.

The relationship between the administration and the church was conditioned almost entirely by Cárdenas's determination to implement Article 3 of the Constitution. There was no doubt that the president was an anticleric; during his campaign he had attacked the church frequently. In the state of Tabasco he had declared, "Man should not put his hope in the supernatural. Every moment spent on one's knees is a moment stolen from humanity."[2] When the PNR met in 1933 to nominate Cárdenas for the presidency, it adopted a platform that, among other things, called for the teaching of socialist doctrine in the primary

---

2. Quoted in Albert L. Michaels, "The Modification of the Anti-Clerical Nationalism of the Mexican Revolution by General Lázaro Cárdenas and Its Relationship to the Church-State Detente in Mexico," *The Americas* 26 (1969): 37.

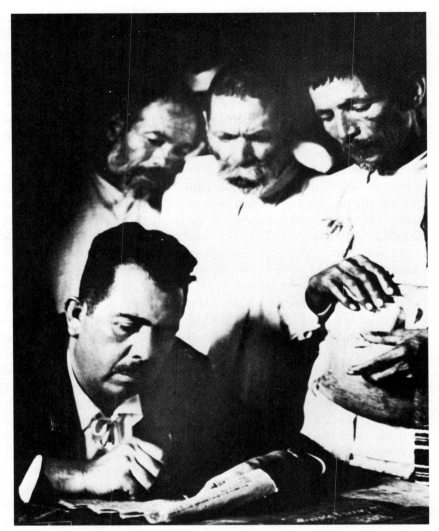

Distributing more land than all of his predecessors combined, Cárdenas here assigns a land title to a group of peasants.

and secondary schools. A new curriculum had previously been developed by the secretary of education, Narciso Bassols. The church was already incensed, but, when the hierarchy learned that sexual education would be offered in the public schools, parents were threatened with excommunication should they send their children to the anti-Catholic schools. Secretary Bassols resigned his position during the controversy, and the administration backed down somewhat on sexual instruction but not on socialist ideals. That another church strike or Cristero Rebellion was avoided is testimony to the good sense of both Cárdenas and the archbishop of Mexico, Luis María Martínez. In an important pastoral letter the archbishop implored the Mexican clergy to show more concern for the socioeconomic welfare of the masses. At the same time Cárdenas allowed that socialist education should be positive—it need not encompass antireligious propaganda in the class-room. Education itself, he believed, would eradicate fanaticism. Nonetheless, his administration's secular reformist goals often clashed with the faith and belief systems of Mexico's rural masses.

The federal expenditure for education in 1936 surpassed ten million pesos for the first time in Mexican history; by 1940 it had reached 11.3 million pesos. Cárdenas earmarked twice as much for rural education as any previous president. But although more Mexicans could read and write than ever before, illiteracy was not curtailed. Inflation coupled with a high rate of population growth outran the educational budget, and, as a result, in 1940 there were two million more illiterates in Mexico than there had been only a decade before.

President Cárdenas also worked hard to strengthen the organized labor movement and to dominate it. Annoyed at the deepseated corruption that had beset organized labor under Luis Morones, the president supported Vicente Lombardo Toledano, a onetime CROM lieutenant, in his effort to form a new national union. Much more intellectually oriented than Luis Morones, Lombardo Toledano embraced the Marxian class struggle as best explaining Mexico's historical reality and called for the establishment of a dictatorship of the proletariat. But, while he held that man was excessively acquisitive and competitive, Lombardo Toledano was no orthodox Communist. He never completely abandoned the humanism he had learned at the feet of Antonio Caso, and when forced to accept an anti-Marxist position he would explain that Mexico's problems were so unique as to require Mexican solutions. While he might have preferred public ownership of all property, he was practical enough to realize that partial socialization was better suited to the Mexican situation in the 1930s.

Lombardo Toledano succeeded in joining together some three thousand unions and six hundred thousand workers to form the Confederación de Trabajadores de México (CTM). The CTM made Lombardo Toledano its secretary general, and although Cárdenas did not give the secretary general a government position, he pledged to support his efforts. Within two years the membership had passed one million.

The CTM in its capacity as spokesman for the workers engaged in many different activities. It sponsored health and sanitation projects and organized a series of sports and recreational programs. But, most important, it concerned itself with improving the wage structure of the country. A survey in 1930 had estimated that the minimum daily wage on which a head of household might adequately support his family was four pesos and revealed, at the same time, that the average minimum wage in Mexico was one peso, six centavos. As Lombardo Toledano sought to rectify the wage structure in the country, he found himself blocked at every step by both Mexican and foreign management. Only by concerted effort did he finally succeed in having a new minimum wage of three pesos, fifty centavos adopted on a nationwide basis.

NATIONALIZATION OF OIL COMPANIES

Without question Cárdenas's most dramatic encounter during his six-year presidential term was the oil controversy with the United States, a matter that had ostensibly been resolved by his predecessors. The dispute began, innocently enough, as a conflict between labor and management within the petroleum industry. In 1936 Mexican workers struck for higher wages and better working conditions. While the oil workers were paid quite well in comparison to other Mexican laborers, the oil companies were extracting huge profits from the country and refused to negotiate seriously with union representatives. Worse yet, company policies more often than not demeaned the Mexican worker. To many, little had changed since the miners struck Colonel Greene's Cananea Consolidated Copper Company in 1906. As the strike in the oil industry began to weaken the Mexican economy, President Cárdenas ordered that the dispute be settled by an industrial arbitration board. The board examined the records of the companies and the living conditions of the workers and issued a decision ordering an increase in wages by one-third and an improved pension and welfare system. The companies, claiming that the order meant an increase in operating costs of over $7 million, appealed the decision to the Mexican Supreme Court, which ultimately upheld the original decision of the arbitration board. When the foreign-owned companies refused to obey the Supreme Court decision in its entirety, President Cárdenas held that they had flagrantly defied the sovereignty of the Mexican state and on March 18, 1938, signed a decree nationalizing the holdings of seventeen oil companies.

The nationalization decree became an immediate *cause célèbre*. Cárdenas received congratulatory telegrams from many other Latin American heads of state and evoked the patriotism of the vast majority of Mexicans. A few days after the decree was signed, a huge celebration was held in Mexico City to honor the stride for economic independence.

Cárdenas was reassured by the support he garnered, for he realized that the reaction would be quite different in the United States. Many United States newspapers expressed outrage, and not a few politicians called for intervention to head off a Communist conspiracy on the very borders of the United States. But there would be no intervention on this occasion, as Franklin D. Roosevelt had come to the United States presidency enunciating a new policy of nonintervention in Latin America. His ambassador to Mexico, Josephus Daniels, did his utmost to ensure that the oil companies negotiated in good faith. The compensation issue was fraught with difficulty, for the companies, led by Standard Oil of New Jersey, bombarded the United States public with articles and pamphlets vilifying Cárdenas and labeling the expropriation as common theft. While the companies claimed the value of the expropriated properties to be in the neighborhood of $200 million (and the British companies claimed an additional $250 million), Cárdenas countered that, since the original investment had been recovered several times and since the subsoil belonged to the Mexican nation, a just figure for the American companies was $10 million. Ultimately a mixed claims commission agreed upon a figure of almost $24 million, plus 3 percent interest effective from the day of expropriation.

A CHANGE IN ORIENTATION

Shortly after the expropriation Cárdenas decided to alter the structure of the PNR, which Calles had created in 1929. Realizing that Mexico was embarking upon difficult economic times, the president wanted an even more broadly based national party and for that reason established the Partido Revolucionario Mexicano (PRM), with representation from four sectors of society: the military, labor, agrarian, and popular. Much like its predecessor, the PRM was the official party and would encounter no serious opposition in either state or national elections.

In 1938 the leftist revolution began to lose some of its thrust, and, in retrospect, the oil expropriations climaxed the socialist and nationalist orientation of Cárdenas's program. The president's last two years were characterized by severe economic difficulty. Wealthy Mexicans, fearful of the establishment of a communist state, refused to invest in the Mexican economy, and foreign capitalists looked elsewhere for lucrative investment fields. Cárdenas created a government oil company, Petróleos Mexicanos (PEMEX), to run the industry, but, inheriting antiquated machinery and a lack of trained technicians, it got off to a shaky start. The situation worsened when Cárdenas learned that he

Mexico's "Women's Workers' Army" supports the Cárdenas oil expropriation decree during the May Day celebration in 1938.

could not buy spare parts in the United States. As oil revenues declined, the national debt rose and confidence in the government lagged. Worst of all, rampant inflation set in. Between 1935 and 1940 food prices alone rose by a staggering 49.39 percent.

The reform program—school construction, benefits for labor, agrarian reform—was expensive, and cuts had to be made somewhere. As early as 1936 the president abandoned his experiments with socialist education. Land redistribution slowed down markedly after 1938 as

Cárdenas implemented agrarian reform only when he needed political support. At the same time, he became more and more sensitive to labor agitation and strikes. Almost imperceptibly, the Mexican Revolution was shifting into a new phase. The change in policy was formalized in 1939 when the recently formed PRM met to choose its presidential candidate. It was expected that Cárdenas would throw his support to his longtime political ally, Francisco Múgica, but instead the president, believing it was time to change the orientation of the Revolution, supported his secretary of war, Manuel Avila Camacho, a conservative. Cárdenas's support assured Avila Camacho of the nomination, and the nomination assured him of victory.

As the Mexican Revolution was about to embark on a new course not all of the old problems had been resolved, but the Cárdenas administration was remarkable, nevertheless, for what it had done. It saw the end of one age and the beginning of another. Cárdenas had finally broken the back of the hacienda system, had fostered an impressive program of rural education, had seen that the labor movement was cleaned up and that it was reorganized into a new, powerful union, and had struck a sharp blow for Mexican economic nationalism when he failed to be bludgeoned by the oil companies. He had demonstrated that reform could progress without bringing the church crashing to its knees and without resorting to strong-arm tactics. With most critics, persuasion, he learned, yielded greater dividends than coercion. But, perhaps most importantly, by avoiding pivotal mistakes and not sacrificing principles to expediency, he won a new respect for the office he held as well as the plans he espoused.

By 1940 most of the goals envisioned by the revolutionaries of 1910 had been reached, and they would have considered Cárdenas's efforts a vindication of their sacrifices. But just as societies are seldom static, revolutions, if they are to be worthy of the name, must be continuing. The thirty years intervening since 1910 had begun to leave a legacy of new problems, and it was now time to reorder priorities and seek new solutions.

RECOMMENDED FOR FURTHER STUDY

Ashby, Joe C. *Organized Labor and the Mexican Revolution under Cárdenas*. Chapel Hill: University of North Carolina Press, 1967.

Bantjes, Adrian. *As If Jesus Walked on Earth: Cardenismo, Sonora, and the Mexican Revolution*. Wilmington, Del.: Scholarly Resources, 1998.

Becker, Marjorie. *Setting the Virgin on Fire: Lázaro Cárdenas, Michoacán Peasants, and the Redemption of the Mexican Revolution*. Berkeley: University of California Press, 1996.

Britton, John A. "Teacher Unionization and the Corporate State in Mexico, 1931–1945." *Hispanic American Historical Review* 59 (1979): 674–90.

Cronon, E. David. *Josephus Daniels in Mexico*. Madison: University of Wisconsin Press, 1942.

Fallaw, Ben. *Cárdenas Compromised: The Failure of Reform in Post-revolutionary Yucatán*. Durham, N.C.: Duke University Press, 2001.

Jayne, Catherine E. *Oil, War and Anglo-American Relations: American and British Reactions to Mexico's Expropriation of Foreign Oil Properties, 1937–1941*. Westport, Conn.: Greenwood Press, 2001.

Michaels, Albert L. "The Crisis of Cardenismo." *Journal of Latin American Studies* 2 (1970): 51–79.

Millon, Robert P. *Mexican Marxist: Vicente Lombardo Toledano*. Chapel Hill: University of North Carolina Press, 1966.

Moreno, Julio. *Yankee Don't Go Home: Mexican Nationalism, American Business Culture, and the Shaping of Modern Mexico, 1920–1950*. Chapel Hill: University of North Carolina Press, 2003.

Schuler, Friedrich E. *Mexico between Hitler and Roosevelt: Mexican Foreign Relations in the Age of Lázaro Cárdenas, 1934–1940*. Albuquerque: University of New Mexico Press, 1998.

Sherman, John W. *The Mexican Right: The End of Revolutionary Reform, 1920–1940*. Westport, Conn.: Praeger, 1997.

Townsend, William Cameron. *Lázaro Cárdenas: Mexican Democrat*. Ann Arbor, Mich.: Wahr, 1952.

Weyl, Nathaniel, and Sylvia Weyl. *The Reconquest of Mexico: The Years of Lázaro Cárdenas*. New York: Oxford University Press, 1939.

Wilkie, James W. *The Mexican Revolution: Federal Expenditure and Social Change since 1910*. Berkeley: University of California Press, 1967.

34

Society and Culture from Obregón to Cárdenas

DAILY LIFE IN COUNTRYSIDE AND CITY

Between 1920 and 1940 the lives of average Mexicans changed more rapidly than they had in any previous twenty-year period. The population decline of the decade of violence stopped, and, with the greater political stability of the 1920s and 1930s, the number of people began to climb rapidly. When Obregón came to office in 1920 the total population of the country was slightly over fourteen million, but when Cárdenas turned over the presidency to his successor twenty years later the total had almost reached twenty million.

Mexico was not yet an urban country when Cárdenas's term ended, although the percentage of population living in communities with fewer than twenty-five hundred people had slipped from about 70 percent in 1920 to some 65 percent in 1940. It was in the rural areas that the change in lifestyle was most dramatic. The percentage of people who wore neither shoes nor sandals declined markedly, as did the percentage of illiterates. By 1940 cultural anthropologists found it difficult to find many of those quaint Indians who spoke a native tongue exclusively.

The new *ejidatario* in rural Mexico, unlike his peón forefather, was no longer bound to the hacienda. He could travel as freely as his pocketbook allowed. It was no longer necessary to purchase daily necessities in the tienda de raya, but if he did shop in the ejido store he would likely find prices somewhat lower than those in the nearby community. The old mayordomos, of course, were gone, and in most cases ejido officials were elected by the ejidatarios themselves.

Thousands of families who had fled their villages in search of security during the early Revolution returned to find that some impressive changes were taking place. Blacktop highways began to supplant bumpy dirt roads, and buses rolled over them with more or less regularity. Bicycles began to push burros off the highways. Tractors challenged the

537

ox-drawn plow. Gasoline engines, rather than mules or horses, turned the mills that ground the corn, and gasoline pumps drew the water from nearby streams. Electricity arrived even in some small towns.

Some of the major changes in Tzintzuntzan, Michoacán, in the 1930s were recorded by the anthropologist George M. Foster.

> The first major cultural impact of modern times occurred . . . in the spring of 1931. General Lázaro Cárdenas, then Governor of Michoacán, sent a Cultural Mission consisting of teachers who specialized in plastic arts, social work, music, home economics, physical education, and "small industries," and a nurse-midwife and an agricultural engineer. . . . Most villagers were reluctant to cooperate, to help find living quarters, and to aid staff members and rural teachers. . . . In spite of such difficulties, however, the Mission had a big effect. A number of the more progressive families agreed to whitewash their houses, to improve the appearance of the village, and the present plaza, then a barren wasteland with a few houses, was cleaned up, sidewalks were marked out, flowering jacaranda trees were planted, a fountain . . . was built . . . and place was cleared for a bandstand. At the end of the first month there was an open house exposition of arts, crafts, sports, and civic betterments, to which General Cárdenas came as guest of honor. . . . Electricity was brought in from Pátzcuaro in 1938 and running water . . . was installed about the same time. . . . In 1939 the new and modern *Escuela Rural 2 de Octubre*, named to commemorate the date of Tzintzuntzan's independence, opened its doors, and for the first time village children had ready access to the full six years of primary schooling.[1]

The rural school in the 1920s and 1930s became a focal point of village life. Economic and social activity centered on programs initiated by the rural teachers, and schools challenged, although not always successfully, the domination of the church over cultural life. Catholic piety and devotion to the Virgin were not readily supplanted. Daily tasks became somewhat easier, and, with the gradual extension of medical facilities into the village, life expectancy improved and the infant mortality rate dropped from 222 deaths per thousand in 1920 to 125 twenty years later. But by no means did all of the essentials of the good life come to rural Mexico between 1920 and 1940. Poverty continued to be the single most pervasive characteristic of rural life. Although it was no longer accurate to suggest that rural Mexicans continued to live as they had since the days of the Conquest, most had not yet really been incorporated into the mainstream of national life.

---

1. George M. Foster, *Tzintzuntzan: Mexican Peasants in a Changing World* (Boston, 1967), pp. 26–29.

City life became more pleasant, at least for some, as the amenities of technology became increasingly commonplace. Mexico's first commercial radio station began transmission in 1923, and scores huddled around each neighbor lucky enough to own or have access to a receiver. Two years later the Department of Education established its own radio station and began beaming educational broadcasts to primary schools recently equipped with receivers. *Radionovelas*, broadcasts of sporting events, and constant streams of music helped relieve the tediousness of daily life. But an even more important revolution in popular culture was around the corner. By the mid-1930s the commercial cinema had begun to challenge the bullfight for pre-eminence in entertainment. The most interesting films were those of patriotic content depicting the glories of the Revolution, like Ezequiel Carrasco's *Viva México* (1934) and Luis Lezama's *El Cementerio de los Aguilas* (1938). But the greatest commercial success was Fernando de Fuentes's musical *Allá en el Rancho Grande* (1936), starring Tito Guízar and Esther Fernández. The extraordinary box office profits of this film led to a cinematographic genre of folk films, soon to be dominated by two towering figures of popular culture, Jorge Negrete and Pedro Infante.

Without question, it was the internal combustion engine that most changed the lifestyle of the urban areas. The motor car had arrived in Mexico shortly before the outbreak of hostilities in 1910, but, because of the tremendous dislocations of that first revolutionary decade, it did

As Mexico left the era of the silent film and moved into the age of sound Fernando de Fuentes's Allá en el Rancho Grande *awoke world interest in the Mexican cinema.*

not begin to transform Mexican life until after 1920. By 1925 fifty-three thousand motor vehicles were digesting thirty-five million gallons of gasoline annually; fifteen years later the number of vehicles had tripled and gasoline consumption had quadrupled. In the early 1920s the motor vehicle was still a prestige symbol, carrying a select few to and from their offices or their families on an occasional weekend outing. Later in the decade motor car racing became popular, and often left a toll of killed or injured. But by the 1930s, with a tremendous increase in the number of trucks and buses, the internal combustion engine had transformed commercial life as well as disrupted staid social patterns. Automobiles, trucks, and buses required an expanded highway network, and Mexican engineers and day laborers completed several thousand miles of new, hard-surface roads during the twenty-year period.

The growth of Mexico City was nothing short of spectacular. The high national rate of population growth, coupled with an internal migration from rural to urban areas, gave Mexico City, with a population of 1,726,858 in 1940, an increase of more than one million in only two decades. The dramatic growth yielded its share of social problems as neither the job market nor the school system could absorb the tremendous influx. The medical infrastructure and public health initiatives were sorely tested as well, as syphilis reached epidemic proportions in the national metropolis in the 1920s and the government sought to control prostitution. Those fleeing to the capital in search of a better life were more often than not disappointed. Rapid growth in other cities also caused difficulties for tens of thousands of recent arrivals. While Mexicans laughed with derision at the prohibition experiment in the United States, alcoholic consumption rose sufficiently in Mexico in the 1920s to cause alarm in the medical and scientific communities.

Life for the Mexican woman was slow to change, and her special burdens inevitably evoked compassion from foreign visitors. Verna Carleton Millan, a North American, was appalled at what she found.

> The American woman who marries into a Mexican family has a gigantic task of readjustment before her; by the mere act of crossing the border, she slips into a world that has many features of the middle ages. . . . Her first psychological shock will take place when she realizes that in Mexico women are still considered inferior beings, unfit to manage their own lives or assume any position of responsibility. . . . The Mexican woman of today, the woman of the towns and larger cities, has this enormous burden of race and tradition upon her shoulders; product of a mestizo culture, she is caught in the mesh of not one but two traditions, both equally repressive. The Spaniards brought to Mexico the strict Catholicism that has held women in a subjective, passive role for centuries. On the other hand, the Indian tribes since time immemorial

have crushed the spirit of their women beneath ironclad taboos and repressions. . . . Within the home, the man reigns supreme. The daughters are taught absolute obedience. If there is a little money in the family, the sons are educated at the expense of the daughters. . . . Marriage
is considered the supreme goal of every woman's life.[2]

The censure was essentially correct, but without the advantage of
historical perspective Mrs. Millan could not have known that change,
albeit almost imperceptible change, was taking place. More and more
women were entering the worlds of business, education, government
service, and medicine. Between 1920 and 1924 only 223 Mexican
women received university degrees; ten years later the figure had doubled. By 1930 women were participating more actively in civic work
than at any previous time, and hundreds of thousands had successfully
rebelled against family-arranged marriages. In 1900 a woman in Mexico City would not have dreamed of carrying a placard of protest in
a parade. By the time Cárdenas left office such activities were
commonplace.

The feminist movement in Mexico was amorphous until 1935, when
the United Front for Women's Rights was founded in Mexico City.
With a membership of more than fifty thousand by 1940, the Front
coordinated the efforts and defined the goals on a national basis. More
important than anything else was the campaign to win for women the
right to vote. Arguing the absurdity of disenfranchising women along
with former convicts, fugitives from justice, and inmates of insane asy-
lums, the Front assumed the offensive and, with Cárdenas's support,
did manage to win the right to vote in a number of states. Woman's
suffrage in national elections would have to wait a few more years, but
the predisposition was clearly set by 1940.

THE INTELLIGENTSIA OF THE REVOLUTION

Mexican culture during the period 1920 to 1940 came to the service of
the Revolution. The artistic, literary, and scholarly communities, with an
abiding faith in the new thrust of Mexican life, supported revolutionary
ideals by contributing their unique talents to awakening the consciousness of the new social order. The process is nowhere better illustrated
than in the cultural achievements of Mexico's most famous painters.

The restlessness of Mexico's artistic community had been apparent
during the late Porfiriato and during the first revolutionary decade,

---

2. Verna Carleton Millan, *Mexico Reborn* (Boston, 1939), pp. 148–58.

but Mexican art came into its own and won world acclaim after 1920. Secretary of education José Vasconcelos commissioned leading artists to fill the walls of public buildings with didactic murals, and Mexico's artistic renaissance combined European training and indigenous motifs in the service of the Revolution. Art was no longer directed to the privileged few who could afford to buy a canvas; it was for the public. If Mexico was not yet able to provide a classroom and a seat for every child in the country, some measure of popular education could be provided by a muralist movement carried out on a scale grander than any the world had yet known.

Vasconcelos, while supplying the government subsidy, was too much the free intellectual to place any constraints on the artists. Coordinating his efforts with the artists' union, the Syndicate of Technical Workers, Painters, and Sculptors, he instructed the artist simply to paint Mexican subjects. To be sure, youthful enthusiasm carried some astray, but giants such as Jean Charlot, Rufino Tamayo, Juan O'Gorman, David Alfaro Siqueiros, Fernando Leal, and Roberto Montenegro emerged in the process as well. Two of the muralists began to dominate the movement and set themselves apart from their talented compatriots.

During the 1920s and 1930s Diego Rivera (1885–1957) became the most renowned artist in the western hemisphere and one of the most

A detail from Rufino Tamayo's Allegories of Music and Song *(1933).*

David Alfaro Siqueiros, Head of an Indian.

Juan O'Gorman, Enemies of the Mexican People.

imposing artists of the twentieth century. A man of boundless talent
and energy, he used the Indian as his basic motif. Rivera's realistic murals did not invite freedom of interpretation as he depicted humanistic messages for the illiterate masses on the walls of the Agricultural
School in Chapingo, the Cortés Palace in Cuernavaca, the National
Preparatory School, the Department of Education, and the National
Palace in Mexico City. The Spaniard during the colonial period, and
his criollo offspring during the nineteenth century, had enslaved the
Indian and had kept him in abject poverty. It was now time to incorporate the Indian into the mainstream of society just as Rivera was in-
corporating him into the mainstream of his murals. Although Rivera
was more interested in content than in form, he was without rival in
technique. His symmetry was near perfect, but his genius emerged
even more clearly in his use of line and color. The Indians were invariably depicted in soft, gentle lines, with earthen red and brown
tones, while the oppressors, white foreigners and white Mexicans, were
portrayed in sharp lines and harsh colors.

Rivera's greatest masterpiece was composed at the Agricultural
School at Chapingo. With esthetic originality and flamboyance, Rivera

spelled out his appreciation of the new revolutionary ideology. Not only did his frescoes display the virtues of land redistribution, but they instructed in the lessons of sociopolitical reality. On one wall he portrayed bad government—the peasants betrayed by false politicians, fat capitalists, and mercenary priests. But the opposite wall was one of revolutionary hope—a scene of agricultural cultivation, a rich harvest, and a liberated peasantry. Nude female figures, and his own pregnant wife, represented the bounty of a productive earth. Just in case the humanist agrarian message might be lost, he painted over the main stairway of the building, "Here it is taught to exploit the land, not man."

Only slightly less famous than Rivera, but no less a genius, was José Clemente Orozco (1883–1949). As the violent decade passed, Orozco abandoned his career as a biting political caricaturist for mural art. Less a realist than Rivera, Orozco could be more forceful, expressive, and passionate. He was willing to experiment with new techniques as well as themes. His brutal and distorted Christs, grotesque depictions of God, and nude Madonnas pilloried all religious piety and brought forth a storm of protest. Some of his frescos were mutilated by angry crowds, but Vasconcelos did not interfere with Orozco's freedom of expression. Orozco's scenes of violence during the Revolution bring to

Details from Diego Rivera's mural in the Agricultural School at Chapingo.

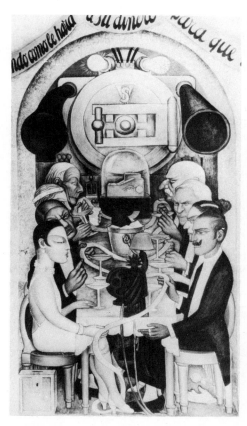

Diego Rivera's Awaiting the Harvest *(1923), a fresco in the Court of Labor, Department of Education.*

Diego Rivera's The Billionaires, *a mural in the Department of Education, satirizes international capitalism.*

mind Francisco Goya's *Horrors of War,* and he might well have had the Spanish master in mind when he conceived them.

Orozco had his tender moments too. During the 1920s, when he could see the first hesitant steps of social progress, some of his murals portray hope. His famous fresco, *Cortés and Malinche,* shows two nude and carnal figures sitting over the figure of the old, prostrate Mexico, and represents the miscegenation process, the biological and spiritual origin of the Mexican people. But in the 1930s, even as the pace of social reform began to accelerate, Orozco became increasingly disillusioned with the progress being made. After spending several years in the United States, he returned to his native Jalisco, and in the Instituto Cabañas in Guadalajara he decided to return to the theme of the Conquest. The new Cortés he portrayed was a powerful, violent con-

José Clemente Orozco's Modern Migration of the Spirit *(1933), from the fresco* Quetzalcóatl and the Aspirations of Mankind, *was painted at Dartmouth College.*

queror in full armor and with sword in hand. The only hope held out is that the spirit whispering in Cortés's ear might convince him to use his power and technology for good rather than for evil.

Also nationalistic, but less public, in her painting was Frida Kahlo (1907–54). Her marriage at the age of twenty to Diego Rivera gave her access to the intellectual avant-garde, but she easily earned recognition on her own as a painter who drew on the tradition of Mexican religious folk art to self-referentially portray human suffering. Her struggle to understand national identity in post-revolutionary Mexico and her battle to overcome debilitating physical impairments are stunningly depicted in the bloody and fragmented bodies of her subjects and her self-portraits. Kahlo also encouraged her students to represent everyday life by painting objects of popular folk art. The ways in which her own production embraced mestizaje and rejected traditional conceptions of gender (and especially of the self-abnegating Virgin Mary) became more fully appreciated in the late twentieth century, both in Mexico and abroad.

The painters were not alone in transforming a national art into a nationalistic one. The literary community contributed as well with its novels of the Revolution. Two of the best came from the pen of Martín Luis Guzmán (1887–1976), who published *El águila y la serpiente* (translated as *The Eagle and the Serpent*) in 1928 and *La sombra del caudillo* the following year. The first constitutes a novelized personal memoir of the young Guzmán, who left the comfortable life of a university student to join the Revolution and found himself a Villista. Captivated by Villa's personality, yet always afraid of his violence, Guzmán sketched the Centaur of the North most vividly in his discussion of revolutionary justice.

> This man wouldn't exist if his pistol didn't exist. . . . It isn't merely an instrument of action with him; it's a fundamental part of his being, the axis of his work and his amusement, the constant expression of his most intimate self, his soul given outward form. Between the fleshy curve of his index finger and the rigid curve of the trigger there exists the relation that comes from the contact of one being with another. When he fires, it isn't the pistol that shoots, it's the man himself. Out of his very heart comes the ball as it leaves the sinister barrel. The man and the pistol are the same thing.[3]

Villa did not turn out to be the ideal man Guzmán had hoped for. The intellectual simply could not communicate with the people's hero and ultimately took his leave. Guzmán never abandoned his revolutionary faith, but he began to wonder whether the goals could be attained without all the violence.

Guzmán's disenchantment with the politics of the Revolution is even more evident in *La sombra del caudillo*, a novel inspired by the presidential election of 1928, which saw opposition candidates Francisco Serrano and Arnulfo Gómez both dead by election day. Mexico's most powerful novel decrying dictatorship, *La sombra del caudillo*, is written with truculence and righteous indignation. But even here Guzmán does not give up on the Revolution. To the contrary, the passionate condemnation was directed against Calles for having betrayed the ideals of the movement.

---

3. Martín Luis Guzmán, *The Eagle and the Serpent*, trans. Harriet de Onís (Garden City, N.Y., 1965), p. 210.

José Clemente Orozco's fresco Cortés and
Malinche.

In a less cynical vein, Nellie Campobello (1900–1986) used short
narrative portraits in *Cartucho* (1931) to portray the violence of the
Revolution, but at the same time to honor the people who sacrificed
their lives for it. *Cartucho* is especially significant because it is the only
testimonial depiction by a woman to have been published in the immediate aftermath of the Revolution. In this work and in *Las manos
de mamá* (1937), translated as *My Mother's Hands*, Campobello also
highlights the changes provoked by the Revolution for women and indigenous peoples in the Mexican north of Pancho Villa.

The Indianist novel of the Revolution reached its apex in 1935 with
Gregorio López y Fuentes's *El Indio*. Without naming a single character or place, López y Fuentes is able to portray the Indian, not as
the noble savage, but as a man beset with social problems that society
can help to overcome. The plot is not intricate, as the author was more
interested in atmosphere. He admirably succeeded not only in illustrating the wide chasm between Indian and white society but also in
making intelligible the deepest suspicions of whites harbored in the
Indian community. López y Fuentes was awarded Mexico's first National Prize for Literature for this perceptive model.

The cultural nationalism focusing on the Indian was carried into the
arena of music by Carlos Chávez (1899–1978). After studying in Europe and the United States, in his late twenties Chávez returned to
Mexico to become director of the National Conservatory of Music and

to begin a brilliant career as a conductor, pianist, musical scholar, and composer. His *Sinfonía India* (1935) and *Xochipili-Macuilxochitl* (1940) were scored for pre-Columbian instruments, but realizing that not all performing orchestras would be able to acquire such esoteric accouterments as strings of deer hooves, he made provision for modern substitutes. But both rhythmically and melodically the compositions were inspired by Mexico's aboriginal heritage. Though Chávez was Mexico's most distinguished musician, he, like the muralists, wanted to reach the people, and he composed two important works, *Llamadas* (1934) and *Obertura republicana* (1935), based upon familiar Mexican tunes. As a result, Chávez enjoyed a popular as well as a sophisticated audience.

Anthropologists led the way among social scientists in the redefinition of cultural values. With the publication in 1922 of Manuel Gamio's highly important three-volume *La población del valle de Teotihuacán*, Mexican archaeologists, ethnologists, and social anthropologists began to take a new look not only at antiquities but at contemporary Indian problems as well. Rejecting theories of racial inferiority and the anti-Indian posture of many nineteenth-century intellectuals, they set out to depict the glories of the Indian past, to restore Indian arts and crafts, and in general to revitalize contemporary Indian culture. Their efforts were greatly facilitated in 1936 when the government established a Departamento Autónomo de Asuntos Indígenas and three years later the Instituto Nacional de Antropología e Historia.

While artists, novelists, musicians, and even anthropologists could mature and prosper with the overriding ideological assumptions of the Revolution, historians encountered problems in their quest for historical truth. Rejecting the positivist tradition that had permeated historical scholarship during the late nineteenth century, the historian of the 1920s and 1930s found no new ideological peg on which to hang his hat. As his discipline was called upon to serve as one of the many vehicles for the apotheosis of the Revolution, he was confronted with an apparently irreconcilable dichotomy: should he serve the interests of the movement or of historical scholarship in those cases in which reality suggested that the two did not converge? The overwhelming majority chose to be loved rather than candid.

Once accepting that the Revolution embodied all virtue, it was necessary to deprecate the real or imagined enemies of the movement in the most scathing terms. The pervading frame of reference thus became prorevolutionary, the historians disagreeing with one another only on the question of which of the many revolutionary protagonists was most orthodox in his revolutionary commitment. Crimes of the Revolution were dismissed on grounds of political necessity, while those of the opposition were portrayed as barbarisms of the worst kind. The Díaz regime, of course, was denounced in the harshest terms with scarcely a redeeming phrase offered in its defense. But the important questions of the day—the goals of the Revolution and the means of implementing these goals—were never brought into sharp focus. One must conclude that historical scholarship did not meet the standards of other cultural endeavors.

Despite the mediocre record of Mexican historians from 1920 to 1940, the country's overall cultural production was remarkable during those two decades. With contempt for convention, the intelligentsia suffused the environment with a new confidence. The illiterate, the petit bourgeois, the pseudosophisticate, and the intellectual could all take genuine pleasure in the tremendous flowering of culture. It was no time for the romantic landscape, the vaporous abstraction, or the unintelligible dream-sequence novel. Art and literature, as well as the social sciences, had to come to the service of the Revolution, repudiating the traditions of the recent past, satirizing the heresies of the present, and commending the material and social conquests of tomorrow.

Unequaled in Latin America, those twenty years of cultural vitality and strength captured the Mexican spirit and yielded a sense of national purpose and pride. The intellectual community did not portray Mexico as an idyllic world or expect a perfect state to arise from imperfect men. But most agreed with the philosopher Antonio Caso, who suggested forcefully in his eloquent *Principios de estética* (1925) that a meaningful morality had to be based on sacrifice and love. The enthusiasm of the intellectuals rested with their realization that after centuries of indelible stigmata, Mexico had embarked upon a compassionate social experiment that drew its strength from the best of human instincts. Although tangible progress was admittedly slow, the system had not proved to be incorrigible. Self-assured by world acclaim, the Mexican intelligentsia could never again feel constrained to look toward Europe for hallowed cultural standards. But, more importantly, the revolutionary beneficence they portrayed penetrated Mexican society deeply. The fighting was now over, and from that sorrow and adversity something positive had been born.

RECOMMENDED FOR FURTHER STUDY

Bliss, Katherine. *Compromised Positions: Prostitution, Public Health and Gender Politics in Revolutionary Mexico City.* University Park, Penn.: Pennsylvania State University Press, 2001.

Brushwood, John S. *Mexico in Its Novel: A Nation's Search for Identity.* Austin: University of Texas Press, 1966.

Buffington, Robert M. *Criminal and Citizen in Modern Mexico.* Lincoln: University of Nebraska Press, 2000.

Campobello, Nellie. *Cartucho and My Mother's Hands.* Translated by Doris Meyer and Irene Matthews. Austin: University of Texas Press, 1988.

Charlot, Jean. *The Mexican Mural Renaissance, 1920–1925.* New Haven, Conn.: Yale University Press, 1967.

Craven, David. *Diego Rivera as Epic Modernist.* New York: G.K. Hall and Co., 1997.

Delpar, Helen. *The Enormous Vogue of Things Mexican: Cultural Relations between the United States and Mexico, 1920–1935.* Tuscaloosa: University of Alabama Press, 1992.

Folgarait, Leonard. *Mural Painting and Social Revolution in Mexico, 1920–1940: Art of the New Order.* Cambridge: Cambridge University Press, 1998.

———. *So Far from Heaven: David Alfaro Siqueiros' The March of Humanity and Mexican Revolutionary Politics.* Cambridge: Cambridge University Press, 1987.

Guzmán, Martín Luis. *The Eagle and the Serpent.* Translated by Harriet de Onís. Garden City, N.Y.: Doubleday, 1965.

Hale, Charles, and Michael C. Meyer. "Mexico: The National Period." In *Latin American Scholarship since World War II*, edited by Roberto Esquenazi-Mayo and Michael C. Meyer, pp. 115–38. Lincoln: University of Nebraska Press, 1971.

Hayes, Joy Elizabeth. *Radio Nation: Communication, Popular Culture and Nationalism in Mexico, 1920–1950.* Tucson: University of Arizona Press, 2000.

Hershfield, Joanne, and David R. Maciel, eds. *Mexico's Cinema: A Century of Film and Filmakers.* Wilmington, Del.: Scholarly Resources, 1999.

López y Fuentes, Gregorio. *El Indio.* New York: Ungar, 1961.

Mora, Carl J. *Mexican Cinema: Reflections of a Society, 1896–1980.* Berkeley: University of California Press, 1982.

Reed, Alma. *Orozco.* New York: Oxford University Press, 1956.

Turner, Frederick C. *The Dynamic of Mexican Nationalism.* Chapel Hill: University of North Carolina Press, 1968.

Vaughan, Mary Kay. *Cultural Politics in Revolution: Teachers, Peasants, and Schools in Mexico, 1930–1940.* Tucson: University of Arizona Press, 1996.

Vaughan, Mary Kay and Steven E. Lewis, eds. *The Eagle and the Virgin: Nation and Cultural Revolution in Mexico, 1920–1940.* Durham, N.C.: Duke University Press, 2006.

Wolfe, Bertram D. *The Fabulous Life of Diego Rivera.* New York: Stein and Day, 1969.

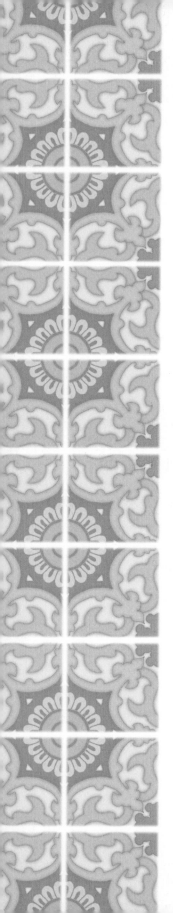

THE REVOLUTION
SHIFTS GEARS AND
RUNS OUT OF GAS

Mexico since 1940

35

From Revolution to Evolution, 1940–58

THE ADMINISTRATION OF AVILA CAMACHO

To some, Mexico's presidential election of 1940 marked the end of the Revolution; to others that same political exercise was simply the harbinger of a new approach to problem solving. Many contemporary political pundits predicted that Cárdenas would give his support to Francisco Múgica, an aging radical with impeccable revolutionary credentials. The conservatives, terrified at the prospect of further socialization of the country, rallied behind Juan Andreu Almazán. A wealthy Catholic landowner who even attracted fascist support to his camp, Almazán won the endorsement of the Partido de Acción Nacional (PAN), a conservative party later to be dominated by urban industrialists. But the official party candidate supported by Cárdenas turned out to be not Múgica but Secretary of War General Manuel Avila Camacho, an honest moderate and scarcely a social revolutionary.

The Mexican citizenry knew little about Avila Camacho prior to the 1940 presidential campaign; in fact, he was nicknamed "the Unknown Soldier." Avila Camacho had joined the Revolution in 1914 and gradually worked his way up through the military ranks. His reputation in the army was one of a compromiser rather than a forceful leader. During the course of the campaign, when asked about his feelings toward the church, he answered with the words, *Soy creyente* (I am a believer). The candid response presaged things to come. It meant specifically, of course, that anticlericalism was not going to be a part of his administration, but more generally it meant that the orientation of the Revolution was about to undergo a fundamental change. No longer would the implementation of Articles 3, 27, and 123 be considered the touchstone of social progress. With the war in Europe threatening the Mexican economy, the leaders of the PRM, like Avila Camacho, felt it was time to change the direction of the movement. Cárdenas himself had recognized the need to slow down during his last year and a half in office.

Official party nomination meant victory on election day. Avila Camacho defeated Almazán soundly and, on December 1, 1940, became the fifty-seventh president of Mexico. His inaugural address suggested that the Revolution was over, and that Mexico was moving from a period of revolution to a period of evolution. To be sure, he took pride in what had been accomplished since 1910, but Mexico could no longer afford to look backward. It was now time to look to a future of economic expansion.

Because the new president was determined to embark upon new programs, he began to phase out some of the old. Land redistribution did not stop entirely, but the pace certainly slowed. Whereas Cárdenas had distributed over forty-nine million acres, Avila Camacho parceled out fewer than twelve million. In addition, because he favored small, private ownership, emphasis was no longer placed on distribution to the ejido but rather to the heads of individual families.

Avila Camacho's educational program also reflected a change of direction. First of all, the ideology of the socialist school was abandoned, and great emphasis was placed on private initiative. Under the slogan "Each one teach one," the president and his secretary of education, Jaime Torres Bodet, had the Congress enact a law exhorting each literate Mexican to instruct one or more illiterates in the fundamentals of reading and writing. The program began amidst great fanfare with the president, his cabinet secretaries, and much of the federal and state bureaucracy setting aside an hour each day to give practical reading instruction. Soon, however, the original enthusiasm lagged, and the program slacked off. Obviously, private initiative was not going to achieve what neither church nor state had been able to accomplish over centuries—the elimination of illiteracy.

The president replaced Marxist labor leader Vicente Lombardo Toledano with the much more conservative Fidel Velásquez. Lombardo Toledano's departing speech was caustic and indicated his anger at the recent turn of events that suggested the victory of the bourgeoisie over the working class. The press, for some time having portrayed Lombardo Toledano as inordinately egotistical, pointed out that he had used the word *I* sixty-four times in the farewell address and took the occasion to dub him "the Yo-yo Champion."

Under Velásquez's leadership, government support of the CTM was held to a minimum. Rejecting what he judged to be Communist domination of the confederation, Velásquez supported moderate elements within the union. Although small increases in wages were won by the new labor leader, they did not keep pace with the rapidly growing in-

COST OF LIVING IN MEXICO CITY
(BASE YEAR 1939 = 100)

Year	Food	Clothing	Services
1939	97.6	104.1	111.8
1940	97.0	114.4	102.9
1941	106.0	127.2	143.3
1942	119.1	156.4	153.9
1943	161.4	217.6	219.7
1944	188.8	241.9	235.7
1945	225.6	261.8	239.9

Source: Jorge Vera Estañol, *Historia de la revolución mexicana: Origenes y resultados* (Mexico City, 1967), p. 737.

flation that engulfed the Mexican economy. All areas of the country were hit, but especially Mexico City. The entire philosophy of the union movement changed. Velásquez did not even protest vigorously when the administration enacted measures limiting the use of strikes. Displeased with the new leadership, in 1942 workers from the textile and building trades industries withdrew from the CTM. The most important potential benefit to accrue to the workingman was the creation of a social security agency, the Instituto Mexicano de Seguro Social (IMSS), in 1943, but the initial coverage was so limited that only a small percentage of the workers fell under the program at this time. When Avila Camacho left office fewer than 250,000 workers were participating.

WORLD WAR II

World War II broke out in Europe while Lázaro Cárdenas was in the last year of his term, and the president left it to his successor to define Mexico's position. After the Russo-German nonaggression pact of 1939, both the Mexican left, led by Lombardo Toledano and Múgica, and the right, led by Almazán, adopted a pro-German position. But when in the summer of 1941 Hitler broke his promises and ordered the Wehrmacht toward Moscow and Leningrad, the Mexican left could no longer support the Axis cause. President Avila Camacho enunciated an unmistakably pro-Allied course of action, and only a few Mexican fascists and neo-fascists failed to support him. One day after the Japanese attack on Pearl Harbor, Mexico broke diplomatic relations with the Axis powers and Secretary of Foreign Relations Ezequiel Padilla took the lead in urging other Latin American countries to support the Allies.

Most Mexicans were satisfied that breaking diplomatic relations was sufficient and that the ultimate step of declaring war was unnecessary. The United States and Mexico appointed members to a joint defense board, and Avila Camacho deported German, Italian, and Japanese diplomats from Mexico. In March 1942, when the president participated in the opening of the new Benjamin Franklin Library in Mexico City, he pointed to the stark cultural contrast between free societies who valued books and the Nazis who burned them. But Mexico would not have entered the war had not Germany forced its hand. On the night of May 14 a German submarine operating in the Caribbean torpedoed and sank the *Potrero de Llano*, a Mexican tanker that was fully lighted and properly identified. On May 24 a second Mexican tanker, the *Faja de Oro*, was torpedoed. Thereupon the president went before the Congress and announced that, although Mexico had tried to avoid war, the country could no longer accept dishonor passively. He asked for and, without serious debate, received his declaration of war.

Many Mexican intellectuals were less shocked at being at war than they were embarrassed at being formally allied with the United States. But on September 16, 1942, on the 132nd anniversary of the Grito de Dolores, an amazing and unprecedented display of camaraderie occurred on the balcony of the National Palace. Six former presidents—Adolfo de la Huerta, Plutarco Elías Calles (invited to return from the United States), Emilio Portes Gil, Pascual Ortiz Rubio, Abelardo Rodríguez, and Lázaro Cárdenas—linked arms with Avila Camacho to indicate that past antagonisms had been forgotten and that Mexico was fully united in time of war.

Secretary of Interior Miguel Alemán was charged with eliminating subversive activity within the national boundaries. Once a stiff espionage act passed the Congress, he began seizing German, Italian, and Japanese properties including banks, drug firms, hardware stores, and coffee plantations to prevent them from being used as bases of propaganda or espionage. Alemán's secret service rooted out several Gestapo agents and other spies operating clandestine radio stations relaying instructions to German submarines in the Atlantic; Mexico's valuable oil fields and munitions factories were placed under strict military control. Some modernization of the Mexican army occurred as military supplies were received through the Lend-Lease program of the United States.

The Avila Camacho administration also moved to provide a small military contingent for service with the Allies. After consultation with the members of the joint defense board it was decided that Air Force Squadron 201 should be prepared for duty in the Far East. Approximately three hundred Mexican aviators and support personnel received their training in the United States and were assigned to the Fifth Air Corps in the Philippines. Using the P47 Thunderbolt as its operating aircraft, Squadron 201 participated in bombing and strafing raids in the Philippines and Formosa in early 1945, and some Mexicans lost their lives. After the war the squadron received commendations from General Douglas MacArthur and a hero's welcome upon return to Mexico.

More important than token military support were the strategic war materials Mexico provided for the Allied war effort. Zinc, copper, lead, mercury, graphite, and cadmium flowed into United States war plants and were transformed into military products. The increased demand for these raw materials could have caused prices to soar, but the Mexican government instituted price controls as further testimony of its cooperation.

The most unique, and ultimately the most controversial, contribution to the war effort was the mutual decision made by Avila Camacho and Franklin D. Roosevelt to allow Mexican laborers (*braceros*) to serve as agricultural workers in the United States. The draft in the United States had depleted the work force, and the Mexicans in many ways picked up the slack as they began to harvest major crops. The terms of the agreement were carefully spelled out: the workers were

May Day demonstrators destroy a Nazi flag in front of a German-owned electric company.

Mexican nurses march in support of the war effort.

to receive free transportation to and from their homes; they were not to displace United States workers or to be used to suppress wages; minimum wages were set at forty-six cents an hour (later raised to fifty-seven cents); and Mexican labor officials were authorized to make periodic inspections to certify that the rules were being enforced. By the spring of 1943, despite the opposition of organized labor in the United States, the program was expanded to include nonagricultural labor as well. When the war ended, the bracero program was well entrenched as some three hundred thousand Mexicans had worked in twenty-five different states, some as far north as Minnesota and Wisconsin. But innumerable difficulties had beset the program, for the regulations were not always enforced and the workers encountered deep-seated prejudices in the United States.

INDUSTRIALIZATION

Although it would be an exaggeration to suggest that Mexico's support during World War II materially influenced the outcome, nevertheless its contribution was more substantial than that of any other Latin American country. Moreover, the war was of singular importance

With thousands of men working as braceros in the United States, Mexican women were called upon to serve the country by working in industry, in the fields, and at home.

for Mexico's internal development. It marked improved relations with the United States and an acceleration of the country's economic development.

Wartime shortages in the United States and Europe deprived Mexico of its normal source of imported manufactured goods and convinced even the doubters of the need for industrialization. The goal was not simply to meet the demands of the domestic market but to produce a surplus of manufactured goods for export to other Latin American countries. Even during the last years of the Cárdenas administration, Mexican social scientists had begun to argue the absurdity of dividing the same pie into smaller and smaller pieces. For the Revolution to realize its ultimate goal of providing a better life for the vast majority of the people, it was imperative that the country's economic base be expanded through a major program of industrialization. The program not only would provide additional employment for a rapidly growing population but, through increased productivity, would generate wealth and improve the standard of living for the masses.

To foster industrial expansion the Avila Camacho administration established the Nacional Financiera, a government-owned bank created primarily to provide loans to industry but also to oversee the industrial

INDUSTRIAL LOANS OF THE NACIONAL FINANCIERA, 1940–45

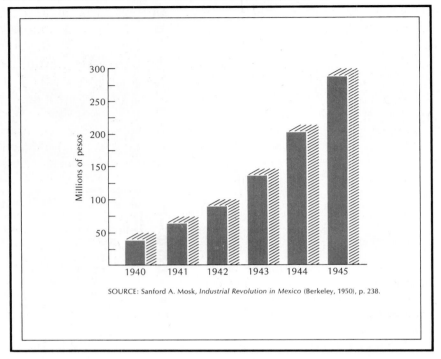

SOURCE: Sanford A. Mosk, *Industrial Revolution in Mexico* (Berkeley, 1950), p. 238.

process. In each year of the administration the favorable loans of the Nacional Financiera increased dramatically, reaching a total of 286.8 million pesos by 1945.

In addition, other incentives, such as tax exemptions and tariff protection, persuaded potential investors that the risks were acceptable. With the CTM in the hands of moderate Fidel Velásquez, the wage structure of the country was not going to change markedly; in fact, Velásquez pledged his support to the new industrialists. Native Mexican capital did begin to pour into new industrial pursuits, but, because the program was such an ambitious one, in 1944 the Congress passed legislation allowing foreign participation in industrialization with the proviso that Mexican capital own the controlling stock in any mixed corporation. Some United States investors jumped at the opportunity. Credits were also extended through the Export-Import Bank in the United States.

The new and often young industrialists took it upon themselves to educate Mexican politicians, and indeed the public, in the virtues of industrial growth. In 1942 they founded the Cámara Nacional de la Industria de Transformación to develop an industrial consciousness in the country and to convince policy makers that without industrialization the masses were doomed to perpetual privation. During the Avila Camacho years industrialization became as important to the national self-conception as agrarian reform had been during the Cárdenas administration. Its lure was irresistible, and stories of new factories pushed political news off the front pages of the newspapers. The Cámara became an effective propaganda agency and lobby, arguing that what was good for industry was good for the nation. Their initial goal was to foster those industries that relied on Mexican raw materials, for example, cereal processing, edible oil from agricultural products, sugar, alcohol, and the manufacture of fibers and chemicals. The ultimate goal was to make Mexico completely self-sufficient in all manufactured goods consumed in large volume and to begin exporting these products as well.

The industrial revolution gathered momentum throughout the war years as a wide range of old industries were expanded and new ones initiated. The textile, food processing, chemical, beer, and cement industries grew rapidly. Pig iron production increased from 99,200 metric tons in 1930 to 240,300 metric tons in 1946, and during the same period steel increased from 142,200 metric tons to 257,900 metric tons. Electrical capacity rose by 20 percent, and the industrial proletariat grew steadily in size.

As predicted, industrialization generated much new wealth. The national income almost tripled, from 6.4 billion pesos in 1940 to 18.6 billion in 1945. Per capita income jumped from 325 pesos the year Avila Camacho was inaugurated to 838 pesos during his last year in office. As social critics quickly pointed out, however, increased per capita income for a growing middle class did not necessarily mean a more equitable distribution of wealth or increased earning power for the poor.

The emphasis of the Revolution had certainly changed. Those who had believed—and with some reason—that the semifeudal society inherited by the Revolution would be replaced by socialism had to reexamine their expectations. It now appeared increasingly certain that the post-Cárdenas period would be typified not by socialism but by industrial capitalism. The agrarian revolution languished. Productivity on most of the ejidos had not lived up to expectations, and government planners decided not to experiment further with communal agriculture.

MIGUEL ALEMÁN INITIATES THE INSTITUTIONAL REVOLUTION, 1946–52

For almost a decade the party had gradually been opened up. By 1946 it was no longer dominated by intellectuals, agrarian reformers, and ardent defenders of the labor movement. The business and industrial communities were now represented, as were economists and technicians. To symbolize that it endorsed the new thrust of the Revolution the party decided to change its name to the Partido Revolucionario Institucional (PRI). In January, the official party for the first time endorsed a civilian, Miguel Alemán, as its presidential candidate. There would now be no turning back. Mexico's conception of modernity had been made synonymous with the industrial state.

The new president reduced the military's share of the budget to less than 10 percent of the total for the first time in the twentieth century, and the generals accepted the decision, scarcely batting an eye. Over the years the military share of the budget was gradually reduced from 70 percent in 1917 to 7 percent in 1952. More successfully than its Latin American neighbors, Mexico curbed the problems of rampant militarism.

With a healthy dollar reserve turned over to him by his predecessor, Alemán launched an impressive number of public works projects designed both to provide work for a steadily growing labor force and to meet a series of crucial developmental needs. Most important was the construction of dams to control flooding, increase arable land acreage, and supply ample power for the modernization impulse. The Morelos Dam on the Colorado River near Mexicali worked agricultural wonders in the northwest as some seven hundred thousand arid acres were reclaimed and converted into a rich truck-farming zone. In the northeast work was initiated, in cooperation with the United States, on the Falcón Dam in the lower Rio Grande Valley. Completed in 1953, the year after Alemán left office, the Falcón project yielded substantial agricultural benefits as well. The major project in the south was the harnessing of the Papaloapan River in the states of Puebla, Veracruz, and Oaxaca. Not only were tens of thousands of acres added to the agricultural base of the nation, but a series of hydroelectric stations contributed to the tripling of Mexico's electrical output capacity by 1952.

Other large-scale public works centered on improving the communications network. In addition to modernizing the railway system, Alemán completed Mexico's segment of the Pan-American Highway. This all-weather road made possible automobile travel between the United States and Guatemala. Of equal importance commercially was the completion of the Isthmian Highway, which connected Puerto México and Salina Cruz across Tehuantepec. To cater to the tourist traffic, an increasingly important source of foreign exchange, Alemán ordered the construction of a four-lane superhighway between the capital and the Pacific resort town of Acapulco, soon to become a playground for the world's rich. In total, paved roads increased from about twenty-five hundred miles in 1946 to over ten thousand by 1952.

Postwar Mexico was prosperous and booming. If the working class did not share proportionately in the benefits of an expansive economy, the middle class continued to grow. Hundreds of small factories, not only in Mexico City but in Monterrey, Guadalajara, Puebla, and San Luis Potosí, took advantage of the cheap and abundant source of electric power and began to transform the economy and also the face of the nation. Low taxes and high rates of profit encouraged both Mexican and foreign capital to continue investing in the industrial sector of the economy. PEMEX expanded its activities; new pipelines and refineries, coupled with accelerated drilling, made it possible for the state-owned corporation to double its production between 1946 and 1952.

The most impressive construction project of all was the new University City built to house the National University of Mexico. Dedicated in 1952, the campus of three square miles was one of the most modern in the world. The architectural and artistic achievements at University City were unparalleled: the plans were conceived by leading artists such as Juan O'Gorman (1905–1982), the buildings designed by talented architects such as Félix Candela, and the walls adorned with anthropological and historical murals by Rivera and Siqueiros. Alemán considered the University a monument to his own presidency, and the first thing visitors encountered when entering the campus in the 1960s was a huge statue of Alemán himself.

Relations between the United States and Mexico continued to be cordial. Accepting an invitation from President Truman, Alemán became the first Mexican head of state to visit Washington. Truman also called upon the Mexican president in Mexico City and delighted his hosts by placing a wreath at the monument of the Niños Héroes, the boy cadets who had fallen fighting United States troops a hundred years before. Both congresses voted to return all trophies of war sequestered in the middle of the nineteenth century. The outward manifestations of goodwill had practical effects as well. The United States was able to count on Mexican support in the cold war, and loans from the Export-Import Bank flowed into Mexico at an accelerated pace. United States tourists (over four hundred thousand in 1952 alone) left hundreds of millions of dollars in the country, and trade relations became more interdependent than ever before.

To some, Mexico seemed a model of health and prosperity. But behind the showy façade Alemán had created, serious problems had begun to sap the vitality of the institutionalized Revolution. As an example, the library at the new University City, while a marvel to gaze at, was embarrassingly short of books. Row after row of empty shelves were symbolic of the building spree that failed to cope with basic issued and emphasized form over content. Corruption beset the

The main library at the National University of Mexico, University City.

administration and many new millionaires emerged between 1946 and 1952. The displays of sprawling mansions, yachts, and airplanes, paid for with bribes, brought to mind the venality of the days of Santa Anna. And to be sure the president himself managed to amass a huge fortune.

While PRI politicians continued to mouth pleasant-sounding revolutionary euphemisms, the little man had been shunted aside. The labor movement was not crushed, but it was intimidated. When in April

*A mural by José Chávez Morado at the Faculty of Science Building,
University City.*

1950 Secretary of the Treasury Ramón Beteta exhorted the industrialists of Monterrey to keep their costs down so that Mexican industry
could become competitive, he was, in effect, inviting them to keep
wages depressed. When petroleum workers struck, army troops were
dispatched to patrol the fields and fifty union leaders were dismissed
from their posts. Despite John Maynard Keynes's revolution in economic theory, the Mexican worker was not yet to be confused with a
consumer.

While new primary and secondary schools were built throughout
the country, teachers' salaries were so paltry that it was almost impossible to staff them with qualified professionals. School attendance remained low. Of the six million schoolchildren in the age bracket six to
fourteen, fewer than 2.25 million attended classes on a regular basis.
Despite the emphasis successive administrations since 1920 had placed
on rural education, the 1950 census revealed that only 5 percent of
rural children finished the sixth grade. Certainly it would be unfair to

President Harry S Truman visits the Pyramid of the Sun during his trip to Mexico City.

hold President Alemán responsible for all of the shortcomings of four decades of Revolution; yet his administration did not move in a direction suited to overcome them.

THE PRESIDENCY OF RUIZ CORTINES

When PRI officials met to choose Alemán's successor, many believed it crucial to rekindle confidence in the integrity of the party. In order to repudiate the peculation of the Alemán administration, they selected sixty-one-year-old Adolfo Ruiz Cortines, whose personal honesty and devotion to service were impeccable. During his governorship of Veracruz and tenure as secretary of interior under Alemán he had garnered a reputation for party loyalty, efficiency, and integrity. With official party support he won over his leading opponent, Miguel Henríquez Guzmán, by a margin of almost five to one.

Ideologically much akin to his predecessor, the hard-working but unspectacular president did not disappoint those who had urged a cleansing of bureaucratic corruption. He announced in his inaugural speech that he would demand strict honesty and ordered all public officials to make public their financial holdings. During the next several years he fired a number of notorious grafters. In an even more significant political reform he pushed through the Congress legislation fully enfranchising the Mexican woman. This long overdue measure culminated years of active campaigning by women's organizations throughout the country.

The Mexican economy remained dynamic during the Ruiz Cortines years as industry continued to receive government support and, in turn, established an entire series of new records for production. A devaluation of the peso in 1953 (to a rate of 12.50 to the dollar) helped stabilize the economy and prompt new foreign investment. United States capital, encouraged by the healthy economic indicators, poured into the country unhesitatingly, and United States visitors in the larger cities saw familiar signs advertising General Motors, Dow Chemicals, Pepsi-Cola, Coca-Cola, Colgate, Goodyear, John Deere, Ford, Proctor and Gamble, Sears Roebuck, and other corporate giants who would not have dared to invest their stockholders' dollars in Mexico twenty years earlier. The new, mixed economy seemed to be working.

Believing that Alemán had overtaxed the idea of public works, the new Mexican president did not initiate many grandiose construction schemes, but he did see hundreds of his predecessor's projects through to completion. Whereas Alemán had built huge dams, Ruiz Cortines sponsored smaller projects; whereas Alemán had built superhighways, Ruiz Cortines paved two-lane roads to help the farmers get their products to a suitable market.

For the first time since its foundation in 1943, the IMSS expanded its coverage sufficiently to constitute an agency of genuine social importance. Ruiz Cortines's director, Antonio Ortiz Mena, not only obtained increased funding but moved the services into the countryside for the first time. The number of IMSS-sponsored clinics rose from 42 to 226 and hospitals from 19 to 105. Rural services did not yet approximate urban ones, but a beginning was at least made as about a hundred thousand rural persons received some kind of social security coverage for the first time. The basic issue of low wages was not resolved. Although salaries did rise by an average of 5 percent a year in the period from 1952 to 1958, the workers lost their increases to inflation, which rose annually at a rate of 7.3 percent.

Throughout his term of office Ruiz Cortines found himself caught up in a situation over which he had no direct control. Mexico's population was growing at a rate that began to alarm not only social scientists but also his political advisers. When Lázaro Cárdenas came to power the population of the country was only about sixteen million. But by 1958 it had doubled to more than thirty-two million. The population explosion was compounded by a concomitant trend toward urbanization. While the national growth rate had reached 3.1 percent a year by 1955 (as opposed to 1.9 from 1930 to 1940), the growth rate of the major cities approached 7 percent a year. The Federal District jumped from 3 million in 1952 to an amazing 4.5 million only six years later.

Drawn by the lure of industry, hundreds of thousands of rural Mexicans flocked to the cities in hope of a better life, but few found it. The industrial revolution required skilled, not unskilled, labor. The need for more jobs, schools, health services, sewage disposal plants, streets, and houses in the cities was now taxing even the extraordinary postwar prosperity. Although by 1958 a million and a half Mexicans were earning their living from industry, the laboring force was growing faster than industry could provide jobs. At precisely the time when the apparent thrust of the country was directed toward modernization, Ruiz Cortines found it necessary to order the use of hand labor rather than machinery on public works just to keep the new work force occupied.

THE REVOLUTION: AN ASSESSMENT AT MID-CENTURY

Ruiz Cortines considered himself a custodian of the Revolution as he announced repeatedly that he had full faith in revolutionary institutions. But surely his policies would have repulsed the heroes of the 1910 movement. The postwar generation of Mexican politicians had redefined priorities and concluded at mid-century that the programs of 1910 no longer had meaning. The burdens of industrial development fell most heavily on those who were least able to bear them. The president's economic advisers were aware of this problem, but they suggested that a temporary lack of equity constituted an important investment in the future. Mexico simply had to continue flexing its industrial muscles.

From the very outset the Revolution had been criticized from both the left and the right. As it turned more conservative in the postwar years, however, the majority of the critics were isolated on the left. More wealth was being generated, but the proceeds were not being distributed. Mexican radicals were alienated by the new trends, but, more importantly, the moderate left was becoming increasingly apprehensive about the burgeoning population and the heavy emphasis on technology as the key to a more abundant life. If something were not done in the near future to arrest the tremendous rate of population growth, all discussion of the quality of life would be beside the point. For the first time in Mexican history social scientists began seriously to ponder the Malthusian theory of impending starvation.

On another important issue the left and right could agree. The official party, the PRI, had pre-empted the political life of the country. Party nomination was tantamount to election. Though the party itself was broadly based and incorporated many segments of society, its complete domination of the political process produced nothing less than a contradiction in terms—a one-party democracy.

As Mexico's distinguished political critic and respected scholar, Daniel Cosío Villegas, pointed out in a brilliant analysis of what was happening to the Mexican Revolution, the shifts of the last decades had produced uneven effects despite economic growth.

> Strictly speaking the only problem of great magnitude is the rate at which the population increase may very well strain the country's physical, human and economic resources, and that if energetic measures are not taken, it may present a very serious problem. . . . The political situation is decidedly less satisfactory. . . . The election [of the president, governors, and local authorities] is far from popular, being decided by personalist forces that rarely or never represent the genuine interests of large human groups. The economic and political power of the president of the Republic is almost all-embracing and . . . it is impossible for one man to know the special needs of each city or town and which person or persons are most suitable to resolve them.[1]

Ruiz Cortines's last message to the Congress was atypical of Mexican politicians of the twentieth century. He, too, had begun to hear the voices of criticism, and rather than exalt revolutionary successes, he took the occasion to pinpoint at least some of the shortcomings. The social imperfections of the system troubled him more than the deficiencies of one-party rule or executive dominance. The Mexican masses, the outgoing president conceded, had not benefited from the revolutionary process as much as he had anticipated. Many of the revolutionary promises were yet to be fulfilled. Illness, ignorance, and poverty had not been overcome. The desired balance between economic development and social justice had tipped in favor of the former.

PRI officials had to agree. The pace of the social movement had slowed and, since 1940, had almost ground to a halt. Perhaps a moderate shift to the left would mute government critics and reinstill some faith in revolutionary ideals. They were willing to give it a try.

---

1. Daniel Cosío Villegas, *Change in Latin America: The Mexican and Cuban Revolutions* (Lincoln, 1961), pp. 30–33.

RECOMMENDED FOR FURTHER STUDY

Brandenburg, Frank. *The Making of Modern Mexico*. Englewood Cliffs, N.J.: Prentice-Hall, 1964.

Call, Tomme Clark. *The Mexican Venture*. New York: Oxford University Press, 1953.

Cline, Howard. *Mexico: Revolution to Evolution, 1940–1960*. New York: Oxford University Press, 1963.

Middlebrook, Kevin J. *The Paradox of Revolution: Labor, the State and Authoritarianism in Mexico*. Baltimore: Johns Hopkins University Press, 1995.

Mosk, Sanford A. *Industrial Revolution in Mexico*. Berkeley: University of California Press, 1950.

Newcomer, Daniel. *Reconciling Modernity: Urban State Formation in the 1940s: León, Mexico*. Lincoln: University of Nebraska Press, 2004.

Niblo, Stephen R. *Mexico in the 1940s: Modernity, Politics, and Corruption*. Wilmington, Del.: Scholarly Resources, 1999.

Paz, Maria Emilia. *Strategy, Security, and Spies: Mexico and the U.S. as Allies in World War II*. University Park: Pennsylvania State University Press, 1997.

Pérez López, Enrique, et al. *Mexico's Recent Economic Growth: The Mexican View*. Austin: University of Texas Press, 1967.

Powell, J. R. *The Mexican Petroleum Industry, 1938–1950*. Berkeley: University of California Press, 1956.

Ross, Stanley R., ed. *Is the Mexican Revolution Dead?* New York: Alfred A. Knopf, 1966.

Schuler, Friederich. "Mexico and the Outside World," in *The Oxford History of Mexico*. Edited by Michael C. Meyer and William H. Beezley, pp. 503–41. New York: Oxford University Press, 2000.

Scott, Robert E. *Mexican Government in Transition*. Urbana: University of Illinois Press, 1959.

Tannenbaum, Frank. *Mexico: The Struggle for Peace and Bread*. New York: Alfred A. Knopf, 1956.

Vernon, Raymond. *The Dilemma of Mexico's Development: The Roles of the Private and Public Sectors*. Cambridge, Mass.: Harvard University Press, 1963.

Wilkie, James W. *The Mexican Revolution: Federal Expenditure and Social Change since 1910*. Berkeley: University of California Press, 1967.

36

The Lull and the Storm, 1958–76

For many, the Mexican Revolution had not achieved its promise. Nonetheless, growing criticism of the PRI and social discontent were temporarily stayed by the presidency of Adolfo López Mateos from 1958 to 1964, only to erupt and then smolder in the next decade. The PRI nominee, López Mateos, the well-educated son of a small-town dentist, won the presidency in 1958 with about 90 percent of the total vote. His conservative, proclerical PAN rival, Luis H. Alvarez, did not fulfill the hopes of his party in capitalizing on the fully enfranchised Mexican women's vote, thought to be influenced by the church. The women's vote increased the total ballots cast but scarcely changed the official party's margin of victory.

DOMESTIC POLICY UNDER LÓPEZ MATEOS

President López Mateos presented a stark contrast to his sixty-seven-year-old predecessor. Only forty-seven at the time of his election, he was dynamic, energetic, and personally attractive. Having served as secretary of labor during the Ruiz Cortines administration, he had won a reputation as a liberal for his management of labor disputes; only a few of the thirteen thousand cases he handled degenerated into strikes. He enjoyed the backing of Lázaro Cárdenas and seemed to be just the right man at the right time. More intellectually oriented than presidents of recent vintage, he indicated during the campaign that he planned to nudge the Mexican Revolution back to the left. Hundreds of thousands of young Mexicans, disheartened with the slow progress in the social field since the Second World War, identified with López Mateos, much as the youth of the United States would, a few years later, identify with President John F. Kennedy.

Shortly after his inauguration the new president was asked to comment on his political philosophy and he answered with the words, "I am left within the Constitution." Mexican Communists, and other radicals whom he judged to be left of the Constitution, were not treated with kid gloves. López Mateos removed Communist leadership from the teachers' union and the railroad union and imprisoned Mexico's internationally known muralist and Communist, David Alfaro Siqueiros, on charges of "social dissolution," an amorphous kind of sedition. But just as local and foreign businessmen and industrialists sat back and relaxed, thinking that they had an unexpected friend in the presidential chair, López Mateos also began to demonstrate that he intended to depart markedly from the conservative, business-oriented policies of his three predecessors.

Land redistribution, almost forgotten as a revolutionary goal by the end of World War II, was stepped up once again, on both an individual and a collective basis. During his six-year term López Mateos parceled out some thirty million acres, more than any president except Lázaro Cárdenas. He also cleared and opened up new agricultural lands in extreme southern Mexico.

State intervention in the economy accelerated from 1958 to 1964 as the administration purchased controlling stock in a number of foreign industries. In 1962, for example, the government gained control of the United States and Canadian electric companies and, not being able to divine a future in which energy would become a luxury, authorized huge, wasteful electric signs proudly announcing *La electricidad es nuestra* (The electricity is ours). At about the same time the government also purchased the motion picture industry, the production and distribution of which had been largely under United States domination. The president pledged to keep the price of tickets low so that all people could avail themselves of this medium of entertainment. Social welfare projects, most notably medical care and old age pensions, were expanded, and the IMSS program for rural Mexico was stepped up markedly. By 1964 public health campaigns had significantly reduced tuberculosis and polio rates, while malaria was almost completely eliminated.

Like his predecessors, López Mateos continued to skirt the issue of birth control, even as a million Mexican babies were born in 1962 and almost a million and a half in 1963. But he did recognize the tremendous dislocations occasioned by rapid urbanization and initiated modest steps to accommodate the dramatically increasing population. For the first time in history the government entered the housing business on a large scale. Low-cost housing projects were initiated in the major industrial cities, many of which had become encircled with shanty towns of indescribable misery and poverty. One of the largest housing developments in Mexico City covered some ten million square feet of a former slum, housed a hundred thousand persons, and contained thirteen schools, four clinics, and several nurseries. The rents were

Even after the emphasis on agrarian re-form programs, life for workers on the maguey plantations of Yucatán remained difficult.

modest: $6.00 a month for a one-bedroom apartment and $16.00 a month for a three-bedroom unit. To complement public housing, the president also developed an incentive program designed to encourage industry to stay away from the greater Mexico City environs. In 1960, on the fiftieth anniversary of the Revolution, Mexico's urban popula-tion surpassed its rural population for the first time.

López Mateos's labor supporters were visibly shaken in 1959 when the president used federal troops to put down a major railroad strike. Arguing that the strike threatened to paralyze the country, he arrested a number of leaders, including Demetrio Vallejo, the head of the union. It was a bad start on the labor front. But in a countermove he decided to implement an almost forgotten article of the Constitution of 1917 that called for labor to share in the profits with management. In 1962 a special commission, the Comisión Nacional para el Reparto de Utili-dades, was convoked to implement the profit-sharing plan. The formula agreed upon was complicated, dependent upon the amount of capital investment and the size of the labor force within each industry. But by 1964 many Mexican laborers were earning an extra 5 to 10 percent a year under the profit-sharing law.

The educational policy of the López Mateos administration renewed the emphasis on the rural school. By 1963 education had become the largest single item in the Mexican budget, and the educational outlay was twice that allocated for national defense. While the percentage of

A major campaign to eradicate malaria in 1962 and 1963 yielded positive results.

Curious villagers inspect the newly completed sewer system in the state of Chiapas.

URBAN–RURAL POPULATION DISTRIBUTION

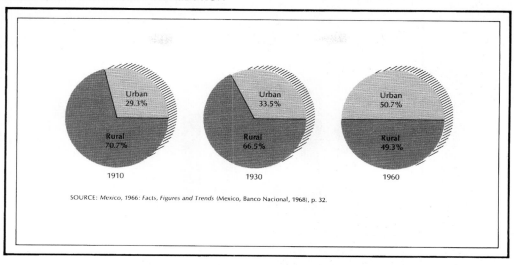

SOURCE: *Mexico, 1966: Facts, Figures and Trends* (Mexico, Banco Nacional, 1968), p. 32.

illiteracy in Mexico had been cut from some 77 percent in 1910 to less than 38 percent in 1960, the population explosion in a very real sense had nullified the results. In absolute numbers there were more illiterates in 1960 (13,200,000) than there had been at the time of the Plan de San Luis Potosí (11,658,000).

To attack illiteracy the president and his secretary of education, Jaime Torres Bodet, who had also served under Avila Camacho, launched a two-pronged assault. Through an ingenious system of prefabricated schools costing only $4,800 per unit, the number of rural classrooms increased rapidly. The government provided the building materials and the technical assistance, and the individual communities were called upon to provide the land and the actual labor. In this way villages were given a genuine stake in the educational process. López Mateos also decided to initiate a system of free and compulsory textbooks. On this program he encountered opposition. Although the books were prepared in consultation with some of the leading scholars in the country, they did reflect the historiographical preconceptions that had grown up with the Revolution, and the Roman Catholic Church took umbrage at the treatment afforded many of its efforts throughout Mexican history. The National Union of Parents Association, a conservative organization supported by the PAN and a number of leading clerics, led demonstrations against the books, insisting that their imposition on a mandatory basis constituted a totalitarian act designed to standardize thought in the Mexican republic. At the same time radical leftists opposed the textbooks because they exalted revolutionary

ILLITERACY, 1910–60

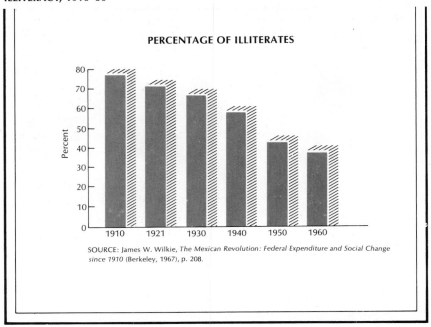

PERCENTAGE OF ILLITERATES

SOURCE: James W. Wilkie, *The Mexican Revolution: Federal Expenditure and Social Change since 1910* (Berkeley, 1967), p. 208.

In an attempt to reduce illiteracy, López Mateos revived the idea of adult reading classes.

accomplishments and overlooked the shortcomings. López Mateos was not intimidated, and the books were adopted throughout the country over the protests.

If Mexico's rate of economic growth under López Mateos did not quite keep pace with that under Miguel Alemán and Adolfo Ruiz Cortines, the economy remained strong. British and French capital poured into PEMEX's new petrochemical division. Private initiative constructed luxury hotels, and tourists came in droves to Acapulco and the newly developed resort town of Puerto Vallarta—and left behind millions of dollars that were put to good use. By 1964 Mexico was self-sufficient in iron, steel, and oil. Local capital no longer felt the need to seek investment fields elsewhere and, indeed, purchased controlling stock in the Mexican telephone network. And in 1963 Mexican bonds were sold on United States and European markets for the first time since the Díaz regime. The country was still in its period of sustained economic growth.

THE FOREIGN POLICY OF THE LÓPEZ MATEOS ADMINISTRATION

Mexico's foreign policy from 1958 to 1964 showed López Mateos not unsympathetic to concerns of the left. Coming to the presidency only a few months before Fidel Castro's July 26 revolution ousted rightest Cuban dictator Fulgencio Batista, López Mateos occupied himself with defining the Mexican position on the most crucial Latin American issue of the postwar period. To the chagrin of the United States, he opted for a policy of total nonintervention in Cuba's internal affairs. Arguing the national sovereignty and juridical equality of all states, Mexico refused to condemn the Castro regime, voted against Cuba's expulsion from the Organization of American States, did not endorse economic sanctions, and, most important, remained the only country in the western hemisphere to retain air service and diplomatic relations with Cuba. But the Mexican government was not prepared to accept dictates from Moscow either, and López Mateos condemned the Soviet Union in 1962 for placing offensive missiles in Cuba. When French President Charles de Gaulle visited Mexico City in the spring of 1964 and was accorded the honor of being the first foreign head of state ever to speak from the presidential balcony overlooking the Plaza de la Constitución, the two leaders congratulated one another on escaping the tutelage of the superpowers. Mexico's independent foreign posture was a theme relayed in a series of trips that López Mateos and his close associates made to Yugoslavia, Poland, Indonesia, India, Canada, and a number of African countries.

By his own reckoning, López Mateos's greatest diplomatic victory concerned the final resolution of a century-old boundary dispute with the United States—the Chamizal controversy. At the end of the war with the United States the boundary had been set at the Rio Grande. But because of the sandy texture of the soil, especially in the area of El Paso, the river periodically shifted its bed. In 1864 it moved suddenly to the south, leaving some six hundred acres of Mexican territory north of the river in the state of Texas. Mexico, of course, claimed that this land, the Chamizal, was part of the national domain, but the various arbitration commissions had been unable to reach an accord suitable to the United States government. When President John F. Kennedy visited Mexico City in 1962, he was informed that the Chamizal continued to be a reminder of Yanqui imperialism and ordered the United States ambassador, Thomas Mann, to enter into new negotiations with the Mexican government for its final resolution. In the summer of 1963 the United States agreed to return the disputed territory to Mexico, to reimburse the El Paso residents for their lost property, and to share the costs of building a new international bridge and a concrete-lined channel to eliminate possible future disputes.

An assassin's bullet took John Kennedy's life before he could sign the agreement, but his successor, Lyndon Johnson, met López Mateos at the Chamizal in September 1964 and formalized the arrangement. Through adroit diplomacy the Mexican president retained the goodwill of the United States and pleased Mexican nationalists.

Mounting Criticism of the One-Party System

Criticism of the PRI's monopoly on government continued to build during the López Mateos administration. His election in 1958 with 90 percent of the total vote marked thirty consecutive years of rule by the official party. The party not only had won every contest for the presidency but also had captured all of the senatorial and gubernatorial races. While electoral fraud might have contributed to some of the early victories, since 1934 there was no need to rig elections. The PRI had succeeded in identifying itself with the Revolution, and the Revolution was practically synonymous with the state. The PRI's colors— red, white, and green—were identical to those on the national flag; they appeared on its symbol on the ballot, and the lesson was not lost on even the illiterate. In addition, the party was able to mobilize bountiful resources to get its message across.

By the early 1960s an increasingly sophisticated electorate began to question the bossism, favoritism, and corruption that had beset the

PRI officialdom. A party without any genuine opposition was accountable to nobody. A party that could embrace the leftist policies of Cárdenas and the business-oriented policies of Alemán was ideologically bankrupt. How could it be expected to embark upon a meaningful redistribution of wealth designed to close the still gigantic gap between rich and poor? Alienation was broadly based, cutting across many class lines and most ideological persuasions. Effective democratization, despite potential obstacles, was deemed crucial. Properly conceived and skillfully channeled, it could lead to a developmental attitude that sought not only to increase the national product but to redistribute it. Pablo González Casanova, a distinguished Mexican social scientist, pinpointed this specific need when he argued in his perceptive *Democracy in Mexico:* "Democracy exists to the extent that the people share the income, culture, and power; anything else is democratic folklore or rhetoric."[1]

López Mateos responded by sponsoring an amendment to the Constitution that altered the electoral procedures in the Chamber of Deputies. To broaden the opposition in the lower house of the legislature, his amendment provided that any party winning 2.5 percent of the national vote was entitled to five congressmen whether or not the candidates actually won their respective races. For every additional .5 percent of the vote these parties would receive an additional congressman, up to a total of twenty, each of whom would occupy a new seat, not replace an elected congressman. Because of the new law the PAN received twenty congressional seats in the 1964 elections and the Partido Popular Socialista (PPS), ten seats. The electoral revision was a step in the right direction but it did not end the debate on the shortcomings of Mexican democracy.

THE COMING STORM

López Mateos is the most fondly remembered president of the postwar era. Like his contemporary in the United States, John F. Kennedy, part of his appeal undoubtedly lies in his style and charisma. But when the occasion demanded it, he exerted forceful leadership. At the same time he was not doctrinaire and appreciated the value of compromise. Yielding to appeals and petitions, he made it a point to pardon muralist Siqueiros at the end of his term. Almost as soon as he left office he suffered a severe stroke and lay in a coma for six years until his death in 1970. He was eulogized as a nationalist who defended Mexican

---

1. Pablo González Casanova, *Democracy in Mexico* (New York, 1970), p. 194.

interests in the world community and a humane statesman who appreciated the concerns of the powerless masses at home. It is not difficult to agree on both counts. Yet new tensions lay just below the surface.

Mexico was not alone in the tumultuous world of the 1960s. Modernization in general, and communications technology in particular, interlaced nations and dramatically shrank the globe. Word of Martin Luther King's assassination reached Angola only minutes after it reached Atlanta, and Robert Kennedy's assassination was known in São Paulo almost as soon as it was known in San Francisco. By the end of the 1960s the entire literate world knew that the United States had dropped a greater tonnage of bombs on Vietnam than the total dropped on all fronts during World War II. Massive marches for peace, for civil rights, and for the right of agricultural workers to organize were reported on the front pages of the world's press.

Mexicans in their living rooms, watching the evening news, saw the destruction of the black ghetto in Washington, the burning of Watts, and riots in Tokyo, Prague, and Berlin; they saw Parisian students pelting police on the Boulevard St. Michel and the senseless killing of students at Kent State University. While the late 1960s did not witness any worldwide conspiracy of the young, there was a youthful commonality of interests that transcended national borders. The international pantheon of heroes, with a few national adaptations, included Che Guevara, Ho Chi Minh, Malcolm X, and Mao Zedong. The intellectually inclined devoured Herbert Marcuse, while others opted for the simpler, more doctrinaire answers of Fidel Castro. Mexico was soon treated once again to the spectacle of violence.

DÍAZ ORDAZ AND POLITICAL DISCONTENT, 1964–70

When the PRI leadership chose Gustavo Díaz Ordaz as the presidential candidate for 1964, it badly misread the temper of the times. Díaz Ordaz had served as secretary of interior in the López Mateos cabinet and was badly tinged with policy decisions that reform-minded groups could not stomach. It had been he who applied the laws of "social dissolution" against David Alfaro Siqueiros and other radicals. Born in Puebla, Díaz Ordaz was reputed to be the most conservative official party candidate of the twentieth century. But after winning the election by the customary official party margin, he pledged to carry out the policies initiated by his predecessor.

The electoral reform law that provided for minority representation in the lower house was interpreted to allow the seating of several minority parties in addition to the PAN—the PPS and, although it did not quite reach 2.5 percent of the vote, the Partido Auténtico de la

Revolución Mexicana (PARM). But the PAN, the only genuine opposition party, received a very unfavorable ruling in the congressional elections. The congressional seats they actually won from PRI candidates would now be subtracted from the total of twenty they were allowed under the constitutional amendment. The decision represented a rejection of the liberalizing tendency, and the trend continued with the sad and disappointing case of Carlos Madrazo.

Shortly after coming to office, President Díaz Ordaz appointed Madrazo, a reform-minded liberal, to be president of the PRI. Championing a series of far-reaching innovations designed to promote internal democratization of the party, increase rank-and-file participation, reduce the vast power of local and state bosses, and bring more women into the organization, he ran headlong into the vested interests. In the spring of 1965, when Madrazo introduced new reforms designed to purify nomination procedures at the local level, the state political machines rose up in rebellion and convinced Díaz Ordaz to fire him. Then, when PAN candidates won the mayoralties of Tijuana and Mexicali in Baja California Norte, the government annulled the elections because of "irregularities." Opposition leaders charged that the PRI was stealing elections with total impunity.

THE OLYMPIC GAMES AND TLATELOLCO

Discontent with the official party spread. Campus after campus exploded with strikes and violence as local university issues merged with national political unrest. A massive strike at the National University in the spring of 1966 resulted in the resignation of the rector. Federal troops were dispatched to restore order on university campuses in Michoacán and Sonora. A major showdown was about to ensue and the students picked their time very carefully. Mexico was planning its greatest extravaganza since the centennial celebrations of 1910.

The International Olympic Committee accepted Mexico's bid to host the summer games in 1968, making it the first Latin American and developing country to have this "honor." Athletes, trainers, representatives of the press, and hundreds of thousands of visitors from the entire world would descend on Mexico and subject it to scrutiny. Construction of athletic facilities, hotels, housing projects, tourist facilities, and a new modern subway system preceded the games, and, amid some amazement, construction workers on round-the-clock shifts finished the major installations on time. To add a unique flavor to the international sports spectacular, a cultural Olympics was scheduled simultaneously, featuring international art exhibitions, book displays, lectures, concerts, and plays. Early charges from critics that the costs were

One of the most modern subways in the world, the Mexico City system was running to capacity and beyond within a few months of its completion. In 1990, more than 5 million Mexico City passengers were using the 87 miles of the metro's double tracks every day. Plans to add an additional 37 miles of track were canceled because of financial exigencies.

Excavation for the subway uncovered hundreds of priceless pre-Columbian artifacts.

exorbitant for a country such as Mexico were fended off by administration spokesmen who argued that not only would the visitors leave behind tens of millions of dollars but the facilities themselves would be put to good use once the Olympic torch was extinguished. The country, they insisted, would show itself as a prosperous and stable republic.

The trouble began almost innocently in July 1968 with a fight between the students of two Mexico City schools, a college preparatory school and a nearby vocational school. The principal of the high school called for police help, and the mayor of the Federal District, General Alfonso Corona del Rosal, erred badly in sending out the *granaderos*, a despised paramilitary riot force. The granaderos stopped the intramural fight but in the process politicized a large portion of the student population in Mexico City. A few days later, as leftist students gathered to celebrate the July 26 anniversary of the Cuban Revolution, they met the granaderos again, and on this occasion a full-scale street riot ensued. But nobody had yet been killed.

August 1968 was a very bad month in Mexico. As city workers were putting the finishing touches on the various construction projects, tensions between the students and the government reached the breaking point. Huge demonstrations were held on the campuses of the National University and the National Polytechnic Institute, and a National Student Strike Committee was formed. A list of demands accentuated tensions; students insisted that all political prisoners be released, that the chief of police be fired, that the granaderos be disbanded, and that the law of "social dissolution" be repealed. Secretary of Interior Luis Echeverría agreed to enter into private discussions with the student leadership, but when the students demanded that the dialogue be broadcast publicly on radio and television, negotiations broke down. On August 27 the National Student Strike Committee brought together in the Zócalo an estimated half a million people, the largest organized antigovernment demonstration in Mexican history. The rally lasted well into the night, and when the government moved tanks and armored cars into the downtown area, violence and the first verified student death resulted.

Under pressure and with the Olympic games fast approaching, Díaz Ordaz took a hard line. Refusing to address student concerns, he stepped up security. In the middle of September, with the capital bedecked with Olympic flags and signs of welcome and the students occupying the campus of the National University, Díaz Ordaz ordered ten thousand army troops, in full battle dress, to seize the campus. Some five hundred demonstrators were thrown into jail, and the new rector of the university, Javier Barros Sierra, resigned in protest of the army occupation of his campus. For two weeks, bands of disgruntled students and other malcontents who were in no way associated with the university roamed Mexico City streets, periodically seizing and burning buses, barricading streets, and pillaging. The climax came on October 2, 1968, at a place that will not be forgotten in Mexican history—Tlatelolco.

Strike organizers called for still another outdoor rally at the Plaza de las Tres Culturas in the District of Tlatelolco. The purpose was to berate the government for its failure to comply with the earlier demands. The rally was not large by recent standards, perhaps only five thousand, including many women, children, and innocent spectators who lived nearby. The speeches were emotional, but the demonstration was peaceful. At about 6:30 P.M., army and police units arrived in tanks and armored vehicles. When the demonstrators failed to disband as ordered, the granaderos moved in and began to disperse them with billy clubs and tear gas. The government's version of what happened, carried the next day in the Mexican press, claimed that terrorists in nearby apart-

ment buildings began firing on the police. Others insisted that the police opened fire first and that only then did snipers in the buildings
begin to shoot. At any rate, when the army units uncovered their high-
caliber machine guns and other automatic weapons, thousands of innocent people were caught in the cross fire. Helicopters dropped flares
into the crowds, and the troops, opting not to err on the side of safety,
sprayed indiscriminately from short range. Official government statistics admitted first eight, then eighteen, and finally forty-three deaths,
but few knowledgeable Mexicans accepted mortality figures under three
or four hundred. Ambulances wailed through the night as hospitals and
clinics filled beyond capacity with the wounded and dying. By the next
morning, Mexico City jails held over two thousand new prisoners. One
has only to recall the trauma that engulfed the United States after Kent
State, a tragedy of much lesser proportion, to appreciate the anger and
despair that Mexicans felt as the story was gradually pieced together
over the next few days. But despair quickly gave way to recriminations
as Carlos Madrazo attributed the killings to police brutality. The decision had been a political one, and it greatly altered public perception
of the country's leadership.[2]

The Olympic Games themselves were notably free of turbulence,
and it appeared that the violence had spent itself. The year that followed was a period of reflection for many Mexicans. But in October
1969, on the anniversary of the tragedy at Tlatelolco, Mexicans became
aware that urban guerrilla groups had been planning to renew their
fight with the administration. Terrorist bombs ripped newspaper offices and government buildings. It was a bad omen as Díaz Ordaz
neared the end of his term. The fire of Tlatelolco had been largely extinguished, but social smoldering would continue to choke the country for years. It would become increasingly apparent that much of the
PRI's legitimacy had been eroded at the Plaza de las Tres Culturas.

Díaz Ordaz had fostered a number of important social and economic
programs during his tenure as president. Federal expenditure for education reached over 26 percent of the total budget, one of the highest
rates in the entire world. Urban renewal projects in the northern border cities catered to the tourist trade, and tourists left record amounts
of money in Ciudad Juárez, Tijuana, Nogales, Piedras Negras, and Matamoros. The economy remained healthy, registering 6 percent annual

---

2. Information made public in December 2001 suggested strongly that the violence
   was orchestrated and conducted by a special government security force known as
   the Olympic Battalion. Although all three branches of the Mexican government
   took steps to facilitate open investigation of the incident, very little has been done
   to bring closure or justice to the issue.

The Plaza de las Tres Culturas, a tourist attraction for thousands, became a battleground for hundreds in October 1968. Courtesy of James W. Wilkie.

increases in the gross national product. Mexico took the lead in international conferences, securing pledges that Latin America should be declared a nuclear-free zone. Under other circumstances, Díaz Ordaz might have been remembered for these accomplishments, but, just as the administration of Richard M. Nixon will be remembered less for finally extricating the United States from Vietnam than for the shame of Watergate, the names of Díaz Ordaz and his successor will always be associated with the unpardonable tragedy at Tlatelolco.

THE PRESIDENCY OF ECHEVERRÍA

The political atmosphere had not returned to normal when Mexico held its 1970 presidential election. PRI candidate Luis Echeverría had been secretary of interior during the recent Olympic trouble, and the Mexican left held him largely responsible for the government's over-reaction. With a reputation for inflexibility and intolerance, he scarcely seemed the man to foster an atmosphere of national consensus. Echeverría decided to campaign vigorously, yet he failed to capture public imagination.

During the first year of his term, President Echeverría showed himself as a man of boundless energy; he put in long hours and demanded the same of those who surrounded him. He nurtured himself on face-to-face dialogue with farmers in dusty villages and workers in urban factories. Not nearly as inflexible as portrayed, he quickly began to counter his reputation by moving to the center and then to the left. To the chagrin of the conservative business community, he began renewing initiatives in rural Mexico and even announced that perhaps industrialization had to slow down. A major emphasis was placed on extending the rural road system and rural electrification. Caught in the worldwide inflation of the early 1970s, he tried to minimize its impact on the poor by ordering rigid price controls of basic commodities; at the same time, luxury items were hit with a new tax of 10 percent, and a 15 percent surtax was added to all bills in first-class restaurants and night clubs. Echeverría even moderated his earlier lack of concern for family planning and halfway through his administration gave a cautious endorsement to birth control. But Echeverría surprised his critics most when he released the majority of Mexico's student prisoners in early 1971.

The transition from Díaz Ordaz to Luis Echeverría seemed to be going well until in late 1971 and early 1972 Mexicans learned that the violent legacy of Tlatelolco was not yet over. Paramilitaries authorized by the president attacked and killed student protesters in the summer of 1971. A series of bank robberies in the fall were traced to revolutionaries of the Movimiento Armado Revolucionario (MAR). Other robberies and political kidnappings followed: Jaime Castrejón, rector of the University of Guerrero, and Julio Hirschfield, director of the nation's airports, both fell into rebel hands. Terrance Leonhardy, United States consul general in Guadalajara, was kidnapped, as were the British honorary consul, Anthony Duncan Williams; Fernando Aranguren, a wealthy Guadalajara businessman; and Nadine Chaval, the daughter of the Belgian ambassador. A wealthy Monterrey industrialist, Eugenio Garza Sada, was killed during a kidnapping attempt, and a train carrying tourists was assaulted in southern Sonora, resulting in the deaths of four travelers. In the summer of 1974, President Echeverría's father-in-law, Guadalupe Zuno Hernández, a former governor of Jalisco, was captured and held for ransom by a group calling themselves the Fuerzas Revolucionarias Armadas del Pueblo (FRAP).

In the mountains of Guerrero, Lucio Cabañas, a flamboyant former schoolteacher, gathered a guerrilla army, had the police chief of

Luis Echeverría (b. 1922). The most active president since Cárdenas, Echeverría was interested primarily in foreign policy, but his energies were directed to the country's serious economic woes.

Acapulco assassinated, and began attacking small army outposts stationed in the state. The eyes of the nation focused on Cabañas when guerrillas under his command kidnapped Guerrero senator Rubén Figueroa, at the time a candidate for governor. Ten thousand army troops were dispatched to Guerrero to capture the guerrillas, but it took them over a year to do the job. Cabañas and twenty-seven of his men were killed in gun battles with the army, but most observers were convinced that another guerrilla leader would simply pick up his banner.

Yet despite the headlines in the morning newspapers, Mexico was not yet falling apart at the seams. Pressures were building, but Echeverría had made some public attempts to accommodate the interests of youth. He brought more young people into important positions in the government than any previous head of state. Laws lowered the voting age to eighteen and reduced the age for holding congressional office. Other administration programs should have been well received by youth. Mexico granted diplomatic asylum to Hortensia Allende, widow of the murdered Chilean president, and accepted other Chilean political refugees. In 1972 the administration nationalized the tobacco and telephone industries. Echeverría's foreign travels opened new avenues of trade and, by extension, sought to lessen dependence upon the United States. Yet all these measures were ineffectual palliatives.

Alienation had set in, and the roots went deep. To be sure, part of the problem could be attributed to the inflation rate, which topped 20 percent in both 1973 and 1974. But to ascribe the alienation simply to the rate of inflation or even to the gradual demise of Mexico's postwar economic miracle would be to miss the point. In at least one sense some of the Revolution's successes, rather than its shortcomings, contributed to the growing tensions in Mexican society as rising expectations engendered by economic and social changes were not met.

By the late 1960s and early 1970s, the young, sophisticated generation of Mexican students had absorbed an incredible amount of revolutionary rhetoric. A not untypical Sunday outing in Mexico City could include a car or taxi ride by the Monument to the Revolution and then on to Avenida 20 de Noviembre, where the book stores carried posters not of Sophia Loren and the Beatles but of Emiliano Zapata and Pancho Villa. Then, on Avenida Francisco I. Madero the walls would be plastered with billboards propagandizing the Partido Revolucionario Institucional. And on Sunday every radio station in the country was required by law to carry "La Hora Nacional," a programming dinosaur that had been born in the 1930s to help foster a national consciousness but had degenerated into blatant progovernment propaganda. It combined musical and cultural presentations with three- to four-minute orations on themes such as "The Pride of Being Mexican," "One Must Defend the Revolution," and "The March of Revolutionary Progress."

The spate of revolutionary euphemisms became more than the young intellectuals could easily accept. Disquieting everyday realities denied the easy revolutionary platitudes. And when late in his term President Echeverría attempted to address a student convocation at the National University, he was driven off the campus by an angry, rock-throwing mob. His successor would inherit a dispirited country, one in which cynicism had become a hallmark. The roots of the problem were economic, but they meshed with ideological postures and social realities to produce an unparalleled crisis of confidence.

The 1970s found Mexico suffering a large balance of payments deficit. The rate of industrial growth had been impressive, but it had rested on the foundation of government protection. Mexican industry was not cost effective and was not generally competitive in world markets. It was unable to turn the balance of payments tide. With imports outstripping exports by almost $3.5 billion in 1975 alone, Echeverría, currying Third World support in a bid for the secretary-generalship of the United Nations, ordered his ambassador in the world organization to cast two votes equating Zionism and racism. Since he had earlier made a speech comparing Yasser Arafat to Benito Juárez, the result shouldn't have surprised him. In early 1976 Jewish groups in the United States organized a tourist boycott of Mexico. Empty resort hotels dramatically testified that a substantial proportion of Mexico's tourist industry of $2.5 billion had been curtailed. Other factors, such as short-ages of electric power, steel, and transportation facilities, contributed to a decline in the rate of economic growth. Echeverría had repeat-edly lectured his citizenry on the need for democratization in Mexico and the value of a free press. As the economic situation deteriorated, however, he found himself attacked on all sides. When criticism from Mexico's largest daily newspaper, *Excélsior*, became too severe, the ad-ministration removed its editor, Julio Scherer García. By the summer of 1976, rumors were rampant that for the first time in twenty-two years Mexico would have to devalue the peso. The president's repeated assurances to the contrary did not prevent the flight of huge amounts of pesos as wealthy Mexicans exchanged their currency for dollars and investment in the United States and Europe. Capital flight in 1976 alone might have topped $6 billion. Mexican pundits quickly coined a new pejorative to deride their unpatriotic countrymen. *Sacadólares* (dollar extractors) would enter the day-to-day parlance.

The decision to devaluate came in September, and the peso fell from 12.50 to 20.50 to the dollar, a 60 percent devaluation. Once the initial shock subsided, Mexicans accepted the devaluation stoically, as they were assured that the resultant reduction of imports and growth of exports would combine to shore up the economy. But Mexican policy makers had not allowed the peso to float long enough to reach its true level. A month later a second devaluation of an additional 40 percent was announced in Mexico City. Psychologically, the second was more painful than the first, for it pointed up financial mismanagement of major proportions.

With the country still in shock, a serious old problem surfaced once again. Thousands of landless Sonora peasants moved onto privately owned lands in the rich Yaqui Valley and seized several hundred thou-sand acres from some eight hundred owners. Although the land seizures were being adjudicated in the Mexican Supreme Court, Echeverría, with not two weeks remaining in his presidential term, took matters into his own hands. He declared the seizures legal and gave the peasants 250,000 acres for communal development. The uproar could have been expected; Mexican industrialists and businessmen joined the former landowners in a huge protest strike. Using populist tactics, Echeverría tried to paper over the failure of the PRI to reform the political system and cover up his own repressive tactics.

The twelve years encompassed by the Díaz Ordaz and Echeverría administrations, 1964 to 1976, were difficult ones in Mexico's post–World War II experience. Since the onset of the institutional revolu-tion in the early 1940s, Mexican confidence had been bolstered re-peatedly by the country's political stability and remarkable economic success. Mexico seemingly had separated itself from the systemic problems of its neighbors to the south. But by 1975 and 1976, it was obvious to Mexicans and foreigners alike that the political system and economic structure had proved themselves to be quite fragile. This fragility would be severely tested in the years to come.

RECOMMENDED FOR FURTHER STUDY

Blough, William J. "Political Attitudes of Mexican Women: Support for the Political System among a Newly Enfranchised Group." *Journal of Inter-American Studies and World Affairs* 14 (1972): 201–24.

Brandenburg, Frank. *The Making of Modern Mexico*. Englewood Cliffs, N.J.: Prentice-Hall, 1964.

Carey, Elaine. *Plaza of Sacrifices: Gender, Power, and Terror in 1968 Mexico*. Albuquerque: University of New Mexico Press, 2005.

Cline, Howard F. *Mexico: Revolution to Evolution, 1940–1960*. New York: Oxford University Press, 1963.

Cochrane, James D. "Mexico's New Científicos: The Díaz Ordaz Cabinet." *Inter-American Economic Affairs* 21 (1967): 61–72.

Eckstein, Susan. *The Poverty of Revolution: The State and the Urban Poor in Mexico*. Princeton, N.J.: Princeton University Press, 1977.

Erb, Richard D., and Stanley R. Ross, eds. *U.S. Policies toward Mexico: Perceptions and Perspectives*. Washington, D.C.: American Enterprise Institute for Public Policy Research, 1979.

González Casanova, Pablo. *Democracy in Mexico*. New York: Oxford University Press, 1970.

Grindle, Merilee S. *Bureaucrats, Politicians, and Peasants in Mexico: A Case Study in Public Policy*. Berkeley: University of California Press, 1977.

Hundley, Norris, Jr. *Dividing the Waters: A Century of Controversy between the United States and Mexico*. Berkeley: University of California Press, 1966.

Johnson, Kenneth F. *Mexican Democracy: A Critical View*. Boston: Allyn and Bacon, 1971.

Liss, Sheldon. *A Century of Disagreement: The Chamizal Conflict, 1864–1964*. Washington, D.C.: University Press of Washington, D.C., 1965.

Lomnitz, Larissa Adler. *Networks and Marginality: Life in a Mexican Shantytown*. New York: Academic Press, 1977.

Ochoa, Enrique. *Feeding Mexico: The Political Uses of Food since 1910*. Wilmington, Del.: Scholarly Resources, 2000.

Paz, Octavio. *The Other Mexico: Critique of the Pyramid*. New York: Grove Press, 1972.

Poniatowska, Elena. *Massacre in Mexico*. New York: Viking Press, 1975.

Ross, Stanley, ed. *Views across the Border*. Albuquerque: University of New Mexico Press, 1978.

Schmidt, Samuel. *The Deterioration of the Mexican Presidency*. Tucson: University of Arizona Press, 1991.

Shapira, Yoram. *Mexican Foreign Policy under Echeverría*. Beverly Hills, Calif.: Sage, 1978.

Williams, Edward J. *The Rebirth of the Mexican Petroleum Industry*. Lexington, Mass.: Heath, 1979.

Womack, John, Jr. "The Spoils of the Mexican Revolution." *Foreign Affairs* 48 (1970): 677–87.

37

The Tensions of Development and Democratization, 1976–88

José López Portillo and Petropolitics

On December 1, 1976, José López Portillo, the presidential candidate of the PRI, replaced Luis Echeverría in the Mexican presidency. While a few Mexicans evidenced optimism on that inauguration day, the vast majority found little cause for celebration. Sixty-six years had passed since Francisco Madero's Plan de San Luis Potosí, but many believed that the same old problems had emerged once again.

Prior to the famous Arab oil embargo in the early 1970s, the world thought little about energy, conservation, or the influence of petroleum and petroleum by-products on inflation and power politics. But these issues dominated the national and international press in the late 1970s and early 1980s. In some circles it became archaic to speak of the First, Second, and Third worlds. It seemed more appropriate to categorize nations as oil producers and oil consumers, and this, in turn, necessitated new conceptualizations of dependency and interdependency.

The large petroleum discoveries made in southeastern Mexico (primarily in the states of Tabasco and Chiapas and offshore in the Gulf of Mexico) antedated the inauguration of President José López Portillo in 1976, but their extent and influence grew markedly during his administration and came to overshadow everything else. The figures for proven and probable reserves have varied tremendously since the discoveries were first announced in 1974. But in 1980, López Portillo verified that proven reserves topped sixty billion barrels, while probable reserves approached two hundred billion.

From the outset, López Portillo followed a policy of gradual, not dramatic, daily increase. Although Mexico had the necessary capital and technology to increase production with great rapidity, it resisted pressures from the United States and other foreign powers to do so. The economic infrastructure was not prepared to digest suddenly huge infusions of foreign capital without negative side effects. More im-

MEXICAN OIL ZONES (Including Off-shore)

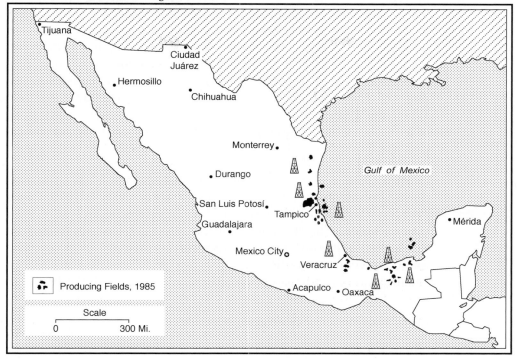

portantly, it then seemed obvious that the price of petroleum in the future was not going to decline. Oil production rose steadily but sensibly during the López Portillo years, growing from about 800,000 barrels per day in 1976 to 2.3 million barrels a day in 1980. In 1981 Mexico became the world's fourth largest producer. The tripling of production during the administration did not reveal the whole story of how petroleum influenced the Mexican economy. For two reasons, Mexico's earning of petrodollars rose much more rapidly than the increased production figures would seem to suggest. First, a large percentage of the increase was destined for the international, not the domestic, market. Even more important was the steadily spiraling price of a barrel of crude. During the same period that production tripled, earnings from petroleum sales increased twelvefold, from $500 million in 1976 to about $6 billion in 1980. Prospects for a healthy and dynamic economy never looked better.

Mexican petroleum wealth had an incalculable impact on how the country viewed itself and how it related to others in the international community. In an energy-hungry world, petroleum production carried unusual international prestige. Mexico's new oil muscle was flexed repeatedly in its relations with the United States. Standing up to Washington and Wall Street, even in the face of threats, was nothing new in the history of the Mexican Revolution. What was different was the self-assurance Mexico carried into the international arena. In a dramatic but symbolic gesture, López Portillo was one of the first Latin American heads of state to announce that his country could not support the Carter administration's boycott of the Moscow Olympics. When the United States and Mexico could not agree on the price of natural gas, the Mexican president brazenly decided to burn off excess gas rather than sell to the United States at a figure judged to be inequitable.

Mexico's new international posture was most graphically displayed during President Carter's goodwill visit to Mexico City in 1979. López Portillo, who thoroughly enjoyed his political vogue and who never tired of berating his northern neighbor, used the occasion to chastise the United States for its historical record in Mexico, to criticize his guest for being insensitive to Mexican dignity, and to warn Carter against "surprise moves or sudden deceits." The new administration of

GROWTH OF THE MEXICAN PETROLEUM INDUSTRY

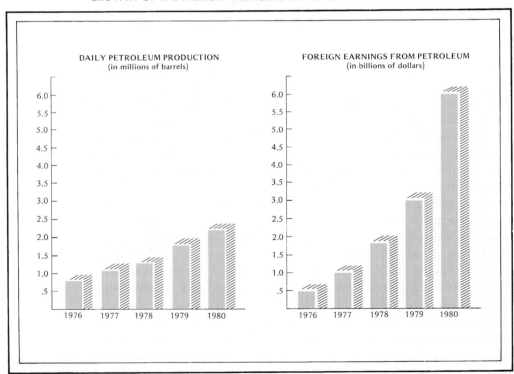

DAILY PETROLEUM PRODUCTION
(in millions of barrels)

FOREIGN EARNINGS FROM PETROLEUM
(in billions of dollars)

Ronald Reagan quickly learned that outward manifestations of friendship and goodwill would not change Mexico's foreign policy. In 1981 Mexico joined France in a declaration recognizing rebel guerrillas in El Salvador as a representative political force. These incidents were less a new hostility than were they a reflection of the new petroleum equation in United States–Mexico relations.

Only the most naïve considered petroleum a panacea for Mexico's sundry social and economic problems, but few realized the dangers that petro-dependency portended for the future. The first indications of trouble were faint and subtle. By the late 1970s, López Portillo was faced with an unemployment rate of almost 25 percent and an underemployment rate of almost 50 percent of the country's work force. Petroleum was a capital-intensive, not a labor-intensive industry. With continuing increased production it could absorb perhaps 150,000 new workers each year, but by 1980, 800,000 Mexicans were entering the job market annually. Jobs would have to be created in other sectors of the economy.

Industry maintained healthy growth during the López Portillo administration, but agricultural production could not keep pace with the increase in population. Fearful that the newly found petrodollars could all be expended on food imports, in March 1980 the president announced the formation of Sistema Alimentario Mexicano (SAM), the Mexican Food System. SAM's goals called for agricultural growth of 4 percent a year and self-sufficiency in basic grains by 1985. A few months after SAM was proclaimed, the World Bank approved a loan of $325 million, the largest loan that agency had ever made, to help implement the program. Increased agricultural production not only promised to improve the standard of living in rural areas, but by eliminating the need for huge food imports would greatly improve Mexico's unfavorable balance of trade. The goals were certainly sound, but the success rate fell short of spectacular. Several years after López Portillo left office, Mexico was still importing about 10 million tons of food annually, and the crisis in the agricultural sector spurred increased immigration to the cities.

Mexico's 1980 census, conducted two-thirds through the López Portillo administration, revealed one very promising trend. In the early postwar years, the percentage of illiterates in Mexico was constantly reduced, but because of the population explosion, the absolute number of illiterates rose. The 1980 census documented not only a decline in the percentage of illiterates from 28 percent in 1970 to 17.1 percent in 1980, but a drop of 1.5 million in the absolute number of illiterates. The education efforts of all the postwar administrations had finally left their mark.

Between 1980 and 1982, Presidents José López Portillo and Ronald Reagan met on four occasions. The public cordiality of the visits notwithstanding, the two countries found it difficult to agree on important issues such as undocumented workers and the revolutionary turmoil in Central America.

THE ECONOMIC SLIDE BEGINS

López Portillo led Mexico on an unparalleled spending spree. Government construction, public works, social welfare projects, and government subsidies of consumer goods all meant an increased government participation in the economy. The number of state-owned enterprises quadrupled during the Echeverría and López Portillo administrations. Although national income was insufficient to cover the costs, Mexico's vast petroleum reserves made the international banking community willing, indeed eager, to extend large loans. Understandably the interest rates were appallingly high and repayment would burden subsequent administrations. Mexico's massive deficit spending was predicated on the supposition that continuing rises in the price of oil would allow the country to generate new wealth and repay its foreign obligations. But contrary to all expectations, petroleum prices did not rise. Because of the world oil glut of the early 1980s, they began to decline. López Portillo was forced to retreat from his assertive foreign policy and adopt a more moderate stance.

In 1982, during the last year of his administration, López Portillo found himself in a position even worse than that of Luis Echeverría in 1976. The Mexican rate of inflation greatly exceeded that in the United States, and the peso was again overvalued in relation to the dollar. As Mexican businessmen lost confidence in the economy, they began investing abroad and opening new bank accounts in the United States. To stop the monetary flight, in February the president ordered the Central Bank to stop buying and selling dollars and to allow the peso to find its true worth. Within a few days, it had lost one-third of its former value as it slipped from twenty-six to thirty-seven pesos to the dollar, and by summer of 1982 had sunk to one hundred pesos, marking the peso's lowest value ever. Concomitant price increases and tight currency controls created near panic in both business and government circles. It was only the tip of the iceberg.

In the last analysis, López Portillo applied the brakes too late, after he had first tried to squander Mexico into prosperity. The oil miracle had become the oil nightmare, and the president came under severe fire for mishandling the economy and demonstrating a lack of judgment and leadership. His response was unanticipated as he accused the country's private banks of looting, greed, and disloyalty for participating in the frenzied flight of Mexican capital in the amount of $22 billion. He had found a perfect scapegoat. In September 1982, without first soliciting any advice from his cabinet, the president dramatically nationalized fifty-nine of the country's banks. The nationalization of the banks was no economic elixir. Many of them were in bad financial shape and assuming their burden was like putting chains on the national economy. The presidential action proved only that clear thinking seldom accompanies clenched fists.

As López Portillo's administration came to an end, Mexicans were incensed to learn that the president, despite his pious incantations about others, had taken care of himself. Failing to keep one eye on history he had constructed four large mansions for himself and his family on prime land. The López Portillo compound was dubbed "Dog Hill," a sarcastic reminder of the president's earlier remarks that he would defend the peso "like a dog." As he departed Mexico for an extended vacation in Europe, he left behind Mexico's worst economic crisis of the twentieth century.

MIGUEL DE LA MADRID: FROM CRISIS TO CRISIS, 1982–88

When forty-seven-year-old Miguel de la Madrid was told that he had won the Mexican presidency, he reportedly quipped to a friend,

"Fraud, fraud!" If he did repeat those words, one could scarcely have blamed him. He faced the sobering prospect of inheriting the leadership of a country beset with economic problems so serious that they threatened to disrupt the social order.

Educated at the Universidad Nacional Autónoma de México and subsequently at Harvard University, Miguel de la Madrid's rise to his country's highest office was nothing short of meteoric. Despite his relative youth, his formal education and previous experience in public administration prepared him better for the tasks that lay ahead than most of his twentieth-century predecessors. He had campaigned on a firm pledge of moral renovation, a promise to eliminate the corruption so endemic in the Mexican public sector. Those who accused him of political posturing were proven wrong. During his first year in office, revelations of corruption during the administration of López Portillo were carried in the front pages of the press almost on a daily basis. Although President de la Madrid did not prosecute his predecessor, he did strike out against other high-ranking government officials. In one spectacular case, Jorge Díaz Serrano, the former director of PEMEX, was indicted for embezzlement of $43 million. Serrano was convicted and sentenced to a ten-year jail term. Even more outrageous were the alleged crimes of Arturo Durazo, Mexico City's chief of police and a friend of López Portillo since childhood. "El Negro Durazo" was charged with fifty murders, trafficking in drugs, and extortion of superlative proportions. His

Elected in July 1982, Miguel de la Madrid succeeded López Portillo as president. He recognized that he would face difficult times but could not have predicted that the country was on the verge of economic collapse.

luxurious residence in the coastal resort of Zihuatanejo was nicknamed "The Parthenon," to which it bore some resemblance. His palatial home near Mexico City came complete with its own discotheque, modeled after New York City's famous Studio 54. Weekend guests, flown to the $2.5 million estate in police helicopters, marvelled at Durazo's string of race horses, nineteen collector's automobiles, casino, gymnasium, and cellar of vintage wines. Not even the most shrewd businessmen, they opined, could have accumulated this kind of fortune on a government salary of $65 per week. But Durazo escaped prosecution by fleeing the country prior to the order for his arrest; after legal delays he was finally extradited in 1986 and subsequently convicted.

The president received his share of accolades for his two highly publicized victories against the egregious dishonesty of Díaz Serrano and Durazo, but there was little euphoria as Mexicans knew that the battle against governmental malfeasance had scarcely been won. The country's comptroller general synopsized the issue perfectly when he stated that Mexican corruption was like garbage: it had to be removed daily.

An equally persistent dilemma was the country's deepening economic crisis. The peso began to slip against the dollar in 1984 and then began a veritable plunge on the free market. Many stood in disbelief as it plummeted from 150 to 200, and then to 380 to the dollar during the summer of 1985, but the bottom had not been reached. By autumn 1986, currency houses and money brokers along the United States–Mexico border were exchanging the peso at an incredible 800 to 1. The year 1987 was even more catastrophic for the peso. When the year opened it took 950 pesos to purchase a dollar, but by December the exchange rate was an incredible 2,300 to 1. The relationship between the two countries' currencies was so out of kilter in the summer of 1987 that a U.S. tourist could ride the Mexico City metro over two thousand times for one dollar or make ten thousand calls on a pay phone for the same amount.

Mexico's foreign debt under Miguel de la Madrid grew in geometric proportion. Although the president was able to arrange a rescheduling of payments on the debt, the pressure on him was tremendous. Political parties, peasant groups, and labor unions of the left, following the lead of Cuba's Fidel Castro, urged him to repudiate the debt or at a minimum to declare a unilateral moratorium on repayment. De la Madrid agreed that the interest rates being paid on Mexico's debt were excessive, but he did realize the necessity of rekindling some degree of confidence in the world's banking community and financial markets. He opted for economic austerity, not repudiation. It was a calculated risk: asking Mexico's beleaguered poor to tighten their belts once again was asking them to accept their miserable squalor.

In late 1987 when it took 11,500 20-centavo pieces to buy one U.S. dollar, Mexicans simply refused to carry the hefty coin. Enterprising owners of hardware stores in Sonora devised an imaginative solution. Not concerned about defacing national currency they drilled holes in the middle of the coins and found brisk business in the good quality washers.

Recognizing that government expenditures had to be drastically reduced, de la Madrid not only curtailed many new projects but also announced reductions in federal subsidies, the sale of inefficient and unprofitable state-owned enterprises, and a freeze on federal employment. Using the considerable influence of the presidential office, he did his best to limit the size of wage increases in the labor force, and he eliminated thousands of federal jobs. The economic reforms were the beginning of a process that would subsequently burgeon under the rubric of neoliberalism. The shift in economic orientation seemed to be paying dividends, for in late 1984 the international banking community not only applauded his efforts but indicated that Mexico was dealing with the debt crisis more effectively than any other Latin American country.

Then, suddenly, tragedy struck during the morning rush hour on September 19, 1985, as Mexico paid the price of sitting at the juncture of three of the earth's tectonic plates. An earthquake registering in excess of 8 on the Richter Scale devastated the capital, leaving more than eight thousand dead, many more injured, and damage estimated at $4 billion. This latest test for the Mexican citizenry was met with many grassroots organizations to deal with the crisis, but the calamity made payments on the foreign debt impossible. Nonetheless, many analysts believe that the earthquake served as a catalyst for the birth

Damage in Mexico City was extensive, and the clean-up task monumental, after the earthquake of September 19, 1985.

of a vigorous civil society in Mexico. A plethora of groups began to advocate for women's and indigenous rights as well as affordable housing and environmental protections.

The last years of the de la Madrid administration saw Mexico slip deeper and deeper into the economic morass. In addition to the collapse of the peso, inflation soared to unprecedented heights. Official inflation rates, released by Mexico's Central Bank, reported 63.7 percent in 1985, 105.7 percent in 1986, and 159 percent in 1987. The person on the street swore that the actual figures were even higher. Increases in the cost of gasoline, corn, wheat, and electricity led the assault on the consumer price index, but no product or service emerged unscathed. The only thing that could match the rapid rise in prices was the rapid growth of the foreign debt. When de la Madrid left office in December 1988, the Mexican government owed foreigners a whopping $105 billion in outstanding debts.

UNITED STATES–MEXICO RELATIONS

Two major problems defying easy solution dominated United States–Mexico relations in the 1970s and 1980s. Both of them concerned movement across the common border, and both of them had national significance that transcended the international line that divides the two countries.

Since the 1950s, the United States–Mexico border region has witnessed one of the most profound demographic shifts in world history not conditioned by either war or epidemic disease. The result of a high birthrate and massive northern migration in Mexico and the equally telling Sunbelt phenomenon in the United States, the population soared unremittingly on both sides of the border. In 1940, only about 16 million persons occupied the four U.S. states and six Mexican states that share the international line. At the beginning of 1990, the estimated population of the same ten states was over sixty million. The swell has been so dramatic that it not only dominates day-to-day human relations of the region but drives international relations as well. The border between the countries is permeable, and not only to people. Disease, polluted water, contaminated air, to cite but a few examples, refuse to respect the artificial line drawn by nineteenth-century politicians to ratify the work of nineteenth-century generals.

Of the major problems growing out of a common international boundary, the most protracted one is that of the undocumented worker. Beginning in the 1970s unemployment, underemployment, persistent poverty, and the undeniable lure of the United States prompted hun-

During most of the post–World War II period, for young and old alike, the chain-link boundary line separating Nogales, Arizona, from Nogales, Sonora, was little more than a daily inconvenience. In 1995, however, United States military troops replaced the chain link with heavy corrugated metal, seeking to make the border more impenetrable. The same process was repeated in town after town along the common border.

dreds of thousands of Mexican workers to cross the border illegally into the United States each year in pursuit of gainful employment. The number of undocumented workers in the United States has grown every year.

The undocumented worker phenomenon is an emotion-charged topic that has precipitated much national and international debate. Everyone agrees that the United States has the right to enforce its immigration laws and to regulate entries into the country. But there is no consensus on precisely what should be done and how.

Realistic solutions have been complicated by the fact that an undocumented worker mythology is current in the United States and is nurtured by vested interest groups. Contrary to popular opinion, the undocumented workers do not constitute a drain on social services. The best evidence suggests forcefully that most of them have federal and state taxes deducted from their wages but do not reap the benefits of the tax system for fear of being detected and reported to immigration authorities. In reality, undocumented workers subsidize social services and use them only infrequently. Equally evident is the myth that a great many displace United States workers and in a major way contribute to unemployment north of the international boundary.

Undoubtedly some United States workers have been displaced, but the large majority of the undocumented fill positions that would remain vacant at wage levels falling below minimum scale. It is true that because many undocumented workers will accept jobs below the minimum wage they tend to depress the labor market. For this reason, a broad spectrum of labor organizations in the United States began calling for tighter controls while an equally broad spectrum of employers, in both rural and urban areas, favored the maintenance of the status quo.

A solution of sorts was reached in 1986 when the United States Congress passed the Immigration Reform and Control Act (the Simpson-Rodino Act). The main features of the legislation provided for a tighter enforcement of immigration policy, sanctions against those who knowingly employed undocumented workers, and an amnesty for those workers who could establish continued residence in the United States since 1982. But Simpson-Rodino did not solve the undocumented worker problem because it addressed only those factors that pulled the Mexican workers toward the United States, ignoring those that pushed them out of Mexico. The undocumented continued to come, albeit in smaller numbers, as there was no shortage of United States employers willing to offer work despite threatened sanctions. The fundamental problems remained. In 1989, Jorge Bustamante, Mexico's leading border specialist, reported that earnings sent back to Mexico by undocumented workers totaled $1.25 billion annually, making this source of income the country's third largest source of foreign exchange.

If Mexican workers were performing useful labor, if they were able to earn money with which to support their families, if they were not contributing in a major way to unemployment in the United States, and if they did not constitute a burden on social services, why were they considered to be a problem? The answer in part rests with the plight of the undocumented workers themselves as revealed in the countless human tragedies that occur each year. Crossing the border illegally immediately converts a law-abiding citizen into a fugitive from justice with no protection from the varied forms of human exploitation. Those Mexicans, called *coyotes*, who contract with individual workers for surreptitious entry and transportation to a job have been known to collect their fees and deliver their human cargo to U.S. immigration authorities. United States employers have been known to set up two-week pay periods, and, after receiving thirteen days of labor from an entire work force, call in the border patrol, thus relieving themselves of the need to meet the payroll. In the Southwest, groups of vigilantes have taken "law enforcement" into their own hands and have terrorized and physically brutalized workers hungry for jobs as object lessons to those who would follow them. Unintended tragedies also abound as many undocumented workers have died in the scorching heat of border crossings.

The second problem that plagued the generally good relations between Washington, D.C., and Mexico, D.F., and that contributed to a politically charged atmosphere, was the unremitting flow of drugs across the United States–Mexico border. The smuggling of contraband between the two countries certainly was nothing new. Arms and ammunition, automobiles, trucks, agricultural equipment, household items, and scores of other products had long evaded the eyes, regulations, and taxing authority of the customs agents. What made the problem so volatile in the late 1980s was the especially insidious nature of the illegal cargo. The international drug traffic, both sides agreed, not only left its legacy of abuse and dependence, but also fostered an entire host of parasitic crimes, especially in the border region. Authorities from the two countries, however, agreed on little else. The public was soon treated to the most bizarre misapplication of the theories of the Scottish economist Adam Smith: United States officials found the problem to be simply one of supply, while their Mexican counterparts retorted that it was simply one of demand.

Following the murder of U.S. Drug Enforcement Administrative agent Enrique Camarena near Guadalajara, in 1986 and 1987 the United States Congress held formal hearings on terrorism and drugs. These hearings prompted the most intemperate statements on Mexico's alleged lack of cooperation on the drug issue despite indications to the contrary from the United States ambassador in Mexico City. By 1988, Mexico-bashing had become a favorite pastime of those who could think of no other reasons for the United States failure to win its much publicized war on drugs. In that year, the U.S. Senate failed to certify Mexico for economic assistance, because it was not doing enough to intercept the flow of drugs before they crossed the border.

As Mexico was about the enter the last decade of the twentieth century, a steadily increasing number of its citizens had become disillusioned with pervasive corruption and with politics as usual. They were not quite ready to reject the official party. Investing in change, they knew, is not without risk. The PRI had, after all, made peace a reality and had scored a series of victories in the social field. But by the 1970s and 1980s the pace of change had slowed so noticeably that even some of the most loyal PRI devotees had become frustrated and had begun calling for the party to strike out on a bold new course, even if they were unsure where the path might lead. Together with fellow Mexicans of the opposition parties they would have an answer sooner than anticipated.

RECOMMENDED FOR FURTHER STUDY

Brannon, Jeffrey, and Eric N. Baklanoff, *Agrarian Reform and Public Enterprise in Mexico: The Political Economy of Yucatán's Henequen Industry*. University: University of Alabama Press, 1987.

Castañeda, Jorge G., and Robert A. Pastor. *Limits to Friendship: The United States and Mexico*. New York: Alfred A. Knopf, 1988.

Domínguez, Jorge I., ed. *Mexico's Political Economy: Challenges at Home and Abroad*. Beverly Hills, Calif.: Sage, 1982.

García-Gorena, Velma. *Mothers and the Mexican Antinuclear Power Movement*. Tucson: University of Arizona Press, 1999.

Gentleman, Judith, ed. *Mexican Politics in Transition*. Boulder, Colo.: Westview Press, 1987.

Grayson, George W. *Oil and Mexican Foreign Policy*. Pittsburgh, Pa.: University of Pittsburgh Press, 1988.

Hellman, Judith Adler. *Mexico in Crisis*. New York: Holmes and Meier, 1983.

Levy, Daniel, and Gabriel Székely. *Mexico: Paradoxes of Stability and Change*. Boulder, Colo.: Westview Press, 1983.

Martínez, Oscar J. *Troublesome Border*. Tucson: University of Arizona Press, 1988.

Purcell, Susan Kaufman. *Mexico in Transition: Implications for U.S. Policy*. New York: Council on Foreign Relations, 1988.

Reynolds, Clark W., and Robert K. McCleery. "The Political Economy of Immigration Law: Impact of Simpson-Rodino on the United States and Mexico." *Journal of Economic Perspectives* 2 (1988): 117–31.

Riding, Alan. *Distant Neighbors: Portrait of the Mexicans*. New York: Knopf, 1985.

Smith, Peter. *Mexico: The Quest for a United States Policy*. New York: Foreign Policy Association, 1980.

Velasco-S., Agustín. *Impacts of Mexican Oil Policy on Economic and Political Development*. Lexington, Mass.: Lexington Books, 1983.

38

Mexico since 1988

THE ELECTIONS OF 1988 AND MEXICAN DEMOCRATIZATION

The 1980s were a decade of democratization or redemocratization throughout much of Latin America. In most of the region, this phenomenon meant replacing military dictatorships with civilian governments chosen in an open or a relatively open electoral process. In Mexico, democratization was something very different. The army had ceased to call the political shots in Mexican politics decades earlier. Democratization in Mexico meant opening up the political system, recognizing that it had systemic weaknesses, and making it more responsive to the Mexican citizenry. The process was so far from innocuous, for it meant that the influential political bosses in the country would have to share their power with others.

The basic problem was not new to the 1980s. Because of Mexico's unique twentieth-century experience, one political party had gained almost absolute dominance. This official party, under different names, had won every election for president and every election for the thirty-one governorships since 1929. If an occasional member of an opposition party could be found occupying a seat in the national Congress, it was probably not because he or she had won a congressional race but because Mexico's electoral law permitted the seating of a limited number of defeated candidates based on the percentage of votes cast for their respective parties in the last election. Mexican democracy had become increasingly diluted and deformed. For most, presidential elections were little more than a tiring ritual.

As the official party became almost synonymous with the government, and thus commanded huge resources as well as incredible patronage, elections became a farce. Mexico's democracy was a one-party system in which the citizens, for all practical purposes, were denied the element of choice, the most fundamental democratic right of all. The most influential television news program in the country, Televisa's "Twenty-Four Hours," hosted for almost three decades by newscaster

Jacobo Zabludovsky, supported PRI and the government through thick and thin. Similarly, much of the print press exhibited little independence. *Excélsior*, a newspaper that had been founded with the Revolution in 1917, gradually lost public confidence for its timid approach to government criticism, even when official scandals begged for full disclosure. Regular "subsidies" to its directors presumably account for such unbecoming journalistic reticence.

In the 1980s, several opposition parties (conservative in the north and leftist in the south), capitalizing on increasing dissatisfaction with the performance of the official party, began to score some modest victories in state and local elections. With some regularity, the official party overturned the electoral results and had its own candidates installed in office. In this process, the PRI began to lose its sense of legitimacy. Even more significant were the proliferating civil society groups—nongovernmental organizations that had turned away from the Mexican state to deal with a host of political and social issues. The growing challenges to the system were clearly evident in the presidential elections of 1988.

The conservative position was articulated by the PAN and its presidential candidate, Manuel Clouthier, a millionaire industrialist. Clouthier ran on a platform calling for a closer relationship with the United States, a more limited role for the government in the economy, a more vigorous private sector, and of course, an end to electoral fraud by the PRI. The leftist opposition came from Cuauhtémoc Cárdenas, the son of former president Lázaro Cárdenas and a former PRI governor of Michoacán. Cárdenas, who had harbored presidential ambitions for some time, broke with the official party over the issue of how presidential candidates were chosen as well as the question of the extent to which Mexico would have to adhere to neoliberal economics. He ran on the Frente Democrático Nacional, a coalition that was able to temporarily unite a broad spectrum of leftist parties. Cárdenas agreed with Clouthier on one platform plank—the need to bring an end to the PRI's electoral fraud—but differed sharply on other issues. He called for greater independence from the United States and indicated that if elected he would declare a moratorium on the repayment of Mexico's gigantic foreign debt.

The PRI candidate, Carlos Salinas de Gortari, was the epitome of the successful technocrat. He had earned a doctorate in economics from Harvard University and in the de la Madrid cabinet was secretary of planning and budget. Never having served in elective office, however, he was unaccustomed to political campaigning, and his effort in this regard was lackadaisical. For the first time in recent memory, the press gave extensive coverage to the opposition. Election day was a surprise even to the most astute political observers. The elec-

MEXICAN PRESIDENTIAL ELECTIONS, 1958–88:
PRI CANDIDATES' PERCENTAGE OF VOTES

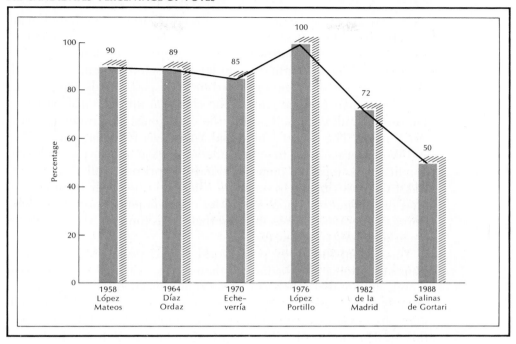

tion was close enough for all three candidates to claim victory. Salinas ultimately was declared the winner in an election many Mexicans believe was stolen from Cárdenas, but his was the worst showing of an official party candidate since 1929. The political stock of PRI had fallen so precipitously that Salinas barely received a majority of the votes cast. The notion of a credible opposition was no longer a whimsical delusion.

The democratizing process continued during the gubernatorial elections of 1989. In an electoral result that shocked everyone, PAN candidate Ernesto Ruffo won the governorship of Baja California Norte, and in the first test of his pledge to fair elections, President Salinas accepted the outcome. More change was to follow. In 1991 blatant electoral fraud cost PRI candidates two additional governorships in the states of Guanajuato and San Luis Potosí. The Chihuahua governorship also fell to PAN candidate Francisco Barrios, the former mayor of Ciudad Juárez in 1992. The president even endorsed a series of political reforms long called for by his political opposition. These included regulation of party finances, limits on campaign expenditures, and greater access to news outlets by opposition parties. Mexican political culture was at the beginning of a remarkable metamorphosis. It would culminate in startling fashion in 2000.

SALINAS BIDS ADIÓS TO THE REVOLUTION

The political education of Carlos Salinas de Gortari, like that of many recently elected heads of state throughout the world, was grounded in a new vocabulary and buttressed with concepts so shocking that politicians even a decade earlier would have considered them sheer madness. As notions of *détente* receded into the past, words like *glasnost* and *perestroika* became part of the common international parlance. The Berlin wall collapsed, as did the communist experiment in eastern Europe. The Soviet Union and Yugoslavia fell apart just as East and West Germany fell together. Fear of nuclear apocalypse no longer dominated political discourse. And most surprising of all, formerly socialist countries began to embrace what had previously been considered the capitalist demon. With Mexico's economic position so deteriorated, President Salinas decided that it was time for Mexico, too, to begin marching to a new cadence.

Throughout the entire post–World War II period Mexican politicians and intellectuals had asked themselves: Is the Mexican Revolution dead? Some morticians had actually consigned the Revolution to an early demise in the 1920s, but others pointed out that only the military phase had ended with the election of Obregón. Still others postulated that the Revolution had succumbed in the 1940s, but a few argued that it was only a coma and called upon a variety of therapists to work with it, nurture it back to health, and instill a new vitality. Salinas's presidency left no doubt that the Revolution was dead.

The intellectual underpinning for Mexico's Revolutionary entombment was neoliberalism. Fundamentally an anti-socialist doctrine, neoliberalism championed the free market by placing stringent limits on all government regulation of economic forces. It enshrined competition, favored free trade as the natural response to the new global economy, and argued that corporations should be given greater independence. Government subsidies for food and transportation should be severely restricted, and trade unions should be more modest in their demands. In short, neoliberalism represented an unambiguous rejection of the solutions Mexico had tested since 1917.

Salinas began to exorcise the ghosts of Mexico's anticlerical past. The process culminated with the president's memorable audience with Pope John Paul II and, in 1992, with the restoration of diplomatic relations between Mexico and Vatican. Those relations had been severed for 130 years. Then came amendments to the Constitution of 1917. Public religious celebrations were legalized, the church could again own property, it could operate religious schools, and foreign priests were welcome to preach on Mexican soil.

Nor were labor rights sacrosanct. During his second month in office, Salinas struck out against the powerful oil workers' union and arrested its leader, Joaquín Hernández Galicia, who was better known by his pseudonym, La Quina. To labor's outrage, the president answered that La Quina and his two leading associates had been arrested because of fraud and corruption in union activities, but some saw the dramatic move as an object lesson to other union leaders who might demand more on the wage front than the government was willing to concede. A few months later the president moved against the dock workers' union in Veracruz. Not yet finished, in January 1992 Salinas ordered the arrest of labor leader Agapito González Cavazo, charging him with tax evasion. It seemed no accident that this arrest occurred only one day before González Cavazo's Union of Journeymen and Industrial Workers was scheduled to go on strike against thirty-three maquiladora plants owned mainly by United States interests.

There was much more to come. Early in the administration the president began mild criticism of the ejido system, the sacred cow of agrarian reformers since the early 1920s. In one speech he had the temerity to call the ejidos unproductive and ultimately concluded that they had been a failure. They no longer represented the hope of a prosperous future for the nation's campesinos; rather, they were the cause of rural poverty. They explained why Mexico in the 1990s was not yet self-sufficient in food production. They explained why rural income was only one-third that of the remainder of the country.

Land redistribution, for Salinas, was a bankrupt solution to a problem with roots in Mexico's ancient past. Its importance as a mechanism to bring social justice to impoverished campesinos had long been overshadowed by lack of agricultural productivity. New laws, unthinkable just a decade earlier, followed quickly. Challenging the sacrosanctity of Article 27 of the Constitution of 1917, they provided for the private ownership of lands formerly owned by the ejidos. Not only were the campesinos given title to their land, but for the first time in the twentieth century, they could trade it, mortgage it, rent it, or even sell it.

All the changes were predicted on a neoliberal reassessment of the proper role of government in addressing society's ills. As Mexico looked toward the twenty-first century, it was clear that the state would exercise a more constricted role than it had in the past. Salinas attributed much of Mexico's economic dilemma to an exaggerated statism, which had seen the government move into the private sector and acquire ownership and control of over a thousand private companies. These the president began to privatize. By early 1992, over 85 percent of these companies had been sold back to the private sector. Among the economic giants quickly purchased by consortia of private investors were BANAMEX (Banco Nacional de México) and BANCOMER (Banco de Comercio), Mexico's two largest banks, and TELMEX (Teléfonos de México), the country's only telephone company. Other investors grabbed up government steel companies, hotels, sugar refineries, steel mills, and mines. Only a few government concerns such as PEMEX, considered crucial to national security, were excluded from divestiture proceedings.

The shift to a free market economy enabled Salinas to lower Mexican inflation to a tolerable 10 percent by 1993 and to reduce Mexico's foreign debt by some $25 billion. But it also served another purpose—it was an integral part of a calculated policy to foster a closer relationship with the United States. From the outset Salinas believed that Mexico's economic malaise could best be addressed by the successful conclusion of the North American Free Trade Agreement (NAFTA) with the United States and Canada. Salinas and his supporters argued that the agreement would herald more capital investment and as a result more well-paying jobs for Mexicans and a more powerful voice for Mexico in international diplomacy. Ultimately this position carried the day. Knowing that Europe would formally enter into its own common market on January 1, 1993, President Salinas, President George H. W. Bush, and Canadian Prime Minister Brian Mulroney recognized that only a new, large, combined North American market would be competitive. The three initialed NAFTA just as Salinas reached the midpoint of his presidential term and shortly before President Bush turned over the White House to Bill Clinton. By the fall of 1993, free trade had become the centerpiece of the Salinas administration. It was a calculated risk because final passage by the United States Congress was far from certain. The sighs of relief were clearly audible when the United States Congress gave NAFTA its final approval in November 1993. The days of a nationalistic economy suspicious of all foreigners now seemed to be over both in Mexico and the United States.

There was a substantial price to pay for declaring the Mexican Revolution dead. On January 1, 1994, a serious antigovernment rebellion broke out in the southern state of Chiapas. Led by a charismatic commander who called himself simply Sub-Comandante Marcos, a Maya Indian army, the Ejército Zapatista de Liberación Nacional, attacked army outposts and captured several towns including San Cristóbal de las Casas, the second largest city in the state. President Salinas sent army troops, rocket-equipped aircraft, and helicopter gun ships to engage the rebels, but ultimately negotiations conducted under the auspices of Bishop Samuel Ruiz—not military might—restored a tenuous peace. The rebellion focused national attention on an ethnic group and a region of the country unfulfilled by the promises of the Revolution.

A still greater shock to the Mexican body politic and to the country's self-image occurred in March 1994. The attractive and energetic

Sub-Comandante Marcos, leader of the Chiapas rebellion in early 1994, is wearing the mask that was the emblem of the rebels. Symbolically the masks represented the faceless indigenous populations of Mexico, but in a more practical sense they afforded the protections of anonymity.

PRI candidate for president, Luis Donaldo Colosio, campaigning on a platform to make his party more responsive to the people, was assassinated during a campaign appearance in the border city of Tijuana. Conspiracy theories, reminiscent of those in the United States following on the heels of the assassination of John F. Kennedy thirty years earlier, surfaced everywhere: in the press, in television commentaries, in the classrooms, and in coffee shop conversation. While the best evidence suggested that a single, perhaps deranged, gunman, Mario Aburto

Martínez, fired the shots, many believed that his actions were part of a wider, politically motivated plot hatched by the PRI old guard or "dinosaurs" who opposed reforms within the party. A second political assassination a few months later was equally disquieting but initially commanded less attention. José Francisco Ruiz Massieu, the second highest ranking official in the PRI and majority leader-elect in the Senate, was shot to death outside a Mexico City hotel. The murdered politician's brother, Mario Ruiz Massieu, was serving as Mexico's deputy attorney general and President Salinas placed him in charge of the investigation. Ultimately it would be this killing, not the Colosio assassination, that would carry public scandal to new heights in the months and years ahead.

TRYING TO KEEP ON COURSE

The PRI candidate chosen to replace Colosio, Ernesto Zedillo, was a career public official and like his predecessor an economist educated in the Ivy League. His campaign speeches indicated that he too was prepared to abandon the Revolutionary legacy in a relentless pursuit of the free market. A rising tide, he suggested, lifts all boats, a concept not comforting to those without a boat. The election was close. The conservative PAN candidate ran a better race than expected but the left, exhibiting a confrontational style and once again honeycombed with sectarian interests, could find no calamity sufficient to unify it. Ernesto Zedillo came out ahead but for the second time in a row the winner of the presidential sweepstakes barely garnered 50 percent of the popular vote. Although the narrow victory cannot be interpreted as evidence of general public acclaim, it was perhaps a cautious vote of confidence for Mexico's embrace of a free market economy and an indication that voters were looking for stability in the uncertain climate of economic difficulties, political assassinations, and the insecurity provoked by the Chiapas uprising.

Zedillo's first months in office coincided with a series of new pressures on the Mexican economy that saw the peso once again begin to slide rapidly against the dollar. It lost 46 percent of its value between December 1994 and January 1995 and continued to fall for the next two months. At the same time the Mexican *bolsa* (the stock market) collapsed in brisk trading. Business closed down and banks began foreclosing on urban and rural properties. Even the state-owned bus company, called Route 101, went into bankruptcy. Inflation, under control for several years, began to rise once again. Interest rates soared, reaching a usurious 100 percent in some areas, and hundreds of thousands were without jobs. The president was anything but decisive in formulating an economic plan to deal with the crisis.

Seeking to cast blame elsewhere President Zedillo uncovered another mariner's metaphor. He claimed that his administration had inherited a leaking boat from his predecessor. A truculent Salinas fired back with his own broadside, charging the new administration with gross mismanagement of the economy. Mexico was not presenting a pretty picture to its own citizenry or to the outside world. The broad panorama of economic pressures combined with the continuing insurgency of Chiapas eroded investor confidence. A tainted PRI gubernatorial "victory" in the state of Chiapas continued to subvert the appeal of Mexico's brand of democracy and reminded its citizens of the still desperate need for political reform.

Realizing the international implications of another Mexican economic collapse, U.S. President Bill Clinton urged a $40 billion loan to rescue the Mexican peso. Political pressures in the United States prompted a reduction to $20 billion, but once extended that sizable loan guarantee, coupled with a series of difficult and unpopular economic reforms, slowed further devaluations of the peso and helped Zedillo place his country on a stabilization path. The vast majority of those who lost their jobs during the economic crisis found new ones within a year, and in 1997 Mexico recorded a 7 percent rate of economic growth. The president also scored one additional victory, even though it proved short-lived. By the late fall of 1995, utilizing a skillful combination of diplomacy and military force, he persuaded the rebels in Chiapas to lay down their arms and work for political solutions to their genuine grievances. Unfortunately negotiations subsequently stalled.

As both political and economic pressures receded Zedillo embarked upon a series of domestic reforms, including the major overhaul of the nation's social security system. Of equal importance was the government's acceptance of PAN victories in several gubernatorial races. The conservative opposition captured the governorship of Guanajuato and a second consecutive governorship in Baja California Norte. By early 1996 it was clear that one-party rule was beginning to collapse as the days of PRI monopoly were ending. Faced with this new reality the president worked hard to convince his fellow Mexicans of his commitment to true democracy and the rule of law. He was not initially successful in this daunting task. Nor was he able to tally notable breakthroughs in Mexico's long war against the country's drug lords. He first tried reorganizing special police units designed to carry out the battle and then created a new federal police force to do the same, but the vast sums of money available to the traffickers enabled them to infiltrate the organizations, bribe high officials, and carry out their nefarious activities almost with impunity.

In many ways Zedillo's biggest problem, one that most eroded confidence in the system and rendered consensus impossible, was a public scandal that made even the most confirmed Mexican skeptic blush and turn away in disbelief. It was of the magnitude of Watergate and, like that public humiliation in the United States, it dominated political discourse and consumed political energy for years.

THE TALE OF FOUR BROTHERS

For at least half a century Mexicans had awaited revelations of corruption each time a new administration replaced an old. But this occasion was different. The news of intrigue, corruption, big money, narcopolitics, and murder that began to surface in February 1995 was not the typical low-grade moral infection. It was a gothic tale that mesmerized the nation. The former president's brother, Raúl Salinas de Gortari, was arrested and charged with masterminding and paying $300,000 for the murder of José Francisco Ruiz Massieu in September 1994. He was sent to the high-security Almoloya prison to await trial.

As the melodrama was pieced together the Mexican public learned that Ruiz Massieu was the former brother-in-law of Carlos and Raúl Salinas de Gortari, having been married to their sister Adriana. Could it be that the president's brother ordered the assassination of their former brother-in-law? Carlos Salinas protested his brother's innocence, claimed that the arrest of his brother was unjustified, and even staged a short hunger strike to drive home his point. Few Mexicans found solace in the ex-president's protestations especially when it was learned that the first official he had placed in charge of the investigation, Mario Ruiz Massieu, the slain politician's brother, did not pursue the investigation vigorously, and perhaps even directed a cover-up. In March 1995 Ruiz Massieu fled to the United States, and although he successfully resisted extradition to Mexico, investigations revealed he had accumulated millions of dollars during his term of office, with the proceeds coming largely from Mexican drug lords. Ruiz Massieu committed suicide in his New Jersey apartment in September 1999.

The detailed investigation into the activities of Raúl Salinas alleged even greater misconduct. In addition to the charge of murder, investigators uncovered evidence of his direct links to both the Gulf coast and Pacific coast drug cartels. He also allegedly accepted huge payments for arranging private access to the president. His corrupt activities earned him the sobriquet Señor Diez Porciento (Mr. Ten Percent), the usual "commission" he charged for facilitating the receipt of lucrative government contracts. President Salinas's massive privatization of profitable government-owned companies also provided his brother with the opportunity to amass a fortune amounting to hundreds of millions of dollars deposited in forty-eight different bank accounts.

The embarrassed former president felt the heat from the beginning and withdrew his name from consideration for the directorship of the World Trade Organization, a prestigious international position that most assuredly would have been his. In March 1995, he went into self-imposed exile, living for a short time in the United States and a short time in Canada before taking up a longer residence in Ireland. The derision directed against him in Mexico befit the magnitude of the scandal that engulfed his presidency. Political cartoonists in both Mexico and the United States had a field day, and dolls depicting the former president, bald, big-eared, and in striped prison clothes, were sold by outdoor vendors on almost every street corner of the capital. T-shirts showing him waving good-bye to Mexico with his middle finger extended could not be manufactured quickly enough to meet the eager demand. From the zócalo to the Zona Rosa street performers lampooned the former president, his presidency, the press that had supported him, and the sycophants who had surrounded him. Cynicism became more entrenched than ever.

Eventually, in the "trial of the century" of January 1999, Raúl Salinas was found guilty as charged and sentenced to fifty years in prison, the maximum allowed by Mexican law. But his conviction did not bring closure to the political speculation about the tawdry episode, especially when an appeals court later reduced the sentence to 27½ years on a technicality. Mexicans could not rid themselves of the perception that Carlos Salinas must have been implicated in some way.

Mexicans had their first opportunity to register their collective displeasure in the summer of 1997. Congressional elections and six gubernatorial elections were scheduled for July 6. In addition, for the first time in Mexican history there was an electoral race for the mayor of Mexico City, heretofore an appointive office. Two open governorships, in the central state of Querétaro and the northern industrial state of Nuevo León, fell to opposition candidates, but that was merely the tip of the iceberg. Cuauhtémoc Cárdenas, twice defeated as a left of center presidential candidate running on the PRD ticket, was elected mayor of Mexico City. Even more startling the PRI was deprived of its congressional majority for the first time in seven decades. If there was a new mandate it came neither from the left or the right. The vote was for change. While the liberal PRD scored strongly in the capital election, the conservative PAN won the two opposition governorships and a majority of the opposition congressional seats—an unequivocal rejection of the official party concept. Mexicans stood up to be counted and they said to the dominant party, "Enough!" The tale of the four brothers, the Salinas de Gortari brothers and the Ruiz Massieu brothers, not only demonstrated how the

When political cartoonists in the United States grew weary of lampooning Whitewater scandals, the fund-raising imbroglios by both Democrats and Republicans, and alleged sexual improprieties in the Oval Office, they found tempting targets in Mexico.

PRI had failed in its repeated promises to curb corruption but, worse, it showed PRI leadership at the very epicenter of all that was wrong in Mexican political culture.

THE ELECTIONS OF 2000

As a result of the PRI debacle, Mexico's first presidential election in the new millennium was quite unlike anything in human memory. It was the fulcrum of Mexico's post-Revolutionary experience, and nobody could be sure where the balance beam would tip, but even President Zedillo never wavered from his pledge to place Mexico on a true democratic course, and he ultimately paved the way for the defeat of his own party. Attention focused not on lackluster Francisco Labastida, the

After capturing the mayoralty of Mexico City, Cuauhtémoc Cárdenas is mobbed by his supporters on election night. Those supporters who anticipated that the triumph presaged a future presidential victory would be disappointed. A mayoral victory that seemed cyclonic at the moment proved to be only a gust of wind.

candidate of the PRI, or on Cuauhtémoc Cárdenas, the mayor of the Federal District and head of the PRD ticket, but on the flamboyant Vicente Fox, running as the candidate of the conservative PAN. Fox, a prosperous rancher, former chief executive of Coca-Cola de México, and popular governor of the state of Guanajuato, ran an outstanding campaign. Often appearing at political events wearing cowboy boots and an open shirt, the physically imposing six-foot-four Fox clearly sought to break out of the stuffy mold carefully fashioned by generations of official party candidates. He was always well prepared and seemed to delight in direct dialogue with the public. His special chemistry with his fellow Mexicans would ultimately pay huge political dividends. Not even when he transgressed revolutionary shibboliths by waving the banner of the Virgin of Guadalupe did most Mexicans recoil.

Throughout much of the campaign political pollsters had Fox and Labastida in a dead heat, with Cuauhtémoc Cárdenas running a distant third. In a nationally televised April presidential debate Fox hit hard on seventy years of PRI incompetence, false promises, and corruption, and polls showed he won the debate in a landslide. From that time forward a Fox presidential victory was no longer unthinkable, although there were still concerns that President Zedillo and the PRI leadership would find a way to overturn the election returns in the event that Fox triumphed.

In the months ahead Labastida's talk of a "new PRI" seemed more and more a contradiction of terms, as he was incapable of divorcing himself from the unpopular policies, major scandals, and minor shenanigans of his predecessors. Mexicans went to the polls in record numbers on July 2, 2000, and handed the heretofore-invincible PRI a stunning defeat. Those anticipating charges of fraud, electoral intimidation, denial of access to ballots, or unfair counting of the vote in an attempt to overturn the results would have to await the United States presidential election between George W. Bush and Al Gore three months later. The Mexican presidential election of 2000 was clean, and, unlike in the United States, the country would not have to endure months of electoral uncertainty.

For the first time in seventy-one years Mexico's president would not represent the PRI. If Salinas and Zedillo had buried the Mexico Revolution by abandoning its most revered principles, Vicente Fox's landmark victory put the final nails in the Revolutionary coffin. While jubilant mobs crowded the streets, President Ernesto Zedillo addressed the nation acknowledging the Fox victory and pledging a smooth tran-

THE 2000 MEXICAN PRESIDENTIAL ELECTION

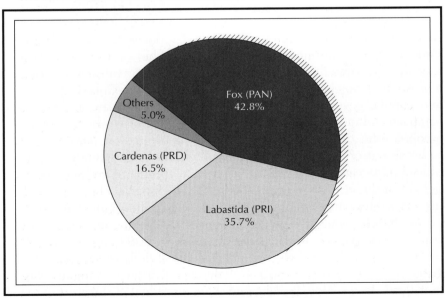

sition. To the chagrin of the distraught PRI leadership, Zedillo was neither defensive nor apologetic about the election. Where they hoped
to find humiliation they spotted only confident satisfaction and even a
measure of pride. Acknowledging the transition to democracy was
Zedillo's finest hour. Historians surely would consider his honest ac-
knowledgment of the dramatic election results his most important political legacy.

In October 2000, after the election but before the inauguration, former President Salinas returned to Mexico City with two purposes in
mind. He wanted to determine if sufficient time had passed to make
a permanent repatriation possible, and, at the same time, he to wanted
to promote his new book, *Mexico: A Difficult Passage to Modernity*.
The book not only referred to the "treason" of President Zedillo but
also blamed him for PRI's defeat in the recent election. Mexicans
wanted none of Salinas's recriminations. His reception was so cold that
he left the country a few days later. The judgmental Mexican public
still held Salinas, his family, and his political cohorts accountable for
the misfortunes that had engulfed the country during the last decade.

VICENTE FOX: A BREATH OF FRESH AIR

Inauguration day, December 1, 2000, found Mexicans basking in democratic legitimacy for the first time in seven decades, and many were
optimistic that the transition to democracy would be accompanied by
economic prosperity and social justice, just as Fox had pledged. On that
memorable day the president-elect conducted a bit of unofficial business prior to receiving the oath of office and donning the red, white,
and green presidential sash. He visited the Basilica of Guadalupe and
joined thousands of other worshippers in paying homage to Mexico's
famous Patroness. The act surely sent shivers down the spines of Mexico's old-line anticlerical revolutionaries, who remembered the many
lives lost in Mexico's difficult struggle to separate church and state.

But Vicente Fox's PAN was not the same conservative, Catholic party
of its origins. Although Fox could please his constituents by publicly
showing his faith, he was still constrained by Mexican political legacies
from the Revolution. His early actions showed how the PAN had moved
toward the center of the political spectrum. Rumors that the new president might further limit already strict abortion rights or privatize
PEMEX proved to be unfounded. He refused to endorse the Archbishop of Mexico's anti-abortion homily, which argued that even in the
case of rape women must accept the mysterious designs of God. Although personally opposed to abortion, the president countered that
he would not introduce any new legislation to change Mexico's abortion laws. Similarly, when President George W. Bush suggested that

United States capitalists might want to invest in Mexican petroleum, Fox rejected the idea politely. The nationalization of the oil industry by Lázaro Cárdenas in 1938 was memorialized every year and still considered an epic event in Mexico's twentieth-century experience. PEMEX, which accounted for about a third of all government revenues, was not yet for sale to foreign investors.

In another move to show that his administration would try to play the political middle, Fox appointed cabinet members from the left and the right. His appointment of Carlos Abascal—a staunch conservative, pro-industrialist, and Catholic heir to a Cristero family—as Secretary of Labor was a concession to the right. At the same time he named Jorge Castañeda, a leftist intellectual and long-time critic of U.S. relations with Mexico, as Secretary of Foreign Relations. His appointment to Mexico's top diplomatic post made it possible for Fox, at least in the short run, to counter arguments that he might be too pro-American in his foreign policy, even as he sought to enhance the new market-driven economy and to attract further U.S. investment.

THE FOX SEXENIO: A LOST OPPORTUNITY?

The optimism that accompanied Mexico's transition to democracy in electoral terms slowly eroded over the course of the Fox presidency because of his failure to deliver on campaign promises, especially those related to economic reform. Some of these shortcomings can be attributed to his own management style and ineptness at statecraft and building coalitions in a situation where his own party did not have a legislative majority. But it was not all his fault. The political immaturity of the multiparty Chamber of Deputies and international factors contributed to a growing malaise. Policy gridlock became evident very early as the PRI and PRD sabotaged a number of his initiatives to reform the tax structure and the energy sector. Political ineffectiveness became even more pronounced when the PRI was the major winner in the congressional elections of 2003. Not only did the tensions between the executive and the legislative branches fester and occasionally flare over the next few years, but the PAN and the administration itself were wracked with internal frictions. Because of his attempts to build coalitions, Fox frequently found himself at odds with his own party. And early investigations into irregularities in his campaign financing from a group called Los Amigos de Fox, accused of illegally funneling money from United States donors, made Mexicans question the president's commitment to fighting corruption.

Abruptly in January 2003, Jorge Castañeda resigned from the cabinet after having been frustrated in his attempts to improve relations with the United States and to reach an accord that would ensure fairer treatment for Mexican laborers. Ironically, given his earlier support for the Cuban revolution, he had also unsettled Mexico's close relationship with U.S. nemesis Fidel Castro. Castañeda was accused of pressuring Castro to make an early exit from a March 2002 United Nations summit on financing for development held in Monterrey, Mexico, in order to please the U.S. delegation and President Bush. He also publicly criticized Cuba for human rights violations and arranged for President Fox to meet with Cuban dissidents on a visit to the island nation. Fox replaced Castañeda with his Secretary of Economy, Luis Ernesto Derbez, and other cabinet shuffles and dismissals of high-level officials followed in 2003. In May 2004, Fox scolded Energy Secretary Felipe Calderón for appearing to launch a rival presidential bid, prompting Calderón to leave the government.

The controversies stirring the most gossip about the Fox administration had to do with "Martita." Fox married his former spokesperson, Marta Sahagún, exactly a year after taking office. Like Hillary Clinton in the United States, the outspoken "Martita" stepped beyond the bounds of activities considered appropriate for a presidential wife. In a move perhaps more reminiscent of Argentina's Eva Perón than Hillary Clinton, she created her own philanthropic foundation, Vamos México, and collected millions from the country's wealthy for projects destined to help the less privileged. Rumors about her political aspirations to succeed her husband as president circulated wildly in the press and made her the object of much derision in political cartoons and rock songs. In 2004, speculation came to an end after Vamos México was accused of siphoning off funds from the National Lottery. Fox's own chief of staff resigned, alleging that the first lady's political ambitions were out of control and that Fox was acting like the autocrats who preceded him. Even though the president finally intervened and announced they would both go home at the end of his term, Marta Sahagún continued to be a lightning rod. After being criticized for having spent too much public money on her wardrobe, the well-heeled first lady donated her favorite outfits to charity.

Fox promised to boost Mexico's annual economic growth to 7 percent. Gridlock and mini-scandals helped subvert this effort, as did a slowdown in the world economy at the beginning of his presidency. Annual economic growth was closer to 1 percent than 7, and certainly less than the 5 percent registered annually between 1996 and 2000. The president's proposal to implement a value-added tax on food, medicine, schoolbooks, and educational fees cost him the support of middle and lower sectors and certainly provided fodder for the opposition parties who charged him with ignoring the less privileged. And, in fact, the inequities in income distribution grew as the lower and middle sectors slipped while the top monopolized modest economic growth.

Fox skirted the political problem of privatizing PEMEX even though it was the most highly taxed and indebted oil company in the world and unable to meet all of Mexico's natural gas and petrochemical needs, but he was able to push through reforms that allowed for some private investment in electricity. Although export growth expanded modestly, in 2003 China replaced Mexico as the third largest exporter of goods to the United States. The president's pledges to boost employment also encountered difficulties as jobs in the maquilas and the Mexican manufacturing industry declined or remained stable.

In the area of social services, Mexico was constrained by lending agencies but, even with slightly higher social spending per capita under the Oportunidades program, the Fox administration made few advances in human capital investment that might ultimately boost productivity—in the areas of education, health, and job training. For many Mexicans, Fox's campaign promises to battle the stubborn causes of persistent poverty rang hollow as the income gap widened. Attempts to orient the school curriculum toward science and technology ran into trouble when it looked as if the curricular innovations would displace an emphasis on Mexico's pre-Columbian past, the "pride" of the nation.

The contemporary predicaments of indigenous people were certainly nothing to boast about. Mexico's native populations, especially those in the south, were counted among the most impoverished groups in the nation. High infant mortality rates, low life expectancy, malnutrition, and appalling rates of illiteracy pervaded Indian communities. But complicating their escape from privation was the fact that they also had been victims of systematic racial discrimination for five centuries. Government programs designed to assist had to be ever mindful of cultural traditions and value systems now more than ever out of step with neoliberal plans for economic growth. In an effort to address the Indian problem throughout the country, Fox named Xochitl Gálvez, an Otomí Indian and highly successful technical consultant, to head the Office of Indian Affairs. The resources at her command were small, however, and the subsequent dismantling of the National Indigenous Institute signaled that the administration would put its efforts into integrating Indian cultures rather than bolstering communal traditions and solidarity. This direction was also evident in the unfolding of the Chiapas situation.

During his campaign, Fox had boldly asserted that he would be able to resolve the Zapatista problem in fifteen minutes. To be sure, his first efforts in freeing Zapatista prisoners from Mexican jails and reducing the military presence in Chiapas indicated that he was sincere in his commitment to find a constructive solution. He also sent to Congress legislation proposed by the Zapatistas themselves to give indigenous peoples more control over their traditional lands and natural resources. To garner support for the legislation, the Zapatistas undertook a march from Chiapas to Mexico City in February and March 2000. They wore their marquee masks but, as previously agreed, left their arms at home. Indigenous Zapatista leaders and Sub-Comandante Marcos addressed

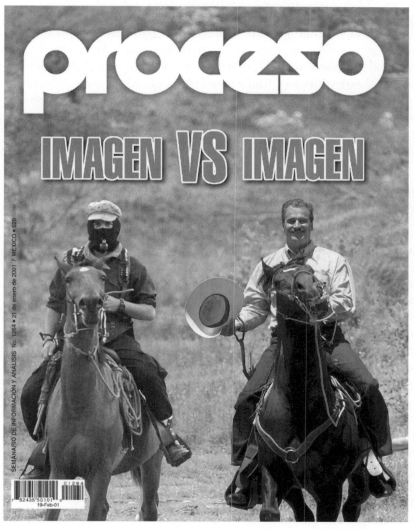

In reality, President Fox never galloped shoulder to shoulder with Sub-Comandante Marcos, but he did create a political track which made possible the Zapatistas' slow trot into Mexico City in March 2000.

a rally of thousands at the *zócalo*, demanding the "people who are the color of the earth" no longer be Mexico's forgotten masses.

They wanted to lay their grievances before Congress, but many PRI and PAN congressmen opposed giving them an official forum. After the president pressured legislators to change their stance, Zapatista leaders, with their spokesperson Marcos conspicuously absent, appeared on March 28 before a two-hour joint session of Congress that was nationally televised. Their chief spokesperson was a Maya Indian woman, Comandante Esther. She enthralled the viewing audience as she argued fervently and persuasively for the passage of the Indian rights bill. The impact of her impassioned plea on Congress was more difficult to determine as many Panistas and hard-liners from the PRI boycotted the session. Ultimately an Indian rights bill passed Congress and was incorporated into the constitution, but it was a greatly watered-down version of the original proposal. From their stronghold in Chiapas, the Zapatista leaders decried its failure to include the crucial measures that would give Indians the tools to revive their communities and promote their economic well-being. The Zapatista movement remained alive but marginalized throughout the Fox administration.

MEXICO AND THE UNITED STATES IN THE AGE OF TERRORISM

As it turned out, the Zapatista impasse was not the issue that monopolized the attention of Mexico in 2001. On September 11, 2001, Vicente Fox and millions of his fellow countrymen stood mesmerized before television sets watching the horrific terrorist attack on the Twin Towers of the World Trade Center in New York City and the Pentagon in Washington, D.C. With Mexico's northern neighbor no longer impervious to terrorist assault, the Mexican president was offered his first opportunity to give tangible meaning to the friendship he had openly professed since the day of his inauguration. Visibly moved, his response was quick and unambiguous. His government expressed condolences, pledged solidarity, and categorically rejected all forms of terrorism. In the days ahead he began actively cooperating with the United States in strengthening border surveillance and bolstering security at the American Embassy in Mexico.

To be sure, a few spokespersons for the Mexican left found in the unspeakable tragedy an opportunity to berate United States foreign policy even while huge plumes of smoke still billowed from collapsed buildings and thousands were unaccounted for and presumed dead. But the vast majority of Mexican citizens rejected outright the notion that the United States somehow got what it deserved. Dozens of Mexicans were among the foreign nationals from seventy-eight countries buried under the rubble at what came to be called Ground Zero. But Mexicans were less concerned with the nationality of the victims than with simple respect for the sanctity of human life. The same thinking also prevailed when Mexico was called upon to support the United States-led invasion of Iraq in 2003.

Whatever Fox's sentiments may have been about supporting the war, polls showed that over 70 percent of the Mexican population opposed an action seen as another manifestation of U.S. imperialism and a thinly veiled attempt by the Bush administration to manage crucial Mideast oil reserves. As the United States pressured Mexico to support its position, the Fox administration assented to the demands of thousands of Mexican protesters, and Mexican diplomats joined Chile, their hemispheric neighbor on the U.N. Security Council, in objecting to the use of military force. Moral solidarity in the face of terrorism was one thing; abandoning diplomacy for military might, and even greed, was another. Mexico, it seems, had not lost its commitment to an independent foreign policy. Fox, however, was not prepared to support former national security advisor and now Mexican ambassador to the United Nations, Adolfo Aguilar Zinser, an important political ally in his contest for the presidency. When the ambassador gave a speech in which he accused the United States of arrogantly regarding Mexico as its "backyard," Fox recalled and dismissed him.

In the final analysis, the September 11th tragedy and the subsequent war in Iraq adversely affected Mexico's relations with the United States. Antiterrorism measures and concerns about the security of United States borders put a damper on the immigration reforms contemplated by the two presidents. When President Bush hosted his Mexican counterpart at the White House less than a week before the terrorist attacks, he called Mexico "our most important foreign relation." Yet Mexico quickly faded into the background (if not the backyard), and the Fox administration's inability to achieve U.S. commitments to immigration reform was seen as another example of failed expectations and unfulfilled promises. By the time George W. Bush proposed in late 2005 to give guest worker visas to illegal immigrants who came to the United States before February 2004 (those who arrived later would be deported), increased anti-immigration sentiment from the United States public and the Congress threatened to subvert it.

With estimates of illegal Mexican immigrants in the United States ranging between ten and twenty million, the immigration problem presented enormous complexities. Undocumented Mexicans were found in every state, and the population burgeoned in the interior Southeast and the western mountain states, where the cost of living was lower. Critics worried about the jobs they were taking from American workers and charged that they depressed wages. Thoughtful citizens were joined by racists in vigilante groups like the Minutemen Project formed on the Arizona border to detain illegal migrants and get them deported. Yet as one observer noted, "If everybody was deported tomorrow, it would be like emptying the equivalent of New York state." Mexican labor was vital to many U.S. businesses. In 2005, the service sector (especially hotels and restaurants) employed about a third of illegal immigrants, followed by the construction industry, food processing, and farming. The Pew Hispanic Center reported that the average family income of undocumented families was about 40 percent below that of legal immigrants. Enforcement of immigration laws was lax, prompting renewed calls for sanctions against employers and a physical fence stretching along the two-thousand-mile border. At the same time, the living conditions of migrants were often substandard, if not abominable, and they faced hazardous work situations and racist retaliation.

The availability of jobs in both the informal and formal economies, which perpetually seek to cut costs, undoubtedly feeds illegal immigration. Experts argue that the situation depicted in the film *A Day without a Mexican,* which comically highlights how the economy and law enforcement would come to a standstill in California bereft of its Mexican population, is exaggerated. But they also believe that with cheap labor no longer available, prices would rise for food, child care, and household maintenance. Businesses would have to pay higher wages, and some would be forced to shut down. With illegal immigrants producing over $900 billion a year in goods and services, 9 percent of the overall U.S. economy, it is difficult to see how the immigration issue will be resolved in the foreseeable future, even if relations between the United States and Mexico improve.

In another arena of cross-border tensions, the Fox administration made aggressive efforts to combat drug trafficking, since the 1980s perpetually abetted by federal, state, and local officials and police. During the first five years of his administration, Fox jailed more top cartel leaders than any previous president, arrested nearly fifty thousand people on drug charges, destroyed numerous clandestine landing strips, and eradicated thousands of poppy and marijuana fields. But the administration's efforts were thwarted not only by escapes of cartel leaders from prison, but by the seeming ease with which they could run cocaine operations from their jail cells. The arrests of drug lords had the effect of prompting bloody battles between rival cartels, while the supply of drugs to the United States and to growing numbers of Mexican consumers did not diminish. Joaquín Guzmán (El Chapo), head of the Sinaloa cartel, escaped from a maximum-security prison shortly after Fox took office. Osiel Cárdenas continued to protect the Gulf cartel's millions of dollars of interests after his incarceration by bribing officials and police in northern Mexico.

In the war between the two cartels, kidnapping and deaths escalated, taking the lives of over a hundred soldiers and federal drug agents throughout Mexico. An all-out gang war erupted on the streets of Nuevo Laredo in 2005, resulting in the bloody executions of scores of people, including the police chief who had pledged to rid the force of police corrupted by drug money or intimidated by threats. Meanwhile, the murders of several hundred young women in Ciudad Juárez over the last decade, widely thought to be connected to police involved in protecting the drug industry, were not investigated forcefully. While drug lords liberally spent money for social serivces in their home communities, grisly crimes took the lives of innocent citizens as well members of organized crime. Although Fox put Nuevo Laredo under federal control, the government seemed to lack resources to forcefully combat the drug problem. The president compared the explosion of killings to the Al Capone era of the 1920s in the United States, and noted that it takes years to get rid of organized crime in an industry worth billions of dollars.

DILEMMAS OF DEMOCRATIZATION

Inadequate efforts to fight the drug trade only contributed to Fox's declining popularity. Nor was the "lame duck president" immune to criticism for intemperate remarks. Mexicans had been used to his shoot-from-the-hip speaking style since Fox's days on the campaign trail. But he shocked many when he stated to a meeting of Texas businessmen in May 2005 that Mexican immigrants in the United States were doing jobs that not even blacks wanted. In November, at the Americas summit in Argentina, he traded insults with South American presidents and a war of words between Fox and Venezuelan populist president, Hugo Chávez, resulted in the recalling of both country's ambassadors.

A more damaging embarrassment to the administration occurred earlier in 2005. Even though the Fox administration had a strong record of supporting free and fair elections throughout Mexico, the president could not distance himself from the machinations of the PRI and the PAN to discredit the PRD mayor of Mexico City, Andrés Manuel López Obrador, known by his initials as AMLO. The left-leaning mayor had garnered enormous popularity in the federal district for maintaining fiscal stability while conducting urban renewal and providing needed social services to the poor and the elderly. As PRI and PAN congressmen saw their parties' hopes for the presidency in 2006 erode, they conspired to have the federal government indict AMLO on a trumped-up charge. He was accused of approving a city project to widen a road to a public hospital on a small piece of land acquired by his predecessor, but whose ownership was in litigation. This highly transparent manipulation was designed to nip AMLO's presidential aspirations in the bud. Since the Mexican constitution prevents anyone under indictment from running for the presidency, AMLO's political opponents planned to have him waiting out the elections in jail.

Their efforts were foiled by the Mexican people, who saw the charges as a throwback to "politics as usual." In April 2005, just after the congressional vote to strip AMLO of the judicial immunity he enjoyed as mayor, an estimated three hundred thousand outraged citizens staged a protest in the *zócalo*. The entire incident had the effect of discrediting the PAN and the PRI, while boosting support for López Obrador. To prevent chaos and further damage to his own party, Fox dissuaded the attorney general's office from prosecuting the mayor. As 2005 drew to a close, the presidential election campaign was in full swing with PRD candidate AMLO leading the polls by a small margin. He was followed by the PRI candidate Roberto Madrazo who, despite being tainted by political corruption himself, had won the nomination in a contentious internal party struggle, and Felipe Calderón from the PAN.

The balance sheet on Mexico's momentous political shift after 2000 has yet to be determined by history, but early analyses based on economic factors were not charitable, as many characterized the Fox presidency as a "lost sexenio" and an opportunity squandered. In the political realm, the first opposition government in seventy years did score some successes in supporting electoral democracy, and perceptions of corruption in Mexico decreased. In defense of Fox, some argued that electoral democracy takes time to mature and, as he prepared to leave office, Mexican polls gave him approval ratings of over 60 percent.

THE MEXICAN REVOLUTION: A RETROSPECTIVE VIEW OF THE TWENTIETH CENTURY

Why did presidents Salinas de Gortari and Ernesto Zedillo signal that the Mexican Revolution had finally ended? Had it been a failure, a myth, a mere invention of historians? Throughout much of the post–World War II period, many alienated Mexicans responded in the affirmative. When U.S. scholar Ramón Ruiz synthesized the movement in a book published in 1980, he preferred not to use the word *revolution* and entitled it *The Great Rebellion: Mexico, 1905–1924*. By that time, some distinguished intellectuals argued forcefully that Mexico was in the throes of a neo-Porfiriato. The government had again become repressive, the scenario continued, and a small group was again enriching itself at the expense of the many. Social priorities, including the redistribution of land, had been laid aside in favor of economic development. Censorship, as evidenced in the celebrated *Excélsior* case, had become political reality once again. Economic exploitation in the form of the multinational corporation was even more pervasive than under the mining and petroleum companies of the early twentieth century. Bourgeois technocrats had replaced the científicos, but all the inadequacies of the closed society remained intact.

These judgments contain many truths, but many flaws as well; they obscure much more than they enlighten. Neoliberalism may have characterized the waning decades of the twentieth century, but it did not assume the guise of neo-Porfirianism. While military force had been used irresponsibly and unpardonably at Tlatelolco, while the army had hunted down and killed Lucio Cabañas, and while political prisoners were taken at the time of the Olympic demonstrations, it is pure folly to imply that presidential tenure in the postwar period rested primarily or even largely on the force of arms, as it had under Díaz. Although private enterprise was flourishing, the state had intervened actively enough to challenge laissez faire economics. Can one imagine Porfirio Díaz, shortly after the turn of the century when rich oil fields were discovered in Mexico, telling a president of the United States "no special consideration for your consumers"? Yet this was precisely Echeverría's message to Gerald Ford when the two met on the Arizona–Sonora border in 1974. The United States would not use Mexico to weaken OPEC. In the 1980s López Portillo and de la Madrid politely informed Ronald Reagan that Mexico's foreign policy, especially regarding Central America, would not be instructed from Wall Street or Pennsylvania Avenue. In addition, the Fox administration maintained Mexico's independent stance when it refused to back the U.S. invasion of Iraq in 2003. While some members of the intelligentsia had been co-opted with largess, in the 1970s Daniel Cosío Villegas could argue the neo-Porfirian theorem and excoriate the administration—indeed, the system—with neither a trip into exile nor a sojourn in a Mexico City prison. Had Díaz's father-in-law, Manuel Romero Rubio, been kidnapped in 1884 rather than Guadalupe Zuno Hernández ninety years later, many innocents would have perished in the search for information and the guilty would have been dispatched without even the formality of trial.

The neo-Porfirian parable continued unabated even after Vicente Fox's stunning presidential victory in 2000. When Sub-Comandante Marcos and his supporters entered Mexico City in the spring of 2001 the Mexican press could scarcely find enough ink and newsprint to equate his arrival with that of the revolutionaries of 1910 following the overthrow of Porfirio Díaz. But this revolutionary equation toppled because of its own grotesque disproportion. Unlike Emiliano Zapata or

Pancho Villa, this new "Zapata" had only won a public relations campaign in reminding citizens and the rest of the world that their democracy still had a long way to go to achieve social justice. In many ways, the grievances of the rebels had not changed much, but their political circumstances were different. In the last analysis, the revolutionaries of 1910 marched into Mexico City because Díaz had refused to allow free elections. Sub-Comandante Marcos, to the contrary, marched into Mexico City because Ernesto Zedillo had presided over free elections and had turned the presidential office over to his freely elected successor.

But all historical analogies tax intellectual sensibilities. The critics might better vent their displeasure on the obvious. The Mexican Revolution simply did not midwife the socialist state, nor did it usher in the millennium. The catalog of shortcomings was far from small. Poverty still abounded to all with open eyes. Studies undertaken in the 1980s indicated that the lowest 20 percent of the population shared only 3 percent of the national wealth, while the upper 20 percent shared a whopping 54 percent. Follow-up analyses in the new millennium indicated that the neoliberal policies of Salinas, Zedillo, and Fox had even widened the gap.

The manifestations of this stilted distribution of wealth were obvious. Millions were still illiterate; wages were low and unemployment was high; housing was inadequate; medical care, especially in the rural areas, was grossly insufficient; and the industrial and vehicular smog of the Federal District choked the Mexican capital and threatened health problems of major consequences. One Mexico City barrio, Ciudad Nezahualcóyotl, with a population of three million, was the largest slum in the world. Children scavenged in huge garbage dumps, where the stench of despair hung in the air. In the rural areas, a million peasants still worked plots too small to sustain themselves and their families. Only one-third of all Mexicans had access to running water in their place of residence. Real income declined in the 1980s and 1990s as inflation consistently outran rises in the minimum wage. Worst of all, as the twentieth century ended, more than a third of all Mexicans still suffered from malnutrition.

But the Revolution had occurred; it had broken the back of neo-feudalism, had eliminated the hacendado class, and had abolished the rurales. After ten years, it had yielded to a system of political stability without the daily use of force, to economic growth with a minimum of foreign participation, and to a broadened political base without the fragilities of traditional democracy or the repugnant liabilities of dictatorship. And in 2000 that system somewhat belatedly yielded to a democratic renaissance in which Mexican votes enjoyed a full measure of dignity for the first time. While the gulf separating the rich and the poor was as wide as ever, Mexico was no longer a country of two social poles. The caloric intake in the average diet doubled between 1910 and 1970; the infant mortality rate (deaths before the age of one year) fell from thirty deaths per hundred children to about five; and, concomitantly, life expectancy soared. The average Mexican lived only about thirty-six years in 1930; in 1996, life expectancy had reached seventy years for men and seventy-six for women, not much below that of the developed countries.

The overall goal of the Revolution had been to ensure a better life for the Mexican citizenry. Despite persistent poverty and multiple imperfections in the system, despite many chores left half finished, more Mexicans were living better in the twenty-first century than ever before. Millions had ascended to the middle class only to share the new bondage of middle-class cohorts throughout the western world: a mortgage on a house; large car payments; and a frightening debt occasioned by small plastic cards. It is naïve to expect that Mexico could completely eradicate the degradations of poverty. Nations that opened the twentieth century far ahead have not succeeded either in an era of globalized liberalism.

The Revolution was brought to an end less because it failed than because it had finally served its purpose. It was a noble experiment that had finally spent itself, both politically and ideologically. The Mexican universe of Carlos Salinas de Gortari and Ernesto Zedillo was totally different from that familiar to Francisco Madero and the revolutionaries of 1910. Vicente Fox capitalized on that difference. Recognizing that Mexico's revolutionary ideology was essentially bankrupt and inappropriate to new and constantly changing problems, his victory marked a bold departure from the political experience all Mexicans knew and understood. He wanted his fellow citizens not to ponder the year 1910 but to envision a Mexican future beyond the year 2000. The democratic transition exposed a multitude of growing pains. Political liberty was not a panacea for achieving social and economic progress or eliminating injustice. Yet as the 2006 elections approached, most Mexicans were characteristically optimistic that the future held promise.

POSTSCRIPT

As it turned out, even the most imaginative Mexican minds did not anticipate the results of the 2006 presidential election held on July 2. Although the PRD's Andrés Manuel López Obrador had run significantly ahead in the polls during the early months of the year, PAN's Felipe Calderón narrowed the lead as the election drew near while Roberto Madrazo of the PRI slipped far behind, illustrating that his party's midterm congressional gains did not presage a dramatic revival of the historically dominant party. More importantly, the election demonstrated that the political transformation of 2000 was not an anomaly.

The leading contenders seemed to represent opposite poles on the political spectrum. AMLO, who hailed from humble origins in Tabasco, had risen through the party ranks of the PRI before becoming a key figure in the newly formed PRD. Building upon his record as Mexico City mayor, he campaigned in a coalition of the PRD and several minor parties called Por el Bién de Todos (For the Good of All). Following leadership trends in Brazil, Argentina, Chile, and Uruguay, he was critical of neoliberal policies that had left many people behind despite general economic growth, vowing instead to work to provide health care and education for the poor, as well as initiate needed infrastructural changes. His support was strongest in Mexico City and in the more indigenous areas of Mexico. The Harvard-educated Calderón, son of a PAN founder from the state of Michoacán, advocated the continuation of neoliberal policies as a means to develop human capital through a competitive economy that would create more jobs and to overhaul the energy and tax sectors. Rallying support from more middle class voters outside the capital, especially in the north, he endeavored to show himself as independent from the lame duck Fox.

The campaign heated up as the candidates traded insults, with Calderón contending that AMLO's performance as mayor demonstrated that he was irresponsible and that his promises to the poor smacked of a messianic complex (while also suggesting that AMLO looked a lot like Hugo Chávez of Venezuela). Calderón's support surged in the polls after the first national televised presidential debate in which AMLO declined to participate. Many analysts believed that this was a mistake; whether true or not, AMLO had clearly underestimated his rival, and he was tardy in mounting a more forceful critique of Calderón's record and the PAN's negative attack ads. Especially damaging was the allegation that López Obrador was *"un peligro para México"* (a danger to Mexico).

On July 2, over 41 million Mexicans (60% of eligible voters) went to the polls. At first the results were too close to call but on July 6, the Federal Electoral Commission declared Calderón the winner, by less than a percentage point of the vote. Chaos threatened as AMLO's supporters took to the streets to cry fraud. López Obrador urged his followers to undertake a campaign of civil disobedience. PRD supporters turned out in the hundreds of thousands to protest in Mexico City's zócalo, charging that big money and crooked politics had skewed the result, and that there was fraud in the tallying of votes (an accusation refuted by international election observers). They also criticized the federal electoral commission for not imposing sanctions on the PAN for overspending and other violations of campaign rules.

Following legal procedures, the Coalition for the Good of All then presented formal complaints before the Federal Electoral Court (Tribunal Electoral del Poder Judicial de la Federación—TEPJF) that charged irregularities in specific voting districts and violations of rules that regulated campaign ads and prohibited direct presidential influence in the elections. To the public, AMLO addressed his call for a total recount of votes.

Meanwhile, Calderón claimed victory and formed a transition team. Although the PAN garnered more seats than any other party coalition in both the Chamber of Deputies and the Senate, it did not win an absolute majority. In the Chamber of Deputies, the PRI's votes would be necessary to give either side a majority.

While the country awaited a decision from the tribunal (by law, the court of last appeal), thousands of PRD supporters set up camps along the main thoroughfare of the Reforma and in the zócalo to mount a systematic protest with daily rallies. When it became apparent that the TEPJF would recount ballots in only a tenth of the voting precincts, López Obrador intensified his attacks on Mexico's flawed institutional structures and called for a "National Democratic Convention" to produce a new governing charter that would provide political, economic, and social justice for all Mexicans. On September 1, with the congressional buildings surrounded by military and police barricades, PRD deputies and senators took over the floor of the congressional session hall and prevented the president from delivering his last annual message in person.

On September 5, the court delivered a verdict, declaring Felipe Calderón Hinojosa the presedent-elect of Mexico. The final count gave him a margin of 233,831 votes (just above a half of a percentage point) over López Obrador. The unanimous judicial decision recognized minor voting irregularities and censured President Fox and the businessmen's council for improper conduct in the campaign, but ruled that none of these violations was sufficient to prevent the free exercise of the vote. Following this announcement, President Bush offered congratulations to Calderón, who stepped up measures to form a cabinet and affirmed that he was open to discussions with all parties. AMLO rejected the court ruling and continued preparations to convene a national assembly of the people.

As the eighth edition of *The Course of Mexican History* goes to press in September 2006, the post-electoral political trajectory remains uncertain. In a situation reminiscent of extremely close and polarized elections in the United States and elsewhere in the world at the outset of the twenty-first century, the embryonic Mexican democratic transition seems to have hit a snag that will make it difficult for either side to claim legitimacy.

RECOMMENDED FOR FURTHER STUDY

Babb, Sarah. *Managing Mexico: Economists from Nationalism to Neoliberalism.* Princeton, N.J.: Princeton University Press, 2001.

Camp, Roderic Ai. *Crossing Swords: Politics and Religion in Mexico.* New York: Oxford University Press, 1997.

Castañeda, Jorge G. *The Mexican Shock: Its Meaning for the United States.* New York: The New Press, 1995.

Collier, George A., *Basta: Land and the Zapatista Rebellion in Chiapas.* Oakland, Calif.: Institute for Food and Development Policy, 1994.

Cornelius, Wayne A., and David Myhre, eds. *The Transformation of Rural Mexico: Reforming the Ejido Sector.* San Diego, Calif.: Center for U.S.–Mexican Studies, 1998.

Foweraker, Joe, and Ann L. Craig, eds. *Popular Movements and Political Change in Mexico.* Boulder, Colo.: Lynne Reinner Publishers, 1990.

Fuentes, Carlos. *A New Time for Mexico.* New York: Farrar, Straus and Giroux, 1996.

Gallagher, Kevin P. *Free Trade and the Environment: Mexico, NAFTA, and Beyond.* Stanford, Calif.: Stanford University Press, 2004.

Harvey, Neil. *The Chiapas Rebellion: The Struggle for Land and Democracy.* Durham, N.C.: Duke University Press, 1998.

Higgins, Nicholas P. *Understanding the Chiapas Rebellion: Modernist Visions and the Invisible Indian.* Austin: University of Texas Press, 2004.

LaBotz, Dan. *Democracy in Mexico: Peasant Rebellion and Political Reform.* Boston: South End Press, 1995.

Levy, Daniel, and Kathleen Bruhn. *Mexico: The Struggle for Democratic Development.* 2d ed. Berkeley: University of California Press, 2006.

Lorey, David. *The U.S.–Mexican Border in the Twentieth Century.* Wilmington, Del.: Scholarly Resources, 1999.

Mattiace, Shannan L. *To See with Two Eyes: Peasant Activism and Indian Autonomy in Chiapas, Mexico.* Albuquerque: University of New Mexico Press, 2003.

Middlebrook, Kevin, ed. *Dilemmas of Political Change in Mexico.* San Diego: UCSD Center for Mexican Studies, 2004.

Morris, Stephen D. *Political Reformism in Mexico: An Overview of Contemporary Mexican Politics.* Boulder, Colo.: Lynn Reinner, 1995.

Needler, Martin. *Mexican Politics: The Containment of Conflict.* Westport, Conn.: Praeger, 1995.

Purcell, Susan Kaufman, and Luis Rubio, eds. *Mexico under Zedillo.* Boulder, Colo., and London: Lynne Reinner Publishers, 1998.

Rubio, Luis, and Susan Kaufman Purcell. *Mexico under Fox.* Boulder, Colo.: Lynne Rienner Publishers, 2004.

Schultz, Donald E., and Edward J. Williams, eds. *Mexico Faces the 21st Century.* New York: Praeger, 1995.

Stephen, Lynn. *Zapata Lives! Histories and Cultural Politics in Southern Mexico.* Berkeley: University of California Press, 2002.

Weintraub, Sidney. "US-Mexico Free Trade: Implications for the United States." *Journal of Interamerican Studies and World Affairs* 34:2 (1992): 29–52.

Williams, Heather. *Social Movements and Economic Transition: Markets and Distributive Conflict in Mexico.* New York: Cambridge University Press, 2001.

Womack, John. *Rebellion in Chiapas.* New York: The New Press, 1999.

39

Society and Culture since World War II

In the period after World War II, Mexico became more fully integrated into the international community than ever before. The country's charter membership in the United Nations at the close of the world conflict symbolized an end to the exclusive concern for parochial matters and a more profound interest in great world issues. Mexican presidents traveled widely carrying Mexico's message to Europe, Africa, Asia, and South America. They were determined to begin exerting leadership in the Third World. This new world outlook effected a basic change in self-image. The strident nationalism of the revolutionary era first gave ground and then surrendered to a new internationalism. Many perceived that the problems faced by the nation—rapid population growth, urbanization with its attendant social dislocations, persistent poverty, serious pollution, and ecological imbalance—were not only Mexican but global. Through science, technology, and economy the world had become increasingly interdependent, and solutions to these problems were scarcely possible within the confines of the national boundaries. Yet globalization of the world's economies posed new dilemmas for Mexico as the twenty-first century dawned.

POPULATION

The social and cultural changes of the postwar years were every bit as dramatic as those that had characterized the Porfiriato. The population growth was nothing short of fantastic, doubling in the twenty-three-year period between 1940 and 1963 and continuing to burgeon in geometric proportion. At the end of World War II, the population of the country numbered some 22 million; by 2005, it had soared to 106 million, three-fourths of them urban dwellers.

The capital had only three million inhabitants in 1950, but in 2000, according to some counts, greater Mexico City had swelled to a de-

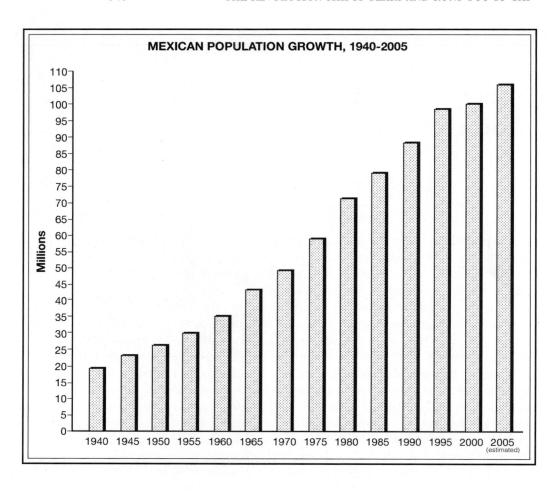

pressing 22.5 million and covered 779 square miles. Like a giant magnet, it draws people from the countryside, adding hundreds of thousands to its population each year, and in the process becomes less uniquely Mexican and more like New York, Paris, or London. Those who enthusiastically approved of the changes argued that the nation's capital had at last become cosmopolitan; those who preferred the simplicity and charm of earlier days suggested that, as each colonial structure was torn down (despite protective legislation) to make room for a skyscraper or a freeway, as cellular phones, that quintessential yuppie symbol, rang during high mass at the main cathedral, the capital had—alas!—ceased to be Mexican. New elegant restaurants and ostentatious nightclubs catered to the thousands of tourists brought in each day by scores of jumbo jets.

Since the 1980s, the sprawling metropolis has lagged behind only Tokyo for the distinction of being the most densely populated region

Arguably the most congested city in the world, Mexico City streets, sometimes twelve lanes across such as the Periférico Norte pictured here, are often paralyzed by gridlock.

on earth, and it has the most acute traffic and smog problems in the western hemisphere. In 2005, more than four million vehicles traveled the crowded streets of the Federal District. In an attempt to relieve traffic congestion on the main thoroughfare of Avenida Insurgentes, the Federal District government of Andrés Manuel López Obrador inaugurated a rapid transit bus line. The entire public transportation system was moving four million people per day. The poisonous atmosphere causes over one hundred thousand deaths annually. In 2000, the World Resources Institute gave Mexico City a dubious distinction: in terms of air pollution it was deemed the most dangerous city in the world for raising children. With visibility sometimes dropping to less than a quarter of a mile, enterprising street vendors walked the sidewalks with tanks strapped on their backs selling individual doses of pure oxygen to sick-looking pedestrians. While some might have marveled at this creative therapy, it obviously did nothing to cleanse the noxious air. Blackouts, brownouts, inadequate telephone service, and low water pressure strained the nerves of virtually everyone. If pharmaceutical sales figures reflect reality, many *capitalinos* added Stresstabs (a dietary supplement made in Mexico) to their shopping lists. In 2005, Mexico ranked tenth in the world in sales of nervous system drugs.

The huge working-class housing projects have brought hundreds of thousands together into closer proximity than they would have imagined possible. Juvenile delinquency and adult crime rates are high. By 1988 Mexico City was recording 242 robberies and thirteen murders every day. Over one million youths belonged to street gangs (the Vikings, Sex Rats, Savages, Street Machine, and the like) that terrorized innocent passersby. In 2003, Mexico recorded the world's second highest number of kidnappings, but the number dropped over the next two years.

As the twenty-first century approached the capital appealed less to those seeking cultural refinement and more to those enthralled by perpetual commotion. With the thought of forestalling some Malthusian tragedy, Mexican urban planners began to consider seriously the building of an entirely new capital, much as the Brazilians had done in the late 1950s. But there was more talk than action as people rationalized that these costs of modernization were inevitable. Even an attempt to move Mexico City's international airport outside of the Federal District failed in 2003. Octavio Paz had synopsized it well when he lamented that after centuries of struggle Mexico was finally a contemporary of all mankind.

Despite the difficulties, Mexico City dominated the entire country as never before. Over 50 percent of the country's industries were located in the capital, and more than 70 percent of the country's daily banking transactions occurred there. Provincial Mexicans resented not only the exaggerated centralism emanating from Mexico City but also what they believed to be the arrogant attitudes of those from the nation's capital. They coined derogatory epithets for them, *Chilangos* and *guachos*, and in the state capitals decorated the walls of buildings with uncharitable graffiti inviting them all to go home.

While the provincial capitals were slightly more successful in retaining some of their local flavor, they, too, fell victim to the homogeneity of technological proficiency conditioned by electronic circuitry, pocket calculators, and large, sophisticated computers. Guadalajara, Monterrey, and Ciudad Juárez followed Mexico City along the path of seemingly uncontrollable pollution, and even the citizens of León, Guanajuato, worried about their health in 1995, when tens of thousands of birds migrating from Canada and the United States died after drinking contaminated water in a local reservoir. They had a right to be concerned, as scientific tests soon revealed that human sewage flowing into the reservoir had turned it into a huge incubator for botulism bacteria. Five years later, a much more sinister and callous ecological disaster was reported directly to the south in Michoacán. Loggers using chemical pesticides purposely killed twenty-two million migrating monarch butterflies. They reasoned that if there were no butterflies there would be no reason to continue setting aside a protected forest as the site of the annual butterfly migration.

Some of the worst environmental conditions exist in the northern Mexico border cities. In 2000, fully 12 percent of the border population lacked access to potable water and a third had no access to wastewater treatment. Air, water, and soils are heavily contaminated by industrial pollution, pesticides, and raw sewage. But since the 1990s, Mexico has seen the proliferation of groups advocating environmental reforms. One had to travel to the small village to escape the cacophony of big city sounds and to encounter some of the charm of an age now past, but there, behind the facade of what seemed quaint to the foreign eye, the disabilities of underdevelopment remained stark. While more rural children were in school than ever before many of those schools had less than six grades and only one teacher. It would not be unusual for the children, at the end of the school's day, to return to hovels barren of comforts.

Diversions for the marginalized urban masses were few and far between. The Sunday bullfight, while still a staple of popular culture, somehow seemed less attractive than a century before. Government subsidies kept the price of movie tickets low, at least until 2000, when prices doubled, enabling many to escape their sobering reality for a few hours of cinema every few months. By the 1960s outside of the isolated rural areas most people had some access to a television set, even if it belonged to a relative or neighbor, making soap operas (*telenovelas*), musicals and traditional sporting events viewing staples. If television did not always make its presence known in isolated nooks and crannies of the Republic, comic books, an often forgotten component of the mass media, did. These *historietas*, directed to adults as well as children, were inexpensive and simple enough that they could be enjoyed even by those whose reading ability was minimal. As they passed from reader to reader to reader their audience was enormous. Often assuming the role of moral mentor, some were steeped in history, others in romance, and still others in family tragedy. Capturing the full spectrum of life's delights, disappointments, and ironies, their appeal was extensive.

A minor sporting attraction of the 1930s became an enthralling public spectacle in the postwar period. The Mexican variant of professional wrestling, *lucha libre*, fascinated hundreds of thousands. Unlike the North American counterpart from which it adapted, almost all of the participants wore masks, enhancing the aura of in-

THE TEN LARGEST MEXICAN CITIES (Estimated 2006)

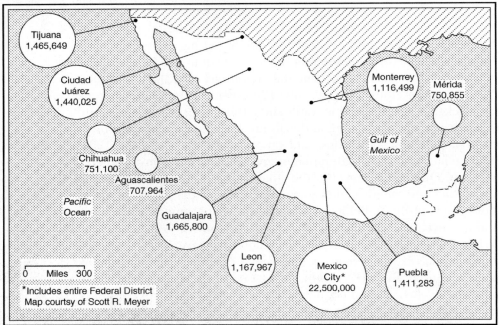

Tijuana
1,465,649

Ciudad
Juárez
1,440,025

Chihuahua
751,100

Aguascalientes
707,964

Monterrey
1,116,499

Mérida
750,855

Gulf of
Mexico

Pacific
Ocean

Guadalajara
1,665,800

Leon
1,167,967

Mexico
City*
22,500,000

Puebla
1,411,283

0   Miles   300

*Includes entire Federal District
Map courtsy of Scott R. Meyer

scrutability. But even with concealed faces, it was clearly impossible to confuse good and evil in these carefully choreographed physical melodramas. Heroes (the *técnicos*) were pitted against villains (the *rudos*) in a metaphor of life's constant struggles. Like any classic melodrama the emotions of the audience were shamelessly manipulated as a series of behemoth scoundrels visited indignities on an equal number of long-suffering heroes. Taunting the crowd with endless gimmicks the *rudos* evoked profound passions, while the *técnicos* inevitably emerged larger than life. It was no accident that the most beloved *técnicos* of the post–World War II period adopted monikers linked to the church. Young and old alike could applaud the heroics of El Angel Blanco or the icon El Santo, while excoriating the outrageous and cheating tactics of the vicious Médico Asesino or the bully Cavernario Galindo. But no match commanded more attention than the 1955 epic when, in virtue triumphant, El Santo unmasked and shamed the *rudo* Sombra Vengadora.

Mexican advocates of population control had their ups and downs in the postwar period. They were crushed by the 1968 papal encyclical banning all methods of artificial contraception, because they recognized the awful truth in the quip that the rich get richer and the poor get chil-

A celebrity of gigantic proportion, El Santo commanded admiration and awe as much for his wholesome image as for his prowess in the ring.

dren. During the presidential campaign of 1970, Luis Echeverría, the father of eight, announced that Mexico did not need to limit family size. In that same year, some six hundred thousand Mexican women underwent illegal abortions, and thirty-two thousand died. In 1972, in face of incontrovertible evidence, the Council of Mexican Bishops performed a remarkable *volte-face* and issued a pastoral letter declaring that Mexican couples should in good conscience make responsible decisions about the size of their families. The president agreed, and government-sponsored clinics began making birth control information available to those who requested it. The program began in a small way; the sell was very soft, but by 1980 López Portillo had earmarked over five hundred million pesos annually for the family planning program and some dividends had been recorded. A population growth rate that had hovered between 3.2 and 3.4 percent during the 1970s had been cut to about 1.7 percent in 2000. Over six thousand family planning centers, funded by the government, were in operation. By

THE TWO-CHILD FAMILY

La familia pequeña vive mejor
decida la suya . . .
(The small family lives better
decide on yours . . .)

Posters such as this, with an unmistakable message, became increasingly common in Mexican cities in the 1970s and 1980s. If conservative Catholics were offended by the modest invitation to consider birth control, they were surely shocked in 1997 when billboards in Mexico City brazenly urged Mexicans to enlist condoms in the war against AIDS.

2005, nearly three out of four women were using some method of contraception, and the overall fertility rate dropped below 2.4 children per woman. Reproduction rates were lower among urban dwellers, educated Mexicans, and people living in northern Mexico and other areas with higher rates of economic development. Demographers were cautiously optimistic that the birth rate would continue to decline. Since the 1970s there has also been a general decline in mortality rates, and life expectancy has increased to 77.9 years for women and 73.4 for men.

The movement for women's rights built up steam during the postwar years. The full enfranchisement of women in 1955 was just the beginning. More important was the feminist victory scored in 1974. While the Equal Rights Amendment languished in the United States, President Echeverría sent a bill to the Congress asking that Mexican men give women their full stake in society. The law that passed promised women equal job opportunities, salaries, and legal standing. Beginning in the 1970s, the feminist movement began seriously to challenge laws and social practices denigrating the role of women. For the first time in its ninety-nine years, the prestigious Mexican Academy of the Language admitted a woman, Dr. María del Carmen Millán. Shortly thereafter Griselda Alvarez Ponce de León became governor of the state of Colima.

In 1984 and 1985, women were incorporated into various municipal police forces, not only because they could perform equally with men, but also because they were thought to be less corruptible than their male counterparts. A few years later, Socorro Díaz, after establishing a brilliant record as a journalist, was elected to Congress and became the first woman to serve as president of the Chamber of

Deputies. She was not alone in Congress. In 1988, ten of the sixty-four Mexican senators and fifty-five of the five hundred members of the Chamber of Deputies were women. By 2003, 24 percent of legislative seats were held by women, and women directed the PRI and the PRD parties. The PRD party leader, Amalia García Medina, was elected governor of Zacatecas in 2004, making her the fifth woman in Mexican history to head a state office. Among professional and technical workers, the percentage of women had risen to 40 percent, but women's income averaged about 38 percent of that of men.

The legal victories scored by the feminist movement were certainly impressive, and women's empowerment had been catalyzed by the formation of politically active groups like Mujeres para la Democracia (Women for Democracy). Women began to undermine the deeply ingrained cultural pressure of Mexican machismo at least at the level of public discourse. But behind a veil of anonymity, male attitudes toward women could be openly insensitive and degrading. The touching, grabbing, and verbal abuse suffered by women on the Mexico City metro became so intolerable in the 1980s that a radical solution was instituted. The Mexico City system became the first subway in the world where the individual cars were segregated by gender.

Mass communication, and most especially television, changed not only patterns of leisure but the information level of the urban citizenry. By the mid-1960s, Mexican television was no longer the sole preserve of the middle and upper classes. Television antennas sprouted from the most decaying of urban slums and attested to the vastness of the audience. In the summer of 1969, millions of Mexicans watched in amazement as Neil Armstrong took his first tentative steps for mankind on the surface of the moon. And although some judged the telecast a gigantic hoax, most would soon have opinions about how nations, weak and strong, should allocate their limited resources. The great educational and cultural potential of the medium was approached no more in Mexico than elsewhere in the western world, but the possibilities were so substantial that in the summer of 1985 the Mexican government contracted with NASA to carry Mexico's first television satellite into space. Successfully launched in an orbit twenty-two thousand miles above the earth, *Morelos I* brought advanced telecommunications to the most remote parts of the country. It was followed shortly by *Morelos II*. Thereafter communications satellites proliferated and were privatized in 1988. In addition, the Internet was eagerly embraced, and Mexico counted 14 million users by 2005. A study in that year reported that more than a fifth of Mexicans spent half of their leisure time playing video games. Internet cafes were ubiquitous.

THE AMERICANIZATION OF MEXICO

United States cultural influences overwhelmed Mexico in the postwar period, occasionally for the better but generally for the worse. If anything, these new cultural inroads were more pervasive than those of the French during the late Porfiriato. Rodolfo Stavenhagen, a distinguished Mexican sociologist, called it a steamroller. To the chagrin of those who prized traditional Hispanic values, advertisements and commercials assumed a distinct United States flavor, and hundreds of Anglicisms invaded the language. Somehow *el jit, el jonron, el extra inin* seemed more palatable, and certainly more understandable, than *okay, bay-bay, chance, jipi, biznes,* and *parquear.* Nobody could explain why Mexican teenagers in Gap jeans began calling up their *suiti* for a date. Linguistic syncretism bequeathed its share of amusing redundancies, such as the cocktail lounge that displayed a sign reading "4:00–5:00, La Hora de Happy Hour" and the tourist restaurant whose menu proudly advertised "Chile con Carne with Meat." Quick lunches (*quik lonches*) and the coffee break (*kofi breik*) replaced heavy noon meals and afternoon siestas; beer supplanted pulque as the favorite alcoholic drink of the lower classes, while Scotch whisky took the place of cognac among the middle and upper classes. For the first time, Halloween, complete with plastic pumpkins and trick-or-treating, began to displace Mexico's traditional celebration of the Day of the Dead, and hand-carved folk toys lost favor to the latest imported crazes.

American-style football did not really challenge the pre-eminence of soccer, but thousands of Mexicans became enthralled with professional football, telecast to Mexico City on Sundays. The January 1988 spectacular, Superbowl XX, between the Osos de Chicago and the Patriotas de Nueva Inglaterra seemed especially to captivate the Mexican sports fan. Mexican businessmen joined the Rotary and the Lions Club. Installment buying on Mexican versions of Visa and MasterCard made possible an orgy of consumption and placed families in a new kind of debt but gave them the opportunity of acquiring furnishings and accouterments for the home that would have been unusual two decades before. *Supermercados* with plastic packaging and individually priced items began to replace the traditional marketplace in all the larger cities. Stocked with corn flakes, Campbell's soup, Heinz 57 Steak Sauce, Cap'n Crunch cereal, and Coca-Cola, Mexican supermarkets were distinguished from their North American counterparts only by the absence of huge parking lots.

Another foreign import, rock music, began to compete seriously with traditional Mexican music forms in the 1960s and by the 1970s had become dominant among the young. Rock bands slowly began to replace the trios and mariachi bands as the Mexican student's music of choice.

After the 1969 Woodstock festival, Mexico produced the Avándaro Music Festival in the Valle de Bravo, outside Mexico City, attracting over 200,000 *rockeros*. The spectacle midwifed a new Latin rock genre known as *la nueva onda* and touched off a new national debate. While purists viewed *rocanrol* as crassly imitative of the worst in United States hippie culture, others, including influential members of the intelligensia, saw it as an significant break with the cultural forms preferred by Mexico's institutional revolution. In its wake, groups such as Los Hitters and Los Johnny Jets enjoyed fleeting fame as well as a measure of financial success. For those who liked hard rock few could compete with the Dug Dugs. While much early Mexican rock was unashamedly derivative (one scholar aptly termed it "Refried Elvis") and some of it even bordered on plagiarism, it eventually developed a distinctive identity, at least to the trained ear. Along with *rocanrol* came the disco, where salsa and other Latin music coexisted with the newer fads. And the 2006 Avándaro festival was planned to include groups like Café Tacuba, Jaguares, Maldita Vecindad, and Maná. Popular singers like Thalía and Paulina Rubio even became known outside of Mexico.

Multinational chains carpeted Mexico City. Residents and tourists alike could rent a car from Avis, Hertz, Budget, or Thrifty; drive on Goodyear, Firestone, or Uniroyal tires to a fast food outlet called Burger King, KFC, or Pizza Hut. When the McDonald's chain opened its first restaurant on the southern edge of the sprawling capital in October 1985, eight Mexico City policemen were kept busy for days directing traffic in front of the golden arches. United States music dominated most of Mexico City's twenty-four radio stations, while television audiences were treated to reruns of "Los Dukes de Hazard" and "The Flintstones." With the proliferation of cable television, Mexican viewers could watch "Law and Order" and "West Wing" only shortly after they aired in the United States. Some cried understandably for spiritual independence, others more modestly for *taco sí, hamburguesa no*. Another slogan would have been more appropriate. In January 1992, in the most bizarre example of gastronomical entrepreneurship, one United States corporation decided it could think of nothing better than to offer Mexicans an example of exquisite Mexican cuisine. Yes, Taco Bell opened its first Mexico City franchise, gagging Mexicans.

But no foreign import could rival Wal-Mart, which operated 710 stores and restaurants by 2005. Having bought up several Mexican supermarket chains, it was Mexico's largest retailer and employer. Many Mexicans were outraged when Wal-Mart, despite loud protests, opened a store in San Juan Teotihuacán in 2004, less than a half mile from the ancient "City of the Gods." Local retailers who decried the desecration that figuratively imposed Mickey Mouse on top of the pyramids, were forced out of business.

Despite the anticlericalism embodied in revolutionary ideology, the faithful continued their pilgrimage to the Basílica de Guadalupe in the postwar period. In 1996 Mexicans were given a less traditional option when the Virgin of Guadalupe opened her own web page on the Internet. The Interlupe can be accessed at http://spin.com.mx/~msalazar.

What did it all mean? It was easy to simply label it all cultural imperialism but that ideologically loaded emblem explained little and resolved less. To the most thoughtful Mexicans the inherent problem was less Americanization than the type of Americanization. By this they meant too much Madonna and Rambo and too little Ernest Hemingway and Leonard Bernstein. But most realized that, in the absence of enveloping the country in a nationalistic cocoon, the process was lamentably inevitable. At the same time, intellectuals like Elena Poniatowska decried the assaults on indigenous folk culture and arts. Others laughed at the absurdity of importing industrial tacos from the United States. In the 1930s when the Mexican philosopher Samuel Ramos assaulted the imitative nature of Mexican culture he had a valid point. But seven decades later, in a world tied ever closer together by the wonders of technological change, most understood that cultural independence everywhere had become increasingly relative.

LITERATURE, ART, AND SCHOLARSHIP

Mexico became a country of vibrant intellectual ferment in the half century following World War II. Mexico City was clearly the cultural capital of the country and in 1985 could boast twenty daily newspapers and 250 periodicals. The television and film industries were based in the capital, as were the most outstanding art galleries and museums.

Throughout the postwar period, new literary journals and magazines of social protest provided the grist for healthy cultural debate. The postwar years saw the demise of both indigenismo and the novel of the Revolution as Mexican writers began their quest for the universal. While nobody could question the Mexicanidad of Octavio Paz, his writing revealed greater concern for ecumenical matters than for the heroes and apostates of the great Revolution. Born in Mexico City four years after the Revolution broke out, he was, by the 1950s, one of the most profound and prolific members of the new intelligentsia. As with many of the great intellects of the postwar period, it was often difficult to pinpoint where his philosophy ended and his literature began. In essays, in drama, and, above all, in poetry, he sought to link the Mexican experience with that of all humanity through the common denominators of suffering and tragedy. His most penetrating study, *El laberinto de la soledad* (translated as *The Labyrinth of Solitude*) (1950), is a psychological study of the Mexican character but was conceived in the United States, where Paz was able to observe Mexicans in a foreign milieu. Solitude for Paz was a condition that Mexicans had to comprehend to understand themselves, but the inquiry into the Mexican psyche revealed his more basic interest in the human condition.

> Solitude—the feeling and knowledge that one is alone, alienated from the world and oneself—is not an exclusively Mexican characteristic. All men, at some moment in their lives, feel themselves to be alone. And they are. To live is to be separated from what we were in order to ap-

proach what we are going to be in the mysterious future. Solitude is the profoundest fact of the human condition.[1]

Paz's criticism of the Revolution was far from mundane. In a work he called *Posdata* (1970) and published in English under the title *The Other Mexico: Critique of the Pyramid,* he critiqued the intellectual paucity of the movement, especially the failure of the intelligentsia to relate the Mexican experience to the human enterprise at large. His literary career culminated in 1990 when he won the Nobel Prize for Literature; eight years later at the time of his death, he was remembered by many as the greatest twentieth-century poet and essayist of the Spanish-speaking world.

While Octavio Paz broke out of the mold many considered properly Mexican, Juan José Arreola (1918–2001) in a number of works turned his back on Mexican themes. Four years younger than Paz, Arreola developed a sharp, biting satire of the bourgeois values of postwar Mexican society. Culturally indebted to Bertolt Brecht and Albert Camus, he was sarcastic, irreverent, hyperbolic, humorous to the point of cruelty, and blatantly sexist. Arreola jabbed mercilessly at the pomposity and deceptions of his world. In one notably wicked short story, he invented a plastic woman and advertised her as would befit the merchandising practices of the new Mexico.

> Wherever the presence of woman is difficult, onerous, or prejudicial, whether in the bachelor's bedroom or in the concentration camp, the use of Plastisex is highly recommended. The army and the navy, as well as some directors of penal and teaching establishments, provide their inmates with the services of these attractive, hygienic creatures. . . . We will furnish you with the woman you have dreamed about all your life: she is manipulated by automatic controls and is made of synthetic materials that reproduce at will the most superficial or subtle characteristics of feminine beauty. Tall and slim, short and plump, fair or dark, redhead or platinum blonde—all are on the market. . . . The mouth, nostrils, inner parts of the eyelids, and other mucous regions are made of very soft sponge, saturated with hot, nutritive substances of variable viscosity and with different vitamin and aphrodisiac contents extracted from sea weeds and medicinal plants. . . .
>
> Our Venuses are guaranteed to give perfect service for ten years— the average time any wife lasts—except in cases where they are subjected to abnormal sadistic practices. . . . Though submissive, the Plastisex is extremely vigorous, since she is equipped with an electric motor

---

1. Octavio Paz, *The Labyrinth of Solitude: Life and Thought in Mexico*, trans. Lysander Kemp (New York, 1961), p. 195.

of one-half horse power. . . . Nude, she is simply unexcelled; pubescent or not, in the flower of youth, or with autumn's ripe opulence, according to the particular coloring of each race or mixture of races.[2]

Perhaps the most creative of the postwar writers was novelist Carlos Fuentes. Born in 1928 to a middle-class family, Fuentes took a law degree at the National University and then studied international law at Geneva. His most famous novel, *La región mas transparente (Where the Air Is Clear)*, published in 1958, is a cynical story of disillusionment with the Revolution. But it is scarcely a novel of the Revolution in the classic sense. While those familiar with the outlines of Mexican history in the twentieth century might find it easier than others to comprehend, more than anything else it is a Marxist critique of human nature and a creative condemnation of capitalism. The names and the places are clearly Mexican, but the major themes—the abuses of power, the self-serving opportunism of the bourgeoisie, the pointless existence of the *nouveau riche*, and the tendency of the new society to accept all things foreign—clearly have an applicability transcending Mexico. The lesson of postwar Mexico for Fuentes was that it reflected the same degenerate bourgeois values that characterized most of the western world. Fuentes went on to have a distinguished diplomatic and literary career. His prolific output in novels, short stories, plays, and essays are known for their cultural, political, and historical insights about Mexico. Many of his works have been translated into English and some have earned national and international prizes.

Critiques of Mexican identity proliferated during the 1950s, 1960s, and 1970s, exposing the failure of the Revolution to incorporate diverse ethnic groups and classes in a national project. Caciquismo, corruption, and moral decay pervade Juan Rulfo's *Pedro Páramo* (1955). Several novels by Rosario Castellanos set in Chiapas, including *Oficio de tinieblas* (1962), and Elena Garro (the wife of Octavio Paz), who penned *Los recuerdos del porvenir* (1963), continued to depict themes of violence and ethnic injustice in rural Mexico, but with the added dimension of gender oppression.

The tragedy of Tlatelolco catalyzed a protracted national debate and spawned its own impressive body of literature in the 1970s. Unified only in its recognition that the terrible evening left scars that would never wholly heal, Tlatelolco literature found expression in the essay, poetry, short story, and novel. While Octavio Paz and Carlos Fuentes dominated the outpouring of perceptive political essays searching for

---

2. Juan José Arreola, *Confabulario and Other Inventions*, trans. George D. Shade (Austin, 1974), pp. 134–39.

accountability, the fictional responses are epitomized by Carlos Monsiváis's *Días de guardar* (1970), Arturo Azuela's *Manifestación de silencios* (1979), Elena Poniatowska's *La noche de Tlatelolco* (1971), Luis Spota's *La plaza* (1977), Gonzalo Martre's *Los símbolos transparentes* (1978) and Fernando del Paso's *Palinuro de México* (1977). No matter what the specific genre, the body of literature itself testified eloquently to the fact that the Mexican intelligentsia insisted that such an untoward episode should be neither repeated nor forgotten. When Poniatowska was awarded the Xavier Villarrutia Literary Prize for *La noche de Tlatelolco* she would not accept it, insisting that the only persons worthy of a prize were those who had given their lives at the Plaza de las Tres Culturas that fateful October evening in 1968. Tlatelolco, in essence, became not only a backdrop, not only a focus of literary discourse, but a major point of departure for the best Mexican literature published in the three decades following the infamous events of 1968. The cultural outpouring combined with political pressure to force the government to declare October 2, 1998, a national day of mourning and to order flags flown at half staff. The modest concession took thirty years.

Under Vicente Fox, however, the attorney general's office made an effort to bring to justice the officials responsible for killing dissidents at Tlatelolco and in its aftermath. Secret security files were opened up, leading to revelations about the roles of key players, including former president Luis Echeverría, who allegedly ordered paramilitaries known as the Falcons (Los Halcones) to attack student marchers in Mexico City in 1971. At least twenty-five protesters were killed. Government prosecutor Ignacio Carrillo Prieto charged Echeverría with genocide (defined as systematic crimes against the lives of members of any national group), but for many, including the Mexican Supreme Court, this tactic was too much of a stretch, and they lamented that the Fox government had not called for the establishment of a truth commission to pursue the matter. Nonetheless, throughout 2004 and 2005, the Mexican public read the lurid details of state-sponsored violence. In June 2006, Echeverría was arrested and charged with crimes related to the 1968 and 1971 killings, but a judge ruled that Mexico's statute of limitations prevented his prosecution.

Political corruption, along with social and environmental concerns, began to displace national identity as the most frequent motif in Mexican narratives of the late twentieth century, as evidenced in José Emilio Pacheco's *Morirás lejos* (1967). The voices of women and gays also emerged more openly in works like Angeles Mastretta's *Arráncame la vida* (1985) and Luis Zapata's *El vampiro de la colonia Roma* (1979). Among the most widely read authors at the turn of the century were the cultural critics, Elena Poniatowska and Carlos Monsiváis, writing in the *crónica* style that crosses the borders between fiction and nonfiction. Monsiváis, who won Mexico's prestigious Juan Rulfo literary prize in 2006, has been described as a kind of "public trickster" who brilliantly describes urban popular culture and seeks to empower his readers through his critiques of official policies.

Sub-Comandante Marcos once again captured public attention in 2004 when he offered Mexican novelist Paco Ignacio Taibo II the opportunity to coauthor a novel with him. Entitled *Muertos incómodos*, the novel was published in installments in the leftist newspaper, *La Jornada*, as the authors alternated chapters in this crime novel featuring a Zapatista detective and a cynical private investigator who expose injustices.

Mexican art in the postwar period also rejected—in fact, rebelled violently against—the nationalistic indigenismo. Although Mexican painters of the 1950s and 1960s never achieved the stature of the great revolutionary muralists, some of the new experiments with abstract expressionism, drip painting, and even op art were exciting to some and completely bewildering to others. Leading the *avant-garde* was José Luis Cuevas, who epitomized the rejection of traditional muralism when he stated that what he wanted for his country's art was "broad highways leading to the rest of the world rather than narrow trails connecting one adobe village to another."[3] Many of his contemporaries agreed, and the new generation, including Olga Costa, Jesús Reyes, Pedro Coronel, and Carrillo Gil, executed paintings that could have been conceived anywhere in the western world. They did not believe it necessary to capture the spirit of an idealized Revolution, to reaffirm their Mexicanidad or to instruct the masses. But it was Juan Soriano who depicted the movement best, and in 1957 a distinguished jury of artists at the Salón de la Plástica Mexicana gave him the first prize ever awarded to Mexican abstract painting. Soriano later articulated his views on the new Mexican art to Elena Poniatowska in a celebrated interview.

> Siqueiros limits himself to one country—Mexico. And to one political idea. I'm interested in ideas that are much broader. . . . Siqueiros . . . wants to create a strongly nationalistic art. And I believe that his art is excellent because it expresses him. But I want, and have always wanted to be universal. . . . Those murals are only tourist bait. They're the same kind of thing as those gigantic posters of the travel agencies: *Visit Mexico*. Furthermore those murals reveal nothing. They're a chronicle and not a poetic creation. Diego Rivera created a completely bureaucratic art. He

---

3. José Luis Cuevas, "The Cactus Curtain," *Evergreen Review* 2 (1959): 120.

made himself a propagandist of the victorious revolution. . . . I reproach him for having completely prostituted the pictorial language, reducing it to little more than a caricature, vulgarizing it. Because, don't you see, the caricature is a creation of the bourgeoisie. . . . I'm not concerned with my nationality. I can assure you I don't carry it like a chip on my shoulder, nor do I have to remind myself daily that I'm a Mexican.[4]

To the amusement of some and to the shock of others, Mexican painting turned iconoclastic in the 1970s and 1980s, first reinterpreting Mexican popular culture motifs within a more personal than national context. Later postmodern tendencies fused past and present styles in often unconventional and innovative ways and media, including installation art. Artistic impiety was epitomized by the sacrilegious work of Rolando de la Rosa. His 1988 art exhibit featured the superimposed face of Marilyn Monroe on the image of the Virgin of Guadalupe and the face of actor Pedro Infante similarly substituted

An architectural and anthropological achievement of gigantic proportions, the new Museum of Anthropology in Mexico City (above and on opposite page) became a prime tourist attraction in the 1970s.

4. Quoted in Elena Poniatowska, "Interview with Juan Soriano," *Evergreen Review* 2 (1959): 144–49.

for that of Christ in his rendition of the Last Supper. A generation or two earlier this type of mocking materialism would have occasioned major outcries, but most viewers simply shrugged their shoulders. If the meaning of this anatomical frolicking was lost on some, no Mexico City resident was confused by the artistic celebration of Earth Day in 1992. The intensity was best captured perhaps by painter Roger von Gunten's depiction of colored smoke from a Mexico City factory. He entitled it *Rainbow of Death*. It reminded many of Carlos Fuentes's depiction of the capital in his 1987 novel, *Christopher Unborn*. He had dubbed it Makesicko City.

Historical scholarship had not fared well in the two decades prior to World War II, for historians often found it impossible to reconcile their faith in the Revolution with documentary evidence available to them. But in the postwar years historical scholarship came of age. Between 1940 and 1951, three important institutions—El Colegio de México, the Escuela Nacional de Antropología e Historia, and the Instituto de Historia of the National University—were founded and devoted major effort to improving historical training. Reacting against the blatant partisanship of the prorevolutionary school that had emerged in the 1920s and 1930s, the new generation of historians was much more concerned with methodology, archival research, careful bibliographical preparation, and documentary publication. The preparation of excellent regional histories and microhistories put the scholarly community on notice that in the future Mexico and Mexico City would not be considered synonymous terms.

Contributing to the maturation of historical scholarship were twelve important conferences in which Mexican historians came together with their United States and European counterparts. Meeting in Monterrey, Nuevo León, in 1949; in Austin in 1958; in Oaxtepec, Morelos, in 1969; in Santa Monica in 1973; in Pátzcuaro, Michoacán, in 1977; in Chicago in 1981; in Oaxaca in 1985; in San Diego in 1989; in Mexico City in 1994; in Fort Worth, Texas, in 1999; Monterrey in 2003; and Vancouver, British Columbia in 2006, historians from around the world who specialized in Mexican history, both established hands and young aspirants, submitted the fruits of their research to one another, tested new ideas, pinpointed lacunae, analyzed historiographical trends, disputed the latest trends in methodology, and published their proceedings. While the conferences were far from barren of vigorous controversy, polemical acrimony was noticeable mainly for its absence. The debates were healthy ones and augured well for the future of Mexican historiography.

One of the most remarkable historical endeavors undertaken in Mexico in the postwar era was the project of Daniel Cosío Villegas. In the late 1940s, he began work on an ambitious, multivolume history of modern Mexico. Twenty-five years later the ninth and final volume appeared, and the project had received acclaim as perhaps the most significant Latin American historical enterprise of the twentieth century. The *Historia moderna de México* covers the years from the restoration of the republic in 1867 to the outbreak of the Revolution, with separate volumes treating the political, economic, social, and international aspects of the period. Cosío planned the project with extreme care, founding in 1950 the Seminar on Modern Mexican History at El Colegio de México. This workshop brought together a group of talented researchers who, under Cosío's direction, prepared extensive bibliographies; compiled statistical data; searched out the major manuscripts, printed documentation, and newspapers; and cooperated in the production of the finished volumes.

Although thirteen scholars contributed sections, Cosío's conception of history permeated the entire enterprise and his guiding hand ensured a high quality. Eschewing the notion that history should be a tool for the apotheosis of the Revolution, Cosío did not find it necessary to excoriate Porfirio Díaz and his regime. He proposed that the birth of modern Mexico was properly attributable to the restored republic rather than to the Porfiriato. He held no special brief for the abuses of the Díaz dictatorship, but, in the tradition of classical nineteenth-century scientific history, he was content to let the facts speak for themselves. When conclusions were offered, however, they were clearly supported by the evidence. The picture that emerged was clear and unflawed by the distortions of prorevolutionary presupposition. The historian Charles A. Hale prepared a penetrating view of Cosío's work in a long review essay. His conclusions are particularly appropriate:

> By breaking through the seemingly impenetrable ideological barrier thrown up by the Revolution of 1910, by eschewing the centennial impulse in historiography, and by basing interpretations on serious research, Daniel Cosío Villegas and his collaborators have given new life to the professional study of modern and contemporary Mexico, both within the country and abroad.[5]

It took a long time for the new scholarship to reach the public, but it did in dramatic fashion late in 1992. Mexico's mandatory school textbooks underwent a major revision. Porfirio Díaz emerged not as a despotic megalomaniac but as a positive actor in the creation of modern Mexico. The Revolutionary icons on the other hand, especially Emiliano Zapata, surfaced as rather less heroic, and not entirely free of warts. In general harmony with the post-Revolutionary political ethic, Mexico's serious national problems were no longer attributed to the imperialistic United States. The books were even silent on the American intervention in Veracruz in 1914. And of equal importance, for the first time Mexican school children were allowed to read a reasonable and accurate accounting of what happened on October 2, 1968, at Tlatelolco. They deserved to know. But the rearrangement of Mex-

---

5. Charles A. Hale, "The Liberal Impulse: Daniel Cosío Villegas and the *Historia moderna de México*," *Hispanic American Historical Review* 54 (1974): 498.

ico's history troubled many. The textbook revisions were very controversial, as many recoiled at the thought that Mexican history should be rewritten to harmonize with the political proclivities of the day. In the most recent reincarnation of the idea that historical interpretation reflects the social milieu of the writer, the Fox administration proposed new changes in school curriculum that de-emphasized the study of Mexico's past in favor of texts that would point Mexico in a more modern, technological direction.

The task of reconciling the past with the future had fallen to Vicente Fox in 2000. Although Mexicans had grown tired of the empty revolutionary rhetoric, they were not ready to eschew all that was Mexican in an increasingly homogeneous and impersonal world. Their vision for the future was perhaps not unlike that of Francisco Madero in 1910—to create a more just and prosperous nation. In 2000 they faced a world in which a different blend of idealism and pragmatism was required to achieve their aspirations for a better life. For many Mexicans, Fox represented the possibility of bridging the gap between promise and reality that had plagued Mexico for decades. By 2005, it was clear that Mexico's new experiment with democracy had been frustrated by an entrenched political culture resistant to change and by an outside world over which Mexico had no control. The 2006 elections highlighted the tensions of a volatile politics in which evolving democratic institutions were challenged by populist initiatives. The next step was scarcely predictable, but no one could doubt that Mexicans would face the future with a deeply ingrained sense of their past.

RECOMMENDED FOR FURTHER STUDY

Arreola, Juan José. *Confabulario and Other Inventions*. Translated by George D. Shade. Austin: University of Texas Press, 1974.

Bailey, David C. "Revisionism and the Recent Historiography of the Mexican Revolution." *Hispanic American Historical Review* 58 (1978): 62–79.

Benjamin, Thomas. *La Revolución: Mexico's Great Revolution as Memory, Myth, and History*. Austin: University of Texas Press, 2000.

Brushwood, John S. *Mexico in Its Novel: A Nation's Search for Identity*. Austin: University of Texas Press, 1966.

Davidson, Miriam. *Lives on the Line: Dispatches from the U.S.-Mexico Border*. Tucson: University of Arizona Press, 2000.

de Beer, Gabriella. *Contemporary Mexican Women Writers: Five Voices*. Austin: University of Texas Press, 1996.

Eagan, Linda. *Carlos Monsiváis: Culture and Chronicle in Contemporary Mexico*. Tucson: University of Arizona Press, 2001.

Fuentes, Carlos. *The Death of Artemio Cruz*. Translated by Sam Hileman. New York: Noonday Press, 1966.

———. *Where the Air Is Clear*. Translated by Sam Hileman. New York: Ivan Obolensky, 1960.

Gilbert, Dennis. "Rewriting History: Salinas, Zedillo, and the 1992 Textbook Controversy." *Mexican Studies* 13 (1997): 271–98.

Goldman, Shifra M. *Contemporary Mexican Painting in a Time of Change.* Austin: University of Texas Press, 1981.

Gutiérrez, Natividad. *Nationalist Myths and Ethnic Identities: Indigenous Intellectuals and the Mexican State.* Lincoln: University of Nebraska Press, 1999.

Hale, Charles A. "The Liberal Impulse: Daniel Cosío Villegas and the *Historia moderna de México.*" *Hispanic American Historical Review* 54 (1974): 479–98.

Hale, Charles and Michael C. Meyer. "Mexico: The National Period," in *Latin American Scholarship since World War II.* Edited by Roberto Esquenazi-Mayo and Michael C. Meyer, pp. 115–38. Lincoln: University of Nebraska Press, 1971.

Irwin, Robert McKee. *Mexican Masculinities.* Minneapolis: University of Minnesota Press, 2003.

Jorgensen, Beth E. *The Writings of Elena Poniatowska: Emerging Dialogues.* Austin: University of Texas Press, 1994.

Joseph, Gilbert M., Anne Rubenstein, and Eric Zolov, eds. *Fragments of a Golden Age: The Politics of Culture in Mexico since 1940.* Durham, N.C.: Duke University Press.

Lewis, Oscar. *The Children of Sánchez: Autobiography of a Mexican Family.* New York: Vintage Books, 1961.

Lipp, Solomon. *Leopoldo Zea: From Mexicanidad to a Philosophy of History.* Waterloo, Ontario: Wilfrid Laurier University Press, 1980.

Lomnitz-Adler, Claudio. *Deep Mexico, Silent Mexico: An Anthropology of Nationalism.* Minneapolis: University of Minnesota Press, 2001.

Lorey, David E. *The University System and Economic Development in Mexico since 1929.* Stanford, Calif.: Stanford University Press, 1993.

Meyer, Michael C. "A Venture in Documentary Publication: Isidro Fabela's *Documentos Históricos.*" *Hispanic American Historical Review* 52 (1972): 123–29.

Paz, Octavio. *The Labyrinth of Solitude: Life and Thought in Mexico.* Translated by Lysander Kemp, New York: Grove Press, 1961.

———. *The Other Mexico: Critique of the Pyramid.* New York: Grove Press, 1972.

Pilcher, Jeffrey. *Cantinflas and the Chaos of Mexican Modernity.* Wilmington, Del.: Scholarly Resources, 2001.

Rubenstein, Anne. *Bad Language, Naked Ladies, and Other Threats to the Nation: A Political History of Comic Books in Mexico.* Durham, N.C.: Duke University Press, 1998.

Steele, Cynthia. *Politics, Gender and the Mexican Novel, 1968–1988: Beyond the Pyramid.* Austin: University of Texas Press, 1992.

Taylor, Kathy. *The New Narrative of Mexico: Sub-versions of History in Mexican Fiction.* Lewisburg, Pa.: Bucknell University Press, 1994.

Vanderwood, Paul J. *Juan Soldado: Rapist, Murderer, Martyr, Saint.* Durham, N.C.: Duke University Press, 2004.

Wilkie, James W., Michael C. Meyer, and Edna Monzón de Wilkie, eds. *Contemporary Mexico: Papers of the IV Congress of Mexican History.* Berkeley: University of California Press, 1976.

Young, Dolly J. "Mexican Literary Reactions to Tlatelolco, 1968." *Latin American Research Review* 20 (1985): 71–85.

Zolov, Eric. *Refried Elvis: The Rise of the Mexican Counterculture.* Berkeley: University of California Press. 1999.

Appendix:
Mexican Heads of State

The Aztec Empire

Tenoch	?
Queen Ilancueitl	1349–75
Acamapichtli and Queen Ilancueitl	1375–83
Acamapichtli	1383–96
Huitzilíhuitl	1396–1417
Chimalpopoca	1417–27
Itzcóatl	1427–40
Moctezuma Ilhuicamina (Moctezuma I)	1440–69
Axayácatl	1469–81
Tizoc	1481–86
Ahuítzotl	1486–1502
Moctezuma Xocoyótzin (Moctezuma II)	1502–June 1520
Cuitláhuac	June–October 1520
Cuauhtémoc	October 1520–August 1521

Immediate Post-Conquest Period

Fernando Cortés	1521–24
Crown Officials	1524–26
Residencia Judges	1526–28
First Audiencia	1528–31
Second Audiencia	1531–35

Source: Adapted from Richard E. Greenleaf and Michael C. Meyer, eds., *Research in Mexican History: Topics, Methodology, Sources and a Practical Guide to Field Research* (Lincoln, 1973), pp. 221–24; and David P. Henige, *Colonial Governors from the Fifteenth Century to the Present* (Madison, 1970), pp. 312–13.

Viceroys of the Colonial Period

Antonio de Mendoza	1535–50
Luis de Velasco (the elder)	1550–64
Gastón de Peralta	1566–68
Martín Enríquez de Almanza	1568–80
Lorenzo Suárez de Mendoza	1580–83
Luis de Villanueva y Zapata	1582–83
Pedro Moya de Contreras	1584–85
Alvaro Manrique de Zúñiga	1585–90
Luis de Velasco (the younger)	1590–95
Gaspar de Zúñiga y Acevedo	1595–1603
Juan Manuel de Mendoza y Luna	1603–07
Luis de Velasco (the younger)	1607–11
Fray Francisco García Guerra	1611–12
Diego Fernández de Córdoba	1612–21
Diego Carrillo de Mendoza y Pimentel	1621–24
Rodrigo Pacheco y Osorio	1624–35
Lope Díaz de Armendáriz	1635–40
Diego López Pacheco Cabrera y Bobadilla	1640–42
Juan de Palafox y Mendoza	1642
García Sarmiento y Sotomayor	1642–48
Marcos de Torres y Rueda	1648–49
Matías de Peralta	1649–50
Luis Enríquez y Guzmán	1650–53
Francisco Fernández de la Cueva	1653–60
Juan de Leyva y de la Cerda	1660–64
Diego Osorio de Escobar y Llamas	1664
Antonio Sebastián de Toledo	1664–73
Pedro Nuño Colón de Portugal	1673
Fray Payo Enríquez de Rivera	1673–80
Tomás Antonio Manrique de la Cerda y Aragón	1680–86
Melchor Portocarrero Lasso de la Vega	1686–88
Gaspar de Sandoval Silva y Mendoza	1688–96
Juan de Ortega y Montañez	1696
José Sarmiento Valladares	1696–1701
Juan de Ortega y Montañez	1701
Francisco Fernández de la Cueva Enríquez	1701–11
Fernando de Alencastre Noroña y Silva	1711–16
Baltasar de Zúñiga y Guzmán	1716–22
Juan de Acuña	1722–34
Juan Antonio Vizarrón y Eguiarreta	1734–40
Pedro de Castro y Figueroa	1740–41
Pedro Cebrián y Agustín	1742–46

Francisco de Güemes y Horcasitas (subsequently first Count Revillagigedo)	1746–55
Agustín Ahumada y Villalón	1755–60
Francisco Cajigal de la Vega	1760
Joaquín de Monserrat	1760–66
Carlos Francisco de Croix	1766–71
Antonio María de Bucareli	1771–79
Martín de Mayorga	1779–83
Matías de Gálvez	1783–84
Vicente de Herrera y Rivero	1784–85
Bernardo de Gálvez	1785–86
Eusebio Sánchez Pareja y Beleño	1786–87
Alonso Núñez de Haro y Peralta	1787
Manuel Antonio Flores	1787–89
Juan Vicente de Güemes Pacheco y Padilla (second Count Revillagigedo)	1789–94
Miguel de la Grúa Talamanca y Branciforte	1794–98
Miguel José de Azanza	1798–1800
Félix Berenguer de Marquina	1800–1803
José de Iturrigaray	1803–08
Pedro Garibay	1808–09
Francisco Javier de Lizana y Beaumont	1809–10
Francisco Javier de Venegas	1810–13
Félix María Calleja del Rey	1813–16
Juan Ruiz de Apodaca	1816–21
Francisco Novella	1821
Juan O'Donojú	did not assume office

Independence Period and Early Republic

Emperor Agustín de Iturbide	1822–23
Guadalupe Victoria (Félix Fernández)	1824–29
Vicente Guerrero	1829
José María Bocanegra (interim)	1829
Pedro Vélez, Luis Quintanar, and Lucas Alamán, triumvirate	1829
Anastasio Bustamante	1830–32, 1837–39, and 1842
Melchor Múzquiz (interim)	1832
Manuel Gómez Pedraza	1833
Antonio López de Santa Anna	variously from 1833 to 1855

Valentín Gómez Farías	1833, 1834, and 1847
Miguel Barragán	1835–36
José Justo Corro	1836–37
Nicolás Bravo	variously from 1839 to 1846
Javier Echeverría	1841
Valentín Canalizo	1844
José Joaquín Herrera (interim)	1844, 1845, and 1848–51
Mariano Paredes Arrillaga	1846
Mariano Salas	1846
Pedro María Anaya	1847 and 1848
Manuel de la Peña y Peña	1847 and 1848
Mariano Arista	1851–53
Juan Bautista Ceballos (interim)	1853
Manuel María Lombardini	1853
Martín Carrera (interim)	1855
Rómulo Díaz de la Vega	1855

The Reform and the French Intervention

Juan Alvarez	1855
Ignacio Comonfort	1855–58
Liberal Government	
Benito Juárez	1855–72
Conservative Government	
Félix Zuloaga	1858 and 1859
Manuel Robles Pezuela	1858
Miguel Miramón	1859–60
Ignacio Pavón	1860
Conservative Junta	1860–64
Emperor Maximilian von Hapsburg	1864–67

Post-Reform Period

Sebastián Lerdo de Tejada	1872–76
Porfirio Díaz	1876–80 and 1884–1911
Juan N. Méndez	1876
Manuel González	1880–84

Revolutionary Period

Francisco León de la Barra (interim)	1911
Francisco I. Madero	1911–13

Pedro Lascuraín (interim)	1913
Victoriano Huerta (interim)	1913–14
Francisco S. Carbajal (interim)	1914
Venustiano Carranza	1914 and 1915–20
Eulalio Gutiérrez (interim, named by Convention)	1914
Roque González Garza	1914
Francisco Lagos Cházaro	1915
Adolfo de la Huerta (interim)	1920
Alvaro Obregón	1920–24
Plutarco Elías Calles	1924–28
Emilio Portes Gil (interim)	1928–30
Pascual Ortiz Rubio	1930–32
Abelardo L. Rodríguez (interim)	1932–34
Lázaro Cárdenas	1934–40

Period of Institutional Revolution

Manuel Avila Camacho	1940–46
Miguel Alemán Valdés	1946–52
Adolfo Ruiz Cortines	1952–58
Adolfo López Mateos	1958–64
Gustavo Díaz Ordaz	1964–70
Luis Echeverría Alvarez	1970–76
José López Portillo	1976–82
Miguel de la Madrid	1982–88

Post-Revolutionary Period

Carlos Salinas de Gortari	1988–94
Ernesto Zedillo	1994–2000
Vicente Fox	2000–2006
Felipe Calderón Hinojosa	2006–

Sources of Illustrations

We gratefully acknowledge the following persons and institutions for the photographs and illustrations in this book.

List of Abbreviations

AMNH	American Museum of Natural History, New York
AIA	Archaeological Institute of America, New York
ASHS	Arizona State Historical Society, Tucson
BL	Bancroft Library, University of California, Berkeley
CENIDIAP/INBA	Centro Nacional de Investigación, Documentación e Información de Artes Plásticas, Instituto Nacional de Bellas Artes
CONACULTA-INAH-MEX	Consejo Nacional para la Cultura y las Artes-Instituto Nacional de Antropología e Historia-México
HRC	Humanities Research Center, University of Texas, Austin
HL	Henry E. Huntington Library, San Marino, California
IADB	Interamerican Development Bank, Washington, D.C.
LC	Library of Congress, Washington, D.C.
MMA	Metropolitan Museum of Art, New York
MNA	Museo Nacional de Antropología, Mexico
MNTC	Mexican National Tourist Council, New York
NA	National Archive, Washington, D.C.
NYPL	New York Public Library
OAS	Organization of American States, Washington, D.C.
SMM	Science Museum of Minnesota, St. Paul
UAL	University of Arizona Library, Tucson

Chapter 1. p. 6, AMNH; 9, left—MMA, Michael C. Rockefeller Mem. Coll. of primitive Art, right—MNA; 10, LC. *Chapter 2.* p. 13, MMA, Rockefeller Coll; 16, AMNH; p. 17, left—AMNH, right—MMA, Rockefeller Coll; 19, MNTC; 20, AIA; 21, MNTC; 23, MNA; 24, Leslie Hughes; 25, Jeffrey House; 28, MMA, Rockefeller Coll; 29, above—AMNH, below—MNTC; 30, MNA; 31, left—MNA, right—Dumbarton Oaks, Washington, D.C. *Chapter 3.* p. 38, AIA; 39, NYPL; 40, Alan Bates; 41, left—MMA, Rockefeller Coll, right—MNTC; 42, CONACULTA-INAH-MEX; 43, 44, Leslie Hughes; 45, above—AIA, below—Bradley Smith; 46, AMNH; 47, MNTC; 48, Thomas Laging. *Chapter 4.* p. 53,

LC; 57, 59, AMNH. *Chapter 5.* 62, Biblioteca, MNA; 63, BL; 65, Dumbarton Oaks, Washington, D.C.; 69, 72, 73, LC; 74, 75, MNA; 76, LC; 79, AMNH; 80, Bradley Smith. *Chapter 6.* p. 91, above left— MMA, Rogers Fund, 1904, right—MMA, Gift William H. Riggs, 1913, below left— MMA, Gift Abraham Silberman, 1937, right—MMA, Rogers Fund, 1921; 92, Hospital de Jesús, México; 98, NYPL.; p. 103, above—Los Angeles County Museum of Natural History, below— MMA, Gift William H. Riggs, 1913; 107, Biblioteca, MNA; 109, above—after a model in the John W. Higgins Armory, Worcester, MA. *Chapter 7.* p. 114, MNTC, 117, Casa Popenoe, Antigua, Guatemala; 119, 121, from Justo Sierra, *Mexico, Its Social Revolution*; 123, BL. *Chapter 8.* p. 141, LC; 142, MMA, Gift William H. Riggs, 1913. *Chapter 9.* p. 147, Pan Amer. Development Foundation; 150, Weidenfeld & Nicolson, London; 151, NA; 155, upper left—Philadelphia Museum of Art, upper right and below—MMA, Gift Mrs. Robert W. de Forest, 1911; 156, from Carlos Nebel, *Viaje pintoresco y arqueológico sobre . . . la República Mexicana . . . 1839*; 157, American Numismatic Society, N.Y. *Chapter 10.* p. 161, LC; 163, Programa Nacional de Arte Popular; 165, LC; 167, Jeffrey House; 168, LC; 171, 172, Vicente Riva Palacios, *México a través de los siglos, 1887–89*; 173, CONACULTA-INAH-MEX. *Chapter 11.* p. 185, CONACULTA-INAH-MEX. *Chapter 12.* pp. 195, 198, from Justo Sierra, *Mexico, Its Social Revolution*, 1900; 203, LC; 205, BL; 206, MMA; 207, Leslie Hughes; 210, 211, Hispanic Society of America, N.Y.; 213, from *México y sus alrededores*, Editorial Valle de México, 1980. *Chapter 13.* p. 222, Bruckman Art Reference Bureau; 230, from *México y sus alrededores*, Editorial Valle de México, 1980. *Chapter 14.* p. 234, OAS; 235, LC; 236, from Carlos Nebel, *Viaje pintoresco y arqueológico sobre . . . la República Mexicana . . . , 1839*; 237, Weidenfeld & Nicolson, London; 240, The Brooklyn Museum; 241, BL; 246, MMA, Bequest Mrs. H. O. Havemeyer, 1929; 248, BL. *Chapter 15.* p. 253, LC; 257, Bettmann Archive. *Chapter 16.* p. 267, from *Gobernantes de México, 1325–1911*, Artes de México, No. 175, año XXI, p. 59. *Chapter 17.* p. 282, from Justo Sierra, *México, Its Social Revolution*, 1900. *Chapter 18.* p. 289, BL; 295, BL; 301, NA; 308, NYPL. *Chapter 19.* pp. 315, 317, from Vicente Riva Palacios, *México a través de los siglos, 1887–89*; 318, 320, from B. Mayer, *Mexico, Aztec, Spanish and Republican, 1852. Chapter 20.* p. 331, BL; 337, BL; 340, ASHS; 343, 347, from M. de los Torres, *El archiduque Maximiliano de Austria en México, 1867. Chapter 21.* p. 353, HRC; 355, NYPL; 357, HL. *Chapter 22.* p. 364, Vicente Riva Palacios, *México a través de los siglos, 1887–89*; 365, BL; 368, *México y sus alrededores*, Editorial Valle de México, 1980; 370, NYPL; 372, from Justo Sierra, *México, Its Social Revolution*, 1900. *Chapter 23.* p. 384, HRC; 385, BL; 386, SMM; 388, ASHS. *Chapter 24.* p. 395, SMM; 397, UAL; 402, HL; 403, SMM. *Chapter 25.* p. 410, ASHS; 411, HRC. *Chapter 26.* p. 423, Hemeroteca Nacional de México; 426, BL; 434, UAL; 436, HRC; 437, ASHS. *Chapter 27.* p. 444, HRC; 450, NA. *Chapter 28.* p. 456, HL; 464, LC. *Chapter 29.* p. 469, HRC; 473, 474, LC; 477, HRC. *Chapter 30.* p. 483, ASHS; 486, LC; 488, above—HL, below—HRC. *Chapter 31.* p. 504, HRC. *Chapter 32.* p. 513, NYPL; 518, Fideicomiso Archivos Calles y Torreblanca. *Chapter 33.* pp. 530, 534, NA. *Chapter 34.* p. 542, 543, LC; 544, Pan Amer. Development Foundation; 545, LC; 546, Dartmouth College Museum, Hanover, NH; 548, National Preparatory School, México. *Chapter 35.* pp. 559, 560, 561, NA; 566, 567, Editorial Photocolor Archives; 568, NA. *Chapter 36.* p. 575, MNTC; 576, OAS; 578, MNTC; 584, 585, MNTC; 588, James W. Wilkie. *Chapter 37.* p. 598, Diego Goldberg/Sygma; 600, Secretaría de Información y Propaganda del Partido Revolucionario Institucional; 602, coin courtesy of Michael M. Brescia; 603, Alejandro Castañeda, México, D.F., 1985; 605, Photography by David Burckhalter, *Journal of the Southwest,* 32 (Spring 1990). *Chapter 38.* p. 615, Juan Miranda, *Proceso*; 620, Dan Fitzsimmons, *Arizona Daily Star*; 621, Archive photos/Daniel Aguilar/Reuters; 627, *Proceso.* *Chapter 39.* p. 641, David Manurian, IADB, 1992; 645, Lourdes Grobet; 650, OAS; 656, 657, MMTC.

Credits for illustrations in color insert, following p. 495.
Pre-Columbian Classic Period. (1) Palenque (North Courtyard of the Palace): Photo by David Hixson. (2) Death Mask (Jade) of Pacal: CONACULTA-INAH-MEX; Photo by Ignacio Guevara/Raíces/ INAH. (3) Anthropomorphic female figurine: Museo Nacional de Antropología, CONACULTA-INAH-MEX; Photo by Marco Antonio Pacheco/Raíces/INAH. (4) Cacaxtla mural: Photo by David Hixson.

Colonial. (5) Cathedral of Oaxaca: Photo by David Hixson. (6) Santa María Tonantzintla church exterior: Photo by Carlos García Calzada. (7) Santa María Tonantzintla church interior: Photo by Carlos García Calzada. (8) Portrait of Sor Juana Inés de la Cruz by Miguel Cabrera, ca.1750: Museo Nacional de Historia, CONACULTA-INAH-MEX. (9) Casta painting by Miguel Cabrera, *De chino cambujo y de india, loba,* 1763: Photo by Camilo Garza (Museo de América, Madrid), oil on canvas. **Nineteenth Century.** (10) José Agustín Arrieta, *La sorpresa,* 1850: Museo Nacional de Historia, CONACULTA-INAH-MEX, oil on canvas. (11) Salvador Murillo, *El Puente de Chiquihuite,* ca. 1875: Colección Banco Nacional de México, oil on canvas. (12) Luis Coto, *La Colegiata de Guadalupe,* 1859: Museo Nacional de Arte; CENIDIAP/INBA, Biblioteca de las Artes, CENART (México), oil on canvas. (13) José María Velasco, *The Valley of Mexico from the Cerro del Tepeyac,* 1894: Museo Nacional de Arte; CENIDIAP/INBA, Biblioteca de las Artes, CENART (México), oil on canvas. **Twentieth Century.** (14) Diego Rivera, from *Día de los Muertos,* 1923–24: Mural, Secretaría de Educación Pública; D.R. © 2006 Banco de México, Fiduciario en el Fideicomiso relativo a los Museos Diego Rivera y Frida Kahlo; Archivo Fotográfico CENIDIAP/INBA. (15) José Clemente Orozco, *Zapata,* 1930: Joseph Winterbotham Collection, "Photography © The Art Institute of Chicago," oil on canvas. (16) David Alfaro Siqueiros, from *El tormento de Cuauhtémoc,* 1951: Mural, Palacio de Bellas Artes; CENIDIAP/INBA, Biblioteca de las Artes, CENART (México). (17) Diego Rivera, *Paisaje zapatista,* 1915: Museo Nacional de Arte; D.R. © 2006 Banco de México, Fiduciario en el Fideicomiso relativo a los Museos Diego Rivera y Frida Kahlo; Archivo Fotográfico CENIDIAP/INBA. (18) Rufino Tamayo, *Dos figuras en rojo,*1973: Couple in Red © Phoenix Art Museum, Arizona/Friends of Mexican Art/The Bridgeman Art Library; D.R. Rufino Tamayo/Herederos/México/2006, Fundación Olga y Rufino Tamayo A.C.

Index